Law and Business

PATTERNS AND ISSUES IN COMMERCIAL LAW

Law and Business

PATTERNS AND ISSUES IN

COMMERCIAL LAW

Jon Patrick McConnell

College of Economics and Business
Washington State University

THE MACMILLAN COMPANY

COLLIER-MACMILLAN LIMITED · London

Fourth Printing, 1971

Library of Congress catalog card number: 66-18768

THE MACMILLAN COMPANY
866 Third Avenue, New York, New York 10022
COLLIER-MACMILLAN CANADA, LTD., Toronto, Ontario

PRINTED IN THE UNITED STATES OF AMERICA

To my wife

Beverly

without whose endless hours of typing
this book would not have been
possible

Preface

WHEN selecting subject matter for a text in business law, the question must be asked, what is the purpose of the course in business law? My answer is this: To convey to the student an understanding of the nature of law and of our legal system.

It may be reasonably argued that this sort of understanding is necessary before any citizen may be considered well informed. But, no doubt, an understanding of the nature of law and of our legal system is particularly important to the businessman.

What should an intelligent person know about law? First of all, he should have some appreciation of the nature of legal problems: Why is discovering and applying the law so much more complex than looking up a word in the dictionary? Why, after continuous development over a period of centuries, should there still be frequent disputes as to the state of the law? What are some of the ways in which law is influenced by, and in turn an influence on, the social, economic, and political forces of our nation?

He should be cognizant of the sources of our law; that is, he should know something of the interaction between common law and legislation and at least something about the nature of the Constitution. Unfortunately, many intelligent people consider law as being synonymous with legislation and do not realize that much of our law is still based upon judicial precedent. Still more are unaware of the extent to which law is written by administrative agencies.

The intelligent person should have some idea as to why our law has come to assume its present form. This requires an examination of some aspects of the history of our law, and of the institutions through which our law is administered and through which our law is shaped.

However, our intelligent person is not greatly helped when he reads that a significant suit in tort or contract is being brought in the trial court if he understands only the nature and role of the trial court. He must also understand the nature of tort or contract. He will comment on current legal issues whether he understands them or not; why not offer him some information in the hope of improving the quality of his comment? Therefore, it seems reasonable that a college student should devote a few weeks of study to some of the more basic areas of the private law.

It need not be true that a course dealing with principles of private, substantive law must be a course intended to make the student his own lawyer. This sort of assumption is no more accurate than a parallel assumption that a course in economics, psychology, or physics can only be for the purpose of enabling the student to be his own economist, psychologist, or physicist. However, we all hope that the understanding that students derive from their college courses may influence their thinking and their decisions at one time or another. And so it is with courses presenting some aspects of our private, substantive law.

In my view, the most important function of a course in business law is to increase the understanding of our world, our nation, our institutions, and our society. But this sort of understanding is complementary, not contradictory, to an understanding of law that may help directly in making business decisions. There is no conflict. Our "legal environment" is relevant to business, and the set of institutions we refer to as business is relevant to our "legal environment." The choice of subject matter follows from these premises.

The purpose of this text, as suggested by the subtitle, is to present a study of patterns and issues relevant to the law, particularly the law of commerce. To do so requires extensive comment about the *nature* of law, yet a time comes when it becomes necessary to commence a study of the law itself. Both perspectives are important and will not be treated in an isolated fashion. In order to present these perspectives and to fulfill the purpose of this text primary reliance has been placed on narrative presentation. However, as an aid to bringing the more important concepts into focus, extensive reliance has been placed upon readings by outstanding jurists, social scientists, and other authorities and upon opinions from decided cases.

In selecting cases, several criteria were used—some of which might not be used in all texts. Of course, the primary criterion was how well the case developed in logical, understandable language the problem under discussion in the supporting text. An effort was made to avoid when possible cases with unnecessarily confusing patterns of fact. The mental effort expended toward unscrambling needlessly complex cases would be of as much benefit to a student of business law as would be memorizing license plate numbers to a student of mathematics. In addition, a deliberate attempt was made to select cases with an element of human interest. The law is interesting. Why select a dull, tedious case when an interesting one may be found to illustrate the same point?

The date of cases has been regarded as largely immaterial, unless the purpose is to illustrate some recent development in the law. In fact, some effort has been made to include cases of varying ages, to demonstrate the continuity in our legal institutions, and to suggest that many of the basic sources of past conflict remain sources of conflict today.

I wish to express my appreciation to a number of colleagues who made substantial contributions to this text. Professor Ted Saldin of Washington State University followed my progress from start to finish and made innumerable contributions both through constructive suggestions and through generously extending the benefit of his own labors in locating a number of readings and cases. Richard Loucks, a solo practioner, and Wallis Friel, of the Pullman, Washington, law firm of Aiken and Friel, both lecturers at Washington State University, contributed important suggestions and located a number of the cases included here.

Professor H. R. Hartzler of the University of Massachusetts provided many helpful comments that served both to reinforce my own views in some instances and to prompt a re-evaluation of my views in others. Professor Andrew J. Coppola, of the City University of New York, and Stuart Macmillan, former Teaching Assistant at the Massachusetts Institute of Technology and presently of the Boston law firm of Hausserman, Davisson, and Shattuck, also furnished detailed, conscientious, and helpful comments upon this text.

Due acknowledgment cannot be extended to all the authors and sources drawn upon in the preparation of this text. However, particularly heavy use was made of *Prosser on Torts,* a superlative text for any purpose, by William L. Prosser, Dean of the School of Law, the University of California at Berkeley; and *Mechem on Agency,* an excellent treatise on that subject, by Phillip Mecham, Professor of Law, University of Pennsylvania. My appreciation is also extended to the *American Bar Association Journal, Columbia Law Review, Harvard Law Review,* and *Christian Science Monitor,* who kindly consented to the use of lengthy quotations under their respective copyrights and to the other journals and publications that consented to the use of lesser quotes.

Finally, it should be stated that despite all the valuable assistance provided me, no one but myself could be expected to have thorough familiarity with all portions of this text. Therefore, what errors there may be are mine alone and responsibility for such errors is willingly assumed.

JON P. McCONNELL

Washington State University
Pullman, Washington

Contents

SECTION FOUR

Limitations on the Right to Contract

SECTION FIVE

Legal Responsibility for the Acts of Others

SECTION SIX
The Transfer of Intangible Legal Rights
(Herein of Assignment and the Negotiable Instrument)

SECTION SEVEN

Business Regulation

APPENDIX

SECTION ONE

Law and Our Legal System

CHAPTER ONE

The Law: Some Popular Misconceptions

. . . It is charged not only that the lawyer is guilty of introducing strange and unwholesome creatures into our linguistic family, but that he is also guilty of leading our familiar members astray. He is a perverter of ordinary speech.[1]

A Myth or Two

THE GENERAL PUBLIC often misunderstands the nature of law and of the legal process. When it does, these misunderstandings often take the following forms.

THE MYTH OF THE MYSTERIOUS ARCHIVES

The nonlawyer is apt to have the notion that law consists of a highly detailed enumeration of do's and don'ts, specific rules that lay down in advance the remedy for every conceivable situation, contained in some mysterious archives. If one is trampled by an escaping circus elephant, the function of the lawyer is thought of as being to conduct a search under *T* for *trample* or *E* for *elephant,* in these archives, the location of which, incidentally, is thought to be a carefully guarded secret among lawyers, for if common access were provided to the archives, lawyers would no longer be necessary.

Consistent with this view is the common assumption that if a lawyer is unable to provide an exact answer to a legal question, he must be incompetent. For what skill could be involved in finding and interpreting a rule of law?

[1] L. I. Fuller, "The Legal Mind," *The Atlantic Monthly* (July 1933), pp. 90–93.

Those with a more sophisticated view may not suppose the sources of legal "answers" to be concealed, but may suspect that "legal technicalities" are deliberately and artificially contrived to foreclose the ordinary man from understanding so fundamentally simple a thing as the law.

THE MYTH OF JUDICIAL CAPRICE

Another view of the law that seems to be widely held assumes the opposite extreme: that rules of law mean nothing; that they are so complex that any judge can justify any decision, and that consequently every legal decision depends upon the personal whim of the judge. Probably there are several reasons for the prevalence of this view, an important one being that almost every party to a lawsuit feels he is in the right. Even though one party must always lose, the human reaction to losing is seldom to accept gracefully the decision that one was in the wrong. Occasionally the reaction is to suspect some plot.

One reason for the prevalence of this view is that many legal questions do depend upon questions of degree—that is, how careless must a party be in order to be negligent? These are by nature questions upon which reasonable men may differ, within a certain range. Legal concepts of this kind are clear enough in black and white, but the gray areas are difficult to sort out. When questions fall within the gray area, individual interpretations may differ.

Finally, students of political science are apt to overestimate the capriciousness of the law for the excellent reason that, to the extent that this condition actually does occur, it probably occurs most frequently and most notoriously in constitutional cases. Because such cases often have important political implications they are naturally of great interest to political scientists. Many important questions of constitutional interpretation were either unprecedented when first heard, or if precedent existed, it occurred at a time and in a context that had little bearing upon the immediate situation. The school integration cases and the reapportionment cases serve as recent examples. When a judge does not have available the usual tools of the law to help him forge a decision, his personal views of right and wrong probably do enter the equation to an important degree. However, this sort of case occurs much less frequently than many imagine.

THE LEGAL LOOPHOLE

One other view of the law, held by a few, assumes that the law is very clear-cut as applied to others, except that no enforceable legal proposition applies to them because there is always a "loophole." Quoting from a friend of ours in private practice: "These people come in after they've already signed a contract and tell me they've changed their mind and want out of the contract. I look the situation over and have to tell them, 'Look, you're stuck. Why didn't you see me before you signed this?" They become very indignant and say, 'You're a lawyer, aren't you? Well, find some loophole, some gimmick. I'll be glad to pay.' The feeling seems to be that for some reason I'm holding out and refuse to help. They can't believe me when I tell them there isn't some loophole made just for them."

Fortunately, there are some settled questions of law, even though they are not contained in a mysterious archive.

SUMMARY

Most areas of law are neither so arbitrary as the adherents to the first view discussed above believe, nor so vague as the adherents of the second view believe, though now and then there may be an extreme situation in which one view or the other provides a fairly accurate description. Most questions would fall along a continuum between the two extremes.

Perhaps this much may be said in clarification: law implies regularity of decision, and legal decisions are usually based to some degree on a rule or precedent previously laid down, though in rare cases there may be no applicable rule or precedent. Even in the usual case, when a rule will provide the basis of decision, some interpretation of meaning is necessary to apply the rule, which is general and abstract in nature, to the particular case, which is concrete. Sometimes more than one interpretation of a rule is possible, and when this is true, a lawyer cannot provide his client with an absolute answer.

Possibly the most important thing to realize is that there are so many different fields of law, and so many types of questions presented within each field, that no adequate description can be given in a few words that will reflect the reality. Undoubtedly the popularity and the persistence of the views of law discussed above lie in their simplicity. Simple explanations are always popular.

Semantic Problems

LEGAL INTERPRETATION

THE LEGAL MIND [2]

> . . . But the business of the lawyer compels him to be "anxious about the sense" of the words he reads. . . . He is forced to discover what slippery, faithless things words are.

. . . It is charged not only that the lawyer is guilty of introducing strange and unwholesome creatures into our linguistic family, but that he is also guilty of leading our familiar members astray. He is a perverter of ordinary speech.

[2] Fuller, *ibid*. Copyright © 1933, by The Atlantic Monthly Company, Boston 16, Massachusetts.

In April, 1932, the *Atlantic Monthly* published an article entitled "Humpty Dumpty's Rule in Law." Many illustrations were given of the tendency of the legal mind to pervert ordinary words, and cases were cited in which courts had declared such incredible things as that a jackass is a horse, a bicycle is an animal, snakes are "tools of trade," a radio is not a "musical instrument," a fence, a tent, and a corncrib are all "buildings." The writer of the article was able to reach no more charitable conclusion than that "the prejudices and predilections of the courts determine the meaning of words." But he overlooked the most striking case of word perversion. According to newspaper accounts, a Brooklyn traffic court in 1927 decided that a hearse is a *pleasure vehicle!*

How could a court reach such a grotesque conclusion? What unspeakable "prejudices and predilections" of the judge led to such a disingenuous and garbled interpretation? The case was very simple. The shortsighted drafter of an ordinance had provided that all traffic on a certain street should be divided between two lanes, one assigned to "pleasure vehicles," the other to "trucks and other commercial vehicles." The court preferred to put the funeral cortege among the picknickers and sightseers, instead of among the garbage wagons and furniture vans. If we were to investigate the cases in which the startling results mentioned above were reached, we should find in each the same explanation: legislative shortsightedness had to be cured by somewhat temerarious interpretation.

Let us for the moment engage in a little adventure of our own in legislative drafting and interpretation. The mechanic's lien statute will serve as a convenient object on which to practice. This statute gives the man (the carpenter, let us say) who has performed work on a "building" a lien for his wages. The lien protects the workman whose employer fails to pay him. Obviously the purpose of a statute creating such a lien is broader than "buildings" in the strict sense. The man who erects a fence, for example, ought to have a lien for his wages by the same right as the man who shingles a roof. Let us exercise the proper legislative foresight and draft our own statute broadly so as to give the lien to anyone who has performed work upon "any building, structure, or any other erection of any kind whatsoever." This sounds not only inclusive but positively "legal." Let me ask the reader to stop at this point and reflect whether he can think of any proper case which would not be covered by this statute. A good many of our statutes have been phrased in this way, and it is unlikely that those who drafted them conceived that there was any possibility of the phraseology proving too narrow.

But unfortunately our statute is not broad enough to cover literally all the cases it should cover. Our thoughts have been on too elevated a plane. We have forgotten the well-digger. There is no good reason for denying a lien to him. But our statute said "building, structure, or any other erection." Does this include a well? Some of our courts have been courageous and sensible enough to declare that a well is a "structure" within the meaning of such a statute. But other courts have lacked the necessary temerity. Let us picture the workings of the mind of the judge faced with this problem. He sees that the general purpose of the statute obviously includes the well-digger, there looms up in his mind the dim picture of some such headline as this mocking him from the news stands? "Isn't law wonderful? Judge says hole in ground is structure." So he resigns himself and does what the unimaginative layman wants him to do. He denies a lien to a well-digger. The result is that some states have been forced to add a page to the immense bulk of their written laws and now have a special "well-digger's lien." And, for aught I know, there is a well-diggers' lobby to keep the statute on the books.

Let me give another illustration of the sort of difficulty which our courts face in interpreting statutes and contracts. Everyone knows what an accident insurance policy is. What is meant by the word "accident" in these policies? The peculiarity here is that we do not have, as in the case of most contracts and statutes, a "general purpose" in the light of which we must interpret (and perhaps pervert) the meaning of the word. The only purpose of the word is to limit the liability of the company. It would seem that if there were any case in the law where we could have a straightforward, literal application of a word, this would be it.

Now obviously the word "accident" as used in these policies would generally exclude death due to disease. No one would suppose, for example, that a case of death from tuberculosis would be included. On the other hand, the word is not confined in its meaning to violent events, such as automobile wrecks and the like, but includes such things as the unintentional swallowing of poison.

We are now ready for an actual case. A workman, who had taken out a policy of accident insurance, is employed in a place where two kinds of water are supplied. One supply is for drinking purposes, the other is for cleaning. Taps supplying the cleaning water are placarded with warnings that the water is unsafe to drink. Certain repairs are made in the plumbing of the building and a careless plumber so connects the pipes that the cleaning water is diverted into the pipes supplying the drinking water. The workman takes a drink from the usual tap, contracts typhoid fever, and dies. His widow sues the insurance company. Can she recover?

If you feel that this was an "accident" and therefore fell within the terms of the policy, consider the following question: Is not typhoid fever always an "accident"? This disease is kept in control by a complicated system of preventive measures, and when it appears it is usually due to a breakdown in this system, to an "accident." And is this not true to some extent of all diseases? In short, what criterion have we for distinguishing between accidents and diseases? I shall not inform the reader how the case was decided; I want him to suffer some of the torture of indecision which is the lawyer's daily lot. And if he finds no great difficulty in disposing of the particular case, does he find it equally simple to give an articulate "reason" for his decision? Can he lay down a "general Principle" which will govern this type of case? For he must remember that this is another demand which he makes on our judges.

John Locke explained many years ago why it is that among laymen the lawyer is known as a perverter of words. It is because the layman himself has so little experience with the complex problem of meaning. "There being no writings we have any great concernment to be very solicitous about the meaning of, but those that contain either truths we are required to believe, or laws we are to obey," we are generally not at all "anxious about the sense of other authors."

But the business of the lawyer compels him to be "anxious about the sense" of the words he reads. In this way he arrives at an insight which is denied to most laymen. He is forced to discover what slippery, faithless things words are.

The layman likes literal interpretations, whatever may be the inconvenience produced by them. This is because he can understand them in cases where he would not have the patience to trace out the reasons justifying a less literal interpretation. Then, too, literal interpretations fit into his ideal of "a government of laws, not of men," and remove from his mind the disquieting suspicion that judges exercise too much power over their fellow men. But until the layman is willing to grant the judge greater freedom in interpretation, he must not complain too bitterly about the volume and complexity of our laws."

When faced with the necessity of deciding a particular case the judge finds himself under pressure both to maintain consistency with the legal pronouncements of his predecessors and to make his decision meet the practical needs of his own day. Since conditions change from era to era he can do both these things oftentimes only by the use of the legal fiction, by maintaining a fictitious consistency with obsolete law.

For a semantic dilemma similar to those mentioned in the preceding article, the student might read the case of *Van Riper* v. *Constitutional Government League*.[3] In this case an insurance policy stated as one of its provisions that the company would not pay for injuries suffered as a result of a "criminal act." The insured was killed upon running a stop sign, a violation of the traffic code that is part of the criminal statutes of any state. The insurer denied liability on the ground that violation of a traffic law obviously is a crime. The court (properly in our view) concluded that the meaning of the word *criminal,* as used in the insurance policy, was the popular meaning of the word, "an intentional, and morally reprehensible act against the law of the land," instead of its technical meaning, as argued by the insurer. Perhaps on hearing of this decision the newspapers carried the headline COURT SAYS NOTHING WRONG WITH RUNNING STOP SIGNS.

CONCLUSION

It is the belief of this writer that, generally speaking, the law makes sense. It makes sense to most people if they are informed of the reasons for apparent contradictions or peculiarities. In some respects law is similar to any other discipline that concerns itself with human behavior. It is not

[3] 96 P2 588. [*Editor's Note:* Because this is the first "case citation" used in this text, perhaps it should be explained that the judges' opinion on every case tried in the state or federal appellate courts is recorded and compiled in volumes for future reference. Each case has an official citation, which is a reference code used to locate the case. In this instance the code indicates the case may be found in Vol. 96 of the Pacific reports, second series, p. 588.]

enough merely to look at what the behavior of past judges, lawyers, and legislators may have produced in cases and statutes; the question must be asked, "Why did the law assume this rather than some other form?"

Just as the existence of law as an institution represents the human response to certain human problems, so each individual rule of law arises in response to some particular problem. It is not realistic to look for coherent patterns in our law, without consideration of the underlying problems. When viewed from the perspective of the particular problem to be solved, law almost always seems reasonable. This does not mean that in some instances the adoption of one solution rather than another may not be debatable, nor that reasonable men may not differ as to the utility of a particular rule, nor that sometimes law may not lag too far behind changing conditions. It is suggested, however, that development of the law has been brought about by decisions that, according to the information available at the time the decisions were made, seemed the best accommodation to the competing demands of a variety of social forces.

POPULAR BELIEF IN THE UNCERTAINTY OF LEGAL PROCEEDINGS [4]

> *People are apt to be angry at the want of simplicity in our laws: they mistake variety for confusion, and complicated cases for contradictory. . . .*

The uncertainty of legal proceedings is a notion so generally adopted, and has so long been the standing theme of wit and good humor, that he who

[4] Sir William Blackstone, *Commentaries on the Laws of England,* 1765 (ed. William Draper Lewis) (Philadelphia: Rees Welsh & Company, 1902), Book 3, 198 pp. *Editor's Note:* Blackstone's life spanned the years 1723–1780. Although he had engaged in the practice of law for only a short period, and was a member of the English Parliament and Solicitor-General of England, he is remembered for his monumental *Commentaries on the Laws of England.*

In this four-volume work, Blackstone undertook not only to portray the major principles of the law of England at that time but, more important, to trace the historical and logical foundations of these principles. In this undertaking, he succeeded well enough to establish the *Commentaries* as one of the important sources of legal authority for at least 100 years.

Although we could find more modern authorities to quote, we prefer to rely upon Blackstone on certain occasions. Partly, this is an attempt to emphasize the persistence, in an historical sense, of certain types of human problems and of the need for solutions to these problems. In some areas, quotations from Blackstone also illustrate the remarkable stability of particular areas of the law—for example, assault and battery, and defamation. We feel that the mere fact that Blackstone wrote his *Commentaries* over 200 years ago and that it still makes sense today is of some interest. In many areas of his writing, it would be difficult to find anyone who has done a better job.

should attempt to refute it would be looked upon as a man who was either incapable of discernment himself, or else meant to impose upon others. Yet it may not be amiss, before we enter upon the several modes whereby certainty is meant to be obtained in our courts of justice, to inquire a little wherein this uncertainty, so frequently complained of, consists; and to what causes it owes its original.

It hath sometimes been said to owe its original to the number of our municipal constitutions, and the multitude of our judicial decisions; which occasion, it is alleged, abundance of rules which militate and thward with each other, as the sentiments or caprice of successive legislatures and judges have happened to vary. The fact of multiplicity is allowed; and that thereby the researches of the student are rendered more difficult and laborious; but that, with proper industry, the result of those inquiries will be doubt and indecision, is a consequence that cannot be admitted. People are apt to be angry at the want of simplicity in our laws: they mistake variety for confusion, and complicated cases for contradictory. They bring us the example of arbitrary governments, of Denmark, Muscovy, and Prussia; of wild and uncultivated nations, the savages of Africa and America; or of narrow domestic republics, in ancient Greece and modern Switzerland; and unreasonably require the same paucity of laws, the same conciseness of practice, in a nation of freemen, a polite and commercial people, and a populous extent of territory.

In an arbitrary despotic government, where the lands are at the disposal of the prince, the rules of succession, or the mode of enjoyment, must depend upon his will and pleasure. Hence there can be but few legal determinations relating to the property, the descent, or the conveyance of real estate; and the same holds in a stronger degree with regard to goods and chattels and the contracts relating thereto. Under a tyrannical sway, trade must be continually in jeopardy, and of consequence can never be extensive: this therefore puts an end to the necessity of an infinite number of rules, which the English merchant daily recurs to for adjusting commercial differences. Marriages there usually are contracted with slaves; or at least women are treated as such: no laws can be therefore expected to regulate the rights of dower, jointures, and marriage settlements. Few also are the persons who can claim the privileges of any laws; the bulk of those nations, viz., the commonalty boors, or peasants, being merely villeins and bondmen. Those are therefore left to the private coercion of their lords, are esteemed (in the contemplation of those boasted legislators) incapable of either right or injury, and of consequence are entitled to no redress. We may see, in these arbitrary states, how large a field of legal contests is already rooted up and destroyed.

In like manner we may lastly observe, that, in petty states and narrow territories, much fewer laws will suffice than in large ones, because there are fewer objects upon which the laws can operate. The regulations of a private family are short and well known; those of a prince's household are necessarily more various and diffuse.

❖

CHAPTER TWO

Law and Custom

. . . Our rules of law are strongly influenced by our society's informal rules of behavior . . . rules of law in turn strongly influence the informal rules of behavior. . . . This process of interaction is a very complex phenomenon. In a general way, however, it may be assumed that the most compelling of the cultural values held by a society will rise to the level of formal rules of law; the less compelling values will be less likely to do so.

The Reasons for Law

THE EXISTENCE of formal legal institutions is invariably found among civilized societies. Why? Some of the more basic reasons are suggested by the following paragraph, an account of a period of lawlessness during the reign of England's King Stephen.

LAWLESSNESS DURING THE REIGN OF KING STEPHEN [1]

. . . You might go a whole day's journey and you would never find a man in a village or land being tilled.

Every powerful man made his castles and held them against the King . . . and when the castles were made they filled them with devils and evil men. Then they seized those men who they supposed had any possessions, both by night and day, men and women, and put them to prison for their gold and silver, and tortured them with unspeakable tortures. . . . Many thousands they killed with hunger. I neither can nor may tell all the horrors and all the tortures that

[1] Winston Churchill, quoting a "monk of Peterborough," *A History of the English-Speaking Peoples* (New York: Dodd, Mead & Company, 1946), Vol. 1, 193 pp.

11

they did to the wretched men of this land. And it lasted the nineteen winters while Stephen was King; and ever it was worse. They laid gelds (taxes) on the villages from time to time and called it "Tenserie"; when the wretched men had no more to give they robbed and burnt all the villages, so that you might go a whole day's journey and you would never find a man in a village or land being tilled. Then was corn dear, and meat and cheese and butter, because there was none in the land. Wretched men starved of hunger; some went seeking alms who at one time were rich men; others fled out of the land. . . . Wheresoever men tilled the earth bare no corn, for the land was all ruined by such deeds; and they said that Christ and his saints were asleep.

✧

In England, during the Middle Ages, all law was held to stem from the sovereign person—that is, the king—and when the king died, all laws were suspended until a new king had been crowned. The same sorts of conditions as described in the reading above always resulted during the interregnum following the death of a king. Even today, under special conditions when the usual rules of civilized living do not apply, as between combatants during war, or when the protection of the law is deliberately removed—as it was from minority groups and prisoners in Europe during the last war—the most horrible abuses seem inevitably to follow.

ESKIMO LEGAL INSTITUTIONS [2]

. . . [feuds] can go on indefinitely, and . . . the . . . state of peace and rectitude is very difficult to arrive at by means of it.

. . . Feud occurs when the principle [of] self-help gets out of hand. In self-help, if I injure you, you kill me. However, my brother is likely to say that the two injuries are not equivalent, and hence he has to take revenge, so he kills you by shooting you in the back. Then your brother says that you killed me in open combat, but my brother killed you by a sneaking low trick, so things are still not evened up, and your brother then kills my brother. This can go on indefinitely, and the feud thus ceases to be a jural mechanism of self-help. You get a new and different series of event. Here is no jural mechanism, because the group or series of social acts that results in correction is never reached. Thus, though feud or threat of feud is a type of counteraction found very widespread throughout the world, it is usually found to be a faulty jural mechanism, because the almost universally desired state of peace and rectitude is very difficult to arrive at by means of it.

✧

[2] Paul Bohannan, *Social Anthropology* (New York: Holt, Rinehart & Winston, Inc., 1963), p. 290.

Law serves the function of aiding us in the pursuit of our personal objectives by providing a peaceful setting in which we may act. Without this peaceful setting, as the previous readings suggest, we would devote most of our effort to defending ourselves, our families, and our property. Very little effort could be devoted to promoting other interests of our own or of our society.

Some conflict is unavoidable within any group, if for no better reason than that man's desires seem to be unlimited, but the means to fulfillment are limited, whether the desire be fame, power, or economic goods. In order to allocate these and other like things among competitors, resort may be to force or resort may be to a set of rules that restrict the types of competition that are permissible to various peaceful means. For a society to progress or even survive the latter alternative must be adopted. It seems to be true that a house divided against itself cannot stand.

Conflict also arises within a society, because although each of us has desires that might be ranked as a series of priorities, not all of the members of the society adhere to the same set of priorities. All members usually agree that they must work together to achieve some goals, but they often differ as to what the goals should be. Thus, most people evidently place a higher priority on national defense than on low taxes; with others the order is reversed. Some individuals place a high priority upon conformity and seek regulation of religious and political views; others place so high a priority upon freedom of action that virtually no regulation of any kind meets with their approval. In order for groups of people with conflicting views to live together in reasonable harmony, it is necessary for them to accept a rule of law, which has attempted to find a balance between divergent views, and for them to accept that rule of law even when not completely agreeing with it.

The fact that people are willing to obey the law even when it is contrary to some of their values or interests means that members of society will be able to work together to solve the major problems of the society: providing for defense, food, clothing, and shelter. In effect, the members of the society are each sacrificing some of their low-priority desires in recognition of the fact that this is necessary if high-priority problems may be jointly solved. When a problem of the highest priority appears, we are usually able to meet it. It is an observable fact that in times of common danger most people are able to forget even major differences and work together to overcome the common danger.

The benefits of living in a society regulated by a well-organized and democratic legal system appear obvious, despite the inherent lack of perfection the legal system may share with all human institutions. And on the whole our legal system would appear to be so successful that the amount of criticism directed at our law and our lawyers seems rather surprising.

Rules and Law

A *rule,* in the sense used here, is a term meaning a prearranged and consistently applied guide to making a decision.

When we speak of a *law* we mean a rule or body of rules that is interpreted and enforced through the machinery of the government. Not all rules are law, but virtually all law is based upon rules. A legal system consists of the procedures devised for formulating such laws, for applying them, and for interpreting them.

Theoretically, and to some extent actually, so long as there is a powerful authority able to dictate to a group of subjects, law could arise solely from arbitrary decrees. In some nations, most law does. Law might, at the opposite extreme, arise solely from a majority or representative vote. But in either case there is some value in informing the populace as to what is expected of it by laying down some rules of behavior. Human organization requires consistency, and law is the formal process by which consistency is obtained.

The first and most obvious advantage of consistency is that of efficiency. Whether we examine a legal system, or some other area of activity, the complexity of most areas of human affairs is such that we cannot afford to analyze every situation and work out a unique means of dealing with it. We comb our hair, brush our teeth, and shave in about the same way every day, leaving our powers of reasoning to cope with new problems. This is also why form letters are used, why assembly lines are set up, why formulas are used in mathematics, and incidentally why precedents are relied upon in dealing with legal problems.

The second advantage in the use of rules is as important as the first but is less widely recognized. Adoption of consistent ways of doing things permits us to predict the behavior of others in instances in which it is important that we do so. We take our place at the rear of a line because it is our expectation that others will do the same rather than trying to crowd ahead. We keep to the right when approaching a car from the opposite direction because we expect that the other car will do the same. Members of a basketball team are able to, and indeed find it necessary to, make very complex predictions as to the reactions both of the referee and of their teammates in various situations. Businessmen may predict that their competition will not ordinarily resort to certain tactics. And they may predict that ordinarily their contracts will be performed by their opposite party.

This aspect of law was discussed by John Dickinson as follows: [3]

"If we examine the bulk of our regulatory legislation, it should be abundantly clear that a great deal of it has no relation whatever to questions of

[3] John Dickinson, "Legislation and the Effectiveness of Law," *American Bar Association Journal* (October 1931), p. 648.

morality or honesty, but is simply designed to insure that particular acts shall be done in a particular way, in one way rather than some other possible way, in order that other persons who are likely to be affected by the acts in question may have a basis for what to expect, may know what to count on, and may thus be enabled to shape their conduct accordingly. This is illustrated, for example, by the vast volume of traffic regulations. No question of morality is involved in whether it is to be lawful for the driver of an automobile to make a left-hand turn at a corner or whether the rear light of a vehicle is to be red or green. The driver is made to do one thing rather than another not because one is morally good and the other morally evil, but in order that other persons may have a reasonable basis for expectation as to which of the two things he will in fact do, and may thus by their own efforts keep out of his way. The same purpose underlies many of the requirements of our corporation laws and laws regulating the marketing of agricultural and manufactured products. Their design is not to make men good, but to supply individuals with a basis of expectation, and therefore with reasonable grounds of action in a world where methods of action change so rapidly that standard types of conduct upon which others can rely have slight chance to grow up and acquire the force of customs."

Of course, not all of our expectations are rational. We do not expect others to eat peas with a knife, and are somewhat upset if they do simply because we are not accustomed to having this "rule" violated. Yet, there are reasons for being ill at ease when engaged in dealings with those operating under rules different from ours. To the degree that their rules are unknown to us we are unable to predict their behavior; we do not know how to reach an understanding, nor can we be sure that an understanding will have the effect we think it will. We realize that those operating under different rules may have the same misgivings in regard to us.

Influence of Culture upon Law

Possibly the most basic reason for law is to maintain order and stability. Even when the needs of order and stability have been met, however, human aspirations go far beyond this. It is possible to live in a stable society characterized by terroristic government, where those in power may condemn on mere suspicion or in order to settle a private grudge. However, most of us, it seems, would prefer to live under a government of law rather than of men, where prosecution may be obtained only when certain defined acts have been committed, and then, only after following a prescribed procedure. And most of us would not feel a procedure was fair unless a conviction were based upon evidence and unless the accused had an opportunity to be heard, and heard before an impartial judge and jury.

These statements apply to the criminal law, but they also apply in principle to all other areas of law as well. We want a legal system that not only assures a stable society but that in addition attains certain more specific ends that we consider desirable. The end discussed above could be described as that of "fair treatment of the accused." But there are a considerable number of other ends we would like our legal system to accomplish.

Speaking of these other ends collectively as *an* end, however, the end of our law, aside from providing stability, is to give effect as much as possible to the ideas of right and morality, the customarily approved behavior patterns, which are generally accepted by our society.

Human societies differ immensely in the various nonlegal codes of behavior to which they adhere, but they are alike in one respect: they have all adopted standards of conduct of one sort or another. These standards are *not* necessarily imposed by some central authority, but in fact often arise spontaneously or to serve some purpose now forgotten, as to express pride in belonging to the group, or to provide an orderly way of carrying out cooperative activities, or merely in response to superstition. These are the informal rules that dictate much of the daily routine of mankind everywhere. These rules are known by such terms as *tradition, custom, mores,* and *habits.* We will refer to all of these types of rules collectively as custom.

Our means of greeting, dressing, eating, and speaking are based on custom. Our attitudes on race, religion, and politics are for the most part the products of the customary attitudes of the groups with which we have identified ourselves. Some customs are even more local, for example, those shared by students of particular colleges or fraternities or those shared by old, well-decorated army regiments. Much of the everyday routine in a business or government office is governed merely by patterns of custom into which the employees have fallen, without specific direction or official enforcement. Some cultural patterns incorporate values to which the group is so strongly attached as to be almost impervious to change. The values incorporated by custom provide the roots that give meaning to the lives of most individuals.

THE SCIENCE OF CUSTOM [4]

> . . . *The life history of the individual is first and foremost an accommodation to the patterns and standards traditionally handed down in his community.*

No man ever looks at the world with pristine eyes. He sees it edited by a definite set of customs and institutions and ways of thinking. Even in his philosophical probings he cannot go behind these stereotypes; his very concepts

[4] Ruth Benedict, *Patterns of Culture* (New York: Mentor Books, 1950), p. 2.

of the true and the false will still have references to his particular traditional customs. . . . The life history of the individual is first and foremost an accommodation to the patterns and standards traditionally handed down in his community. From the moment of his birth the customs into which he is born shape his experience and behaviour. By the time he can talk he is the little creature of his culture, and by the time he is grown and able to take part in its activities, its habits are his habits, its beliefs his beliefs, its impossibilities his impossibilities. Every child that is born into his group will share them with him, and no child born into one on the opposite side of the globe can ever achieve the thousandth part. There is no social problem it is more incumbent upon us to understand than this of the role of custom. Until we are intelligent as to its laws and varieties, the main complicating facts of human life must remain unintelligible.

❖

Custom undoubtedly influences the type of rules to which official sanction is given and which therefore emerge as laws: ideas of right and wrong are largely determined by our culture, and the law ordinarily promotes the generally accepted ideas of right and wrong.

It would be strange were it not true, and it appears certain to be true, that our rules of law are strongly influenced by our society's informal rules of behavior, and that, on the other hand, rules of law in turn strongly influence the informal rules of behavior. No doubt this process of interaction between law and custom is a very complex phenomenon. In a general way, however, it may be assumed that the most compelling of the cultural values held by a society will rise to the level of formal rules of law; the less compelling values will be less likely to do so. Interestingly, certain values that were at one time more important than at present may persist as formal rules of law but go unenforced.

As ideas of right and morality change over time, the direction of the law may be expected to follow. Change may occur either through legislation or through common-law judicial interpretation. But when law attempts to compel custom rather than to follow it, the experience is poor, as witness the prohibition experiment. When the end of the law sought does not receive strong support from society, even though a slight preponderance of opinion may desire it, difficulties in consistent enforcement may be predicted. An illustration is our antitrust legislation, which is opposed by many observers besides monopolists, and which has been undercut in the past through legislators' voting budgets inadequate to provide adequate enforcement as well as through lukewarm prosecution by some administrations. Another illustration is our body of law requiring racial integration. Strict implementation of judicial decisions calling for racial integration is made difficult by the fact that the courts in the areas most involved tend to reflect the mores of their local society, and the ideas of right and wrong as their local society sees them. The mores of the nation as a whole are in conflict with those of a region. The result is a series of legal problems that no formula can resolve with complete satisfaction. Law in the short run may guide policy, but in the long run law is a tool of policy. When there is no consistent or reasonably clear-cut policy to be implemented, devising a patchwork of law to make up for this lack is never very successful, though sometimes necessary.

QUESTIONS

1. What does the common law of Morrison County (in the reading that follows) have to do with custom?

2. What does the common law of Morrison County have to do with law?

3. What do custom and law have to do with one another?

THE COMMON LAW OF MORRISON COUNTY [5]

> *The common law of Morrison County is inconsistent at times. It suspects lawyers and "their" law represent a triumph of technicalities over common sense, but the common law of Morrison County treasures technicalities far more technical—witness the rule of the ballpoint pen.*

"There are three great branches of the law," the senior member of the Bar told me when I first arrived at the county seat. I listened respectfully, but also somewhat skeptically, as befitted a man fresh out of law school. He then elaborated: "First, there is the statutory law, the law enacted by the legislature, found in the codes and statute books; second, there is the common law, the law handed down in court decisions since before the days of Coke and found in the reported court cases; and finally, and most important, there is the common law of Morrison County."

It is now ten years later and, oh, 'tis true, 'tis true. Not all the law is in the books.

There are eighty-seven counties in Minnesota alone, each with its own distinctive common law. Each day new precedents are being set down in every county by real estate agents, bankers, justices of the peace, constables, auction sale clerks, notaries public and other prominent jurists. . . . Justice Holmes observed that the life of the common law is experience, not logic. Undoubtedly he had Morrison County in mind.

It was the common law of Morrison County that first established that no legal document signed with a ball-point pen is legal. Nobody knows who first

[5] John E. Simonett, "The Common Law of Morrison County," *American Bar Association Journal*, 49 (March 1963), pp. 263–265. Reprinted by permission of *American Bar Association Journal*.

made the ruling or why, but it stubbornly persists, and, as I understand it, the rule has spread as far east as Massachusetts.[6]

A will, of course, should not be executed on a Sunday, nor should a deed except in the direst emergency, although it is legally permissible to execute an earnest money contract on Sunday. Apparently the law succumbed to the temptation of the earnest money. Assuredly some day it will happen, human nature being what it is—the dream case—somebody will sign a will on Sunday with a ball-point pen. This will mean going to see a lawyer and paying money, which might have otherwise been used for worthwhile pursuits, to get the whole mess straightened out.

Also a will does not have to be probated. Where this notion originated has never been adequately explained. Like much of the common law, its origin is shrouded in mystery, in the legends and mores of past generations. Some say the doctrine evolved from a logical rather than a historical basis; that it was reasoned by the people of Morrison County that if a man paid a lawyer once for making the will it could hardly be expected that he, or more accurately his estate, should have to pay the lawyer a second time for probating it.

Perhaps the first legal crisis any married couple faces is when, having purchased their home, the lawyer asks how the deed should be drawn—with the husband's name alone or with both husband and wife as grantees. If the wife's name is not included on the deed, won't she, the keeper of the hearth, be without any legal rights to her own home?[7] This is at best a sticky situation, and, unless love is strong, domestic tranquillity dictates both spouses hold title. This explains why so much property is held in joint tenancy in Morrison County, or to put it more precisely, why husbands and wives hold property with an "or" between their names.

True, there is the academic objection that joint tenancy disinherits the children, that upon the father's death the property goes outright to the wife, evading any provision the father might have contemplated for his offspring. The objection is academic because it is firmly believed in Morrison County that a surviving spouse will not remarry and will always cherish the children in a pecuniary as well as a maternal, or, in the unheard of instance where the wife dies first, paternal way.

. . . [A] Morrison County jury is never influenced by sympathy for an injured plaintiff unless the defendant is insured. Since the Minnesota Supreme Court has held that it is prejudicial error to disclose to a jury that a litigant has liability insurance, local law has established the presumption that all defendants are insured. This is an irrebuttable presumption because it is usually objectionable in Minnesota to tell the jury that the defendant is not insured.

What gives the common law of Morrison County its zest and vitality is its great capacity to adapt to changing conditions. One illustration, the local law of fixtures, will suffice. It has always been understood in Morrison County that the

---

[6] Note that the author is writing tongue in cheek. This and the other "rules" that follow are the custom, not necessarily law as it would be enforced in court. But these practices may never be challenged in court!

[7] As a matter of law, this supposition is incorrect.

corn crib goes with the land and the Venetian blinds with the house. When my aunt sold her house a few years ago, she unscrewed and took with her all the light bulbs, leaving the new tenant in darkness. When I protested, she told me, first, that she was surprised her nephew had learned nothing in law school, and, second, that everybody knows the light bulbs never go with the house.

This last decade, however, presented a new and vexing problem, when television antennas began sprouting ubiquitously on rooftops. Is the television antenna, or is it not, a fixture? For several years the law was unsettled, with some real estate agents claiming the antenna stayed with the house, others disagreeing, and notaries public generally refusing to venture any opinion on the reasonable assumption that, as soon as all homes had antennas, the problem would solve itself. In any event the question today is at rest. The television antenna is a fixture which stays with the house; any realtor or notary in the county will tell you this is the law.

. . . In Morrison County administrative law is very old and there is much to say about it. There is much to say, for example, on such sensitive matters as how to call a creamery board meeting to order, how to find out when the town board will meet and where, and when not to speak at a village council meeting.

The common law pronounced by judges in reported court decisions and the common law of Morrison County are, at the same time, closely related and far apart. Both draw on the vast fund of common sense, prejudice, habits and customs of the community, and though the routes at times appear to go in different directions, they criss-cross and seek the same destination. The common law of Morrison County is aware that a set of rules and order is necessary for a community to carry on its daily business. The arena of the common law is the lawyer's office, the courtroom and the appellate judge's chambers; the arena of the uncommon law is the realtor's office, the sales barn and the street corner.

The common law is made, or at least announced, by lawyers and judges. The common law of Morrison County avoids lawyers on the grounds that lawyers cost money and why should a man consult a lawyer about something so uncomplicated as to what is right and wrong—unless he knows he is wrong.

The common law of Morrison County is inconsistent at times. It suspects lawyers and "their" law represent a triumph of technicalities over common sense, but the common law of Morrison County treasures technicalities far more technical—witness the rule of the ball-point pen.

Yet one should not think harshly of the common law of Morrison County for it serves a useful function and discharges a ready justice. Much of it is good common sense, although I have dealt here mostly with its uncommon aspects. If at times the rules are arbitrary, it is sometimes better to have an arbitrary rule than none at all, and, if at times its doctrines seem irrational, it may be because people do not always act rationally, even in Morrison County.

The common law of Morrison County recognizes, as someone once said, that the law is too important to leave to the lawyers alone. Yet lawyers need not feel slighted. Indeed, the system pays the lawyer the supreme compliment, for in matters of great moment, where an appeal is taken from the decision of the insurance agent or the notary, the appeal is taken to the attorney's office, the court of last resort. This is, in truth, a matter of trust as well as a compliment, and if at times here I have sounded a plaintive cry, it is only because each year of law practice has brought with it an increasing realization of my vast ignorance of the third great branch of the law, the kind that is not to be found in the books.

✧

LAW IN ANTE-BELLUM MISSISSIPPI [8]

> . . . the prosaic rules of the common law were not allowed to interfere with the rules of honor.

A vivid picture of society in Mississippi before the war is presented in a recent book by Mr. Reuben Davis, *Recollection of Mississippi and Mississippians,* the sole survivor of the bar of Mississippi of fifty years ago. It was the Age of Chivalry, and the prosaic rules of the common law were not allowed to interfere with the rules of honor. The result is that many things in this book give our ideas of the majesty of the law a rude shock. Murder seems to have been regarded as rather laudable than otherwise. Mr. Davis resigned his position of District Attorney to avoid prosecuting his friends for killing their fellow-citizens. He defended over two hundred charged with murder, no one of whom was hung. Perhaps this spirit of leniency was fostered by the grand carousal in which the judge and jury participated, which followed an acquittal; but of course the great reason was that every one was expected to kill those with whom he quarreled, and none would vote to hang another for doing what he himself would have done under the same circumstances. One marvels, however, that the district attorneys did not tire of indicting. Even in the presence of the court the haughty Southerner could with difficulty curb his fiery spirit. Mr. Davis, one of the most courteous, refined, and popular men in the State, tried to cut the throat of a judge for whom he had the highest respect, but whom he thought had fined him unjustly. In a case in which the passion of the spectators became aroused the position of the judge was precarious if his rulings displeased them. We read that a certain ruling as to the admissibility of evidence was received with a storm of indignation by the spectators. "Yells, curses, and even tears attested the fervor of their emotions. The court saw its danger and hastily recalled the witness." We must be careful, however, not to assume that justice was administered after the frontier style. Cases like the above were the rare exception. All the technicalities of the common law pleading were in full force; the law, except in the case of homicide, was effectively administered, and we are assured that fraud and corruption of all kinds were detested.

✧

[8] Editors, *Harvard Law Review,* Cambridge, Mass. (1891), 4, p. 90.

FRONTIER JUSTICE [9]

No culprit has ever been known to remain after a second visit.

[*The narrator is an Englishman who is describing his tour in 1822 through Indiana, Illinois, and Missouri*]

After leaving Carlyle, I took the Shawnee town road, that branches off to the S.E., and passed the Walnut Hills, and Moore's Prairie. These two places had a year or two before been infested by a notorious gang of robbers and forgers, who had fixed themselves in these wild parts, in order to avoid justice. As the country became more settled, these desperadoes became more and more troublesome. The inhabitants therefore took that method of getting rid of them, that had been adopted not many years ago in Hopkinson and Henderson counties, Kentucky, and which is absolutely necessary in new and thinly settled districts, where it is almost impossible to punish a criminal according to legal forms.

On such occasions therefore, all the quiet and industrious men of a district form themselves into companies, under the name of "Regulators." They appoint officers, put themselves under their orders, and bind themselves to assist and stand by each other. The first step they then take is to send notice to any notorious vagabonds, desiring them to quit the State in a certain number of days, under the penalty of receiving a domiciliary visit. Should the person who receives the notice refuse to comply, they suddenly assemble, and when unexpected, go in the night time to the rogue's house, take him out, tie him to a tree, and give him a severe whipping, every one of the party striking him a certain number of times.

This discipline is generally sufficient to drive off the culprit. But should he continue obstinate, and refuse to avail himself of another warning, the Regulators pay him a second visit, inflict a still severer whipping, with the addition probably of cutting off both his ears. No culprit has ever been known to remain after a second visit. For instance, an old man, the father of a family, all of whom he educated as robbers, fixed himself at Moore's Prairie, and committed numerous thefts, etc. etc. He was hardy enough to remain after the first visit, when both he and his sons received a whipping. At the second visit the Regulators punished him very severely, and cut off his ears. This drove him off, together with his whole gang; and travellers can now pass in perfect safety where it was once dangerous to travel alone.

There is also a company of Regulators near Vincennes, who had broken up a notorious gang of coiners and thieves who had fixed themselves near that place. These rascals, before they were driven off, had parties settled at different distances in the woods, and thus held communication and passed horses and stolen goods from one to another, from the Ohio to Lake Erie, and from thence

[9] W. N. Blane, *An Excursion Through the United States and Canada, 1822–1823* (London: 1824), p. 233, as quoted in John H. Wigmore, *A Kaleidoscope of Justice* (Washington, D.C.: Washington Law Book Company, 1941), pp. 520–522.

into Canada or the New England States. Thus it was next to impossible to detect the robbers, or to recover the stolen property. . . .

This practice of *Regulating* seems very strange to an European. I have talked with some of the chief men of the Regulators, who all lamented the necessity of such a system. They very sensibly remarked, that when the country became more thickly settled, there would no longer be any necessity for such proceedings, and that they should all be delighted at being able to obtain justice in a more formal manner. I forgot to mention that the rascals punished have sometimes prosecuted the Regulators for an assault. The juries, however, knowing the bad characters of the prosecutors, would give but trifling damages, which divided among so many amounted to next to nothing for each individual.

✧

QUESTION

1. May it not have been dangerous to be a stranger, or even merely an eccentric, when the Regulators were in sway? Note the complete absence of any attempt to establish guilt, aside from deciding that someone qualified as a "notorious vagabond."

ESKIMO JUSTICE [10]

. . . the injured party goes about and asks permission from the individual members of the community to kill the outcast. . . .

There is one other sort of concerted counteraction an Eskimo community may take: it may decide that a wrongdoer must be thrown out of the local community—either by exile or, more definitively, by execution. This state is brought about by one of two means. Either the injured party goes about and asks permission from the individual members of the community to kill the outcast, or else the informal leader of the community—either the greatest hunter or the diviner . . . initiates the action, gets the permission from the entire community, and then proceeds to tell the closest kinsmen of the condemned man that they must carry out the execution, thus making sure that no feud will develop. Here, in an informal, unorganized way, is a situation that we may liken to a court. There is no officially recognized body of men enacting certain roles; nevertheless, here is organized community action. Let us call such a group a "moot" and save the word "court" for organized bodies responsible to officials in a statelike social organization. The word "moot" is an ancient Anglo-Saxon word for a group of men of the community in a sort of town meeting. It leans on community consensus. A court is a specialized and duly constituted body, appointed by the state.

✧

[10] Bohannan, *op. cit.*, p. 291.

The Reasons for Criminal, Constitutional,
and Private Law

THE SPHERE OF THE CRIMINAL LAW

The first rules or laws enforced by societies are usually those designed to protect the society from serious harm. In primitive society this sometimes took the form of punishing an individual for violating some taboo that might be expected to bring the wrath of God upon the group. This area of law, which restrains the individual from antisocial acts, is known to us as the criminal law. The criminal law consists of an elaboration of acts that are not permitted, sanctions to be evoked if the acts are committed, and a body of procedure by which the acts are proved and the punishment imposed.

In the Western world, the earliest criminal laws were designed to prevent, or at least reduce, direct physical conflict between members of the society. Not only did physical conflict reduce the possibility of cooperation toward attaining group objectives, but it actually reduced, through an occasional killing or maiming, the armed strength that the society could mobilize. And, as mentioned earlier, conflict then as now had a tendency to spread. An injury or death can lead to a feud.

Physical security in and of itself is important to us, and most of us are willing to forego our opportunity to impose upon our neighbor, in return for a means of placing a curb upon his opportunity to impose upon us. Up to the national level we and many nations have almost solved the problem of violence. It seems reasonably apparent that if we could solve this problem at the international level, by devising an effective international law, we could devote much more effort to fulfilling our other aspirations.[11] Conflict is wasteful, and law is the rational substitute for armed conflict. However, if devising a workable system of international criminal law effective against nations were not much more easily said than done, this would have been done long ago.

As a society becomes more complex, there is usually greater interdependence between members of the society and greater opportunity to injure other members of the society. More responsibility tends to be required of the individual. This, at any rate, has been the trend in the United States. Although the traditional felonies—for example, murder, arson, burglary, robbery, and rape—have been retained as part of our criminal law, all sorts of regulations involving traffic, business conduct, sanitation, hunting, and maintenance of pets, to cite a few areas affecting the ordinary citizen, have been added to our body of criminal law. Criminal law used to be restricted in its applications to deliberate wrongdoers. Today, any of us may run

---

[11] At present, about two thirds of our federal budget is spent for defense.

afoul of the regulations that are included, technically, as part of the criminal law.

Innovations seem to lead to greater regulation. Without the automobile, we would all be regulated much less, for surely traffic regulation is one of the most pervasive areas of the law at the present time. On the other hand, our activity would be sharply curtailed in other ways if we did not have the automobile or if we had the automobile but no traffic regulation at all. Possibly, as the reading that follows seems to suggest, the impact of culture upon law tends to be overestimated. The exact relationship between our culture and our law may be debated, for the subject is not accessible to objective proof. The reader will therefore have to form his own opinion.

THE LIMITS OF CUSTOM AS A MEANS OF REGULATION [12]

So far as custom can operate, it is certainly a more reliable and effective agency for guiding expectations of conduct than law can ever be, but we do not sufficiently realize that custom is essentially the product of a small-moving and static society and that its effectiveness is paralyzed when change goes forward at such a rate that customs have no time to form, much less to take root.

In a simple society where most men are engaged in the same types of activity, and where these remain stereotyped from generation to generation, standards of conduct can become rooted as customs so that no deliberate and artificial regulations by enacted law are necessary. But in a changing society where individuals are constantly shifting from one narrowly specialized activity to another, and where the methods and technique of any given activity are subject to constant alteration and improvement, customs have small opportunity to become well-established, and individuals are not in a position to have customs ingrained in them by habit. We often hear it said that many matters which we attempt to deal with by law should properly be left to custom. So far as custom can operate, it is certainly a more reliable and effective agency for guiding expectations of conduct than law can ever be, but we do not sufficiently realize that custom is essentially the product of a slow-moving and static society and that its effectiveness is paralyzed when change goes forward at such a rate that customs have no time to form, much less to take root.

Are there there any considerations which enable the legislator to determine in advance what standards of conduct can be made effective by governmental action and what standards on the other hand men will refuse to conform to in spite of the threat of penalties?

[12] Dickinson, *op. cit.,* pp. 648–649.

On this point it is usual to say that no legal standard will or can be effective which is in advance of the general and customary habits and practices of the community—that law, in other words, cannot be in advance of usage. I suggest that here again we are in the presence of an oversimplification. In a rough way, the view just stated is sound, but only if reduced to the tautology that a law cannot be enforced if it cannot be enforced. Consider the difficulty of determining what we mean when we talk of the existing practice or usage beyond which law cannot advance. In a complex modern society, made up of numerous layers of individuals differing widely in training, intelligence and occupation, there is the widest range of usage on many of the matters with which law has to deal and a wide variety of views and opinions as to what is just and fair and careful in any given set of circumstances. How shall we tell which special brand of usage or opinion out of this variety and diversity is the "normal" one beyond which law may not advance? Shall we try to count noses and allow a temporary majority always to prevail? Is not the usage of an active and aggressive minority often on the way to being imitated and thus becoming the usage of next year's majority? How shall we say that there is a usage at all where the matter in question concerns only a small part of the community and where there are differences of usage within even that restricted group? In short, when we talk of usage we are not dealing with something fixed and stable, but with a fluid, changing, complex phenomenon which alters under our eyes while we are attempting to ascertain it, and this is why we get so little real or substantial aid when we seek the proper standard of the effectiveness of law in a supposed "normal" standard of extra-legal practice.

It is well that this should be so. Where customary practice is so uniform and stable on the part of practically the entire community as to amount of custom in the real and effective sense of the word, then it is true that there is little possibility of improvement or change through the medium of law, or for that matter by any other means. This is why custom-ridden societies always become stagnant and tend, as Walter Bagehot long ago pointed out, to be eliminated in the struggle for survival. If the world they live in alters, the strength of custom keeps them from adapting themselves by law or otherwise to their new environment. By way of illustration we can note the case of British India where this seems to be one of the principal sources of difficulty at the present time. The cake of custom in such instances is encased in so hard a rind that there is no opening for any force making for improvement to insert an effective entering wedge. On the other hand in a society already mobile and diversified like the industrial nations of western civilization, the varieties and layers of usage existing side by side and competing for adoption create an opening for law to put its force behind one usage rather than another, and thus to enter the field as one of the factors, and a very powerful factor, making for the promotion of certain practices and the abandonment of others. The diversity of existing practices, at the same time that it prevents there being any norm of practice to which law is compelled to conform, makes it possible to employ law as an agency for supporting and extending the practice which ethically or economically seems in advance of the others.

✧

THE SPHERE OF CONSTITUTIONAL LAW

A grant of power to the public authorities for the purpose of maintaining the peace through the enforcement of the criminal law creates new problems. A police force must be built up to deal with crime. Control of the police is usually control of the state. What is to prevent the authorities from arbitrary and capricious actions in the exercise of their power? What is to prevent the authorities from using the police as a means of perpetuating their power? As a matter of fact, misuse of police power is common in many parts of the world. Men in power usually attempt to remain in power, by fair means or by the usual methods. When they do not, we must concede that something remarkable has occurred. There are not very many functioning democracies in the world today.

The evidence seems to demonstrate that no man is good enough to govern any other, yet anarchy does not seem to be an ideal solution to the problems of governing. The best solution to the dilemma presented by the evils of government on the one side, and the evils of anarchy on the other, has been the development of a system of limitations upon governmental power. The ruler may rule, but he must rule according to prescribed rules, not by prerogative. This is the meaning of the statement *a government of law, not of men.* Men may be in offices of power, yet they may exercise their power only along certain established channels. The limitations to the power of those governing our nation are set out in our state and federal constitution. Our constitutional law consists largely of a description of the channels by which the powers of government may be utilized and the extent of these powers. In addition, it sets out the basic rights of the governed. More is said on this subject on page 60 and following.

THE SPHERE OF PRIVATE LAW

Assuming a system of criminal law has been developed through which a government prevents private citizens from abusing one another, and a system of constitutional law has been developed to prevent excesses on the part of the govenment, how are private citizens to resolve their disputes? Prior to adoption of a criminal law, disputes between individuals could be resolved by pure physical power, or through intimidation based on physical power.

If power is removed as a structuring force, what is to take its place? The answer must be the creation of a body of law designed for the express purpose of settling private disputes. Rules are established to regulate the distribution and acquisition of property, to define marital relations, to enforce contracts between parties, to provide a means of compensation for injuries inflicted by one private person upon another, and to settle most of the other questions that commonly bring men at odds with one another.

In summary, the role of our private law is to reduce conflict between individuals, by setting up standards, in the form of laws, that may be applied to decide a dispute in favor of one party or the other. In fact, the existence of rules of law provides the parties with a means of ascertaining their rights in advance, so that they may arrange their affairs in conformance with the law, and settle their affairs without recourse to formal hearings. The details of these laws are strongly influenced by the particular cultural milieu.

LAW AND MORALITY [13]

The problem of the legislator is misconceived . . . by simply saying that law cannot make men honest or moral. . . .

So far we have been speaking of legislative regulations which have no direct reference to issues of morality, but much of our regulatory legislation does go further and concerns itself with questions of fair dealing, justice, honesty, carefulness and the like. Admitting that these moral qualities cannot be legislated into human beings by *fiat* of the state, does it necessarily follow that such legislation is futile and meddlesome? In other words, where legislation holds men to certain standards of conduct which have moral implications, must it be said that the purpose of such legislation is to instill into them the moral qualities on which such standards are based, and that since moral qualities cannot be created by law, the legislation is therefore bad? I know of no subject on which there is more widespread confusion than this, or where over-simplification of thought is more in evidence.

Perhaps the most direct way of clarifying the issue is to consider the ordinary common law rules as to fraud and negligence. The conception of fraud certainly carries with it strong moral implications, just as the conception of negligence carries with it an implication of the mental attitude which we describe as carelessness. Is it proper to say that the object of the legal rules which establish liability for fraud and negligence is to instill into individuals the qualities of honesty and carefulness? Even if indirectly and in the long run they may possibly have some tendency to promote that result, it seems clear that their primary object is a different one. Primarily, their object is simply to provide that certain types of external conduct shall be followed by certain legal consequences of a deterrent character. They do not aim, in other words, to produce an honest frame of mind on the part of dishonest persons. They merely give notice that if conduct does not measure up to a certain external standard of honesty or carefulness, consequences will ensue of a character probably regarded as undesirable by the person who fails to meet the prescribed standard. In other words, the aim of the law is not to accomplish the hopeless task of altering human character, but merely to insist on conformity of conduct to a

[13] Dickinson, *ibid.,* pp. 648–649.

standard deemed advisable for the protection of the other individuals who compose the community. If an individual fails or refuses to measure up to that standard, all that the law can do and all that it undertakes to do is to make him pay a penalty in the form of damages or otherwise. There is no reason to suppose that this last is impossible, or that the resulting protection to the community is rendered nugatory, simply because it happens to be impossible for the law to instill morality into the culprit.

The problem of the legislator is misconceived, and the central difficulty of regulatory legislation obscured, by simply saying that law cannot make men honest or moral, and letting the matter go at that. The real difficulty is a different one. It is the difficulty of determining how high a standard of conduct regulatory legislation can reasonably require with any hope of being effective. It is impossible for law to hold men to conformity with a standard so much more strict than that to which they are willing to conform that the difficulties of enforcement will prove insuperable. This is the problem of what may be called the effectiveness of law.

✧

CHAPTER THREE

The History and Characteristics
of the Common Law

*. . . The common law, therefore, is not a written law. . . .
In each decision, the judges profess to decide according to the
view reported in a similar case. They do not claim to decide
according to abstract justice. . . .*[1]

Origin and Use of the Term *Common Law*

THE TERM *common law* is sometimes used to suggest the presence of
democratic institutions. Strangely, however, the origin of the term has
nothing to do with the common man. The adjective *common* came to be
adopted when, some years after the Norman invasion of England and following the creation of a central judicial system by Norman kings, the same
body of law began for the first time to be applied uniformly in all the
realms of England, by the judges of the king's courts. This body of law,
being common to all of England, was called the common law.

The term *common law* is confusing because it is used in two different
ways. First, it is used to describe the legal system that originated in England
and spread to the United States, Canada, New Zealand, Australia, and
some of the new British dominions. Used in this sense, the term distin-
guishes our legal system from the other major legal system, the civil law, a
system based largely upon detailed written codes, traceable to Roman origin though extensively modified and supplemented since the days of Impe-
rial Rome. The civil law is presently in force in the Continental European

---

1 Henri Levy-Ullman, *The English Legal Tradition* (London: Macmillan and Co.,
Ltd., 1935), p. 4; quoting Jeremy Bentham as he was quoted by Etienne Dumont in
De l'Organisation judicaire et de la codification, from a section headed "De l'Incon-
venient des lois non escrites" ("The Inconvenience of the Unwritten Law").

countries and their colonies past and present, including all of South America, and, in addition, in Japan and Turkey.

The term *common law* is also used to describe that component of our law that is based upon judicial precedent rather than upon legislation. The ordinary citizen tends to think of the "law" in terms of legislative enactments. This may therefore strike some as surprising, but, in fact, large areas of our law (tort and contract, for example) are still mainly the product of judicial precedent rather than statutes. For centuries almost all of the English law was based upon judicial precedents. Only in comparatively recent times has legislation begun to eclipse our common law in significance. Our body of common law is also known as our "unwritten law." The term *unwritten* is not strictly accurate, because every precedent is explained by a written opinion that is compiled for reference in the large volumes that line the walls of lawyers' offices. It is not "written" as a precise statute, however, as is our legislation.

Confusion occasionally results because today, when one refers to "common law," he may be referring to the entire Anglo-American legal system or he may be referring to our body of "unwritten law" as distinguished from our legislation.

Common Law and Civil Law: A Contrast of Legal Systems

There has been considerable debate between proponents of the common law and those of the civil law as to which provides the better approach to the solution of legal problems. Much of the argument reminds one of a debate between a theoretical scientist and a practical engineer. The civil code jurist is the more theoretical of the two. His ideas of law begin with philosophical ideas of the nature of law, from which certain abstract principles of justice are derived and applied to particular cases. The civil law is deductive in orientation and based to a large extent on pure reason.

The common law is more pragmatic. A common-law jurist begins his inquiry into the law by searching for precedents [2]—that is, authoritative reports on how the courts have decided similar cases in the past, the earliest case decisions often being based upon the custom of the people. After enough precedents have been set to clearly delineate the legal problem involved, a general legal principle begins to evolve that may be applied directly or by analogy in deciding other cases. Thus, the common law is inductive, reasoning from the particular to the general.

The civil law may boast of greater logical symmetry; the common law may

[2] Our system of precedents is often referred to as the doctrine of stare decisis, which, translated from Latin, means "to abide by or adhere to decided cases."

be, however, more in tune with the needs and desires of the people, less autocratic in philosophy, concerned more with adjusting the law to the living patterns of the governed rather than forcing society into a preconceived mold.

What is your custom? Do the precedents based upon your custom still make sense? These are the inquiries of the common-law jurist. It might be argued that the civil law judge, given the power and the responsibility for determining "God-like" what is just, would naturally tend to develop a more authoritarian law than the common-law jurist. The tendency appears to have been in this direction.

To give the flavor of the debate between the two great legal systems, the civil law and the common law, various writers are quoted below. Because the readings were selected by a writer strongly biased in favor of the common law, it is no coincidence that the exponents of the common law may seem to get the better of the argument.

IMPRESSIONS OF JAPANESE LEGAL TRAINING [3]

> . . . We Japanese . . . are capable of systematizing and philoso-
> phizing. You Americans . . . deal with concrete cases, which are
> small and simple, rather than with ideas, which are big and diffi-
> cult.

A Japanese friend once expressed to me his conclusion about Japanese and American law professors. "We Japanese," he told me, "are thinkers. We are capable of systematizing and philosophizing. You Americans, by contrast, are immature. You deal with concrete cases, which are small and simple, rather than with ideas, which are big and difficult." "I do not assert," he added graciously, "that Americans are wholly incapable of thought. Rather, they simply avoid it."

Now, I do not deny that some Americans (including me) avoid the hardest of all work, namely, thinking. And I do not deny that some Japanese do systematize and philosophize. But my friend overstated his case at both ends. Many Japanese do not think, and a few Americans do. Nevertheless, it is probably fair to say that a large number of Japanese jurists (though not all) like to regard themselves as philosophers and a large number of American jurists (though not all) like to think of themselves as "practical" men. Japanese legal scholars, it seems to me, tend to base their conclusions on deductive reasoning, enriched by their own meditation or (more often) their recollection of some scholar's meditation. By contrast, American legal scholars often, though far from invariably, aspire to be "legal scientists" and to use the scientist's method of organizing facts on the basis of the observed or supposed

[3] Walter Gellhorn, "Impressions of Japanese Legal Training," *Columbia Law Review* (1958), pp. 1239–1240.

relationships among these facts. This involves no less thought (in my estimation) than does "philosophizing." It means merely that the scholar proceeds from the particular to the general, rather than the other way around.

Both of these methods have much merit. In my opinion, however, the deductive approach can be overdone, and, especially, can be too readily counterfeited by men who in fact are not thinking at all, though they talk as if they were. . . .

Stung by the remarks of the Japanese friend whom I quoted earlier, I snapped back at him in impolite words like these: "The trouble with a lot of your Japanese legal philosophers is that they do not systematize anything for themselves but simply follow some earlier 'authority's' systematizing. They do not think; they merely echo other men's thought. They are abstract, to be sure, and they prefer to deal with generalities rather than specifics. But they too readily confuse abstractness with thought, instead of recognizing that it is merely an avoidance of the world's realities. They can deal in generalities—and thus seem to be 'theoretical'—when all they are doing is to be theoretically descriptive of things that do not actually exist. They would be better off if they exposed themselves to some fresh material, and tried to discover its significance." Of course, I was being very rude, and just as unfair as my friend had been.

THE ENGLISH LEGAL TRADITION [4]

> . . . [The judges] claim to be mere mouthpieces of law derived from previous decisions.

The law of those two countries [England and English-speaking America] is divided into two unequal parts: one is called the common law (loi commune), an odd way of describing a body of legal rules assumed rather than known to have a legitimate basis, which has again and again been put forward by the judges as the source of their decisions. These decisions in turn, treated as precedents, have come to form a body of juridical rules which has served as the basis for later decisions. . . . The common law, therefore, is not a written law. . . . In each decision, the judges profess to decide according to the view reported in a similar case. They do not claim to decide according to abstract justice; on the contrary, they would reject the suggestion as insulting to their office; they claim to be mere mouthpieces of law derived from previous decisions. Readers are now in possession of the facts and in a position to understand the arguments against this method of judging. . . .

✧

[4] Levy-Ullman, loc. cit., p. 30.

METHODS OF DETERMINING LEGAL DISPUTES [5]

. . . Thus often arises secret intimidation, enforced confessions, torture, and blackmailed pleas of guilty. These sinister dangers were extinguished from the Common Law of England more than six centuries ago.

. . . The English speaking peoples began to devise methods of determining legal disputes which survive in substance to this day. A man can only be accused of a civil or criminal offense which is clearly defined and known to the law. The judge is an umpire. He adjudicates on such evidence as the parties choose to produce. Witnesses must testify in public and on oath. They are examined and cross-examined, not by the judge, but by the litigants themselves or their legally qualified and privately hired representatives. The truth of their testimony is weighed not by the judge [but] by twelve good men and true, and it is only when this jury has determined the facts that the judge is empowered to impose sentence, punishment, or penalty according to the law. All might seem very obvious, even a platitude, until one contemplates the alternative system which still dominates a large portion of the world. Under Roman law, and systems derived from it, a trial in these turbulent centuries, and in some countries even to-day, is often an inquisition. The judge makes his investigation into the civil wrong or the public crime, and such investigation is largely uncontrolled. The suspect can be interrogated in private. He must answer all questions put to him. His right to be represented by a legal adviser is restricted. The witnesses against him can testify in secret and in his absence. And only when these processes have been accomplished is the accusation or charge against him formulated and published.

Thus often arises secret intimidation, enforced confessions, torture, and blackmailed pleas of guilty. These sinister dangers were extinguished from the Common Law of England more than six centuries ago. By the time Henry II's great-grandson, Edward I, had died, English criminal and civil procedure had settled into a mold and tradition which in the mass govern the English-speaking people to-day. In all claims and disputes, whether they concerned the grazing lands of the Middle West, the oilfields of California, the sheepruns and goldmines of Australia, or the territorial rights of Maorise, these rules have obtained, at any rate in theory, according to the procedure and mode of trial evolved by the English Common Law.

[5] Winston Churchill, *A History of the English-Speaking Peoples,* Vol. 1 (New York: Dodd, Mead & Company, 1946), pp. 222–223. Reprinted by permission of Dodd, Mead & Company from *A History of the English-Speaking Peoples—Volume I: The Birth of Britain* by Winston Churchill. Copyright © 1956 by The Right Honourable Sir Winston Churchill, K.G.O.M., C.H., M.P. Permission also granted by Cassell and Company, Ltd., and McClelland and Stewart Limited.

A Historical Sketch of the Common Law

In order to understand the nature of the common law, some discussion of its historical development is necessary. A complete history would require hundreds of pages. The ensuing discussion will confine itself to mentioning a few of the turning points.

First, when did the history of the common law really begin? Britons, Romans, Britons again, Anglo-Saxons, Danes, and more Anglo-Saxons in turn controlled England before the period of the Norman kings, under whom the common law became a recognizable institution. Did any substantial body of the common law come from those earlier sources? So far as formal legal institutions—court organization, procedure, and rules of jurisdiction—the answer appears to be that virtually nothing in existence now can be traced back before the Norman Conquest in 1066.

Conceivably, some of the customs that later became absorbed into the rules of the common law dealing with property, marriage, or trade may have already been a part of the traditions of the Anglo-Saxons during the centuries in which they were establishing themselves in England, at the expense of the Britons. This is, of course, difficult to establish. Although custom did play a significant part in the formation of the common law, tracing particular rules of law back to particular customs is not an easy matter.

We will begin with a discussion of the legal institutions as they were during the later days of the Anglo-Saxon kings, about 100 years before the Norman Conquest.

By this time the courts fell into a reasonably definite pattern. England was organized into shires, and each shire was composed of two or more "hundreds." The hundred did not consist of a definite number of persons but varied considerably from one section of England to another. The hundred was simply the smallest administrative unit.

The hundred had a court attached, and certain of the landowners had an obligation to appear as a body for the purpose of hearing and settling disputes of their neighbors. A court was also attached to the shire, a larger administrative unit presided over by the head of the shire, the sheriff. This was called the county court. The court of the hundred and the county court were not a lower court and a court of appeal, strangely enough. The less important folk patronized the court of the hundred, and the more important, the county court. Both courts relied heavily upon local custom in their decisions, but also incorporated legislation enacted by the king into the law they administered. Both courts were seriously defective in that appearance for trial was practically voluntary in civil cases, and could be avoided by the rich and powerful. Certain pressures against those refusing to submit to the jurisdiction of the court were available. The king's protection might be removed from those refusing to appear, or permission might be extended to the other party in the suit to seize the recalcitrant party's property and retain it until he appeared in court. Such remedies would obviously be less effective against the powerful men of the community than against the common folk.

Means of proof were also primitive, consisting of such tests as requiring a litigant to hold a hot iron—if three days later no burn was evident he was presumed truthful; or he was thrown into a pond—if he sank, it was presumed his Maker was willing to receive him and he was truthful. (He was not required to drown, only to sink momentarily.) In later years the Normans, under whom these courts continued to function, introduced trial by battle and wager of law. The latter provided that litigants could prove their case by getting various witnesses to swear that the litigant was truthful. The one with the most, and the most important, witnesses won. Neither of these institutions was much of an improvement. (The jury was not adopted as a fact-finding body until later.)

During the ascendancy of the Anglo-Saxons, legislation was enacted by the king, or by the king supported by an assembly of the leading nobles, termed the Witan. The Witan was nearly the only organ of administration developed by the Anglo-Saxon kings. It provided a forum in which policies common to kings and nobles might be devised, and cooperation of the nobles begged or coerced by the king, depending upon his strength. Most legislation, however, consisted of little more than lists of forbidden acts and the corresponding penalties.

Following the Norman invasion in 1066, the Norman kings were also dependent in varying degrees upon the new nobility—a Norman nobility placed in power after the conquest. The Norman kings, too, frequently summoned the leading nobles for meetings of state. The meetings came to consist of a definite body of nobles who more or less represented the interests of the nobility as a whole. It met at regular intervals. The group was at first similar to the Anglo-Saxon Witan, but came to be a much more elaborate organization. This body became known as the King's Council, or the *Curia Regis*.

At the time of the Norman Conquest the problems of government certainly demanded better governmental organization than had been previously known in England. Peaceful accommodation had to be made between the Norman aristocracy and the Anglo-Saxon majority. War with France was practically chronic. Welshmen, Scotsmen, and Irishmen had to be dealt with by war or by guile. Although the king and the nobles together represented most of the political power of England, their interests coincided only in some respects and collided head-on in others. The king was almost totally dependent upon the nobles for levies of money and men; the nobles needed the king to maintain some degree of internal harmony and to lead the country against foreign invaders or in foreign military ventures. Each viewed an attempted increase in power of the other with suspicion. The king was more powerful than any single noble but much less powerful than a coalition of nobles. The English kings had to play off one noble against the other in order to retain a degree of central authority. Much of the legislation resulting from meetings of the King's Council was an expression of balances struck between the interests of king and nobility.

One of the most important gifts the Norman invaders brought to England was an aptitude for administration. As the problems of the King's Council became more complex, an efficient body of clerks and administrators became a permanent, full-time addition to the Council. This group was directly responsible to the king and soon found itself doing much of the work toward carrying out his policies.

Thus, practically all the machinery of government centered about the King's Council. (Later that part composed of the nobles evolved into a more distinct group called the Parliament. Still later, rich merchants, in a position to strike a bargain with king or nobles, became a group advisory to the Council, and eventually the commoners were formed into a separate division, ancestor to the House of Commons.)

During the first hundred years or so of the Norman rule, the kings took an active part in the judicial administration of England. They permitted the county courts and the courts of the hundred to remain essentially intact, but the kings assumed jurisdiction over crimes committed on the king's highways, settled feuds between nobles, enforced taxes and levies of men for the army, and investigated and punished treason. All of these duties were performed with the assistance of, or altogether by, the administrators of the King's Council, who developed remarkably effective means of carrying out the king's will, even in contests with the nobility. A body of legal specialists developed within the Council, steeped in knowledge of tradition and legislation. Members were soon traveling the length and breadth of the realm, in order to cope with special legal problems.

The common law was born when Henry II, to extend his authority and further unify his realm, managed to broaden the recognized power of the king to encompass all criminal acts. To hear such cases he provided a national system of courts, which, incidentally, would also hear civil cases.[6] He extended the right of trial by jury to these new courts and the jury was instantly recognized as a vast improvement over the primitive means of fact finding used in the traditional courts. Heretofore, the function of the jury

---

[6] In this usage, *civil* refers to noncriminal cases—that is, disputes between two private individuals. Unfortunately, the same word is used to refer to Continental European legal systems, thus causing much confusion.

had been solely that of special fact finding on matters of royal concern. The king was the only one with authority to empanel a jury. Technically in extending the jury system to all the king's courts, Henry was merely delegating the king's prerogative to empanel a jury to those members of his Council acting as judges in the new court.

The superiority of the king's courts, due to their freedom from local pressures and therefore their greater impartiality, sounder and more uniform rules of law, use of the jury, and better-trained judges, soon had the effect of drawing litigants from the older courts, even in civil cases. The king's courts offered a better product. This new judicial machinery continued for a while as a branch of the King's Council. Eventually, however, the court became entirely free from the king's administrative machinery and later defied kings, recognizing no authority higher than the law itself.

Bear in mind there was little legislation extant at this time. Any rules of law announced by the judges had to be based either on the prevailing custom, which the county courts and the courts of the hundred had relied upon, or upon the sheer discretion of the judge. The rules of law adopted by the king's courts came from both of these sources, and the second is not to be minimized. With active, intelligent, professional judges, equipped with the perspective that came from traveling throughout the land and viewing a variety of local rules, much local law was no doubt discarded and much new law devised. The doctrine of stare decisis, which means that the rule of law applied to one case will be applied to like cases arising in the future, was not formally accepted until many years later, but with the adoption of this doctrine, the foundations of the common law were laid.

The effect of the king's courts upon the development of the common law was therefore profound. The fact that a tightly knit, professional judiciary was created raised the caliber of judicial interpretation. The fact that it was a coherent group, responsible for deciding cases all over the realm, resulted inevitably in the gradual abandonment of purely local rules, still in sway in many counties, in favor of law common to all the counties of the realm. The feature of commonality, a goal approaching realization at the death of Henry II, gave rise to the term *common law*.

THE COURT OF EQUITY

The most important single development following the reign of Henry II was the evolution of *equity* as a branch of our jurisprudence. In ordinary conversation, the term *equity* is used synonomously with *right* or *just*. In the law, aside from being used in this sense on occasion, the word *equity* is used also to identify an entire branch of our law, distinct in historical origin and in other respects from the bulk of our common law. Equity was the product of the English *Court of Chancery*, though the term *Court of Equity* is more frequently applied to our American counterpart.

As early as the days of the Anglo-Saxon kings, a certain amount of judicial power was recognized as residing in the sovereign rights of the king. The king's right to dispense justice provided a means of righting wrong outside the usual scope of the law. This function seems to have been performed by most kings throughout history. Vestiges of this type of executive justice remain even today, in the power of the president or governor to pardon convicts.

After the formal separation of the common-law courts from the King's Council, the king retained the power to dispense justice upon special petition. Over the years, such petitions became so numerous that a specific official of the King's Council, the chancellor, came to perform the function of dispensing the king's personal justice, and a formal court was organized in which to perform this function. This special court became known as the Court of Chancery, and the law it administered, as *equity*. Just as the common-law courts had done at an earlier date, the Chancery gradually became a separate institution, independent from the King's Council. It continued to be an important judicial institution, however, because it offered different, and in some instances more adequate, legal remedies than the common-law courts. The remedies at common law were confined almost exclusively to awards of money damages. The Chancery went beyond this remedy, and would order parties to do, or to refrain from doing, certain things. The exact nature of equitable remedies is discussed at greater length in the chapter on legal remedies (page 85).

Probably a tendency toward rigidity in the common law during certain periods encouraged the growth of equity. If the common-law courts did not offer an adequate remedy for many wrongs, and equity did, naturally equity grew and prospered. One of the main characteristics of the Chancery, in fact, was a decreased emphasis on strict adherence to rules of law and greater reliance on discretion and individually tailored justice. The main advantage of equity jurisprudence, aside from certain special remedies, was greater flexibility. Yet inevitably a body of rules came to be worked out and adhered to that were almost, if not quite, as binding as those of the common law. Even in equity, the necessity of deciding like cases in a like manner had to be recognized. To treat every case as completely unique was found to place an impossible administrative burden upon the judges—there was simply not time to evolve a new, ingenious solution to every problem presented; besides, attempting to do so forced parties into court, because they could not guess what their rights would be without a court test.

The rules adopted by the Chancery differed substantially from those in effect in the common-law courts. For one thing they were heavily influenced by the Roman law; a continental education was in vogue even then, and the educated men in the Council had usually been trained in Roman law. One of the early differences between the law of equity and common law remains today. Cases in equity are not tried before a jury. Decisions of fact were and still are decided by the chancellor, as was usual under Roman law.

With two alternative, competing court systems applying differing rules of law, conflict between the two was inevitable. The situation became chaotic when the two courts began countermanding one another's decisions. One had to be found supreme, and some rule had to be devised to delineate which cases should go to the Chancery and which to the common-law courts.

The battle between the two courts was finally joined and resolved in 1616, when one of the most famous English jurists, Lord Coke, was chief justice of the King's Bench, a common-law court. The historic decision was made by King James I, and he decreed the Chancery supreme on occasions when the two courts were in dispute: Equity could set aside or interrupt proceedings of a common-law court and hear the matter itself in certain circumstances. However, the jurisdiction of the two courts was divided so that ordinarily there would be no conflict between the two. The jurisdiction of the two courts was divided along these lines: so long as an award of money damages was an adequate remedy, then a case could be heard only before a common-law court. This disposed of most cases. But, whenever the facts indicated that damages would not be an adequate remedy, then a plaintiff might apply to equity. Thus, the potential area of conflict between the two courts was narrowed down to differences over the question, When is money damages an adequate remedy? Differences over this question, though they did arise, never presented an overwhelming problem.

There were, in addition, certain instances in which a defendant could succeed in having a case transferred from a common-law court to one of equity, because the Chancery alone could consider the so-called equitable defenses, which included fraud, mistake, misrepresentation, duress, and undue influence.

Having resolved the question of conflicting jurisdictions, the Chancery and the common-law courts existed side by side for a long period of time. One might reasonably ask the question, Is there a need for two separate courts, even though each may hear somewhat different types of cases? There would seem to be no need for separate courts, and in fact, the two have merged in almost all American jurisdictions as well as in England. Today we still have the equitable remedies, discussed in detail in Chapter 7 of this text, and when one of these remedies is involved, the case is still normally heard without a jury. Nevertheless, it is almost invariably heard in the same courtroom and before the same trial judge as would be a comparable case in which money damages were sought. In other words, the rules of equity have now been incorporated into our common law, and are considered merely one branch of our law.

THE LAW MERCHANT

One other body of law was absorbed into the English common law. This body of law is the law merchant, the law by which commercial disputes are settled. The law of Admiralty, by which maritime disputes are settled, has had a history substantially parallel to that of the law merchant. The law merchant is the direct lineal ancestor of our modern commercial law.

THE LAW MERCHANT [7]

Markets and fairs had their own machinery for carrying out commercial law; most famous of them are the courts of piepowder, which were specially concerned with wandering merchants who traveled from market to market. . . . These mercantile courts [administered] . . . a peculiar type of law called the law merchant. It was not until the eighteenth century that the law merchant became completely absorbed in the common law.

Markets and fairs had their own machinery for applying commercial law; most famous of them are the courts of piepowder, which were specially concerned with wandering merchants who travelled from market to market. The word seems to have been at first a nickname referring to the "dusty feet" of its clients, but was later accepted as the official style of the court. The English courts of piepowder closely resembled similar courts on the continent, but just as the royal Admiralty superseded the local maritime courts, so a system of royal courts was set up by statute at various times in the fourteenth century which competed seriously with the local mercantile courts. These were called courts of the staple.

For a long time the administration of maritime as well as commercial law rested in the hands of local jurisdictions. Seaport towns had their own maritime courts sitting on the seashore from tide to tide, but the only ones which survived in active working in England into modern times was the jurisdiction of the group of five towns called the Cinque Ports, which is the oldest existing maritime jurisdiction in England. The other local maritime courts in the end were largely superseded by a newer and more centralised jurisdiction, the courts of Admiralty, held in the name of the Lord High Admiral, who was appointed by the Crown.

As soon as mercantile and maritime jurisdiction seemed desirable, the common lawyers began to covet it. The local courts felt the attack first. Fair courts were being hampered both by statute and by decision even in the fifteenth century; in the sixteenth, the local maritime courts waged a losing fight with Admiralty, and in the late sixteenth century Admiralty itself came into conflict with the courts of common law.

[7] Theodore F. T. Plucknett, *A Concise History of the Common Law,* 5th ed. (Boston: Little, Brown and Co., 1956), pp. 660–663.

At the close of the fifteenth and the beginning of the sixteenth centuries we had in England a Reception of the Italian mercantile law; and yet, a century later, in the first years of the seventeenth century, Coke asserted that "the law merchant is part of the law of this realm."

✧

Commercial law continued to be part of the common law in the United States—that is, based almost purely upon judicial precedent until the advent of the model uniform laws, particularly the Uniform Sales Act and the Uniform Negotiable Instruments Act. These acts were simply model drafts prepared by a group of experienced men under the auspices of the Commissioners on Uniform Laws, and these two acts were adopted by the legislatures of the great majority of American states.

A more recent act, the Uniform Commercial Code, supplants the above-mentioned acts and provides in addition uniform law governing a great many other commercial relationships. The Uniform Commercial Code has already been adopted by about one half of the states, and probably all states will adopt it within the forseeable future. The pages tinted gray in this volume contain quotations from or elaborations on the Uniform Commercial Code, and the sections of the code covering the law of sales and the law of negotiable instruments is included in full in the appendix. Throughout the remainder of this text, the Uniform Commercial Code will be designated by the abbreviation UCC.

CHAPTER FOUR

The Sources of
Our Rules of Law

---

*The chief cause of the success of our common law doctrine of
precedents as a form of law is that it combines certainty and
power of growth as no other doctrine has been able to do.*[1]

Judge-Made Law: The Doctrine of Precedent,
or Stare Decisis

AS HAS BEEN SAID, the common law is a system of judge-made law.
The earliest common-law cases were based upon varying considerations of custom, of practical utility, and of what might promote the interests of the Crown. Before long, a large body of cases had been decided, and
when the doctrine of *stare decisis* was officially adopted, these cases acted
as precedents. Cases somewhat similar, but nonetheless different in some
respects, frequently arose and were often decided by analogy to a decided
case. Thus the body of case law grew, almost every decided case adding
something new to the common law. One might think that after several centuries had elapsed there would be a workable precedent for every conceivable situation. To think so is to underestimate the complexity of human
affairs, as well as to ignore the fact of change. New situations, anticipated
neither by legislation nor by previous case law, continue to arise every
year. In such a case, the judge bases his decision on grounds of reason and
policy, which is another way of saying he attempts to make it logical within
the context of commonly accepted customs and traditions.

[1] Roscoe Pound, *The Spirit of the Common Law* (Boston: Marshall Jones Company, 1921), p. 182.

43

As more and more cases involving a new problem are ruled upon, the boundaries of the new legal concept become more and more clearly defined. With a large number of cases to elaborate the dimensions of a new legal concept, a well-established rule may eventually be devised, summarizing the treatment of the problem in question. This is the way general rules of the common law arise.

There is an element of efficiency in the application of precedents. From the point of view of the judge, efficiency results in being able to apply previous decisions without always going into a detailed study of the underlying policy considerations. From the point of view of society, efficiency results in being able to predict the outcome of future cases with a fair degree of accuracy, because we may presume that the present rule will not be changed and that we may rely on the validity of past decisions.

However, legal disputes are often not so stereotyped that one may say positively that a case is governed by certain precedents or that it is not. Frequently a case is like one set of precedents in some respects and like another set in other respects. Much of the skill of the attorney is devoted to explaining why one set of precedents should be controlling rather than another. In such a case, even today, the argument may well be as to which precedent most nearly appears to reflect our custom or which will result in the least social dislocation.

One other aspect of stare decisis must be mentioned in this discussion. A precedent is always subject to being overruled. So long as the use of a line of precedents seems to produce desirable results, there is no reason for changing it; unnecessary change in the law produces unnecessary confusion. However, few rules of law remain valid forever. Conceptions of right and wrong, social relationships, business practices, modes of government —all change over the years. Often, lines of precedent change almost imperceptibly, so that the law bends gradually as the world changes. Sometimes, however, the existing law must be flatly repudiated. This is within the authority of the judge. When a judge overrules a precedent, if other judges agree with his reasoning, his case will constitute a new precedent and will be followed when the same type of case arises in the future. If other judges disagree, they will follow the older authority, and the departure will be recognized as merely a faulty statement of law.

In summary the common law attempts to balance the two competing considerations of stability and change. When the world is changing slowly, the common law can evolve gradually, making slight adjustments from case to case. If abrupt change is necessary, however, to keep the law in conformance with the views of our society, fairly sharp changes may be made by overruling precedents.

It must be conceded that the processes of the common law cannot shape whole new codes of law in the way that legislative acts do. For one thing, a rule of the common law can be changed only when a case involving that rule is before the court. This may not happen for years after a rule becomes out of date. Then, only that particular rule may be changed. Many other rules in the same general area may be in need of change, but a court may decide only the rule applicable to the case before it. The legislature knows none of these limitations, and this is why the legislature is our main instrument for effecting sweeping change and for inaugurating new policy. The common law tends to stay rather close to tradition, mores, and custom. The legislature may overrule or change existing legislation or the then existing common law. In case of a conflict between the two, legislation always prevails.

The following series of readings provide several viewpoints concerning the dynamics of change and the development of the common law.

EVOLUTION OF THE LAW [2]

Courts have a creative job to do when they find that a rule has lost its touch with reality and should be abandoned or reformulated to meet new conditions and new moral values.

More than ever social problems find their solution in legislation. Endless problems remain, however, which the courts must resolve without benefit of legislation. The great mass of cases are decided within the confines of stare decisis. Yet there is a steady evolution, for it is not quite true that there is nothing new under the sun; rarely is a case identical with the ones that went before. Courts have a creative job to do when they find that a rule has lost its touch with reality and should be abandoned or reformulated to meet new conditions and new moral values. And in those cases where there is no stare decisis to cast its light or shadow, the courts must hammer out new rules that will respect whatever values of the past have survived the tests of reason and experience and anticipate what contemporary values will best meet those tests. The task is not easy—human relations are infinitely complex, and subtlety and depth of spirit must enter into their regulation. Often legal problems elude any final solution, and courts then can do no more than find what Cardozo called the least erroneous answers to insoluble problems.

[2] Judge Roger J. Traynor [of the Superior Court of California], *University of Illinois Law Forum*, **1956**, No. 2, p. 232.

JUDICIAL EMPIRICISM [3]

. . . the limits of [a legal] principle . . . are discovered gradually by a process of inclusion and exclusion as cases arise which . . . prove how far it may be made to do justice in its actual operation.

The chief cause of the success of our common law doctrine of precedents as a form of law is that it combines certainty and power of growth as no other doctrine has been able to do. Certainty is insured within reasonable limits in that the court proceeds by analogy of rules and doctrines in the traditional system and develops a principle for the cause before it according to a known technique. Growth is insured in that the limits of the principle are not fixed authoritatively once and for all but are discovered gradually by a process of inclusion and exclusion as cases arise which bring out its practical workings and prove how far it may be made to do justice in its actual operation. If the last century insisted overmuch upon the predetermined premises and fixed technique, it did not lose to our law the method of applying the judicial experience of the past to the judicial questions of the present and of making that experience yield principles to be developed into working and workable rules of justice by a process of judicial experimentation.

There is a common element in the two fundamental doctrines of the common law, the doctrine of precedents and the doctrine of the supremacy of law. The same spirit is behind each. The doctrine of precedents means that causes are to be judged by principles reached inductively from the judicial experiences of the past not by deduction from rules established arbitrarily by the sovereign will. . . .

LAW IN SCIENCE AND SCIENCE IN LAW [4]

. . . Because I believe that the claim of our especial code to respect is simply that it . . . is the one to which we have become accustomed . . . I am slow to consent to overruling a precedent. . . .

. . . Inasmuch as the real justification of a rule of law, if there be one, is that it helps to bring about a social end which we desire, it is no less necessary that those who make and develop the law should have those ends articulately in their minds. I do not expect or think it desirable that the judges should undertake to renovate the law. That is not their province. Indeed precisely because I believe that the world would be just as well off if it lived under laws that differed from ours in many ways, and because I believe that the claim of our especial code to

3 Pound, *loc. cit.*

4 Oliver Wendell Holmes, *Harvard Law Review,* Cambridge, Mass. (1899), **12,** p. 460.

respect is simply that it exists, that it is the one to which we have become accustomed, and not that it represents an eternal principle, I am slow to consent to overruling a precedent, and think that our most important duty is to see that the judicial duel shall be fought out in the accustomed way. But I think it most important to remember whenever a doubtful case arises, with certain analogies on one side and other analogies on the other, that what really is before us is a conflict between two social desires, each of which seeks to extend its dominion over the case, and which cannot both have their way. The social question is which desire is strongest at the point of conflict. The judicial one may be narrower, because one or the other desire may have been expressed in previous decisions to such an extent that logic requires us to assume it to preponderate in the one before us. But if that be clearly so, the case is not a doubtful one. Where there is doubt the simple tool of logic does not suffice, and even if it is disguised and unconscious the judges are called on to exercise the sovereign prerogative of choice.

✧

The following is the first of many appellate court opinions included in this text. The function of the appellate courts and the purpose of the opinion are discussed in more detail (pages 72–74). For the present, suffice it to say that the opinion is a statement of the reasons supporting a decision.

Every appellate opinion stems from a request for review, or appeal, from the decision of the trial court. Only questions of law are considered on appeal, the facts having been decided in the original trial, usually by a jury.

The appellant is the party seeking review, and therefore, normally, the loser in the original trial. Of course, the appellant may have been either plaintiff or defendant in the original hearing, because sometimes a plaintiff loses and sometimes a defendant, but in either case the party who loses is apt to be dissatisfied. However, in either case the appealing party must specify some grounds for his appeal, must allege that in some way an error of law was made to his prejudice and that it may have been responsible for his adverse decision.

The party against whom the appeal is taken is known as the appellee in some states and the respondent in others. He is the party who won in the lower court and who is seeking to have that decision affirmed.

The case at hand provides an excellent illustration of common-law change. Despite precedents that probably go back for hundreds of years holding a hospital immune from tort suits, the court finds that conditions have changed, and the precedents are no longer applicable to modern conditions. Under these circumstances it is in the power of the court to change the law, and that is exactly what it does here.

such insurance would as necessarily be involved in the operation of its business as any other legitimate expense.

The writers of these articles occupy a position with respect to the advancement of the judicial body of the law similar to that of the corps of engineers to an advancing army. Unfettered by precedent and stare decisis these gentlemen are always in the vanguard of the progressive march of the body of the law, constructing bridges, as it were, and clearing the way for advanced positions which may be safely contained when surrounded by new and changing social, political and economic conditions. They are quick to recognize the development of a social policy and are instrumental in crystallizing it into a fixed concept which the legislature and the courts denominate "public policy."

(7, 8) The declaration of "public policy" is primarily a legislative function. The courts unquestionably have authority to declare a public policy which already exists and to base its decisions upon that ground. But in the absence of a legislative declaration of what that public policy is, before courts are justified in declaring its existence such public policy should be so thoroughly established as a state of public mind, so united and so definite and fixed that its existence is not subject to any substantial doubt. . . . It is equally true that when the reason for the existence of a declared public policy no longer obtains that the courts should without hesitation declare that such public policy no longer exists.

During the past two decades both the Federal Congress and the legislatures of practically all of the states have in various forms declared a public policy to exist in this country that is diametrically opposed to that invoked in these cases to sustain the immunity of charitable institutions from liability for damages for the torts of their servants. As examples practically every state in the Union has enacted a workmen's compensation law; occupational disease disability laws making employers liable to workmen if the injury or illness arises out of and in the course of their employment regardless of any question of negligence; employment security acts designed to take care of individuals during periods of enforced idleness, and even in cases of voluntary strikes under certain circumstances thus relieving the unfortunates of the burdens of misfortune and shifting such burdens to the shoulders of the public at large. In addition to these laws Federal legislation has encompassed the entire field of welfare and social security.

We believe that these legislative declarations of public policy which relieves the individual from the burden of his misfortunes and makes the general public bear the load levying taxes directly or indirectly to carry out such policy, completely repudiate the rule of nonliability of charitable institutions for the torts of their servants based on public policy.

(9) For the above reasons we are of the opinion that if public policy ever required that charitable institutions should be immune from liability for the torts of their servants, that public policy no longer exists. We therefore expressly overrule the holding in the Wilson cases, supra, and now hold that charitable institutions are liable for the torts of their servants from which injury proximately results to a third person, whether stranger or patient and whether

the patient is a paying or nonpaying patient. In this view of the case the question of the burden of proof becomes immaterial.

Judgment reversed and remanded for a new trial in accordance with the views hereinabove expressed.

UDALL, C.J., and STANFORD, DE CONCINI and LA PRADE, JJ., concur.

✧

QUESTIONS

1. What does this court have to say concerning "cultural lag" (a time period following change in conditions, before the law changes accordingly)?

2. What institution is said to be the primary enunciator of "public policy"?

3. What does this court view to be the role of legal writers?

Legislation as a Source of Law

In an earlier section of this text, we observed that much law is deliberately enacted for the purpose of dealing effectively with new problems. Law that is formally enacted through some recognized process of government is termed *legislation*. We have noted that in earlier days this function was served by a king or the king in cooperation with his Council. Today, legislation is enacted by a majority vote of elected representatives, at least in the common-law nations and most noncommunist European nations.

The United States government and most state governments have an upper house, usually designated a Senate, and a lower house, usually designated a House of Representatives. A majority of each house must approve a measure and the chief executive sign it for proposed legislation to become law.

We have alluded previously to the quickness with which change may be effected through legislation. Although change effected through departures from judicial precedent is evolutionary, permitting slow, orderly adjustment in response to gradually changing conditions, legislation may be revolutionary, wiping whole areas of law off the books and substituting something completely different. As social and economic change becomes more rapid, the role of the legislature must inevitably expand in order to cope with new conditions. This trend has been evident in the United States during the last hundred years.

The ability to make rapid, revolutionary change is important in an organized society that is itself subject to forces requiring quick adjustment. Certainly the United States today, along with most other nations, is in the hands of such forces. Consequently, legislation is an exceedingly important component of our law. In earlier days legislation was much less important.

Although an increase in legislative activity was probably an inevitable by-product of the Industrial Revolution and modern technology, the leading early apostle of the active legislature was Jeremy Bentham. Bentham, a student of both law and economics, led a group known as the Utilitarians in late eighteenth-century England. He was a strong advocate of legal reform of all kinds and a bitter critic of the legal status quo. He made a penetrating analysis of the English common law as it then stood, recommending legislation as the means of correcting most of the defects he found. English law at that time was in fact very resistant to departures from precedent and therefore unyielding to the forces of change. Quite likely, Bentham failed to recognize many of the strong points of the common law, and possibly he overestimated some of the defects. Experience has proved that legislation, although effective, has its limitations and is not as complete a cure for social ills as Bentham assumed. Nevertheless, in many ways he anticipated things to come, and he certainly made an important contribution in paving the way for modern legal reforms.

An essential difference between legislation and judge-made law is that the former is very often and quite frankly an expression of political sentiment; the latter is presumed not to be—on the whole, correctly. The judge-made law deals most effectively in providing a basis for the settlement of disputes between private individuals.

Areas in which common-law rules are of greatest importance involve such questions as what is required to hold a party liable for negligence and what is required in order to prove a contract. Questions of this type may be of great importance to individuals; yet they are not political issues, because they do not usually affect one large group at the expense of another. The impact is about the same on everyone.

The legislature on the contrary is an arena in which the power struggle between differing groups, whether professional, economic, or geographic, may be fought out and at least temporarily resolved by comparatively peaceful means. Some typical subjects of legislation are assessing the amount and the burden of taxes to be levied; regulation of professional, business, labor, or economic groups; and expenditure of money for public services or improvements. We need not state that these are often emotionally charged political issues.

Much of what the legislature does is by compromise, logrolling (you scratch my back and I'll scratch yours), and other forms of mutual accommodation. Although many an upright citizen may deplore such tactics as "dirty politics," it is precisely through this media that the interests of competing groups are accommodated and, therefore, armed coups and rebellion are avoided.

The power struggle is carried on through pressure groups and lobbies rather than with bombs and cannons. We have agreed to substitute the ballot for the bomb, and the fruit of victory is in the form of favorable legislation. Anyone who wishes may support the lobby that promotes his interests, and he is not wrong in doing so. The battle is fought in a scramble for votes of the legislators, and may be refought at the next general election when the legislators themselves are elected.

All legislation is deemed to represent the public policy. Realistically, it is difficult to argue that all legislation really does represent public policy, if this term is construed to mean awareness and approval by the general public. Much frivolous and inconsequential legislation is passed and soon forgotten. Occasionally, small, hard-lobbying groups pressure measures through the legislature that are contrary to both the interests and the desires of the majority. Nevertheless, there is no rational basis for deciding that some legislation should not be law (aside from constitutional limitations). The legislature is for the purpose of deciding policy, and any measure passed by the legislature and signed by the Chief Executive becomes the public policy of the state, except as limited by the state and federal constitution or by federal legislation.

It is true that the legislature is free to change rules of the common law even in matters of little or no public interest, and often does. Any time the legislature enacts a statute contrary to the common law, the legislation is controlling, and the common law is to that extent annulled. Some traditional areas of the private law, especially commerical law, have looked to legislation in an attempt to provide uniformity through the states, and again, to permit rapid adjustment to change.[5]

Although the importance of legislation vis-à-vis the common law has no doubt increased in recent years, judicial decision is an important factor in the interpretation of legislation. Attorneys approach most new legislation with little confidence as to its meaning until a test case or two has provided clarification. Legislation will always be vague to a degree for several reasons. Language is by its nature subject to differing shades of meanings, so that ambiguity is to some extent inevitable. No one could foresee all possible problems that might arise in the application of an act, so that spaces will need to be filled by judicial interpretation. The problem is often to determine what the legislators intended, when in truth the question under consideration might never have occurred to them. Finally, legislation is usually a compromise between two or more opposing factions, who have differing ends in mind. When no other form of compromise is available,

---

[5] Practically all phases of commercial law have recently been codified in a model code, the Uniform Commercial Code, which has been passed by the legislatures of nearly half of our states, and is under consideration in many others. See page 41 and Chapter 16 *et seq* for further discussion of this code.

legislators have sometimes deliberately left an act in hazy language. In such a case each party may cherish a hope that his view will be favored in the judicial interpretation. Moreover, if the interpretation is not favorable to everyone, voters may be informed that the courts and not the legislator is to blame.

The judicial decisions explaining and embellishing legislation are themselves precedents, and after a time a sort of common law grows up around legislative enactments. These are looked to in addition to the statute in order to determine the law.

One of the most frequent complaints leveled against American legislators concerns the abundance of their product. British jurists, having to follow only one Parliament, with a comparatively modest flow of legislation issuing from it, are often amazed at the great flood of legislation gushing not only from the Congress of the United States but from 50 separate state legislatures, each producing different laws.

The following excerpt suggests some reasons why the problem may not be as serious as it may seem at first glance. Nonetheless, there is a problem. For example, although most legislation does not apply directly to any one businessman, it is often difficult for a businessman embarking upon a new venture to discover all of the legislation that does apply to him. This is complicated by the fact that many state codes are badly indexed.

Furthermore, acts are often passed which, because of lack of more than temporary enthusiasm (if any) on the part of the general public or anyone else, die a quiet death through nonenforcement. Yet this situation presents a difficult problem: will the acts stay dead? Should the legislation be ignored by those affected, on the theory that it will continue not being enforced? Or should a businessman put himself at a competitive disadvantage by obeying all legislation, whether enforced or not, on the theory that someday enforcement may suddenly commence?

IS LEGISLATION TOO VOLUMINOUS? [6]

> . . . It seems abundantly clear that the corpus of private law as a whole, the corpus of law which governs the great mass of commonplace everyday dealings of the business world, is only slightly affected by the output of even a legislative session so prolific in the total number of its enactments as the Pennslyvania Legislature of 1929.

If we would estimate the actual meaning and burden of legislation, apart from federal legislation, we must limit ourselves to the legislation of some particular state and ask ourselves whether its legislation is excessive.

[6] John Dickinson, "Legislation and the Effectiveness of Law," *American Bar Association Journal* (October 1931), pp. 646–647.

Pennsylvania lawyers are in an advantageous position to ask this question because our own state is certainly an offender if quantity and bulk of legislation be regarded as offense. Let us by way of example, take up for somewhat detailed examination the statutory output of the Pennsylvania Legislature of 1929. The statutes passed at that session fill a volume of more than 1,800 pages, exclusive of resolutions, and amount to a total of 601 acts. In this bulky output of a single legislative session, we have an excellent specimen for analysis to determine how far the charge is justified that our legislative bodies are passing too many laws. I have, accordingly, examined these 601 statutes with some care to determine the nature of the subject matter dealt with, and the extent to which they impose a burden on the individual and introduce uncertainty and confusion for the practicing lawyer.

The first result of the analysis is that of the total of 601 statutes, 362 relate to the conduct and organization of the government of the Commonwealth and its local subdivisions and have practically no bearing on the activities and interests of private individuals. Thus, a very considerable part of the bulk of the statute book is accounted for by the so-called "administrative code" (Laws of 1929—No. 175) which defines the organization of the various administrative branches of the state government, and which runs to a total of 165 pages; by the "fiscal code," which defines the organization and duties of the department of Revenue and other agencies concerned with the collection and disbursement of public moneys (Laws of 1929—No. 176), and by "general county law" (Laws of 1929—Act. No. 447), which runs to 230 pages. Of course, many of the provisions of the fiscal code are of direct concern to taxpayers but, on the whole, the vastly greater part of all these statutes have a direct bearing and interest only for public officers and employes, and this is still more true of the remaining 359 enactments of this class which the 1929 statute-book contains. Thus, we have an act "for the purchase of digests and law books for the offices of district attorneys of the Commonwealth by the boards of commissioners of counties" (No. 193); an act "requiring county commissioners to provide at the expense of the county telephone, typewriter and stenographic services for the county superintendent of schools" (No. 204); an act "authorizing the register of wills in counties of the fifth class to appoint a solicitor" (No. 206); an act "providing for the purchase by the Commonwealth of a building in the City of Harrisburg for the use of the department of property and supplies" (No. 233); an act "authorizing recorders of deeds in counties of the fourth class to appoint a solicitor" (No. 393); an act "requiring the county commissioners of the respective counties to furnish the county comptroller with an official seal" (No. 437); an act "empowering the salary board of counties of the fourth class to fix the salary of the prison warden" (No. 439); besides numerous acts relating to the conduct and management of schools, the construction and maintenance of highways, the conduct of public penal and charitable institutions, and the like.

In short, the chief bulk of the Pennsylvania legislation of 1929 is accounted for by the character of the state government as a vast operating agency for the management of certain enterprises like roads, schools, poor relief and the administration of justice; which, in a community of the size of Pennsylvania, call for the organization on a tremendous scale of the agency which is to conduct them. Viewed simply as an operating agency for the performance of these elementary functions of government—functions which no one would suggest should be taken away from the state—the government of a state like Pennsylvania necessarily exceeds in size and complexity the largest business corporations which have emerged in even this era of business-giants; and the greatest part of the legislation which the biennial sessions of our legislature add to the statute book are concerned simply with the organization and conduct of the machinery charged with the performance of these tasks and with the provision of funds for their support. Such statutes are of concern to the private individual only in so far as they increase or impede the efficiency of the services which the state performs for the community and which no one today would argue could be satisfactorily performed except by the state. Whether or not the efficient performance of these services calls for the large amount of legislation by the lawmaking body which under our American system of government we are accustomed to devote to it, is, of course, open to question and I shall say something about it at a later point in this paper; but at any rate it is clear that such legislation is not of a character which imposes new restrictions on individual liberties or places burdens, except possibly by way of increased taxes, on the private citizen.

If we deduct from the total output of the legislature of 1929 these 362 acts which are concerned with the organization and operation of governmental agencies, there remain approximately 239 other enactments to be accounted for. Of these, about 30 are tax statutes. The greater number of these apply in each instance to only a simple narrowly defined class of taxpayers, such as banks, insurance companies, public utilities, coal mines, amusement enterprises, dealers and brokers in various types of merchandise, and the like. Perhaps ten statutes, those dealing with the personal property tax, the inheritance tax, tax liens and procedure in tax cases, are of general concern to a large proportion of the tax-paying public. It is open to argument that our tax laws stand seriously in need of simplification and that ten alterations are too many for a single session of the legislature to make without creating confusion and uncertainty. However, when we face this question and realize the importance and great complexity of the question of taxation for a commonwealth of the size and economic diversity of Pennsylvania, it is desirable that we should have an accurate picture of the situation in mind and should understand that the number of legislative changes effected in the year in question was no greater than it really was.

Eliminating tax statutes and statutes dealing with governmental organization, there remain approximately 200 enactments of the 1929 legislature. These may be grouped into two classes, each including about 100 acts: the class of enactments which may be roughly described as regulatory, and, on the other hand, amendments of the basic corpus of general law.

Of the regulatory statutes, approximately twenty relate to the protection of fish and game, conservation, and to such agricultural matters as the grading of grapes, the certification of seed potatoes and the elimination of forest-fire hazards. Two relate to amusements, motion pictures and boxing. Twelve relate to the regulation of traffic, motor, air and water, including the basic "Aeronautics Act" (Act No. 316). Ten are building and zoning statutes and regulations for fire protection, including the municipal building code for cities of the first class, which runs to 120 pages in length (Act No. 413, pages 1063–1182). Fifteen statutes are primarily for the protection of public health, including regulations of milk selling, drugs, medical practice, undertakers, bakers, barber shops, and the practice of optometry and midwifery. There are thirteen statutes dealing with labor relations, four relating to child labor, three to hours of labor and the remainder, for the most part, to the safety of labor in mines. As might be expected, the largest number of the enactments falling in the class of regulatory statutes are regulations of various kinds of businesses. These amount to twenty-six in all. Six relate to insurance, eight to banks and trust companies, three to building and loan associations, three to the sale of corporate securities, and the balance are scattered statutes dealing with real estate brokers, employment agencies, power companies, pipe lines and title insurance companies.

In assessing the burden which this mass of regulatory statutes places on the individual, two facts must be kept in mind. The first is that the vast majority of these statutes are merely amendments and, for the most part, comparatively brief amendments, of existing regulatory legislation. They involve a slight modification of existing requirements rather than an addition of new requirements. It may be said, of course, that even such a mere change of requirements adds to the difficulties of the individual who desires to keep within the law, since it places on him the burden of becoming acquainted with the new enactments and thereby increases uncertainty and inconvenience. In this connection arises the importance of the second fact which it is necessary to take into account, the fact, namely, that any single individual or business concern is subject to only a very inconsiderable portion of the total number of these statutes. Banks have no direct concern with statutes dealing with the safety of mines, the grading of potatoes or the rules of air navagation, laboring men are not required to conform to statutes imposing regulations on insurance companies, optometrists and medical practitioners. In short, the effect of this body of regulatory legislation is not cumulative on the individual citizen, and while a certain burden is doubtless placed on the processes of the community as a whole, it may well be that the beneficial results in the way of added protection to any given individual against the conduct of others is greater than the additional burden which happens to be placed on him as member of one of the groups subjected to regulation.

When we turn from the class of regulatory statutes to those which are amendments of, or additions to, the corpus of ordinary private law, we find that out of a total of approximately 100 enactments, 83 affect the field of civil and 18 that of criminal law. Of the 83 civil statutes, 31 relate to the law of private corporations, 10 to the law of such corporations in general, and the remainder to the law of special kinds of corporations, insurance corporations, natural gas corporations, agricultural cooperatives and various kinds of non-profit corporations. Six statutes relate to the powers and liabilities of banks. Four are amendments of the Workmen's Compensation Act, two relate to bonds of contractors engaged in public works. Four deal with the subject of eminent domain. Thirteen deal with civil procedure, the process of selecting jurors, fees of witnesses, fees of Justices of the Peace, jury fees in Allegheny County, all of relatively restricted importance. More important are the statutes affecting practice in *assumpsit* and trespass, Orphans' Court practice, practice on appeals and entry and recording of judgments.

The statutes so far considered account for approximately two-thirds of those dealing with the general civil law of the state. The remainder, amounting to twenty-three, deal with guardians and fiduciaries, divorce, adoption of children, bulk-sales, warehouse receipts, checks and notes, mechanics' liens, mortgages, partition, and damages for conversion. Of these subjects the only ones on which more than two statutes were enacted are mortgages and guardians and fiduciaries, each of which was the subject of five enactments.

The scheme of classification resulting in the figures which I have just given is necessarily a rough one. Any classification is bound to be somewhat arbitrary and a different scheme might result in slightly different figures for the various classes of acts. This, however, is of no great significance for our present purposes. The important point is the relative ratio of the different broad categories of legislation. From this standpoint it seems abundantly clear that the corpus of private law as a whole, the corpus of law which governs the great mass of commonplace everyday dealings of the business world, is only slightly affected by the output of even a legislative session so prolific in the total number of its enactments as the Pennsylvania Legislature of 1929. The great body of these enactments relate to more or less specialized departments of activity and therefore, affect the interests and conduct of only a relatively small portion of the community.

BACKGROUND ON THE UNIFORM COMMERCIAL CODE [7]

Hitherto most commercial transactions have been regulated by a number of uniform laws prepared and promulgated by the National Conference of Commissioners on Uniform State Laws. These acts, with the dates of their promulgation by the Conference, are:

Uniform Negotiable Instruments Law	1896
Uniform Warehouse Receipts Act	1906
Uniform Sales Act	1906
Uniform Bills of Lading Act	1909
Uniform Stock Transfer Act	1909
Uniform Conditional Sales Act	1918
Uniform Trust Receipts Act	1933

Two of these acts were adopted in every American State and the remaining acts have had wide acceptance. Each of them has become a segment of the statutory law relating to commercial transactions. It has been recognized

[7] Excerpts from the *Uniform Commercial Code, 1958 Official Text with Comments* (Philadelphia: The American Law Institute, 1958), pp. 2–5.

for some years that these acts needed substantial revision to keep them in step with modern commercial practices and to integrate each of them with the others.

The concept of the present Act is that "commercial transactions" is a single subject of the law, notwithstanding its many facets.

A single transaction may very well involve a contract for sale, followed by a sale, the giving of a check or draft for a part of the purchase price, and the acceptance of some form of security for the balance.

The check or draft may be negotiated and will ultimately pass through one or more banks for collection.

If the goods are shipped or stored the subject matter of the sale may be covered by a bill of lading or warehouse receipt or both.

Or it may be that the entire transaction was made pursuant to a letter of credit either domestic or foreign.

Obviously, every phase of commerce involved is but a part of one transaction, namely, the sale of and payment for goods.

If, instead of goods in the ordinary sense, the transaction involved stocks or bonds, some of the phases of the transaction would obviously be different. Others would be the same. In addition, there are certain additional formalities incident to the transfer of stocks and bonds from one owner to another.

This Act purports to deal with all the phases which may ordinarily arise in the handling of a commercial transaction, from start to finish.

Because of the close relationship of each phase of a complete transaction to every other phase, it is believed that each Article of this Act is cognate to the single broad subject "Commercial Transactions," and that this Act is valid under any constitutional provision requiring an act to deal with only one subject. See, for excellent discussions of the meaning of "single subject": House v. Creveling, 147 Tenn. 589. . . .

The Chief Reporter of the Code was Professor Llewellyn, and the Associate Chief Reporter was Professor Soia Mentsehikoff. Final editorial preparation of the 1952 edition was in the hands of Professor Charles Bunn of the University of Wisconsin Law School. The Coordinators for the revisions leading to this edition were Professors Robert Braucher and A. E. Sutherland of the Law School of Harvard University, Professor Braucher doing the final editorial preparation for this edition.

The actual drafting was done in some cases by practicing lawyers and in others by teachers of various law schools. The customary procedure required that before a draft was submitted for discussion to the general memberships of the American Law Institute and of the National Conference of Commissioners, it was successively approved by three groups.

The first group were the so-called "advisers," consisting of specially selected judges, practicing lawyers and law teachers. The advisers met with the draftsmen on frequent occasions to debate and iron out, not only the substance but the form and phraseology of the proposed draft.

After the draft was cleared by the advisers, it was meticulously examined by the next two groups—the Council of The American Law Institute and either the Commercial Acts Section or the Property Acts Section of the Conference of Commissioners.

When these bodies had given their approval to the draft, it came before the general membership both of the Institute and of the Conference for consideration.

In addition in the final stages leading to this Edition each article was reviewed and discussed by a special Subcommittee for that article. Recommendations of the Subcommittee were reviewed and acted upon by the Enlarged Editorial Board, pursuant to authority from the sponsoring bodies.

The Constitution as a Source of Law

CONSTITUTIONAL RESTRAINT ON LEGISLATIVE ACTION [8]

"When an act of Congress is appropriately challenged in the courts as not conforming to the constitutional mandate the judicial branch of the Government has only one duty—to lay the article of the Constitution which is invoked beside the statute which is challenged and to decide whether the latter squares with the former."—Justice Roberts, in United States v. Butler, 297 U.S. 1 (1936).

"While unconstitutional exercise of power by the executive and legislative branches of the Government is subject to judicial restraint, the only check on our own exercise of power is our own sense of self-restraint."—Justice Stone (dissenting), *ibid.*

Legal rules stemming from a constitution are a third source of law. The meaning of the word *constitution* is somewhat different in Great Britain than in the United States and the British dominions. In Great Britain, the constitution is unwritten in the same sense that the common law is unwritten. The British constitution embodies the fundamental, unchanging, legal propositions that are central to the common law and to English tradition. There is nothing except tradition and public opinion to prevent legislative amendment, encroachment, or repudiation of the legal propositions of the British constitution. They are contained not in one document but in a series of documents, common-law cases, and traditions. A constitution of this type is termed "flexible," because it really has no more force than does law from

[8] Edward S. Corwin, *The Constitution and What It Means Today* (Princeton, N.J.: Princeton University Press, 1954), 13 pp.

other sources except to the extent that jurists and legislators choose to give it greater force. Nevertheless, the forces of tradition supporting the British constitution seem to be very strong.

The United States on the other hand has a formal written document for its constitution. This document prescribes a general blueprint to which the various organs of government must adhere, allotting certain powers to executive, legislature, and judiciary, and providing in most instances for the selection of the incumbents. In addition, our Constitution attempts to delineate the respective limits and powers of the state and the federal governments. Lastly, in the bill of rights and some later amendments are provisions guaranteeing to the citizens certain rights and liberties. The traditional common-law notions of the rights of Englishmen greatly influenced our Constitution, especially the bill of rights.

Unlike the British constitution, the American Constitution has greater force than the general run of our law. It is the supreme law of our land. It cannot be contravened, and it is difficult to amend. Any legislative enactment, judicial decision, or executive order that is counter to some provision of the Constitution may be set aside. Just as legislation must be interpreted by someone, and in our legal system that someone is the judge, so the Constitution must be interpreted, and the body having the final authority to do so is the United States Supreme Court. Surprisingly, the designation of who is supposed to interpret our Constitution does not appear in that document, although the Supreme Court itself is created by Article III of the Constitution. One of the most interesting and significant chapters in our history is that in which our Supreme Court first asserted the right to set aside an act of one of the other branches of government on the ground that the act was contrary to the Constitution.[9] Practically all authorities agree that this indeed is what the framers of the Constitution intended, for if the Supreme Court is not to be the final Constitutional authority, who is? There is no other body sitting permanently, in a position to lend its services for solving difficult questions of interpretation. Furthermore, the legislature, under direct pressure from whatever shade of the electorate happens to have a temporary majority, is in a poor position to resist popular demands for encroachments into the basic rights of a temporary minority.

In a practical sense, one of the greatest single functions of the Constitution may be to resist the severity of cyclical swings in public opinion. Temporary national overenthusiasm for any political point of view meets a restraining hand in the Constitution. When this happens, as we see when we examine the history of the past 50 years, the Supreme Court may become a target for abuse, but this does not mean that it has not performed its function.

[9] *Marbury* v. *Madison* (1803), 1 Cranch 137.

Inevitably there have been differences in interpretation of the Constitution. To what extent this is due to differences in personnel on the Supreme Court or to differences in conditions over long periods of time is difficult to determine, and no doubt both factors are involved. It is safe to assume that some variations in interpretation will continue to occur in the future.

Besides our federal Constitution, each of the states of the United States has its own constitution. Most of these are similar in many respects to the federal Constitution, but each has its own variations. Each is interpreted by the Supreme Court of the state.

CHAPTER FIVE

The Organization and the Operation of Our State Courts[1]

Because of the large number of cases decided by our trial courts, it is necessary to have a well-established, commonly understood, step-by-step procedure to which the parties must adhere in presenting their case. This is purely in the interest of providing some order for what would otherwise be chaos.

Introduction

OUR COURTS are sometimes referred to as the machinery of justice, and the analogy is apt. In one end of the machine go all the elements of a dispute: masses of facts, important and otherwise; misunderstandings: poor memories; biased memories; events so complex that no one could really understand them; witnesses, reliable and unreliable; and lies, varnished and unvarnished. The issues between the parties must be brought into focus, the facts sorted out and decided, the law applied to the facts, and a final decision announced. The final decision, the end product of the machine, is a product of all of the difficult decisions of fact and law made along the way.

Some formal organization must exist to provide an orderly means of

[1] The court organization here described is that apt to be found in one of our smaller and perhaps newer states. The larger or older states, aside from having an intermediate layer of appellate courts, often have two trial courts, one of general jurisdiction and one with a more limited jurisdiction but still higher than the justice of the peace court or its equivalent. Some states have a special court to handle probate matters.

hearing and disposing of the great number of legal disputes that arise. As is true with most forms of organization devised for the purpose of gathering and evaluating information and making decisions based thereon, our courts are organized in the form of a hierarchy.

The Justice and Municipal Courts

The courts lowest in authority deal with the least important and most routine cases, and are the most numerous. These courts are known by a variety of names: justice of the peace courts, police courts, traffic courts, and municipal courts. The exact type and name of the lowest-level court varies from place to place. The courts we have enumerated are not identical. Traffic courts are restricted to traffic cases, whereas police courts are usually restricted to minor criminal matters. Both traffic courts and police courts are usually confined in their jurisdiction to a particular city, as is the municipal court, which differs by having jurisdiction of both criminal and private cases in a particular city. The justice of the peace court has jurisdiction of both criminal and private cases, and its jurisdiction is usually extended throughout a county.

Frequently the judge presiding over one of the lowest courts has no legal training. Usually no verbatim transcript of the proceedings is made, although it is not true, as some have concluded from the designation "courts not of record," that no records whatever are maintained. In many states either party may, on appeal, have the case retried at the next higher court, regardless of the decision of the lower court. The main advantage of these lower courts is that they provide a speedy, cheap means of disposing of minor controversies. The procedure is very informal in most cases. Citizens', not lawyers', views of justice are apt to predominate.

The Trial Courts

Next on the scale is the trial court, usually at the county level and known by various names—for example, district court, superior court, or county court. All proceedings in this court are noted by court reporters, and it is therefore termed a court of record. The atmosphere is quite formal. The jury trial is the outstanding characteristic of this court. This is the court that is usually portrayed in entertainment media.

Because of the large number of cases decided by our trial courts, it is necessary to have a well-established, commonly understood, step-by-step procedure to which the parties must adhere in presenting their case. This is purely in the interest of providing some order for what would otherwise be chaos. Through following a well-established procedure the litigant, the opposing party, and the judge can ascertain what step will be next in the proceedings and prepare themselves accordingly.

THE PLEADING

The first steps are for the purpose of bringing the issues of the dispute into focus. It is necessary to establish in outline the major facts and rules of law each party is claiming in support of his position, and of sorting out the aspects upon which they agree. Then the points on which the parties really are in contention, and only those points, can be presented before judge and jury. These steps, preliminary to the trial, are called the pleading.

The pleading is not done in open court but in the form of documents prepared by the attorney for one adversary and delivered to the other by process servers. They are usually drawn up with care, and ample time is afforded in which to respond.

The document sent by the plaintiff to the defendant, and thereby initiating a lawsuit is termed appropriately the *complaint.* (It is called the declaration in some states.) In earlier days, pleading used to be a highly technical undertaking. Today considerable leeway is given to the plaintiff in wording his complaint. If evidence is uncovered that necessitates some restatement of the defendant's alleged wrong, the complaint may be changed before, usually during, and sometimes even after the evidence is presented. Today the law is fairly flexible in this regard. Some limitations on the plaintiff's right to change his complaint must be imposed, however, because the rights of the defendant must also be considered. He is entitled to reasonable and timely notice of what the plaintiff's charges are, and should not be harried by sudden, tactical changes in the allegations basic to the plaintiff's case. A balance has been struck that attempts to be, and usually is, reasonable.

Upon receiving the plaintiff's complaint, the defendant has a period of time to file his answer, which is termed appropriately the *answer*. The defendant may admit such items contained in the complaint as he may wish to admit. He may wish to do so either because the admission does him no damage or because he feels the matter can be proved by the opposing party so easily there is no point in denying it. If he admitted everything alleged, the plaintiff would simply secure a judgment for the damages requested and go home, so this almost never happens. The defendant normally contradicts one or more significant points in the plaintiff's case. Thus, the controversy is narrowed to specific issues.

If a defendant fails to act upon receipt of a complaint, the plaintiff may go to court (on a date designated in the complaint) and secure a judgment by default—that is, an uncontested judgment.

Occasionally, the situation will arise where the plaintiff's complaint contains nothing to which the defendant disagrees but which at the same time is no basis for recovery at law. As an example, the plaintiff might outline a cause of action complaining that the defendant honked his horn for no reason, badly startling the plaintiff and resulting in emotional distress, to the value of $5,000. Because of the flood of lawsuits that could arise from this type of action, there is at present no legal basis for a suit of this nature. The defendant would not deny any of the plaintiff's allegation under these circumstances. His objection is not that the facts are misstated. His objection is that the facts, though true, do not constitute a legal wrong on his part. The issue, therefore, is whether or not the undisputed facts provide a legal basis for recovery by the plaintiff. Under these circumstances, instead of filing an answer, the defendant files a *demurrer*. The demurrer admits (at least for the sake of argument) all facts pleaded, but denies the existence of any legal remedy. It is also possible for the plaintiff to file a demurrer in reply to the answer of the defendant. By this device, the plaintiff admits the truth of some new fact pleaded in the defendant's answer as a defense but denies that the fact, even if true, constitutes a valid legal defense.

No jury is needed when the issue is joined over a demurrer; juries determine only facts, and when a demurrer is being decided there is no issue of fact. Because the issue is joined on a question purely of law, the judge makes the decision. Use of the demurrer is fairly rare. Most cases go to court on the basis of issues framed by a complaint and an answer.

The basic purpose of all of these pleadings is to select from the infinite number of points that either side might present the significant ones that are central in importance and are in dispute. When the case goes to trial, the evidence admitted is confined to whatever has a bearing on the issues defined in the pleading. The purpose of the pleading stage is to narrow the issues. Although in some cases the court may be criticized for preferring to remain blind to matters outside the pleading, the greater good is undoubtedly served by having a process by which the parties may screen the wheat from the chaff. When the complaint and answer have both been submitted, the next step is for the parties to appear in open court, before the judge and jury.

THE JURY TRIAL

When the pleading stage is completed and the issue is joined, a date is then set for trial. Usually the court has empaneled a group of jurors to hear a series of cases over a period of time as long as several weeks. From this panel 12 jurors will be selected to hear a particular case. Each attorney has a right to question each prospective juror to see if there are any grounds for his rejection, as, for example, prejudice. Either attorney may disqualify as many jurors as he may wish, providing reasonable grounds indicating bias or incapacity may be shown. He is also entitled to disqualify a restricted number of jurors without grounds other than his own hunch that the juror might be unsatisfactory from his point of view. Any disqualified jurors are replaced by ones found qualified; then when 12 suitable jurors are found the trial begins.

The first step in the trial proper is the opening statement of the plaintiff's case, which is merely an oral summary of the nature of his complaint and what he intends to prove. The defendant may make his opening statement either following the plaintiff's opening statement or after the plaintiff has finished presenting his evidence.

After the defendant's opening statement, if he makes one, the plaintiff presents his evidence. Most evidence is introduced in the form of oral statements from witnesses, usually in answers to interrogation by the plaintiff's attorney, though occasionally a witness may be asked to testify in the form of a narrative. Most witnesses are called to testify because they have specific knowledge of specific happenings in relation to a case, but some are called because they have expert knowledge pertinent to some issue in question. The psychiatrist, the economist, or the engineer, to state only a very few examples, may be asked to testify simply because he may have skill and knowledge pertinent to the question of what happened in some situation, even though he witnessed none of the events leading to the dispute.

During the period that a witness testifies, the opposing attorney stands by to object to any immaterial or prejudicial testimony. If he objects to an improper question and the judge feels the objection is valid, he will instruct the witness not to answer. Sometimes the jury is dismissed from the courtroom while the judge determines if a question is proper. The reason for this is that to make a ruling on the admissibility of testimony the judge often has to have more information as to what the testimony will be. If the jury hears the possibly immaterial or prejudicial testimony, the damage is largely done.

In most cases, one improper statement is not going to determine the outcome of a case, and when a witness has blurted out something objectionable the judge usually warns the jury to disregard the statement and the trial proceeds. The common interpretation of this procedure seems to be that judges are so far removed from reality that they do not realize the jury might consider the statement, even though instructed that they should not. Ignorance on the part of judges is not the correct explanation for this procedure. The problem is, conceding that the jury might be influenced, what should be done? There are only two alternatives: to proceed, and hope that the jury will do as instructed and not be influenced by the improper statement, or to throw the case out of court and start all over again. Obviously the dangers of any particular improper statement must be weighed against

the inconvenience of declaring a mistrial. In cases where substantial prejudice might result, a retrial may be required.

After each of the witnesses for the plaintiff has completed his testimony,
the opposing attorney may cross-examine him, usually hoping to lessen the
credibility of the witness's testimony in the eyes of the jury.

After all the witnesses for the plaintiff have been examined and cross-
examined the same procedure is followed with witnesses for the defendant.

The jury decides all questions of fact. Typical questions of fact are these:
Did Perry Mason's client kill the victim? If so, was it self-defense? An accident? Deliberately, with malice aforethought? Some of these questions are
highly subjective, but all must be determined on occasion. Turning to areas
of law other than the criminal, questions of fact might be these: Did the
parties intend to contract, or was their agreement in jest? Did the speeding
of one driver *cause* an accident, or would the accident have occurred anyway because the other driver ran a red light?

When all the evidence is in, the judge provides a statement of the law, by
which the jury is to be guided in arriving at its decision. This statement of
the law is termed the judge's *instructions*. The task for the jury is to decide
what the facts of the case actually were, to apply to the facts the law as
stated in the judge's instructions, and then to arrive at a verdict.[2] If they
are unable to do so, the case is retried before another jury.

There are, it is true, some limitations upon the discretion of the jury.
Although a jury verdict is accepted in all cases where reasonable men
might differ on the outcome, a jury is not permitted to be utterly unreasonable. If a jury brings in a verdict that has no supporting evidence, in the
eyes of the judge, the trial judge may countermand the verdict and decide
the case in favor of the other party. (This is not true in a criminal case,
however.) This is termed a judgment "not withstanding verdict," or
"N.O.V." (which stands for the Latin words *non obstante veredicto*.[3] This
power is used very sparingly by trial judges, and in fact it requires a rather
unusual situation where one may say that there is so little evidence on one
side that reasonable men could decide only in one way.

What are the advantages and disadvantages of the jury system? As the
jury presently functions, it frees the judge from deciding many questions,
often of a nature that one man is as capable of deciding as another. Sometimes the despair of literal-minded attorneys and judges, the jury (which
was referred to by some cynic as "twelve citizens with no evident qualifications") nevertheless serves other functions aside from the primary one of
deciding facts. The jury prevents a concentration of legal power in the

---

2 In criminal cases the jury must reach a unanimous verdict. In civil cases, many
states accept less than unanimity, in many states agreement of 10 out of 12 jurors
often being the requisite for a verdict.

3 The judge also has the privilege of dismissing a case after hearing the plaintiff's
case, if the plaintiff's evidence is so weak that there seems to be no basis for recovery.

hands of government officials. Rather than having a legal system completely in the hands of judges who are a part of a tight, centrally controlled hierarchy, as is true in some countries, much of our legal administration is responsive to the public simply because members of the jury are selected at random from the public, and the law is actually applied by the jury.

There is a substantial amount of intelligent criticism directed at some aspects of the jury as an institution. Perhaps the best basis for criticism is the fact that many types of cases are simply too complex for a jury to comprehend. Many disputes between private businessmen, for example, dealing with esoteric questions of corporation mergers, or high finance, can only be understood by those having some background in the particular area. Furthermore, because these types of cases do not involve a criminal prosecution, there is no important reason for a trial by the litigants' peers. Indeed, some authorities have advocated that the jury be dispensed with in all commercial litigation. One result of dissatisfaction with jury trials in this area, as well as dissatisfaction with the expense and delay involved in law suits, has been an increasing resort to arbitration as a means of settling disputes.[4]

In cases decided according to the rules of equity, no jury is empaneled to decide the questions of fact. The judge decides the facts, as well as applying the law to these cases. The reasons for this difference are mainly historical. (See pages 38–40.)

In any case, the parties may, if they wish, agree to dispense with a jury and assign the task of deciding the facts to the judge. It even happens occasionally that parties are able to agree to the facts but disagree as to the law. In this event, the parties file an agreed statement of facts, called a stipulation, and present the case to the trial judge for his decision on the questions of law.

THE TRIAL JUDGE

It would seem that when men engage in almost any type of complex, organized activity, someone has to be in charge. The trial judge is in charge of the proceedings in a jury trial.

Depending upon the political unit selecting the judge, he may either be elected or appointed to his post. If appointed he usually has tenure for life, which has the merit of removing him from the political arena, and thereby reducing the possibility of his decisions being influenced by political considerations. If elected, theoretically at least, the judge may be removed from office by the electorate any election. Although it is probably true that most persons who have considered the question carefully favor appointment rather than election of judges, the theoretical objections to the election of judges are often not borne out in practice.

[4] See pages 38–40 to 234–242 in this text for further discussion of this point.

In the first place, it seems to be traditional in many parts of the country for an incumbent judge facing retirement to resign in mid-term. This means that his immediate successor will be appointed to fill out the term. Usually the appointment is made by the governor, but on the advice of the *local bar association*. In effect, the local bar, consisting of the attorneys who are going to practice before the appointed judge, are instrumental in choosing the judge, and considering that they are going to have to practice before whomever is selected, they may be expected to consider the integrity and ability of candidates very carefully.

The judge appointed with the endorsement of the local bar association rarely finds himself opposed when his term expires. Even if he is, the active support of the bar association usually assures his reelection, and therefore he is not likely to be opposed. Even in cases where an incumbent judge resigns at the end of his term, usually the endorsement by the bar association of one candidate can secure his election. Most citizens do not take very much interest in the judicial elections, and rely, wisely in all probability, on their lawyer friends for advice as to the merits of different candidates.

Perhaps we should stop to consider what qualifications a judge should have. Above all he should have integrity. The function of the judge is to decide like cases, or issues within cases, in a like manner and to be consistent and impartial in his application of rules. Consistency is important not only because it is central to our ideas of justice but because if decisions are not consistent, there is no way of predicting who will win a dispute other than by going to the time and expense of bringing the dispute to trial.

Some citizens appear to believe that the judge should be politically accountable for the outcome of cases he decides. This view is particularly liable to be expressed when a party to the case is identified with some political view or interest, or when a defendant has been accused of a particularly unpopular crime. To argue that a judge should be held accountable at the polls if he does not arrive at the popular decision is simply to argue that prejudice, rather than rules, should be relied upon in deciding; or stated differently, that law should not be the basis for decision in cases involving strong public feeling. The public is in fact not qualified to comment upon many judicial decisions, because in most cases it is not aware of the rules the judge was following that caused him to arrive at the outcome. It undoubtedly happens on occasion that a judge, applying the rules that are supposed to be followed, arrives at a decision in a case contrary to what he or the public would have preferred. However, given the choice of adhering to the dictates of the law or arriving at a popular verdict, in all probability the public is much better served in the long run by adhering to the law. When the public demands decisions be made to satisfy mob instinct rather than rule, there is no reason why all decisions should not be made in this way. History provides instances in which this has occurred.

Of course a judge must be well versed in the law. If he is to make decisions between differing interpretations of law, advocated by opposing attorneys, he obviously should know at least as much and preferably a good deal more of the subject than they. Otherwise, the judge will find it difficult to retain the respect of the attorneys practicing before him.

Finally, the judge should be both open-minded and imaginative. After all, he has to know not only what the law is but often what it should be. When deciding whether it is time to overrule a precedent, or in deciding which of two equally logical ways a precedent should be interpreted, imagination is required to determine what the social effects would be. At the same time, he must be open-minded enough to see that the conventions to which he personally adheres may not be those that are best suited to present conditions.

Let us now look at the specific functions the trial judge performs. We have already said that he is the party in charge of the proceedings. He maintains orderly proceedings and forbids undue bickering or unduly demonstrative outbursts by anyone in the court. He has authority consistent with his responsibility, and if his order is violated with regard to the conduct of a trial, the judge may hold the offending party guilty of contempt of court and may fine or imprison that party.

In addition to his function of providing leadership during the conduct of a trial, the judge decides all questions of law that arise.

We have previously discussed how the attorneys elicit evidence in the form of testimony of witnesses for consideration by the jury. The primary function of the judge, meanwhile, is to rule out evidence that is prejudicial or immaterial to the case in issue.

Evidence may be ruled out because it consists of matters not placed in issue by the original pleading or matter not directly bearing on the point in issue. Some categories of evidence, such as hearsay, are untrustworthy and therefore excluded. In every case, the burden is upon the attorney wishing matter to be suppressed to make a timely objection, upon which the judge will then make a ruling.

Criticism by laymen is often directed at the rules of evidence for ruling out too much. The line may occasionally be drawn too closely; perhaps now and then matter is excluded that could fairly be presented to the jury. Lines drawn on the basis of principle cannot always correspond to everyone's view of the ideal, but having some limits as to what may be considered valid evidence is clearly essential. The law of evidence, a large and complex field of law, seems to be workable.

Last, but not least, the judge provides the statement of law that will guide the jury in reaching its decision in a statement termed the *instructions*.

The Appellate Courts

When a case is appealed from the trial court, it goes to an appellate court, the highest courts in the state hierarchy. Some states have only one appellate court, the State Supreme Court, whereas others have an intermediate layer of appellate courts. If the latter is the case, an appeal may go from the trial court to the intermediate appellate court. The loser on this appeal may then carry his case to the State Supreme Court.[5] The intermediate appellate court serves to reduce the load of the State Supreme Court, because many litigants would tire of litigation after one appeal, and in cases where the trial court and the appellate court emphatically agree, it is often obvious that there is no basis for reversal.

The immediate function of the appellate court is to serve as a check upon the trial courts—to provide an avenue for the losing party whereby any doubtful decision of the trial judge may be reviewed. The possibility of appellate review also serves to maintain a consistent interpretation of the law throughout the various trial courts under the supervision of the appellate court, because any interpretations of law contrary to those previously enunciated by the appellate court are likely to be appealed by the losing party and the trial court reversed. It should be borne in mind that the reputation of a trial judge depends partly upon having a low rate of reversals. Probably we may assume that most trial judges strive to keep their decisions consistent with the announced legal interpretations of the court having appellate jurisdiction over them.

From what has been said above, we see there is a second function of the appellate courts, somewhat related to the function of providing a check upon the trial courts. This function is in providing authoritative pronouncements as to what the law of the particular jurisdiction is. In each of our 50 states today, the appellate courts of that state are the forum in which the state's common law is molded. The appellate courts are also the forum in which legislation is authoritatively interpreted.

CONDITIONS FOR BRINGING A CASE FOR APPEAL

Complaints against the findings of fact made by the jury are almost never considered as being adequate ground for appeal. The findings of fact will be reviewed only in cases where the verdict appears so obviously faulty that the judge may be said to have erred because he did not overrule the verdict of the jury. In other words, appeal is still placed in the context of whether the judge made an error. In practice, appellate courts almost never find a judge guilty of error in not overruling the jury, reasoning that the

---

[5] In a few states the highest appellate court goes by some other name, notably in New York, where the highest appellate court is termed the Court of Appeals.

trial judge, having himself viewed the witnesses, is in a better position to evaluate the validity of the jury's finding than an appellate court.

The allegations of judicial error on questions of law are usually of two types; either (1) that the judge made an error of law in screening the evidence, either admitting that which should have been excluded or excluding that which should have been admitted; or (2) that the judge gave faulty instructions to the jury about the law governing the subject in issue.

In either case, the issues to be considered on appeal are narrowed in several ways. For one thing, no assertion of error may be made if the attorney for the party did not object at the time an error was committed. There has been much reasonable criticism of this requirement. What is or is not admissible is a highly technical question; the right to appeal may depend more upon the quick-wittedness of the attorney than on generally accepted ideas of justice. The issues to be raised on appeal are also narrowed by requiring that a written statement of the alleged errors be provided the appellate court, along with legal authorities supporting the position of the party appealing. This seems a legitimate requirement, even though the appellant is foreclosed from later introducing any points not considered in the written statement. The judges are entitled to advance notice of the issues involved so they may study those points and be prepared to question the counsel raising those points.

THE OPINION

The legal analysis of every appellate decision, including a discussion of the salient facts, the issues, and the rules of law used in deciding the case, and the reason why those rules and not others were applied, are contained in a written memorandum called the opinion. Such a statement is inherently necessary in a system of common law, because if a decision is based upon precedents the question naturally follows, what precedents? If the precedent is not followed, why not? Furthermore, because the case being decided itself becomes a precedent to be relied upon in the future, it is of great use to later judges to know why the precedents selected to decide the instant case were thought to apply rather than other, different precedents.

The opinion has the effect of requiring a judge to keep his decision in accord with precedent, or if departing from precedent, to state the reasons for the departure. If the reasoning is faulty, the record is open for the world to see, and subsequent judges will not adopt the faulty decisions as a precedent. Scholars, in the comfort and leisure of their ivory towers, may write scholarly articles criticizing the unfortunate judge. There is little leeway for authoritarian dictates in the common law, because the decision stands or falls depending upon the strength of the supporting reasons. When, as is often the practice under the Civil Codes, the reasons may be given in generalities or not at all, these checks are lacking.

At the present time the opinions of all cases brought before appellate courts in this country are printed, indexed, and made available for study by attorneys. Compilations of these opinions make up most of the volumes that overawe visitors to attorneys' offices. Many opinions are included for study in this text. These opinions in total make up our expanding case law.

A Word Concerning the System of Adversaries

Law is unique among the professions in relying upon adversary proceedings. Every lawyer representing a client in a lawsuit is pitted against the lawyer on the opposing side. Each is required by professional ethics, though also by personal inclination in most instances, to represent his client as forcefully as his abilities permit.

Much criticism is directed at the practice of adversary proceedings, terming the practice a trial by combat rather than a search for truth. Writers have stated that, after all, physicians attempting to save a patient, or businessmen attempting to make a sound decision, merely review the evidence and make a (presumably wise) decision. Why, then, cannot lawyers get together, examine the evidence, and quietly dispose of a client's life or property in a more philosophic manner?

Of course, this type of analogy misses its mark. A team of lawyers working to save a man from the electric chair can work together just as objectively as a team of physicians attempting to save a patient, for the same reason: they are united in their goal. The physicians are combating, not cooperating with, a disease; the lawyers are combating the electric chair, in the immediate form of a prosecuting attorney, who in turn has been furnished evidence convincing him of the probability that the accused is guilty. The prosecutor's job is to present this evidence before judge and jury because the interest of society demands that crime be punished. The defense attorney has heard from his client information that, if believed, may constitute a defense. We mention the probability of doubt about facts on the part of both attorneys, because surely the suggestions that the attorneys not act as adversaries stems from a belief that in some way the attorneys really do know or can in some way discover the absolute truth. If they did, then perhaps they could after all get together as reasonable men and decide what to do. In cases where the defendant admits his crime, often his attorney and the prosecutor do agree on a sentence and so recommend to the judge.

However, because the exact truth is usually unattainable, each attorney is assigned the task of developing his side of the case as energetically as possible, and because no partisan can be impartial, the decision is left in other hands.

There is no more sense in the attorney's accommodating to the danger threatening his client than there is in the physician accommodating to the disease. As for the businessman, when he is deciding which of two products to buy, very likely the representatives of two companies he is considering as his supplier, in attempting to sell their products, act very much like attorneys. The businessman would probably do well to consider such objective evidence as is presented, just as a jury does. Would the businessman prefer that his suppliers get together to decide who should sell to him?

Personal experience as a judge has convinced this writer, at least, that an impartial party could not possibly be expected to conduct inquiry into the defects in the opposite party's case with the zeal that a partisan will. It does not seem humanly possible for an impartial party to manufacture, in some artificial manner, the zeal of a partisan. At the same time, the partisan cannot decide with the objectivity of a neutral party. Although this zeal may introduce some tension into the courtroom, it has resulted in discovery of evidence that has determined cases that would otherwise have been decided improperly.

To abandon adversary proceedings is really a suggestion that the defendant's right to defense be waived, for someone would have to present the evidence of a defendant's crime whether the defendant was represented or not. It seems doubtful if a change of this sort would represent a step forward.

CHAPTER SIX

Our Federal System of Government

The power of the state does not stem from its constitution, as is true of federal power; rather the state constitution merely limits the power of the state. The state government has the power to pass any legislation . . . unless specifically forbidden by the state constitution, or the federal Constitution, or unless in conflict with federal legislation.

Our System of Dual Sovereignty

THE ADMINISTRATIVE and legal organization of the United States is unusual among nations in the sense that it is a system based upon dual sovereignty. That is, we have two coexisting governmental structures. The federal government is the supreme political and legal authority in regard to some areas of activity; [1] the individual state governments retain supremacy in other areas. [2]

On one hand, we have a federal legislature (Congress), a federal Constitution interpreted by the United States Supreme Court, and a system of lesser federal courts, including both trial and appellate courts. To complete the picture, we have a Chief Executive of the United States, the President. heading a federal executive department.

In general outline, this organization is duplicated in each of our 50 states. Each state has its own legislature, its own constitution, its own supreme court and lesser state courts, and its own chief executive, the Governor. Each state has, in addition, its own common law. *There is no federal*

---

[1] See Article VI, Section 2, and Article I, Section 8, of the United States Constitution.

[2] See Article X of the United States Constitution.

common law. All federal law is based on legislation, which in turn must be authorized by our federal Constitution.[3] (But see note page 82.)

The reasons for our system of dual sovereignty are largely historical. The original 13 colonies existed before the formation of the United States government. Leaders of the colonies conceived of their unification into the United States essentially as a surrender of certain powers by the then sovereign states to the proposed federal government. Most of these powers are enumerated in Article I, Section 8 (see below), of the Constitution. Powers not granted the federal government in the Constitution were to be retained by the states. The federal government, theoretically at least, was to have no powers except those expressly granted to it in the Constitution and, as later established, those powers necessary and proper to carrying out the powers expressly granted. Therefore, the federal Constitution is often referred to as being a *grant* of powers.

The state governments retained all powers of government except those granted to the federal government. The power of the state does not stem from its constitution, as is true of federal power; rather the state constitution merely *limits* the otherwise almost unlimited police power of the state. The state government has the power to pass any legislation aimed at promoting the health, safety, welfare, or morals of the state, unless specifically forbidden by the state constitution or the federal Constitution, or unless in conflict with federal legislation.

CONSTITUTION OF THE UNITED STATES

ARTICLE I, SECTION VIII

1. The Congress shall have power to lay and collect taxes, duties, imposts and excises, to pay the debts and provide for the common defense and general welfare of the United States; but all duties, imposts and excises shall be uniform throughout the United States;

2. To borrow money on the credit of the United States;

3. To regulate commerce with foreign nations, and among the several States, and with the Indian tribes;

4. To establish an uniform rule of naturalization, and uniform laws on the subject of bankruptcies throughout the United States;

5. To coin money, regulate the value thereof, and of foreign coin, and fix the standard of weights and measures;

6. To provide for the punishment of counterfeiting the securities and current coin of the United States;

7. To establish post offices and post roads;

8. To promote the progress of science and useful arts by securing for limited

[3] Rules and regulations of administrative agencies are another source of law both at the state and federal levels. This subject is considered in Chaps. 38 and 39.

times to authors and inventors the exclusive right to their respective writings and discoveries;

9. To constitute tribunals inferior to the Supreme Court;

10. To define and punish piracies and felonies committed on the high seas and offenses against the law of nations;

11. To declare war, grant letters of marque and reprisal, and make rules concerning captures on land and water;

12. To raise and support armies, but no appropriation of money to that use shall be for a longer term than two years;

13. To provide and maintain a navy;

14. To make rules for the government and regulation of the land and naval forces;

15. To provide for calling forth the militia to execute the laws of the Union, suppress insurrections, and repel invasions;

16. To provide for organizing, arming and disciplining the militia, and for governing such part of them as may be employed in the service of the United States, reserving to the States respectively the appointment of the officers, and the authority of training the militia according to the discipline prescribed by Congress;

17. To exercise exclusive legislation in all cases whatsoever over such district (not exceeding ten miles square) as may, by cession of particular States and the acceptance of Congress, become the seat of the Government of the United States, and to exercise like authority over all places purchased by the consent of the legislature of the State in which the same shall be, for the erection of forts, magazines, arsenals, dockyards, and other needful buildings;

18. To make all laws, which shall be necessary and proper for carrying into execution the foregoing powers, and all other powers vested by this Constitution in the Government of the United States, or in any department or officer thereof.

✧

Respective Role of Federal and State Governments

THE LEGISLATIVE BRANCH

The power of the state to legislate in order to promote health, safety, welfare, or morals is termed the *police power*. The federal government has no police power in the technical sense of that term; that is, theoretically, at least, Congress cannot legislate except in areas where the constitution grants it the power to do so. The areas in which the federal legislature (Congress) may act are enumerated above.

Probably one may say that in sheer volume, more federal legislation stems from the commerce clause than any other single source. The federal government regulates interstate commerce in myriads of different ways. Regulation of labor relations, the safety of food and drugs, virtually all forms of transportation and communication, electric power, stocks and bonds, and monopoly are some of the forms of federal regulation that stem from the commerce clause.

A large amount of federal legislation is also concerned with taxes, especially the income tax and the estate tax. Aside from the commerce clause and the tax clause each provision of Article I, Section VIII, has been the father of some federal legislation. Hardly anyone denies that over the years the federal government has extended its authority to the extent that it might reasonably be said to exercise police power in the traditional sense of legislating for the health, morals, and general welfare of the United States. This expansion of federal power has been justified under a liberal interpretation of the commerce clause. For example, federal legislation makes kidnaping a federal crime (if the victim is taken over a state line) on the theory that this involves interstate commerce.

The fact that the Constitution gives the federal government the power to legislate in certain areas does not mean that the states are entirely precluded from exercising their jurisdiction in these areas. Not until Congress actually has passed legislation dealing with these subjects are the states excluded, and even then only to the extent that their exercise of power would in some way conflict with the exercise of federal power. Many difficult questions have been presented regarding the rights of a state to exercise its police power when Congress has entered one of the areas of jurisdiction to a limited extent.

Stated very broadly, the role of the state legislature is to determine the directions in which the police power of the state will be exercised. The legislature levies taxes, imposes such criminal and regulatory laws as seem needed, and maintains such services as the legislators deem necessary. Highways, schools, welfare schemes, police protection, and health measures are illustrations of matters to which legislatures devote their attention, but these, as well as those mentioned earlier (page 51–60) are by no means all. Many of these activities are delegated to smaller units of the state— for example, cities, counties, and school districts. These are considered branches of the state government.

THE EXECUTIVE DEPARTMENT

In very simple terms, the function of the federal executive, the President, is primarily to enforce and administer the laws of the United States. Of course, it is not really that simple. The process of enforcing and administering is so complex that the executive branch of our government practically defies description. To assist the President in this task there is first of all the Cabinet (Departments of State, of Defense, of the Treasury, of Commerce, of Labor, of Agriculture, of the Interior, and of Health, Education, and Welfare, and of the Office of the Attorney-General, for example). In addition, there is a sizable agglomeration of boards (Federal Reserve) and independent administrative agencies (Interstate Commerce Commission, Fair Trade Commission, National Labor Relations Board, to state a few), which are to a large extent independent of the Chief Executive and whose responsibilities are often legislative and judicial as well as executive. Almost all the departments, boards, and agencies operate within the confines of a grant of federal legislation, but most are given some, and often very wide, power to supplement the enabling legislation with their own rules and regulations. This is a matter of simple necessity. The affairs being administered by the executive branch are so complex that Congress lacks the time and the expert knowledge required to provide continuing supervision, and to devise the rules and regulations needed to meet the current and often shifting problems. There is an assumption that such rules and regulations are valid, though they may be attacked in the courts on the ground of being beyond the scope of the enabling legislature, or of being unreasonable and therefore a denial of due process of law. (See Chapter 39, dealing with administrative agencies.)

In addition to supervising this complex administrative machinery the President is given certain specific powers under the Constitution, notably, those of the Commander-in-Chief of the Armed Forces and the power to make treaties with foreign powers, though the latter must be ratified by a two-thirds vote of the Senate. He also usually takes an active part in proposing new legislation.

Each of our states has a Chief Executive, the Governor, and has much the same types of administrative organs—departments, boards, and agencies—as the federal government.

THE JUDICIARY

Although the United States Supreme Court is the only federal court created by the Constitution, authority is given Congress in Article III of the Constitution to create a system of inferior federal courts, and this has been done. The federal trial courts are termed Federal District Courts. The appellate courts are termed Circuit Courts of Appeal, and from these Courts one may appeal to the Supreme Court. However, because of time limitations the Supreme Court is unable to hear all cases it is requested to hear, and in fact it tends to consider a case only if it is in some way particularly significant.

The system of federal courts created by Congress is similar to that of one of the larger states.

In that the federal government and the states maintain coexisting judicial systems, what criterion determines whether a case will be heard before a state or a federal court? In general, the state courts hear cases based upon civil disputes or violations of the state criminal law occurring within the particular state, or involving disputed rights to property within the state, (title to land for example.)

The federal courts hear only certain well-defined types of cases. Certain parties to a case will give federal jurisdiction. These include cases in which (1) the United States is a party, and (2) cases between citizens of different states involving more than $10,000, as well as a few very rare situations we need not consider here. As to subject matter of a suit, regardless of who the parties may be, the federal courts will hear cases concerning questions arising under the federal Constitution, or arising under the laws of the United States, or under a treaty, or involving maritime or admiralty jurisdiction.

CONSTITUTION OF THE UNITED STATES
ARTICLE III, SECTION II, PART (1)

The judicial power shall extend to all cases, in law and equity, arising under this Constitution, the laws of the United States, and treaties made, or which shall be made, under their authority; to all cases of admiralty and maritime jurisdiction; to controversies to which the United States shall be a party; to controversies between two or more States; between a State and citizens of another State; between citizens of different States; between citizens of the same State claiming lands under grants of different States, and between a State or the citizens thereof, and foreign states, citizens, or subjects.

The federal and most state Supreme Courts consist of nine judges, and intermediate appellate courts often consist of a panel of three judges. Because the facts of a case are not in issue on appeal, the appellate court has no jury attached. The issues are issues of law, and the judges are there in order to review questions of law.

Relative Importance of State and Federal Government

Despite the paramount importance of our federal government, the importance of our state governments must not be underemphasized.

State law encompasses most criminal law, the law of marriage and divorce, the law of wills and inheritance, and the law of personal wrongs (torts). Most of what is usually thought of as business law, including the law of contracts, sales, negotiable instruments, real-estate transactions, partnerships, corporations, suretyships, and insurance, is devised and administered by the states. In addition, of course, each state has its own educational, correctional, and charitable institutions, as well as the duty to provide roads, bridges, and other services. Taxes are assessed and collected for these purposes.

Every state at present has its own common law (traceable back to English common law, but now derived from the appellate court decisions of that state) as well as its own legislature. Of course, in arriving at a judicial decision, state courts do tend to consider the decisions of other states, particularly when there are no local precedents on a question. However, virtually all federal law is based on legislation. There is no federal common law, except in isolated instances.[4]

As would be expected, there are both advantages and disadvantages to the decentralization that characterizes the organization of our government. The principal advantages are essentially those inherent in any form of decentralization. Local control means that the wishes of the local population may be more readily given effect. Each state may devise laws that seem to it most appropriate to local conditions. Certainly our states vary widely in terms of economic base, size, ethnic composition, population, and even history, and these differences are reflected to some degree in their law.

On the other hand, the multiplicity of jurisdictions found in the United States leads to difficult problems for those involved in transactions that are not confined to one state but are regional or national in scope. It is not surprising that businessmen have attempted to devise one commercial code, one which it was hoped would be adopted uniformly by all the states. (The Uniform Commercial Code, discussed elsewhere in this text, represents the latest attempt toward achieving uniformity in business law.) Commercial transactions are made exceedingly difficult when uniformity of law is lacking. Another chronic source of problems and even injustice has been the wide disparity in the law of marriage and divorce. Failure of some states to recognize divorces granted elsewhere has resulted in innocently contracted bigamous marriages, as well as the anomaly of marriages valid in one state but not in another. We do not even know for certain what the traffic laws will be when we enter another state.

Naturally, there is pressure for greater uniformity of state law, but the areas where divergence is most significant are often areas in which the emotional commitment to a local rule is strongest, the law of marriage and divorce being an example.

---

[4] See *Clearfield Trust Company* v. *United States,* 318 U.S. 363 (1943), where the law to delineate rights controlling negotiable instruments issued by the United States was deemed a question for federal case law.

CHAPTER SEVEN

Legal Remedies

Whether the basis for suit is contract or tort, the usual remedy is a sum of money, determined by the jury as being adequate compensation for the injury.

Money Damages

WE MUST NOT forget that the entire detailed, expensive apparatus of the law exists as a means of providing a remedy for an injured party in a particular case. The time-consuming process of trial is only a means to an end. When a criminal case is in issue, the end is determination of guilt or innocence and, if the party is found guilty, assessment of punishment. In this text we shall be concerned much more with cases between private individuals. In these cases the end is the determination of whether or not the plaintiff has been wronged, and if it is found that he has been, determination of the amount of compensation for the wrong.

Most private wrongs fall within two areas: breach of contract and torts. A contract, roughly described, is an agreement made between two parties that the law will enforce by awarding damages if the agreement is not performed. The wrong, therefore, consists in one party's not living up to the agreement. Torts are a varied group of acts which we as a society consider wrong and which have in common merely the fact that none are based on contract. Assault and battery, libel and slander, and negligence are torts with which the general reader is at least somewhat familiar, though there are others.

What remedies are available to compensate the plaintiff for the defendant's wrong? Whether the basis for suit is contract or tort, the usual remedy is a sum of money, determined by the jury as being adequate compensation for the injury. This appears to strike many as odd. The comment is often made that actually money cannot fully compensate for loss of limb, excruciating pain, or emotional scars. Although comments along these lines are admittedly sound, the fact that an award of money is not a perfect remedy is not the issue. The question is, what *can* compensate for such injuries? The answer in every case, literally, is nothing. However, awarding nothing by way of compensation does not seem to be the ideal solution either. Money appears to be the least inadequate of several inadequate alternatives.

Another related question often raised is, how can a monetary value be placed upon serious injuries? The procedures used in determining the amount of damages appropriate to an injury are the same as those used in determining any other fact. Most evidence will be introduced in the form of testimony from witnesses in a position to describe the nature and extent of the injury. In the case of a bodily injury, much of the testimony relating to damages will probably be by physicians, because they are especially qualified to assess the severity and probable long-term consequences of the particular injury. Having heard testimony from both sides on a question of damages, the jury will be instructed that the damages should be considered in two parts. *Special damages* are those to which an exact dollar-and-cents value can be ascribed. Medical bills, hospital bills, and loss of wages already encountered are examples of special damages, and may be calculated without much difficulty. *General damages* are those that may not be calculated with precision. Pain and suffering in a personal injury case are the most common examples of general damages.

In calculating general damages, the jury is cast at sea. The calculation is not an exact science, and the remarkable thing is that jury awards are as consistent as they are. As a matter of fact, experienced insurance adjusters can often predict within a reasonable range, though almost never exactly, the amount a jury will award. Probably the fact that a jury consists of 12 citizens has the effect of tempering the judgment of the occasional juror whose thinking is considerably more generous, or more parsimonious, than the general run of citizens. In any event, this sort of decision must be made if plaintiffs are to be compensated for wrongs inflicted, and giving the issue to a jury seems to be about as sound a basis for decision as any other. Whether this is the soundest possible system for measuring damages or not, this is in fact the system for measuring damages, in all the trial courts in the United States and in many foreign countries.

The problems in assessing damages in contract actions are usually less imposing than in the case of torts. The estimate to be made in a contract case is how much financial loss came about as a direct and foreseeable result of the breach. Usually this resolves into an evaluation of how much profit a businessman would have realized if the contract were performed, compared to the actual profit (or loss). Often there is reasonably reliable accounting data to guide the jury in its decision.

Suppose that a defendant in a private action has no money. What may be done to secure damages in that event? The answer is, practically nothing. We have eliminated debtor's prisons, and even when we had them, they did not noticeably increase the creditor's prosperity. As stated by Mr. Micawber, in *David Copperfield,* you can't get blood out of a turnip. If a defendant is without property and penniless, even though the plaintiff has secured a valid judgment, that plaintiff is probably no better off than he was at the start of the trial. His one hope may be that the defendant will accumulate some assets. Even when a defendant has minor assets, such as household possessions, going through the necessary legal forms of seizing and selling the property often involves enough expense to make the game not worth the candle.

The inability to recover from a penniless defendant is one of the greatest practical defects in the working of our legal system. Yet what can be done? Forcing debtors into indentured servitude seems unacceptable, and there seems to be no sentiment toward having the government underwrite this type of loss. In some types of cases, notably automobile accident claims, legislation is being devised to correct the situation. Various schemes are being invented to force drivers to secure liability insurance, so that a victim of another's negligence will be able to recover against an insurer. In most areas of the law, however, the problem of the impecunious defendant presents an unresolved problem.

Equitable Remedies

In Chapter 3, *equity* the body of rules derived from the English Court of Chancery was discussed. Today, these rules have been absorbed into the common law, and are almost universally applied by the same judge, and in the same courtroom, as are the more traditional rules of the common law. Nevertheless, the impact of equity jurisprudence upon the common law has been substantial. The remedies devised by the courts of equity are still part of our law and serve to provide a suitable remedy in many cases when money damages would be inadequate. These remedies may be relied upon only after a showing that a *sum of money would not adequately reimburse the plaintiff.* The mere fact that a defendant will probably not be able to pay a judgment is not enough to warrant recourse to an equitable remedy. There has to be a showing that damages (the traditional remedy at common law) even if paid would not right the particular wrong.

The essential difference between the traditional common-law remedy of damages and the equitable remedies is that damages provide recourse only against the defendant's property. Means are provided whereby a plaintiff may seize property belonging to the defendant with which to satisfy a judgment. The equitable remedies, however, provide recourse against the defendant personally. The plaintiff, if he prevails in his suit, may secure an order from the court in which the defendant is personally ordered to do or not to do something. If the defendant violates the order, he is subject to punishment for contempt of court.

The three most common types of equitable relief are probably the injunction, specific performance, and rescission. An *injunction* is an order of the court commanding a party not to do a certain act. A repeated, minor trespass by an individual presents a case where damages are inadequate, because the cost of bringing suit is greater than the money damages provable, and such an award furnishes no protection against future trespasses. However, an order of the court commanding the party not to trespass will prevent future trespasses. Violation of the order will constitute contempt of court. In earlier days, the party in contempt of court could be seized and tortured until he agreed to sin no more. Presumably, this worked. Today, violation of a court order is enforceable by fine or imprisonment.

Almost any unlawful act for which damages cannot fully compensate a party may be the subject of an injunction. The injunction is probably most famous in modern times for its use, or misuse, in labor disputes. Acts of common-law courts or of executive officers may be enjoined, as was the seizure of the steel industry by the President during the Korean War.

Although we have not yet studied contracts, we assume the student has some notion that a contract is a type of agreement entered into that the law will enforce. The usual remedy for breach of contract is an award of money damages. However, this remedy is sometimes inadequate. The most common instances where money damages are an inadequate remedy arise when there is a contract involving performance that is in some way unique. Under these circumstances, the equitable remedy of *specific performance* may be obtained, which means that instead of awarding money damages, a court will order the reluctant party to the contract to proceed with his performance or face fine or imprisonment. Of course, the petitioning party must then perform his side of the bargain.

A unique performance by definition is one for which the desired performance cannot readily be obtained on the open market, nor duplicated, nor otherwise acquired through the expenditure of money. In other words, money damages cannot compensate for breach of contract if a performance is unique, and this is why the court requires that the contract actually be performed.

Perhaps because real property [1] in English law tended to imply manors

---

1 Real property is land, buildings, and other structures attached to land and property intended to remain permanently attached to the buildings and other structures. Personal property does not refer to personal articles—that is, comb, toothbrush, razor, and so on—but in general refers to any property that is intended to remain movable. In most

or castles, all real property was considered unique, and though this tenet seems of doubtful validity today, any parcel of land is still generally considered unique. Consequently, contracts for the purchase or sale of real property fall within the scope of the equitable remedy of specific performance.

When there is a contract for the sale of land and the seller refuses to perform by giving the buyer a deed, the buyer may get an order from the court ordering the seller to transfer title and possession to the property. If the seller refuses to perform he is in contempt of court. The buyer, of course, is required to pay the agreed sum of money.

Aside from land, other articles that have been considered unique are rare paintings, heirlooms, or almost any article that has a substantial claim to individuality. In one case, a manufacturer made a contract to be supplied for a period of time with an essential commodity (coal) that could not reasonably be obtained elsewhere. The supplier refused to abide by the agreement, and a court order requiring specific performance on the contract was obtained.

An important exception to the general rule is that specific performance will never apply to enforce a contract for personal services. This would apply to maids, butlers, and employees of all kinds. Forcing one individual to perform distasteful personal services for another would be contrary to the traditional common-law ideas respecting individual freedom. If specific performance were granted in such cases, hard-pressed debtors might be induced to enter long-term employment contracts under disadvantageous terms. If contracts of this type could be enforced, the result would in effect be peonage.

Rescission is a third type of equitable relief. The remedy sought through rescission is the cancellation of a contract, because inequitable means were used to procure it. Both parties will be returned to their original condition. Examples of the inequitable means on which rescission may be based are fraud, mistake, and duress. These, by the way, are called *equitable defenses*. We will see a number of instances in which rescission is sought in the section on contracts.

In most American jurisdictions today, a case involving one of these equitable remedies is not tried in a separate court nor before a special judge. Today the case will usually be tried in about the same way as any other case, but the special rules of law characteristic to equity still apply. Thus, even today equity cases are not tried before a jury. The judge makes the findings of fact.

---

cases, whether property is real or personal is obvious, but close cases must depend upon the apparent intent of the party involved. After all, buildings may be moved, and a house trailer can be permanently attached to the land. The status in each of these cases depends upon the apparent intent of the parties in control.

[EDITOR'S NOTE: Further discussion relating to problems of damages may be found in the following cases and in the text treatment after the cases: *Poplar* v. *Bourjois,* pages 153–154, concerning the extent of damages in tort; *Hadley* v. *Baxendale,* pages 405–407, concerning the extent of damages for breach of contract. Also see *Gagne* v. *Bertran,* concerning the measure of damages in fraud, and discussion, pages 287–290.]

The Declaratory Judgment

One of the traditional limitations upon the capacity of a court to hear and decide an issue has been the requirement that the issue present an actual case or controversy. Existence of a case or controversy implies that the parties must be engaged in a genuine dispute and that a judgment or order against one of the parties will result from the determination. There are several reasons for this requirement. For one thing, most courts have always had enough of a workload settling actual disputes to keep them more than busy. If parties could go to court merely to satisfy their curiosity as to how a hypothetical case might be decided, at the very least our society would have to divert far greater resources to hiring judges and building courthouses.

Furthermore, our courts rely upon the presence of adverse interests between parties to assure that the facts and the law applicable to a certain case will be adequately explored and presented. It is left to each of the parties in a lawsuit to present the issues of fact and of law upon which he may choose to rely. If two parties lack adverse interests and in fact both wish for the same result, it may reasonably be doubted that an adequate presentation of both sides will be given to provide the judge with the thorough exploration of competing considerations he needs in order to render a judgment. The judgment rendered in the "friendly suit" would then become a bad precedent. In summary, there are good reasons for requiring a case or controversy before a case may be eligible for judicial determination.

However, whether or not there is sufficient adversary interest between the parties as to assure vigorous exploration of the issues need not be a black-and-white question. Frequently cases arise in which a prospective plaintiff is not yet in a position to claim damages but in which if events run their natural course, he undoubtedly will suffer serious losses sooner or later. One might well wonder, under these circumstances, why the parties should be required to wait until the situation becomes aggravated before they might have their rights adjudicated.

For this reason, an exception to the older rule, that a case must be one subject to a judgment or order, has been modified. Although the requirement that the parties must present adverse interests remains, nevertheless, in almost all states, suits may be brought for the purpose of determining the rights of the parties, and informing them as to those rights, even if a loss has not yet materialized. This form of remedy is called the *declaratory judgment*. Thus, for example, the validity of an insurance policy that is questioned by the insurer may be decided in advance of a loss. Rights under a lease may be determined in advance of eviction by the landlord or abandonment by the tenant.

The declaratory judgment is an exceedingly valuable tool in determining the rights of the parties in many business disputes, as well as other disputes, in advance of and as a means of avoiding serious escalation in the dimensions of a dispute.

Torts

CHAPTER EIGHT

The Difference between
Tort and Crime

Crime is an offense against the public pursued by the sovereign, while tort is a private injury which is pursued by the injured party.[1]

IT WAS MENTIONED in earlier reading that the law serves two different functions in governing citizens' relationships. One function of the law is to provide a standard by which disputes between private citizens may be settled. The other function is to define and interpret the commands of the sovereign [2] and the limitations upon the power of the sovereign. These commands of the sovereign restrain the citizen from certain acts, or sometimes require affirmative acts, in the public interest.

The body of law that fulfills the first function is called the private law, and embodies such fields as contracts, torts, and property. The second body of law includes our criminal law as well as constitutional and administrative law. This is our public law.

Criminal law is that branch of the public law that defines the duties of the citizen to the sovereign, and the penalties to be imposed if the citizen does not live up to these duties. Treason is a crime because it is a wrong directed against the sovereign. Murder is also a crime. The sovereign knows it cannot be strong if citizens are permitted to kill one another. This must be prevented; therefore killing is outlawed. The killing is looked upon

[1] *State* . . . v. *Cobb* (North Carolina, 1939) 2 SE 2d 565.

[2] *The sovereign,* as used in discussions of law, refers to the powers of the government. This is an historical usage springing from the time when, in fact, most governmental authority did repose in kings and could be identified as a person. Today, sovereignty cannot be identified as one individual or body, but is a useful abstraction representing the power of government.

93

as a wrong against the sovereign; the sovereign regulates society. So, in the same sense, robbery, assault, negligent driving, and overparking are all wrongs against the sovereign, and are punished through government action. They are crimes.

Obviously, in instances in which an individual is murdered, or injured, or his property is stolen or destroyed, not only has a wrong been committed against the sovereign, but also against the individual. The wronged person or his heirs should have the opportunity to collect for their loss of income, hospital bills, and other expenses, and in addition an injured person should receive compensation for his suffering. He is not permitted simply to seize the wrongdoer's property, because this would result in a breach of the peace. For this reason our law provides for private actions. Our private law exists for the purpose of determining whether one private party has injured another, and if so, the amount of damages owed. The sovereign provides the forum, the judge, and the legal principles, but aside from this is neutral. The sovereign is promoting an orderly society by providing the means by which the individuals may settle their claims against one another.

Probably the two largest areas of private law are contracts and torts. Contract problems are usually identifiable, being based upon a claim by one party that the other did not live up to an agreement made between them. The right to legal recovery depends upon the existence of a legally recognized agreement. Torts consist of other types of acts that society recognizes as private wrongs. Tort and contract cases, if successfully concluded, usually provide compensation by money damages,[3] an award entitling the wronged party to collect a sum of money from the wrongdoer. This award is called a judgment. The amount is normally decided by the jury.

Loosely translated, the word *tort,* in the Latin, means "wrong." The law of torts is composed of several diverse groups of acts that have in common the fact that the law has deemed each of these acts "a wrong." Examples we shall study are assault, battery, libel, slander, and negligence. A tort is a private—that is, noncriminal—wrong, and is not based upon any agreement or breach of contract between the wrongdoer and the wronged.

The distinction between a tort and a crime is sometimes difficult for a beginning student to understand. The difference is exceedingly important. The confusion between the two arises from the fact that the same act may be, though need not always be, both a tort and a crime.

Because a crime is considered to be an act directed against the sovereign, a criminal act is prosecuted in the name of the state. *People* v. *Jones,* or in some states *State* v. *Jones,* may be the title of a criminal prosecution for the crime of assault and battery. The actual prosecution is handled by a district attorney, representing the state, and the police or sheriff's office will usually have conducted the investigation and secured the evidence.

[3] See Chapter 7.

Let us suppose that all of the above has occurred following an attack by Jones against Smith, in which Smith received a concussion. Jones may well be sentenced to a term in jail and may proceed to serve his sentence. The state is satisfied; Jones presumably will not attack others, having learned his lesson; and the public, viewing the example of Jones, will refrain from similar acts. Smith, however, still has a sore head and has not been reimbursed for his doctor bill. He may bring a private action against Jones and collect for damage suffered. Smith must retain his own attorney, he or his attorney must marshal the evidence, and the name of the suit will be entitled *Smith* v. *Jones*. (Remember, the party being sued is the *defendant;* the party bringing suit, the *plaintiff*.)

In this tort action, Smith is suing because of the same act for which Jones was previously jailed. If he wins, Smith may collect an award of money damages to compensate him for his doctor bills, loss of wages, and all other out-of-pocket losses (special damages) and, in addition, for his pain and suffering, humiliation, and anguish (general damages). In the case of a deliberate and malicious act such as this he may even get exemplary damages, which are assessed by the jury to make an example of Jones. As we know, the amount of damages are within the province of the jury, within certain limitations.

A more common, if less dramatic, example of interrelationship between the area of tort and crime often presents itself in the case of an automobile accident. Suppose Jones runs a stop sign and damages Smith's automobile. Quite likely, Jones will receive a traffic citation from the police for running the stop sign. (Generally, for minor traffic offenses a party may post a sum of money as bond, and the authorities will not require the party to appear in court but will merely consider the sum deposited as a forfeit in lieu of an appearance, conviction, and fine. Still, this results from a violation of the criminal law; the fine or forfeit is imposed by government officials.)

Again, payment of a fine by Jones is not of much help to Smith. Smith may, however, bring a tort action against Jones, for damages inflicted upon his automobile. Smith is entitled to the reasonable cost of restoring the car to its original condition. If Jones is insured, perhaps his insurance company will wish to negotiate a settlement rather than to litigate or for that matter Jones may be willing to pay without suit. Nevertheless, the decision of whether or not to pay is determined by reference to tort law. In this case, the tort involved is termed the *tort of negligence*. We undertake a study of this tort beginning with Chapter 11.

The fact that two trials may result from the same act—one criminal, and one in tort—is in no sense exposing the defendant to double jeopardy. Double jeopardy refers only to cases where a person is tried twice before the *criminal court* for the same act. (Even this prohibition is the subject of many exceptions.)

For historical reasons, there is considerable similarity between crimes and the deliberate torts; in fact, at one time the distinction between tort and crime did not exist.[4] Even today, the basic elements of criminal assault and battery and of tortious assault and battery remain very similar in many states. In the case of most other wrongful acts the similarity is less striking.

Despite similarities between torts and crimes, remember that not all acts that give rise to a tort action are crimes, and all acts that give rise to a criminal action are not torts. Slander, for example, is not a crime in some states but is invariably a tort. Perjury and treason are crimes everywhere but not torts. In fact, aside from assault and battery, concurrent elements of crimes and torts are not too common.

Why are the acts presently recognized as torts considered wrongs, whereas other acts are not? In the final analysis this must be considered a reflection of the moral judgment of the community plus some considerations of the practicalities of judicial enforcement. In other words, public policy is the long-run determinant of what wrongful acts warrant a recovery: those acts are then defined as torts. A legal wrong is a "wrong" merely because we agree that it is, and the law has taken cognizance of our attitudes.

Therefore, failing to yield the right of way (unless an injury results) is not of itself a tort, because the general concensus of opinion does not consider the damages—mere loss of a few seconds—important enough to justify a private remedy.[5] Because of the danger in such an act, it *is*, however, a criminal offense. The state will punish the violator. Some types of mental injury, such as swearing at another, are not torts because of the frequency of such incidents and the relatively slight damage usually inflicted. Actually, some very sensitive individuals might be seriously upset by such an event, and there have been some cases in the advance guard of the law that have awarded damages in this type of case. The deliberate infliction of mental suffering is a type of wrong, presently almost unrecognized, that appears to be gathering momentum and may eventually blossom forth into a well-recognized tort. Some states regard swearing at another as a crime, because of the danger that the party verbally abused may retaliate physically.

Some wrongful acts that are clearly tortious will not support an action in special cases because of a particular policy of overriding importance to the public welfare, contradicting the general policy underlying tort law.[6]

---

[4] The rules of law in the "Code of Hammurabi," a Babylonian king, in 2250 B.C., provide an example of this. See sections of this code in this text, page 100.

[5] But if an accident *does* result in which a party is injured, a tort probably has been committed.

[6] "Privilege" in assault, battery, or defamation cases is an example. See pages 133 and 136.

The immunity given legislators, protecting them from suit in slander when speaking before the legislature, is an example. The right of police to use force in apprehending criminals is another.

Thus, the process of selecting which acts shall be legally actionable as a tort seems to involve a balancing of competing interests. On the one side is weighed the social benefits that stem from the act; on the other side is weighed the social detriment. Every act that is considered a tort is an act which when placed on the balance between benefit and detriment has been found substantially detrimental. The same sorts of decisions, of course, are involved in deciding whether or not an act should be considered criminal. However, in deciding whether an action should or should not be considered criminal, the question is not merely whether a victim is entitled to compensation, but whether the act is so dangerous to the community that it should be punished by the sovereign.

QUESTIONS

1. In a criminal action, in order to obtain a conviction the state is required to prove guilt "beyond a reasonable doubt." In a private action, the plaintiff need only prove his case by a "preponderance of the evidence." Are there any good reasons for this difference in proof required?

2. Considering the above, would it seem possible that a person might be found innocent of a criminal battery but liable for damages in a private action arising from the same incident?

3. Are there any good reasons for deciding criminal guilt and private damages in two different suits? Any disadvantages?

STATE . . . v. COBB (North Carolina, 1939)
2 SE 2d 565

> Crime is an offense against the public pursued by the sovereign, while tort is a private injury which is pursued by the injured party. . . . The state . . . does own property and has property rights which might be the subject of invasion. If a wrong is committed against it in the nature of a tort, it must be with respect to such a right. . . . No crime against the . . . state violates any of its property rights. . . .

The State brought this action to recover the expenses of the recapture and return to the State Prison of one Eddie Cobb, who had escaped from custody during the year 1937. The amount sued for was $1,134.21.

SEAWELL, J.

This interesting case is admittedly novel in the history of jurisprudence in so far as the attorneys concerned, and the Court as well, are aware. Without precedent to guide us, we do not find in the argument of the able counsel for the plaintiff sufficient legal ground to sustain the judgment of the trial court.

The plaintiff bases its action on tort. It is difficult to see how an actionable tort could arise out of defendant's criminal offense in effecting his escape from custody, or his status as a fugitive from justice. The step from one to the other is a bit too long for the judicial stride. "The distinction between a tort and a crime with respect to the character of the rights affected and the nature of the wrong is this: A tort is simply a private wrong in that it is an infringement of the civil rights of individuals, considered merely as individuals, while a crime is a public wrong in that it affects public rights and is an injury to the whole community, considered as a community, in its social aggregate capacity."

"Crime is an offense against the public pursued by the sovereign, while tort is a private injury which is pursued by the injured party."

If a tort is pursued by the sovereign, it must be with respect to the same sort of right and in the same way as may be allowed a private citizen. This is a part of the definition. A sovereign, who is also a natural person, may, of course, bring an action for tort in his individual capacity and with respect to his individual and proprietary rights. Authorities are somewhat divided as to where sovereignty lies in a Republican State, Story on the Constitution, paragraph 270; *Filbin Corporation* v. *U.S.;* but the term is still useful in providing categories affecting rights and liabilities. . . .

The State constitutes a sort of intangible sovereignty. Legally speaking, it cannot be assaulted, slandered, or injured as an individual with respect to a personality that it does not possess. But it does own property and has property rights which might be the subject of invasion. If a wrong is committed against it in the nature of a tort, it must be with respect to such a right.

It does not appear that the defendant has invaded any property right of plaintiff except that which may be involved in the expenditure of the State's public funds for his apprehension after his escape. Since his recapture was a public duty required by law under a general system which the State has established, the position of the sovereign towards such a public expenditure can scarcely be that of a private individual who has been compelled to spend money because of the tortious conduct of another. Indeed, in point of legal logic, defendant's yen for the open spaces and his heeding of the call of the wild was rather the occasion than the cause of the expenditure, or, at least, did not afford the compulsion. While his flight was contrary to the will of the sovereign, as expressed in its law, the expenditure for his recapture was voluntary.

No crime against the sovereignty of the State violates any of its property rights and no governmental expenditure paid out for apprehension of a criminal or the maintenance or recovery of his custody incident to the punishment or correction of such a crime can be construed into a tortious invasion of the property rights of the State, since it is voluntarily made by the State, although a mandatory duty on the custodial agency, for the protection of the people of the State at large in preserving the integrity of the penal system. The offense was against the sovereignty of the State, the penalty fixed by law, and the exactions because of it do not go to the sovereign in any proprietary capacity justifying any application of the law of torts.

The most that can be said in behalf of the plaintiff is that it is endeavoring to protect public funds given into its custody. These funds were legitimately spent for a public purpose, and there is no statute law, and certainly no common law principle, authorizing their recovery from this defendant.

The judgment of the court below is reversed.

Reversed.

✧

What issues of policy are involved here? What would the effect be of charging convicts for the expenses incurred in effecting their capture?

An opposite decision would have opened the door to countless suits against convicts. Could not the costs of imprisonment be just as easily assessed against the convicted? If this included the jailer's salary, food, cost of prison, as well as investigation costs and expenses to the state for the trial, the sum would in most cases be very large indeed. In fact, such a policy would probably amount to confiscation of the convict's estate in the case of all but the most wealthy convict. This of course would amount to punishment of the convict's dependents. Confiscation of the convict's assets actually was at one time a part of the common law and seems to persist in some parts of the world even today.

We must conclude that wise policy lies behind the insistence upon confining liability to the private law and leaving the punishment of crime to the public law.[7]

Therefore, though this may not appear from a casual scanning of the case, this case is in one sense an affirmation of civil rights. There is rather clearly a choice between governmental power on the one hand and individual rights on the other.

QUESTIONS

1. Would the outcome have been different if the defendant had wrecked a state automobile during his flight?

2. What does the court mean when it refers to a "personal sovereign" in the case?

---

[7] Note, however, that vague speculations of policy, though possible, are not necessary to decide this case. Adherence in this case not to precedent but to established policies of the law provides the correct answer.

CHAPTER NINE

Assault and Battery

The tort of assault was developed to insure our interest in being free to live without fear of impending attack, and the tort of battery to insure us against actual physical attack. These torts provide a basis both for securing financial compensation for the fear and outrage likely to result from an assault or battery, and for providing the victim with a private, orderly way of securing revenge in place of physical retaliation.

Why the Torts of Assault and Battery?

THE CODE OF HAMMURABI (2250 B.C.) [1]

If a son strike his father, they shall cut off his fingers.

If a man destroy the eye of another man, they shall destroy his eye.

If one break a man's bone, they shall break his bone.

If a man knock out a tooth of a man of his own rank, they shall knock out his tooth.

If a man strike another man in a quarrel and wound him, he shall swear: "I struck him without intent," and he shall be responsible for the physician.

If he die as the result of the stroke, he shall swear as above, and if he be a man he shall pay one-half manna of silver.

✧

QUESTION

1. What happens if a toothless man knocks out another's tooth? Is it fair to impose the same penalty for eye-gouging upon a one-eyed man as upon a two-eyed man? What happens if a tooth is knocked out, or an eye destroyed, in a quarrel when the injury was

[1] Robert Francis Harper, *The Code of Hammurabi, King of Babylon* (Chicago: University of Chicago Press, 1904), p. 73.

unintended (compare the last statement above to the others)? Was some study of the law necessary or desirable for a judge in Hammurabi's day? Observe that no distinction is made between the private and public (criminal) law. What criticism might be made of these statements of law? Is this law better than none?

BLACKSTONE ON ASSAULT AND BATTERY [2]

. . . The law cannot draw the line between different degrees of violence, and therefore totally prohibits the first and lowest stage of it. . . .

. . . The absolute rights of each individual were defined to be the right of personal security, the right of personal liberty, and the right of private property. . . .

As to injuries that affect the personal security of individuals, they are either injuries against their lives, their limbs, their bodies, their health, or their reputations . . . and these may be committed. . . .

By . . . assault; which is an attempt to beat another, without touching him; as if one lifts up his cane, or his fist, in a threatening manner at another; or strikes at him but misses him; this is an assault, insultus, which Finch described to be "an unlawful setting upon one's person." This also is an inchoate violence, amounting considerably higher than bare threats; and therefore, though no actual suffering is proved, *yet the party injured may have redress . . . whereof he shall recover damages as a compensation for the injury.*

By battery; which is the unlawful beating of another. The least touching of another's person willfully, or in anger, is a battery; for the law cannot draw the line between different degrees of violence, and therefore totally prohibits the first and lowest stage of it; every man's person being sacred, and no other having a right to meddle with it in any the slightest manner.

❖

Today, when people speak of civil rights, they usually speak of such rights as the right to vote or to practice their own religious beliefs. The torts of assault and battery, however, represent devices for insuring certain basic human rights that are as important as human rights can be.

The tort of assault was developed to insure our interest in being free to live without fear of impending attack, and the tort of battery to insure us against actual physical attack. These torts provide a basis both for securing financial compensation for the fear and outrage likely to result from an as-

[2] Sir William Blackstone, *Commentaries on the Laws of England,* 1769, William Draper Lewis (ed.) (Philadelphia: Rees Welsh & Company, 1902), Book 3, p. 119.

sault or battery and for providing the victim with a private, orderly way of securing revenge in place of physical retaliation. In addition, the victim of a battery may, of course, recover for any medical expenses, loss of wages, or pain and suffering connected with the battery.

Although these torts may take a great number of forms, and the severity may vary accordingly, the form of the assault and battery and the severity are considered by the jury in deciding the extent of the damages.

There is abundant reason for providing legal safeguards designed to inhibit the more aggressive members of our society. Nevertheless these safeguards themselves must have some limitations. We cannot say that an assault is committed every time someone is frightened, because some people become frightened without good reasons. We cannot prevent people from becoming angry by legal means, and perhaps it is desirable that some latitude be allowed for citizens to "blow their stack," so long as they do not go beyond reasonable bounds and place their fellow citizens in reasonable fear of immediate physical attack. In this type of question, as in all legal questions, there are competing interests: in this case freedom of action must be balanced against regulation of action. The law is an expression of the balance at which our society has arrived.

The general rules defining assault and battery came about through the process of common-law decision—that is, the principles were evolved one case at a time, and were followed as precedents in later cases. However, the principles have remained basically unchanged for well over a hundred years: one may see that they were essentially the same in the eighteenth century, when Blackstone wrote the paragraph quoted above.

Elements of Assault and Battery

ASSAULT

The legal elements of the tort of assault are these: (1) that there must be a *present apparent* ability on the part of the perpetrator to carry out the threatened act—hence a threat made by one behind bars, or over the telephone, is not enough to constitute an assault. (2) There must be *some* movement, or act, indicating an offer or attempt to carry out a battery. Mere words alone do not constitute an assault. (3) The threatening offer or act must be intentional, and not merely negligent, as careless handling of firearms. (4) The act or offer must be such as would put a reasonable person in fear of impending attack, though not necessarily of actual injury.

The complainant is required to be reasonable in his apprehensions and cannot complain of acts that would not create apprehension in a reasonable person. The jury would decide the question of whether or not one was reasonably in apprehension, this being a question of fact.

BATTERY

Means of injuring our fellow man have advanced greatly over the last few score years. Yet the flexible, workable, definition of a battery laid down by common-law jurists centuries ago has proved adequate to the tests of changing times and conditions.

Although Blackstone's definition referred to a "beating," [3] the general interpretation of the elements of a battery has been more broad, being simply, "any intentional, unpermitted contact."

This definition helps to illustrate the difference between two different types of legal rule, although the differences between the two types is merely one of degree. Contrast the rules by which we determine the existence of a battery with the excerpts from Hammurabi. As you can see, the latter rules dealing with injuries consist of an enumeration of extremely narrow points, leading in application to arbitrary results, not necessarily attuned to either the severity of the injury or the intent of the responsible party. Furthermore, the narrowness of the definitions would tend to encourage a wrongdoer to devise means of injury not prohibited at all.

Narrow rules of this type are termed *precepts* and are especially characteristic of a legal system that is still in a fairly early stage of development, though no legal system is without them. Some individuals who have never put much thought to the matter seem to consider our present law an enumeration of specific do's and don'ts and assume there is a particular rule covering every possible point.

In order to provide a rule of law to cover points that cannot even be anticipated, broad rules or "principles" are needed. We mention this point here because the definition of *battery* provides an excellent illustration of a legal principle.

Relying on intelligent application of principle a battery may reasonably be found not only when striking with the fist but with a sword, whip, or club. A battery may be found when striking with a spear, stone, arrow, or bullet. No exact precedent is required. Such actions as spitting on an enemy or kissing an unwilling maiden are deliberate unpermitted contacts and therefore batteries, as is offering poisoned candy which is then eaten or intentionally infecting another with a disease. It is easy enough to see that wrongs not yet perpetrated (intentionally exposing to radioactive materials) may in the future be decided by the application of this principle.

The most important test in determining if a battery occurred is, did the

---

[3] *Ibid.* [*Editor's Note:* One reason for specifically mentioning beating is that at that time more aggravated forms of assault were treated in a slightly different manner, as the tort of "wounding" or of "mayhem."]

intentional act of the defendant directly cause the unpermitted contact with the plaintiff? [4]

By utilizing a principle that can be applied widely to effect the policy desired, theories are available to apply to unforeseen problems, though more imagination and training is required to apply general principles than to apply specific precepts. Reason in the application of general principles, rather than the application of masses of particular precepts, is the basis of much of our law. Of course, the very general principle and the very specific precept are but two poles on a continuum of rules.

QUESTION

1. Try devising a better principle than those evolved by the common law to regulate the acts encompassed within assault and battery. What acts would you restrict that are not restricted under the traditional formula, and what acts would you permit that are not presently permitted? (Assuming the law should reflect the present mores of our society, there is always the possibility you are correct and the common law is outdated.)

HOWELL v. WINTERS (Washington, 1910) 108 P 1077

An assault is an attempt, with unlawful force, to inflict bodily injury upon another, accompanied with the apparent present ability to give effect to the attempt if not prevented. . . . Every person has a right to complete and perfect immunity from hostile assaults that threaten danger to his person; "A right to live in society without being put in fear of personal harm."

Appeal from a judgment of the superior court of Chehalis County, Sheeks, J., entered December 29, 1909, upon the verdict of a jury rendered in favor of the plaintiffs, in an action for damages for an assault. Affirmed.

RUDKIN, C.J. On the 7th day of July 1909, the plaintiff Julia Howell visited

[4] In *Commonwealth* v. *Stratton,* 114 Mass. 308, 19 Am. Rep. 850 (a criminal case involving poisoning), the court stated: "Although force and violence are included in all definitions of assault or assault and battery, yet, where there is physical injury to another person, it is sufficient that the cause is set in motion by the defendant, or that the person is subjected to its operations by means of any act or control which the defendant exerts. . . ." It is there further said: "If one should hand an explosive substance to another, and induce him to take it, by misrepresenting or concealing its dangerous qualities, and the other, ignorant of its character, should receive it, and cause it to explode in his pocket or hand, and should be injured by it, the offending party would be guilty of a battery, and that would necessarily include an assault. . . . It would be the same if it exploded in his mouth or stomach. If that which causes the injury is set in motion by the wrongful act of the defendant, it cannot be material whether it acts upon the person injured externally or internally, by mechanical or chemical force."

a store conducted by the defendant, John Winters, and his brother, in the city of Hoquiam, for the purpose of returning a corset purchased by her husband a few days before, and securing a return of the purchase price. The defendant and his brother denied that the purchase was made in their store, and refused to accept the corset or refund the money. In the controversy that arose between the parties over the return of the money, the plaintiffs contend that defendant assaulted the plaintiff Julia Howell and used vile and opprobrious language towards her, for which damages were sought in this action. The jury returned a verdict in favor of the plaintiffs. . . . Judgment was entered for [$700], from which this appeal is prosecuted.

In its charge to the jury the court defined an assault as follows:

"An assault is an action, or conduct, on the part of the defendant—for instance, if you believe her testimony that he shook his fist in front of her face angrily and unlawfully, when he was in such proximity to her, as that he could or might have struck her, also near enough to produce a feeling on her part that she might be struck—that would be an assault. Then of course if he did strike her that would be an assault and battery. She may recover in case you only find assault, or in case you find assault and battery, if you find it was made unlawfully and under the circumstances I have mentioned."

Upon this instruction the first error is assigned. It may well be doubted whether an erroneous definition of the term *assault* would be prejudicial in this case, for all the testimony on the one side tended to show an actual battery, while the testimony on the other side tended to refute either an assault or a battery. But regardless of this, we think the definition as given is substantially correct. An assault was formerly defined by our statute as, "An attempt in a rude, insolent, and angry manner unlawfully to touch, strike, beat, or wound another person, coupled with a present ability to carry such an attempt into execution." Rem. & Bal. Code. sec. 2746. This section was repealed by the new criminal code, and so far as we are able to discover, the term *assault* is not defined in the latter act. We must therefore look to the common law for a definition. Cooley defines the terms thus:

"An assault is an attempt, with unlawful force, to inflict bodily injury upon another, accompanied with the apparent present ability to give effect to the attempt if not prevented. Such would be the raising of the hand in anger, with an apparent purpose to strike, and sufficiently near to enable the purpose to be carried into effect; the pointing of a loaded pistol at one who is within its range; the pointing of a pistol not loaded at one who is not aware of that fact and making an apparent attempt to shoot; shaking a whip or the fist in a man's face in anger; riding or running after him in threatening and hostile manner with a club or other weapon; and the like. The right that is invaded here indicates the nature of the wrong. Every person has a right to complete and perfect immunity from hostile assaults that threaten danger to his person; 'A right to live in society without being put in fear of personal harm.' " Cooley, Torts (3d ed.), p. 278.

. . . The presence or absence of an assault depends more upon the apprehension created in the mind of the person assaulted than upon the undisclosed intentions of the person committing the assault.

It is next contended that the court refused to define or explain the right the appellant would have to remove the respondent Julia Howell from his store. In this connection the court charged the jury as follows:

"I will instruct the jury that he would have a right to request her to depart, but the fact that she did not comply with the request would not justify him in making an assault. He might, after proper request, use sufficient force to put her out of the store; he would have a right to do that, but he would have no right to make an assault of the kind I have described nor an assault and battery as I have described."

It seems to us this charge is correct and was ample and sufficient for the guidance of the jury. Furthermore, if an assault or an assault and battery was actually committed, there is no pretense that it was committed in the removal of this woman from the store.

FULLERTON, GOSE, MORRIS, and CHADWICK, JJ., concur.

There are unusual aspects of this opinion. For one thing, in only a few areas of the law may the criminal law be cited to support a proposition of tort law. Here we get the impression that the judge would have relied on the statute defining criminal assault had not that statute been repealed.

Second, textbooks are occasionally but not usually cited as a source of the common law. This is a much more common practice in the civil law of Europe. Of course, if the judge had wished he could have found plenty of cases defining assault and battery, and the authors on whom he relied have no doubt based their statements on those of previous judicial decisions.

CROUCH v. RINGER (Washington, 1920) 188 P 782

The law is well settled that the proprietor of a place of business to which the public is invited generally, may request one making a disturbance to leave, and upon noncompliance, may use such force as is necessary to eject the disturber.

Plaintiff brought this action against the defendant, Pavlik, manager of the Pacific Meat Company, alleging that, while in the store owned and conducted by the defendants, on lawful business, she was assaulted by defendant Pavlik. From a judgment for $200 in favor of the plaintiff, after trial before the court sitting without a jury, this appeal is prosecuted.

. . . Plaintiff testified in chief to the effect that she ordered a pound of fish by telephone from defendant's store; that, when her order came, she paid for it and unwrapped the parcel, and the odor from the fish was such that she did not want it; that she telephoned to the store and said: "The fish is not fresh, I do not want it," and was answered: "All right, bring it back," and that immediately a man's voice sounded over the telephone, and after she had repeated her complaint, he said: "We don't want your trade and you need not come here any more." Plaintiff thereupon went in person to the store with the fish for the purpose of returning it, gave the fish to the cashier with the remark that it was not fresh, received back the twenty cents she had paid for it, and thereupon the manager, Pavlik, who was standing near, said: "We don't want any more of your trade. We would like to have you keep away from this store."

[EDITOR'S NOTE: Thereafter she refused to leave, but instead followed Pavlik around the shop talking excitedly and arguing. After repeated requests by Pavlik for her to leave, he took her by the arm and shoulder and escorted her out the door.]

The law is well settled that the proprietor of a place of business to which the public is invited generally, may request one making a disturbance to leave, and, upon noncompliance, may use such force as is necessary to eject the disturber.

The facts here shown would have justified such an ejection.

The judgment is reversed, with directions to dismiss the action.

✧

QUESTIONS

1. From a reading of this case and the previous one, may we state as a legal proposition that a woman returning an undergarment who is ejected from a store will succeed in an action based upon assault but one returning fish will not? If not, what is the explanation for the differences in those two cases, both occurring in the same state and both somewhat similar as to the facts?

2. Every legal dispute involves a choice between two competing interests. Express clearly the interest being asserted by each of the parties to this case.

The Proof of Intent

LAW AND MORALS [5]

By 1400 self-defense had become a bar to an action for a battery. Pardons for killing in self-defense became a matter of course. . . .

Primitive Law regards the word and the act of the individual; it searches not his heart. "The thought of man shall not be tried"; said Chief Justice Brian, one of the best of the medieval lawyers, "for the devil himself knoweth not the thought of man."

As a consequence early law is formal and unmoral. Are these adjectives

[5] James Barr Ames, *Harvard Law Review*, Cambridge, Mass. (1908), **22**, p. 97.

properly to be applied to the English common law at any time within the period covered by the reports of litigated cases? To answer this question let us consider, first, the rule of liability for damage caused to one person by the act of another. Not quite six hundred years ago an action was brought in the King's Bench for a battery. The jury found that the plaintiff was beaten, but that this was because of his assailing the defendant who had acted in self-defense, and that the action was brought out of malice. It was nevertheless adjudged that the plaintiff should recover his damages according to the jury's verdict, and that the defendant should go to prison. The defendant had committed the act of battery; therefore he must make reparation. He was not permitted to justify his act as done in protecting himself from the attack of the plaintiff. That attack rendered the plaintiff liable to a cross action, but did not take away his own action.

The case we have just considered was an action for compensation for a tort. Suppose, however, that the defendant, instead of merely injuring his assailant, had killed him in self-defense, using no unnecessary force. Did the early English law so completely ignore the moral quality of the act of killing in self-defense as to make it a crime? Strictly speaking, yes. An official reporter of the time of Edward III and Lord Coke were doubtless in error in stating that prior to 1267 a man "was hanged in such a case just as if he had acted feloniously." But such killing was not justifiable homicide. The party indicated was not entitled to an acquittal by the jury. He was sent back to prison, and must trust in the King's mercy for a pardon. Furthermore, although he obtained the pardon, he forfeited his goods for the crime. *But the moral sense of the community could not tolerate indefinitely the idea that a blameless self-defenser was a criminal,*[6] or that he should have to make compensation to his culpable assailant. By 1400 self-defense had become a bar to an action for a battery. Pardons for killing in self-defense became a matter of course; ultimately the jury was allowed to give a verdict of not guilty in such cases; and the practice of forfeiting the goods of the defendant died out.

From the following cases, an idea of the legal meaning of *intent* should emerge. "The end desired" is close to the meaning, not the end a particular individual desired but the end a reasonable person would presume would result from an act. Furthermore, there must be convincing *evidence,* based on objective actions, that the course of events does clearly indicate, at least to a reasonable man, a probable result. If an act and the consequent result are clearly deliberate, such as when a surgeon operates upon an ear though the wrong ear, intent is present. (Mohr *v.* Williams, supra.)

Shooting at a person or striking at a person is clearly an intentional act, and a battery results even if a third person intercepts the bullet or blow. Thus, intent does not need to be directed against any particular person, and such acts as throwing a brick out a window into a crowded street, firing a

6 The italics are those of the author.

gun into a crowd, or driving an automobile into a crowd of people would each constitute a battery.

Surely a safe conjecture as to the reason "intent" came to assume its present importance in the common law can be made. The effect of the requirement of intent is to divide wrongdoers into two catagories; those who are willful wrongdoers and those who are not. The distinction seems to reflect an acknowledgment, in our law, of the responsibility of the individual and of his free will.[7] Intent is therefore a reflection of a policy to hold the individual responsible for his willful acts. It is a necessary element of most crimes.

Most of us are accustomed to think of intentional injuries as much more evil than those unintended, though it is not clear that judges of Hammurabi's time thought this to be the case, and based upon the preceding reading, this may not have been felt universally even during the early days of the common law.

Today, the policy of the criminal law is toward distinguishing between intentional and unintentional acts, at least as to the major crimes. Due to obvious problems of administration, such minor crimes as running stoplights, speeding, and overparking often do not consider the question of intent. Some major crimes are in this category. In the crime of statutory rape (having intercourse with a girl below a designated age) a party having committed the defined act is guilty of a felony regardless of how convincing the evidence may have seemed to the defendant of the girl's having attained the required age, if in fact she had not. Many laws regulating the sale of liquor to minors operate in the same fashion. Not surprisingly, there is a strong dissenting opinion as to the desirability of these laws.

PERKINS v. *STEIN* (Kentucky, 1893) 22 SW 649

> *A battery is the actual infliction of violence on the person. . . .*
> *We do not think that mere acts of negligence in any of its degrees are assaults and batteries in the meaning of the statute. . . .*

HAZELRIGG, J., delivered the opinion of the court:

The petition of Perkins averred that the appellees were the owners of a large brewery in Louisville, Ky., and of numerous brewery wagons, used for the purpose of delivering beer; that while so engaged the agents and drivers of the appellees carelessly, negligently, and recklessly ran into, over, and upon the

---

[7] Also remember this classification completely vindicates a person who in a direct sense may have caused an injury but who had no control over the circumstances. If a would-be suicide leaps in front of a moving car, the driver is not liable if he had no way of avoiding the injury.

plaintiff, and bruised and injured him externally and internally, the wagon running over his left ankle, and the shafts striking in the breast; that thereby he was knocked down, and trampled upon by the horses of the defendant's wagon, and confined to his room, etc.; all to his injury in the sum of $5,000. While the action was pending, the plaintiff, Perkins, died and thereupon his administratrix, the appellant here, moved to revive the action, filing the proper evidence of her qualification. The court overruled the motion. She has appealed to this court, and the sole question presented is, does the action survive to the personal representative?

Section 1, Chap. 10, Gen. Stat., provides that "no right of action for personal injury, or injury to real or personal estate, shall cease or die with the person injuring or the person injured, except actions for assault and battery . . . but for any injury other than those excepted an action may be brought or revived by the personal representative, or against the personal representative, heir, or devisee, in the same manner as causes of action founded on contract." [8]

It is contended by the appellees that the negligent act of their servant or driver in running over the plaintiff was . . . an assault and battery in the meaning of the statute; and that for the injury growing directly out of this act an action would lie at the common law, even against the master. Such an action they contend, under the authority of *Anderson* v. *Arnold,* 79 Ky. 370, dies with the person.

The vital question then is, what is an assault and battery in the meaning of the statute? "An assault is defined to be an inchoate violence to the person of another, with the present means of carrying the intent into effect." . . . "The intention to do harm is of the essence of an assault."

"An assault is an attempt with violence to do a person some bodily harm, as by holding up a fist, striking at another with a stick which does not touch the latter, or throwing anything at a person which misses him, or by any similar act of inchoate violence showing an intention to do injury, and the aggressor being within such distance from the party assaulted that the intention might possibly be executed."

Mr. Greenleaf says: "A battery is actual infliction of violence on the person. . . . The degree of violence is not regarded in the law. . . . Thus, any touching of the person in any angry, revengeful, rude, or insolent manner; spitting upon the person; jostling him out of the way; pushing another against him; throwing a squib or any missile or water upon him; striking the horse he is riding, whereby he is thrown; taking hold of his clothes in an angry or insolent manner, to detain him—is a battery. So, striking the skirt of his coat or the cane in his hand is a battery; for anything attached to the person partakes of its inviolability."

"A battery is more than an attempt to do a corporal hurt to another; but any injury whatsoever, be it ever so small, being actually done to the person of a

---

[8] *Editor's Note:* Here we see an illustration of the vital importance of knowing exactly what type of suit is being brought. If this is a battery, no action may be brought after the death of the injured party. In other words, the statute dictates that the survivors have no remedy against the plaintiffs if this is found to be a battery.

man in an angry or revengeful or rude or insolent manner, such as spitting in his face, etc., is a battery in the eye of the law. It should be observed that every battery includes an assault."

Bishop, in his work on Criminal Law, says that to constitute a battery "there must be some sort of evil in the intent." We are therefore prepared to say that to constitute an assault and battery under the foregoing definitions the act complained of must be done with a hostile intent.

. . . Undoubtedly cases of extreme recklessness, as furiously riding or driving into or upon a crowd, may be instanced, indicating or implying an evil or hostile design, but such is not the case under consideration.

Under the petition as drawn, the plaintiff is entitled to recover upon showing any degree of negligence, whether ordinary or gross, and we do not think that mere acts of negligence in any of its degrees are assaults and batteries in the meaning of the statute. . . .

✧

In this case we find a forerunner of much of our automobile accident litigation, the only difference being that here we had a horse-drawn beer-wagon.

The exact issue on which this case went to trial was somewhat complex, but is worth going into in detail. For one thing, we again have an instance in which a statute enters directly into our problems.

"Section 1, Chap. 10, Gen. Stat." is the citation to the Kentucky statute quoted. The statute, as the reader noticed, states in effect that certain types of suit may not be brought after the plaintiff has died. What the common law of the state was prior to the statute cannot be ascertained without further research, but the question is immaterial. After the legislature has acted, the common law is to that extent nullified.

Because we find that in this state (at the time of this action, at least) suits in assault and battery died with the wronged person, it is essential to determine whether this wrong was an assault and battery. This in turn depends upon the definition of intent.

QUESTION

1. Even aside from the statute involved in this case, most litigants faced with circumstances that might amount either to a battery or negligence would probably bring suit in the latter. Why?

Defenses to Assault and Battery

CONSENT

Consent to be touched is a defense to the torts of assault and battery. Thus, an agreement between two brawlers to go into an alley and settle their differences is consent by each to permit blows struck by the other, in many states. Such an agreement would not constitute consent to be knifed or shot.

Consent prevents an action in assault and battery by prizefighters when struck by their opponents, by children injured at play, and by football players injured during a game, but in all of these cases, the consent is assumed to extend only to the normal contacts inherent in the particular activity. Football players would not be presumed to consent to opponents' deliberately fracturing their bones to put them out of the game, as has happened on occasion.

All of us are presumed to consent to the normal contacts that are unavoidable in our society, as the customary crowding in subways, even when strictly speaking such acts are intentional. This is a version of the legal fiction (discussed in the next case) "implied consent."

PRIVILEGE

Another limitation to the scope of assault and battery is that of privilege. Privilege implies that under certain circumstances, factors that would otherwise constitute a valid case in assault or battery will not do so, because of social necessity. Therefore, a policeman making an arrest may touch the party arrested without permission, so long as no more force is applied than necessary. Reasonable force may be used in defense of life and property, though means likely to result in serious injury or death may not be used to deter mere trespassers or others interfering with property alone. This rule is consistent with the policy of the common law holding life more important than property. Parents may punish their children, but the same limitations of reasonableness apply, and brutally beating one's own child is an actionable tort in some states. Husbands are no longer permitted to apply such force as is reasonably necessary to correct the defects of their wives, but did have this privilege until rather recently. Whether or not the policy of the law supports corporal punishment by schoolteachers is an area in which there is much disagreement from state to state even today.

MOHR v. WILLIAMS (Minnesota, 1905) 104 NW 12

> The patient must be the final arbiter as to whether he will take his chances with the operation, or take his chances of living without it. Such is the natural right of the individual, which the law recognizes as a legal one. Consent, therefore, of an individual, must be either expressly or impliedly given before a surgeon may have the right to operate.

Appeal from District Court, Ramsey County; OLIN B. LEWIS, J. Affirmed. Action by Anna Mohr against Cornelius Williams. From an order denying a motion for judgment notwithstanding the verdict, defendant appeals; and from an order granting a new trial, plaintiff appeals. Affirmed.

BROWN, J.

Defendant is a physician and surgeon of standing and character, making disorders of the ear a specialty, and having an extensive practice in the city of St. Paul. He was consulted by plaintiff, who complained to him of trouble with her right ear, and at her request, made an examination of that organ for the purpose of ascertaining its condition. He also at the same time examined her left ear, but, owing to foreign substances therein, was unable to make a full and complete diagnosis at that time. The examination of her right ear disclosed a large perforation in the lower portion of the drum membrane, and a large polyp in the middle ear, which indicated that some of the small bones of the middle ear (ossicles) were probably diseased. He informed plaintiff of the result of his examination, and advised an operation for the purpose of removing the polyp and diseased ossicles. After consultation with her family physician, and one or two further consultations with defendant, plaintiff decided to submit to the proposed operation. She was not informed that her left ear was in any way diseased, and understood that the necessity for an operation applied to her right ear only. She repaired to the hospital, and was placed under the influence of anaesthetics; and, after being made unconscious, defendant made a thorough examination of her left ear, and found it in a more serious condition than her right one. A small perforation was discovered high up in the drum membrane, hooded, and with granulated edges, and the bone of the inner wall of the middle ear was diseased and dead. He called this discovery to the attention of Dr. Davis—plaintiff's family physician, who attended the operation at her request—who also examined the ear, and confirmed defendant in his diagnosis. Defendant also further examined the right ear, and found its condition less serious than expected, and finally concluded that the left, instead of the right, should be operated upon; devoting to the right ear other treatment. He then performed the operation of ossiculectomy on plaintiff's left ear; removing a portion of the drum membrane, and scraping away the diseased portion of the inner wall of the ear. The operation was in every way successful and skillfully performed. It is claimed by plaintiff that the operation greatly impaired her hearing, seriously injured her person, and, not having been consented to by her, was wrongful and unlawful, constituting an assault and battery; and she brought this action to recover damages therefor. The trial in the court below resulted in a verdict for plaintiff for $14,322.50.

It is contended that final judgment should be ordered in his favor for the following reasons: (a) That it appears from the evidence received on the trial that plaintiff consented to the operation on her left ear. (b) If the court shall find that no such consent was given, that, under the circumstances disclosed by the record, no consent was necessary. (c) That, under the facts disclosed, an action for assault and battery will not lie; it appearing conclusively, as counsel urge, that there is a total lack of evidence showing or tending to show malice or an evil intent on the part of defendant, or that the operation was negligently performed.

We shall consider first the question whether, under the circumstances shown in the record, the consent of plaintiff to the operation was necessary. . . . The evidence tends to show that, upon the first examination of plaintiff, defendant pronounced the left ear in good condition, and that, at the time plaintiff repaired to the hospital to submit to the operation on her right ear, she was under the impression that no difficulty existed as to the left. In fact, she testified that she had not previously experienced any trouble with that organ. It cannot be doubted that ordinarily the patient must be consulted, and his consent given, before a physician may operate upon him. It was said in the case of *Pratt* v. *Davis* . . . : "Under a free government, at least, the free citizen's first and greatest right, which underlies all others—the right to the inviolability of his person; in other words, the right to himself—is the subject of universal acquiescence, and this right necessarily forbids a physician or surgeon, however skillful or eminent, who has been asked to examine, diagnose, advise, and prescribe (which are at least necessary first steps in treatment and care), to violate, without permission, the bodily integrity of his patient by a major or capital operation, placing him under an anaesthetic for that purpose, and operating upon him without his consent or knowledge." 1 Kinkead on Torts, 375, states the general rule on this subject as follows: "The patient must be the final arbiter as to whether he will take his chances with the operation, or take his chances of living without it. Such is the natural right of the individual, which the law recognizes as a legal one. Consent, therefore, of an individual, must be either expressly or impliedly given before a surgeon may have the right to operate." There is logic in the principle thus stated, for, in all other trades, professions, or occupations, contracts are entered into by the mutual agreement of the interested parties, and are required to be performed in accordance with their letter and spirit. No reason occurs to us why the same rule should not apply between physician and patient. If the physician advises his patient to submit to a particular operation, and the patient weighs the dangers and risks incident to its performance, and finally consents, he thereby, in effect, enters into a contract authorizing his physician to operate to the extent of the consent given, but no further. It is not, however, contended by defendant that under ordinary circumstances consent is unnecessary, but that, under the particular circumstances of this case, consent was implied; that it was an emergency case, such as to authorize the operation without express consent or permission. The medical profession has made signal progress in solving the problems of health and disease, and they may justly point with pride to the advancements made in supplementing nature and correcting deformities, and relieving pain and suffering. The physician impliedly contracts that he possesses, and will exercise reasonable care and exert his best judgment to bring about favorable results. The methods of treatment are committed almost exclusively to his judgment, but we are aware of no rule or principle of law which would extend to him free license respecting surgical operations. Reasonable latitude must, however, be allowed the physician in a particular case; and we would not lay down any rule which would unreasonably interfere with the exercise of his discretion, or prevent him from taking such measures as his judgment dictated for the welfare of the patient in a case of emergency. If a person should be injured to the extent of rendering him unconscious, and his injuries were of such a nature as to require prompt surgical attention, a physician called to attend him would be justified in applying such medical or surgical treatment as might reasonably be necessary for the preservation of his life or limb, and consent on the part of the injured person would be implied. And again, if, in the course of an operation to which the patient consented, the physician should discover conditions not anticipated before the operation was commenced, and which, if not removed, would endanger the life or health of the patient, he would, though no express consent was obtained or given, be justified in extending the operation to remove and overcome them. But such is not the case at bar. The diseased condition of plaintiff's left ear was not discovered in the course of an operation on the right, which was authorized, but upon an independent examination of that organ, made after the authorized operation was found unnecessary. Nor is the evidence such as to justify the court in holding, as a matter of law, that it was such an affection as would result immediately in the serious injury of plaintiff, or such an emergency as to justify proceeding without her consent. She had experienced no particular difficulty with that ear, and the questions as to when its diseased condition would become alarming or fatal, and whether there was an immediate necessity for an operation, were, under the evidence, questions of fact for the jury.

The contention of defendant that the operation was consented to by plaintiff is not sustained by the evidence. At least, the evidence was such as to take the question to the jury. This contention is based upon the fact that she was represented on the occasion in question by her family physician; that the condition of her left ear was made known to him, and the propriety of an operation thereon suggested, to which he made no objection. It is urged that by his conduct he assented to it, and that plaintiff was bound thereby. It is not claimed that he gave his express consent. It is not disputed but that the family physician of plaintiff was present on the occasion of the operation, and at her request. But the purpose of his presence was not that he might participate in the operation, nor does it appear that he was authorized to consent to any change in the one originally proposed to be made. Plaintiff was naturally nervous and fearful of the consequences of being placed under the influence of anaesthetics, and the presence of her family physician was requested under the impression that it would allay and calm her fears. The evidence made the question one of fact for the jury to determine.

The last contention of defendant is that the act complained of did not amount to an assault and battery. This is based upon the theory that, as plaintiff's left ear was in fact diseased, in a condition dangerous and threatening to her health, the operation was necessary, and, having been skillfully performed at a time when plaintiff had requested a like operation on the other ear, the charge of assault and battery cannot be sustained; that, in view of these conditions, and the claim that there was no negligence on the part of defendant, and an entire absence of any evidence tending to show an evil intent, the court should say, as a matter of law, that no assault and battery was committed, even though she did not consent to the operation. In other words, that the absence of a showing that defendant was actuated by a wrongful intent, or guilty of negligence, relieves the act of defendant from the charge of an unlawful assault and battery. We are unable to reach that conclusion, though the contention is not without merit. It would seem to follow from what has been said on the other features of the case that the act of defendant amounted at least to a technical assault and battery. If the operation was performed without plaintiff's consent, and the circumstances were not such as to justify its performance without, it was wrongful; and, if it was wrongful, it was unlawful. As remarked in 1 Jaggard on Torts, 437, every person has a right to complete immunity of his person from physical interference of others, except in so far as contact may be necessary under the general doctrine of privilege; and any unlawful or unauthorized touching of the person of another, except it be in the spirit of pleasantry, constitutes an assault and battery. In the case at bar, as we have already seen, the question whether defendant's act in performing the operation upon plaintiff was authorized was a question for the jury to determine. If it was unauthorized, then it was, within what we have said, unlawful. It was a violent assault, not a mere pleasantry; and, even though no negligence is shown, it was wrongful and unlawful. The case is unlike a criminal prosecution for assault and battery, for there an unlawful intent must be shown. But that rule does not apply to a civil action, to maintain which it is sufficient to show that the assault complained of was wrongful and unlawful. . . .

The amount of plaintiff's recovery, if she is entitled to recover at all, must depend upon the character and extent of the injury inflicted upon her, in determining which the nature of the malady intended to be healed and the beneficial nature of the operation should be taken into consideration, as well as the good faith of the defendant.

Order affirmed.

JAGGARD, J., took no part.

❖

Note the court's statement that consent to operate could be implied if a person were unconscious (pages 114–115). This is an example of a "legal fiction." Because it would be poor policy for doctors to be prevented from operating on anyone unconscious, no matter how critical their condition, something must be invented to avoid that result. The device suggested by the court is "implied consent." Courts will imply that an unconscious party in serious and immediate need of an operation, who is operated upon, wanted the operation. This would be true even if the patient later insisted he did *not* want the operation that saved his life.

However, it is not suggested that the fiction of implied consent may be used sporadically, at the judge's whim. A reasonably clear-cut type of situation is projected by the court as requiring that solution. The principle must be applied intelligently and consistently to effect a desired policy.

Lastly, one of the principles of stare decisis is that only those principles actually needed to solve the case at hand are binding as precedent. Others are termed *dicta* and are not binding. The discussion here regarding "implied consent" is dicta, and therefore not *really* binding on *future cases,* but still serves to communicate a good idea to subsequent judges.

In the preceding case we do not see why there is any question of intent, much less negligence, in that the physician *intended to perform the operation.* Because it was an unpermitted contact, and there was no consent, the element of battery seems clearly established. There was no intent to do harm, but there was certainly an intent to do the unpermitted act complained of, which is all that is required to establish that element.

The student may be surprised to find that even today, cases in this pattern (a physician performing a different operation than he was supposed to) are occasionally sources of litigation.

QUESTIONS

1. List the advantages and disadvantages implicit in holding a physician liable for battery if he performs work other than that originally agreed upon. Are the advantages enough to convince you of the validity of the decision?

2. Would it be possible for physicians to protect themselves by securing permission in advance of an operation to perform such work as seemed necessary?

Assault and Battery by Agents of the Government

The existence of remedies for assault and battery constitute an important phase of our basic civil rights. By providing us with a peaceful substitute for revenge and a means for securing compensation for damages, these tort remedies contribute to our personal security, supplementing criminal sanctions.

But while the government provides us with remedies against our neighbors, what remedies have we against our government?

We will consider two aspects of the legal relations between the government and individual: (1) the right to sue the sovereign and (2) other limitations imposed upon the sovereign.

SUIT AGAINST THE SOVEREIGN

As a matter of common knowledge, and as we have touched upon earlier, any problem concerning government is apt to involve two different sovereigns. One is the state government and the other is the federal government.

Thus we have two sets of sovereigns to contend with: the states, the primary source of police power, and the federal government, with the power to act in specified though admittedly expanding areas. Let us ask the broad question, under what circumstances may a sovereign be sued according to the common law? The answer is, only when the sovereign has given its consent. Various theories are advanced to explain this situation. In effect, the interest of permitting government to govern without interference has been placed above the personal rights of the governed to the extent of not providing the governed with a civil remedy against the sovereign. Our state and federal governments are all sovereign for this purpose; thus they may not be sued without their consent.

However, Congress has passed legislation that gives blanket consent to be sued in certain types of cases. Contract claims may be brought against the federal government much as against any other party. Tort claims have been governed by the Federal Tort Claims Act.[9] According to the latter act, suits in negligence may be brought, suits in deliberate torts may not. Not only is the government itself not subject to suit, but even the individual responsible for an intentional tort is granted immunity if the act was discretionary rather than purely ministerial (that is, routine). The reason for this distinction is to protect government employees from constant suit when using their discretion. The distinction is difficult. Litigants are hard put to show that some of the most mundane acts do not require discretion. This concept is closely allied to the usual sorts of privilege normally attached to the intentional torts. Whether justified or not on grounds of policy, we must admit that our remedy for torts inflicted by employees of the federal government is far from adequate.

State governments vary considerably in their willingness to submit to suit. Most states have at least some provisions for suit against them by a private party, but most are even less generous than the federal government in extending consent to be sued.

STEPP v. UNITED STATES (CCA Virginia, 1953)
207 F 2d 909

> *Private Cotham aimed at Stepp with the intention of hitting him. . . . This amounted to assault and battery, since it involved the use of excessive force in making an arrest under the existing circumstances. . . . The action was therefore barred by . . . the Federal Tort Claims Act.*

DOBIE, CJ.

This is an appeal from a judgment of the United States District Court for the Eastern District of Virginia dismissing for lack of jurisdiction a civil action

9 28 USCA 1952 Supp. §§1346, 1402, 1504, 2110, 2401, 2402, 2411, 2412, 2671–2680.

instituted against the United States under the Federal Tort Claims Act, 28 U.S.C. subsection 1346 (b). The lower court held that the action was barred by the provisions of 28 U.S.C. subsection 2680 (h), which provides in part: "The provisions of this chapter and section 1346 (b) of this title shall not apply to . . . (h) Any claim arising out of assault, battery. . . ." The action was instituted by William V. Stepp, Sr., as Administrator for his deceased son, William V. Stepp, Jr.

On June 4, 1948, the deceased was a civilian seaman serving on an L.S.T. operated by the Army Transport Service. On that date his ship was docked at Anchorage, Alaska, and deceased had gone ashore. About two A.M. Stepp approached the entrance to the dock for the purpose of going aboard his ship. This entrance was guarded by a check point, which consisted of a sentry shack with a guard on duty. When Stepp approached this check point, he was met by Private Cotham, who was the guard on duty.

Cotham had been instructed to let none of the members of a ship's crew go upon the dock carrying intoxicating beverages. On the night in question he had been given special orders to be on the alert for seamen approaching the dock with whiskey. Stepp had a package in his hand as he approached this guard hut, upon being questioned, told Cotham it contained laundry. Cotham told Stepp that it would be necessary to investigate the package and to see Stepp's identification papers.

At this point, the phone in the guard shack rang and Cotham answered it. While so engaged, he looked out and saw Stepp running towards the dock. Cotham immediately gave chase, calling upon Stepp on three occasions to halt. When Cotham had closed the gap separating the two from 300 to 45 feet, he drew his gun and fired two shots into the ground, again calling upon Stepp to halt. Stepp still continued to run and Cotham thereupon aimed his gun at Stepp, and fired two shots, both of which hit Stepp, resulting in his almost instantaneous death. Cotham carried a night stick with him in addition to his gun.

The case came on for trial on February 5, 1953. The only evidence introduced at the hearing was the deposition of Donald Cotham, taken on behalf of the United States. On the day after the hearing but before judgment, the United States was allowed to file an amended answer. This amended answer contested the jurisdiction of the court under Section 2680 (h), Title 28, U.S.C. on the ground that the deceased's claim was one arising out of assault and battery. The District Court found that Private Cotham aimed at Stepp with the intention of hitting him: that this amounted to assault and battery, since it involved the use of excessive force in making an arrest under the existing circumstances: and that the action was therefore barred by Section 2680 (h) of the Federal Tort Claims Act.

(2–4) It is well established that an intentional use of excessive force in making an arrest amounts to an assault and battery. . . . There was sufficient evidence to support the District Court's finding that Cotham intended to hit Stepp and that this shooting constituted the use of excessive force under the circumstances. The District Court did not err in holding this to be an assault and battery and, as such, barred by Section 2680 (h), Title 28, U.S.C.

For these reasons we think there was no error committed in the trial below and the judgment of the District Court is, accordingly, affirmed.

Affirmed.

❖

EXCERPTS FROM THE FEDERAL TORT CLAIMS ACT

Subsection 2674. Liability of United States.

The United States shall be liable, respecting the provisions of this title relating to tort claims, in the same manner and to the same extent as a private individual under like circumstances, but shall not be liable for interest prior to judgment or for punitive damages. . . .

Subsection 2680. Exceptions.

The provisions of this chapter and section 1346 (b) of this title shall not apply to—

(a) Any claim based upon an act or omission of an employee of the Government, exercising due care in the execution of a statute or regulation, whether or not such statute or regulation be valid, *or based upon the exercise or performance or the failure to exercise or perform a discretionary function or duty* on the part of a federal agency or an employee of the Government, whether or not the discretion involved be abused.

(h) Any claim arising out of assault, battery, false imprisonment, false arrest, malicious prosecution, abuse of process, libel, slander, misrepresentation, deceit, or interference with contract rights.

❖

The problem of the plaintiff's attorney was obvious in this case. The wrong was assault and battery, but assault and battery along with an array of other wrongs was specifically excluded by the terms of the federal statute. He therefore attempted to bring the suit in a tort we have mentioned, the tort of *negligence*. (The case of *Perkins* v. *Stein* was found to be the tort of negligence.) Unhappily for the plaintiff, the court correctly held the wrong here to be assault and battery instead of negligence, and found in favor of the United States.

Other Limitations against Violation of Personal Rights by the Sovereign

Although compensation for torts committed by government officials is difficult and in many cases impossible to obtain, there are some restrictions upon their powers. These restrictions are contained in the state and federal constitutions, one of which is illustrated by the following case.

ROCHIN v. CALIFORNIA (U.S. Supreme Court, 1951)
342 US 165, 96 L ed 183, 72 S Ct 205, 25 ALR 2d 1396

> . . . This course of proceeding by agents of government to obtain evidence is bound to offend even hardened sensibilities. They are methods too close to the rack and the screw to permit of constitutional differentiation.

Mr. Justice FRANKFURTER delivered the opinion of the court [the United States Supreme Court].

Having "some information that [the petitioner here] was selling narcotics," three deputy sheriffs of the County of Los Angeles, on the morning of July 1, 1949, made for the two-story dwelling house in which Rochin lived with his mother, common-law wife, brothers and sisters. Finding the outside door open, they entered and then forced open the door to Rochin's room on the second floor. Inside they found petitioner sitting partly dressed on the side of the bed, upon which his wife was lying. On a "night stand" beside the bed the deputies spied two capsules. When asked, "Whose stuff is this?" Rochin seized the capsules and put them in his mouth. A struggle ensued, in the course of which the three officers "jumped upon him" and attempted to extract the capsules. The force they applied proved unavailing against Rochin's resistance. He was handcuffed and taken to a hospital. At the direction of one of the officers a doctor forced an emetic solution through a tube into Rochin's stomach against his will. This "stomach pumping" produced vomiting. In the vomited matter were found two capsules which proved to contain morphine.

Rochin was brought to trial before a California Superior Court, sitting without a jury, on the charge of possessing "a preparation of morphine" in violation of the California Health and Safety Code, 1947 subsection 11,500. Rochin was convicted and sentenced to sixty days' imprisonment. The chief evidence against him was the two capsules. They were admitted over petitioner's objections, although the means of obtaining them was frankly set forth in the testimony by one of the deputies, substantially as here narrated.

On appeal, the District Court of Appeal affirmed the conviction, despite the finding that the officers "were guilty of unlawfully breaking into and entering defendant's room and were guilty of unlawfully assaulting and battering defendant while in the room," and "were guilty of unlawfully assaulting, battering, torturing and falsely imprisoning the defendant at the alleged hospital." . . . One of the three judges, while finding that "the record in this case reveals a shocking series of violations of constitutional rights," concurred only because he felt bound by decisions of his Supreme Court. These, he asserted, "have been looked upon by law enforcement officers as an encouragement, if not an invitation, to the commission of such lawless acts." Ibid. The Supreme Court of California denied without opinion Rochin's petition for a hearing. Two justices dissented from this denial, and in doing so expressed themselves thus: ". . . a conviction which rests upon evidence on incriminating objects obtained from the body of the accused by physical abuse is as invalid as a conviction which rests upon a verbal confession extracted from him by such abuse. . . . Had the evidence forced from the defendant's lips consisted of an oral confession that he illegally possessed a drug . . . he would have the protection of the rule of law which excludes coerced confessions from evidence. But because the evidence forced from his lips consisted of real objects the People of this state are permitted to base a conviction upon it. [We] find no valid ground of distinction between a verbal confession extracted by physical abuse and a confession wrested from defendant's body by physical abuse." . . .

This court granted certiorari . . . because a serious question is raised as to the limitations which the Due Process Clause of the Fourteenth Amendment imposes on the conduct of criminal proceedings by the States.

In our federal system the administration of criminal justice is predominantly committed to the care of the States. The power to define crimes belongs to Congress only as an appropriate means of carrying into execution its limited grant of legislative powers. . . . Broadly speaking, crimes in the United States are what the laws of the individual States make them, subject to the limitations of Art. 1, subsection 10 (1), in the original Constitution, prohibiting bills of attainder and ex post facto laws, and of the Thirteenth and Fourteenth Amendments.

These limitations, in the main, concern not restrictions upon the powers of the States to define crime, except in the restricted area where federal authority has preempted the field, but restrictions upon the manner in which the States may enforce their penal codes. Accordingly . . . "we must be deeply mindful of the responsibilities of the States for the enforcement of criminal laws, and exercise with due humility our merely negative function in subjecting convictions from state courts to the very narrow scrutiny which the Due Process Clause of the Fourteenth Amendment authorized." . . . Due process of law, "itself a historical product," . . . is not to be turned against the States in the administration of their systems of criminal justice.

However, this Court too has its responsibility. Regard for the requirements of the Due Process Clause "inescapably imposes upon this Court an exercise of judgment upon the whole course of the proceedings (resulting in a conviction) in order to ascertain whether they offend those canons of decency and fairness which express the notions of justice of English-speaking peoples even toward those charged with the most heinous offenses." . . . These standards of justice are not authoritatively formulated anywhere as though they were specifics. Due process of law is a summarized constitutional guarantee of respect for those personal immunities which, as Mr. Justice Cardozo twice wrote for the Court, are "so rooted in the traditions and conscience of our people as to be ranked as fundamental" . . . or are "implicit in the concept of ordered liberty." . . .

The Court's function in the observance of this settled conception of the Due Process Clause does not leave us without adequate guides in subjecting State criminal procedures to constitutional judgment. In dealing not with the machinery of government but with human rights, the absence of formal exactitude, or want of fixity of meaning, is not an unusual or even regrettable attribute of constitutional provisions. Words being symbols do not speak without a gloss. On the one hand the gloss may be the deposit of history, whereby a term gains technical content. Thus the requirements of the Sixth and Seventh Amendments for trial by jury in the Federal courts have a rigid meaning. No changes or chances can alter the content of the verbal symbol of "jury"—a body of twelve men who must reach a unanimous conclusion if the verdict is to go against the defendant. On the other hand, the gloss of some of the verbal symbols of the Constitution does not give them a fixed technical content. It exacts a continuing process of application.

When the gloss has thus not been fixed but is a function of the process of judgment, the judgment is bound to fall differently at different times and differently at the same time through different judges. Even more specific provisions, such as the guaranty of freedom of speech and the detailed protection against unreasonable search and seizures, have inevitably evoked as sharp divisions in this Court as the least specific and most comprehensive protection of liberties, the Due Process Clause.

The vague contours of the Due Process Clause do not leave judges at large. We may not draw on our merely personal and private notions and disregard the limits that bind judges in their judicial function. Even though the concept of due process of law is not final and fixed, these limits are derived from considerations that are fused in the whole nature of our judicial process.

Restraints on our jurisdiction are self-imposed only in the sense that there is from our decisions no immediate appeal short of impeachment or constitutional amendment. But that does not make due process of law a matter of judicial caprice. The faculties of the Due Process Clause may be indefinite and vague, but the mode of their ascertainment is not self-willed. In each case "due process of law" requires an evaluation based on a disinterested inquiry pursued in the spirit of science, on a balanced order of facts exactly and fairly stated, on the detached consideration of conflicting claims, . . . on a judgment not ad hoc and episodic but duly mindful of reconciling the needs both of continuity and of change in a progressive society.

Applying these general considerations to the circumstances of the present case, we are compelled to conclude that the proceedings by which this conviction was obtained do more than offend some fastidious squeamishness or private sentimentalism about combatting crime too energetically. This is conduct that shocks the conscience. Illegally breaking into the privacy of the petitioner, the struggle to open his mouth and remove what was there, the forcible extraction of his stomach's contents—this course of proceeding by agents of government to obtain evidence is bound to offend even hardened sensibilities. They are methods too close to the rack and the screw to permit of constitutional differentiation.

. . . It would be a stultification of the responsibility which the course of constitutional history has cast upon this Court to hold that in order to convict a man the police cannot extract by force what is in his mind but can extract what is in his stomach.

On the facts of this case the conviction of the petitioner has been obtained by methods that offend the Due Process Clause. The judgment below must be Reversed.

✧

False Imprisonment

The tort of false imprisonment, like that of assault and battery, repre-sents a device for insuring certain basic human rights. This tort is similar to assault and battery in requiring intent. However, the germ of the action rests upon an unlawful restraint of the person rather than threatened or ac-tual contact.

Most people have heard of "false arrest." A false arrest is merely a spe-cial class of false imprisonment. A false imprisonment apparently made under valid legal process, but actually unlawful, is often termed a false ar-rest. The difference in nomenclature is not important.

This tort presents difficulties to the retailer who has problems with shop-lifters. Generally a citizen does have the right to arrest another citizen who has committed a misdemeanor in the presence of the first citizen or who has committed any felony. However, if the arrested party is found not to have committed a crime, he may bring suit against the arresting citizen for false imprisonment. (This is not true if the arresting party is a police offi-cer who has seen the misdemeanor committed *or* who has a valid warrant.) In jurisdictions with this view, the retailer is in a difficult position. If he arrests a suspected shoplifter himself, he may face a suit in false imprison-ment if he cannot prove his allegations. If he sends for a police officer to procure a warrant, and make the arrest, the officer may arrive too late, and if he simply ignores the situation, the shoplifter may, of course, simply proceed with his shoplifting. Therefore, some states have modified the law so as to give the retailer the right to arrest upon reasonable suspicion that shoplifting has occurred.

MONTGOMERY WARD & COMPANY v. *WICKLINE,* 50 SE 2d 387, 1948

False imprisonment is restraint of one's liberty without any suffi-cient legal excuse therefor by word or acts which he fears to disregard, and neither malice, ill will, nor the slightest wrongful intention is necessary to constitute the offense.

EGGLESTON, J.

Melvin Wickline, hereinafter called the plaintiff, instituted an action against the defendant, Montgomery Ward & Company, a corporation, by notice of motion for judgment in the court below, seeking damages for false imprison-ment. The notice alleged that on the evening of November 30, 1946, while the plaintiff and a friend, James C. Taylor, were leaving the defendant's store, where they had been shopping, they were, "at the suggestion of the defend-ant's servants, agents and employees," "without any sufficient legal excuse," "placed in restraint" and searched by a police officer and charged with the theft of a small article of merchandise of the approximate value of seventy-five cents.

It further alleged that later, at the request of the defendant's servants, agents and employees, the plaintiff and Taylor were arrested and taken by the officer to the police station where they were held until they were released upon bail for their appearance in the police court.

The defendant filed a plea of not guilty. The trial before a jury resulted in a verdict of $750 for the plaintiff, upon which the lower court entered judgment.

The first assignment of error is that the lower court erred in failing to set aside the verdict, because, it is said, it is contrary to the law and the evidence and without evidence to support it.

In the main the evidence is not in dispute. Montgomery Ward & Company operates a store in the city of Alexandria, which was at the time under the charge of Charles R. Wells, as manager, and Herman A. Jacoby, as assistant manager.

The plaintiff testified that on the night of Saturday, November 30, 1946, he and Taylor were shopping in the store, where they had been regular customers for some time and where each had a charge account. As they passed through the front door of the store and reached the sidewalk they were accosted by a police officer who had been notified by Jacoby that one of the two men had stolen a small tool from a counter in the hardware department. In the presence of both Wells and Jacoby the two men were searched. During the progress of the search, Wells told the officer that the plaintiff [Wickline] had passed or delivered the tool to Taylor as the two customers were leaving the store. The tool was found in Taylor's pocket.

Jacoby testified that he had seen Wickline take the implement from the counter a short while before the two men left the store. Wells testified that he had seen Wickline pass the implement to Taylor as the two men were leaving.

Both Wickline and Taylor denied that either had stolen the tool. Taylor said that he had purchased it earlier during the day on a previous trip to the store. Taylor was taken into the store and asked to identify the saleswoman who had sold him the article. He was unable to do so. When found on his person the tool was unwrapped and unaccompanied by a sales ticket.

It is admitted that the officer came to the store at the request of Jacoby, who notified him of the incident and was authorized to call him. It is uncontradicted that Wickline and Taylor were searched by the officer in the presence of Wells and Jacoby and at their direction.

Both Wickline and Taylor were taken by the officer to the police station where, for the first time, a warrant was issued for their arrest, charging them with petty larceny.

Over the objection of the defendant it was shown that at a hearing in the police court they were acquitted of the charge.

(1) In Burks Pleading and Practice, 3d E., subsection 143, p. 246, it is said: "False imprisonment is restraint of one's liberty without any sufficient legal excuse therefor by word or acts which he fears to disregard, and neither malice, ill will, nor the slightest wrongful intention is necessary to constitute the offense." . . .

(2) "The gist of the action is the illegal detention of the person, without lawful process, or the unlawful execution of lawful process." . . .

(3) It is firmly settled that a peace officer may legally arrest, without a

warrant, for a misdemeanor committed in his presence, but that a warrant is necessary where the offense is not committed in his presence. . . .

Moreover, to justify the arrest for a misdemeanor not committed in his presence, the officer must have the warrant with him at the time. . . .

(4) In the case before us the alleged misdemeanor or theft of the article from the store was not committed in the presence of the officer, and hence the arrest of the plaintiff without a warrant was illegal and constituted false imprisonment.

(5) Since it further appears, without contradiction, that the arrest of the plaintiff was at the instance and direction of the defendant's employees, who acted within the scope of their authority, the plaintiff's evidence made out a case against the defendant company. See *Long* v. *Eagle 5, 10 and 25¢ Store Company,* where the circumstances of the detention and search were quite similar to those in the case before us.

(6) The defendant company argues that the circumstances were such as to justify the arrest of the plaintiff and his companion, if not to show that they were guilty of the charge which was placed against them. This is beside the point. It confuses an action for false imprisonment with an action for malicious prosecution.

(7) In an action for false imprisonment, as distinguished from an action for malicious prosecution, the good faith of the defendant in causing the arrest, or probable cause therefor, is no defense to a claim for actual or compensatory damages sustained in consequence thereof. . . . The plaintiff makes out a case for compensatory damages when he shows that he has been illegally detained without lawful process.

(8) Where punitive damages are claimed, evidence of want of probable cause is admissible to enhance the damages, and, conversely, a showing of probable cause is admissible to mitigate the damages. . . . But here there was no claim for punitive or exemplary damages.

(9) In our opinion the evidence before us amply supports the verdict in favor of the plaintiff for compensatory damages.

QUESTIONS

1. There are valid considerations for restricting the right of the retailer to detain persons suspected of shoplifting. What are these considerations?

2. Jones is riding an elevator in a department store when due to a power failure the elevator stops and Jones is trapped between floors for three hours. Why is this not a case of false imprisonment?

3. Smith is walking down the street when Green accuses him of being a pickpocket. Green demands that Smith remain there while police are sent for, threatening to hit Green if he attempts to leave the scene. Smith is cleared of the charge of being a pickpocket. Why is this a false imprisonment, despite the fact that there is no enclosure?

CHAPTER TEN

Defamation

Everyone has the right to the enjoyment of good reputation, of which no one may deprive him through falsehood or malice without liability therefor.[1]

Why the Torts of Libel and Slander?

THE CODE OF HAMMURABI (2250 B.C.) [2]

If a man bring an accusation against a man, and charge him with a [capital] crime, but cannot prove it, he, the accuser, shall be put to death.

If a man point the finger at a priestess or the wife of another and cannot justify it, they shall drag that man before the judges and they shall brand his forehead.

If a man charge a man with sorcery, and cannot prove it, he who is charged with sorcery shall go to the river, into the river he shall throw himself and if the river overcome him, his accuser shall take to himself his house [estate]. If the river show that man to be innocent and he come forth unharmed, he who charged him with sorcery shall be put to death. He who threw himself into the river shall take to himself the house of his accuser.

✧

QUESTIONS

1. Enumerate some of the loopholes in this set of laws, so far as protecting reputation is concerned.

2. Observe in the last section here the combination of penalty and reimbursement for damage.

[1] *Freeman* v. *Busch Jewelry Company* (USDC Georgia, 1951) 98 F. Supp. 963, quoting 53 CJS.

[2] Robert Francis Harper, *The Code of Hammurabi* (Chicago: University of Chicago Press, 1904), p. 11 and p. 45.

3. May not the last section be the origin of the expression "Go jump in the lake"?

BLACKSTONE ON SLANDER [3]

> . . . *If the defendent be able to . . . prove the words to be true . . . the law gives no remedy.*

. . . Injuries affecting a man's *reputation* or good name are, first, by malicious, scandalous, and slanderous *words,* tending to his damage and derogation. As if a man maliciously and falsely utter any slander or false tale of another. . . .

. . . Words of heat and passion, as to call a man a rogue and rascal, if productive of no ill consequence . . . are not actionable;

. . . Also, if the defendant be able to justify, and prove the words to be true, no action will lie even though special damage hath ensued; for then it is no slander or false tale. As if I can prove the tradesman a bankrupt, the physician a quack, the lawyer a knave, and the divine a heretic, this will destroy their respective action: for though there may be damage sufficient accruing from it, yet, if the fact be true . . . the law gives no remedy.

A second way of affecting a man's reputation is by *printed* or *written* libels, pictures, signs, and the like; which set him in an odious or ridiculous light, and thereby diminish his reputation.

✧

Next to our right to go about free from physical attack, or from the threat of physical attack, perhaps nothing is so important to us as our reputation. Consequently our law provides safeguards designed to protect the individual from unfair vilification.

Although the torts of assault and battery involve a balancing of freedom of action against regulation of action, the torts of libel and slander (which together are termed the twin tort of *defamation*) involve a balancing between the communities' right to freedom of speech and the individual's right to an untarnished reputation. Slander consists of an oral attack upon another's reputation; libel, of an attack in print or other permanently recorded form.

Many difficult questions of policy are presented in drawing the line between these competing interests. As was true of assault and battery, the lines have been drawn case by case through common-law decision, and ad-

---

[3] Sir William Blackstone, *Commentaries on the Laws of England,* 1769, William Draper Lewis (ed.) (Philadelphia: Rees Welsh & Company, 1902), Book 3, p. 1121.

justments will no doubt continue to be made in the same manner, though some state legislatures have also taken an active hand in modifying the law of defamation.

Elements of the Torts of Libel and Slander

Let us now examine these requirements in more detail. The first requirement to an action in defamation is that the statement be false. The spirit of the common law is tough and moralistic: one familiar with the common law might guess that no policy would be devised to soften the impact of the truth. An injurious statement, if proven true, is not defamatory.

In order for a statement to be defamatory, it must adversely affect the subject's reputation. This is often expressed in the cases by such a statement as "tending to expose one to hatred, ridicule, contempt, or obloquy," but simply means that those hearing the statement might be expected to have substantially less respect for the subject as a result of hearing the statement. Therefore, trivial statements, even if untrue, are not defamatory.

Nevertheless, the line between what does or does not adversely affect one's reputation is a fine one, and many cases turn on that point alone. This is primarily a question of fact, not of law, and may even vary from one community to another.

In order for any defamation, either libel or slander, to exist there must be communication of the injurious false statement to at least one person aside from the defamer and the defamed. This is logical enough, because no statement confined to the ears of the defamer and the defamed could affect the latter's reputation. The requirement of communication to an outside party is termed *publication*. In slander, the publication is oral; in libel it is printed or permanently recorded. The test of publication is whether or not the defamatory statement is actually transmitted from one mind to another. Thus, statements made to persons who cannot hear could not be defamatory (unless overheard by others). Writing a letter containing false and injurious statements about the recipient and which is opened and read by the recipient's secretary or wife could constitute a defamation.

Intent to falsify is not an element of defamation. Statements thought true but actually false will nevertheless give rise to an action. This is true when the publisher of the defamation is merely repeating statements made to him by another and supposedly accurate source. Anyone repeating defamatory gossip may be held liable, assuming the other elements are present. Furthermore, the burden is always on the defendant in a defamation action to prove that the statement was true. Uuless the defendant has evidence sufficient to convince a jury of the truth of a derogatory statement, truth will not be a defense. If every damaging statement had to be proved false by the plaintiff before being actionable, these torts would afford little protection to our reputation. As the law stands, making any statement damaging to another's reputation is dangerous, unless clear proof of the truth of the statement is available.

FREEMAN v. BUSCH JEWELRY COMPANY
(USDC Georgia, 1951) 98 F. Supp. 963

Libel has been defined as a malicious publication, expressed either in printing or writing, or by signs and pictures, tending either to blacken the memory of one dead or the reputation of one who is alive, and to expose him to public hatred, contempt or ridicule.

HOOPER, CJ.

In this action plaintiff seeks to recover $25,000 damages for wounded feelings and marital difficulties growing out of this transaction. It appears without dispute that the plaintiff, a young married man of LaGrange, Georgia, and his wife purchased from defendant company a radio for the sum of $19.95, on which payments of $1.25 per week were made for many weeks, there remaining on September 16, 1948, a small balance of $4.20.

Plaintiff at the time of the purchase was living at 912 Todd Street and working at Almond's Service Station, and continued to work and reside at the same places on September 15, 1948. On that date there came to plaintiff's residence through the mail, a postal card from defendant company bearing the following writing: "Dear Milford, I'll be in LaGrange next week. Call me at 9693. Love, Mary." Defendant was then at work. On returning home for lunch his wife showed him the post card. He attempted to explain to her that he did not understand its contents, that he knew no girl by the name of Mary and that he had had no affair with any person. After lunch he went to defendant company and caused its agent to phone his wife and make an explanation which, at that time, she apparently accepted. Upon further reflection, however, the wife, who was then in a delicate condition, worried considerably over the matter and later in the evening packed up her personal belongings, and, taking their child with her, went to live with her mother. Some two weeks later plaintiff was able to induce his wife to return home, she being then sick and apparently in need of help.

Prior to the receipt of this postal card this young couple were living happily together with no other than the usual trivial domestic disagreements. After this time, however, things began to change. The wife could not free her mind from the thought that plaintiff might have been unfaithful to her and she did not trust him as before. When he would come home after being out, she would ask him questions, and he, being irritated at her distrust, would decline to answer. His drinking, before this time only moderate, tended to increase, as sometimes happens under the same or similar circumstances. He even struck his wife on one occasion. There have been other separations. It so happened that prior to the receipt of this postal card, plaintiff had been pursuing studies in Atlanta under the G.I. Bill of Rights, and, on two week-ends, instead of returning to his home, he remained in Atlanta, explaining to the satisfaction of his wife that he was busy studying.

There is no evidence that his stay in Atlanta over the week-end was anything but innocent. However, coupled with the other circumstances, it caused his wife to worry and distrust the husband. It does not appear that even to this time the confidence of his wife which plaintiff formerly enjoyed has been restored.

Plaintiff's wife sworn as a witness by defendant gave a fair and plausible account of her mental reactions. She trusted her husband prior to September 16th, and since that time on some occasions thought that she continued to trust him, and on other occasions, including the time of the trial, stated very frankly she just doesn't know what to think.

From the evidence in the case it is clear to the court that the receipt of this postal card was definitely the beginning of plaintiff's marital difficulties, that it caused plaintiff's wife for the first time to distrust him, and to leave him, that her distrust of plaintiff was the source of great annoyance and disappointment to plaintiff, and that subsequently thereto plaintiff has been more addicted to drink, according to his wife's own testimony, than previously.

While the parties have resumed their marital relationship and their cohabitation along with their two small children, it seems clear that the status of mutual respect and affection existing prior to September 16th does not now exist, though it is possible that the husband's exoneration by the judgment in this case might assist in its restoration in the future; at least the Court hopes so.

Defendant was guilty at least of a great degree of negligence in sending to this husband at his home an open postal card which on its face would convey to his wife no other impression than that the husband had a clandestine relationship with some person named Mary. The reactions of plaintiff's wife were to be reasonably anticipated. There are circumstances of aggravation: The radio which defendant sold had been practically paid for, a payment had been made shortly before; defendant had retained title and could have collected this small balance by retaking the radio, or other legal means.

Defendant contends that a bill sent to plaintiff came back with the notation by the post office that plaintiff had moved, but the bill in question was not produced in court.

The court finds that defendant committed a tort and that plaintiff's damages are in the sum of $5,000, although injuries and damages suffered by plaintiff are such as are not easily computed by any monetary standards.

While not necessary to rule that the action arises from a libel, attention is called to the following citations from 53 CJS, subject Libel and Slander.

Libel has been defined as a malicious publication, expressed either in printing or writing, or by signs and pictures, tending either to blacken the memory of one dead or the reputation of one who is alive, and expose him to public hatred, contempt, or ridicule. . . .

Everyone has the right to the enjoyment of good reputation, of which no one may deprive him through falsehood or malice without liability therefor.

Various publications concerning relations of men and women, which, although not imputing a want of chastity, yet tend to disgrace the party charged or to render him ludicrous or ridiculous, have been held libelous per se.

A communication to plaintiff's spouse ordinarily is a public one within the contemplation of law.

Suffice it to say, the implication of the postal card was libelous in that it conveyed the impression of infidelity on the part of the husband, it was published in that the wife was given every opportunity to read it, and actually did read it, and it caused damage to the plaintiff as herein set forth.

✧

The purpose of the communication in the above case does not appear, but perhaps it was merely intended to harass the debtor, in the hope he could thereby be prodded into paying his debt.

Ordinarily we think of a libel as a statement in which a person is called something or accused of something. Strictly speaking, the statement in this case did neither. However, any communication, no matter how stated, that tends to injure the reputation of another may be defamatory, providing the other elements are present.

QUESTIONS

1. Some courts have had difficulty in determining whether a communication is offensive enough to warrant legal action. After all, everything said that might conceivably affect someone's reputation cannot be considered defamatory. What standard would you suggest by which to measure whether or not a statement is serious enough to be considered defamatory?

2. According to the rule extant in most states, slanders (depending upon the type of statement) are not actionable unless some money damages are proved. Is there a necessary connection between the amount or even existence of money damage and the damage occurring to one's reputation?

Defenses to Libel and Slander Actions

MISCELLANEOUS DEFENSES

The defense most commonly asserted in cases of libel or slander is simply that one of the elements to a case was lacking. In particular, truth is often asserted as a defense to actions in defamation. The assertion that the statement was not really injurious to reputation is also frequently made.

ABSOLUTE PRIVILEGE

Privilege is another important defense. The torts of libel and slander constitute an infringement on absolute freedom of speech, even though we consider the extent of the infringement a reasonable limitation. Inevitably, situations arise in which the need for public information is so important as to be paramount to the need for protecting the private citizen.

For the same reasons that actions normally constituting assault and batteries were privileged under certain well-defined circumstances, types of statements that would normally be defamatory are privileged. Each class of privilege excusing a party from liability for defamation rests upon reasons of policy deemed so important as to override the policy of merely protecting an individual's reputation.

In some instances privilege is considered absolute—that is, in force regardless of the good faith of the publisher. This is true in the case of public officials: judges on the bench, legislators in their chambers, and executive officers of the state.

It is generally conceded that the reputations of private individuals actually have been damaged on occasion by malicious public servants hiding behind their absolute privilege. Nevertheless, the interest in leaving legislators, judges, and executive officials free to speak openly, and even bluntly, in the exercise of their public functions is considered to overshadow the possible harm to the individual. This is one example of the private interest being sacrificed to some extent in the public interest.

SALOMON v. MAHONEY (New York, 1946) 66 NYS 2d 598

The immunity of judges for statements made and acts done in their judicial capacity is for sound reasons of public interest and policy a fundamental principle of our jurisprudence on which rests the independence of the administration of justice. . . .

(2) The complaint read with the exhibit shows that the statements were made by defendant in the Magistrate's Court, City of New York (Felony Court, Borough of the Bronx), over which defendant was actually presiding in his official capacity as a judicial officer. The court was in session and the Magistrate on the bench was endeavoring to procure before the court proper attendance of persons after he had been obliged to suspend for 15 minutes because of their prior non-attendance in the courtroom and loitering in the corridor of the courthouse. . . . The court said, "If I find anybody is soliciting, I will punish him," but did not undertake to punish plaintiff. . . .

(3, 4) On the facts and circumstances disclosed, the claimed defamatory statements were absolutely privileged and accordingly the complaint is insufficient. The immunity of judges for statements made and acts done in their judicial capacity is for sound reasons of public interest and policy a fundamental principle of our jurisprudence on which rests the independence of the administration of justice. . . . In that case Chief Justice Kent, directing entry of judgment in favor of the defendant, said: "The doctrine which holds a judge exempt from a civil suit or indictment, for any act done, or omitted to be done by him, sitting as judge, has a deep root in the common law. It is to be found in the earliest judicial records, and it has been steadily maintained by an undisturbed current of decisions in the English courts, amidst every change of policy, and through every revolution of their government. A short view of the cases will teach us to admire the wisdom of our forefathers, and to revere a principle on which rests the independence of the administration of justice."

This immunity extends even to defamatory statements made by a judicial officer in the course of his official acts. . . . In that case, reversing a judgment on the law and dismissing the complaint, the court said: "The public mischief which would ensue from permitting civil actions of this sort to be brought against judicial officers far outweighs the private inconvenience or damage to individuals who may deem themselves aggrieved by judicial conduct."

In *Scott* v. *Stansfield*, L.R., 3 Exch. 220, 222, 223, sustaining the defense of absolute privilege in reference to a county judge, Chief Baron Kelly held: "The question arises, perhaps for the first time with reference to a county court judge, but a series of decisions uniformly to the same effect, extending from the time of Lord Coke to the present time, establish the general proposition that no action will lie against a judge for any acts done or words spoken in his judicial capacity in a court of justice. This doctrine has been applied not only to the superior courts, but to the court of the coroner and to a court martial, which is not a court of record. It is essential in all courts that the judges who are appointed to administer the law should be permitted to administer it under the protection of the law independently and freely, without favour and without fear. This provision of the law is . . . for the benefit of the public, whose interest it is that the judges should be at liberty to exercise their functions with independence and without fear of consequences."

Here the statements were made by defendant in the course of his official duties which included the right to preserve order and prevent interruptions of the court's proceedings through non-attendance of persons. . . .

All concur.

✧

To fully understand the above case, one must realize that to accuse an attorney of soliciting clients is a most serious accusation. An attorney may be disbarred if he is found seeking out clients and attempting to persuade them to bring suit, which is what is meant by "soliciting." *Ambulance-chasing* is a less dignified term for the same practice.

QUALIFIED PRIVILEGE

There are a number of situations in which a private individual, under well-defined circumstances, has a privilege to make statements that ordinarily would give rise to an action in defamation. However, this type of privilege is in effect only when the publisher is in good faith. Again the exceptions are based upon reasons of social policy.

For example, the individual has a privilege analogous to his privilege of self-defense in the case of a battery. Just as the victim of a battery is entitled to fight back within reasonable limits, when the individual has been defamed, he is permitted to attack the veracity of the defamer within reasonable limits.

One of the most consistent policies of the common law is that of encouraging business activity. It is through business, after all, that most of our goods and services are produced and distributed, and it is business that provides employment for most of our working population. This policy of encouraging business activity accounts for several different types of situations in which a qualified privilege exists.

Perhaps the most controversial qualified privilege is that afforded to dispensers of credit information (in many states, though not all). Through this privilege, the dispensers of credit information are not liable for distributing incorrect data. This is true despite the fact that not only may the reputation of an individual be affected, but his business may be jeopardized because of ensuing difficulties in obtaining credit. This privilege does not extend to malicious injury; it applies only to honest mistakes by the informant.

The specific rationale behind the privilege extended to credit agencies is that credit information is fundamental to many business decisions, and the free flow of such information should remain unimpeded. It might easily be argued, however, that dispensing this type of information is itself a business; that the occasional party who is injured should be compensated by the business responsible, just as the occasional party who is assaulted and battered by a store clerk should be compensated by the particular business employing the clerk.

Closely related to the one just discussed is a privilege permitting full and frank discussion in writing letters of reference. Basically the same rationale, free flow of important business information (in this case relating to prospective employees' capabilities and defects), is behind this form of privilege. The same limitation applies; the information conveyed may actually be incorrect, but the privilege does not apply if the false statements are malicious.

Last, internal business communications are privileged. Interoffice memoranda of a corporation or conversations between partners, dealing with some third party in a business connection, are privileged. Here, again, the policy is that of encouraging the free flow of business information. Again the statement may not be malicious, and the privilege only applies so long as the information is confined to members of the particular business organization.

WATWOOD v. *STONE'S MERCANTILE AGENCY*
(CCA District of Columbia, 1952) 194 F 2d 160

. . . A mercantile agency's credit report to an interested sub-scriber is qualifiedly privileged; unless it is made in bad faith or for an improper purpose. . . . The harm that such statements occasionally do . . . is believed small in relation to the benefits that subscribers derive from frank reports. . . .

EDGERTON, CJ.

Appellant's second amended complaint for libel includes substantially the following statements. Appellee Mercantile Agency sent to a subscriber a credit report about appellant that had been read by several members of appellee's staff. It contained this language: "Watwood, Miss Susie V. . . . claims to be single. . . . Miss Watwood is reported to have one child attending school. According to information the child's name is Gwen Cohen. . . . D.C. Civil Suit, 3/27/42: *Susie V. Watwood* v. *Jacob M. Cohen* for damages for breach of promise to marry, $50,000. D.C. Civil Order, 11/4/42: *Susie V. Watwood* v. *Jacob M. Cohen,* order for dismissal." According to the complaint, this language implies that appellant is the mother of a child born out of wedlock, but the facts are that appellant is married to Jacob M. Cohen and is not a mother. She uses her maiden name in business.

Appellee's answer to the complaint says appellee furnished the report in good faith to a subscriber, in response to his request, for use in his business, and that this subscriber forwarded it unread to appellant's attorney, at whose instance the subscriber had obtained it from appellee. The District Court awarded summary judgment to appellee on the ground that the pleadings and depositions showed there was no genuine issue as to any material fact and that appellee was entitled to judgment as a matter of law.

(1–3) A jury might well think appellee's report suggested that appellant was unmarried and a mother. The fact that she is neither does not prevent a suggestion that she is both from being defamatory. But the usual rule, which we think should prevail in the District of Columbia, is that a mercantile agency's credit report to an interested subscriber is qualifiedly privileged; unless it is made in bad faith or for an improper purpose, the fact that it contains erroneous unfavorable statements about the plaintiff does not make the agency liable. . . . The harm that such statements occasionally do to applicants for credit is believed to be small in relation to the benefits that subscribers derive from frank reports. . . . Since marital status and number of dependents bear on credit, the qualified privilege is broad enough to cover the statements in appellee's report.

(4, 5) The agency need not show that the subscriber was actually interested in the plaintiff's credit. It is a general rule of the law of defamation that "while a misguided notion as to the defendant's moral obligation or justification to make the statement will not exonerate him, he is privileged to publish it to any person who reasonably appears to have a duty, interest, or authority in connection with the matter." . . . The principle is not confined to the law of defamation. "In practically all cases of privilege in the law of torts the existence of a privilege depends upon the facts as they reasonably appear to the person whose liability is in question. The privilege of self-defense and the defense of property, for example, are available if the defendant believes on reasonable grounds that defensive efforts are necessary. . . . Privilege is of little value if it depends upon the existence of facts that are unknown or unknowable to the person affected." . . .

(6) The fact that the report was handled by more than one of appellee's employees in the ordinary course of business does not destroy the privilege. . . .

Affirmed.

✧

Note the similarity between the privilege to arrest a suspected shoplifter, given to a retailer by statute in some states and the privilege accorded the credit agency. Probably the objections to be raised against these types of privilege would be the same in each case. Obviously, here is a question of social policy and one which could be changed regardless of precedent if a court felt strongly that the policy no longer was supported by good reasons.

There is a qualified privilege permitting comment upon the work of all sorts of public figures and celebrities. Thus, the capability of outstanding athletes, the dramatic ability of actors, the literary worth of authors, and the vocal talents of opera singers, to mention a few types of celebrity, may all be the subject of the critics' scorn or praise. However, comment directed at the personal life of the public figure is not privileged. Thus, it is permissible to call a public figure a poor writer or singer, if this is his field; it is not permissible to call him immoral or a criminal, unless, of course, the accusation can be proved.

In this way, the public may hear opinions of experts as to what books are worth reading, what concerts worth hearing, yet at the same time the private life of the public figure is not exposed to unfair comment.

LIBEL AND CRITICISM [4]

Criticism in good faith of an author's work is allowed almost without restriction; but the law guards the private individual as distinguished from the man in his public capacity. It does not permit the critic to go behind the book to attack the author as a private person.

A scientific man has written a book in which he attempts to disprove the existence of the force of gravity. A scientific newspaper, in reviewing the

[4] Editors, *Harvard Law Review*, Cambridge, Mass. (1897), 11, p. 53.

book, attempted to show by way of criticism that the author does not know enough to be able to appreciate the force of the argument by which the law of gravitation is proved. The author says that this is a false and malicious libel, and that it has damaged him to the extent of thousands of dollars.

Criticism in good faith of an author's work is allowed almost without restriction; but the law guards the private individual as distinguished from the man in his public capacity. It does not permit the critic to go behind the book to attack the author as a private person. On these principles Mr. Ruskin, in speaking of Mr. Whistler's paintings, was able with impunity to charge the artist with the "cockney impudence" of asking two hundred guineas for "flinging a pot of paint in the public's face." But when he accused him of "willful imposture," he overstepped the mark, and had to pay a farthing in damages. In the present case, the question is whether the imputation of ignorance has a legitimate bearing as criticism upon the book. If the imputation of ignorance is made as an inference from the book itself, it seems to have a clear connection with the credit to which the book is entitled. It is true that in an English case, *Dunne v. Anderson,* 3 Bing. 88, it was held to be libel for one, in criticising a petition to Parliament by a physician, to reflect upon the physician's knowledge of chemistry. But that case is to be distinguished from the present one, in that in presenting the petition the physician is not so distinctly before the public as the author in publishing a book. As Lord Cockburn says in *Strauss* v. *Francis,* 4 F & F. 1114, "a man who publishes a book challenges criticism." The critic is strictly accountable for any damaging misstatement of fact; but here there is no such misstatement. If there were nothing in the book which might lead a reasonable man in the critic's position to take the same view, it might be held that this was not fair criticism. But the force of gravity is well enough established for the courts to take judicial cognizance of it; and they are hardly likely to hold that this statement, if made merely as a deduction from the author's treatment of his subject, was so unfounded as to be a libel, rather than a fair though strong criticism.

✧

CHAPTER ELEVEN

Negligence

Negligence involves unreasonable conduct on the part of the defendant leading to injury to the plaintiff. Therefore, there must be a cause and effect sequence between the unreasonable conduct and the injury.

Preface to Negligence

IN THE CHAPTER on assault and battery, an important difference was noted between the legal system codified by Hammurabi in 2250 B.C. and most modern legal systems. The former law consisted of a list of very specific prohibitions with equally specific sanctions. Modern legal systems have developed broader, more flexible principles. This difference was illustrated in previous discussions by comparing the acts of violence outlawed by Hammurabi and their remedies with our torts of assault and battery.

Why do we find specific prohibitions characteristic of earlier legal systems and the use of broader principles a later development? We might guess that something has to come first, and that as in any process of evolution the simpler forms will give birth to the more complex. We might also note that even today many nonlawyers assume that there is an exact rule of law, precisely answering every legal problem that may arise. Certainly specific rules of law are easy to communicate and to understand. "Do not put out another's eye or tooth" is a very clear and precise command, though somewhat inadequate as a guide in a variety of circumstances. A command that one avoid deliberate, unpermitted contacts is not so clear and precise, though more adequate as a device for regulating conduct. Being highly specific in defining prohibited acts results in a high degree of certainty as to the acts prohibited; yet, broader principles are necessary to meet the unforeseen needs of a changing society. What about all the wrongs that are not expressly prohibited by Hammurabi's Code? And if we say other acts are prohibited by implication, which others? What test is applied?

To validate the more specific approach to lawmaking, the dogged student may attempt to expand a list of wrongs and remedies to include every conceivable possibility. If this strikes the reader as plausible, he is invited to try. Legal scholars have seriously attempted to do this, but cannot be said to have been successful.

When principles rather than specific rules are relied upon as a basis for deciding cases, the area of judgment in applying the principles is necessarily enlarged. Although the advantage of a principle is that properly understood and utilized it will solve an array of problems, application of a legal principle to a specific case requires skill and imagination.

The advantages and disadvantages of applying a legal principle to the solution of specific cases may be considered by the student throughout the discussion concerning the tort of negligence. One broad principle is central to this body of law: *whatever a person does, he is required to use reasonable care under the circumstances to avoid injury to others.*

Why Negligence?

THE CODE OF HAMMURABI (2250 B.C.) [1]

Negligence [2]

If a builder build a house for a man and do not make its construction firm, and the house which he has built collapse and cause the death of the owner of the house, that builder shall be put to death.

If it cause the death of a son of the owner of the house, they shall put to death a son of that builder.

If it cause the death of a slave of the owner of the house, he shall give to the owner of the house a slave of equal value.

If it destroy property, he shall restore whatever it destroyed, and because he did not make the house which he built firm and it collapsed, he shall rebuild the house which collapsed from his own property [that is, at his own expense].

Accident

If a man hire an ox or an ass and a lion kill it in the field, it is the owner's affair.

If a man hire an ox and a god strike it and it die, the man who hired the ox shall take an oath before god and go free.

If a bull, when passing through the street, gore a man and bring about his death, this case has no penalty.

✧

1 Robert Francis Harper, *The Code of Hammurabi; King of Babylon* (Chicago: University of Chicago Press, 1904), pp. 81–87.

2 Hammurabi was to be commended for distinguishing negligence from accident. Many primitive legal systems do not draw this distinction.

Most of us feel intuitively that intentional wrongs, as those encompassed within the torts of assault and battery, should warrant a legal remedy. With a few exceptions grounded on reasons of public policy, we have seen that intentional injuries are indeed provided with a legal remedy. However, not all injuries are intentional. In modern times, over most of the world at least, injuries to persons and property are usually unintentional. Therefore, some body of principles must be devised to aid us in deciding when compensation should be forthcoming to victims of unintentional injuries.

Although is is apparent that in general, intentional injuries should be compensated, through legal action if necessary, it is not so apparent that *all* unintentional injuries should be compensated. Though primitive societies often adopt the principle that a person is responsible for all injuries attributable to his actions, however fortuitous, this runs contrary to our sense of justice. Holding a person responsible regardless of fault would mean that the driver of a car under which a suicide leaps could be held responsible, as for that matter, could a physician under whose care a patient died despite competent medical treatment. Measured by the values of our society, it is neither necessary nor desirable to provide a legal remedy in these cases.

Our law, along with that of other Western nations, usually requires that a person must be at fault before he may be held responsible.[3] What is needed, therefore, is a principle that can be applied to unintentional injuries, by which we may measure whether the person causing the injury is at fault or not. Only if we find that he is at fault do we hold him liable. The question, then is, what do we mean by fault?

Essentially what we mean is conduct that is avoidable and that carries with it an unreasonable risk of injury to others as compared to the social benefits of the conduct. When an injury is caused by conduct that carelessly exposed others to unreasonable risk, our law provides a remedy in tort. This remedy is known as the tort of negligence. The principle underlying the tort of negligence is very broad, but being broad it can be applied to a wide variety of situations.

Although the torts of assault and battery and defamation encompass a comparatively small and well-defined set of acts, the tort of negligence involves human conduct about as diverse as the sum total of human activity. Almost everything that may be done at all may be done negligently and result in some form of injury to others. The tort of negligence may be thought of as occupying the area of conduct bounded on one side by the deliberate torts and on the other by unavoidable accident. What is left constitutes the area of unintentional wrongs, and the tort of negligence provides us with the legal vehicle by which we may secure redress for those wrongs.

---

[3] Though we do hold parties for certain wrongs of their employees, as discussed throughout Section 5.

SCHULTZ v. CHENEY SCHOOL DISTRICT
(Washington, 1962) 371 P 2d 59

> . . . *It was for the jury to determine whether his action in lower-*
> *ing his head and endeavoring with one hand to remove the bee*
> *was instinctive or whether reasonable care required him to main-*
> *tain control of the bus in spite of this painful distraction.*

Appeal from a judgment of the Superior Court for Spokane County, RAYMOND F. KELLY, J., entered November 2, 1959. Affirmed.

Action for personal injuries. Plaintiff appeals from a judgment entered upon a verdict in favor of the defendant.

This is a personal injury action in which the jury returned a verdict for the defendant. The evidence showed that the plaintiff fell or was thrown from her seat in the defendant's school bus when it was driven off the highway into a ditch. This occurred because the attention of the driver was diverted momentarily from the road when a bee flew in the window and stung him on the neck. He ducked his head and tried with his left hand to extricate the bee from under his collar. While he was thus engaged the bus veered to the left and onto the shoulder of the road, a distance of about 75 feet.

At this point the driver raised his head and perceived what had happened. He endeavored to turn the bus back onto the road, but because of the soft condition of the shoulder, he was unable to do so and the bus went down into a shallow ditch, tilting first to the left and then to the right before it could be stopped. It was this motion of the bus that caused the plaintiff to fall into the aisle.

There was no contention that the driver was operating the bus in a negligent manner before the bee stung him. But the plaintiff urged in the trial court, and now urges here, that the evidence showed that he was negligent as a matter of law in failing to keep the bus under control after that incident. The testimony was that only a few seconds passed between the moment of the bee sting and the moment the driver discovered that the bus had veered across the highway. He testified that the sting startled him and that the bee continued to buzz under his collar after it had stung him.

We think the trial court correctly decided that it was for the jury to determine whether his action in lowering his head and endeavoring with one hand to remove the bee was instinctive or whether reasonable care required him to maintain control of the bus in spite of this painful distraction. It is not a question that can be decided as a matter of law.

The defendant, by its answer, denied negligence and affirmatively alleged that the accident was unavoidable. Error is assigned to the giving of an instruction defining "unavoidable accident."

. . . It is well established in this jurisdiction that an instruction on unavoidable accident is proper when the evidence shows or justifies an inference that an unavoidable accident has occurred, as that term has been defined.

In this case, the defendant was not negligent as a matter of law. It affirmatively alleged and introduced evidence that the accident was unavoidable. The jury could find the defendant liable if it found that the accident was the result of the driver's negligence, or it could find, as it did, that the driver lost control of his vehicle momentarily because of his instinctive reaction to the sudden and unexpected attack of the bee, and that his acts under the circumstances were not negligent. Implicit in this finding is a determination that the accident was unavoidable in the exercise of due care. The instruction was proper under the evidence.

The judgment is affirmed.

✧

Was the driver of the school bus at fault? Was he guilty of unreasonable conduct that carried a risk of injuring others? This determination is left to the jury in all but the most obvious cases, and as we see, the jury found that under the circumstances the conduct was not unreasonable.

QUESTION

1. Considering that another jury, under these facts, might have found the defendant liable for negligence, does not this seem a rather inexact way of making important determinations? What is the purpose in leaving such wide scope to the finding of a jury in cases of this nature?

The circumstances under which negligence cases might arise are so diverse as to defy enumeration. Undoubtedly automobile "accidents" are the most frequent source of negligence litigation in the United States. (The cases when damage results from a genuine accident—that is, when neither party is at fault—are rare.) Even a simple fender denting brings the law of negligence into play. Often it is reasonably clear which driver was responsible for damage, and the driver is insured, and his insurer settles out of court on the basis of an independent estimate of the damage. Liability insurance protects the driver only from legal liability. The insurer is not liable for damage by their insured unless the insured *was* negligent. Of course neither is the insured liable unless he was negligent.

Trains, buses, airplanes, and ships crashing, colliding, or otherwise negligently damaging persons or property provide their share of negligence litigation. Another type of negligence suit of particular interest to the businessman is that involving liability for the condition of business premises. Department stores, grocery stores, and theaters seem to attract the most publicity in this respect, but anyone occupying real property whether for business purposes or not could be involved in a negligence suit based upon an injury resulting from unsafe conditions on the property.

Still another form of negligence suit of special interest to the businessman is the suit for malpractice. In this type of suit a professional, tradesman, or businessman, in a calling requiring special training, skill, or experience, is alleged to have performed duties at a level below the standard required of his calling. Physicians seem to be the most common target for this type of suit. However, lawyers, accountants, skilled tradesmen, and many other specialized callings might be held for malpractice. In one case an insurance broker was found liable for failing to recommend a form of coverage. The omission had caused a disastrous loss to the customer. The loss was in effect shifted to the broker, because of the latter's negligence in overlooking the need for insurance. Appraisers have been held for negligence in making a faulty estimate of value. (See case on page 287, where a tradesman was found liable for negligence in performing his calling.)

These are only a few of the more common categories in which liability based on negligence may be a danger. Every business has its particular problems. Because the details of one's business are usually better known to the executives in the business than to attorneys with whom the executives may consult, the executives must assume much of the responsibility for identifying situations that carry an undue exposure to suit, and must take steps to minimize the danger as well as to shift the burden through insurance when this seems desirable.

Elements of the Tort of Negligence

As has already been stated, the tort of negligence provides a remedy for injuries resulting from acts that are not intentional but that are within the control of the actor.

Therefore, three elements must be found in order to constitute an actionable case in negligence:

1. The careless, or "negligent," act of the defendant. This, as has been seen, involves a difficult value judgment about what is or is not unreasonable conduct under the circumstances.

2. The act must result in an injury. The injury may be either to the person, to the property, or otherwise to the financial interests of the plaintiff. However, it must be reasonably tangible. An injury to the plaintiff's feelings, for example, will not ordinarily constitute the basis for a negligence action, though most jurisdictions do recognize an injury if a sudden emotional impact, especially fear, causes an actual physical injury, as, for example, a miscarriage.

3. There must be a direct causal connection between the act and the injury. This requirement is termed *proximate cause.*

Requirements (1) and (3) are discussed in more detail below.[4]

4 EDITOR's NOTE: The above discussion varies from the usual analysis of negligence in that it does not include a discussion of duty. (Two aspects of duty are, however, considered subsequently. The limitation of the duty of a manufacturer for defects in

UNITED STATES v. *FOLK* (CCA South Carolina, 1952) 199 F2 889

> . . . *We think there was no negligence in Cecil's pursuing Hammond with Cecil's pistol in his hand, cocked and with the safety catch off. . . . The split second saved by having the pistol completely ready might well have meant the difference . . . between Cecil's physical safety and serious physical harm.*

Shortly after daylight on Saturday, January 13, 1951, Roy L. Cecil, Criminal Investigator, Alcohol Tax Unit, of the United States Treasury Department, acting within the scope of his employment, and while in the active discharge of his duties, accompanied by Criminal Investigators of the Alcohol Tax Unit, together with South Carolina State Constables, conducted a raid on an illicit distillery for the manufacture of whiskey, in Edgefield County, South Carolina. At the still, John Henry Hammond, a colored man, was working, along with three other persons.

Cecil alone walked into the distillery site and observed four men, none of whom he knew, working at the distillery. He drew his forty-five caliber automatic army pistol, which he was then carrying, and called to the men, "A Federal Officer—don't run." Immediately after hearing these words, the four men at the distillery fled, with John Henry Hammond and another colored man, later ascertained to be Ernest Holmes, running up the embankment side-by-side near Cecil.

When Cecil started running after Hammond he took the safety off of his loaded forty-five caliber army automatic pistol, and while continuing to hold it in his hand cocked, with the safety off, pursued John Henry Hammond and Ernest Holmes through the woods and up the hill. A short distance up the hill Ernest Holmes turned to the left, ran into Criminal investigator Cecil Martin and was apprehended.

his products is considered briefly—page 153—and the limitations upon the duty of owners and occupiers of land is considered—page 175.) Conventional treatment of the elements of negligence requires (1) the existence of a duty of care on the part of the defendant, (2) violation of that duty, (3) injury, and (4) proximate cause. Normally we do owe a duty to exercise care for the safety of our fellow man. It is true that in some cases a duty of due care is not owed—for example, against a burglar ransacking one's house; and some cases have held that no duty is owed for completely unpredictable results of an act even if performed carelessly—as when a person seemingly not in danger is injured through unforeseeable events (see *Palsgraff* v. *Long Island Railroad,* 162 NE 99, 1928).

In the final analysis, this requirement provides a means of limiting liability in unusual cases. A finding of no duty is a finding that under the circumstances a defendant should not be held liable, regardless of the fact that he may not have exercised care. We feel that a brief and necessarily superficial treatment of torts is better presented without much consideration of this confusing and difficult subject. It is safe to state that in the overwhelming majority of instances in which an injury to defendant is proximately caused by negligence of the defendant, an action will lie.

Hammond continued up the hill with Cecil still in pursuit. At a point approximately one hundred yards from the distillery, and when Cecil was "20 or 25 steps" behind him Hammond jumped over a ditch. As Cecil attempted to jump the same ditch in pursuit, he fell, accidentally discharging the pistol in the direction in which Hammond was fleeing. The bullet entered the right forearm of Hammond, from the back of the arm, severing an artery. Hammond proceeded up the hill, with Cecil following him to the crest of the hill, a distance of about sixty-five yards from the place where the pistol was discharged. Upon his arrival at the crest of the hill, Cecil fired two shots from his pistol as signal shots to his associates.

After looking for Hammond about "five or ten minutes," Cecil returned to the site of the distillery. He remained in the vicinity of the distillery, with the others associated with him in the raid, approximately three hours.

The following Sunday afternoon, January 14, 1951, Hammond's body was found by friends, who were searching for him at the instigation of members of his family, after he had failed to return home. The body was found in a ditch at the bottom of the hill, one hundred and ten yards from the crest of the hill, where Cecil had stopped in his pursuit of Hammond. Hammond had bled to death from the bullet wound in his arm. The next day, blood was found by another officer on several trees at the crest of the ridge at or near the point where Cecil ceased his pursuit of Hammond.

The terrain from the distillery site to where the body of Hammond was found, and along the course of his flight, consisted of woodland from which all large timber had been cut, with some undergrowth, with visibility unhampered, except by the hill and a few small scattered pine trees.

We quote from the Findings of Fact and Conclusions of Law on the part of the District Judge the following extracts which seem to us of primary importance in this case:

> . . . he [Cecil] knew or should have known that he had no right to pursue the fleeing Hammond through the woods, over rough terrain, with a cocked, loaded automatic pistol in his hand with the safety off and his finger inside the trigger guard and his hand over the grip-safety. Such action on the part of the officer, in my opinion was negligence. He should have foreseen that such handling of his highly dangerous pistol could or would cause injury or death to plaintiff's intestate.
>
> After his pistol was discharged while he was "20 or 25 steps" behind Hammond, he should have known that the pistol was discharged in the direction in which Hammond was fleeing and he owed him the duty to make a reasonable search of the entire area to ascertain if any injury or death had been inflicted. Although he remained at the distillery site more than three hours he did not look for Hammond more than "five or ten minutes." With the assistance of all the six other officers he could have found Hammond and probably saved his life. Other officers, after Hammond's body was discovered the next day, found blood on the ground and on two of the trees in the vicinity. His failure to make a reasonable search under all the circumstances and his failure to notify the other officers of his pursuit and of the discharge of his pistol during the pursuit of Hammond was negligence.
>
> The defendant's employee, while acting within the scope of his employment, was guilty of actionable negligence, which was the direct and proximate cause of plaintiff's intestate's death.

The negligence of defendant's employee was such that the defendant, if it had been a private person, would be liable to the plaintiff in both cases under the law of South Carolina, where the injuries and death occurred.

With the conclusion that Cecil was guilty of negligence, we cannot agree. Since that was the only basis of liability on the part of the Government, the judgments below must be reversed. . . .

This seems to be the law of South Carolina. . . .

No case has been cited to us disclosing just what measure of care, under the South Carolina law, was owed here by Cecil to Hammond. Hardly could this measure be higher than the care owed to a mere trespasser. . . . For here, Cecil a federal officer, had detected Hammond in the very act of committing a federal crime and Hammond, when called on to surrender, had fled. It was clearly Cecil's job to pursue Hammond and to make every reasonable effort to arrest him.

Under these circumstances, we think there was no negligence in Cecil's pursuing Hammond with Cecil's pistol in his hand, cocked and with the safety catch off. Cecil did not know what course of conduct Hammond might adopt. Had Hammond resisted arrest when caught, or attacked Cecil, the split second saved by having the pistol completely ready might well have meant the difference between Hammond's escape or his arrest, or between Cecil's physical safety and serious physical harm. With sympathy for Hammond, we must not too strictly limit what a federal officer should do in carrying out a dangerous duty imposed on him here by virtue of his office. There was certainly nothing wilful or wanton about Cecil's conduct.

Nor can we agree with the District Judge's finding: "He [Cecil] should have foreseen that such handling of his highly dangerous pistol could or would cause injury or death to plaintiff's intestate." In the case of an accidental discharge of the pistol, it was highly improbable that the bullet would hit Hammond, a rapidly moving target. No one else was visible on the landscape. The real danger from an accidental discharge was to Cecil himself.

Nor do we find any negligence in the failure of Cecil, and the other officers, to make a more extended search for Hammond. Cecil was partly stunned by his fall and Hammond, when last seen by Cecil, was rapidly disappearing over the crest of the hill. Cecil testified that he had no idea that the bullet had wounded Hammond.

The Federal Tort Claims Act exempts the United States from liability resulting from an assault and battery. The Government strongly contends that there was no liability here under that exemption. Since our decision of lack of negligence here completely disposes of this case, we need not pass on this rather difficult question. . . .

It follows from what has been said that both the judgments below must be reversed, and these cases are remanded to the District Court with instructions to enter judgment for the defendant, United States, in each case.

Reversed.

✧

QUESTIONS

1. Was the officer in danger of criminal prosecution in the above case? Why or why not?

2. A reasonable, prudent revenue agent may pursue a moonshiner with his gun cocked and loaded. However, in *Stepp* v. *United States* (page 118) we found that the court stated categorically that an assault and battery had occurred under slightly similar circumstances, even though the government won (under a provision of the Federal Tort Claims Act excepting the government from liability for assault and battery). May we say it is permissible to shoot persons suspected of manufacturing illicit liquor but not those suspected of carrying it aboard ship? Explain the difference between these two cases.

3. In *Hartley* v. *Lasater* (Washington, 1916) 165 P 106, the judge stated: "Men who act in emergencies are not to be held to the strict accountability that the law demands of those who act deliberately. Nor are they to be penalized because they did not do what, in the light of subsequent events, or in theory, would have avoided the accident. The instinct of self-preservation and the instinct to refrain from harming others are always present in emergent situations affecting personal security. These impulses prompt that which is done, and what is done is usually that which should have been done, or all that could have been done. Hence the law will excuse an act which if done deliberately or after a lapse of time sufficient for reflection would make the actor answerable as for a willful tort."

The "Negligent" Act of the Defendant and the Test of the Reasonable Prudent Man

Perhaps because the question of which conduct is "negligent"—that is, unreasonable under the circumstances—is largely one of social values; the determination of whether conduct is "negligent" or is not is left to the jury. In order to present this question to the jury in a concise manner, some concise way of stating the test to be applied had to be devised. This need resulted in the invention of the fiction known as the "reasonable prudent man."

The reasonable prudent man is a fictitious person. This fictitious person is endowed with certain characteristics. Perhaps his paramount virtue is care. He always ponders whether or not his actions may in the normal course of events lead to injury of others or their property. He never commits errors without good cause, nor is he guilty of momentary lapses. He is *not,* however, held to superhuman foresight or to superhuman responses in emergency situations. He is always held to normal foresight and normal responses.

The value of this fictitious reasonable prudent man is that he represents a standard to which a jury may compare the act of a real defendant. If on comparison the acts of the defendant seem to be consistent with those of the reasonable prudent man, the defendant is not guilty of negligence. The reasonable prudent man represents a principle, though a more abstract and more difficult principle than "unpermitted contact" does in relation to battery.

Often, a defendant in a particular case will be handicapped, as, for example, a blind man. The question then is not, did that defendant act as the ordinary man with sight? But rather, did he act as the reasonable prudent blind man? Physical and mental defects of a particular defendant are incorporated into the makeup of the reasonable man as he is defined in a particular case. Ordinarily a person with a handicap must exercise a higher degree of care to compensate for his handicap. Often too, special training or skill is required for proper performance of certain acts. Although we do not hold a physician liable because his patient dies, we do hold him to a high standard in the performance of his duties. A physician, in practicing his profession, is held to the standard of a reasonable prudent physician, not merely to the standard of any reasonable prudent layman.

Minors are the beneficiaries of a public policy extending special treatment to them in almost every contact with the law. In the law of negligence, account is taken of a minor's immaturity and lack of judgment. Essentially, a minor is held to the standard of a reasonable prudent minor with the mental characteristics of the particular subject. Young children are considered incapable of negligence both because they need extra protection and because they are in fact not able to appreciate dangers obvious to more mature persons, nor are they able to weigh causes and effects accurately. On the other hand, late teenagers would in most instances be treated as adults. In each case involving minors, the question of the standard to be applied to the minor is a question for the jury. There are not arbitrary ages fixed for determining the minor's degree of responsibility.

The Test of Proximate Cause

Negligence involves unreasonable conduct on the part of the defendant leading to injury to the plaintiff. Therefore, there must be a cause-and-effect sequence between the unreasonable conduct and the injury.

Speeding down a crowded street at a high rate of speed does constitute unreasonable conduct, but it does not constitute the tort of negligence, because there is no injury. (It may well constitute the *crime* of negligent driving.) The same act followed by an individual falling into a manhole in another part of town does not constitute the tort of negligence. There is no cause-and-effect relationship between the negligent act and the injury. If the car hits a pedestrian under these circumstances, the tort of negligence does exist. The act and injury are directly connected, and we say that the act was the proximate cause of the injury.

Problems in causation sometimes become difficult, because very frequently a number of different factors, some often unknown, work together to produce a result. After all, if the victim of an auto accident had left home earlier, and hence not been at an intersection when the defendant hit him, the accident would not have occurred. If he happened to arrive at the intersection when he did because a train's earlier negligence had blocked his way, is the railroad liable? If a clerk at the victim's place of employment negligently made out the vacation schedules, thus arranging for the victim to be in town and therefore to sustain the accident, is this the cause of the victim's accident? How about the fact that the victim had been crowded into another lane a block earlier by a taxicab, so that presumably the defendant would have hit the taxi had the plaintiff not been crowded out? Is the taxi liable for the accident?

The requirement, proximate cause, is first an attempt to confine liability only to acts that are "direct" or "immediate" causes of injury.

One of the tests of whether a defendant is liable for results that can be traced back to his negligent act is the test of foreseeability. Is it reasonably foreseeable that a train delaying a motorist would set the stage for a motorist being struck by another car some blocks later? Is it foreseeable to a taxicab, forcing the motorist into another lane, that the motorist will be struck by another car some blocks later? In both cases the answer is no. In both cases, proximate cause is lacking, even though a cause-and-effect relationship may in fact exist. The perpetrator is not held for completely unpredictable consequences of his act. He is held, however, to understand the ordinary dangers, if any, that a reasonable man would associate with an act. He need not be able to predict exactly what injury may result from creating a particular danger. The Southern Utilities Company case below is a good illustration of this point.

SOUTHERN PUBLIC UTILITIES COMPANY v. THOMAS
(CCA North Carolina, 1935) 78 F 2d 107

We agree that in determining what was the proximate cause of the accident, the test is whether the injury was a reasonably foreseeable event, or the natural and probable consequences of the omission of the defendant's workmen. . . .

Appeal from the District Court of the U.S. for the Middle District of North Carolina, at Winston-Salem. Action by Melvin Thomas, through his guardian A.S. Thomas, against the South. Pub. Util. Co. Judgment for P, D appeals. Judg. affirm.

SOPER, CJ.

Melvin Thomas, a child not quite five years of age, was seriously burned in May, 1933, when he poured into the fire in his mother's kitchen stove some gasoline which workmen in the employ of the Southern Public Utilities Company, defendant in the court below, had unintentionally left on the porch of the Thomas home, after they had repaired a washing machine sold by the Utilities Company to the father of the child. The question in the case is whether the failure of the workmen to take the gasoline away with them when they had finished the job constituted negligence which was the proximate cause of the accident.

The washing machine was on the back porch, and it was there that the work was done. The crankcase of the machine was drained and washed out with gasoline, which the workmen had brought with them in a gallon tin can, supplied with a screw cap. After the machine was cleaned, more than a pint of gasoline remained in the can. The cap was replaced and the can set down upon the porch. In gathering up their tools, the men overlooked the can and went away without it.

While the men worked on the porch, three children, including the infant plaintiff, stood by and watched them. One child picked up a knife and was made to put it down. Two of the children went off to school before the work was finished, but Melvin remained. After the men had left, he accompanied his mother when she went to drive the cow into a lot a short distance from the house. Upon their return, he preceded her. He found the gasoline, poured some of it into a fruit jar, and then, entering the kitchen, poured it into the stove because he thought it was lamp oil and "wanted to make mamma's fire burn better." Previously, Mrs. Thomas had used kerosene in building fires.

The verdict below was for the plaintiff, and the defendant complains of the action of the District Judge in refusing to direct a verdict in its behalf. It is said that a person of ordinary prudence in the workmen's place could not have foreseen, as a natural and probable result of their omission to take the gasoline away, that the boy would remove the cap from the can and pour some of the contents into the fire. Hence it is contended that the proximate cause of the injury was not the negligent act of the defendant, but the child's own conduct.

We agree that in determining what was the proximate cause of the accident, the test is whether the injury was a reasonably foreseeable event, or the natural and probable consequence of the omission of the defendant's workmen. . . . On this point there is no disagreement. The controversy arises in the application of the rule to the facts of the case. In similar situations it has been deemed pertinent that explosive substances have been left unguarded and accessible to children in a place where they had the right to be, and whither they might be expected to come.

Bearing in mind that gasoline is a substance inherently dangerous . . . we are unable to conclude that there was no actionable negligence in the instant case. We cannot say, as the defendant argues, that there was nothing about the gasoline can to attract the child, or that his conduct was so unexpected that it could not have been reasonably foreseen. Quite the contrary seems to be the tendency of the evidence. The workmen had come into the child's own home, bringing with them a volatile liquid, highly inflammable when contact with fire is established. It was noticed that the curiosity of the child . . . was provoked by the [washing machine] repairing. Thoughtlessly the dangerous substance was left behind (where the child was most likely to play). What more probable than that he should find the can (or more natural than that he should dangerously handle it). In our opinion, the District Judge was right in submitting the question to the jury, and the judgment of the District Court is affirmed.

✧

The problem in this case is not only one of causation. Although it is true that this particular accident would not have occurred if the child had not thrown the gasoline into the fire, it is also true that the accident would not have happened if the workmen had not left the gasoline behind. Furthermore, they were in a position to know the dangerous propensities of the gasoline, whereas the minor was not. Of course, a five-year-old could not be held for contributory negligence.

The defendants were found liable because the general danger was foreseeable, even though the particular type of accident that resulted was not.

Would it have affected the outcome of this case if the child's parents were negligent as well as the employees of the utility company? Almost certainly not. The child is the one injured, and the suit is for his benefit. The fact that parents of an injured child *are* negligent (which does not imply that they were in this case) does not mean that another party is absolved from negligence. The fact that parents allow a child to wander in the streets doesn't mean that a driver need not use due care to avoid hitting the child or that the driver can't be held for his negligence if he negligently injures the child.

POPLAR ET AL. v. BOURJOIS, INC., ET AL.
(New York, 1948) 80 NE 2d 334 (Part One)

As a general proposition, liability for negligence turns upon the foreseeability of any harm resulting from the careless conduct, not upon the foreseeability of the exact nature and extent of the injury which does in fact ensue. . . .

FULD, J.

A day or two after Christmas, 1940, as Myrtle Poplar was showing her sister perfumes and cosmetics which her husband had given her, she pricked her finger on the point of a silvery metal star that adorned the gift box in which they were contained. A serious streptococcus infection developed, she became gravely ill, and the infected finger had to be amputated. . . . This negligence action was brought against Bourjois, Inc., by Mrs. Poplar to recover for her injuries and by her husband for the loss of her services and for medical expenses.

Bourjois is a producer of perfumes, cosmetics and kindred articles. In 1940, it bought a large quantity of boxes from Lorscheider Schang Co., Inc., which manufactured them according to the former's specifications. Each was of cardboard overlaid with a silk fabric, about a foot square and three inches deep; the two cover lids were quilted, and to each was glued a thin and sharply pointed metal star some three inches from point to point. In anticipation of the 1940 Christmas trade, Bourjois packed about 10,000 of these cardboard boxes with its products, stamped its name prominently upon the cover, and marketed the entire package as its own. It sold some of them to a department store in Baltimore, Maryland, and it was one of those that Mr. Poplar, living in nearby Havre de Grace, bought for his wife.

The charge of negligence leveled at Bourjois was that it had failed to have the injury-producing star fastened securely to the box, and there was evidence that the point of the star had become slightly upturned so that it was not flush with the cover. It was claimed that defendant Bourjois' carelessness rendered the article "dangerous to life and limb." For its part Bourjois denied the charge of negligence. . . . A trial was held; the jury returned a verdict in favor of plaintiffs against Bourjois. . . . The Appellate Division reversed the judgment in plaintiff's favor and dismissed the complaint.

As a general proposition, liability for negligence turns upon the foreseeability of any harm resulting from the careless conduct, not upon the foreseeability of the exact nature and extent of the injury which does in fact ensue. . . . If a negligent act be the reasonable and proximate cause of an injury—that is, if the plaintiff's injury is traceable to the defendant's negligence without the intervention of any other independent, legally operative event—the injured person is entitled to recover for the harm actually suffered, even though the precise nature and extent of those injuries, as they finally developed, were more severe than could ordinarily have been foreseen. . . . In other words, a defendant is chargeable for all the harm and suffering which his negligent act brought on even though the plaintiff's injuries were aggravated by his own predisposition or weakness. . . . or by the intervening mistake or negligence of a physician who treated the original injury. An infection, unquestionably connected to, and flowing from an injury carelessly caused, should be and is equally chargeable to the careless defendant. . . . So, in the present case, if Bourjois owed a duty to ultimate purchasers and could be held liable to plaintiffs for marketing the box in a defective condition, it would likewise be liable for all the proximate results of its negligence, including infection and amputation of the finger. It would be legally inconsequential that amputation was less clearly to be foreseen than a simple scratch or pin prick.

The judgment of the Appellate Division should be affirmed, with costs. Judgment affirmed. [for the Defendant, on other grounds]

LOUGHRAN, C.J., and LEWIS, CONWAY, DESMOND, THACHER and SYE, JJ., concur.

✧

Here, the court seems to take the position that if a reasonable person should foresee injury (and that the defendant should have is not so obvious here as in some situations), there is no limit to the damages that may be assessed. Here, this talk is merely dicta, because as it happened the judge had already found for the defendant on other grounds. Nevertheless this case dramatizes the issue: What if a more serious disability had resulted? Would it seem fair to assess almost limitless liability on the basis of such slight negligence? On the other hand, would it seem fair to refuse full compensation for injuries suffered by the plaintiff, as a result of negligence by the defendant, no matter how slight?

No satisfactory solution has been found to this dilemma, but some courts have tended to limit the extent of damages under the guise of a limited duty.

Wishing to emphasize the issue of foreseeability and proximate cause, we deleted the discussion relating to other questions from the preceding case. However, the court held for the defendant because the applicable law (that of Maryland) recognized no duty of reasonable care for injuries resulting from a manufacturer's product, except toward purchasers of the product. Only in the case of inherently dangerous articles is the manufacturer's responsibility extended to noncustomers. The article in question here did not meet the test of being inherently dangerous, and the plaintiff was not a customer but the recipient of a gift.

Of course, finding no duty in a case such as this is another way of saying that as a matter of policy the courts will restrict the liability of the manufacturer. His liability extends not to the general public but only to those bearing a certain relationship with the manufacturer—namely, only to customers.

As for inherently dangerous goods, the policy is different. The manufacturer is liable to anyone injured, probably on the theory that being on notice of the dangerous propensities of the article in question, the manufacturer is also on notice that he must take steps to assure the safety of any member of the public who might be affected. Therefore, when inherently dangerous articles are involved, the duty of the manufacturer is more broad.

QUESTION

1. What arguments can you propose for imposing *some* limitation on either class of individuals, time, or distance on the liability of a manufacturer for injuries purportedly arising from negligent manufacture of products?

Intervening Causes

One pattern of factual events that has occurred often enough to merit special consideration may be illustrated by the following example. Speedy accommodates Scared by giving the latter a ride to Metropolis, 60 miles away. Speedy drives 90 miles an hour all the way and narrowly averts disaster several times. Then he slows down to 60 miles an hour. They actually meet disaster when a bridge collapses as they are driving over it. The collapse of the bridge had nothing to do with Speedy's driving (except that it would have collapsed before they arrived if Speedy had been traveling at a normal speed). This is an illustration of an intervening cause. An intervening cause, in general, exists when a defendant has been careless but some extraneous and unforeseen event has caused an injury. In practice, many cases require more careful analysis to determine whether or not a cause should qualify as intervening. In our example it obviously did. Often, the cause of the injury is more or less related to the defendant's act, the problem again being to separate the borderline cases on a logical basis. Causes that the defendant might have reasonably forseen as arising would not be considered intervening. The best test of whether a cause is intervening or not seems to be that of foreseeability. If foreseeable, a cause is not intervening.

Contributory Negligence

For a negligence action to succeed, an act of the defendant must have been the proximate cause of the defendant's injury. If the injury can be traced to a negligent act of the *plaintiff,* an action should not succeed. This is the actual state of the law. Negligence by the plaintiff, without which his injury would not have occurred, is termed *contributory negligence.*

The relative degree of negligence on the part of the plaintiff versus that of the defendant is immaterial.[5] The only important fact is: Would the injury have occurred if the plaintiff had not himself been negligent? No matter how slight the degree, if the plaintiff's negligence was a proximate cause of the injury, he will lose. For example, despite the defendant's negligence in proceeding well in excess of the speed limit on a dark, rainy night, if the fact of the plaintiff being in the road, in dark clothing and for no good reason, was a proximate cause of the accident, no recovery would be possible.

By the same token, however, mere careless or even illegal acts of the plaintiff will *not* constitute a defense, if the acts *cannot* be shown to be a proximate cause of the accident. Thus, the fact that a plaintiff's taillight was out of operation would not constitute a defense when the plaintiff had been hit head on, in his own lane, by a defendant in the wrong lane. Lack of a taillight might have been carelessness and a violation of the criminal law, but it was certainly immaterial. When jurisdictions have a right-of-way law, giving the driver to the right (termed the favored driver) the right of way in uncontrolled intersections, decisions often state that speed moderately in excess of the speed limit by a driver with the right of way is not contributory negligence in an accident with a driver lacking the right of way. The driver with the right of way could reasonably proceed without looking to see if a driver lacking the right of way was approaching. The disfavored driver had the obligation of watching for and yielding to the favored driver. If the disfavored driver failed to perform this obligation, why should it matter that the favored driver was exceeding the speed limit by a small amount?

In other words, the favored driver was careless, he might get a speeding ticket, but his speeding was not a proximate cause of the accident; the failure of the disfavored driver to yield the right of way was. In cases where the favored driver's speed was considerably above the speed limit, there is a tendency on the part of judges to instruct that excessive speed could be a proximate cause and for juries to find that it was. This, of course, only defeats the favored driver's claim against the disfavored driver. He still has no suit against the other driver.

The result of an accident involving negligence, on the part of both parties, each party's negligence being a proximate cause, is a standoff. Each is barred from judgment against the other by the defense of contributory negligence, regardless of the extent of injuries suffered. However, what would be the result in an auto collision in which both drivers were negligent but each driver had passengers? Normally passengers are not guilty of negli-

---

[5] A very few jurisdictions consider "comparative negligence" and hold that contributory negligence does not bar a suit but merely reduces the amount of the verdict.

gence despite the acts of their drivers.[6] In such a case, each passenger in car *A* might recover from driver *B,* and each passenger in car *B* could recover against driver *A.*

CARAGLIO v. FRONTIER POWER COMPANY
(CCA New Mexico, 1951) 192 F 2d 175

> . . . In determining whether an injured person has been guilty of contributory negligence the standard of conduct to which he must conform is that of a reasonably prudent man under the circumstances. The reasonably prudent person will be presumed to possess those qualities of attention and perception which are possessed by mankind in general.

PICKETT, CJ.

Enes Caraglio, administratrix of the Estate of her husband, John Caraglio, deceased, brought this action against the Frontier Power Company, a corporation, in the District Court of Colfax County, New Mexico, to recover $25,000 damages for deceased's death. The defendant removed the cause to the United States District Court for the District of New Mexico, where it was tried. At the conclusion of all the evidence, the District Judge directed a verdict for the defendant upon the grounds that the defendant had not violated any duty owed the deceased and that the deceased was guilty of contributory negligence. This is an appeal from the judgment entered in favor of the defendant.

The essential facts are not in dispute. The deceased, with his family, operated a rural store and bar in Colfax County, New Mexico. The premises were leased and had been in possession and control of the deceased for more than three years. The Caraglios also raised turkeys and chickens and for this purpose used a shed at the rear of the premises. In 1931, the defendant, having a right of way and easement; installed poles to carry an electric transmission line which crossed the property near the shed. Extending away from the shed was a high board fence and a heavy gate. The posts at each end of this gate were high and there had been placed on top of these two posts a plank which extended across the opening made by the gate. Near one of these gate posts the defendant had placed two poles which were approximately 25 feet in height and were used to carry the wires of the electric transmission line. Twelve feet above the ground between the two poles was constructed a narrow platform upon which a transformer had been placed to reduce the high voltage of the transmission line sufficiently for service to the premises occupied by the deceased.

Late in the afternoon of December 18, 1949, a number of turkeys belonging to the deceased had flown onto the electric poles and the transmission lines. The deceased and his two daughters were attempting to get the turkeys off the poles

---

[6] However, a passenger could be negligent by failing to warn the driver of a condition the passenger was aware of and the driver was not.

and lines and into the shed. One persisted in remaining on one of the poles. The deceased directed his sixteen-year-old daughter to climb upon the fence, then onto the transformer platform to remove this turkey. When the daughter refused the deceased told her to get down off the fence and that he would ascend to the platform, which he did. As there were no pikes or ladders on either of the poles, deceased accomplished this by climbing upon the fence, then to the cross-plank over the gate, and stepping across onto the platform, he received an electric shock which caused his death. There was no fence around these poles, nor were there any signs warning that it was dangerous to ascend to the transformer platform.

The deceased was 54 years old and he had had a fourth grade education. Prior to moving onto the premises in question, he had worked a short time for a power company and for a number of years in a mine where high voltage electricity was used extensively.

On numerous occasions the fuse on the poles above the transformer in question had been burned out by lightning. Employees of the defendant suggested that they leave fuses with Caraglio so that he could replace them when necessary. This he refused to do, stating that he would not accept this responsibility. None of the family of the deceased had been on the platform before. The only indication that anyone else had ever been on the platform except employees of the defendant was testimony by the deceased's uncle, who owned the premises and built the buildings thereon, that he climbed up there once to chase some of his turkeys off the wire; and by the deceased's daughter that on one occasion she saw some children there. There is no suggestion that the deceased was upon the platform with the permission or invitation of the defendant or that it or any of its agents knew of his presence there. Without the knowledge, consent or inducement of the owners, he voluntarily went upon property belonging to others upon a mission of his own and for his own purposes and interests. . . .

A power company engaged in distributing electric current over its wires to consumers is not an insurer of the safety of the consumer or anyone else, although the company must exercise a high degree of care to protect those likely to come in contact with its wires. The care required is that commensurate with the dangerous character of the business and consistent with its practical operation, and it extends not only to the erection, maintenance, and operation of the company's plant and apparatus, but also to an inspection thereof and to the discovery of defects. Under the conditions here, the defendant was bound only to anticipate the normal use of the territory surrounding its transformer and to place it at a distance above the ground where the current would not interfere with the normal and proper use of such surroundings. The plaintiff contends that the defendant was negligent in not providing adequate protection and insulation on the transformer platform. It owed no such duty to the deceased. The transformer was situated where his presence could not have been reasonably foreseen.

The failure to fence the posts or to put warning signs thereon was not negligence. The transformer had been in the same location since the line was constructed. It was higher above the ground than required by the National

Electric Safety Code. It was on the property of the defendant and in a place where the deceased had no right to be. The injuries were not caused by the transformer being too low but by the deceased voluntarily climbing up to the transformer and placing himself in a perilous situation. The defendant could not have foreseen that the deceased would climb up onto the platform.

Even an infant trespasser generally cannot recover from an electric company for injuries suffered on an electric transmission tower or pole unless something in the immediate surroundings has some characteristic which would attract the infant so that his presence on the premises and exposure to the danger could be reasonably anticipated.

If we should assume that the defendant was guilty of primary negligence then we are convinced that the deceased was guilty of contributory negligence which would bar a recovery by his administratrix. We said in *Saindon* v. *Lucero* . . . . : "Generally it has been said that contributory negligence is the neglect of the duty imposed upon a person to exercise ordinary care for his own protection and safety which is legally contributing cause of an injury. . . . In determining whether an injured person has been guilty of contributory negligence the standard of conduct to which he must conform is that of a reasonably prudent man under the circumstance. Restatement, Torts, p. 464. The reasonably prudent person will be presumed to possess those qualities of attention and perception which are possessed by mankind in general. . . . If a person, by his own actions, subjects himself unnecessarily to danger which should have been anticipated and is injured thereby, he is guilty of contributory negligence and may not recover for his injuries. . . ."

The deceased here was a mature man who had had considerable experience in a mine and there had worked around electrical equipment. He had lived on the property near the electrical lines for three years prior to his death. On the day he sustained the injuries which caused his death, he climbed 12 feet up to a transformer connected with 13,800 volts of electricity. He did this after his daughter had refused. Neither he nor any of his family had previously been on the platform. The deceased had on a prior occasion refused to accept the responsibility of changing a fuse located on the poles. We think a proper inference from all the evidence is that the deceased knew of the dangerous condition and did not exercise the degree of care of a reasonably prudent man, and unnecessarily subjected himself to danger which he should have anticipated. . . .

The trial court properly directed a verdict in favor of the defendant.

Judgment is affirmed.

✧

This case is no doubt before the federal court on the basis of diversity of citizenship. In all probability, an investigation would reveal that the power company was incorporated in some state other than New Mexico. Therefore, despite the fact that the particular facility was in New Mexico, the defendant is considered a resident of another state.

Probably the reason the plaintiff lost is sufficiently obvious. The fault leading to the injury was clearly that of the plaintiff. Furthermore, there is no evidence that the defendant was negligent.

We find some discussion relating to a point not previously considered: the trespasser. Although in general we are bound to avoid conduct that might lead to injury to others, we are not bound to anticipate trespassers. This leads into the subject of duty. Usually we do owe a duty to avoid injuring others. In certain classes of cases, this being one, we are not bound to anticipate injury to others or to guard against such injury. If there is no duty, there can be no recovery by the injured party.

QUESTIONS

1. Granted that the power company's liability can be gauged in terms of a lack of duty to a trespasser, could not the test of the reasonable, prudent man be used just as well? Could not the power company as a reasonable, prudent man assume that parties would not climb upon its electrical equipment?

2. Could this case have been decided under the rules of assumption of risk (see page 167) rather than contributory negligence? If so, does it matter which are used?

UNITED STATES v. DOUGLAS AIRCRAFT COMPANY
(CCA California, 1948) 169 F 2d 755

> It is well settled that, where there is uncertainty as to the exist-
> ence of either negligence or contributory negligence, the question
> is not one of law, but of fact, and to be settled by a jury; and
> this whether the uncertainty arises from a conflict in the testi-
> mony, or because, the facts being undisputed, fair-minded men
> will honestly draw different conclusions from them.

STEPHENS, CJ.

The United States brought an action to recover the sum of $10,589.61 as damages to a government-owned airplane, resulting from a collision with an airplane owned and operated by Douglas Aircraft Co., Inc., Thomas W. Scott, the pilot, being joined as defendant. The jury brought in a verdict for the defendants, judgment was entered, and the United States appeals.

On November 11, 1943, at the Los Angeles Municipal Airport, Los Angeles, California, on a diagonal runway, a collision occurred between a P–51 airplane having a 37-foot wingspread, owned and operated by the plaintiff-appellant, and a S.B.D. airplane having a 42½-foot wingspread, owned and operated by the defendant-appellees.

The airport consists of two main runways which are 300 feet wide, with macadamized strips running the length of the field, parallel to each other but separated by a clear plot of ground. Diagonally from the four corners of the field 150 feet wide, macadamized runways bisect the main runways.

At the time of the accident, the airport was managed by employees of the City of Los Angeles. The plaintiff-appellant was a tenant of the City, as was the Civil Aeronautics Authority, an agency of the government, whose employees operated the air traffic control tower.

On the day of the accident, A. W. Pitcairn was assigned to make a test flight for plaintiff-appellant in the P–51 airplane. According to custom and usage, the air traffic control tower was informed of the test, and as customary the plane was towed to its starting point where it took off on a test flight. The plane returned to the field and landed with permission of the control tower on the main runway, 25–L, parallel to the runway 25–R. According to practice in tests, the pilot cut the motor and coasted down the runway to the intersection of the diagonal runway, turned left and parked on the right side of the diagonal runway 22, near the edge of the runway. There is conflicting evidence whether it was parked entirely within the runway or partially off the runway. Before landing, Pitcairn, the pilot, requested the tower to send a tractor to meet him and tow the plane to the parking area. He remained parked approximately ten minutes when the Douglas S.B.D. plane, piloted by Scott, collided with his plane.

Scott was employed by Douglas Aircraft Company as a test pilot. Returning to the field from a test flight and while in the air, the signal tower gave him permission to land. He landed on runway 25–R, coasted down to the diagonal runway, and turned left into the diagonal runway 22, diagonal runway and the main runway 25–L. After waiting for a plane to take off from the main runway, he taxied across the main runway with permission of the tower and entered diagonal runway 22. As he was not in a position to see ahead clearly, due to the shape of the plane, he S-ed or zigzagged the plane at 15° angles, so he could see in front of his plane. He testified that he looked down the diagonal runway, but did not remember whether he actually did look all the way down it, but knew that he could see all the way down or to the end of it. According to the record it was a clear day, but there was a haze; the hills in back of the parked plane were brown or sand color and the building and plane were painted a brown camouflaged army color. Also, the runway was painted several colors of paint and the grass alongside was dry and brown in color. He did not see the parked plane and ran into it.

Just after the collision, according to Scott, Pitcairn said: "I am glad you cut the switch." Scott replied: "I am sorry, I didn't see you." Pitcairn replied: "I am sorry. I had no business being here. I have been here for about ten minutes. I called for a truck and they haven't come after me yet." There was conflicting evidence as to whether it was customary for the traffic tower to notify pilots of obstructions on the field. No notice was given Scott as to the parked plane.

After the evidence was in, appellant made a motion for a directed verdict upon the ground that the defendant-appellee pilot was negligent as a matter of law in failing to see the parked plane before the collision, but the court declined to grant it, and submitted this issue to the jury.

Appellant contends that the failure of Scott in looking and not seeing what was in plain sight constituted negligence; plaintiff-appellant's acts did not constitute contributory negligence; before contributory negligence on the part of the appellant can be established, it must be shown that his purported negligence concurred or cooperated with the negligent act of the appellee; there was no evidence of an unavoidable accident present to warrant an instruction thereon; and the court erred in not granting the motion for a directed verdict or a new trial.

Defendant-appellees contend that Scott exercised due care under the circumstances, and that the collision was caused by the negligence of appellant's agents, the pilot of the parked plane, and the employees in the control tower. It is argued that the record shows that Scott did all that could be expected of him.

In *Brinegar* v. *Green et ux.*, the court set forth a test often used: "The determination of the existence of negligence where the evidence is conflicting or the undisputed facts are such that fair-minded men may draw different conclusions from them is a question of fact for the jury and not one of law for the court." Measured by this test, we think the question of negligence was properly left to the jury.

Appellant argues that looking and not seeing something in plain sight constitutes negligence as a matter of law. It is not, however, clear that such a situation existed. We cannot say, as a matter of law, that Scott violated the duties of a reasonable man in the circumstances.

Appellant contends that there was no basis for an instruction on contributory negligence—that no evidence was present to warrant such an instruction. It is also urged that such a question was one for the court, that is, that there was no contributory negligence constituting a proximate cause of the accident as a matter of law. The reasoning urged is that the evidence is such that it is not in conflict on the facts and that from these facts reasonable men can draw but one inference. It is also argued, quoting from the brief, "Before negligence of the plaintiff can rise to the heights of contributory negligence that negligence must concur or cooperate with the negligent act of the defendant, both being the proximate cause of the injury or damage complained of."

It is stated in *Basler* v. *Sacramento Gas & Elec. Co.* . . . that ". . . the contributory negligence which will bar a recovery must be such as to establish that the person by failure to exercise the required amount of care proximately contributed to produce the injury complained of 'so that but for his concurring and co-operative fault the injury would not have happened.' . . ."

Appellant made a motion for an instructed verdict to the effect that it was not guilty of contributory negligence, which was overruled, and appellant claims error. Appellee argues that there was ample evidence to sustain a finding of contributory negligence on the part of appellant. In *Snipes* v. *Southern Rd. Co.*, affirming language by the Supreme Court in *Richmond & Danville Rd. Co.* v. *Powers*, 149 U.S. . . . the court states: "It is well settled that, where there is uncertainty as to the existence of either negligence or contributory negligence, the question is not one of law, but of fact, and to be settled by a jury; and this whether the uncertainty arises from a conflict in the testimony, or because, the facts being undisputed, fair-minded men will honestly draw different conclusions from them."

Pitcairn's conduct plus his statement substantiating possible lack of care could lead reasonable men to draw different conclusions and thus become a question of fact for the jury. The evidence in regard to the parked plane's position, its right to be where it was parked, and the custom and practice of the Air Traffic Tower and its duties, is in conflict. The Air Traffic Tower agency of plaintiff had authority and control over traffic, and would appear to be in the best position to take precautions for the removal of parked planes as hazards to traffic or to warn and advise appellee's pilot of the parked plane's position. Whether or not the action or non-action of the traffic tower in any instance was customary, its operation may constitute negligence. See *Robinet* v. *Hawks.* . . . Since more than one reasonable deduction can be drawn from the evidence, the issue is for the jury.

In Zibbell v. *Southern Pacific Co.* . . . the court rejected an argument that the court should instruct the jury that plaintiff was contributorily negligent as a matter of law: " 'It is only where no fact is left in doubt, and no deduction or inference other than negligence can be drawn by the jury from the evidence, that the court can say as a matter of law, that contributory negligence is established. Even where the facts are undisputed, if reasonable minds might draw different conclusions upon the question of negligence, the question is one of fact for the jury.' " . . .

We are of the opinion that the trial judge properly instructed the jury on the proximate cause doctrine and did not ignore the above rule. Want of ordinary care on the part of appellant could have concurred as a proximate cause and not a remote cause in producing the injury, and defendant would not be liable, although in fault, and so long as this possibility existed, the trial judge did not err.

The court instructed the jury upon the subject of unavoidable or inevitable accidents. The appellant claims error because, he asserts, there is no evidence in the case from which it can be determined that the accident was unavoidable or inevitable.

The circumstances, other than the collision itself, are practically without dispute. It was a clear day with haze. The pilot of the parked plane had landed at a proper place and took the precaution to pull over to the side of the landing strip, if not entirely off it. His plane was camouflaged and could well have blended almost imperceptibly with the brown background. It was ten minutes from the time the pilot requested a tractor in sending a machine to pull him to the hanger before the collision, but there was considerable activity upon the field by other planes. Scott, the Douglas test pilot, landed at a proper place, looked up the landing strip, and noticing no obstruction taxied forward but with the customary caution of S-ing or zigzagging his plane. These facts may well have convinced the jury that the accident happened notwithstanding all concerned used due and proper care throughout.

It is apparent from what we have already said that we do not agree with plaintiff-appellant's contentions that the court erred in denying its motion for a directed verdict or for a new trial or that the evidence is insufficient to sustain or support the verdict.

Affirmed.

✧

More than anything else, this case, in our opinion, illustrates the great complexity inherent in even a simple, well-defined accident. All that happened is that one airplane ran into another. Despite the fact that this happened on a clear day and it was the job of several people to watch the airplanes, the simple fact of whether or not the parked plane was entirely or only partially on the runway is not clear. Whether or not it was customary for a traffic tower to notify pilots of obstructions on the field is in dispute. Whether a pilot zigzagging down a runway in a plane with obstructed vision should see a camouflaged plane on, or partially on, his runway is not so obvious a question as it first appears.

To come to their decision, the jury had to conclude either (1) that the defendant's pilot was not negligent, or (2) that an employee of the plaintiff, either in the control tower or the pilot, was contributorily negligent. We do not know the exact basis for the jury's finding.

On this appeal, the appellant was claiming that the trial judge should have taken the case from the jury and decided for appellant as a matter of law. Trial judges *can* take a case from the jury, or even enter a finding contrary to that of the jury. Although the jury acts as a check upon the government's control of the judicial machinery, the right of the judge to take some cases from the jury is a check upon possible excesses of the jury. But this may be done *only* in instances when reasonable men could come only to one conclusion. Only when all evidence points to a conclusion may the judge substitute his judgment for that of the jury. In this case the defendant had at least as valid an argument as the plaintiff. Certainly there was no basis for the judge to take the case from the hands of the jury; he would have been abusing his discretion had he done so.

QUESTIONS

1. Would it be reasonable to consider the employees of the control tower negligent for not notifying the approaching SBD airplane of the presence of the P–51 airplane, even if it was established that the general practice of control towers was not to do so?

2. Should the fact that it was necessary to zigzag the SBD airplane in order to see after landing be considered negligence in and of itself?

CITY OF CLEVELAND v. KAUFMAN
(Ohio, 1952) 116 NE 2d 446

Whether the pedestrian involved in the accident was negligent or not is no defense to the question of the guilt or innocence of the defendant.
[Query: Why not?]

SKEEL, PJ.

This appeal comes to this court from a judgment of guilty entered against the defendant, who was charged in the Municipal Courts of Cleveland with violating Section 2417–1 of the Traffic Code of the City of Cleveland.

Section 2471–1 of the Traffic Code provides:

Pedestrians Right of Way at Crosswalks:
(a) It shall be the duty of the operator of any vehicle, street car or trackless trolley, to yield the right of way to a pedestrian lawfully crossing the roadway within any crosswalk.

On the 7th of March, 1952 at 6:45 A.M. two school girls were attempting to cross over Fulton Road and West 41st Street at the intersection of said streets with Bush Avenue. The intersection is controlled by a traffic control signal light. At the time the girls were attempting to cross from east to west over the north crosswalk of Bush Avenue, the defendant was driving north on Fulton Road and as he came into the intersection his automobile struck one of the girls on the crosswalk. It is the claim of the state that as the little girls started across Fulton Road they were moving with the traffic signal, that is, it was green for east and west traffic over Bush Avenue and red for north and south traffic over Fulton Road and West 41st Street.

It is the claim of the defendant that just as he came into the intersection, the traffic light which had been green for north and south traffic on Fulton Road turned to yellow or caution, as it went out of his vision and as he passed through the intersection the little girl ran into the side of car.

This is a criminal prosecution. Whether the pedestrian involved in the accident was negligent or not is no defense to the question of the guilt or innocence of the defendant. The question presented, therefore, is, was there credible evidence that the little girl was crossing on a crosswalk with the green or "go" traffic signal in her favor, and if so, did the defendant fail to yield the right of way to her while thus rightfully crossing the street? The defendant's claim is that there is no evidence to support the allegation of the affidavit upon which this prosecution is founded. The traffic guard gave the following testimony:

A: There were two little girls standing on the curb, and the green light come on Bush Avenue for the children, and I went out and blowed the whistle and put my sign up, and the bus coming out Fulton Road to Crile Hospital stopped, but this fellow coming down Fulton Road—he put on his brakes and he couldn't stop, and he swerved over and hit the little girl. She tried to get back on the curb.
Q: Assuming Fulton Road runs north and south, where was the girl standing? On which corner? A: They were standing and the bus stopped. They come down Bush Avenue toward Fulton. That is, on the other side of Fulton. I live on the west side of Fulton.

The testimony of the school guard with respect to his conduct is fully corroborated by the testimony of a transit system bus driver who was driving south on Fulton Road and had stopped at Bush Avenue because the signal light was red. According to the bus driver's testimony, the traffic light turned red for north and southbound traffic when he was about 40 feet from the center of the intersection and he stopped about 15 feet from the crosswalk and was at a standstill when he saw the two girls enter the crosswalk and saw one of them being struck by defendant's automobile, which came to a stop about 15 feet north of and beyond the crosswalk. He further testified that the light indicated red or "stop" for Fulton Road north and south traffic at the time the little girl was struck by defendant's automobile.

From the evidence quoted and cited, the defendant's claim that there is no evidence that the defendant failed to yield the right of way to the little girl while on the Bush Avenue crosswalk with the green light in her favor cannot be supported. A question of fact was presented to the trial court which the court resolved against him. With this conclusion, which is fully supported by credible evidence, we are bound.

A further claim is presented by the defendant that because there is no evidence that the little girl looked in both directions as provided by Sec. 2417–5 of the traffic ordinances, before she stepped into the street, she was not lawfully on the crosswalk. Such a requirement is not provided for when the pedestrian is acting under the direction of a traffic control signal light.

The provision of Sec. 2402–10 of the Traffic Code of the City of Cleveland provides:

> Whenever traffic is controlled by trafficcontrol signals exhibiting the word "go" "caution" or "stop" or exhibiting different colored lights successively one at a time, or, with arrows, the following colors only shall be used and said terms and light shall indicate and apply to operators of vehicles, street cars and trackless trolleys and pedestrians as follows:
> (a) Green alone, or "go."
> (1) Pedestrians facing the signal may proceed across the roadway within any marked or unmarked crosswalk.

If this was a negligence action, circumstances could conceivably arise where failure to look might consitute contributory negligence. But here we have the simple question, was the little girl on the crosswalk with the green light in her favor, and did the defendant fail to yield to her the right of way? There being credible evidence to support the conclusions of the trial court, the judgment must be affirmed.

Judgment affirmed. Exceptions noted.

HURD and THOMPSON, JJ., concur.

✧

The subject matter of this case is clearly related to, but in an important way distinct from, the negligence cases and concepts presented up to this time. It deals not with tort law but with the criminal law.

This case concerns the violation of a traffic code. As is true of most of our present-day criminal law, it is based upon legislation, in this case an ordinance of the City of Cleveland. There is no question of contributory negligence, proximate cause, or even injury. The ordinance requires operators of vehicles to adhere to certain conduct. The only pertinent question is whether the defendant's act fell within the required conduct. If not, he is guilty of a crime.

Upon examining the act of the defendant it becomes clear that his conduct was in violation of the city ordinance, and he was accordingly found guilty.

Although statutes have been described as acts of a state legislature, we have not met with an ordinance before. An ordinance is similar to a legislative act, except that it is passed by the duly constituted authorities of a city government, and is effective only within the particular city. Often, ordinances are passed by the City Council. The city itself is actually a corporation, created by the state. Legally an arm of the state, certain types of legal authority are delegated to the city at the time of its creation. These are spelled out in the city (corporation) charter, but in some instances are matters of common law, or state legislation.

In this particular case, because it is a criminal action no award of damages will go to the injured girl as a result of this decision. However, she may well have brought her own suit in negligence, either before or after this contest.

Assumption of Risk

Closely allied to the defense of contributory negligence is that of assumption of risk. Assumption of risk arises when a party with full knowledge that he is engaged in a risky activity nevertheless elects to pursue the dangerous activity. In so doing he is assumed to have consented to the risk attached to the activity. Thus, one accepting a ride with a driver who is obviously drunk would ordinarily be barred from suit, in the event of injury, by the defense of assumption of risk. Patrons of baseball parks electing to sit under a portion of the bleachers unprotected from foul fly balls have been held to assume such a risk. Assumption of risk will never be found, however, unless the danger supposedly assumed is apparent. This defense is quite similar to the defense of "consent" in the areas of the intentional torts.

KAVAFIN v. SEATTLE BASEBALL CLUB ASSOCIATION
(Washington, 1919) 181 P 679

> It matters not whether one designates his act in this regard contributory negligence or . . . assumption of risk, the result is the same. . . . If there was a chance of danger, the respondent took it.

PER CURIAM

The facts in the case show that the respondent entered the grandstand, owned and operated by appellant, during the progress of a baseball game; that he was familiar with the manner in which baseball games are conducted, having been a frequent spectator thereof; that the grandstand had a screen in front of a portion of it, back of the home plate, and that in this screened portion there were a great number of vacant seats, any of which he was entitled to take under his admission ticket; that he voluntarily took a seat outside of the screened area; and that, having gone there to see a baseball game, it must be true that, before many minutes had elapsed, he became conscious of the fact that between him and the balls no screen existed, if he was not aware of that fact at the very moment of taking his seat. Conscious of the fact that balls are very often hit "foul," and that wild throws sometimes result in the ball falling among the spectators, and conscious of the fact that there was no protection between the balls and himself, he continued to occupy a seat in that unscreened portion until he received his injury.

It matters not whether one designates his act in this regard contributory negligence or views it as in the nature of assumption of risk, the result is the same. The place in which he could have taken a seat would have fully protected him against the ordinary and usual hazards incident to witnessing the game in question, but he chose to sit elsewhere and substitute for that safety the compensating vacility of vision. If there was a chance of danger, the respondent voluntarily took it. Having purchased a ticket which offered him a choice of two positions, he, with full knowledge of the risk of injury, chose the more dangerous position.

The judgment of the lower court is reversed and the cause dismissed.

❖

The question of policy presented here would seem to be, how much care must we require of the owners of ball parks in insuring the safety of their patrons? Obviously, ball parks could be constructed so that no one would be hit by foul balls. On the other hand, it would be very expensive to do so, but probably more important, most customers evidently prefer not to watch a baseball game through a screen, but rather prefer to take their chances, and perhaps to nurture the hope that they might catch a fly ball of their own.

For these reasons, so long as a place is provided where spectators who wish protection may obtain it, the conduct of the ball park in maintaining unprotected bleachers is not unreasonable.

QUESTION

1. How would you decide this case if the plaintiff had attempted to sit in the protected area, but all the seats in that area were filled, thus leading him to sit in the unprotected section? What other facts would you like to know in order to answer this question?

Last Clear Chance

Last clear chance is a doctrine of tort law that in general outline seems reasonably clear as to both purpose and application. In practice it has become fraught with excruciating multiplicities of distinctions, subdivisions, and conflicting decisions. This being the case, we shall confine our discussion to the most superficial aspects of this doctrine.

Consider a situation where a person becomes intoxicated and falls unconscious in the middle of a busy street. Certainly, the possibility exists that such a party, if injured, might be barred from recovery in tort by contributory negligence. Suppose that a driver injuring the drunk had a clear view of the street and could have easily stopped or passed around him. Can we say that the driver is not liable? This would amount to declaring open season upon parties in exposed or helpless positions.[7]

Should there be any difference if a plaintiff is not drunk but merely engrossed in thought and crossing a busy highway oblivious to heavy traffic? The doctrine of last clear chance permits a plaintiff who was negligent to recover against a defendant when that defendant comprehended or should have comprehended that the plaintiff was in a position of peril from which he could not extricate himself, or was unaware of any peril, and the defendant failed to exercise ordinary care in avoiding injury to the plaintiff. The fact should be emphasized that last clear chance can only be applied when the defendant *actually did have a clear chance to avoid the injury*. He cannot be held when he merely failed to respond to an emergency with superhuman reflexes. If he had only a split second in which to avoid an injury he would typically be guilty of no negligence whatever, and his defense would be simply lack of negligence on his part. Even if he had been negligent but was faced with a situation where the plaintiff was also negligent, and the defendant had only a split second in which to avoid injury, the defense of contributory negligence would remain good, and last clear chance alleged by the plaintiff would fail.

Remember: Contributory negligence is asserted by the *defendant* as a defense. Last clear chance is asserted by the *plaintiff*, as a vehicle to secure a judgment despite his own careless acts.

---

[7] Perhaps this is an overstatement, because contributory negligence has been held not to apply if an injury is *deliberate*. As we have seen earlier, however, the line between extreme carelessness resulting in injury and intentional injury is a fine line.

FLOECK ET AL. v. HOOVER (New Mexico, 1948)
195 P 2d 86

> *It must appear (1) that plaintiff has been negligent, (2) that as a result of his negligence he is in a position of peril from which he cannot escape by the exercise of ordinary care, (3) that defendant then had a clear chance, by the exercise of ordinary care, to avoid the injury, and that he failed to do so. . . .*

COMPTON, J.

Plaintiff's intestate, Gerald M. Floeck, was killed as a result of a collision between a bucking horse he was riding, and an automobile driven by defendant, at a point on highway 66 near the Cory-Penn Filling Station, immediately west of Tucumcari, New Mexico. The case was submitted to a jury upon the issues of the negligence of the defendant and the contributory negligence of the deceased. The trial court refused to instruct the jury on the issue of last clear chance. The jury returned a verdict for the defendant and following the overruling of a motion for a new trial, judgment was entered in accordance with the verdict.

Three grounds are urged for a reversal of the judgment. First, the refusal of the court to instruct the jury on the doctrine of last clear chance. . . .

Since we are called on to determine whether the trial court committed error in its refusal to give an instruction on the doctrine of last clear chance, it is well to announce those factual matters as will present such an issue. It must appear (1) that plaintiff has been negligent, (2) that as a result of his negligence he is in a position of peril from which he cannot escape by the exercise of ordinary care, (3) that the defendant knows or should have known of plaintiff's peril, and (4) that defendant then had a clear chance, by the exercise of ordinary care, to avoid the injury, and that he failed to do so. . . .

A review of the facts is necessary. The deceased was riding in borrow pit on the south side of the highway, traveling in an easterly direction. The defendant also was driving in an easterly direction, at a speed of 30 to 35 miles per hour. About the time the defendant passed the filling station, and about 35 feet before he had overtaken the horse and its rider, the horse began to buck. It bucked out of the borrow pit onto the highway. The defendant, becoming aware of the deceased's perilous position, immediately applied his brakes, and at the same time swerved the automobile abruptly to the left, or north side of the highway. The horse continued bucking in the direction of the defendant's on-coming automobile, and bucked into the automobile at about the center of the black top or middle of the highway. The force of the impact dented the right front fender, the right door, and broke the glass out of the right front door. Defendant's car came to a stop about 20 or 30 feet east of the impact on the north side and parallel to the highway, with both left wheels off the black top.

It is further shown in evidence that the widow of the deceased, an eyewitness to the accident, immediately thereafter stated that the defendant pulled to the left and tried very hard to get out of the way of the horse; that the defendant did everything he could to avoid being hit by the horse, and that she was afraid that the defendant was going to turn his car over or wreck it in trying to get out of the way of the horse.

From a consideration of this evidence, it clearly appears that an issue on the last clear chance doctrine is not presented. The law does not require a defendant to exercise a greater care than that required of plaintiff for his own safety. Nevertheless, the evidence shows that the defendant exercised more than ordinary care, yet failed to avoid the injury. Consequently, the fourth element, as a basis of the doctrine is absent.

Affirmed.

✧

QUESTION

1. The landmark case in last clear chance occurred over a hundred years ago in England. The plaintiff, a farmer, had hobbled a donkey, and the donkey had somehow made its way onto a nearby highway. A stagecoach, failing to observe the donkey, which was in plain sight, ran over the donkey. How was the case decided?

HUMPHRIES v. *BOERSMA ET AL.* (CCA Florida, 1951) 190 F 2d 843

> . . . *"proximate cause," and . . . "last clear chance," are not absolutes. . . . The reviewer may frequently conclude that the evidence would also support a contrary finding.*

(5, 6) Experience has established, and daily confirms, that "proximate cause," "sole negligence," "contributory negligence," "concurring negligence," and "last clear chance" are not absolutes. It is the exceptional case when they can be determined and enforced as a matter of law. Determination of the existence or nonexistence of these elements in a given case generally must be made upon consideration of all the facts, with the result usually influenced and controlled by the comparative weight that the trier of facts accords the acts of the parties when compared with what would have been done in the same or similar circumstances by the law's "prudent man." It is only natural, then, that, upon review of such findings, the reviewer may frequently conclude that the evidence would also support a contrary finding.

✧

Res Ipsa Loquitur ("The Thing Speaks for Itself")

A case in negligence should succeed when the defendant is shown to be guilty of conduct unreasonable under the circumstances, which resulted in injury to the plaintiff. However, proof of facts demonstrating what the defendant's acts were, and demonstrating in what way the defendant failed to conform to the standard of the reasonable man, must normally be presented in order to establish a case.

It became obvious, in the early development of the tort of negligence, that situations do occur in which all circumstances point to the defendant's negligence, yet no proof of specific acts of negligence is possible. In such a case, the defendant is often the only party who has the means of explaining, or even discovering, the actual cause of an injury to the plaintiff. Stated differently, cases arise in which there is circumstantial evidence of negligence, but the only party able to ascertain the true facts is the defendant.

The first case in which this problem was recognized occurred in an English case in the year 1863. The fact pattern was uncomplicated: a barrel fell out of a factory window upon the plaintiff. No specific acts of negligence could be established, the owner claimed to have no idea what caused the accident, but the result indicated negligence on the part of someone, and the barrel and the premises were clearly within the control of the defendant, through his employees. Proof of these facts, all consisting of circumstantial evidence of negligence, was held to constitute a case that might be presented to the jury for their consideration. The defendant, in turn, is permitted to introduce any evidence he may muster to negate a finding of negligence.

The peculiar set of rules applicable to cases falling within the pattern described above are designated as a particular doctrine of tort law known as the doctrine of *res ipsa loquitur*. Translated from the Latin, res ipsa loquitur means, "the thing speaks for itself."

The right of the plaintiff to take circumstantial evidence to the jury without proof of the exact nature of the defendant's negligence is the essential feature of *res ipsa loquitur*. However, the jury is not bound to find for the plaintiff despite the presentation of some circumstantial evidence. The evidence is considered to create an inference, but not a presumption that the defendant was negligent. The defendant may introduce evidence to rebut the inference, but even if he does not, the jury is under no obligation to consider inference as binding them to a verdict for the plaintiff. The duty of the jury is to weigh the evidence according to the particular facts and their own experience and judgment and to arrive at a verdict according to the weight of the evidence.

HUDSON v. BENNETT (Ohio, 1952) 115 NE 2d 20

> *One of the principle reasons for the application of the res ipsa loquitur rule that the proof of the cause of the injury is more accessible to the person against whom the rule is applied than it is to the other party.*

HORNBECK, PJ.

This is an appeal on questions of law from a judgment of the Common Pleas Court in favor of the plaintiff, against the defendant and in the sum of $1,265.99.

Plaintiff alleges that on the 10th day of June 1949 plaintiff's wife was driving his Chrysler sedan in a northerly direction on Olentangy River Road at or near premises described in the petition, which were in the possession and control of defendant Capitol Motor Car Company. It is further averred that on said date the defendant company had on its premises, whereon was being conducted an automobile auction, a certain 1949 Chevrolet convertible automobile belonging to and in the control of such defendant; that "at the southerly part of said premises a private driveway or passageway runs from the premises to the said Olentangy River Road, and that at said point the said Olentangy River Road is lower than the said premises, and that the said driveway or passageway has a sharp decline from said premises to the said Olentangy River Road.

It is further averred that while plaintiff's wife was operating his autombile in a northerly direction on Olentangy River Road and as she approached the premises of defendant company, at the point where the driveway from the premises runs to Olentangy River Road, the Chevr)let convertible ran wild, without a driver, down the private driveway a with force and violence crashed into plaintiff's automobile, causing the damage of which complaint is made. . . .

At the conclusion of plaintiff's case in chief, defendant company moved for a directed verdict, which motion was overruled, and elected to offer no testimony in its behalf, whereupon the court charged the jury and submitted the cause upon the theory that the *res ipsa loquitur* rule applied. The jury returned a verdict for the plaintiff, a motion for new trial was overruled, judgment was entered on the verdict, and a motion for judgment *non obstante veredicto* was overruled.

There are five errors assigned, all of which but one are directed to the question whether the facts pleaded and developed at the trial justified the submission of the evidence to the jury to determine the negligence of the defendant by applying the *res ipsa loquitur* rule. The other error assigned is that, if the doctrine was applicable, the charge was not correct.

Specifically, it is the claim of defendants that the plaintiff is not entitled to invoke the rule of *res ipsa loquitur* because it does not appear that the agency, i.e. the automobile which struck plaintiff's car, was, at the time of the collision, in the exclusive control of defendant company. Defendant company cites in support of its position [several cases]. . . .

From the facts in this case it is obvious that the collision would not have occurred had ordinary care been employed in the handling of the Chevrolet automobile. It was placed on an incline, where unless held by its brakes an automobile would have rolled down the incline onto a driveway which might reasonably have conducted it to the public thoroughfare where plaintiff's wife was driving his automobile.

The testimony discloses that it was the practice of the defendant company through its employees to apply the brakes and leave a car in gear when parked, but it is not testified that this was done at the time that the Chevrolet was parked. It appears also that this Chevrolet was somewhat unusual and attracted many observers, but it does not appear that any one got into the car, that the motor was started, or that the car was driven. It is the reasonable inference that the sole cause of the collision was the inadequacy of the brakes or the failure to properly apply the brakes of the Chevrolet. But it is said that, inasmuch as any prospective purchaser had the right to inspect the car and drive it if desired, it may not be concluded that the defendant company was in exclusive control. We doubt if it may be inferred that some person other than the employees of defendant company actually operated the car at any particular time after it was parked for sale. However, it is evident that, if any one inspected the car, operated it, released its brakes, or drove it, such act or acts were contemplated by and with the acquiescence and consent of defendant company which had the sole right to control such use.

In the instant case, it might be inferred that the defendant company in permitting prospective purchasers to inspect and drive a car should anticipate that they might not apply the brakes at all when leaving the car or might not apply them effectively. The fact that it was the practice of the defendant company to not only apply the brakes to the car but leave it in gear is convincing that it realized that it was necessary to use every precaution to hold the car when parked on the incline.

(1) One of the principal reasons for the application of the *res ipsa loquitur* rule is that the proof of the cause of the injury is more accessible to the person against whom the rule is applied than it is to the other party. . . .

In the instant case, plaintiff's wife was moving along on a public thoroughfare when suddenly, without any warning, an automobile with no driver crashed into the side of the car she was driving. She was utterly without fault and entirely unable to determine the specific cause of the collision. The defendant company which last had the possession and control of the driverless auto was in the better position to explain and account for the occurrence. But it is suggested that the defendant company could not know because there were 100 or 150 prospective purchasers, any one of whom, conceivably, might have caused the condition which brought about the accident. However, the defendant company knew of this possibility and had the opportunity (and it is inferrable that such was its obligation) to take all reasonable steps to prevent such an occurrence as caused the collision. Although the company, no doubt, did not know who failed to properly brake the car, it had the means at hand of making sure that such braking or other safety measure would be taken, and it was its obligation to exercise care commensurate with the danger. At the time the Chevrolet left its place at the parking lot, in all probability it was unoccupied because it was without a driver when it struck plaintiff's car. Who then had control of the car when at rest and as it left the parking lot? The most logical conclusion is that the defendant company had such exclusive control.

(2) It is our judgment that the facts developed in this case warranted the application of the *res ipsa loquitur* rule, and that the court committed no error in charging on it and in holding against the defendant company on its motions for a new trial and a directed verdict.

We have examined the charge of the court in the particular in which it is challenged and do not find that the claim of such error is well made.

The judgment is affirmed.

Judgment affirmed.

WISEMAN and MILLER, JJ., concur.

✧

The circumstantial evidence here, of course, was the fact of the auto rolling downhill. Apparently the jury believed the evidence presented to be adequate, though they could have held to the contrary had they wished.

QUESTION

1. Is this case authority for the proposition that if someone should unbrake your car while parked on a hill and damage results you can be held for the damage under the doctrine of *res ipsa loquitur?* If not, why not?

Owners and Occupiers of Land

IN GENERAL

Liability for injuries resulting from negligent maintenance of real property is in most instances imposed upon the person in possession of the property. The reason for this state of the law is that regardless of who owns the property, the person in actual possession is usually the person able to control conditions upon the premises. Of course, frequently the owner is in possession of real property. Aside from the owner, the person in possession will most frequently be a tenant (lessee).

The problems involved in applying the principles of negligence to owners and occupiers of land are somewhat more difficult than in most other types of negligence case. Because of the particular sanctity that has traditionally surrounded real property under the common law, we consider a man's home, whether owned or leased, his castle, and we dislike interfering with the private enjoyment of real property, particularly to accommodate persons who have little or no business there anyway. However, if a landowner or tenant were free to do anything he pleased with his land, without any restrictions of social policy, there would be no legal problems to concern us. The policy of the common law is also to protect human life, so a balance must be struck between these competing considerations. The question remains, to what extent should our humanitarian concerns impinge upon our policy favoring enjoyment of private property?

To provide a standard for balancing these interests, plaintiffs who are suing for injuries suffered upon another's real property are placed into one of three categories. The category into which the plaintiff falls largely determines his opportunity for a successful case, because the duty of the owner or occupier varies in each of the three categories.

The least promising of these categories is the trespasser. He has not obtained permission to enter upon the land, either expressly or impliedly. His act may be innocent, in that he may have lost his way or entered under a mistake of fact. Nevertheless, the duty owed the trespasser is merely to refrain from deliberately injuring him and to refrain from setting traps. There is also a duty to warn him if he is visibly about to walk into or upon something that will probably result in his injury.

On the other hand, the owner or occupier is entitled to use as much force as is reasonably necessary to remove a trespasser from the premises. The trespasser may also be held legally accountable for any property damage inflicted during his trespass.

The second category is that of the licensee, which includes those who have been given permission to enter upon real property or in whose presence the owner or occupier seems to have acquiesced. The possessor is under no duty to maintain reasonably safe premises for a licensee, but does have a duty to warn him in advance of the presence of dangerous conditions and to take reasonable steps to prevent his being injured because of these dangerous conditions. Household guests and persons permitted to use the land for picnicking, hunting, or other forms of recreation are licensees. Uninvited visitors who have entered frequently upon the property in the past have been held to be licensees rather than trespassers on the theory that the failure to eject them constituted an implied permission. Therefore, possessors of land are placed in the position of being forced to eject trespassers in order to avoid the possibility that they might be considered licensees.

The third category of entrants upon real property is the business invitee. An entrant upon real property is a business invitee if he has been expressly or impliedly invited onto the premises for some business purpose. The most common instance of a business invitee is a customer of a retail establishment, but about any situation in which one person enters upon the premises of another for the purpose of transacting business gives that person the status of a business invitee.

The possessor of real property owes an affirmative duty to invitees to maintain the premises in reasonably safe condition. He is not an insurer, even to an invitee, and is therefore not responsible for every injury suffered on his premises. For example, if one customer creates an unsafe condition without the occupant's knowledge, and another customer is injured before the occupier has a reasonable opportunity to discover the danger, there is no basis for liability. Even as to invitees, liability is based upon fault, though the fault may be of omission rather than commission. The question is, did the possessor know, or in the exercise of reasonable care, should he have known of the defect? If the answer to this question is no, he should not be held liable for negligence.

Most cases involving business invitees are probably brought against commercial establishments frequented by the public: department stores, grocery stores, movie theaters, and the like. Nevertheless, the courts have, in some cases, stretched very far to find a business relationship. The occupant of a private residence is liable to the same extent as is a commercial establishment whenever an injured party is actually found to be on the premises as a business invitee.

ATTRACTIVE NUISANCE

Although the general rule is that an occupier of land is not liable for injuries to trespassers, there is an important though narrow exception. This exception has been termed the *attractive nuisance doctrine*. It applies only to children, and even as to children it is circumscribed so as to apply only in carefully defined situations.

The attractive nuisance doctrine results from an attempt to impose liability upon an occupier of land in instances when it is apparent that children may invade the premises, but at the same time an attempt is made to avoid imposing a blanket liability for all situations where children may be injured on someone else's premises.

The main requirement of attractive nuisance is that there must be some object of exceptional interest to children drawing them onto the property. Usually, but not necessarily, this has been some form of machinery. Swimming pools have also been frequently involved in suits based on this doctrine. Prosser [8] summarizes the requirements of attractive nuisance as follows: (1) the place where the condition is maintained must be one upon which the possessor knows or should know that young children will come upon his premises; (2) the condition must be one which the occupier should recognize as involving a reasonable risk of harm to such children; (3) the child because of his immaturity either does not discover the condition or does not in fact appreciate the danger involved; and (4) the utility to the possessor of maintaining the condition must be slight as compared with the risk to children involved.

[8] William L. Prosser, *Law of Torts* (St. Paul, Minn.: West Publishing Co., 1955), pp. 440–445.

CHAPTER TWELVE

Workmen's Compensation

It is the conditions of the modern industrial world which have completely altered the situation. The old law of master and servant did no great injustice so long as all industry and manufacturers were carried on by little bands of apprentices and workmen who might be looked upon as the family of the employer. Up to the eighteenth century the work of the craftsman was as a rule not especially dangerous. But all this has changed.[1]

Historical Background of Workmen's Compensation

THE COMMON LAW, feeling its way along from case to case, is at its best when dealing with areas of law undergoing a slow evolutionary process. The vast number of precedents presently available offer a stable base for meeting old conditions, and act as analogies through which the law can be changed gradually to conform to new conditions. But when sudden, dramatic change is needed, legislation works better. The body of precedents is not too helpful if the conditions the law is supposed to regulate are in a state of flux, because the entire body of precedents may be outmoded. A detailed description of the desired changes, supplied by the legislature, will function better in this type of situation. Thus the common law of negligence could keep up with new conditions created by the automobile and airplane because the precedents from horse-and-buggy days were applicable. Negligence law could not keep up with the social and economic conditions resulting from the rise of factories during the Industrial Revolution. There was no precedent to which the new conditions could be compared.

---

[1] F. P. Walton, "Workmen's Compensation and the Theory of Professional Risk," *Columbia Law Review*, 11 (1911), p. 36.

Legislation was needed. Workmen's compensation acts, which we will now discuss in detail, were one result of the need for new legislation that arose from the Industrial Revolution.

Probably no area in our law provides a better illustration of social and economic conditions changing too fast for the common law than that dealing with the employer's liability for his employee's injuries.

Until recent times, even the word *employee* was practically meaningless. Persons hired by others were "servants": maids, butlers, liverymen, and the like. Goods were produced not by employees but by independent craftsmen assisted by apprentices, in small shops. Crowded, dangerous factories were nonexistent.

Servants were practically an extension of the master's own household. The master assumed certain responsibilities in regard to the care and welfare of his servants. Their period of employment was indefinite and often for life. As a matter of custom, at least, each owed obligations to the other. The same was true as between the apprentice and his master.

As a consequence the law provided little in the way of legal recourse to the servant for injuries arising from his employment. Suit against one's own master being unthinkable, why should any special rules be provided granting a means of recovery for an injured servant?

This whole picture changed drastically with the advent of the machine. No longer was there a personal relationship between the master and the servant. One factory might employ hundreds of workers, perhaps none of whom the owner could recognize on sight. The employer, under these circumstances, felt no responsibility for the welfare of the worker, beyond his obligation to pay his wage. In addition, the work became considerably more dangerous. Untried and untested machines run by laborers unaccustomed to working on or near machinery combined to maim and kill at unprecedented rates, often without being caused by actual negligence on the part of anyone.

The only law available to apply to these emerging problems, however, was the then existing law of negligence. The many defenses available to a master in the unlikely event of a suit brought against him by one of his servants had not presented serious problems in earlier days, but became a source of injustice in the industrial age.

Three defenses disposed of most claims against employers. These were "assumption of risk," "contributory negligence," and the "fellow-servant doctrine." Assumption of risk and contributory negligence have already been considered in the context of the ordinary negligence suit. About the only additional comment that need be made is that assumption of risk was held to apply to instances in which the employee was working in the area of an obvious danger. The more obvious the danger, and therefore in one sense the more blameworthy the employer, the easier it became to establish that the employee assumed the risk. If he did not like the risk, he had the alternative of seeking another job. Of course there was often no other job and if there was, often it was even more dangerous than the first, but legally this made no difference.

The fellow-servant doctrine had the effect of protecting a master against suit by one of his servants for injury sustained because of the negligence of another of the master's servants. This is contrary to the usual rule. (See Chapter 26.) Ordinarily the employer is liable for injuries resulting from negligent acts of his servants (employees) while the latter is within the scope of his employment. A customer or a member of the general public who was the victim of such negligence could obtain a recovery. A fellow employee could not.

Thus a special and probably unfair rule discriminated against servants (employees): they were the only group who could not recover against the employer because of an injury negligently inflicted by another subordinate acting within the scope of his authority.

These defenses were so good that in the long run they could not be tolerated. Not only these defenses, but the entire law of torts was discarded, so far as compensating employees for accidents suffered in the course of their employment. Of course, the existence of these defenses is not the only reason for chucking out the law of torts as applied to accidents arising from employment. A different theory, insurance, rather than reimbursement based upon fault, was deemed appropriate.

Legislation is needed to meet drastic change. However, even legislation requires a corresponding change in public sentiment, because the views of the legislators must be presumed to reflect to a large degree the views of their constituents. It is perhaps surprising how long a time some nations, the United States in particular, took to correct the imbalance between actual conditions and the law. Some authorities argue that the delay was the result of a deliberate policy of assisting the infant industries at the expense of the working force. Those supporting this thesis maintain that capital by which to initiate and nourish industry was scarce at best; that both public sentiment and the judiciary recognized the long-run benefits to society of industrialization, and that inadequately protecting the working man was thought to be less of an evil than impeding the development of industry. The argument may or may not be valid, and is difficult to prove one way or the other. The fact is, most of the industrial nations of continental Europe, England, and elsewhere in the world adopted programs of workmen's compensation during the last decades of the nineteenth century. The United States did not adopt such a program until the early years of the twentieth century.

The following article was written before any of the United States (except New York) had adopted any form of workmen's compensation plan.

Nevertheless, it outlines with remarkable foresight many of the problems that became difficult and pressing in this country following the adoption of workmen's compensation by our states. Many of the problem areas anticipated in this article remain a source of difficulty today.

WORKMEN'S COMPENSATION AND THE THEORY OF PROFESSIONAL RISK [2]

An Early View of Workmen's Compensation

> *The manufacturing countries have become vast noisy workshops full of whirring wheels, of electric wires, and of dangerous explosives. . . . Millions of workmen pass their lives in continual danger. . . . Is it fair that the workman should bear this professional risk? His employer may not be negligent, but, at any rate, the work is being carried on for his profit. Opponents of this principle are in the habit of saying that the workman is paid at a higher rate just because his work is dangerous. There might be some force in this argument if it did not suffer from the misfortune of resting upon no basis of solid fact. . . .*

During the last few years few subjects have occupied the attention of social reformers and of members of the various legislatures in the United States more than that of a modification of the law of the liability of employers to their employees for injuries sustained in the course of the employment.

During the last thirty years one European country after another has become convinced of the inadequacy to modern conditions of the fundamental rule of the old law that an employer was not liable to compensate his employee for injuries received in an industrial accident unless some fault had been brought home to the employer. . . .

If the countries of Europe, divided as they are from each other by immemorial prejudices and jealousies, conspire to legislate in the same sense, and if the principle of this new legislation is adopted in distant lands, such as New Zealand, South Australia, The Transvaal, Newfoundland, and, now, Quebec, not to mention many other countries, this is surely a fact calculated to awake doubts even in the most conservative minds with regard to the justice of the old principles of law applicable to this matter.

Few people who have much experience of the actual working of the present system can regard it as satisfying the notions of natural justice. It is a nightmare to the employer without being by any means a sure protection to the workman. It combines the maximum of cost with the minimum of gain to everyone except the lawyers. Their interest is of course important, but it is hardly the primary interest to consider. The employer whether he wins or loses has heavy costs to

[2] *Ibid.*

pay. When he wins, his recourse against the plaintiff is worthless. As the Scotch proverb says, "You cannot take the breaks from a Highlander," and you cannot get ten thousand dollars of costs from a poor workman. Very often an employer, grasping this truth, compromises a threatened action though he believes he has a good legal defense. In other cases employers who are insured against claims are compelled for the sake of preserving their recourse against the insurance company to dispute demands which they know to be just. The employer has learned by a long and sad experience that juries are "uncertain, coy and hard to please"; that in awarding damages they are swayed by every passing gust of sentiment, and that they are but little embarrassed by want to evidence of fault on the part of the employer.

On the other hand, the workman has, with slender or no resources, to face a long and uncertain litigation, with a vista of appeals and new trials even if he succeeds in getting a verdict. His witnesses, simple and unlettered, are unfitted to bear the brunt of skillful cross-examination, even when the tale they have to tell is plain and unvarnished. He may be bowled over by the defense of common employment.[3] That doctrine was in my opinion admirably described by Mr. Birrell in a speech in the House of Commons in these terms:

> The doctrine of common employment was only invented in 1837, Lord Abinger planted it, Baron Alderson watered it, and the devil gave it increase.
> Workingmen who had never heard of one another, nor had the faintest relation with one another, were held to be in common employment, and if one was injured by the negligence of the other there was no title to compensation. A plate-layer going home after his day's work was refused damages when he jumped on to a train, and was injured by the gross negligence of the engine-driver, on account of supposed common employment.

Even when the workman succeeds in breaking down every defense, and is able to hold the verdict which he has won, he finds that a large part of the damages recovered goes into the pockets of his lawyer.

The English common law rules as to the remedy in accident cases, especially after the doctrine of fellow-servant has been developed, were not really worth transplanting to the American Continent, and now that they have been given up in the country of its origin it is inconceivable that the United States, where democracy is said to be triumphant, should long remain contented with them.

It is the conditions of the modern industrial world which have completely altered the situation. The old law of master and servant did no great injustice so long as all industry and manufacturers were carried on by little bands of apprentices and workmen who might be looked upon as the family of the employer. Up to the eighteenth century the work of the craftsman was as a rule not especially dangerous. But all this has changed.

The manufacturing countries have become vast noisy workshops full of whirring wheels, of electric wires, and of dangerous explosives. Before the days of steam, electricity and dynamite the workman could as a rule protect himself by the exercise of ordinary care. His tools were few and simple. None of them

---

3 That is, the fellow-servant doctrine, discussed earlier.

moved except when he handled them and no one was in a hurry. It is, therefore, not to be wondered at that the law gave him no claim for damages unless some fault, at least of omission, could be clearly brought home to the employer. Under modern conditions, on the other hand, millions of workmen pass their lives in continual danger. They have to deal at close quarters with complicated machines, to handle terrible explosives, to run the risk of coming in contact with live wires, and, in a word, to face a thousand perils. Even the strictest care cannot always save them. A boiler may burst or some other accident occur, the precise cause of which can never be discovered. Thousands of lives are lost every year by this terrible *accident anonyme,* as French writers have well called it. In many kinds of employment the workman knows that he is exposed to mysterious and sudden danger.

He has to take the risk. It is inherent in the nature of the occupation. The master may have the best and newest plant. He may spare no expense and may employ all vigilance in adopting every means for protecting his men. The workmen may always be on the watch. But all this cannot prevent the accident.

Is it fair that the workman should bear this professional risk? His employer may not be negligent but, at any rate, the work is being carried on for his profit.

Opponents of this principle are in the habit of saying that the workman is paid at a higher rate just because his work is dangerous. There might be some force in this argument if it did not suffer from the misfortune of resting upon no basis of solid fact. Every-day experience shows that many of the most dangerous occupations are the least well paid, and that there is in fact no correlation between the rate of wages and the danger of the occupation.

The workman under all these acts has no longer to prove fault on the part of the employer, but otherwise the general rules in regard to onus of proof still apply. The plaintiff has to prove that the incapacity for which he claims compensation was caused by an accident happening to him as a workman in one of the protected occupations and that the accident happened to him by reason of, or in the course of, his work. . . .

The meaning of the term "accident" has been much discussed, and the courts of France and of England have arrived independently at pretty much the same conclusions. In England the courts have avoided definitions, but the House of Lords has held that the word "accident" was to be taken in its ordinary and popular sense, and some of the noble and learned lords explained it as meaning "a mishap or untoward event not expected or designed." In France "accident" has been authoritatively explained as "a bodily lesion coming from the sudden action of an external cause." One of the best French writers on the subject adopts a very similar definition, "an injury to the human body produced by the sudden and violent action of an external cause." . . .

Even a disease may be an accident if due to a sudden infection which can be assigned to some determinate fact connected with the employment, as ,if a workman contracts anthrax in handling wool. There is here the sudden and unexpected element. It is an accident that the bacillus is present and it is an accident that it strikes at a spot where there is some abrasion of the skin which permits its entrance into the system. The French and the English decisions agree upon this point also.

Moreover in estimating the compensation to which the victim of an accident is entitled, it appears that the sole element for consideration is the reduction of his earning power by the accident, and that no account is to be paid to his previous state of health or bodily condition. So if a one-eyed man loses the sight of his one eye by an accident, he is as much entitled to claim compensation for absolute and permanent incapacity, if this is the effect of his total blindness, as if he had been deprived by the same blow of the sight of both eyes. It makes no difference that the previous infirmity was one for which his present employer was in no way responsible. It may have been congenital, or it may have been due to an accident suffered in another employment. With such considerations the court will have no concern; the only question is by how much has the earning power of the workman been reduced in consequence of the accident.

When an accident is caused by any defect in the machinery or equipment there is no doubt that compensation is payable, and the same is true in general in accidents caused by the negligence of a fellow workman of the victim, although this fellow workman may not have been at the time engaged in the course of his work. This at any rate is the accepted view in France, and two very equitable reasons are given for such a construction. In the first place, the enforced contact with a number of fellow employees, some of whom are sure to be careless, makes industrial employment especially dangerous, and in the second place, a workman whose attention is occupied by his work, cannot at the same time keep a watch on things going on around him. So in a number of French cases where a workman has been shot, owing to the imprudence of a fellow workman in handling firearms, it has been held that the Act applied.

✧

The Adoption and Operation of Workmen's Compensation in the United States

NEW YORK CENTRAL RAILROAD v. WHITE
(U.S. Supreme Court, 1916) 243 US 188, 61 L. ed 667, 37 Sup. Ct. Rep. 247

> . . . It cannot be pronounced arbitrary and unreasonable for the state to impose upon the employer the absolute duty of making a . . . compensation in money to every disabled employee. . . .

Mr. JUSTICE PITNEY delivered the opinion of the court:

A proceeding was commenced by defendant in error before the Workman's Compensation Commission of the State of New York, established by the Workmen's Compensation Law of that state, to recover compensation from the New York Central & Hudson River Railroad Company for the death of her husband, Jacob White, who lost his life September 2, 1914, through an accidental injury arising out of and in the course of his employment under that company. The Commission awarded compensation in accordance with the terms of the law; its award was affirmed, without opinion, by the appellate division of the supreme court for the third judicial department, whose order was affirmed by the court of appeals, without opinion.

The errors specified are based upon these contentions: . . . (2) that to award compensation to defendant in error under the provisions of the Workmen's Compensation Law would deprive plaintiff in error of its property without due process of law, and deny to it the equal protection of the laws, in contravention of the 14th Amendment.

[EDITOR'S NOTE: Thus, we find that the decedent's widow has brought her case before the Workmen's Compensation Commission of New York, the Supreme Court, and the Court of Appeals of New York (corresponding to the Supreme Court of most states). The trial now related is before the Supreme Court of the United States. The employer contends that the Act is unconstitutional.]

We turn to the constitutional question. The Workman's Compensation Law of New York established forty-two groups of hazardous employments, defines "employee" as a person engaged in one of these employments upon the premises, or at the plant, or in the course of his employment away from the plant of his employer, but excluding farm laborers and domestic servants; defines "employment" as including employment only in a trade, business, or occupation carried on by the employer for pecuniary gain, "injury" and "personal injury" as meaning only accidental injuries arising out of and in the course of employment, and such disease or infection as naturally and unavoidably may result therefrom; and requires every employer subject to its provisions to pay or provide compensation according to a prescribed schedule for the disability or death of his employee resulting from an accidental personal injury arising out of and in the course of the employment, without regard to fault as a cause (with some minor exceptions). . . .

[EDITOR'S NOTE: The bare essentials of coverage are now outlined. "Employee" has been defined, and certain types of employment excluded. "Employment," "injury" and "personal injury" have also been defined. We will find in our reading elsewhere that the precise meaning of all of these terms, even today, remains an almost chronic problem.]

Provision is made for the establishment of a Workmen's Compensation Commission with administrative and judicial functions, including authority to pass upon claims to compensation on notice to the parties interested. The award or decision of the Commission is made subject to an appeal, on questions of law only, to the appellate division of the supreme court for the third department, with an ultimate appeal to the court of appeals in cases where such an appeal would lie in civil actions. A fund is created, known as "the state insurance fund," for the purpose of insuring employers against liability under the law, and assuring to the persons entitled the compensation thereby provided. The fund is made up primarily of premiums received from employers, at rates fixed by the Commission in view of the hazards of the different classes of employment, and the premiums are to be based upon the total pay roll and number of employees in each class at the lowest rate consistent with the maintenance of a solvent state insurance fund and the creation of a reasonable surplus and reserve. Elaborate provisions are laid down for the administration of this fund.

[EDITOR'S NOTE: We now see some of the particulars of how the Act is to be administered. The legislature (who could not possibly hear each case, or determine the contribution to be made by each employer) has delegated the actual administration of the act to a board entitled the Workmen's Compensation Commission. This board has the final authority for determining the amount of award if any to be made in each death or injury case. Appeal to the courts is provided, *but only as to questions of law*. The decision as to the facts is solely up to the Commission, in about the same sense that it is up to the jury in a common-law case. There are also provisions governing the contribution by the employers to the fund from which the employees are paid. The New York Act gives the employer several alternatives as set out above. Some states require the employer to pay into a state administered fund and provide no other choice. Note below the history of this workman's compensation legislation in New York; especially the Ives case, the subsequent constitutional amendment, and the enactment of the statute now in question.]

In a previous year, the legislature enacted a compulsory compensation law applicable to a limited number of specially hazardous employments, and requiring the employer to pay compensation without regard to fault, Laws 1910, chap. 674. This was held by the court of appeals in *Ives* v. *South Buffalo R. Co.* . . . to be invalid because of conflict with due process of law provisions of the state Constitution and of the 14th Amendment. Thereafter, and in the year 1913, a constitutional amendment was adopted, effective January 1, 1914, declaring:

"Nothing contained in this Constitution shall be construed to limit the power of the legislature to enact laws for the protection of the lives, health, or safety of employees; or for the payment, either by employers, or by employers and employees or otherwise, either directly or through a state or other system of insurance or otherwise, of compensation for injuries to employees or for death of employees resulting from such injuries without regard to fault as a cause thereof . . . provided that all money paid by an employer to his employees or their legal representatives, by reason of the enactment of any of the laws herein authorized, shall be held to be a proper charge in the cost of operating the business of the employer."

In December, 1913, the legislature enacted the law now under consideration (Laws 1913, chap. 816), and in 1914 re-enacted it (Laws 1914, chap. 41) to take effect as to payment of compensation on July 1 in that year. The act was sustained by the court of appeals as not inconsistent with the 14th amendment in *Jensen* v. *Southern P. Co.* . . . and that decision was followed in the case at bar . . .

[EDITOR'S NOTE: In this section the court sets out some of the history of the concept of Workman's Compensation in the State of New York. Note that the original act was declared in conflict with the Constitution of the State of New York, but that the constitution was then amended, removing that barrier. The allegation is made in the instant case that the present act is in violation of the United States Constitution. We will see how this argument is disposed of.]

These are the charges being made as to alleged violations of the Federal Constitution:

. "The scheme of the act is so wide a departure from common-law standards respecting the responsibility of employer to employee that doubts naturally have been raised respecting its constitutional validity. The adverse considerations urged or suggested in this case and in kindred cases submitted at the same time are: (a) That the employer's property is taken without due process of law, because he is subjected to a liability for compensation without regard to any neglect or default on his part or on the part of any other person for whom he is responsible, and in spite of the fact that the injury may be solely attributable to the fault of the employee; (b) that the employee's rights are interfered with, in that he is prevented from having compensation for injuries arising from the employer's fault commensurate with the damages actually sustained, and is limited to the measure of compensation prescribed by the act; and (c) that both employer and employee are deprived of their liberty to acquire property by being prevented from making such agreement as they choose respecting the terms of the employment.

[EDITOR'S NOTE: The first two objections are simply to the fact that the legislation departed from the common law. Whether liable for negligence or not, the employer must meet the payment designated by the Commission. Negligence is no longer the test, nor is contributory negligence a defense against the employee. Liability results from the fact of being an employer. At the same time, the worker loses his right to sue in negligence. This is a loss of some substance, because awards under common-law tort suits generally run much higher than a workmen's compensation award for the same injury. The reason is that compensation for pain and suffering tends to make up a large part of common-law tort awards. No compensation for pain and suffering is included in Workmen's Compensation awards. In effect, the workman is given a bird in hand in preference to two in the bush. He is almost certain to be compensated for his injury, but his award is almost certainly smaller than it would be if he could establish negligence and overcome the common-law defenses.]

In support of the legislation, it is said that the whole common-law doctrine of employer's liability for negligence, with its defenses of contributory negligence, fellow-servant's negligence, and assumption of risk, is based upon fictions, and is inapplicable to modern conditions of employment; that in the highly organized and hazardous industries of the present day the causes of accidents are often so obscure and complex that in a material proportion of cases it is impossible by any method correctly to ascertain the facts necessary to form an accurate judgment, and in a still larger proportion the expense and delay required for such ascertainment amount in effect to a defeat of justice; that, under the present system, the injured workman is left to bear the greater part of industrial accident loss, which, because of his limited income, he is unable to sustain, so that he and those dependent upon him are overcome by poverty and frequently become a burden upon public or private charity; and that litigation is unduly costly and tedious, encouraging corrupt practices and arousing antagonisms between employers and employees.

The close relation of the rules governing responsibility as between employer and employee to the fundamental rights of liberty and property is, of course, recognized. But those rules, as guides of conduct, are not beyond alteration by legislation in the public interest. No person has a vested interest in any rule of law, entitling him to insist that it shall remain unchanged for his benefit. . . . The common law bases the employer's liability for injuries to the employee upon the ground of negligence; but negligence is merely the disregard of some duty imposed by law; and the nature and extent of the duty may be modified by legislation, with corresponding change in the test of negligence.

The immunity of the employer from responsibility to an employee for the negligence of a fellow employee is of comparatively recent origin, it being the product of the judicial conception that the probability of a fellow workman's negligence is one of the natural and ordinary risks of the occupation, assumed by the employee and presumably taken into account in the fixing of his wages. . . . The doctrine has prevailed generally throughout the United States, but with material differences in different jurisdictions. . . . It needs no argument to show that such a rule is subject to modification or abrogation by a state upon proper occasion.

The same may be said with respect to the general doctrine of assumption of risk . . .

So, also, with respect to contributory negligence . . . it is plain that the rules of law upon the subject, in their bearing upon the employer's responsibility, are subject to legislative change; for contributory negligence again involves a default in some duty resting on the employee, and his duties are subject to modification.

[EDITOR's NOTE: Judging from the following discussion, how would you describe the constitutional limitations, if any, upon the process of substituting legislation for common-law rules? Would constitutional restraints operate mainly against the degree of change or the specific nature of the change?]

The statute under consideration sets aside one body of rules only to establish another system in its place. If the employee is no longer able to recover as much as before in case of being injured through the employer's negligence, he is entitled to moderate compensation in all cases of injury, and has a certain and speedy remedy without the difficulty and expense of establishing negligence or proving the amount of the damages. Instead of assuming the entire consequences of all ordinary risks of the occupation, he assumes the consequences, in excess of the scheduled compensation, of risks ordinary and extraordinary. On the other hand, if the employer is left without defenses respecting the question of fault, he at the same time is assured that the recovery is limited, and that it goes directly to the relief of the designated beneficiary. And just as the employee's assumption of ordinary risks at common law presumably was taken into account in fixing the rate of wages, so the fixed responsibility of the employer, and the modified assumption of risk by the employee under the new system, presumably will be reflected in the wage scale. The act evidently is intended as a just settlement of a difficult problem, affecting one of the most important of social relations, and it is to be judged in its entirety. We have said enough to demonstrate that in such an adjustment the particular rules of the common law affecting the subject-matter are not placed by the 14th Amendment beyond the reach of the lawmaking power of the state; and thus we are brought to the question whether the method of compensation that is established as a substitute transcends the limits of permissible state action.

We will consider, first, the scheme of compensation, deferring for the present the question of the manner in which the employer is required to secure payment.

Briefly, the statute imposes liability upon the employer to make compensation for disability or death of the employee resulting from accidental personal injury arising out of and in the course of the employment, without regard to fault. . . .

. . . Reduced to its elements, the situation to be dealt with is this: Employer and employee, by mutual consent, engage in a common operation intended to be advantageous to both; the employee is to contribute his personal services, and for these is to receive wages, and, ordinarily, nothing more; the employer is to furnish plant, facilities, organization, capital, credit, is to control and manage the operation, paying the wages and other expenses disposing of the product at such prices as he can obtain, taking all the profits, if any there be, and, of necessity, bearing the entire losses. In the nature of things, there is more or less of a probability that the employee may lose his life through some accidental injury arising out of the employment, leaving his widow or children deprived of their natural support; or that he may sustain an injury not mortal, but resulting in his total or partial disablement, temporary or permanent, with corresponding impairment of earning capacity. The physical suffering must be borne by the employee alone; the laws of nature prevent this from being evaded or shifted to another, and the statute makes no attempt to afford an equivalent in compensation. But, besides, there is the loss of earning power—a loss of that which stands to the employee as his capital in trade. This is a loss arising out of the business, and, however it may be charged up, is an expense of the operation, as truly as the cost of repairing broken machinery or any other expense that ordinarily is paid by the employer. Who is to bear the charge? It is plain that, on grounds of natural justice, it is not unreasonable for the state, while relieving the employer from responsibility for damages measured by common law standards and payable in cases where he or those for whose conduct he is answerable are found to be at fault, to require him to contribute a reasonable amount, and according to a reasonable and definite scale, by way of compensation for the loss of earning power incurred in the common enterprise, irrespective of the question of negligence, instead of leaving the entire loss to rest where it may chance to fall—that is, upon the injured employee or his dependents. Nor can it be deemed arbitrary and unreasonable, from the standpoint of the employee's interest, to supplant a system under which he assumed the entire risk of injury in ordinary cases, and in others had a right to recover an amount more or less speculative upon proving facts of negligence

that often were difficult to prove, and substitute a system under which, in all
ordinary cases of accidental injury, he is sure of a definite and easily ascertained
compensation, not being obliged to assume the entire loss in any case, but in all
cases assuming any loss beyond the prescribed scale.

In excluding the question of fault as a cause of the injury, the act in effect
disregards the proximate cause and looks to one more remote—the primary
cause, as it may be deemed—and that is, the employment itself. . . . Viewing
the entire matter, it cannot be pronounced arbitrary and unreasonable for the
state to impose upon the employer the absolute duty of making a moderate and
definite compensation in money to every disabled employee, or, in case of his
death, to those who were entitled to look to him for support, in lieu of the
common law liability confined to cases of negligence.

This, of course, is not to say that any scale of compensation, however
insignificant, on the one hand, or onerous, on the other, would be supportable.
In this case, no criticism is made on the ground that the compensation prescribed by the statute in question is unreasonable in amount, either in general or
in the particular case. Any question of that kind may be met when it arises.

We conclude that the prescribed scheme of compulsory compensation is not
repugnant to the provisions of the 14th Amendment.

Judgment affirmed.

✧

Continuing Problems in Workmen's Compensation

Usually, in order to qualify for an award of workmen's compensation,
two basic facts need to be established: (1) that an accident occurred, and
(2) that the accident arose out of and in the course of employment.

Therefore, a good share of the cases appealed by or from the decision of
a workmen's compensation commission involve a dispute as to one or the
other of these points. The following two cases are concerned with these
issues.

NICHOLS v. CENTRAL CRATE & BOX COMPANY
(Michigan, 1954) 65 NW 2d 706

*The aggravation of a previously existing nonoccupational disease
is not compensable under part 2 of the workmen's compensation
law unless the aggravating injury is accidental in character.*

DETHMERS, J.

Plaintiff, 73 years of age, worked for defendant as head sawyer for eight
days. His job consisted largely of pushing a level back and forth to operate a

carriage on a saw and of drawing logs by tractor from a yard to skids leading to the saw. Generally, some other employee placed the logs on the skids so that they could roll down to the saw. On the last day of his employment, when no other employee was immediately available for that purpose, plaintiff undertook to slide or roll a log onto the skids. For that purpose he took a cant hook and attempted to raise the log from the ground with a steady pull, but it did not come, so then he gave it a jerk and there was more of a load than he had anticipated and it "came up solid." At that instant he felt as if a bee bee shot had hit him in the back of the head. He continued working the rest of the day. The next morning when he awoke it was discovered that he was partially paralyzed due to a stroke. According to medical testimony he had had a pre-existing bradycardia and arteriosclerosis and the strain involved in or resulting from plaintiff's attempt to move the log with the cant hook could have aggravated that pre-existing physical condition to cause a stroke. The workmen's compensation commission found that plaintiff had sustained an accidental injury in that connection and awarded compensation accordingly. Defendants appeal, contending that plaintiff did not suffer an accident.

(1, 2) Plaintiff says that a disability under part 2 of the act is compensable when due to an injury arising out of and in the course of employment, even though not caused by accidental means and, further, that if an accident be deemed prerequisite as an aggravation of a pre-existing physical condition, that requirement is met if the result suffered by plaintiff is unexpected, unusual or fortuitous even though the cause thereof was not. Such theories run counter to our holdings in [cases]. . . . In all of these cases it was held that to be compensable there must be an accident or fortuitous event which aggravates the pre-existing physical condition to cause a disability. Typical is the statement . . . that "the aggravation of a previously existing nonoccupational disease is not compensable under part 2 of the workmen's compensation law unless the aggravating injury is accidental in character." . . . This Court there said:

> It is not sufficient that there be an unusual and unanticipated result; the means must be accidental—involuntary and unintended. There must, too, be some proximate connection between accidental means and the injurious result.

(3–6) Was plaintiff's pre-existing condition aggravated by an accident or fortuitous event arising out of and in the course of his employment by defendant? Plaintiff says yes, contending that there were two fortuitous events of that character, namely (1) that plaintiff was doing what was ordinarily done by some other employee when he attempted to move the log onto the skids; (2) that the log did not respond to plaintiff's cant hook operation as he had expected. In this connection plaintiff cites 18 Michigan cases. . . .

In Grove, St. Clair and Smallegan the plaintiff was doing the work ordinarily done by two or more men. In La Veck plaintiff had been subjected to unusual and excessive heat. In Robbins the Court found that while plaintiff and another were pulling and lifting a 600-pound engine the plaintiff "was suddenly, and accidentally, put at a disadvantage by the act of his fellow workman and the sticking of the engine on the concrete floor." In Shroetke plaintiff died of heart failure resulting from nervous shock caused by the excitement and disturbing events attending the unexpected and accidental breaking out of fire on the employer's premises. In Schlange the plaintiff was jerked or thrown against a machine and, in addition, was required to do a job in an unusual manner causing an unusual strain not ordinarily or common to the doing of that job. In Watson this Court said "plaintiff's leg gave way and he fell." Such were the facts, respectively, which this Court deemed, in those cases, to constitute fortuitous events. In the case at bar the plaintiff was not shown to have done alone what was customarily done by some other man on that same job, even though under the division of labors plaintiff had not ordinarily done that particular part of the work. It was not shown that an unusual or excessive strain was imposed on plaintiff's physique or that he exerted himself in a manner unusual to or greater than is ordinarily the case in the general field of common labor, that being the test of the existence of an accident or fortuitous event in these cases as we expressed it in [case]. This case is in that respect likewise distinguishable from La Veck. Plaintiff was not jerked or required, as in Schlange, to exert himself in a manner unusual or to a greater degree than was ordinary and common to the work in which he was engaged when the aggravation is alleged to have occurred, namely, that of moving a log onto skids. He was not suddenly and accidentally put to a disadvantage and compelled by a fortuitous event to lift more than expected or than was otherwise done by one man as in Robbins and in Smallegan. There was not here the accidental circumstance of excitement attending the breaking out of a fire, as in Schroetke, or the sudden giving way of a member and consequent falling, as in Watson. Here plaintiff was doing what was customarily done by one man on such job. Nothing slipped, nothing unusual occurred. He testified that in his years of experience with timber he often had attempted to move a log with a cant hook and found that it would not yield to his exertion. There is no showing that plaintiff's condition was aggravated to any greater degree in his use of the cant hook by reason of the failure of the log to respond thereto than would have been the case had the log actually moved as desired in response to his employing of an equal amount of exertion. At all events, the mere fact that he had expected the log to move and that it failed to do so was not such an unusual, unexpected or fortuitous event as to constitute an accident. Experience, such as plaintiff had had in the moving of logs, and an examination of its size and shape must have made it apparent that the log would not yield to such pressure as plaintiff would be able to exert against it with a cant hook. In attempting to move it he was performing the kind of hard work customarily performed by men on such jobs, which, as in McGregor, "required a degree of physical exertion not shown to have been unusual to or greater than that ordinarily experienced in the general field of common labor. Exertion to that extent did not constitute a fortuitous event." Plaintiff is not entitled to compensation.

Reversed with costs to defendants.

BUTZEL, C.J. and CARR, BUSHNELL, SHARPE, BOYLES, REID, DETHMERS and KELLY, JJ. concur.

✧

This case cannot be considered authoritative on the question of what is and what is not an accident under workmen's compensation statutes. The answer varies from one jurisdiction to another. Possibly this might have been considered an accident, for workmen's compensation purposes, in some states. More than anything, the case illustrates the fact that the term *accident* is impossible to define with perfect clarity. No matter where the line is drawn, or how "accident" is defined, there are bound to be border-line cases.

QUESTIONS

1. What merit is there in restricting coverage to accidental injuries received on the job, rather than extending coverage to any injury received on the job?

2. The plaintiff in this case had suffered from preexisting conditions which when aggravated resulted in serious impairment. If the aggravation had resulted from the negligence of another party, say a slight jar in an auto accident would the negligent party be held for the consequent impairment, regardless of the preexisting conditions? Review *Poplar* v. *Bourjois* (page 153).

3. Are the two situations, (1) the Nichols case, and (2) the situation postulated in question number 2, really comparable? Explain.

ANDERSON v. KROGER GROCERY & BAKING COMPANY (Michigan, 1949) 40 NW 2d 209

> *An injury arises out of and in the course of the employment when it occurs while engaged in the duties of the employment and it has a rational causal connection to the work.*

BUTZEL, J.

Defendants appeal from an order of the department of labor and industry awarding to plaintiffs dependency compensation and also medical and funeral expenses. The controlling question is whether the decedent's presence on the street at the time of the fatal accident arose out of and in the course of his employment, as found by the commission.

Robert V. Anderson was the manager of the Kroger Grocery & Baking Company store in the village of Grant, Michigan, for eleven years up to and until the time when he met with fatal injuries upon being struck by an automobile while he was returning from Johnie's restaurant to the Kroger store. Plaintiffs, widow and minor children of decedent, claim that the injury arose out of and in the course of his employment. Defendants claim that decedent was injured while on a personal mission not within the ambit of his employment.

The duties of decedent varied and the manner in which he performed them was left largely to his discretion. He was often on the street on business errands, including trips to the bank and to the postoffice. Among his other outside activities for the store were visits to the creamery to purchase and pick up butter, the occasional delivery of groceries to a few nearby farms and to the restaurant, and the purchase of vegetables and fruits. He was not engaged in these particular activities at the time of the accident.

In the village of Grant, Front street and M–37 run north and south parallel to each other and a block apart, with M–37 on the east. The Kroger store is located on the northwest corner of Front street and Lincoln street. Johnie's restaurant is on the east side of M–37, about a block and a half from Kroger's. Across from Johnie's restaurant is a short-cut through vacant property and a well-worn, traveled path that runs to the store.

Testimony shows that the main business in and about Grant is the raising and selling of fresh vegetables, particularly onions; and further, that about 75 per cent of the area's transactions in onions, as well as some of those in other vegetables, were made in Johnie's restaurant over a cup of coffee.

Decedent opened the Kroger store, in which there was no telephone, at about 8 o'clock each morning and customarily each morning went to Johnie's restaurant at about 9 o'clock or shortly thereafter to have toast and coffee, his first food of the day. He did not take breakfast at home. He would transact any business that could be done while there, including the occasional purchase of vegetables and the solicitation of grocery orders. John Morrison, proprietor of Johnie's restaurant, would give him grocery orders on the average of twice weekly. The evidence does not indicate that the company had any objection to his trips to the restaurant. The testimony shows that the company's district manager would go there with him when he was in Grant.

On the morning in question decedent remained in the restaurant for about 7 or 8 minutes, partook of his usual fare, and received a grocery order from the owner. He was in a hurry to return to the store and was offered a ride back by a friend who had a car parked across M–37. He was run down while crossing the highway. The facts are not clear as to whether he intended to accept the ride or walk across the short-cut.

(1, 2) An injury arises out of and in the course of the employment when it occurs while engaged in the duties of the employment and it has a rational causal connection to the work. . . . The proper test to be applied in this and similar cases is concisely stated by Chief Justice Cardozo . . . as follows: "We do not say that service to the employer must be the sole cause of the journey, but at least it must be a concurrent cause To establish liability, the inference must be permissible that the trip would have been made though the private errand had been canceled. . . . The test in brief is this: If the work of the employee creates the necessity for the travel, he is in the course of his employment, though he is serving at the same time some purpose of his own. . . . If, however, the work had had no part in creating the necessity for travel, if the journey would have gone forward though the business errand had been dropped, and would have been canceled upon failure of the private purpose, though the business errand was undone, the travel is then personal, and personal the risk."

(3) The commission found that decedent had a two-fold purpose in going to the restaurant, one to have breakfast and the other to do business for his employer, in accordance with the well-established custom acquiesced in by the employer; that the causes were concurrent and so closely related that it would be impossible to conclude that either one was the primary reason for his absence from the store. As the business aspect was found not to be merely incidental, it follows that the injury arose out of and in the course of the employment, and is compensable. The requisite causal connection was present.

(4) This is a borderline case. Were we the trier of facts, it is possible that we might have inferred that the causes of the trip were not both of major importance and found that it would not have been made in the absence of the personal desire for the morning repast. However, there is some competent evidence to support the finding . . . provides in part that: "The findings of fact made by the compensation commission acting within its powers, shall, in the absence of fraud, be conclusive. . . ."

(5) It has been repeatedly held that this court may not disturb the findings of the department of labor and industry when there is competent evidence to support them . . .

Defendants contend that the finding that the two causes of travel were so closely related that it would be impossible to conclude that either one was the primary cause for the trip automatically defeats plaintiff's case, citing [a case] as authority. In the former the claimant failed to sustain the burden of proof when it was impossible for the commission to determine whether the fatal peritonitis resulted from the repair of a hernia or an appendix removal. In the latter the inference that the injury resulted from an existing condition was as strong as the one that it resulted from a fortuitous event. Both these cases dealt with the proximate physical cause, not with whether the employee's activity at the time of injury was within the ambit of his employment.

Defendants cite in support of their claim that the injury was outside the ambit of employment. The facts of those cases distinguish them from the instant one. In the Murphy case the injury occurred after the working day, while claimant was on the way home. She was not at the time engaged in any specific mission for her employer. The other three cases deal with injuries sustained while on a deviation from the route for the sole purpose of carrying out a personal mission.

We are not entirely in accord with some of the statements contained in the opinion of the commission, which have not been mentioned herein, but these are not pertinent to our determination of the main issue.

The award is affirmed, with costs to plaintiffs.

SHARPE, C.J. and BOYLES, RIED, NORTH, DETHMERS, CARR and BUSHNELL, JJ. concur.

✧

The question of when a party is or is not in the course of employment is at least as difficult to answer precisely as the question of when a party is or is not acting as a reasonable prudent man. No one rule can be applied to all or even most of the fact patterns that arise. The same problem, in a different setting, is discussed in Chapter 26.

QUESTION

1. It was said in paragraph (5) above, "It has been repeatedly held that this court may not disturb the findings of the department of labor and industry when there is competent evidence to support them. . . ." Why not?

Intent in Contractual Relations

CHAPTER THIRTEEN

Preface to the Study of Contracts [1]

Reliance upon honor alone was found long ago to be insufficient protection. The only alternative, providing legal means of enforcing certain types of promises, was therefore developed. These legally enforceable promises are termed contracts. *Promises that do not meet the requirements of a contract are not enforceable except in a few special cases. . . .*

Introduction

THE LAW of contracts is one of the more important areas of commercial law. At the same time, the law of contracts transcends commercial law. Although most commercial transactions involve contracts, many contracts, as we will see, have nothing to do with commercial transactions (using *commercial transactions* in the sense of transactions between merchants or other businessmen).

One of the most important types of contract is the sales contract. The sales contract is a specialized type of contract in which personal property is transferred in exchange for a price. It combines aspects of the general law of contract with certain variations designed to cope with peculiar problems that arise in commerce. Some features of the law of personal property are

---

[1] EDITOR'S NOTE: The following discussion reflects the traditional view of the role of contracts, and a view that until recent years almost certainly has been accurate. According to recent findings, discussed further on pages 244–247, the contract may no longer be fulfilling its traditional role, especially in some industries characterized by large size, stability, and repeated contacts between sales personnel of buyer and seller.

also incorporated into the law of sales, because every sale involves a transfer of personal property.

The general law of contracts, to which primary attention is devoted in the following sections, is a product of the English common law, as influenced by the law merchant and modified by the common law and the legislation of our states. The law of sales contracts is based upon all of these sources, but at present, state statutes are the most important source. The first extensive codification of the sales contract was under the Uniform Sales Act, which was adopted in all American jurisdictions. The Uniform Commercial Code is a more recent codification, and at point of writing it has been adopted in about one half of our states.

The Uniform Commercial Code is the last word on sales law, and to all indications it is destined to be the main source of sales law in the near future. Wishing to do justice both to the general law of contracts, and to the sales contract, we have followed the plan in the succeeding chapters of first presenting a phase of the general contract law, then setting out the particular rules of the Uniform Commercial Code dealing with the sales contract. This plan is followed throughout the chapters dealing with contracts.

Importance of Contracts in Our Society

Probably it is evident that the economy of the United States is based upon the exchange of goods and services rather than upon home production of the necessities of life. Goods and services are generally exchanged for money—so much per hour for services, so much per ton for goods, though less frequently a barter may be arranged. Even when bartered, the value of each item exchanged is generally expressed in terms of money.

Except when the simplest and smallest transactions are involved, it is fairly rare for payment and exchange of goods or services to be made immediately upon striking a bargain. Usually one or both sides to an agreement are performed at a later date. In order for an exchange to be arranged at one time, with the performance to come later, the parties either have to rely upon one another's honor to insure performance, or there has to be a legally enforceable obligation to perform the agreement. Reliance upon honor alone was found long ago to be insufficient protection. The only alternative, providing legal means of enforcing certain types of promises, was therefore developed. These legally enforceable promises are termed *contracts*. Promises that do not meet the requirements of a contract are *not* enforceable except in a few special cases, considered later. The creation of a contract is the most common means of rendering a promise enforceable.

The contract is essential to a complex economic system. Pause a moment and consider the commitments that must be filled for any modern industry to operate. A multitude of raw materials and semifinished products must be available at a certain time and place in a concern's manufacturing process. Dependable electric, water, and telephone service must be provided; highly skilled and highly paid executives must be hired, often under complex arrangements involving options, retirement programs, and other fringe benefits. Machinery must be leased, and often serviced by the lessors. Regular and adequate transportation services must be arranged; the land that the plant is operated on must be either purchased or leased, as must buildings. Some agreement as to wages, hours, and working conditions must be reached between the labor force and the management. The finished product of the operation must be sold to customers, and finally, the profits must be distributed by some established scheme to the stockholders. Each of the diverse arrangements enumerated above is normally defined by a contract.

Every business concern relies upon the promised performance of the other concerns with which it deals. If most of these contracts were not performed according to their terms, most of the time, complicated transactions and manufacturing processes in business and industry would be impossible.

Any commercial establishment, therefore, tends to consist of a mass of separate activities linked together into an effective whole by a multitude of contracts. The contract is a cement that holds our economic system together.

The fact that promises, when in the form of contracts, are legally enforceable does not insure performance, but undoubtedly does substantially increase the probability of performance being made according to the agreed terms. A party, knowing he may face a legal action if he does not perform, is more likely to perform, and if performance is not forthcoming, the fact that a suit may be brought may be enough to secure a satisfactory out-of-court settlement. If a satisfactory settlement is not possible, as a last resort, damages may be obtained through legal action.

In this text, we devote more space to the study of contracts than to any other subject area. There are several reasons for this. For one, the study of contracts is a difficult field in which to generalize. A number of problems cannot be clarified in any way other than through careful distinction and comparison. In addition, there is probably some merit in studying one area of the law with particular care, if only to give possible insight into the nature of some detailed legal problems. Finally, the basic importance of contracts to the ordinary citizen, in helping him understand the functioning of the world around him, justifies detailed attention.

CHAPTER FOURTEEN

The Nature
of Assent

The test as to whether the second party really accepted an offer is very similar to the reasonable-man test of negligence. Would a reasonable man in the position of the offeror have concluded on the basis of all the circumstances that the other party accepted?

Definitions

ANSON[1] DEFINES a contract as an "agreement enforceable at law, made between two or more persons, by which rights are acquired by one or more to acts or forebearances on the part of the other or others." This definition has the merit of emphasizing first things first. In the logical development of contracts attention must first be focused upon "the agreement." In fact, shortening Anson's definition to "an agreement enforceable at law" would serve to distinguish contract from other types of legal relationships, which is about all that could be expected of so few words in reference to so large a topic.

The excessive use of definitions in this discussion is regrettable, but the problem remains, what is an agreement? Williston's[2] simple statement on this score is clear and concise enough to merit quoting: An "agreement is nothing more than a manifestation of mutual assent." The implications of this statement are broad. Above all, observe that assent is not the most important thing but rather the *manifestation,* or *appearance,* of assent by each party.

[1] Sir William R. Anson, *Principles of the Law of Contracts,* Thomas H. Patterson (ed.) (Chicago: Callaghan and Company, 1939), pp. 10–11.

[2] Samuel Williston, *Williston on Contracts,* Walter H. E. Jaeger (ed.) (3d ed.; Mount Kisco, N.Y.: Baker, Voorhis and Company, Inc., 1957), I, p. 6.

The reason for the difficulty in pinning down the term *agreement* can be traced to a problem with which the reader is familiar by now: assent presumes an intent. Intent is subjective and can only be ascertained exactly by mind readers. While in most crimes, and in the deliberate torts, intent must be proved, even in these cases objective evidence, being all that is available, is used to prove intent.

For analyzing contracts, (the subject of many more transactions than intentional torts, and less important than crimes, at least in the sense of not exposing parties to imprisonment, or death), an even more expedient test is desirable. The test for finding an agreement to contract does not consider the ultimate question of assent (which implies an intent to agree). In contract problems the only question is, was there *manifestation* (or appearance) of assent? Strictly speaking, intent is not an element of contract. *Apparent* intent to agree—that is, manifestation of assent—is.[3]

The Test of Apparent Assent

By what test, in an actual case, do we measure the presence or absence of conduct by a party that might constitute a manifestation of assent? In general the problem arises in this way. One party offers to contract. The other party accepts this offer, or so it appears, to the first party. The test as to whether the second party really accepted is very similar to the "reasonable man" test of negligence. "Would a reasonable man in the position of the offeror have concluded on the basis of all the circumstances that the other party accepted?" If so, there is a valid manifestation of assent. The test, in other words, is the conduct of the acceptor, not his secret intent.

The same test is applied to the offer: thus, the question is, did the offeror appear to a reasonable man to be making an offer? Not: did he really *intend* to make an offer?

This test succeeds in reflecting our ideas of justice, or good policy, in this way. It represents a compromise between expediency, on the one hand, by leaving the difficult problem of proof of the secret intent unnecessary. On the other hand, it avoids the hardships that might result from a completely arbitrary test. If the person accepting an offer is obviously joking, so that any reasonable person could see that he was not serious, the interpretation is not so arbitrary as to ignore the joke. An oral statement of acceptance would not be binding even though his words alone might suggest an accept-

[3] EDITOR'S NOTE: It is not at all uncommon to find courts, when dealing with other contract problems, speaking of "intent to contract" rather than "manifestation of assent" as one of the elements of a contract. While dealing directly with this problem, few if any courts would speak of intent to contract. The only explanation can be that it is difficult to be completely precise about one aspect of a problem when another aspect is under particular scrutiny.

ance. However, what if he was accepting in jest and had confided this to all the witnesses around except to the person making the offer? Assume that to the latter, as a reasonable man, the acceptance appeared sincere. In that case, the party making the offer would have a right to rely upon the manifestation of assent as an acceptance. A contract (other requirements being present) would result. A reasonable person *in his position* would have no notice of the jest, and the manifestation of assent conveyed by the other party would be binding upon that party.

LEO F. PIAZZA PAVING COMPANY v. BEBEK AND BRKICH ET AL. (California, 1956) 296 P 2d 368

> *If from a promise, or manifestation of intention, or from the circumstances existing at the time, the person to whom the promise or manifestation is addressed knows or has reason to know that the person making it does not intend it as an expression of his fixed purpose until he has given a further expression of assent, he has not made an offer.* [Restatement of Contracts, Section 25.]

[EDITOR'S NOTE: Previously, attention was drawn to the importance of the contract as a means of eliminating uncertainties of business. That is what the plaintiff in the following case (Piazza Paving Company) was attempting. Plaintiff requested that the defendants (Bebek and Brkich) submit a bid stating their price on a subcontract to do pipeline work, so that plaintiff could then bid with confidence on the prime contract, a road construction project for the State of California. Some confusion followed, but let us see what happened to the plaintiff in this case, and more important, why.]

Breach of contract action. The Superior Court, Santa Clara County, Leonard R. Avilla, J., rendered judgment for defendants, and plaintiff appealed. The District Court of Appeal, Peters, P.J., held that evidence sustained finding that defendants had not made an offer, or intended to make an offer, to perform pipe line work in connection with road construction project for which plaintiff had submitted bid to state.

Affirmed.

(1) On this appeal both sides agree that for a valid contract to exist the consent of the parties must be free, mutual, and communicated by each to the other, and that consent is not mutual unless all the parties agree upon the same thing in the same sense. . . . Both sides also agree that in determining whether there has been a mutual consent to contract the courts are not interested in the subjective intent of the parties, but only in their objective intent—that is, what would a reasonable man believe from the outward manifestations of consent? . . . .

This general rule, approved in California, is expressed in section 25 of the Restatement of Contracts as follows:

"If from a promise, or manifestation of intention, or from the circumstances existing at the time, the person to whom the promise or manifestation is addressed knows or has reason to know that the person making it does not intend it as an expression of his fixed purpose until he has given a further expression of assent, he has not made an offer."

Comment "a" to this section reads:

"It is often difficult to draw an exact line between offers and negotiations preliminary thereto. It is common for one who wishes to make a bargain to try to induce the other party to the intended transaction to make the definite offer, he himself suggesting with more or less definiteness the nature of the contract he is willing to enter into. Besides any direct language indicating an intent to defer the formation of a contract, the definiteness or indefiniteness of the words used in opening the negotiation must be considered, as well as the usages of business, and indeed all accompanying circumstances." . . .

(2) Thus, the basic question involved is whether, measured by the objective standard, there is any substantial evidence to support the finding that defendants did not make an offer, or intend to make an offer, to perform the work.

Plaintiff argues that while there was some uncertainty as to the intent of the parties up until the last meeting between Piazza [Plaintiff] and Bebek [Defendant], such uncertainty was completely removed when Kappetanich [Defendant's agent], several days later, knowing that Piazza intended to use them in his bid, handed Piazza plaintiff's Exhibit One, containing price quotations on the items requested. It is argued that, tested by the objective standard, this led plaintiff as a reasonable man to believe that defendants were making an offer to contract. Plaintiff also places some reliance on two letters written by defendants in October and November, 1952, telling plaintiff that they could not perform the work due to "pressing difficulties" and "circumstances beyond our control," contending that since such letters did not deny the existence of the contract they amounted to recognition of its existence.

If these were all of the facts there might be some merit in plaintiff's position. But these are not all of the facts. All of the surrounding circumstances must be considered. When Bebek told Piazza that he would furnish figures for the bid, he stated: "I can't give no bid, because I don't trust those 'specs,' but if you want to take a chance (of jetting) . . . quotation can be used about $1.25 a yard for the dirt, using the same dirt back . . . sand or selected material would be $2.00 a yard." Bebek made it quite clear that he was not giving a figure at which he would do the job, but merely giving to Piazza "some kind of an idea to use" in making his bid, and he was specific that "but it is O.K. if he wants to use this quotation and it is O.K. if he don't want to use it." This was corroborated by Kappetanich, who also testified that when Piazza later called at defendants' office and copied the work sheet containing a quotation of prices, he, Kappetanich, told Piazza that they could not give him a bid because the jetting was in question, but they would give him a figure so plaintiff could bid on the job. This occurred the very same day the quotation of prices was handed to plaintiff. This quotation of prices contains no promises, and it specifies no place or time of performance. Reasonably interpreted it is what its name implies, a mere quotation of prices given to plaintiff by defendants in fulfillment of Bebek's promise to give Piazza a quotation of prices to aid him in preparing his bid for the State.

Under these circumstances, it is apparent that the trial court was justified in concluding that Bebek actually communicated to Piazza that his intent was not to make an offer, but was to submit a mere quotation of prices. The finding of the trial court to this effect is amply supported.

Nor is there any material significance in the October and November letters relied upon by plaintiff as a recognition of the existence of a contract. Although they do not specifically deny the existence of a contract, it must be remembered that in fact no contract then existed. In these letters defendants declined to do the work, which is compatible with a construction of the letters as a rejection by defendants of plaintiff's offer to contract at the prices quoted by defendants. There is nothing in these letters acknowledging the existence of a contract. In fact, defendants' refusal to do the work can be interpreted as an assertion that there was no binding contract. . . .

The judgment appealed from is affirmed.

BRAY and WOOD, JJ., concur.

The moral may be stated succinctly. A reasonable man does not consider the delivery of a list of specifications as an offer, when he has previously been told that the figures submitted are *not* intended as an offer. The entire question revolves around the question of manifestation of assent, but assent (in this case, to offer) can hardly exist when express language negates any intent to contract.

QUESTION

1. Compare the "reasonable man" of torts, to that referred to in the first paragraph of the preceding case. Are the two concepts identical? Why do we meet the reasonable man so frequently in the legal setting?

Implied and Express Contracts

Although contracts usually are made manifest by oral or written communication, sometimes a contract is entered into purely on the basis of acts. A party with long hair seating himself into a barber chair may be held to be contracting to have his hair cut, for example. Contracts in which the manifestation of assent is purely acts rather than words are termed *implied contracts*. Contracts formed by oral or written communications are express contracts. Observe that the only difference between the two types of contract is the method of communication. They are equally valid, though express contracts are more common.

CARON v. ANDREW (Farm Service Company, surety for Andrew, actually the appellant) (California, 1955) 284 P 2d 550

Express and implied contracts both are based upon the intention of the parties and are distinguishable only in the manifestation of assent. The making of an agreement may be inferred by proof of conduct as well as by proof of the use of words.

[EDITOR's NOTE: Defendant, and now appellant, Farm Service Company, had issued a contractor's bond, guaranteeing that Andrew Brothers would satisfactorily complete a construction job for Grimes and Picchi. (This, again, is a device for assuring certainty in business affairs.) Grimes and Picchi were thus assured that if Andrew Brothers did not complete the contract, Farm Service Company would assume responsibility.

Andrew Brothers withdrew from the job, and Farm Service Company took over completion of the contract. In so doing, they took possession of equipment leased to Andrews Brothers by plaintiff-respondents, Caron and Oliver.]

This appeal is from a judgment rendered in favor of respondents Caron and Oliver, copartners, against Farm Service Company, a corporation. The judgment rests upon breach of an implied contract for the payment of the reasonable rental value of two pieces of equipment suitable for use in leveling land. The equipment had been leased by repondents to Andrew Brothers.

Andrew Brothers entered upon the performance of the land leveling contract and moved the subject machinery to the work, where it was used for a period extending from August 15, 1950, to October 25, 1950. At that time Andrew Brothers ceased work on their contract and, as the court found, appellant Farm Service Company took over the work of completing the leveling contract with the consent of Grimes and Picchi. Pursuant to those arrangements appellant went upon the property. The subject machinery was there. Some repairs were needed to fit the machines for further use and appellant undertook to make them.

Appellant returned one piece of equipment to respondents on February 10, 1951, but did not return the other until August 10, 1951. Prior to that date and on March 5, 1951, respondents began this action to obtain compensation for the retention and use of its equipment.

(1–10) It is the contention of appellant that the evidence is insufficient to support the trial court's findings that an implied contract was entered into between appellant and respondents whereunder appellant agreed to pay respondents the reasonable rental value of the two machines, or the findings that it took and retained the machines pursuant to that contract for the periods fixed in the findings. This contention cannot be sustained. The rules to be applied in determining whether or not an implied contract has been entered into are well settled.

"A contract is either express or implied."

"An express contract is one, the terms of which are stated in words."

"An implied contract is one, the existence and terms of which are manifested by conduct." . . .

"Contracts are often spoken of as express or implied. The distinction involves, however, no difference in legal effect, but lies merely in the mode of manifesting assent." Restatement of the Law of Contracts, sec. 5.

"It is generally held that the existence of an implied contract is usually a question of fact for the trial court. Where evidence is conflicting, or where reasonable conflicting inferences may be drawn from evidence which is not in conflict, a question of fact is presented for decision of the trial court. . . .

"Further, on appeal we must draw all reasonable inferences in favor of the judgment." . . .

"Express and implied contracts both are based upon the intention of the parties and are distinguishable only in the manifestations of assent. The making of an agreement may be inferred by proof of conduct as well as by proof of the use of words. . . .

". . . Before a contract may be implied, however, it must be determined as a question of fact whether the parties acted in such a manner as to provide the necessary foundation for it, and evidence may be introduced to rebut the inferences and show that there is another explanation for the conduct. Such a contract is inferred from the conduct, situation, or mutual relation of the parties and enforced by the law on the ground of justice. It is implied where facts and circumstances show a mutual intention to contract, and without such mutual intention there can be no contract in fact. . . .

"Both express contracts and contracts implied in fact are founded upon an ascertained agreement, or, in other words, are consensual in nature, the substantial difference being in the mode of proof by which they are established."
. . .

(11) When appellant, with the consent of Grimes and Picchi, undertook to complete the leveling contract, the first requisite, of course, was that Grimes and Picchi make available to it such possession of the subject land as was necessary for the performance of its undertaking. Into such possession of the land appellant entered and upon the land was the equipment in question. Not only did it also take possession of the equipment that had been rented to Andrew Brothers, but it also exercised dominion over it, declared its intention to use it as Andrew Brothers had used it and embarked upon making repairs to it to fit it for such use. Certainly the trial court could hold that appellant expected to pay for it, and in the absence of appellant's having made any other arrangements with respondents, the court could find appellant expected to pay the reasonable rental value of the machinery while possessing and retaining it. It is true that inclement weather, followed by floods, prevented any actual use of these machines in leveling work, but that does not detract from the evidence that appel-

lant intended to keep and use the machines. This concept is further strengthened by the fact that it did return the machines to respondents, one within a short time, the other after a long time. The trial court could certainly suppose that machinery of the type here involved would not be taken and retained by appellant without appellant expecting to pay substantial sums for its retention, even though in fact being unable, because of weather and flood conditions, to make the intended use of it. If appellant was not satisfied with the reasonable rental value standard of pay it should have undertaken to make an express bargain. It did not take or attempt to take an assignment to it of the contract which Andrew Brothers had on the machines and the court could, therefore, find that it had no intention of making, and did not make, any promise, measured by the provisions of that agreement. The evidence sufficiently supports the findings.

The judgment is affirmed, save that it is reduced in the conceded sum of $158.30. Respondents will recover costs.

SCHOTTKY and PEKK, JJ., concur.

✧

Q U E S T I O N

1. Does an implied contract require an agreement between the parties? Explain.

Many students beginning the study of contracts believe that contracts must be in writing to be enforceable. This view is almost totally wrong. (The significance of writing will be examined in detail later, under the heading "Requirements of Form.") We find in this case that a contract need not be written or even oral. The pertinent question remains: what is the intent of the parties? Here that intent was expressed by actions, not by words either written or oral.[4]

[4] EDITOR'S NOTE: Mention should be made of still another concept, the contract implied by law, or quasi contract. The quasi contract is not really a contract, and it is not based upon an agreement between two parties, but it is treated as though it were both.

The quasi contract is conjured up by a court, in order to work justice. For example, Jones embezzles $10,000 from his employer. Obviously, Jones was not thinking in terms of making a contract. The employer, however, may bring suit for return of the money, in quasi contract, asking the court to imply or pretend an agreement by Jones to return the money. Despite Jones' vigorous protest that he neither agreed nor intended to return the money, a quasi contract could be found. In general, the quasi contract is utilized as a device for compensating a party for services rendered or goods used, when the other party should be obligated to pay, but no actual agreement, express or implied, can be found.

QUESTION

1. What then is the sole difference between expressed and implied assent?

GRAVES v. *NORTHERN N.Y. PUBLISHING COMPANY, INC.* (New York, 1940) 22 NYS 2d 539

> . . . [*as*] *it was . . . apparent to the plaintiff that the alleged offer was printed in a "joke column" . . . we conclude . . . there was no meeting of . . . minds . . . essential to a valid contract.*

Action by James G. Graves against the Northern New York Publishing Company, Inc., to recover $1,000 allegedly offered to any person who would give to defendant's newspaper the telephone number of the Western Union in the City of Ogdensburg. From an order denying defendant's motion for summary judgment, defendant appeals.

Order reversed and motion granted.

Argued before CROSBY, P.J., and CUNNINGHAM, DOWLING, HARRIS, and McCURN, JJ.

PER CURIAM.

There was no valid contract upon which to base plaintiff's cause of action. The affidavits leave no issue of fact as to the defendant's contention that the alleged offer was published through mistake or error. It is clear from such affidavits that the defendant never actually intended to offer $1,000 to the person who would furnish it with the telephone number of the Western Union. The mistake was corrected as soon as it was discovered and the plaintiff was put to no loss or disadvantage on account of it. It is a matter of common knowledge that the Telephone Company will, upon request from "information," furnish the telephone number of a business subscriber like the Western Union free of charge. It was also apparent to the plaintiff that the alleged offer was printed in a "joke column" in defendant's newspaper. We conclude therefore that there was no such meeting of the minds as is essential to a valid contract.

❖

Exactly what happened in this case is not completely clear, and does not appear to have been clear to the judges either. At one point they speak of a joke, at another they speak of the item appearing through mistake. Whether joke or mistake or both, the outcome should be the same. Parties reading the advertisement should not, as reasonable men, believe this to be an offer to enter into legal relations.

Judges and lawyers are often accused of being "legalistic." Yet in cases such as this, the public often feels the law should be much more literal than does the judge. Laymen often feel that anything phrased as an offer *is* an offer, therefore, when accepted results in a contract. The answer is that anything phrased as an offer is *not* necessarily an offer. In every case judgment must be used to decide whether a communication suggests an assent to enter legal relations or not.

Note that in all the cases presented in contracts so far, the basic issue could be summarized as follows: As a matter of common sense, what should each party have understood the other's intent to be. The party most in tune with common sense has consistently won.

CHAPTER FIFTEEN

Elements of Offer
and Acceptance

*Questions of judgment will never be completely absent from
any type of legal problem, but contracts, being a relationship
voluntarily entered into, can afford to have rules which are more
rigid, and which depend more upon mechanical—that is, a
geometric type of reasoning. . . . The technical rules governing
offer and acceptance are illustratons of an area of law in which,
though there may be minor variations between states, the law
tends to be clear-cut.*

Introduction

WE HAVE HARDLY begun to explore the different types of problems
involving manifestation of assent in contractual relations. However,
before considering some related problems in more detail, we must digress
for a moment to consider the more technical features of the formation of a
contract.

First we would like to make an observation. Contractual rights are an
important form of right. The contract once made is an assurance that a
thing will be done, and if it is not, that compensatory damages will be
awarded by a court. The conduct of any type of business or industry is almost impossible without the assurance that commitments for materials,
machinery, and utilities will be met and that commitments for payment of
the service or product will be honored.

Nevertheless, contracts protect a different type of interest than torts.
There is no element of choice presented to the victim of a tort; a person
may enter a contract or not as he chooses. It is important that people deliberately or negligently injured shall have a remedy, and to see that they do,
the law must remain highly flexible, leaving many questions in a rather

vague state. Negligence law in particular includes very few precise rules and requires very broad exercise of judgment both by judge and jury.

Questions of judgment will never be completely absent from any type of legal problem, but contracts, being a relationship voluntarily entered into, can afford to have rules that are more rigid and that depend more upon mechanical—that is, a geometric type of reasoning. In fact, with many types of contract question, one might argue that the more rigid the law, the more clearly one's rights may be stated. Anyone wishing to contract may see his lawyer and ascertain his rights before he begins to negotiate. Some aspects of contract law are in that happy state in which answers may be rather definitely and concisely given. If the facts are not disputed between the parties, a prediction can usually be made of the probable disposition of a case after problems arise, improving the possibility of the parties compromising their differences rather than resorting to the courts to settle any dispute.[1]

The technical rules governing offer and acceptance are illustrations of an area of law in which, though there may be minor variations between states, the law tends to be clear-cut.

The Offer

The agreement necessary to a contract arises when one party (the offeror) makes an offer that is accepted in its entirety by the other party (the offeree). At this time, the contract itself arises. Thus, to find a contract, we look for an offer, and an acceptance of the offer. (The fact that both offer and acceptance must be in the form of words, conduct, or both in order to manifest assent has already been discussed. A manifestation of assent is assumed to be present in the following examples.)

The offer consists of two parts: (1) a promise by the offeror, coupled with (2) a request addressed to the offeree for something in return. The promise the offeror makes is not binding upon him until the offeree unconditionally assents to the terms contained in the offer. Then a contract results. Often, the terms of the offeror are simply that the offeree make a return *promise* to perform some acts in the future.

This is not as complicated as it sounds. As an example of an offer, I will promise you $5 *if* (my terms) you will promise to mow my lawn. The promise to pay $5 is binding as soon as you promise to mow the lawn. Until then I am free to withdraw the offer.

Aside from a few considerations of illegality or of public policy, which we will consider later, there is no limit to what terms the offeror may re-

---

[1] Why should the ability to predict the outcome of a case improve the chance of the parties agreeing to a compromise?

quest from the offeree as a price for his own promise. Of course, if too much is asked the offeree will simply refuse to accept the offer, and no contract will result. Nevertheless, the power is in the hands of the offeror to dictate what the offeree must do to accept the offer, and in what manner.

Depending upon the manner of acceptance requested by the offeror, contracts are divided into two groups. These are bilateral contracts and unilateral contracts.

THE BILATERAL CONTRACT

The bilateral contract is the more usual arrangement. In a bilateral contract, the term submitted by the offeror is merely that the offeree extend a certain promise (as in the above example) in return for the promise contained in the offer. Making the requested promise constitutes acceptance of a bilateral contract, and instantly results in a mutually enforceable contract. The prefix bi in bilateral suggests two of something; actually it refers to the fact that there are two promises.

To illustrate, in an employment contract, the offeror promises a salary of $500 per month in return for the promise of the employee to work for a month. In a sales contract, a seller may promise to deliver his car to the buyer in return for the buyer's promise to pay $1,000. In each of these examples, the promises form a binding contract as soon as the return promise (the acceptance) is made.

THE UNILATERAL CONTRACT

Unlike the bilateral contract, described above in terms of an exchange of two promises, the unilateral contract contains only one. The offeror makes a promise, but the request attached to his promise requires performance of an *act* instead of a return promise. The assent consists in actually performing the act requested by the offeror. Until the requested *act* is performed, neither party is bound. Therefore the performance and the acceptance are one and the same.

Some strange implications relating to the unilateral contract stem from the rule stated earlier, that the offeror may dictate what the offeree must do to accept the offer, and in what manner.

The peculiar result of a unilateral contract is that the contract is not binding nor technically even in existence until the offeree has fully completed his performance. If the acts to be performed by the offeree of a unilateral contract are relatively simple in nature, and are performed quickly, no particular problem need arise. On the other hand, if a long, involved performance is contemplated, what is to prevent the offeror from withdrawing his offer after the offeree has begun performance of the required acts, or even when he has almost completed them? We will discuss this problem in the following paragraphs.

TERMINATION OF THE OFFER

Whether we are speaking of bilateral or unilateral contracts, the question arises, how long does the offer remain valid? A brief answer to this question is, an offer remains valid until it is terminated. We will now examine specific ways in which an offer may be terminated.

1. An offer is terminated by revocation (cancellation) of the offer by the offeror, providing the revocation is communicated to the offeree before the latter has accepted. What may be required to constitute an acceptance varies, being dependent upon the terms set out by the offeror, but no matter what type of contract, the basic rule remains that the revocation is only effective if communicated before acceptance. If the revocation is not communicated until after acceptance, a contract results regardless of the wishes of the offeror. The rule of law that a revocation may be made any time before acceptance by the offeree presents no serious problem in the case of the bilateral contract. However, the unilateral contract is another matter. Because a unilateral contract is not accepted until the acts required by the offeror are actually performed (rather than when merely promised, as in the case of a bilateral contract) there can be a long period of time between the offer and the performance-acceptance. If the offer contains a request to do something requiring a large expenditure of time or effort, quite possibly an offeree might have greatly extended himself in an effort to accept. Yet, applying the usual rules dealing with acceptance, the offeror is still free to revoke his offer until the performance is completed. Clearly, this may work an injustice in some cases. The question is what to do? Certainly there is a dilemma. On the one hand we like to think the individual is free to contract as he sees fit. Following this principle, if an individual unwisely enters into performance of a unilateral contract and the other party embarrasses him by revoking just before completion, there should be no remedy. This was the view at common law. On the other hand, most of us feel that simple justice requires better treatment of the offeree, and many courts have gone along with this feeling. Some require the offeror to reimburse the offeree to the extent of the value of the latter's performance up to the date of revocation. Other courts treat the contract as a bilateral contract, holding the offeror and offeree bound to one another as soon as the offeree has performed enough to reasonably demonstrate his intention to complete the contract, and then permit the offeree a reasonable time in which to complete his performance. The unilateral contract presents difficult questions and probably no method of dealing with them will completely answer all objections that might be raised.

Whether an offer is unilateral or bilateral in form, one troublesome aspect of the revocation of offers arises when the offeror promises the offeree to hold his offer open for a stated period of time. This type of promise is termed an option. May the offeror change his mind, and inform the offeree that the option is revoked before the stated time has expired?

The traditional view is that, despite a promise contained in the offer to keep the offer open, an offer may be revoked any time before acceptance. On purely logical ground this makes sense: it is merely consistent with the rule already stated that any offer may be revoked prior to acceptance. Logical or not, this rule seems to run so strongly contrary to ordinary views of justice that it has been modified to some extent under the Uniform Commercial Code. (See page 254.)

(A contract may be made by which one party extends a payment of money, or other benefit, in return for a promise by the other party to leave an offer open for a stated period of time. If accepted, the offer is enforceable. The difference is that while in the first example above we merely had a *promise* to keep an offer open, under the present arrangements we have a *contract* by which a party is bound to keep some offer open. This type of contract is discussed elsewhere in this text. See page 323.)

2. An offer will be terminated by expiration of a reasonable time, if not first accepted by the offeree. We are back to a question of judgment. The answer to the question of what constitutes a reasonable time will vary with the circumstances of the case: a short period for an offer to sell items with rapidly fluctuating prices, intermediate for such items of personal property as an automobile or appliances, and longer for items with a more stable value, such as real estate. The validity of any of these examples could be destroyed by the facts of a particular case. No doubt circumstances arise when an offer to purchase securities would remain open for a long, though unstated, period. No doubt offers to buy real estate, because of circumstances known by both parties, could expire within hours or minutes. As with any other question of judgment, all the circumstances must be considered. This is a question of fact and is for the jury to decide.

3. An offer will be terminated by expiration of a time period stated in the offer or upon occurrence of any other terminating condition included as part of the offer. Practically any event could be stated in an offer as terminating the offer. A provision stating that the offer to sell an article would terminate immediately even without notice, if the article were purchased by someone else before acceptance by the offeree, would be valid in most jurisdictions.

4. Rejection by the offeree terminates the offer. Not only does a flat no act as a rejection, but any response demanding modification of the terms of the offer is treated as a rejection. This is true even when the answer claims to be an acceptance. A response of this type is called a counteroffer, acting both as a rejection and a new offer to the original offeror. If the offeror accepts the terms suggested in the offeree's counteroffer, a contract results.

5. Impossibility to contract because of death of either of the parties, de-

struction of the subject matter, or intervening illegality[2] of the offer will terminate it. Parties cannot contract after their death, so acceptance of an outstanding offer of a deceased offeror will not be binding upon his estate; nor may an offer extended to a party who subsequently dies be accepted after death by the decedent's estate.

Although not directly on the subject, some confusion may be avoided by our explaining at this time that when a contract has been made and *then* one of the parties dies, the contract may well be binding upon the estate of the decedent.[3] The possible difference in outcome depends upon whether a contract exists before death. A contract cannot be *formed* once one of the intended parties has died. When a contract does exist, it may well survive the death of one or both parties.

6. When the terms of the offer are rendered physically or legally impossible of performance for any other reason, the offer is also terminated.

7. Last, and of great interest to the student, an offer may be terminated by the unconditional acceptance of the offer by the offeree. Then, of course, a contract results, and from the instant of the acceptance both parties are bound.

Acceptance

The acceptance, as has been stated, consists of an unconditional assent to the request of the offeror. If the offer is for a unilateral contract, acceptance consists in performing a requested act. If a bilateral contract, acceptance consists in making a return promise as requested by the offeror. In either case, to constitute an acceptance there may be no material deviation from the mode of performance dictated by the offeror.

How must the acceptance be signified by the offeree of a bilateral contract? Again, this is determined by the terms of the offer. Often no restriction is imposed in the offer, and any reasonable means of communication would generally be deemed adequate. But any sign, act, or form of notice that the offeror insists be used to manifest acceptance must be adopted by the offeree. Of course, various ways may merely be suggested by the offeror without being mandatory. In some cases it is difficult to determine whether a method of assent suggested by the offeror of a bilateral contract is mandatory or is merely optional. The decision in such a case requires the exercise of judgment, taking into account all the known facts bearing upon the

[2] *Intervening illegality* refers to a change in the law subsequent to the offer, rendering the proposed transaction illegal.

[3] An obvious exception would be a contract requiring personal services of the decedent or containing some other term making performance impossible by reason of the decedent's death.

offeror's apparent intent. Because the offeror is entitled to designate the means of acceptance, it is conceivable though not usual for him to dispense with actual notice of acceptance. He may wish to designate some sign or act other than notice to him as signifying acceptance. However, usually it is assumed that notice of acceptance will be sent to him.

In addition, a number of legal presumptions concerning the effective time of communication between offeror and offeree have an important bearing upon when and whether an acceptance is valid. These will be considered in the following section.

BYFORD v. GATES BROS. LUMBER COMPANY
(Arkansas, 1950) 225 SW 2d 929

> . . . If the offeree proposes new conditions he is really making a counter offer that must in turn be accepted by the other party. But it is well settled that the offeree's acceptance is not conditional merely because it recites terms that would in any event have been implied from the original offer. . . .

Gates Bros. Lumber Company and L. J. Boatner sued Mrs. L. G. Byford to enforce a contract whereunder defendant bound herself to settle debts owed to plaintiff by defendant's daughter.

The Circuit Court, St. Francis County, ELMO TAYLOR, J., directed a verdict for plaintiffs and from the judgment defendant appealed.

Judgment affirmed.

[*Editor's summary of the facts.* Dorothy Cole and her husband were in financial difficulty. They owned a house and restaurant, both of these being in the process of foreclosure by creditors. Mrs. Byford, Dorothy Cole's mother, made an offer to the creditors. The offer provided that she would give Gates Lumber $3,000 and some unused building materials against their claim if, in return, Gates Lumber and another creditor would agree not to satisfy their claims against the Cole house until the other assets of the Coles were exhausted. Mrs. Byford hoped that the other assets would be sufficient to pay off all the claims, and that the house would in this way be saved.]

. . . The letter [communicating Mrs. Byford's offer to the Gates Brothers' attorneys] concluded, "Please advise whether or not this is acceptable to your client."

On November 19 the attorneys for Gates Brothers replied: "We are authorized by Gates Bros. to accept the settlement offered in your letter to us dated the 16th inst., provided, the cash settlement is paid promptly and a reasonable time is allowed for removal of the lumber from the skating rink, which I suggest should be 90 days in view of the season of the year we are in. We assume that you will prepare whatever papers you consider necessary for modification of the decree and we will co-operate for Gates Bros. however may be necessary."

[It soon became evident that the other assets would *not* be sufficient to satisfy the claims, and that the house would be sold regardless of payment of $3,000 by Mrs. Byford. This meant she was losing her $3,000 without really helping her daughter.]

. . . On the day before the sale Mrs. Byford informed her attorney that she would not continue with the proposed settlements. . . .

[This suit is against her, for her breach of the contract entered into with Gates Lumber.]

The appellant's most forceful argument is that the Gates Brothers' letter did not amount to an acceptance of the proposed settlement for the reason that additional terms were suggested. We recognize the familiar rule that if the offeree proposes new conditions he is really making a counter-offer that must in turn be accepted by the other party. But it is well settled that the offeree's acceptance is not conditional merely because it recites terms that would in any event have been implied from the original offer. . . . Gates Brothers asked that the money be paid promptly and that a reasonable time be allowed for removal of the lumber. Since the sale that Mrs. Byford sought to avert was only eleven days away, it is evident that the offer itself contemplated prompt payment by Mrs. Byford. And the law would allow a reasonable time for removal of the lumber; so this requirement in the acceptance added nothing to the contract. Even though Gates Brothers "suggested" that ninety days would be a reasonable time, there still came into existence a binding contract by which Gates Brothers could remove the lumber within a period fixed by law as reasonable, whether greater or less than ninety days. . . .

Upon this point our earlier cases are controlling. In *Bushmeyer* v. *McGarry*, an offer to sell land provided that the abstract of title would be left with an Oklahoma bank, but the letter of acceptance directed that the abstract be forwarded to the vendee in Arkansas. The seller did forward the abstract but later attempted to avoid the contract on the theory that the vendee's counter-proposal had not been accepted. We upheld the contract, saying: "It is true the letter of acceptance introduces a change in details, in that . . . it is asked in this letter that the abstract be forwarded for inspection. Now, that was not a substantial change in the terms, but merely a detail which the defendant promptly acceded to by forwarding the abstract as requested. It was not such a change as amounted to a qualification of the originial offer." To the same effect is *Skinner* v. *Stone*. . . .

There were several objections to rulings upon matters of evidence, but we find no semblance of prejudicial error. The testimony adduced by both sides is entirely free from material conflict. It is shown without dispute that the contracts were made, that the appellees tendered performance, and that the appellant defaulted. The obligation being to pay money, there is no question as to the measure of damages. (Gates Brothers bought the lumber at the sale; its value is not involved here.) *Leach* v. *Smith*. Only issues of law were presented below, and the court's peremptory instruction for the appellees was a correct determination of these issues.

Affirmed.

✧

The question presented in the preceding case is whether a minor departure from the language of the offer constitutes a counteroffer or qualifies as an acceptance. This question, in the final analysis, must be determined upon the basis of whether reasonable people would consider the departure as being significant. The court found there was no significance to the new language, merely clarification of implicit terms, and therefore the acceptance had not departed from the terms of the offer.

We have not departed from our initial inquiry: "What did the parties seem to intend by their communications?"

GARRISON v. WARNER BROTHERS PICTURES
(CCA California, 1955) 226 F 2d 354

If a bona fide offer is made and accepted within a reasonable time without conditions and without varying its terms a contract may arise. There can be no contract if the offer is revoked before a valid acceptance. The evidence showed that Garrison never performed acts that would have constituted an unqualified acceptance of the alleged offer.

WILG, DJ.

Garrison appeals from an adverse judgment in his action for breach of contract against Warner Brothers Pictures, Inc., a corporation. Trial was had before the district court, sitting without a jury, and judgment was entered based upon the court's findings of fact and conclusions of law.

The breach of contract was predicated on offers made by Warner Brothers through the media of a newsreel and newspaper stories, that it would pay $1,000,000 to anyone who could prove that actor Burt Lancaster, the star of a motion picture entitled "The Flame and the Arrow," did not perform all the daring stunts he was shown doing in the motion picture. Garrison saw the newsreel and the motion picture. He then had two telephone conversations with an attorney for the corporation. In the first conversation he told the attorney he "felt sure," "thought," or "believed" he could prove that Lancaster had not done all of the stunts in the picture. Three days later, Garrison told the attorney he could prove his claim. (No effort, however, was made to prove it until the trial of the action, about three years later.) Garrison, a resident of Los Angeles, California, also told the attorney that if he would "arrange for Warner Brothers to buy me a ticket to New York and a suit of clothes and some change to put in my pocket I will go to New York" and "forget about it." The attorney told

Garrison it was his position that no offer had been made but that if Garrison thought one had been made it was withdrawn. Later, Garrison, through his own attorney, wrote Warner Brothers that Garrison had accepted the offer and had given proof that Lancaster "did not do all of the stunts he is shown doing in the picture."

(1) The illusory offer apparently confounded Garrison's trial attorney. The complaint alleged, among other things, that Warner Brothers offered to pay the sum of money to anyone who could prove Lancaster "did not do or perform all of the stunts he was shown doing *or purported to perform*" in the motion picture. (Emphasis supplied.) A careful examination of the record fails to reveal any evidence in support of the making of an offer in the words or language alleged in the complaint. The trial court's finding that no offer as set forth in the complaint was ever made was clearly correct.

(2, 3) If a bona fide offer is made and is accepted within a reasonable time without conditions and without varying its terms, a contract may arise. There can be no contract if the offer is revoked before a valid acceptance. The evidence showed that Garrison never performed acts which would have constituted an unqualified acceptance of the alleged offer. At the most, he indicated only that he thought he could prove Lancaster did not do all the daring stunts shown in the motion picture.

(4) Garrison urges that the attempt to revoke the offer by direct communication with him was ineffectual because the revocation must have been made by the same means as used in making the offer—newsreels and newspapers. This unique contention is not supported by any authority or reason. As to the remaining members of the public, the same media would have to be used in order to revoke the offer, but as to Garrison, direct personal notice that it had been withdrawn was sufficient.

(5) In connection with the issue as to whether Lancaster performed all his daring stunts in the motion picture, Garrison proved that in three episodes a substitute actor appeared in the film portraying the character played by Lancaster. By the use of trick photography in a scene wherein this character was shown carrying a young boy along the crest of a roof, it would appear to a viewing audience that the action was daring or dangerous. However, in the motion picture set, a platform two feet wide was erected behind the false front of the building. Approximately four feet below that platform, there was another platform three feet wide protected by a hand rail three and a half feet high. None of this, of course, was shown in the film, but it was along the upper platform that the actor actually ran carrying the youth. In the second episode, the substitute actor entered a courtyard on horseback, came to a stop, stepped down to the bed of a stationary two-wheel cart, cut a rope by which another character was suspended, and then drove the horse, pulling cart away from the courtyard. In a sword fight or duel, two short views showed the arm and shoulder of the substitute actor. To the audience, the action portrayed actual combat. This illusion was dispelled by testimony of a fencing instructor, who described himself as a "motion picture choreographer of fencing," to the effect that all the action was laid out, memorized and practiced in advance in the same manner as the choreography of a ballet. The trial court found that the foregoing did not

constitute stunts. We have viewed the film and examined the record, and affirm the trial court's finding in this respect.

Garrison urges that the picture itself defined the term "stunt" and what is daring or dangerous through its representation to the public that what the public saw on the screen was real. Warner Brothers answers by saying: "This disregards entirely the fact that any motion picture in its entirety is an illusion," and adds that: ". . . what constitutes a 'daring stunt' cannot be tested by the apparent danger created through the ordinary practices of the dramatic acts." We accept the answer.

The judgment is affirmed.

✧

No reference is made to unilateral contracts in this case. Nevertheless we hope the student associated what he has read concerning unilateral contracts with one of the issues above. Assuming there was an offer, the offer in this case was to be accepted by an act—that is, providing proof of a certain nature—*not* by *agreeing* to provide proof at some later date. The offer (if any) was therefore to enter into a unilateral contract. Before the proof was submitted, the offer had been revoked. Communication of a revocation may be by any means, and need not, as was alleged, in this case, be transmitted in the same form as the offer.

Another aspect of this case may remind the reader of the case on page 210, concerning an offer to pay $1,000 for the telegraph company's phone number. We should not take purported offers of this kind seriously. The intent must seem doubtful to any reasonable man. We know of no legal maxim that says the reasonable man is also a reasonably sophisticated man, but we suspect that most courts assume this to be true. We all know that pioneers in a western movie are not *really* in danger of being scalped. The bullets fired at the hero are not real, and almost nothing that takes place on the screen does literally occur. We also know that an offer promising a reward if one can prove these sorts of things are not really happening is a publicity device, not an attempt to contract.

QUESTION

1. Assuming that the court would have enforced the contract if the acceptance had been performed properly (the assumption is doubtful), what would Garrison have had to do in order to accept, considering that the defendant seemed primed to revoke their offer at the slightest hint that it might be accepted?

Negotiation of Contract Terms: Contrasted with Offer and Acceptance

Granting that a contract arises upon the acceptance by the offeree of the terms of the offeror, in actual practice, the situation is often not so clear-cut as one might think. Defining the essentials is easy enough, but deciding in a particular case whether the facts fall within a definition is much more difficult.

One of the first problems to arise is that of distinguishing between negotiations and offers. Frequently, if not usually, a period of bargaining will precede any actual offer. The only objective difference between a party negotiating and one actually making an offer is the apparent intent of the party and therefore, to distinguish the two, reliance must be placed on all the objective evidence. Did the statement in question sound like an offer rather than a mere bargaining proposition? [4]

To decide this question, such evidence as past dealings between the parties involved, trade practices in the particular line of business, and other evidence bearing on the case should be considered. The greater the degree of equivocation attached to a proposition, the greater the likelihood that a statement is intended merely to sound out the position of the opposite party. On the other hand, if two parties clearly understand one another to be merely negotiating and not making firm commitments, quite possibly some statements taken out of this context would sound like offers.

Advertising is a common type of communication that often sounds like an offer but is usually held not to be. Advertisements are generally assumed to constitute "invitations to trade" rather than offers, based no doubt on considerations of commericial expediency. Otherwise, what would happen if a retailer advertised goods for sale but sold out before the day was half over? Other difficulties could be imagined. Yet in particular cases, where the circumstances point convincingly to the conclusion that an offer was actually intended, an advertisement will be treated as an offer. Offers for rewards serve as an example. We may assume that without convincing evidence to the contrary, commercial advertisements are not offers.

FORMATION OF CONTRACTS: AN ILLUSTRATION

What must transpire before an agreement in the legal sense is reached?
Essentially, both parties must manifest their agreement to the same thing at the same time. Let us follow a simple set of proposals and counterproposals as an illustration.

JONES: "I'm thinking of offering you $500 for your car." (*No legal effect, preliminary negotiation.*)

SMITH: "Good deal." (*Also no legal effect.*)

JONES: "Well, it's a wreck, but I'll give you $500 for your car." (*We assume the parties clearly understand what car is the subject of this conversation. This is an offer.*)

SMITH: "Nothing doing you cheapskate, you know it's worth $600."

[4] See the last paragraph of part (1) in the case of *Piazza* v. *Bebek and Brkich,* page 204 (b) for a discussion on this point. In that case the proposition was construed as a negotiation.

(We must consider this a rejection. It is not a counteroffer because he did not say, "I'll sell for $600," but merely mentioned that it was worth that. A rejection, as you recall, terminates the offer, so even if Smith should reconsider and offer to sell for $500, a contract would not result until Jones accepted this specific offer.)

JONES: "I'll go $550." *(Not too specific, but under the circumstances a reasonable man would consider this an offer. Out of this context it might not be.)*

SMITH: "Go $575." *(Above comments apply. Here we have a counteroffer, which you may recall has the effect of rejecting the offer, but is at the same time an offer by Smith which Jones may accept.)*

JONES: "You robber, how could you have the nerve to ask $575 for that clunker? I'd walk first." *(This is a rejection.)*

SMITH: "O.K. $550." *(In the context clear enough.)*

JONES: "I'll give you $550."

Query: At what point was the contract formed in this case?

Although in this simple illustration, the only term expressly bargained over was the price, in many offers a multitude of terms are included, sometimes in great detail.

Generally speaking, the offeree, in accepting, must accept the offeror's terms as stated, and any material variation in the terms of the acceptance will constitute a counteroffer, thus rejecting the contract. This principle is easy enough to apply in the above example, where the only term subject to discussion was the price. In more complex offers, statements sometimes included in an offer are merely explanatory or statememts of preference (possible examples would be preferred shipping route and method of labeling cartons). What happens if one small term is varied in the acceptance? The whole key lies in the question, was the variation material? How do we tell what is material? Isn't it the right of the offeror to decide what he thinks is material and what he does not? The answer is a qualified yes. When examining an acceptance to see if it conforms to the offer, our main concern is the offeror's manifest intent. Looking at their statements objectively, did the term in question appear to be material to the offeror? The answer must be based upon judgment, taking into account all the facts of the case as well as custom, trade practice, and anything else shedding light on the case.

TRUSTEES OF FIRST PRESBYTERIAN CHURCH v. HOWARD COMPANY JEWELERS (New Jersey, 1953) 97 A 2d 144

> . . . An offer to constitute a contract must be in a form which is intended of itself to create legal relations on its acceptance.

[EDITOR's NOTE: Because the role of the respective parties in this case is somewhat confusing, we think it desirable to provide an index of characters. The plaintiff-appellants were the Trustees of First Presbyterian Church, owners of the building in question. Schwebemeyer was their renting and managing agent. They claimed a contract was formed, and they won at the trial court. On appeal to the superior court, appellate division, they lost. They have now taken the case to the New Jersey Supreme Court.

The defendant-respondents are Howard Company Jewelers, represented by Linder, who denied having made a contract. They lost at the trial court, won on appeal, and have been taken to the Supreme Court of New Jersey. I. Hausman and Sons, Inc., was a mere bystander, having been the tenant up to the time it was released from the lease following negotiations between plaintiff and defendant.]

The appellant board of trustees is the owner of the premises located at 813 Broad Street, Newark, New Jersey. A store at that location was occupied by I. Hausman & Sons, Inc., under a lease which was to expire on April 30, 1952. The Hausman concern desired to terminate the lease and so informed Ralph B. Schwebemeyer, appellant's renting and managing agent. Negotiations then were had between Schwebemeyer and Mr. Linder, president of the defendant-respondent, respecting the leasing of the premises. On May 2, 1950, Linder signed a letter addressed to Schwebemeyer in which it was stated that "We now advise we are prepared to enter into a lease for the store premises . . . , provided we can do so on the following basis": the terms were thereafter set out. The letter also stated: "If this proposal be approved, it is our intention to take a lease in the name of The Howard Company, Jewelers. . . . Inasmuch as we are now in process of deciding upon our future course of action, it is essential that we have your early advice with respect to the foregoing."

At a special meeting of the appellant-trustees held on May 4, 1950, a resolution was adopted, stating that they "accepted the proposal and authorized Mr. Schwebemeyer to [arrange] leases embodying the terms of the proposal." The respondent was informed of the "acceptance" by Mr. Schwebemeyer on May 11, 1950, and the Hausman Company was released from its lease by the appellant. [An attorney] on behalf of the trustees then prepared a "proposed lease" and Mr. Schwebemeyer submitted it to the respondent's attorney with a covering letter which states "Should you like me to do so, I will be glad to join you in consideration of its contents at your convenience."

The proposed lease contained the usual clauses of the long form lease which were not included or discussed in the correspondence, such as those relating to repairs, insurance, subordination to the mortgage, inspection of the books, assignment of the lease, use of sidewalk, termination by vacation of the premises, bankruptcy, etc. Mr. Linder, respondent's president, refused to sign the proffered lease and it was never executed. The premises remained vacant until October 1, 1950, and the plaintiff appellant instituted this action seeking to recover in damages (1) $6,000 for the loss of rent, (2) $5,124.16 for real estate agent's commissions, and (3) $250 in counsel fees and costs.

The trial court held the letter of May 2 from Mr. Linder was an offer and that the resolution adopted by the trustees on May 4 was an acceptance of that offer which resulted in a binding contract, and accordingly entered judgment for the sum demanded.

The Appellate Division reversed on the ground that the respondent's letter was not an offer to contract but a proposal to enter into a lease the terms of which would be settled after negotiation between the parties, and it found as a fact from the circumstances that neither party intended a contract until the many terms involved in such a letting for a long term of such a valuable piece of property were agreed upon and embodied in an executed writing.

The question therefore presented for our determination is whether there was such an offer and acceptance out of which a binding contract between the parties arose, despite the fact that the formality of a written lease was within the contemplation of the parties. Our decision will turn on the application of the elementary principles of contract law to the circumstances of this case.

It is a well-established principle of contract law that to constitute a binding contract in such circumstances the proposition of one party must be met by an acceptance of the other, which corresponds with it entirely and adequately; and that until the actual completion of the bargain, either party is at liberty to withdraw his consent and put an end to the negotiation. . . .

The question is primarily one of intention, and an offer to constitute a contract must be in a form which is intended of itself to create legal relations on its acceptance. It must contemplate the assumption of legal rights and duties and must show a clear intention to assume liability. . . .

Under the facts and circumstances of this case we cannot bring ourselves to a conclusion that the respondent intended by its offer that an acceptance thereof would constitute the full contractual expression of the parties with respect to the liabilities and duties to be assumed under the proposed lease. From all the circumstances it seems reasonably clear that both parties considered that many terms remained to be agreed upon despite the fact that the basic terms, the length of the lease and the amount of the rent, had been definitely settled. It is common experience that the lease of a valuable piece of property such as this is never based solely upon the length of the term or rental alone, and until there is an agreement as to the other essential terms usually found in such a lease and ordinarily formalized in the writing, no binding contract exists.

A few of the terms in the proposed lease were such that ordinarily would be implied if they had been omitted from the lease, but many of the other terms were important items which could not be implied into the contract and which had to be settled by agreement, and as to these we cannot spell out from the respondent's offer an intention of complete acquiescence with respect to such terms. The minds of the parties never met in the sense required by the rule above quoted from *Water Commissioners of Jersey City* v. *Brown*, supra.

The judgment of the Appellate Division is affirmed.

✧

Note the wording of the alleged offer made in this case: "If this proposal be approved, it is *our intention* to take a lease in the name of The Howard Company Jewelers. . . . Inasmuch as we are now in process of deciding upon our future course of action, it is essential that we have your early advice with respect to the foregoing."

This is a good example of an offer to negotiate, but should not be, and was not construed to be an offer that would mature into a contract if accepted. The terms were too general under the circumstances, as evidenced by the fact that the "acceptance" contained many terms not previously discussed. Thus the decision of the court, "From all circumstances it seems reasonably clear that both parties considered that many terms remained to be agreed upon despite the fact that the basic terms, the length of the lease and the amount of the rent, had been definitely settled. It is common experience that the lease of a valuable piece of property such as this is never based solely upon the length of the term or rental alone. . . ."

In determining the apparent intent of the parties, regard must be given to the usual commercial practices pertinent to a particular type of contract. Some types of contract are entered into much more casually than others. It happens that leases for commercial properties are usually entered into after detailed, cautious negotiation. This does not mean that parties could not agree on a detailed lease after a two-minute chat. It merely means that if their intent is later subject to dispute, the fact that parties do not usually do this is likely to enter into consideration. This illustrates one form of interaction between common practice and the law.

QUESTION

1. When parties intend to employ a formal document such as a lease to reflect their final agreement, is it not almost inevitable that the agreement be a two-stage affair? That is, first agreement as to the common objective of reaching a certain type of agreement must be reached, then a detailed agreement as to the precise provisions to control.

Communication of Offer and Acceptance

In order for an offer to be accepted by the offeree it must be communicated to him. To cite an example, no contract comes into existence when A advertises a reward for his dog, and B, not having seen the advertisement, returns the dog as a favor. Remember, the first requirement of a contract is an agreement. There cannot be an agreement unless an offer was communicated to the offeree. An acceptance cannot occur except in response to an offer. In our example concerning the dog, B had no intention of accepting an offer, and thus creating a legal obligation when he returned the dog. Merely because he happens to do something that *A* wishes done does not mean that a contract comes into existence. This may seem unfair, but could we live with the rule that every time *X* does something that makes *Y* happy, *Y* is therefore legally bound on a contract?

This does not imply that all the *terms* of the offer must be understood or even communicated to the offeree. For example, where an offeror gives a sales talk to an offeree and then presents a long, detailed contract to the offeree who signs it without reading, a contract usually results.[5] Technically, there may not have been communication of all the terms. What is required, then, is communication of the *fact* of the offer. If the offeree is willing to make a carte blanche acceptance, that is his business. The manifestation of assent controls, not actual assent to all terms.

Though mistakes of interpretation may occur, the question of whether or not there has been communication does not usually present much of a problem when parties are dealing face to face. Confusing situations may arise when the parties are dealing from a distance. Questions are likely to arise as to when an offer, counteroffer, revocation, rejection, and acceptance are effective.

Is a communication effective when it is sent or when it is received? Because parties frequently do not specify their intentions, a set of presumptions has been devised to settle those questions as a matter of law. These presumptions apply only when parties do not specify their intent. If the parties through previous dealings or agreements wish to deal according to rules contrary to those presumed by the law to govern this phase of contracts, they may do so by specifying exactly what their intention is. The apparent intent of the parties is paramount.

To give order to the complicated patterns that may arise when a series of communications are exchanged from a distance, crossing one another, or as sometimes happens, being lost en route, a legal fiction is utilized. According to the fiction, the means used by the offeror to communicate his offer is presumed to be his agent. Accepting this fiction, it follows that if an offer is telegraphed, the telegraph is the offeror's agent. Therefore, when the acceptance is delivered by the offeree to the telegraph office, the offeror's agent has received the acceptance, and a contract arises immediately. Thus an acceptance can be effective and a contract arise prior to notice of acceptance to the offeror. Another result that logically follows is that if the telegram is lost or delayed before delivery to the offeror, a contract exists nevertheless, because the offeror's agent received it. On the other hand, if the offeree decided to answer by another means—private messenger, for example—the offer is not accepted until the message is actually delivered to the offeror. The messenger, of course, is not the offeror's

---

[5] Assuming no actual misrepresentations by the offeror to secure the signature.

agent. If the messenger fails in his duty and never delivers the acceptance, a contract never arises.

As you see, this system of reasoning is a means of determining which party bears the embarrassment and losses arising from a failure of delivery. It also determines the exact time a contract is formed. If a different system were adopted it would not matter greatly. The important thing is that there be a definite, agreed principle by which the outcome of court cases may be made easily predictable by the parties to a dispute. This is a situation in which one of two innocent parties often must suffer a loss. When the law is not able to work perfect justice, the next best thing is to reach consistent results.

Although an acceptance is binding as soon as delivered to the offeror's messenger, this is not true of either a rejection, a counteroffer, or a revocation. These must be actually communicated to the other party before being effective, as, for that matter, the original offer had to be.

An illustration may be in order:

(1)

Offer (mail) 5/2/61	Offer received 5/3/61
Revocation of offer mailed 5/3/61	Offer accepted (mail) 5/4/61
Acceptance received 7/11/61	Revocation received 5/5/61

Here, the revocation is of no effect: a contract came into existence as soon as the acceptance was mailed by the offeree. Date of receipt of the acceptance by the offeror is immaterial when the offeror's "agent" is used by the offeree.

Let us vary the facts.

(2)

Offer (mail) 5/2/61	Offer received 5/3/61
Revocation of offer mailed 5/3/61	Offer accepted (telegraph) 5/4/61
Acceptance received 5/8/61	Revocation received 5/5/61

Here no contract would result. The acceptance, because it was not communicated by the offeror's agent (the mail), would not be effective until received. The revocation terminated the offer prior to the receipt of the acceptance.

This one should be easy:

(3)

Offer (mail) 5/2/61	Offer received 5/3/61
Acceptance received 5/5/61	Offer accepted (telegram) 5/4/61
Rejection received 5/4/61	Offer rejected (telephone) 5/4/61

Because this offer also would not result in a contract until actually received, and because the rejection was received first, the offer would have been terminated (by telephone) before being accepted (by receipt of the telegram). Therefore, no contract.

One last situation, which is perplexing, follows almost the same pattern as above.

(4)

Offer (mail) 5/2/61	Offer received 5/3/61
Acceptance received 5/5/61	Acceptance (mail) 5/4/61
Rejection received 5/4/61	Rejection (telephone) 5/4/61
	(later in day)

Plainly, the acceptance was effective May 4 when the acceptance was mailed and a contract should arise. However, the offeror in this case received the rejection first. If this was a contract by which the offeror was to sell an item of which he had only one—a house, for example—he might easily have sold it to someone else before receiving the acceptance of the offeree. Would it be fair to permit the offeree to insist upon his contract when his own action in sending the rejection led to the offeror's selling? Clearly not. Presumably, in this type of situation the offeror would be permitted to escape from the contract, because he had been misled by the offeree, but if on the other hand he wished to insist on performance and was still in a position to do so, he could.

[EDITOR'S NOTE: (1) Contrast the type of reasoning used in determining whether a purported offer or acceptance was a manifestation of assent to contract, with that used to determine at what time a communication caused a contract to result.

In determining whether or not there was manifestation of assent, there is no guide other than judgment, or, stated differently, common sense. Much the same approach must be used in determining whether or not a person was negligent.

In determining when a communication becomes effective, we have a precise, mechanical test. For example, we start with a rule (an acceptance by the same mode of transmission as the offer is effective immediately), and by applying the rule, we can determine the exact time the contract resulted. No difficult lines need be drawn.

The advantages of a simple, mechanical test of this sort are obvious. Therefore, why do we not use some test of this kind to determine whether a party made manifest his assent or whether a party was guilty of negligence?

(2) The rules relating to communication were adopted before it was possible to stop delivery of material already mailed. In 1913 it first became possible to stop delivery, and in following years some courts reversed their position, on the theory that delivery to the mails was no longer an irrevocable acceptance. In a dissenting opinion in the case of *Dick* v. *United States* (182 F. Supp. 326) Judge Madden stated his support for the traditional rule as follows:

"Some occasion or event must be selected by the law as the one which converts negotiation into contract. The law has, in fact, selected the overt act of delivering an acceptance to the post as that occasion. I think it is a mistake for the court to introduce confusion into a satisfactorily settled legal situation. The court's [meaning the majority from whom Judge Madden is dissenting] decision would mean, quite certainly, that a contractor who had mailed his acceptance of an offer made to him by the Government would still be subject to losing his contract if the Government should, before it receives his letter of acceptance, telephone or telegraph him withdrawing the offer. That has not been the law and I think it should not be."]

Special Modes of Acceptance

If no contrary intention is expressed, a problem involving communications of offer, acceptance, revocation, and rejection will be dealt with as discussed above. However, the offeror may expressly state that other principles shall apply, and proceed to define rules that will decide a controversy, should any arise. The terms to be contained in the offer are strictly the affair of the offeror. The offeror is entitled to include in his offer a provision to the effect: "No contract shall arise until acceptance is received in this office." This is in fact a very good idea on the part of an offeror, because this protects him from the possibility that a contract may be accepted by delivery to the "agent" (the mail, for example) but subsequently lost and thereby bind him to a contract without his even knowing it. An offer may go even further and state that the promises constituting the acceptance shall be deemed binding upon the occurrence of some event.[6] As one illustration, it could be agreed that the acceptance shall become binding when and if a buyer accepts certain goods, as in the case on page 233, or when an executive approves a contract, as in the following case. Observe that in both of these cases the requirement of communication is being voluntarily discarded.[7] If the parties agree that a contract becomes effective upon approval of an executive, the contract is formed at that time.

UNION INTERCHANGE, INC. v. SIEROTA
(Colorado, 1960) 355 P 2d 1089

> *The offeror has the right to prescribe the time, place, form or other condition of acceptance, in which case* the offer can be accepted only in the way prescribed by the offer.

PER CURIAM

The parties are here in the same order as they appeared in the trial court; namely, Union Interchange, Inc., as plaintiff and Simon Sierota as defendant. The action was originally brought by the plaintiff in the Municipal Court of

---

[6] This must not be confused with the unilateral contract, where an act is the performance requested. Here the act merely signifies that he will perform some other acts requested by the offeror.

[7] Some courts disagree, however, and refuse to find a contract without *actual* communication of the acceptance, regardless of the terms of the offer.

the City and County of Denver on March 22, 1957, upon a contract demand by the plaintiff against the defendant in the amount of $187.50. On May 3, 1957, that court entered a judgment of nonsuit on the plaintiff's claim. On May 13, 1957, the plaintiff filed an appeal bond which was approved and appeal taken to the Superior Court of the City and County of Denver.

The matter was there tried on September 10, 1958, to the court. There were no written pleadings in the case.

Exhibit A was offered in evidence by the plaintiff as a contract between the parties to establish the liability of the defendant. This exhibit is an authorization to advertise the defendant's business in the next issues of two publications and an agreement to pay $150 therefor. The instrument contained the following clause: "This agreement shall become effective only when accepted by your office in Los Angeles, California. You (plaintiff) shall notify me (defendant) of such acceptance."

Over defendant's objection Exhibit A was received in evidence.

Witness Renell further testified that payment was overdue and had not been received. The plaintiff thereupon rested.

The defendant testified that a salesman for the plaintiff company had approached him and asked if he wanted to sell his store; that the salesman told the defendant he had a customer for the store and that if he wanted to sell it to sign the paper which is Exhibit A; that defendant signed the paper believing it to be a listing which required him to pay when the plaintiff sold the property.

At the conclusion of the evidence, the court found that the plaintiff had failed to prove a contract between the parties, holding that no acceptance, or notice thereof as required by the contract, had been established.

(1) Ordinarily, in contract law notice of acceptance is not a requisite, but here it was expressly required by the terms of the instrument that the acceptance must be made and that there must be notification of such acceptance.

Illustrative of the law on this matter are the following cases:

Brach v. *Matteson:*
". . . If the offer requires an acceptance to be made in writing, no other form of acceptance can be made. Page on Contracts (2d Ed.) paragraph 185."
Shortridge v. *Ohio:*
" 'Acceptance of an offer is an expression of assent to the terms thereof made by the offeree in a manner requested or authorized by the offeror.' Restatement, Contracts, Vol. 1, Sec. 52, p. 58. Sec. 61 of the same Restatement reads: 'If an offer prescribes the place, time or manner of acceptance its terms in this respect must be complied with in order to create a contract. If an offer merely suggests a permitted place, time or manner of acceptance, another method of acceptance is not precluded.' In *Hunt* v. *Jeffries,* the court said: 'The general rule . . . is stated in Lawson on Contracts, 3d Ed., Section 23, page 38, as follows: "The offeror has the right to prescribe the time, place, form or other condition of acceptance, in which case *the offer can be accepted only in the way prescribed by the offer.*" ' See Williston on Contracts, Rev. Ed., Vol. 1, Sec. 76, p. 218. The text in 17 C.J.S., Contracts, paragraph 42, p. 381, reads in part as follows: 'An offer in writing need not be assented to by signing the offer, but may be accepted orally, unless the offer requires its acceptance to be in writing, in which case it must be thus accepted and a verbal acceptance is insufficient unless it is assented to by the offerer. . . .' "

Barnes Cycle Company v. *Schofield:*
"An instrument in the form of a contract between two parties, signed by one of them and by an agent of the other, with a clause reciting that 'this contract shall not be considered as binding upon the first party until approved in writing by' the second party, is only a proposal to contract, submitted by the party of the first part to the party of the second part."

(2) The trial court was correct in its ruling and the judgment is affirmed. SUTTON, C.J., and HALL and FRANTZ, JJ., concur.

✧

Although there is no limit to the procedures that may be required of an offeree in order for him to accept, one thing is definite: in order to accept, the offeree must adhere to whatever the terms of the offer demand.

QUESTION

1. Why do we not permit a contract to be accepted by any reasonable means indicating acceptance, rather than by requiring strict adherence to the demands of the offeror?

For development somewhat along this line see pages 587–588, UCC section 2–204, 2–206, 2–207.

BELLMORE DRESS COMPANY v. *TANBRO FABRICS CORPORATION* (New York, 1952) 115 NYS 2d 11

> *An offer to contract may be accepted in any way provided by the parties. Here the writings expressly provide how they are to be accepted. Petitioner took in the goods either knowing or charged with knowledge that he was thereby making a contract in the terms set out in the order.*

[EDITOR'S NOTE: This case involves a "battle of the forms," a situation often arising when two firms deal with printed forms containing contradictory provisions, each blandly ignoring the provisions of the other's form.

Here, there could be some question as to who made the offer. Probably the analysis used, however, was that the buyer made an offer, the seller, by using a contradictory form, made a counteroffer, and then we see what happened. See the further discussion of this question after the case following this one.]

Proceeding in the matter of the arbitration of controversies between Bellmore Dress Company, Inc., and Tanbro Fabrics Corporation. A Special Term, ARON STEUER, J., held that a contract existed between the parties.
Order in accordance with opinion.

STEUER, J.

The facts as stated in the petition are that the parties negotiated orally for the purchase by the petitioner, hereinafter called the buyer, of three certain lots of goods from the respondent, hereinafter called the seller. The buyer gave purchase orders for these goods and informed the seller that these would be the only documents it would recognize. Thereafter the seller sent contract forms to the buyer, one for each order. These forms contained the words, prominently printed on their faces:

> This order embodying the terms on the face and on the reverse side hereof is acknowledged to be correct by buyer but it shall become a contract either when signed and delivered by buyer to seller and accepted in writing by Seller or when Buyer or his agent has accepted delivery of the whole or any part of the goods herein described.

These orders were never signed but delivery was accepted. The orders contained clauses providing for arbitration. A dispute having arisen seller served a notice in accord with the arbitration clause. Buyer, by this petition, seeks a stay of the arbitration until a jury has passed on the question of whether there is a contract to arbitrate.

Petitioner states a number of propositions in which confidence is used as a substitute for accuracy. Its position is that the orders being unsigned can not be deemed contracts. This is untrue. An offer to contract may be accepted in any way provided by the parties. Here the writings expressly provide how they are to be accepted. Petitioner took in the goods either knowing or charged with knowledge that he was thereby making a contract in the terms set out in the order.

. . . The motion is denied.

QUESTIONS

1. What should the buyer do if he is not satisfied with the terms of the agreement as set out by the seller's form?

2. Is this contract bilateral, unilateral, or unclassifiable? Is the distinction important?

[EDITOR'S NOTE: Both this and the next case involve questions of arbitration.

Arbitration is a process by which two parties to a dispute refer the issue to a third party or parties for settlement. Labor disputes, for example, are sometimes arbitrated by having the union and management each appoint a representative who together select a third. The three work out a settlement. Labor and management agree in advance to accept whatever agreement the parties reach.

Many fields of business, among them real-estate brokerage and stock brokerage, have established arbitration machinery. Disputes between members of these businesses are usually settled through arbitration rather than through courts of law. Arbitration may in fact be advantageous. In some states, the courts are so crowded that cases may not come to trial for several years. Arbitration is apt to be cheaper; and the arbitrators will probably be more conversant with the particular trade practices and usages involved than the court. However, there is probably more danger of favoritism or pressure upon the arbitrators from very important dealers. The courts are probably more predictable at least as to what evidence will be considered, and as to the criterion by which their decision will be judged. Probably speed is the most important advantage of arbitration.

In older days, when court costs were one source of income to the judge, the law discouraged arbitration. In modern times, the law has encouraged arbitration in order to lighten the load on our courts. Thus, we find in this case and in the next case, the court upholding agreements to arbitrate and decreeing that the parties should proceed with arbitration.]

RULES OF LAW OR LAISSEZ-FAIRE IN COMMERCIAL ARBITRATION [8]

> . . . Do the advocates of arbitration feel, as did the middle age ecclesiastics, that business affairs are too mundane for our courts, or do they feel that the law of business disputes is too far above the level of our judges? Do they want a separate, independent system of self-administered business jurispudence and tribunals? We thought the latter idea was exploded by the venerable Lord Coke. . . . What real function have our courts if it is not to pass on, adjudicate, and assist in the law of commerce and industry?

Self-regulation in industry extends back to the earliest periods of our law. The old merchants' courts practiced the essentials of arbitration, and even before their existence guilds required their members to submit disputes to the guild tribunals before they could go to court. It has been a growing custom of modern trade associations to require their members to submit their disputes to arbitration and since 1920 such requirements have become common. Newly adopted standardized contracts will contain arbitration provisions. Trade associations not compelling arbitration will probably recommend its use.

However, the "arbitration process" contemplated by these various arrangements covers many different types of proceedings, ranging from mediation and compromise to something almost analogous to a legal trial. The courts profess to recognize only the latter as true arbitration. One's view is apt to be tempered by his fundamental conception of the process. Professor Isaacs has pointed out two concepts, one that the arbitrators are judges whose powers are limited by judicial authority, the other that arbitrators are agents whose powers are limited only by the authority given them by the parties to the arbitration. Many conflicting decisions on the process can be thus explained.

[8] Phillip G. Phillips, "Rules of Law or Laissez-Faire in Commercial Arbitration," *Harvard Law Review*, Cambridge, Mass. (1934), **47**, pp. 590–623.

The courts, however, classify arbitrations as common-law and statutory. In the former the rules of the common law, centuries old, govern the proceeding; in the latter, for the moment, we may assume that the proceeding is governed by statutory provisions. At common law an award of arbitrators could be enforced legally only by suit. But no time could be saved by arbitrating if a suit had to be brought on the award, so statutes were early passed by which an award could be enforced by speedy process. In many jurisdictions the award, when filed in court, could automatically be made the basis of a judgment; in others, of a motion to confirm, after which judgment would be entered.

In order to gain the benefits of the statutory method, certain words of art had to be used in the arbitration agreement or certain formalities had to be gone through with. Comply with these formulae, and the "open-sesame" to a statutory process was obtained. In addition to the benefits of speedy enforcement of an award, various statutes provided the arbitrators with powers not possessed by their less fortunate common-law brethren. They could, for example, summon witnesses, obtain depositions, administer oaths, and the like, thus strengthening the arbitration proceeding itself. Of recent years, more and more statutes have made the arbitration agreements complying with the terms of the statutes irrevocable, and under some statutes a clause in a contract providing for the arbitration of disputes thereafter arising will be specifically enforced. Except for their enforcement provisions, however, the modern statutes do not depart from the principles of the older ones. The formulae have disappeared in many states; until now the only requirement that is insisted upon is that the agreement be in writing. Nevertheless, except in one state, it is still said to be possible to have a common-law arbitration, and the proceeding may be considered such in the event that the parties have not used the proper statutory formulae. The use of the statutory process has been stimulated by the fact that most trade associations provide elaborate instructions for their members, so drawn that their proceedings will fall under the statutes, even though a great many enforce arbitration agreements and awards by their own methods of discipline. In some states it is difficult to know what could now be a real common-law arbitration, but the courts are constantly using the distinction, and we must bear it in mind.

At first glance such a distinction would seem to make for simplicity, but such is not the case. The number of statutes pertaining to arbitration seems limited only by the ingenuity of man. Many state constitutions provide for arbitration, though the only practical effect of such provisions seems to have been in the sustaining of the Kentucky Workmen's Compensation Law! It must be recalled that the many modern arbitration statutes are the result of business propaganda. A whole new arbitration statute is passed which repeals "all acts inconsistent therewith." Unfortunately, there is no inconsistency between the old arbitration act and the new one, with the result that in four states there seem to be at least two different methods of statutory arbitration, each complete in itself. Kentucky has had two complete arbitration statutes for many years; Louisiana seems blessed with three and Pennsylvania with at least four, each complete and differing from each other in many ways. In addition, there are in seven states long, complete statutes besides the general arbitration act, providing for arbitration of small claims or claims originally brought in Justices Courts; Georgia has codified its common law regarding arbitration, as well as its statutory law; Delaware has an arbitration act applying to arbitration of an equitable nature, and another for those of a legal one. Besides, many general statutes apply to arbitration situations, and as no arbitration statute is complete on all matters of arbitration and procedure, the rules of the common law must be brought into play even in the arbitrations under statutes. In such a situation, the desirability of "statutory" arbitration becomes a much more doubtful question. It is needless to add that the multiplicity of general arbitration acts has made for confusion in decisions.

In a common-law arbitration nothing could be done to correct errors in law made by an arbitrator. His decision was final, his law unassailable; he was a law unto himself. And today, under a great many statutes, the arbitrator's decision as to matters of law is final. Under other statutes, however, the arbitrators must decide according to law. In England, as a general rule, unless the errors of law appear on the face of the award, it will not be set aside. Under some American statutes not requiring the arbitrators to decide according to law, an error in law appearing on the face of the award may vitiate it, but, on the other hand, some states which require the arbitrators to follow the law will not set aside the award unless the error appears on its face. It is even possible that arbitrators may disregard statutory law, though it is probable that when the statutes lay down law of great public policy they will be required to follow it. Court decisions shed little light on the subject.

In all states, if the parties provide in their arbitration agreement that the arbitrators must decide according to law, the courts will hold the arbitrators to that agreement and will review their law on appeal. But it takes very strong language to achieve that result, and courts do not thus construe an arbitration agreement unless clearly forced to do so. If, however, the arbitrators intend to follow the law, and err in so doing, the court will set aside their award. But up to the time of the courts' thus passing on the award they will not advise the arbitrators of the law. In fact, even if the parties or arbitrators should agree that the courts might do so and request it, they cannot.

The mere fact that there is a lawyer on the arbitration board does not necessitate their following the law; in fact, not even if the lawyer is one of three arbitrators, and has the sole decision on questions of law. There is some intimation, however, that if the arbitrators know the law, and deliberately choose to disregard it, their awards may be set aside. Of course, the presence of counsel at an arbitration will in many ways help the arbitrators follow the law unless the point is obscure and the lawyers help obscure it. There is a conflict of decisions as to whether the arbitrators may exclude counsel from the hearings. Arbitration rules, however, often make provision for the presence or exclusion of counsel, and these will be respected by the courts. Formerly it was common practice to exclude them from the hearings, and older rules frequently so provided. Lawyers, however, were found to be generally the determining factor in deciding whether or not parties would arbitrate, and to place them in a favorable mood towards arbitration, rules allowed them to attend the hearings.

The Commissioners' Arbitration Act provides that none but an attorney may represent a party to an arbitration. Some believe that "presence of counsel fortified with . . . legal maxims and some legal anachronisms" will only confuse the arbitrators, but it is submitted that wise attorneys know better than to thus antagonize lay arbitrators not drawn from the ordinary rank and file as are jurymen. In England it is common to have a legal assessor present to advise the arbitrators regarding points of law. It might be a splendid idea for us to copy; the businessman could still present business facts, and the arbitrator also be informed of the law. Several trade associations in the United States, which do not allow counsel for the parties to appear before arbitrators, have their own counsel, who are unbiased, advise the arbitrators regarding points of law.

Arbitration rules frequently prohibit the use of precedents in arbitration. As a matter of fact, awards are generally not only private, but the arbitrators are encouraged not to give any reasons for their decisions in the award. On the other hand, certain trade associations not only customarily give reasoning in their awards, but publish them in well-indexed and -digested volumes. But how can we build up a unified system of commercial law and practice and code regulation unless they are used? Without them we have a hodgepodge of nothingness, and business is not helped nor arbitration aided by the mistakes or wisdom of others.

But an arbitration clause in a contract can forestall any attempt to learn the actual effect of a disputed point or what the particular arbitrators decide it to be. Until the actual arbitration for each case is held no one will be able to ascertain any disputed rights. Business security demands the alleviation of such a condition, and the substitution of definiteness for the unascertainable, unpredictable, unappealable will of individual arbitrators.

Recall that the often-irrevocable agreement to arbitrate is made, in most instances, far in advance of any controversy, at a time when the parties are unable to foresee the issues which may be involved. The propagandist's argument that if, after a dispute arises, a real question of law presents itself the parties can choose a lawyer as an arbitrator is an admission of weakness. It may be a good sop thrown out to the legal profession, but it is unwanted, and points to a danger in the use of a general arbitration. Do the advocates of arbitration feel, as did the middle age ecclesiastics, that business affairs are too mundane for our courts, or do they feel that the law of business disputes is too far above the level of our judges? Do they want a separate, independent system of self-administered business jurisprudence and tribunals? We thought the latter idea was exploded by the venerable Lord Coke; certainly it would be as wasteful and out-of-date in our fast-moving political philosophy as the utilization of oxen to propel a subway car. In a nation dedicated to improvement by regulation and control of commerce and industry, what real function have our courts if it is not to pass on, adjudicate, and assist in the law of commerce and industry?

Occasional arbitrations are carried on in the offices of attorneys or businessmen wherein there is no agreement between the parties as to exactly how the arbitration is to be conducted, and there may be agreements between parties to arbitrate wherein no method of selecting arbitrators is provided and no manner of determining the place and time for a hearing is set forth. Even the most earnest advocates of arbitration admit that these casual proceedings are unsuccessful. At present it is customary to agree in advance for rules to govern the arbitration, and many trade associations and codes of fair practice provide for arbitration according to definite rules. These rules are a clear index of what businessmen desire in arbitrations; a brief examination of certain points laid down in them ought to shed light on our problem.

It should not be imagined that these rules are like Roberts' Rules of Order, merely laying down a procedural guide to be followed at a hearing. They are rather a combination of Rules of Court and Rules of Law. In many instances they are self-executory, and, for example, in the appointment of arbitrators, if the parties fail to follow the procedure outlined, the trade association administering them will do so on their behalf. Unless contrary to a well-defined rule of law, an agreement to arbitrate according to rules will be respected by the courts, and the rules considered as a vital part of the contract to be followed by the arbitrators, and by the courts in passing on the proceeding, though it is possible that the authority of the trade association to appoint arbitrators, unlike an arbitration agreement, might be revocable in all jurisdictions. Unfortunately, confusion exists in the use of the word "rule." Many general rules and regulations (often known as by-laws) of trade associations provide that all disputes must be arbitrated, or that members must place an arbitration provision in their contracts. In addition, these associations have Arbitration Rules, governing the conduct of the proceeding itself. Unless otherwise indicated, it is the latter type of rule to which we refer.

Many contracts are so drawn that it is difficult to ascertain exactly what procedure the parties intended to apply to the arbitration. Certain trades in New York use a clause providing for arbitration "in the usual manner," and the courts, while condemning such clauses, have held that the rule of a particular trade association would apply if customarily used in the trade. But there must be some mention of arbitration in the contract, and the mere fact that an order blank provides that "all sales be governed by the Rules of the X Association," and it is shown that the Rules among other things provide for arbitration will not be standing alone, suffice to obtain an order compelling arbitration.

It is quite customary for the parties to contract to arbitrate in accordance with rules existing, not at the time of making the contract, but at the time of the dispute. This may become important, for the rules are generally amendable by the arbitration committees of the particular trade association. Interpretation of the rules is generally for the arbitrators, in the first instance, though occasionally the arbitration committee assumes this function. Usually, if the arbitrators are unable to agree on the interpretation of the rules, the arbitration committee acts, and may even determine the procedure in the event that the rules do not cover the particular matter. Quite often the rules lay down standards for their own interpretation, but these are usually of a general nature, high-sounding phrases—advertising slogans, and not legal guides. Expediency has doubtless dictated many of these rules (and rightly, too), but justice and permanency of arbitration demands court control, advice, and check. As pointed out previously, a few rules make provisions for the reference of questions of law to counsel for the trade associations. The British Rules, of course, make provisions for the reference of questions to the courts in a stated case, and in Illinois and Massachusetts special rules have been adopted to facilitate this. No hardship seems thus vested upon the rule makers in states adopting the English procedure.

One is immediately struck in examining the trade association rules by the larger number providing for an appeal after an arbitrator's decision to another board of arbitration. One may doubt whether these provisions can be legally enforced, especially in jurisdictions providing a definite method of enforcing an award. But of what use an appeal unless there is a definite standard of law laid down? Their significance lies in showing that businessmen are not always satisfied with the results of arbitration, and need some appellate review of them. So great is the tendency to appeal that there are provisions forbidding more than one appeal in any particular case.

✧

LEVEL EXPORT CORPORATION v. *WOLZ, AIKEN & COMPANY* (New York, 1953) 111 NE 2d 218

> . . . *When a party to a written contract accepts it as a contract he is bound by the stipulations and conditions expressed in it whether he reads them or not. Ignorance through negligence or inexcusable trustfulness will not relieve a party from his contract obligations.* . . .

LEWIS, J.

Incidental to a commercial transaction between the parties to this proceeding, there has emerged the question, now decisive in this litigation, whether each of the two contracts, which fixed the obligations of the parties, validly incorporated an agreement that "Any controversy arising under, or in relation to, this contract, shall be settled by arbitration."

As to facts: The petitioner-respondent, Level Export Corporation, to which reference will be made as the buyer, is engaged in the purchase and export of a variety of commodities including textiles. On January 22 and February 14, 1951, the buyer executed two written contracts, practically identical in text, by which it agreed to purchase from the respondent-appellant, Wolz, Aiken & Company, hereinafter referred to as the seller, a total quantity of 135,000 yards of leno——a light-weight cotton fabric used in making summer garments. Each of the two agreements contained the names of the parties, the quantity of fabric sold, the delivery dates and the terms of payment. The balance of each contract —covering a substantial portion of the single page upon which the agreement was printed—consists of the following paragraph:

"This Salesnote is subject to the provisions of Standard Cotton Textile Salesnote which, by this reference, *is incorporated as a part of this agreement and together herewith constitutes the entire contract between buyer and seller. No variation therefrom shall be valid unless accepted in writing.* . . ."

The standard cotton textile salesnote which—by the words italicized above —is incorporated by reference in each of the two agreements here involved contains ten subdivisions. . . . The tenth subdivision, relating to "Arbitration," provides as follows: "Any controversy arising under, or in relation to, this contract, shall be settled by arbitration. If the parties are unable to agree respecting time, place, method, or rules of the arbitration, then such arbitration shall be held in the City of New York in accordance with the laws of the State of New York and the rules then obtaining of the General Arbitration Council of the Textile Industry and the parties consent to the jurisdiction of the Supreme Court of said State and further consent that any process or notice of motion or other application to the Court or a Judge thereof may be served outside the State of New York by registered mail or by personal service, provided a reasonable time for appearance is allowed."

When a dispute subsequently arose between the parties with regard to performance under the two purchase agreements, the seller instituted arbitration proceedings in accord with the rules of the General Arbitration Council of the Textile Industry. Thereupon the buyer, when requested to do so, refused to appoint an arbitrator and has thus far successfully opposed arbitration by motion for a stay made at Special Term upon the ground that no agreement to arbitrate exists between the parties. . . .

The buyer admits that it executed the contracts of purchase mentioned above, each of which by its terms incorporates the standard cotton textile salesnote containing the provision upon which is based the seller's demand for arbitration. The ground upon which the buyer resists arbitration, viz., that no arbitration agreement exists between the parties, is stated in the affidavit by the buyer's secretary and treasurer, read in support of its motion in this proceeding, as follows:

"At no time was the petitioner informed in any way that the provisions of the Standard Cotton Textile Salesnote contained any provision requiring arbitration of any controversy between the parties."

"Neither the petitioner nor any of its officers or directors is a member of any association or any textile group; none of us has ever seen the Worth Street Rules; we have never been provided with a copy thereof. Arbitration was mentioned for the first time by the attorneys for the respondent on September 14, 1951, which was several months after the controversy arose. At the time that the petitioner signed the contracts . . . neither the petitioner nor any of its officers or directors was aware of . . ." any provision requiring arbitration under the contracts. . . .

"The petitioner [buyer] did not know, if it is the fact, that by signing the agreements annexed hereto that it had agreed to arbitrate any disputes with respondent. No arbitration clause was ever called to the attention of the petitioner."

The question thus presented is whether the factual allegations contained in the buyer's affidavit, quoted in part above, serve to raise ". . . a substantial issue as to the making of the contract," thereby entitling the buyer to a stay of arbitration. . . . That question is one of law. . . .

Mindful that "No one is under duty to resort to arbitration unless by clear language he has so agreed," . . . we are unable to find in the record legal justification for the buyer's present claim that it is not obligated, by each of the purchase agreements to which it was a party, to arbitrate the disputes which have arisen in the course of performance of those agreements. Each of those contracts contains the statement that it is made "subject to the provisions of Standard Cotton Textile Salesnote" which, as we have seen, was expressly ". . . incorporated as a part of this agreement and together herewith constitutes the entire contract between buyer and seller." Difficult it would be to find words more clearly to express the contractual intent of the parties. There is no evidence that an attempt was made to limit the application of the standard cotton textile salesnote; nor was there indication that any one of the ten subdivisions of salesnote was not intended to apply. Indeed, a contrary intention is indicated by the sentence which immediately follows the contract provision last quoted above: "No variation therefrom shall be valid unless accepted in writing."

The effect of the foregoing contract provisions was to adopt, and to integrate into each purchase agreement, the terms of the standard cotton textile salesnote. Among those provisions is the tenth subdivision, bearing the caption "Arbitration," beneath which is the printed statement "Any controversy arising under, or in relation to, this contract, shall be settled by arbitration," followed by procedural provisions in the event arbitration should become necessary.

In view of the documents to which reference has been made—which, when integrated, form the contracts executed by buyer and seller . . . we regard the buyer's contention—that no contract to arbitrate exists between the parties—as being at variance with the plain language of its agreements.

There is no allegation by the buyer of misrepresentation by the seller either with respect to the effect of the two purchase agreements, or with respect to provisions of the standard cotton textile salesnote. Nor does the buyer claim to have been innocently misled by words or conduct of the seller which indicated that disputes between the contracting parties would be settled by means other than by arbitration. The buyer's sole contention is that through its own ignorance of the provisions contained in the standard cotton textile salesnote it failed to understand the significance and effect of those provisions of the purchase contracts to which reference has been made. Upon that phase of the case we note in the record a statement by an officer of the buyer that the business of that corporation ". . . consists of the purchase of commodities and their export to customers throughout the world" and that the commodities purchased and exported comprise a wide variety of items including textiles. In those circumstances we may assume that the buyer—an exporter of wide experience—dealt with the seller with knowledge that the provisions of the purchase agreements here involved were to have legal effect and were thus enforceable.

. . . this court had occasion to state the rule which we believe to be applicable to the present case: ". . . when a party to a written contract accepts it as a contract he is bound by the stipulations and conditions expressed in it whether he reads them or not. Ignorance through negligence or inexcusable trustfulness will not relieve a party from his contract obligations. He who signs or accepts a written contract, in the absence of fraud or other wrongful act on the part of another contracting party, is conclusively presumed to know its contents and to assent to them, and there can be no evidence for the jury as to his understanding of its terms." . . .

Our examination of the present record leads us to conclude that it does not raise a "substantial issue" as to the making of the two purchase agreements in suit so as to avoid their legal consequences. . . .

Accordingly, the orders should be reversed and the matter remitted to Special Term for further proceedings not inconsistent with this opinion, with costs to appellant in all courts.

✧

The terms of the offer were contained on a printed form provided by the seller. The dispute is over the following term: "This salesnote is subject to the provisions of Standard Cotton Textile Salesnote which, by this reference, is incorporated as a part of this agreement and together herewith constitutes the entire contract between buyer and seller. No variation therefrom shall be valid unless accepted in writing."

This paragraph means that the terms of still another document (Standard Cotton Textile Salesnote) are included in the contract of the parties. The provision regarding arbitration, which the buyer claims does not bind him, was a part of the Standard Cotton Textile Salesnote, and therefore was incorporated into the contract by reference.

The above being true, the case may be reduced to the proposition that a party apparently agreeing to a contract is bound by its terms. If he did not understand the reference to the Standard Cotton Textile Salesnote, he should have inquired before signing.

This case is included at this time to illustrate other possibilities for disagreement as to whether or not a binding acceptance has been made. It might have been included in the later section on unilateral mistake, for that is one aspect of the issue.

The underlying issue here is the same as in the first case in this section: What does the intent of the party appear to be? If commerce is to function at all, we must assume that people who read and sign a contract intend to be bound by its terms. The policy being implemented is simply commercial expediency.

[EDITOR'S NOTE: The preceding discussion probably reflects the most widely accepted view concerning the role of contracts in business. Recent studies appear to contradict this view to some extent. (See the following reading.) Results of that study seem to indicate that at least in some areas of business, agreements are thought of in terms of "orders" rather than of "contracts," with orders presumably being subject to cancellation by either party. Further, despite the fact that these orders are usually in the form of legally enforceable contracts, a party who actually resorts to the courts to enforce such an "order" is apt to be thought of as unsporting, to say the least. Statistics on the type of cases (cited in the following reading but not reproduced here) appealed in Federal Courts suggest that contract disputes do not result in much litigation.

Possibly the importance of binding contractual agreements to businessmen is understated in the article under question owing to the nature of the concerns under study. (The contracts under study were mainly between large concerns and their suppliers.) Any concern that deals mainly with one or only a few major customers is not apt to take too strong a position against these customers. Usually the danger of losing a customer is of greater economic significance than the possibility of a loss on a particular transaction. In many areas of business, contracts are probably enforced more rigidly. Insurance, real-estate transactions, and retail sales appear to be areas of business in which the ultimate legal rights of the parties tend to loom rather large.

However, it may be, as suggested by Evan (page 247), that patterns of business dealings are changing and that changes in the law of contracts may be expected in time to follow. In fact, some changes in the law of sales under the Uniform Commercial Code appear to follow the patterns of businessmen as described by Macaulay in the following reading.]

NON-CONTRACTUAL RELATIONS IN BUSINESS [9]

> . . . *The purchasing agent would use his company's form with its 24 paragraphs printed on the back. . . . However, the seller may fail to read the buyer's 24 paragraphs of fine print, and may accept (on his own form). . . . Typically this form will have ten to 50 paragraphs favoring the seller. . . . This practice . . . is called the "battle of the forms."*

Most larger companies, and many smaller ones, attempt to plan carefully and completely. Important transactions not in the ordinary course of business are handled by a detailed contract. For example, recently the Empire State Building was sold for $65 million. More than 100 attorneys, representing 34 parties, produced a 400-page contract. Another example is found in the agreement of a major rubber company in the United States to give technical assistance to a Japanese firm. Several million dollars were involved and the contract consisted of 88 provisions on 17 pages. The 12 house counsel—lawyers who work for one corporation rather than many clients—interviewed said that all but the smallest businesses carefully planned most transactions of any significance. Corporations have procedures so that particular types of exchanges will be reviewed by their legal and financial departments.

More routine transactions commonly are handled by what can be called standardized planning. A firm will have a set of terms and conditions for purchases, sales, or both printed on the business documents used in these exchanges. Thus the things to be sold and the price may be planned particularly for each transaction, but standard provisions will further elaborate the performances and cover the other subjects of planning. Typically, these terms and conditions are lengthy and printed in small type on the back of the forms. For example, 24 paragraphs in eight point type are printed on the back of the purchase order form used by the Allis-Chalmers Manufacturing Company. The

[9] Stewart Macaulay, *American Sociological Review,* Rochester, N.Y., 28:1 (February 1963), pp. 56–61.

provisions: (1) describe, in part, the performance required, e.g., "Do Not Weld Castings Without Our Consent"; (2) plan for the effect of contingencies, e.g., ". . . in the event the Seller suffers delay in performance due to an act of God, war, act of the Government, priorities or allocations, act of the Buyer, fire, flood, strike, sabotage, or other causes beyond Seller's control, the time of completion shall be extended a period of time equal to the period of such delay if the Seller gives the Buyer notice in writing of the cause of any such delay within a reasonable time after the beginning thereof"; (3) plan for the effect of defective performances, e.g., "The buyer, without waiving any other legal rights, reserves the right to cancel without charge or to postpone deliveries of any of the articles covered by this order which are not shipped in time reasonably to meet said agreed dates"; (4) plan for a legal sanction, e.g., the clause "without waiving any other legal rights," in the example just given.

In larger firms such "boiler plate" provisions are drafted by the house counsel or the firm's outside lawyer. In smaller firms such provisions may be drafted by the industry trade association, may be copied from a competitor, or may be found on forms purchased from a printer. In any event, salesmen and purchasing agents, the operating personnel, typically are unaware of what is said in the fine print on the back of the forms they use. Yet often the normal business patterns will give effect to this standardized planning. For example, purchasing agents may have to use a purchase order form so that all transactions receive a number under the firm's accounting system. Thus, the required accounting record will carry the necessary planning of the exchange relationship printed on its reverse side. If the seller does not object to this planning and accepts the order, the buyer's "fine print" will control. If the seller does object, differences can be settled by negotiation.

Businessmen often prefer to rely on 'a man's word' in a brief letter, a handshake, or 'common honesty and decency'—even when the transaction involves exposure to serious risks. Seven lawyers from law firms with business practices were interviewed. Five thought that businessmen often entered contracts with only a minimal degree of advanced planning. They complained that businessmen desire to 'keep it simple and avoid red tape' even where large amounts of money and significant risks are involved. One stated that he was 'sick of being told, "We can trust old Max," when the problem is not one of honesty but one of reaching an agreement that both sides understand.' Another said that businessmen when bargaining often talk only in pleasant generalities, think they have a contract, but fail to reach agreement on any of the hard, unpleasant questions until forced to do so by a lawyer. . . .

Moreover, standardized planning can break down. In the example of such planning previously given, it was assumed that the purchasing agent would use his company's form with its 24 paragraphs printed on the back and that the seller would accept this or object to any provisions he did not like. However, the seller may fail to read the buyer's 24 paragraphs of fine print and may accept the buyer's order on the seller's own acknowledgment-of-order form. Typically this form will have ten to 50 paragraphs favoring the seller, and these provisions are likely to be different from or inconsistent with the buyer's provisions. The seller's acknowledgment form may be received by the buyer and checked by a clerk. She will read the face of the acknowledgement but not the fine print on the back of it because she has neither the time nor ability to analyze the small print on the 100 to 500 forms she must review each day. The face of the acknowledgement—where the goods and the price are specified—is likely to correspond with the face of the purchase order. If it does, the two forms are filed away. At this point, both buyer and seller are likely to assume they have planned an exchange and made a contract. Yet they have done neither, as they are in disagreement about all that appears on the back of their forms. This practice is common enough to have a name. Law teachers call it "the battle of the forms."

Ten of the 12 purchasing agents interviewed said that frequently the provisions on the back of their purchase order and those on the back of a supplier's acknowledgment would differ or be inconsistent. Yet they would assume that the purchase was complete without further action unless one of the supplier's provisions was really objectionable. Moreover, only occasionally would they bother to read the fine print on the back of suppliers' forms. . . .

A large manufacturer of packaging materials audited its records to determine how often it had failed to agree on terms and conditions with its customers or had failed to create legally binding contracts. Such failures cause a risk of loss to this firm since the packaging is printed with the customer's design and cannot be salvaged once this is done. The orders for five days in four different years were reviewed. The percentages of orders where no agreement on terms and conditions was reached or no contract was formed were as follows:

1953	75.0%
1954	69.4%
1955	71.5%
1956	59.5%

It is likely that businessmen pay more attention to describing the performances in an exchange than to planning for contingencies or defective performances or to obtaining legal enforceability of their contracts. Even when a purchase order and acknowledgment have conflicting provisions printed on the back, almost always the buyer and seller will be in agreement on what is to be sold and how much is to be paid for it. The lawyers who said businessmen often commit their firms to significant exchanges too casually stated that the performances would be defined in the brief letter or telephone call; the lawyers objected that nothing else would be covered. Moreover, it is likely that businessmen are least concerned about planning their transactions so that they are legally enforceable contracts.

Business exchanges in non-speculative areas are usually adjusted without dispute. Under the law of contracts, if B orders 1,000 widgets from S at $1.00 each, B must take all 1,000 widgets or be in breach of contract and liable to pay S his expenses up to the time of the breach plus his lost anticipated profit. Yet all ten of the purchasing agents asked about cancellation of orders once placed indicated that they expected to be able to cancel orders freely, subject to only an obligation to pay for the seller's major expenses, such as scrapped steel. (See the case studies on cancellation of contracts in *Harvard Business Review*, 2 (1923–24), pages 238–240, 367–370, 496–502.) All 17 sales personnel asked reported that they often had to accept cancellation. One said, "You can't ask a man to eat paper [the firm's product] when he has no use for it." A lawyer with many large industrial clients said, "Often businessmen do not feel they have 'a contract'—rather they have 'an order.' They speak of 'cancelling the order' rather than 'breaching our contract.' When I began practice I referred to order cancellations as breaches of contract, but my clients objected since they do not think of cancellation as wrong. Most clients, in heavy industry at least, believe that there is a right to cancel as part of the buyer-seller relationship. There is a widespread attitude that one can back out of any deal within some very vague limits. Lawyers are often surprised by this attitude."

COMMENT ON MACAULAY [10]

> . . . *Mercantilists and early entrepreneurs . . . [developed an] elaborate system of law [which their] . . . modern-day successors . . . find it convenient to disregard. . . .*

Historically, it is noteworthy that as mercantilists and early entrepreneurs came into conflict with one another they gradually developed a body of law in England called the "law merchant." This body of private self-regulatory law was eventually incorporated into the common law of England and subsequently into the common law of the United States. After giving rise to this elaborate system of law, the modern-day successors to mercantilists and entrepreneurs—as Macaulay has discovered—often find it convenient to disregard the labors of their predecessors in going about their daily transactions. Will some of the non-contractual norms that are evolving as part of the "occupational morality" of businessmen lay the groundwork for a new body of law for the regulation of business?

[10] William M. Evan, "Comment" (on a paper entitled "Non-Contractual Relations in Business" by Stewart Macaulay, presented at the annual meetings of the American Sociological Association, August, 1962, in Washington, D.C.), *American Sociological Review*, 28:1 (February 1963), p. 69.

CHAPTER SIXTEEN

Formation of the Sales Contract under the Uniform Commercial Code

A contract for sale of goods may be made in any manner sufficient to show agreement, including conduct by both parties which recognizes the existence of such a contract.

Definitions

UNDER the Uniform Commercial Code (hereafter referred to as the UCC) a sale is defined as follows:

> UCC—SECTION 2–106 (1): A "sale" consists in the passing of title (of goods) from the seller to the buyer for a price.
>
> UCC—SECTION 2–105 (1): "Goods" are defined as all moveables except things in action and money, but specifically including the unborn young of animals and growing crops, and objects to be severed from realty.

The price referred to in the definition of the sale need not be money, but may be anything of value including other personal property or even real property (both discussed earlier, page 86). In other words, under the UCC, a trade is a sale. Any transfer of title to tangible, personal, property in exchange for something of value, money or otherwise, is a sale under the act.

In the usual context, title refers to ownership rights, and one should most emphatically not think of title solely in terms of a formal written document. When one buys a pack of gum, the title to the gum passes; that is, the ownership rights pass, and because money has been given in exchange for the title, the transaction was a sale.

From the definition quoted above, it should be apparent that the word *sale* is not synonomous with *contract*. *Sale* refers to the instant in time when title passed. The contract of sale is the preceding set of arrangements that determined which goods will be exchanged for what price. Of course, in the instance of buying a pack of gum, the contract and the sale are simultaneous. In many if not most instances, however, the arrangement —that is, the contract of sale—comes first; then some time later the actual sale occurs. As defined in the UCC the distinction is as follows:

UCC—SECTION 2–106 (1): "Contract for sale" includes both a present sale of goods and a contract to sell goods at a future time. . . . A "present sale" [as in the case of the gum] means a sale which is accomplished by the making of a contract.

Formation of a Sales Contract

One or two things must be said about the purpose of the UCC in general and of the section on sales in particular. The UCC was drawn primarily for the purpose of regulating the transactions of merchants. However, sales between nonmerchants will also be determined according to the provisions of the UCC. The problems, the manner of doing business, the particular trade practices of merchants, and their needs were carefully considered in drawing up the act. As we will see, the most outstanding feature of the rules governing offer and acceptance is the ease and informality with which such contracts may be made. Great flexibility is permitted in the formation of sales contracts. Apparently, the sentiment among merchants, as found by the framers of the UCC, was in favor of reducing formal requirements and of increasing the ease in which a legally binding agreement may be formed.

We may as well begin with the UCC definition of *merchant,* because certain sections are restricted to merchants in their application.

UCC—SECTION 2–104: Definitions: "Merchant"; "Between Merchants"; . . .

(1) "Merchant" means a person who deals in goods of the kind or otherwise by his occupation holds himself out as having knowledge or skill peculiar to the practices or goods involved in the transaction or to whom

such knowledge or skill may be attributed by his employment of an
agent or broker or other intermediary who by his occupation holds himself out as having such knowledge or skill.
(3) "Between merchants" means in any transaction with respect to
which both parties are chargeable with the knowledge or skill of merchants.

Turning again to the UCC on sales:

UCC—SECTION 2–204: Formation in General.
(1) A contract for sale of goods may be made in any manner sufficient
to show agreement, including conduct by both parties which recognizes
the existence of such a contract.

A sales contract will result from an apparent agreement of the parties
whether expressed by the parties or implied from the conduct of the parties. The fact of the UCC stating that conduct may indicate agreement is
not really a departure from the general law of contracts (see *Piazza Paving
v. Bebek and Brkich,* page 204). But at least this provision of the act
serves to remind merchants that their conduct alone may bind them in
contract.
    The question of conduct also appears in other sections of the UCC.

UCC—SECTION 2–207 (3): Additional Terms in Acceptance or Confirmation.
(3) Conduct by both parties which recognizes the existence of a contract is sufficient to establish a contract for sale *although the writings of
the parties do not otherwise establish a contract.* In such a case the terms
of the particular contract consist of those terms on which the writings
of the parties agree, together with any supplementary terms incorporated
under any other provisions of this act.

    By this section, legal defects in the offer and acceptance clearly were
cured by subsequent *conduct* of the parties. In a situation where two parties have exchanged communications over a period of time without arriving
at a position where the writings alone would demonstrate a contract, there
still might be a contract under the UCC. The written communications may
have been supplemented by acts of the parties.
    Moreover, inconsistent as this may seem, the exact time at which a con-
tract was legally formed need not be clear or even ascertainable. If a course
of conduct between the parties gradually led to a relationship that clearly

indicates a contract, exactly when the agreement first came about is immaterial to the question of the validity of the contract. This follows from
2–204 of the UCC:

> UCC—SECTION 2–204: Formation in General.
> (2) An agreement sufficient to constitute a contract for sale may be
> found even though the moment of its making is undetermined.

So far as the physical means of communicating an acceptance is concerned, the rule under the UCC is identical with the general law of contracts. (Remember, any reasonable means of communication is acceptable
at contract law; however, by adopting the offeror's method, an acceptance
is usually made immediately upon receipt by the communicating agent.)

> UCC—SECTION 2–206:
> (1) Unless otherwise unambiguously indicated by the language or
> circumstances (a) an offer to make a contract shall be construed as in-
> viting acceptance in any manner and by any medium reasonable in the
> circumstances. . . .

In contract law an offer is normally construed to be a promise contingent
upon the offeree's promising something that has in turn been requested by
the offeror. This describes the offer for an ordinary bilateral contract. It is
also possible to make an offer with the acceptance depending upon actual
performance rather than a mere return promise, this arrangement being a
unilateral contract. In cases of doubt, the presumption has been that a contract is bilateral rather than unilateral. *The UCC practically obliterates the
difference,* with the following language:

> UCC—SECTION 2–206:
> (1) (b) an order or other offer to buy goods for prompt or current ship-
> ment shall be construed as inviting acceptance *either* by a prompt prom-
> ise to ship *or* by the prompt or current shipment of . . . goods. . . .

This section means not only that an offer in bilateral form may be accepted by the shipment of goods instead of by return promise (there was
prior authority that this would be the case) but much more revolutionary,
an offer in unilateral form may be accepted by a promise to deliver! This
might actually defeat the intent of a party making an order in some instances, but at the same time aids the party filling an order placed in uni-

lateral form. By communicating an acceptance to such an order, the party wishing to fill the order is protected from irresponsible revocation by the offeror.

UCC—SECTION 2–206:

(2) Where the beginning of a requested performance is a reasonable mode of acceptance an offeror who is not notified of acceptance within a reasonable time may treat the offer as having lapsed before acceptance.

So, not only may a party to whom an offer is made in unilateral form accept by merely communicating his acceptance, in fact, he had better do so. Or at least he had better notify the offeror that he has undertaken the performance, because under this provision if the offeree does nothing more than undertake to perform, the offeror who has received no notice is entitled to treat his offer as lapsed. Apparently, the offeror need not even give notice of revocation in order to terminate the offer, under these circumstances. Notice is not generally necessary to terminate an offer when the offer is terminated by the expenditure of a reasonable period of time.

Terms of Acceptance or Confirmation

Where under the common law of contracts an offer results when, and only when, it is met by an unqualified acceptance, even this rule has been liberalized. Under the UCC, an acceptance is effective even though it *does* state new or different terms than were contained in the offer. Exactly what effect the new and different terms will have becomes a rather complicated question. Let us examine this portion of the act:

UCC—SECTION 2–207:

(1) A definite and reasonable expression of acceptance or a written confirmation which is set within a reasonable time operates as an acceptance *even though it states terms additional to or different from those offered or agreed upon,* unless acceptance is *expressly made conditional* on assent to the additional or different terms.

(2) The additional terms are to be construed as proposals for addition to the contract. Between merchants such terms become part of the contract unless:

(a) the offer expressly limits acceptance to the terms of the offer;

(b) they materially alter it; or

(c) notification of objection to them has already been given or is given within a reasonable time after notice of them is received.

Thus, if the transaction is between merchants, the additional terms become a part of the contract, unless the original offeror gives reasonable notification that the additional terms are not acceptable. In effect, traditional contract law regarding the presumption of the offeror's intent is reversed under this provision of the UCC. In ordinary contracts, any actual departure from the terms of the offeree's acceptance has been presumed to be a counteroffer and hence a rejection. For a contract to result, the offeror would have to communicate his acceptance to the new or different terms. Under the UCC, new or different terms added by the offeree are presumed accepted by the offeror unless he specifically rejects them.

These generalizations have their qualifications. First, if the variations *materially* alter the contract, the reply will be considered as a rejection (2b). What is or is not material is simply a question of judgment. Second, in 2a we find that if the "offer expressly limits acceptance to the terms of the offer" additional terms elaborating upon an acceptance will not be binding. Phrases limiting the terms of the acceptance to the offer will no doubt find their way into the order blanks and other commercial forms of many business concerns, in order to take advantage of this provision.

Section 2–207 (3) makes clear, if it was not clear before, that a formal written contract is by no means essential to create a contract for sale, and gives some standards by which informal contracts will be interpreted:

UCC—SECTION 2–207: Additional Terms in Acceptance or Confirmation. (3) Conduct by both parties which recognizes the existence of a contract is sufficient to establish a contract for sale although the writings of the parties do not otherwise establish a contract. In such case the terms of the particular contract consist of those terms on which the writings of the parties agree, together with any supplementary terms incorporated under any other provisions of this Act.

The Option

One matter of contract law on which the various jurisdictions have been unable to agree involves the offer that the offeror has agreed to leave open for a specified period of time. An offer of this kind is known as an option. Probably the majority of our jurisdictions permit the offeror to revoke his offer any time prior to acceptance, unless something is promised in return for holding the offer open. The reasoning in support of this position is logical. Strictly speaking, how can a promise be binding unless there is a contract, and how can there be a contract until something is promised in return for holding the offer open? However, some states have made a special exception, making such promises binding in deference to commercial convenience. This matter is expressly covered under the UCC as follows:

UCC—SECTION 2–205: Firm Offers.
An offer by a merchant to buy or sell goods in a signed writing which by its terms gives assurance that it will be held open is not revocable, for lack of consideration, during the time stated or if no time is stated for a reasonable time, but in no event may such period of irrevocability exceed three months; but any such term of assurance on a form supplied by the offeree must be separately signed by the offeror.

The minority position of contract law on this point is adopted under the UCC, with special modifications. Firm offers are binding only between merchants and only for a reasonable period of time with an outside limit of three months. Finally, a promise of this sort can be incorporated on an order form provided by the offeree only if there is a special signature of the offeror acknowledging this part of the agreement. Obviously, this provision is designed to call the offeror's attention to the provision and to avoid his carelessly consenting to a provision for a firm offer when this was not really his intent.

CHAPTER SEVENTEEN

Certainty
of Terms

No arbitrary test may be applied to determine whether or not a contract is certain enough to be enforceable. Short of anticipating every conceivable course of dealings and every conceivable resulting contract, a precise test, applicable to every case, is impossible. Certainty is a matter of degree.

General Background

UNTIL NOW, our primary question has been, did the parties in a course of dealing reach an agreement upon the same thing at the same time? The phrase *certainty of terms* is applied to a set of problems relating to the formation of agreement but which must be distinguished from the question of whether or not the parties did reach an agreement.

When problems relating to certainty are under consideration, the fact that the parties agree to *something* is assumed and is beside the point. Now the question is, were the terms of their contract specific enough to enable a court to define what was meant? Was their agreement definite enough that it could be given effect even if we do know approximately what they meant?

As an extreme case, consider a contract worded as follows: "*A* promises to do a favor for *B*, upon *B*'s agreement to compensate *A*." This could never be enforced because the obligation of neither party could be determined. If the obligation of *A* were stated, and if the nature and amount of *B*'s compensation were stated, the requirements of certainty would then be met.

No arbitrary test may be applied to determine whether or not a contract is certain enough to be enforceable. Short of anticipating every conceivable course of dealings and every conceivable resulting contract, a precise test, applicable to every case, is impossible. Certainty is a matter of degree. However, a number of guides are in use. The maxim "That is certain which may be made certain" is always applied. That is, if reference to any outside source will give the contract a clear meaning, it will be interpreted accordingly. For example, if such outside evidence as trade practice or previous dealings will clarify the meaning of a contract, that evidence will be considered. In addition, many cases stand as precedents to guide the courts and certain patterns have become reasonably clear. For example, a contract will *not* ordinarily be deemed uncertain because of a failure to state *when* a contract should be performed. If no time of performance is stated, the time limit for performance shall be "a reasonable time." If a contract is not performed within what a jury finds to be a reasonable period of time, the party failing to perform may not defend on the ground of uncertainty, and will be held for breach of contract, assuming no other defects in the plaintiff's case. As to the question of *duration* of time, the American jurisdictions are split. By duration is meant the type of situation that arises in an employment contract. A party is employed under some vague term as "permanent employment," but no particular period is set. Shortly thereafter the employee is dismissed without cause. Some American courts refuse enforcement on the ground of uncertainty; others instruct the jury that *permanent* means a reasonably long period of time, and instructs the jury to decide how long *permanent* was intended to mean in the particular case. We note that all courts are willing to let the jury tackle the question "What constitutes a reasonable period of time?" in cases involving *duration of an offer*. There is no reason why they should shy away from essentially the same type of problem, that of deciding duration of performance once a contract is made.

Contracts that are silent as to price involve more difficult problems. If the product being considered is one with an ascertainable, going price—as, for example, items on the commodity market or wholesale items as to which the market price is highly standardized, or securities quoted on an exchange—the going price would ordinarily be controlling and the contract would not fail for lack of certainty.

The treatment of items in a rather vague middle zone appears to vary widely. Contracts for items commonly sold at retail outlets—medium- or low-priced appliances, cars, and other items with a wide market and fairly consistent price structure—seem to be enforced in some jurisdictions, leaving the price to be ascertained by the jury. Other jurisdictions declare these types of contracts unenforceable for lack of certainty because of the failure to state a price.[1]

Contracts for items that clearly do not have a going price—real estate,

---

[1] Much of the inconsistency in treatment of these types of items will probably be cleared up by a widespread adoption of the Uniform Commercial Code.

works of art, antiques, and the like—will fail for uncertainty if the price is omitted. The judge may not impose terms upon which the parties themselves seemingly did not reach agreement.

Although the details of this discussion have centered mainly upon contracts for the purchase of property, the same considerations will control in other types of contract. For example, an employment contract will not fail because of uncertainty if the employee is hired for a job at which there is a reasonably well established going wage rate, as is usually true in the case of hourly workers. Contracts for top executives where no salary is stated would probably fail because the salary variation in the top executive brackets are wide.

The fact that the total amount to be paid under a contract cannot be ascertained at the time a contract is made does not mean a contract will fail. As a simple illustration, a contract to pay a person a dollar an hour to mow a lawn will not fail merely because there is some uncertainty as to how many hours the job will require. Nevertheless, many students are confused by similar situations: suppose a trucking company agrees to buy from a gasoline company all the gas it will need for the coming year at 25 cents a gallon. If gasoline goes up (or down) in price, could either party avoid the contract as being uncertain? The answer is no, because although the total amount to be paid over the year is not certain, that amount can be easily calculated by multiplying the number of gallons actually used by the agreed price.[2]

PULLIAM v. SCHIMPF (Alabama, 1896) 19 So 428

> A contract, void on its face for uncertainty or other cause will not be enforced, and hence will not furnish a cause of action which will support a judgment.

Appeal from circuit court, Mobile county; JAMES T. JONES, J.

Action by Jarrett T. Pulliam against Charles Schimpf for damages for breach of contract. From a judgment for defendant, plaintiff appeals. Affirmed.

The contract sued upon by appellant, Pulliam, as averred in the first count, was that he and appellee (defendant below) agreed to establish and run a shooting gallery in a certain specified building in Mobile, which was then in possession of defendant, the business to be managed and conducted by plaintiff, under which agreement plaintiff was to fix up the room and necessary partitions

---

[2] The question of whether or not there is consideration in this type of contract (there is) is discussed later in the section on consideration (page 321). The possibility that contracts of this sort may be contrary to the Clayton Act is discussed in the section "Business Regulation."

in a manner suitable for a shooting gallery, and to furnish the rifles and targets and other necessary apparatus, and the defendant was to furnish the building, and the net profits arising from said business were to be divided between the plaintiff and defendant. By the terms of the agreement (which was made February 24, 1892) the business was to continue until about the 1st of April, or at least until after Mardi Gras Day; and shortly after Mardi Gras Day, and about the 1st of April, it was agreed between the parties that the business should continue upon the same terms, and under the said agreement, so long as the business paid expenses; and the plaintiff, in addition to what he had already done, was to paper the walls of the room in which the business was carried on. The plaintiff averred performance of the agreement on his part until May 15th, following, when defendant broke it, on his part, by terminating the business, in a manner specified, causing a loss to the plaintiff of profits which he alleges he would have realized from a continuance of the business.

A contract void on its face for uncertainty or other cause will not be enforced, and hence will not furnish a cause of action which will support a judgment. We think there can be no doubt that the contract in the present case is of that character. By its terms the business was to continue so long as the business paid expenses, or was profitable. If the business should, so long, prove either profitable, or merely sufficient to pay expenses, both parties were, if the agreement is valid, bound to keep it going, without limit. The defendant was bound, for a lifetime, to furnish his house for carrying on the business, though he may receive but a farthing of profit as compensation for its use, or though he receive nothing at all, if the business proved sufficient to pay the expenses of its operation. Not only this, but he imposed a perpetual, indefinite restraint upon the alienation or other disposition or use of the house. The plaintiff bound himself for a lifetime, if the business should so long yield enough to pay its expenses, to furnish his guns, etc., and his own personal labor and services, to the carrying on of the business, for which he might receive a bare farthing, or no compensation at all. How was the end of the contract to be ascertained? Let us suppose the parties at a disagreement as to whether the business was profitable, or sufficient to pay expenses, the solution of which was necessary to determine whether it should proceed or be dissolved. The plaintiff, we will say, contends that upon a fair consideration and estimate of the assets and liabilities, and of repairs, replenishments of stock, and other expenses necessary to be incurred, the business is not paying expenses, to say nothing of the loss of his own time and services and use of his property. The defendant contends, upon like considerations, that the business is paying expenses and ought to proceed. Is there a conceivable remedy in a court of justice of the difference, which would be finally determinative of the right to have the business continue for any definite time, or be dissolved? Suppose a resort to equity to dissolve and settle it, and after the law's delays—after the court shall have taken an account of its internal workings, its successes and failures, in order to determine whether or not it was paying expenses at the institution of the suit—it is determined that it was paying expenses, and the bill is consequently dismissed, and thereafter a new disagreement arises every week or month, shall there be as many suits as there are disagreements, until it shall be decided that the business does not pay expenses and may be dissolved? Suppose, pending the first or any subsequent suit, the business in fact ceases to pay expenses; shall it nevertheless continue until a new bill can be filed, and a decree establishing the fact obtained. Then, again, upon what principle shall the court proceed? What is meant by "paying expenses?" Will the dullness of the trade for a day or a week or a month or a year, causing for that time an excess of expense over receipts, which may be compensated by the better success of the following day or week or month or year, terminate the contract? How long must the failure continue? Who, or what court, has the right to fix the limit?

Again, in all human conception, what is the measure of damage for the breach of an agreement like this? The only measure alleged is the loss of anticipated profits. Conceding that past profits are legal criteria by which to judge the future, for or upon what period of time must the future profits be computed? Does the plaintiff, in his declaration or proof, point us to a time certain, or in the remotest degree probable, when the business would have ceased to pay expenses? Shall the court arbitrarily assume that it would have paid expenses, and therefore be entitled to continue, as a going concern, for the residue of the plaintiff's life, and that profits such as the business had earned should be awarded him for the entire period of his life expectancy? His personal services, under the contract, entered largely into his profits. Shall he remain idle the rest of his days, and require the defendant to pay him the value of his services, or shall he utilize his services while he lives, and earn, possibly, more than they would have realized in the shooting business, and make the defendant no allowance therefor? How are these alleged rights, the outgrowth of such indefinite duration and unknown circumstances, to be ascertained upon any sort of practical or tangible basis? The plaintiff's loss, manifestly, rests in the idlest conjecture. In *Erwin* v. *Erwin,* and *Howard* v. *Railroad Company,* we laid down the principle that, when no breach of a contract could be assigned which could be compensated by any criterion of damages to be furnished by the contract itself, the contract is void for uncertainty. That principle is decisive of this case. . . .

Affirmed.

QUESTIONS

1. What steps might have been taken to make this contract certain enough to be enforceable?

2. One problem may appear insurmountable here: How can damages be assessed in the event of a breach, even if all of the other terms are made sufficiently certain?

Actually, parties may agree in advance what damages shall be in the event of a breach. A provision in a contract specifying the amount of damages is termed *liquidated damages*. This type of provision is enforceable so long as the "liquidated damages" bear some reasonable relationship to the amount of money damage that would probably be incurred. A liquidated damage provision is not valid if the amount agreed upon is so excessive as to constitute a penalty.

By including a provision for liquidated damages, the uncertainty regarding the amount of recovery could have been resolved.

NATIONAL AIRLINES v. PORT OF NEW YORK AUTHORITY (New York, 1955) 142 NYS 2d 518

> An agreement to agree in the future upon vital and essential terms is, in law, no agreement at all.

[EDITOR'S NOTE: National Airlines is attempting to secure permanent space in the Permanent Terminal Building, on the ground that the facilities in the temporary building, presently undergoing demolition, are becoming inadequate; even though not yet removed. The part of the case included herein concerns only the question as to whether National Airlines had an enforceable contract right to demand facilities in the Permanent Terminal Building at the present time.]

SCHREIBER, J.

National occupies certain space in the temporary terminal building at Idlewild Airport under a lease from the Authority, dated January 1, 1953, and expiring September 30, 1974. The lease gives National, in addition, the right to common use of the airport and of various facilities. The lease states that it is the Authority's intention to erect a permanent terminal building and related facilities at the airport . . . and it authorized the Authority to terminate the lease "if the Authority tenders to the Airline a Lease Supplement covering the use and occupancy of comparable space in the Permanent Terminal Building." . . . National is, however, given no enforceable right to comparable space, or any space, in the permanent terminal building, when erected, except as a condition of a termination of its lease by the Authority. The closest the lease comes to giving National a right to space in the permanent terminal building, independent of a termination of its lease by the Authority, is the provision in Section 5.02, that on completion of the permanent terminal building the Authority "shall lease . . . and the Airline shall hire . . . such space in Permanent Terminal Building as *may at the time be mutually agreed upon by the parties to this lease (which space need not be comparable space as defined in Section 15.02)* on such terms and conditions (other than rent) which shall be fixed in accordance with Section 5.03 *as may at the time be mutually agreed to by the parties to this lease.*" (Italics supplied) The section continues with a provision that nothing in Section 5.02 shall be construed to limit the Authority's right *"in its sole discretion"* to terminate leases of space in the temporary terminal building by tendering leases of comparable space in the permanent building.

(1, 2) It is thus clear that, except as a condition of termination of its lease by the Port Authority, National is entitled to space in the permanent terminal building only if the Authority and National are able to agree upon the space to be occupied by National and upon the terms and conditions of the lease, other than rent. An agreement to agree in the future upon vital and essential terms is, in law, no agreement at all.

✧

An agreement to agree will not be enforceable as a contract. If the parties can reach a subsequent agreement, thereby clarifying the situation, the contract would then be enforceable. If they cannot, there is no reason why a court should intervene and invent a series of rights and duties to which at least one of the parties had not assented. To do so would be contrary to the purpose of contracts, that purpose being to carry out mutually agreed rights and duties.

QUESTION

1. In what way is this case similar to the First Presbyterian Church case on page 225?

Certainty of Terms in Sales Contracts under the Uniform Commercial Code

CERTAINTY IN FORMATION

UCC—SECTION 2–204: Formation in General.
(3) Even though one or more terms are left open a contract for sale does not fail for indefiniteness if the parties have intended to make a contract and there is a reasonably certain basis for giving an appropriate remedy.

UCC—SECTION 2–311: Cooperation Respecting Performance.
(1) An agreement for sale which is otherwise sufficiently definite (subsection 3 of section 2–204) to be a contract is not made invalid by the fact that it leaves particulars of performance to be specified by one of the parties. Any such specification must be made in good faith and within limits set by commercial reasonableness.

As we have observed when dealing with the question of uncertainty in our study of the general law of contracts, some jurisdictions arrived at a position fairly close to the provisions of the UCC, at least as to some patterns involving uncertainty. Nevertheless, by prescribing "a reasonably certain basis" as the mode of settlement for all problems of indefiniteness, this subsection will probably insure a greater inclination toward enforcing somewhat indefinite contracts of sale. It may even result in a major shift in policy on the part of jurisdictions hitherto applying a stringent policy concerning enforcement of somewhat uncertain contracts.

The question of price is dealt with at considerable length, as follows:

UCC—SECTION 2–305: Open Price Term.
(1) The parties if they so intend can conclude a contract for sale even though the price is not settled. In such a case the price is a reasonable price at the time for delivery if
(a) nothing is said as to price; or
(b) the price is left to be agreed by the parties and they fail to agree; [3] or
(c) the price is to be fixed in terms of some agreed market or other standard as set or recorded by a third party or agency and it is not so set or recorded.
(2) A price to be fixed by the seller or by the buyer means a price for him to fix in good faith.
(3) When a price left to be fixed otherwise than by agreement of the parties fails to be fixed through fault of one party the other may at his option treat the contract as cancelled or himself fix a reasonable price.
(4) Where, however, the parties intend not to be bound unless the price be fixed or agreed and it is not fixed or agreed there is no contract. In such a case the buyer must return any goods already received or if unable so to do must pay their reasonable value at the time of delivery and the seller must return any portion of the price paid on account.

In summary, under the UCC provisions, failure to state a price in a sales contract usually will not result in a failure of the contract on the basis of uncertainty. The main criterion as to whether a contract should fail because of failure to state a price is the intent of the parties: if they intend to be bound but left the price to be determined later by any of several possible means, a reasonable price will be implied if it is not set otherwise. If they do not as yet intend to be bound and no price is as yet determined, no contract will result.

ABSENCE OF SPECIFIED PLACE OF DELIVERY

The possibility that a contract of sale may fail to state a place of delivery is also dealt with in the UCC as follows:

[3] Note that this provision in effect reverses the present law and makes an agreement to agree enforceable if the parties so intend. However, part four of this section must also be considered when dealing with this question.

UCC—Section 2–308: Absence of Specified Place for Delivery.
Unless otherwise agreed
(a) the place for delivery of goods is the seller's place of business or if he has none his residence; but
(b) in a contract for sale of identified goods which to the knowledge of the parties at the time of contracting are in some other place, that place is the place for their delivery. . . .

UNCERTAINTIES IN DURATION AND TIME OF PERFORMANCE

As one might have anticipated, questions involving time, both as to time of performance and time of duration in the event of a long-term contract, are largely settled by provisions in the UCC.

UCC—Section 2–309: Absence of Specific Time Provisions; Notice of Termination.
(1) The time for shipment or delivery or any other action under a contract if not provided in this Article or agreed upon shall be a reasonable time.
(2) Where the contract provides for successive performances but is indefinite in duration it is valid for a reasonable time but unless otherwise agreed may be terminated at any time by either party.
(3) Termination of a contract by one party except on the happening of an agreed event requires that reasonable notification be received by the other party and an agreement dispensing with notification is invalid if its operation would be unconscionable.

From these provisions it is clear that contracts of sale will not fail for failure of a stated time of performance. A reasonable time will apply if no other provision for time of performance is made.

The provisions in regard to duration of a contract requiring long-term performance do seem somewhat confusing. The gist of the matter seems to be that a contract involving repeated performances (as, for example, a contract with a dairy to deliver milk) will be presumed binding for a reasonable period of time if nothing is said by either party, but may be terminated upon reasonable notice to the other party.

Termination of an offer by the occurrence of an event is theoretically possible, even without notice of the termination, but such a provision would not be effective if working an unfair hardship on the other party. Therefore, it would seem that a provision of this type could not be depended upon by the offeror. It would be better for him to give notice of termination even if a contract states that this is unnecessary.

UNCERTAINTY OF TIME AND PLACE OF PAYMENT

UCC—SECTION 2–310:
   Unless otherwise agreed
   (a) payment is due at the time and place at which the buyer is to receive the goods even though the place of shipment is the place of delivery. . . .

This section would seem to foreclose any uncertainty concerning a question of when and where payment is due.

Is There a Trend Toward Flexibility in the Interpretation of Contracts?

Thus far in the study of contracts, we have seen little evidence of dispute among legal authorities as to the aims of contract law. Few questions of morality or of political or social values are involved in formulating rules to govern offer and acceptance. The law governing the mechanics of entering a contract does not usually promote heated dispute as to what is right and what is wrong. Mainly, what is required is utility—that is, rules that are clear enough to permit the outcome of a case to be predicted. When this is true, cases may usually be resolved without the necessity of litigation.

The purpose of contracts is often stated as giving effect to the intent of the parties. This, of course, refers to the intent at the time the contract was made. (Presumably, if a contract has become the subject of dispute, either the intent of one or both of the parties has changed, or there was a misunderstanding between the parties when the contract was formed.) It seems reasonable to assume that by increasing formal requirements, the number of contract disputes would tend to decrease. To the extent that a contract is written, adheres to standard form, uses words and phrases with well-understood legal meanings, and in general follows patterns that are well established and traditional in legal documents, then the greater the likelihood that the parties will understand each other, and the greater the likelihood that a court will be able to divine the original meaning of the parties.

In summary, the practical interests of promoting certainty and predictability, and thereby of facilitating ease of decision by a court, would militate toward the same end—an emphasis on adherence to formal requirements in the formation of contracts.

On the other hand, businessmen and others who contract frequently, feel the need for a high degree of flexibility, permitting them to make contracts expeditiously and simply. Perhaps reviving the formal requirement of placing sealing wax on a document, as was done in bygone days, would provide indisputable evidence that legal relations were intended, but how many businessmen wish to carry sealing wax wherever they go? Businessmen wish to be free to give effect to their intent with a minimum of bothersome technical requirements.

The interests of certainty and predictability are promoted by imposing formal requirements, but those of flexibility and speed are advanced by eliminating formal requirements. These interests are in conflict. What seems to be the trend in deciding between these alternatives?

In order to form the agreement, the law is most flexible and is becoming more so. All that is required is to have the promise requested by the offeror accepted in the same terms by the offeree. No particular formalities, such as standard wording, witnessing, or sealing, are required in the ordinary contract. As a result, occasionally disputes arise as to whether there was an intent to contract or merely to negotiate. This type of misunderstanding could be avoided by relying on formal requirements, but the interest of flexibility has won out in this case. The ability to make contracts on the spur of the moment, without being reduced to writing or any other formalities, has evidently been deemed the more important of the two interests and has seemingly prevailed.[4]

When parties are communicating from a distance, a set of mechanical, highly certain rules determine whether offers and acceptances, or subsequent revocations and rejections, will be effective. Nevertheless, this arbitrary and workable set of rules does not encroach too much upon the interest of flexibility. If the parties make their intent known, their intent will supersede the effect of the usual rules of law, and in fact, even the requirement of communication of acceptance can generally be supplanted by prior agreement.

As to the interpretation of contracts, the trend appears clearly to be toward requiring less and less certainty. As has been noted, the UCC contains a provision that contracts shall not fail for lack of price, presumably resulting from pleas by commercial sources for even greater flexibility and less emphasis on exactitude in contractual dealings. The UCC, in fact, has gone to remarkable lengths in permitting the formation of sales contracts with a minimum of formality. If, as is probably the case, the UCC does reflect the needs and desires of businessmen, it seems clear that the businessman is in favor of less, and not more, formality.

---

[4] Some types of contracts must be in writing, however, and these are dealt with in the section on formalities.

CHAPTER EIGHTEEN

Further Problems in Intent: Mistake, Fraud, Misrepresentation, and Related Problems

. . . When an agreement had been reached, but one party realized that the other entered into the contract because of a mistake, this contract could be rescinded. . . . The case where a false statement of one party causes the false impression presents a more extreme case . . . than . . . where one party was merely aware of an error by the other. . . .

Valid, Void, and Voidable Contracts

DEFINITION

FOR THE PURPOSE of classifying contracts as to the possibility of their enforcement, they are divided into the categories of valid contracts, void contracts, and voidable contracts.

A contract is valid if it is not subject to successful attack by either party. This implies that all the legal requirements of a contract have been met, and if either party seeks to avoid performance, a legal remedy is available to the other. This remedy will usually be damages, assuming a monetary loss may be proved, but sometimes specific performance may be invoked. A valid contract is the usual result when two parties have bargained and apparently arrived at an intended legal agreement.

A void contract lies at the opposite extreme. Technically, the words *void contract* are a contradiction in terms. A void contract is *not* a contract. It is a legal nullity. Therefore, either party may successfully attack the claimed agreement, the understanding, or whatever course of action was claimed as a contract, and neither may enforce it through any means. Despite the semantic inconsistency in using the words *void contract,* they provide a useful label for describing the situation that arises when a contract is claimed but in fact does not exist.

In the following sections, void contracts are most often met when there has been a complete absence of assent on the part of one of the parties to an agreement alleged to exist by the other. This condition might result, for example, when negotiations are completed and formal signing is to take place but one party by trickery substitutes, and acquires a signature on, an entirely different document than the one under discussion. Of course, the resulting "agreement" is void. To be distinguished is the instance where a contract is signed or otherwise accepted because one party, through carelessness, fails to read or comprehend the proposed contract, though it was submitted in good faith by the other party. In the latter case, we ordinarily have a manifestation of assent on which the second party reasonably relied, and therefore a valid contract.

An "agreement" secured through threat of physical harm (duress) also results in a void contract because of the total absence of assent by one party. We will find in later sections that contracts requiring illegal acts, and some cases in which performance was impossible at the time of contracting, because of facts unknown by either of the contracting parties, may also result in void contracts.

Voidable contracts lie in a middle zone between valid and void contracts. They arise in a variety of circumstances in which the assent by one of the parties was present in a general way, yet the party's assent was for some reason incomplete or legally defective. Often the defect in assent arises through a misapprehension created in the mind of one party by some misleading act or omission by the other party. Misrepresentation or concealment relating to a significant term of the contract by the second party, and some forms of mistake on the part of the first party, may sometimes, though not always render a contract voidable. In addition, contracts with those under mental or legal incapacity are usually voidable under the theory that the assent, although not necessarily made under any misapprehension, was nevertheless questionable because of the party's mental or legal defect. Contracts with minors are almost always voidable by the minor.

Because the agreement to which assent was manifested corresponded to the actual agreement in a general way, or was with a person having some degree of contractual capacity, the party who was misled or under a disability may rely upon the contract if he so desires, and if necessary may bring suit to enforce it. However, because of the defect either in the assent or in the party's capacity to assent, he may declare the agreement void, if he so desires. In that event the other party may not enforce the agreement.

EXECUTED CONTRACTS AND EXECUTORY CONTRACTS

One other classification of contracts must be introduced at this time. There are important differences in legal effect between contracts in which the promises have actually been performed and those in which performance is still pending in some degree. Therefore, labels have been provided to designate the current state of a contract in this respect. Contracts that have been performed on both sides are termed *executed contracts*. Contracts that have not been performed, or have been only partially performed on one or both sides, are termed *executory contracts*. Many contracts are designed to be executed quickly, as in the sale of a specific article of personal property, whereas others are designed to run for long periods of time, perhaps indefinitely, as executory contracts. An example of the latter might be a contract between a manufacturer and a seller of the *manufacturer's* goods operating under an exclusive franchise. A contract of this type would anticipate regular sales of merchandise from manufacturer to seller over a period of years. The agreement could be perpetually executory—that is, not providing for any termination date. Naturally, the problems arising under this type of contract tend to be different from those involving one transaction.

RESCISSION AND WAIVER AND THEIR SIGNIFICANCE TO VOIDABLE CONTRACTS

When a party enters into a contract and subsequently discovers that he may be entitled to avoid it for some reason, he is faced with certain options. One option is simply to proceed with the performance according to the terms of the agreement. In that case, assuming the contract to be voidable and not void, he may demand that the opposite party perform, and may take legal action if the opposite party does not. If the contract is void, of course, neither party may secure performance.

However, if he is dissatisfied with the contract, he will probably seek means to avoid performance. One possibility in this event is to refuse to perform, and if the opposite party brings suit for damages, he may defend on the ground that the contract is voidable: he would have to present the legal basis for his allegation that the contract is voidable—that is, fraud, misrepresentation, and so on, and the particular facts supporting this defense. In the case of many wholly executory contracts this approach may be satisfactory. However, if the contract is executed, or if it is partly executory, he is faced with the necessity of undoing something that is already to some extent done, and the flat refusal to perform further is not a satisfactory means of adjusting the rights of the parties.

In this situation, the usual remedy for the party seeking to avoid a contract is to bring suit requesting the equitable remedy of rescission. A decree by a court granting rescission cancels a contract—that is, it has the effect of completely abrogating the contract, retroactively. Each party is restored to his position before the contract was made. Not only is this remedy often relied upon in cases of executed and partly executory contracts, but it is also useful in avoiding contracts wholly executory. The reason is that it permits the wronged party to seek an early adjudication of his obligations under a doubtful contract. If he were required to wait until the other party brought suit, the affairs of the party wishing to repudiate the contract might be seriously confused by his not knowing whether or not he would be held to the contract.

A party should, in fact, act promptly to rescind because there is some danger that the right to rescission may be lost to a party through the operation of waiver. *Waiver* is defined as "the intentional or voluntary relinquishment of a known right; or such conduct as warrants an inference of the relinquishment of such right. . . ." [1] In general, when a party discovers, or should as a reasonable man discover, that he has grounds for avoiding a contract but takes no steps to do so, he may find that he has waived his rights to avoid it. This is especially likely when the other party has himself continued to perform in some material way.

It should be mentioned at this point that waiver is a very broad concept and has applications in many areas of the law. In criminal law, for example, a defendant may waive the right to a preliminary hearing or to an extradition proceeding. Waiver is superficially related to estoppel (considered later in the text—see page 335) and is often difficult to distinguish from that concept.

Another way in which a party may lose his right to rescission concerns cases involving a transfer of title. When title to property is passed from one party to another under a voidable contract, the party taking title can pass valid title to a third party (who lacks knowledge of any wrong committed by his seller). The second transfer cannot be rescinded by the party who passed the property under the original, voidable contract. The party who was wronged under the original contract has rights against the party with whom he contracted but not against a subsequent innocent party with whom the first taker of the property might deal. However, if the contract were void, no title can be passed, and any later taker under a void contract could be required to return the property thus acquired.

Mistake

GENERAL BACKGROUND

Should the reader be seeking guidance as to how to conduct his legal affairs relating to this topic, the advice is straightforward. Try to avoid mis-

---

[1] Henry Campbell Black, *Black's Law Dictionary* (4th ed.; St. Paul, Minn.: West Publishing Company, 1953), p. 1751.

takes when entering contracts. Strict adherence to this advice will avoid litigation arising from contractual mistakes, but this, unfortunately, is more easily said than done. By definition, mistakes are not made intentionally.

There are two fundamentally different ways in which mistakes in entering contracts may occur. First, one party alone, because of inattention, preconceived ideas, or for any of the dozens of reasons for error, may be mistaken in his understanding of a contract, while the other party to the contract is not laboring under any mistake. This situation is described as a *unilateral mistake*.

There is also the possibility that both parties to the contract are mistaken as to some important element of a contract. They may have assumed the existence of an object that no longer exists, or they may be mistaken as to the ownership, nature, or identity of something bearing a crucial relationship to their contract. This type of mistake, involving both parties, is called a *mutual mistake* or *bilateral mistake*. The approach to problems of unilateral mistake is substantially different from that of bilateral mistake. The latter will practically always result in a void contract. The former will result in a voidable contract under certain circumstances, to be considered later, but in most cases a contract will be valid and therefore enforceable despite the unilateral mistake.

Either type of mistake must relate to present or past circumstances in order to meet the legal requirement of mistake. A mistake as to future prospects of a venture could not ordinarily be the basis for any judicial relief. If the reverse were true, any contract that did not yield the expected or hoped-for profits could be set aside on ground of mistake. This is not the case.

From the experience the student has already gained in analyzing similar problems, he will probably see immediately that in a contract with a number of terms, mistake may or may not be important. The mistake could relate to a matter of no significance to either party, or a mistake could be crucial.

Just as a contract will not fail for lack of certainty unless the uncertainty is substantial, so a contract will not fail even because of mutual mistake unless the mistake is substantial. The question is one of degree, but in any particular case a court must hold that the mistake either is or is not substantial enough to be material.

A mistake must be distinguished from an error in judgment or a failure to appreciate values. Thus a seller who does not appreciate the value of his own real estate cannot seek to have his sale set aside because he sold for too little, unless he was induced to sell through actual misrepresentations going beyond mere statements that it was not worth what he was originally asking. We are permitted to haggle for a low price if we wish. To hold otherwise in general would render bargaining almost impossible. To hold otherwise even in the occasional case when a speculator makes a large profit on a shrewd buy would undermine the position of experts of all kinds whose main stock in trade is an expert eye for values. Such dealers perform an important economic function in buying property in relative disuse and selling to those who will utilize it more intensively.

A sale based upon a clerical error, for example, incorrectly multiplying the number of acres times the price per acre, would constitute a mistake. Where an ignorance of value is involved, the selling price would probably have been the same a week before or a week after the transaction. It was not the result of a momentary lapse. In the case of an error in arithmetic, the mistake was clearly the result of a momentary lapse that would not be repeated. Therefore, error of a clerical nature, even though relating to value, may be treated as mistake.

Even though the fact is established that a party entered into a contract because of a mistake it does not necessarily follow that he will be able to avoid his contract. However, at least the door is left open for proof of additional circumstances that may provide ground for avoiding the contract. The owner who sold too cheaply because of a failure to appreciate values is usually in a completely hopeless position so far as voiding his contract is concerned.

UNILATERAL MISTAKE

The law relating to unilateral mistake is complex in particular application, but not so complex in general outline.

The law of unilateral mistake is relatively simple in outline because it consists of little more than an application of the test with which we are already familiar for determining the existence of an agreement. The test as we know it is that of "apparent assent." If one party makes a mistake, assents to a contract under the influence of that mistake, the important question is whether he *appeared* to assent in the eyes of a reasonable man in the position of the other party. If the answer is yes, why should the contract not be enforced? By the same token, if the mistake is outrageous enough that the other party should have realized the mistake of the first party (or did realize it), the manifestation of assent in the eyes of a reasonable man is lacking and the contract should not be enforced. In that event the result is a voidable contract, and the mistaken party has the option of performing or of escaping the contract, providing that the rights of innocent third parties are not adversely affected—as, for example, when a party has innocently taken title to property to which the seller had a voidable title.

The law of unilateral mistake is complex in particular application due to the fact that exceptions based upon mutually inconsistent policies have been adopted, and the law sometimes is characterized by vacillation between one policy and the other. We may define these competing ends as consisting of "the rule" that is the test of apparent assent, as discussed above, and the "exceptions to the rule" that we will now consider.

One commonly adopted exception provides that a contract apparently assented to may still be set aside if founded upon a clerical error of one party and if notice is given to the other party before the latter has actually relied on it. An example of reliance would be using the figure submitted as a basis for a contract bid to a third party.

Another common exception is applied in cases where a contractor has submitted a bid on a project, and a contract is made on that basis, but due to subsequent unforeseen circumstances performance is much more expensive than originally contemplated. In some instances courts have virtually rewritten the contract in order to allow for the unforeseen circumstances. The parties are said to be mistaken because they assumed the unforeseen circumstance would not occur.

There are also cases that seem to be based upon nothing more than the feeling that a harsh result would accrue if the contract were enforced, or that the mistake affected the "very substance" of a contract and therefore the performance delivered was not that bargained for at all.

The main trouble with these exceptions is that usually there is no way of telling very clearly whether there really was a mistake or merely a desire to avoid the contract. If every unilateral mistake is to release a party from his contract, it will be very difficult for businessmen to know whether they can rely upon their contracts or not, because usually they have no way of knowing whether those with whom they deal have made an error. And there will be little to discourage a party from carelessness in his dealing; indeed, he might be encouraged to incorporate some indication of error into his bargain as an escape valve in case he should wish to rescind.

Undoubtedly, exceptions of the kind noted do work justice in particular cases. But these exceptions also pierce large holes in the objective theory of contracts, and predictability of result is lost when contracts may be avoided according to such vague standards. The resulting situation illustrates the truth of the legal maxim "Hard cases make bad law." That is, in a case apt to be harsh in its impact, the tendency is to find an exception that in the long run will only confuse the law. We submit that on this question the harsher rule is the better rule, and that a manifestation of assent should be binding regardless of unilateral mistake, assuming the mistake was not of such magnitude as to put the other party on notice and that in fact the other party had no reasonable notice of the mistake. If exceptions are to be made, they should be clearly defined, so as to prevent them from developing into a contradictory rule.

MUTUAL OR BILATERAL MISTAKE

Entirely different considerations come into play when we consider mutual mistakes. Even if both parties did manifest their assent, there is no reason based on policy or otherwise why they should be bound to a contract that neither intended. Consequently, the usual result of a contract created while dealing under the influence of a mutual mistake is that it is void—that is, unenforceable by either party.

Occasionally a mistake occurs in a written instrument whereby the parties had clearly agreed to one thing, but the instrument stated terms to the contrary. A high degree of proof is required for a plaintiff to establish the fact that the writing failed to reflect the actual agreement of the parties, but if the burden of proof is met, the equitable remedy of reformation is available. Thereby, the written instrument is altered to conform to the agreement actually proved, or realistically, the agreement is upheld despite the written evidence to the contrary. Assuming the high burden of proof concerning the original agreement is met, granting reformation would not seem to be much of an inroad into the objective theory of contracts.

As has been stated, mutual mistakes ordinarily result in a void contract. This means that no legal effects at all arise from the contract. If possession of an object being sold should be transferred under a void contract, the person receiving the article has no title, nor would anyone to whom the transferee may sell it. As can be seen, the difference between a void and a voidable contract is most significant. A voidable contract becomes valid if action is not taken. A void contract remains a legal cipher.

GENERAL ELECTRIC SUPPLY CORPORATION v. REPUBLIC CONSTRUCTION CORPORATION (Oregon, 1954) 272 P 2d 201

> To grant a complainant rescission on account of a unilateral mistake it is necessary that the mistake be basic and known to the other party, or that circumstances are such that the other party, as a reasonable person, should have known of the same. . . .

Appeal by Republic Construction Corporation, defendant, from a decree rescinding a written contract entered into between plaintiff General Electric Supply Corporation and defendant, wherein plaintiff agreed to sell to defendant certain apartment house kitchen equipment for the sum of $93,503.27, and from a judgment against the defendant in the sum of $30,150.

The amended complaint is predicated on two causes of suit, the first being that plaintiff made a unilateral mistake in submitting its bid to defendant with actual or constructive knowledge on the part of defendant for which rescission is prayed, and secondly, that there was a mutual mistake in the execution of the contract between the parties for which reformation is asked.

The facts are that defendant had a contract to build the Ione Plaza apartment house in Portland for the sum of two and one-half million dollars. Prior to the awarding of such contract, and on December 7, 1949, defendant procured from plaintiff a written statement offering to furnish the equipment in question for the sum of $126,531.90. Later on, negotiations were had between plaintiff and defendant, defendant urging plaintiff to bring its bid down because its competitors were "away lower," when finally on or shortly after July 7, 1950, after certain changes were made in the plans and specifications concerning such equipment, plaintiff verbally offered to sell to defendant such equipment for the sum of $93,503.27. Thereupon, on July 11, 1950, in conformity with the verbal understanding, plaintiff prepared a written contract itemizing the various units involved and submitted it to the defendant. The contract was then formally entered into between the parties, plaintiff agreeing to sell to defendant the units in question for the sum of $93,503.27. Deliveries of the kitchen equipment thereupon ensued. . . .

On May 3, 1951, plaintiff notified defendant in writing that it had made an error and mistake in submitting the bid of $93,503.27 and that on account thereof elected to and did rescind the contract entered into between them and tendered back to the defendant $83,664.14 theretofore paid to plaintiff by defendant and demanded a return of the equipment in question, which demand was refused by defendant.

Since the equipment went into the building, which placed it beyond the power of defendant to return, the court, in addition to rescinding the contract, entered judgment against defendant for the amount of the discrepancy.

(1) There is no evidence in this case of mutual mistake between the parties warranting reformation, that being the basis of plaintiff's second cause of suit. The written contract between the parties truly reflected their oral agreement, and, in such circumstance, there can be no mutual mistake that would justify reformation. . . . The trial court evidently took this view of the matter since the decree ordered rescission rather than reformation.

Plaintiff's first cause of suit is predicated on a unilateral mistake for which it asks rescission of the contract. The basis for such mistake is that in preparing the kitchen equipment work sheet on July 7, 1950, a mistake was made in figuring a subtotal. This work sheet consisted of 26 units, unit prices, subtotals and a grand total. One of the units consisted of 100 Pullman kitchens listed at $335 per kitchen. The subtotal carried forward was $3,350 instead of $33,500.

(2) To grant a complainant rescission on account of a unilateral mistake it is necessary that the mistake be basic and known to the other party, or that circumstances are such that the other party, as a reasonable person, should have known of the same. . . .

(3) There is no evidence of actual knowledge of the alleged mistake on the part of defendant. The question posed, then, is whether or not defendant, as a reasonable person, under the circumstances, should have known of the same.

It is first contended by plaintiff that the disparity between its preliminary bid of December 7, 1949, of $126,531.90 and the final bid of July 7, 1950, of $93,503.27 was so great as to put defendant on notice of plaintiff's mistake.

The evidence discloses that on a number of occasions defendant told plaintiff to get his bid down to meet competition and plaintiff suggested that if certain changes were made in the plans and specifications such end might be attained. These changes were effectuated, and Mr. David D. Seeley, the employee handling builder and apartment sales projects and builder activities, who negotiated the deal, and Mrs. Marion Hughes, who did the kitchen planning, checked dealers, made up and helped to price the equipment list, and Mr. Paget, general sales manager, all of whom were plaintiff's employees, thought that such changes were accountable for the disparity in price.

Since plaintiff thought that the changes were responsible for the reduced price, defendant could reasonably indulge in the same belief.

It is claimed that Mr. Leveck, vice president of defendant corporation, urged an immediate signing of the contract after he saw the work sheet in question and by thus snapping up the bargain an inference should be drawn that Mr. Leveck was cognizant of the mistake. We do not believe that such an inference is warranted. Mr. Seeley's testimony discloses that the $93,000 bid was submitted to Mr. Leveck between July 7 and July 11, the contract being signed on the latter date; that Mr. Leveck at that time requested Mr. Seeley to reduce the bid further; and that thereupon Mr. Seeley returned to his office and rechecked the figures with the assistance of his comptometer employees and returned the next morning to Mr. Leveck's office, the day before the contract was signed. Thereupon the bid was accepted and Mr. Seeley returned to his office and prepared the contract that was executed on the General Electric Company form. The record shows that at the request of Mr. Leveck a contract dated July 12, on defendant's form, was signed by the parties. It is practically identical to the General Electric contract of July 11.

The claim is made that on the occasion of the last meeting Mr. Seeley went over the figures and prices with Mr. Leveck and Mr. Seeley handed Mr. Leveck the work sheet in question; that thereupon he absented himself to his inner office for a period of ten or twelve minutes and upon returning announced that he would accept the bid. There is no evidence as to what occurred in the private office excepting the testimony of Mr. Leveck and Mr. Bellerby, his assistant, that the only matters discussed were the number of units and the lump sum bid. It will be noted that Mr. Seeley fixed the date of this meeting as the day before the contract was signed, and, further, that Mr. Seeley prepared the July 11 contract on the General Electric Company's form. We do not believe that this evidences a snapping up of the bargain.

How the plaintiff could charge defendant with notice of the mistake from such circumstances, when it claims it did not know of the same, is beyond comprehension. It will be remembered that such work sheet was dated July 7, 1950, some four days before the execution of the contract. It was in the possession of the plaintiff during this period of time. The evidence discloses that not only did Mr. Seeley and Mrs. Hughes check and recheck the same but that Mr. Paget and plaintiff's comptometer operators also went over the figures. It occurs to us that with so many fingers in the pie someone should have plucked out the plum. Therefore, if defendant should have had knowledge of the mistake a fortiori plaintiff should have had knowledge.

The view we have taken of this case makes it unnecessary for us to go into the matter of the alleged negligence on the part of plaintiff, its inability to place defendant in statu quo, or the affirmance of the contract by plaintiff after the discovery of the mistake by cashing the check of defendant and delivering materials to the job.

Reversed.

✧

The seller's offer was accepted. Yet after the contract was made the seller attempted to repudiate his offer.

Although it might seem one could argue that this mistake was mutual because both failed to catch the clerical error, the fact remains that it is the seller's responsibility to name his price, the buyer's merely to decide if he is willing to buy at that price. Therefore the error was made by the seller. At most, the buyer merely failed to catch the seller's error.

The mistake could have been in the other direction; that is, due to a clerical error the buyer could have accepted at too high a price. Presumably, this would have been considered a unilateral mistake on the part of the buyer. Having indicated his willingness to be bound at a certain figure, he would be held to his manifested assent regardless of the fact that some error entered into his decision to pay the named price.

Cases involving unilateral mistake are very closely allied, if not identical in principle, to the early cases in manifestation of assent. The reasonable person assumes an offeror to mean what he says when he makes an offer. The integrity of contracts demands that agreements made be enforceable, except in the most extreme circumstances. Thus the competing interests that must be resolved are again commercial expediency versus the desire to avoid penalizing a person for an honest mistake. The former interest usually prevails.

BOND ET AL. v. CHALFANT (Oklahoma, 1949)
208 P 2d 535

It is well settled that where due to a mutual mistake of fact the minds of the contracting parties failed to meet, equity may rescind the apparent contract.

Action by Rollin E. Greene, grantor, against Alpha N. Bond and Josephine Bond, a minor, grantees, to cancel a deed executed in consideration of marriage, and to quiet title. The plaintiff died before the case was tried, and the action was revived in the name of A. V. Chalfant, administrator of the estate of Rollin Greene, deceased. Judgment for plaintiff, and defendants appeal.

The court found that Rollin E. Greene had understood that he was to convey the land in question to Alpha N. Bond only, in consideration of marriage, and that she refused to marry him after the deed had been executed, delivered and recorded; that Rollin E. Greene did not know that Josephine Bond had been named as a grantee in the deed until after it was delivered and recorded, and had no agreement with her, and that there was no meeting of minds between Rollin E. Greene and Alpha N. Bond as to the consideration for the execution of the deed, and concluded that the deed was null and void and should be cancelled for a total lack of consideration, and the fact that there was no meeting of the minds of the parties as to the agreement covering the conveyance of the home of Rollin E. Greene. The court did not specifically find that any fraud had been practiced or that the deed had been obtained by fraudulent means or methods.

(3) The trial court found that there was no meeting of minds between the parties as to what consideration Mr. Greene was to receive for the execution of the deed to Mrs. Bond. The court found Mr. Greene understood Mrs. Bond was to marry him. Mrs. Bond asserted that she never intended to marry Mr. Greene and was not going to marry him. There was sufficient evidence in the record to justify the finding of the trial court that the minds did not meet on the consideration, and that Mr. Greene executed the deed in question under the mistaken belief that Mrs. Bond would marry him. Mr. Greene testified on direct examination as follows:

"*Q:* Tell the court, why you signed this deed. *A:* Well, the consideration was that—my understanding was that she was to become my wife."

"*Q:* If you had known that she was not going to become your wife, would you have signed the deed? *A:* No, sir."

On cross-examination he testified:

"*Q:* Then you never did ask her to marry you before you executed the deed? You never did say, 'Mrs. Bond, I want you to be my wife'? *A:* To be my life's companion."

"*Q:* Did you ever ask her to be your wife? *A:* Well, I think I made that plain to her."

(4) It is well settled that where due to a mutual mistake of fact the minds of the contracting parties failed to meet, equity may rescind the apparent contract. The rules as to the cancellation of instruments for mistake of fact find frequent application to deeds. The Supreme Court of Alabama properly expressed this idea in *Glenn* v. *City of Birmingham,* 223 Ala. 501, 137 So. 292, as follows: "To correct or cancel deeds on the ground of mistake, when the mistake is clearly shown, is one of the familiar duties of a court of equity." . . .

The trial court in this case found that the minds of the parties did not meet on the question of whether marriage was to be consummated between the parties. We are unable to say that the finding and judgment are clearly against the weight of the evidence.

Judgment affirmed.

✧

The circumstances seem most confused here. The evidence as to what the parties agreed to is vague, and the case is actually decided on the theory that one party intended one thing and one party another.

Perhaps each was mistaken about the intent, or possibly Alpha Bond had simply led the decedent to convey his land, never intending to marry.

This would have been fraud. Or she may have had second thoughts about marrying him after receiving the deed to the land. This would have been breach of contract. However, the remedy would have been the same in any of the three cases. Obviously Greene could not have legally forced Alpha Bond to marry him. Whether mistake, fraud, or breach of contract, the remedy would be rescission—that is, the return of the land to Greene, or in this case his heirs.

Because the remedy for all three possibilities would be the same, undoubtedly the safest, and most charitable, decision was to conclude that there had been a mutual mistake. Actually, there was no clear evidence of deliberate fraud, and the contradictory evidence is easier to interpret as a mistake than as a breach of contract.

Because the remedy sought was rescission, this case was tried in equity. The interests of commercial expediency—that is, maintaining the validity of contract—is here overcome by the opposing interest of fairness. Whether the contract resulted from fraud, breach of contract, or mutual mistake, either of these is sufficient to destroy any semblance of mutual assent, real or apparent. Here is a set of facts strong enough to justify setting the contract aside.

Observe that there may be different types of mutual mistake.

(1) The case where *A* believes one thing to be true or to be agreed; *B* believes another thing true or agreed. Each has some basis for his belief, or at least neither can be proved incorrect. This was the situation in *Bond* v. *Chalfant*.

(2) Another type arises when both parties assume some fact to be true, but in reality they are both incorrect in their assumption. This could be the case when, unknown to either party to a sale, the subject matter of the sale has been destroyed.

A famous case of the first type [2] concerned a London merchant who ordered cotton to be shipped aboard a ship in Calcutta, India, named the *Peerless*. Unknown to either buyer or seller, there were two ships at anchor by that name. The cotton was placed aboard the wrong *Peerless*, one that arrived in England two months later than the *Peerless* the first party had in mind. The court held the contract void. Certainly, this illustrates a mutual mistake where neither party could be blamed. The result, of course, placed each party's loss on his own shoulders.

Misrepresentation

In the previous section we advanced the principle that when an agreement had been reached, but one party realized that the other entered

[2] *Raffles* v. *Wichelhaur* (England, 1864), Court of Exchequer. 2 Hurlstone and Coltman, 106.

into the contract because of a mistake, this contract could be rescinded.

If we apply the reasoning behind that rule to the similar situation in which one party's *false representation* caused the other party to enter into a contract, we see that the same answer should result. The case where a false statement of one party causes the false impression presents a more extreme case of wrongful and deceptive conduct than the previous example, where one party was merely aware of an error by the other but did not cause the error. If the mistake was caused by the misrepresentation of one party to the contract, we certainly do not need to let that party profit from his misrepresentation. Therefore, a contract secured through misrepresentation is voidable. It may be avoided by an action in rescission.

There are some limitations even in this case. The statement must be of material importance to the contract. Furthermore, if the statement was obviously untrue, so that no reasonable person would have relied on it, we must assume that the party objecting to the contract did not rely on the misrepresentation but is merely using this as an excuse for getting out of a disadvantageous contract. For misrepresentation to be a defense against liability on a contract it must have induced the contract. And when contracting parties are dealing at arms length, one party may boast of his wares so long as his claims are only opinion—that is, "best in the world," "worth double its price," "will give good service," and the like. These are recognizable as only opinions and are within the leeway given businessmen in praising their wares. Statements of this type are termed *trade puffs*. On the other hand, direct, supposedly factual but false statements relating to a significant term of the contract, reasonably relied upon by the other party, will give that party grounds for rescission. This is true *regardless* of whether the person making the statement knew that the statement was false or not, but if he did, the term *fraud* is applied. A detailed discussion of that subject follows.

Fraud

In the same sense that an innocent misrepresentation provides a clearer ground for rescission than mere knowledge by one party that the other party has made a mistake, so *deliberate* misrepresentation provides a clearer case than *innocent* misrepresentation.

Securing a contract through deliberate misrepresentation has been labeled with a special and well-known name: fraud.

Terminology aside, we are still pursuing the logical ramifications of "apparent assent." The contract secured through fraud is one in which one of the parties is misled because the other party misled him through deliberate misrepresentation. The person guilty of the deliberate misrepresentation knows, or ought to know, that the person misled is, as a consequence, contracting in reliance upon a set of facts that do not exist in reality. The person guilty of fraud has no reason, therefore, to believe as a reasonable person that the other party's assent is genuine. Therefore the victim of the fraud may not be held to his contract.

There are two types of fraudulent contract: in most cases of fraud, a voidable contract results. This is the case when the general type of contract intended by the innocent party is actually made but certain important aspects have been misrepresented. This type of fraud is called *fraud in the inducement*. In the other type a void contract results. This will occur when there is no assent by one party at all, as when he is tricked into signing a document, having been told that it is a writing of a substantially different nature. In this case, even the awareness of having made the contract is apt to be lacking, and of course no legal validity whatever would attach. Fraud of this sort is termed *fraud in the factum*. Aside from providing the basis for rescinding a contract, fraud may also provide a recovery in damages. This is discussed on page 283.

In order to prove fraud, the following things must be established: (1) false statement, (2) of a material fact, (3) made with knowledge of its falsity, or with complete disregard of its truth or falsity, (4) that the other party relied on, (5) to his detriment.

Assuming that there is a good reason for undertaking the burden of proving fraud, which requires proof of intent, all of the five elements previously alluded to must be proved.[3] An elaboration of these elements follows:

(1) Although in general a false statement is necessary to constitute fraud, cases occur in which it is possible to misrepresent without any actual statement. Deliberate actions to conceal a defective condition are just as effective. One well-known example was the action of a seller in rolling over a valuable teak log so that the rotten inside of the log was concealed. Other examples are turning back an auto speedometer to deceive purchasers who might rely on it as a means of checking the mileage.

(2) Whether the fact misrepresented or concealed is material or not involves exactly the same issues as the question of whether a mistake is material or whether an innocent misrepresentation is material. What is material or not to a contracting party is a question of his intentions and preferences, but without a specific evidence of these, the standard of the reasonable man will be applied.

(3) What we mean by *intentional* misrepresentation is usually clear enough. A slightly more difficult question is defining a "statement made

---

[3] These elements are the same as in misrepresentation, summarized briefly in the preceding discussion, except that proof of intent to misrepresent is unnecessary to secure rescission or to defend an action in breach of contract. Therefore, misrepresentation should usually be easier to prove than fraud.

with complete disregard to its truth or falsity." A party makes a statement, not knowing it to be false, but having no idea of whether it is true or false. His claiming knowledge of a fact when actually he knows he does not have such knowledge is a misrepresentation in its own right: he is claiming to have knowledge, when in fact he is merely speculating, if the facts are contrary to his claims. If his claim to knowledge is relied upon, he is guilty of fraud. A minority of jurisdictions go further and find fraud when the defendant *in good faith and with some reason thought a fact was true* but a more prudent man would have known better. In other words, in cases of a negligent statement, fraud may be found in these jurisdictions (see case on page 287).

(4) When a contracting party is aware that a statement by the other party is false, but still feels the proposed bargain is advantageous, there is no reason to permit rescission or damages if he should later change his mind. This is the rationale behind the requirement that a party must really be deceived before he may defend or bring an action on the basis of fraud. The agreement cannot be attacked if the party, being aware of the "fraud," nevertheless did agree to the bargain. Looking at this from another perspective, the policy behind providing relief from contracts induced by fraud is to permit compensation for the party misled, rather than to punish an evildoer. If a party was not misled, but rather accepts a bargain with full knowledge of the facts, he has no reason to complain of his bargain.

(5) There are two schools of thought as to the proper measure of damages for fraud. One is the "out-of-pocket" approach, which permits a defrauded party to recoup the losses or out-of-pocket expenses attributable to the fraud. The second is the "benefit of the bargain" theory. Under this theory, if a certain return from a contract was promised but not forthcoming because the promises were fraudulent, the plaintiff is entitled to recover the amount promised, the "benefit of the bargain." The former is no doubt the rule adopted by the majority of jurisdictions.

The trouble with this theory is that an innocent party might be persuaded to buy a $200 ring for $200, having been convinced it was of a size and quality making it worth $400. Being a poor man, and not a dealer in rings, he would never have bought it except for the false statements. Under the out-of-pocket-loss rule he has no remedy, under the benefit of the bargain rule he has.

The essential difference between fraud and misrepresentation is the third item, "made with knowledge of its falsity. . . ." All of the five elements of fraud enumerated must be proved, but the knowledge of falsity, being strictly a matter of intent, is often most difficult to establish. Consequently, as a general proposition, if all that is being sought is rescission, misrepresentation could be asserted in every case that was actually fraud and would be easier to prove, because proof of intent would be unnecessary. However, often the party claiming fraud also wishes to collect damages, obtainable only by alleging and proving fraud, which does require proof of intent.

The student must retain his perspective as to what is and what is not fraud. For example, is it necessarily fraud to sell a $200 ring for $400? The answer is no, unless false statements have been made. If such a sale can be effected on the basis of trade puffs—that is, "Your girl will love you for it," and "No other ring like this," and even, we would venture to say, "The price is $400 and it's worth every penny of it"—this is "good business" and not fraud.

The common law has always stressed the independence of the individual, permitting him to bargain as he pleases within certain bounds. Our law, historically, has not placed much of a burden on one party to come forth and outline to the other party the possible disadvantages in a proposed bargain. So long as neither misrepresentation nor deliberate concealment are resorted to, the parties are expected to be their own judge of whether or not a contract is advantageous. As already stated in the section on mistake, the mere fact that a party's judgment is bad and things do not turn out as hoped is not ground for rescission, nor is it proof of fraud.

Assuming that a person has been led into a contract through fraudulent practices, the question becomes, what remedies are available? The answer to this question varies somewhat from state to state but may be summarized as follows:

(1) If the party wants nothing more than to avoid the contract, because of fraud rescission may be obtained, though as stated, proof of innocent misrepresentation should be easier to establish than of fraud. In most jurisdictions, in order to seek rescission the fraud must be objected to at the time it is discovered; otherwise the fraud is deemed to be waived. "Waiver" resembles estoppel but is said to be the surrender of a right, rather than a legal bar to changing one's position, as is true of estoppel. By continuing one's own performance after fraud is discovered or should have been discovered, the right to rescission is deemed to be waived.

If rescission is granted, the contract is, of course, canceled retroactively, and no further remedy in contract could be allowed.[4] However, if damages did occur owing to the defendant's false statements, the plaintiff may bring still another action, this time for damages, in the common-law tort of deceit. The elements of the tort of deceit (often simply called *fraud*) are the same as in other fraud suits. The difference between deceit and other suits in fraud is that deceit is not even based directly on the contract but is brought as a tort suit, the essence of the tort being the misleading statement and not the fact that there was a contract. Many types of fraud are not

---

[4] Traditionally, courts have felt there would be a logical inconsistency in rescinding a contract, so that technically it is rendered a legal nullity, and at the same time awarding damages for breach of the nonexistent contract.

based on contract at all (false statements or concealment involved in influencing a will, false dealings by an agent damaging to his principal, false statements by corporation directors damaging to the stockholder), but may provide an action in the tort of deceit.

There is yet another alternative. If a plaintiff decides not to try for rescission or, for that matter, if acts constituting a waiver have already occurred barring any chance for rescission, the plaintiff may elect to "affirm" the contract. *Affirming the contract* means giving notice that the contract will be performed according to its terms. Having affirmed the contract, the plaintiff is entitled to bring a suit in contract based upon the damages arising from the defendant's false statement.

There can be no general rule for stating which remedy would be the best in a particular case between the choices of obtaining rescission, and perhaps suing for deceit, or of affirming a contract and suing in contract. The answer would depend upon circumstances—for example, the ease of proof, amount of damages, importance to the plaintiff that the contract be performed, and other subjective considerations.[5]

In a few special types of situations, fraud will be found without any false representation having been made or conveyed. For the most part, these situations depend upon a special relationship between the parties, termed a *fiduciary relationship*. The broad rule may be stated that where a special duty of care and confidence exists, there is a fiduciary relationship, and therefore there is an affirmative duty to disclose all pertinent details. When a fiduciary relationship exists, any failure to reveal pertinent data is termed *constructive fraud*.

In some types of relationships, as between a guardian and his ward, there is a presumption of fraud attached to any contracts made between the two, so that if any question arises the burden of proof is upon the guardian to prove he dealt fairly. The reason for the rule is, of course, to serve to protect the weak and dependent. There is no particular reason why a guardian has to make contracts with his ward, and although he is not absolutely forbidden from doing so, he is on notice that he had better be scrupulously fair, and keep good records in addition.

The question arises in applying the special liability against fiduciaries, when is a party a fiduciary to another?[6] Clearly the guardian is a fiduciary to his ward, the attorney is to his client, the trustee is to his beneficiary, and usually the agent is a fiduciary to his principal. That a physician is a fiduciary to his patient would not seem necessarily to follow, though that

---

[5] Often, a contract provides that one party will pay attorney's fees for the other or provide some other type of unusual benefit. If so, to claim the benefits under the contract, the suit would have to be in contract rather than in tort.

[6] Fiduciary relationships have been subdivided into legal and confidential. No doubt the former requires a somewhat higher standard of conduct than the latter.

he is seems to be the general rule. That one friend is presumably a fiduciary to another seems rather surprising. The whole question is whether the purpose is to protect persons in a dependent position, who are in very great danger of being victimized, or whether the policy should extend to making ingratitude or faithlessness to friends a form of fraud. It might be argued that the latter goes too far, but the majority rule seems to hold friends as fiduciaries.

McWILLIAMS ET UX. v. BARNES (Kansas, 1952)
242 P 2d 1063

A party, induced by fraudulent representations to enter a contract which has been partly performed before the discovery of the fraud, does not waive the fraud by an election to affirm the contract, complete its performance, and retain what was received under it, and is not precluded from recovering damages sustained by reason of the fraud because of delay.

This was an action to recover damages for misrepresentations made in connection with a sale of real estate, and from a judgment in favor of plaintiffs the defendant appeals.

The action was commenced on August 18, 1950, in the city court of Kansas City. In their bill of particulars plaintiffs alleged that on November 18, 1947, they entered into a written option purchase contract for certain described real estate at an agreed price of $4,500, and at that time defendant stated and represented to them that the drainpipes in the house situated on the real estate were connected to and emptied into the city sewer system; that about the latter part of September, 1948, plaintiffs discovered that the drainpipes were not so connected but drained into a pit on the rear of the property, and at the time of discovery the pit was overflowing and sewage lay on top of the ground; that plaintiffs could not have discovered the falsity of defendant's statement about the drains connecting with the city sewer by ordinary inspection of the property; that such statements were wilfully, maliciously, and wantonly made for the purpose of defrauding plaintiffs; that the actual value of the real estate at the time of plaintiffs' purchase was $3,800, instead of $4,500 and plaintiffs had been damaged in the sum of $700; that by reason of the false statements and the wanton and malicious manner in which they were made with deliberate attempt to injure the plaintiffs, they were entitled to punitive damages in the sum of $250; and they prayed judgment for these sums.

Without detailing the evidence of any witness the proof tended to show that prior to the execution of the contract appellees inspected the house on the real estate, inquired about the drains from the bath, toilet and kitchen sink and were informed by appellant the drains were connected with the sewer in the street; that in September, 1948, the sewer stopped up and on inquiry then made it was found the drains connected with the cesspool in the back yard and not with the sewer; that efforts to secure settlement were unavailing and action for damages was commenced. Other evidence tended to show the value of the premises with and without sewer connections. Other evidence tended to show that appellant was warned by a third party that if she sold the property she had better tell the buyers the property was not connected with the sewer and appellant replied it was on the sewer. We note further that appellant, testifying in her own behalf, stated that one of the appellees asked her if the property was connected to the sewer and that she answered, "The sewer is across the street."

The appellant presents four grounds that the trial court erred in overruling her demurrer to the evidence.

(1) I. She first asserts that if there was any fraud the appellees have waived it by continuing to make the payments due under the contract after they had discovered the fraud, and in support she directs attention to *Bell* v. *Keepers*. . . . Examination of those decisions discloses that in each the action was not one on the contract to recover damages, but was one to rescind. Such cases are not in point here. The general rule applicable here is that a party defrauded in the making of a contract, who discovers the fraud after having partly performed, may continue with performance and also have his action for damages. See annotation on "Proceeding under executory contract after discovering fraud as waiver of right to recover damages for the fraud" in 13 A.L.R. 2d 807, 815. The rule above-stated is the rule in Kansas. See *Bushey* v. *Coffman,* where it was held: "A party, induced by fraudulent representations to enter into a contract which has been partly performed before the discovery of the fraud, does not waive the fraud by an election to affirm the contract, complete its performance, and retain what was received under it, and is not precluded from recovering damages sustained by reason of the fraud because of delay, if his action is begun within the period fixed by the statute of limitations." (Syl. 3.)

(2) II. Appellant also contends that the statute of limitations commences to run from the date of the contract. The gist of the contention is that nothing prevented appellees from making a full and complete inspection of the premises, and, inferentially that they did make inquiry concerning the sewer and cannot now be heard to say they were damaged by something concerning which they sought information and which, by the exercise of more diligence, they might have learned. It seems to us this contention is entirely without merit. Appellees made inquiry from appellant, who knew but concealed the fact. We know of no rule of law that would compel the appellees to have made inquiry throughout the neighborhood to determine whether appellant had told the truth, nor to have searched records, if any were available and there is no showing there were any, to discover whether a sewer connection had been made, nor to have conducted an excavating expedition to have learned the fact. Without further discussion, we hold that appellees' cause of action accrued when they discovered the fraud on the occasion when the drains from the house to the cesspool in the back yard clogged and the fact they were not connected to the sewer then became known.

(8) Appellant also contends that the evidence did not justify any award of

punitive damages against her, her contention being there was no evidence of concealment on her part. No complaint is made as to the instructions of the court to the jury for its guidance in determining whether such damages should be allowed, nor the amount. There is no contention the jury disregarded the court's instructions, nor that the verdict was excessive. Appellees' evidence tended to show concealment and appellant's own testimony tended to show, if not concealment by affirmative act, a statement tending to deceive. The jury, by its verdict, found that appellant was guilty of wilful misrepresentation. The trial court not only approved the verdict, but denied the motion for a new trial. By analogy this case is quite like that considered in *Martin* v. *Hughes*. . . . What is there said as to when punitive damages are recoverable need not be repeated, but that decision and those cited therein demonstrate that the award in this case was proper.

No error of the trial court has been made to appear and its judgment is affirmed.

The *statute of limitations* is a legislative act, found in every jurisdiction, requiring that suits be commenced within a certain period of time. After that time has elapsed, the remedy is simply barred. A suit can then be defeated merely by the defendant's establishing that the time period has elapsed. The purpose of a statute of limitations is to require a plaintiff to bring suit with reasonable promptness, before the witnesses die, memories fade, and the evidence otherwise becomes stale. All that the plaintiff needs to do to stop the running of the statute is to file suit. Delaying tactics of the other party after filing of suit will have no effect on the running of the statute.

Waiver is a voluntary surrender of a legal right. Some authorities hold that when fraud is disclosed, a plaintiff must decide almost immediately whether he wishes to rescind the contract and sue in tort or affirm the contract. Perhaps in this case the right to rescind was lost, but this did not prevent the plaintiff from continuing to perform his side of the contract and bringing suit in fraud on the contract. The fraud suit here is based on the fact that the real estate was not as represented by the defendant. In other words, plaintiff is affirming the contract and suing on that contract. The misrepresentation in this case is so clearly repugnant to our sense of justice that few would argue that such a misrepresentation should not warrant assessment of damages.

The movement of the law of fraud is clearly in the direction of stricter standards on the part of those making representations, and the extension of greater protection to those relying upon representations. To put it another way, there is a trend toward emphasizing one interest (ability to rely on statements) at the expense of another (right to speak with complete freedom, whether what you say is strictly true or not). This trend may be seen in cases similar to this one.

[EDITOR'S NOTE: The McWilliams case involves a particularly clear case of fraud, in that there was a careful inquiry by the purchaser and a false answer by the seller. Is it true that without the deliberate, false statement the seller would have won? Actually, a number of cases have held that a duty lies on the part of a seller to disclose any latent defects that would endanger life or health. Because an accumulation of sewage in the back yard would surely be considered a danger to health, probably this case would have been won by finding an obligation of the seller to disclose this danger, even without the element of misrepresentation.

A recent case held that a sale of real property infested with termites was fraud, even though the buyer had never inquired as to the presence of termites, and the seller never claimed the property to be free from termites. The court found fraud on the theory that sooner or later the termites, if unchecked, could have weakened the building until it collapsed and therefore the seller had a duty to volunteer the information that the building was infested. (*Olde v. Schlemeyer*, 56 Wn 2 449, 353 P 2 672.) The danger was one that would not have become critical except over the very long run, and then could have been checked or at least retarded by scientific exterminating methods. Similar cases around the country were noted in the opinion. The area in which fraud may occur without any actual deceptive statement seems to be widening.]

QUESTION

1. Why, in this case, would a suit in misrepresentation even if successful have been inadequate as a remedy?

GAGNE v. *BERTRAN* (California, 1954) 275 P 2d 15

> *Moreover, even if defendant's statement was an opinion, plaintiffs justifiably relied thereon. Defendant held himself out as an expert, plaintiffs hired him to supply information concerning matters of which they were ignorant, and his unequivocal statement necessarily implied that he knew facts that justified his statement. . . . The cause of action for deceit was therefore established by the evidence.*

The evidence in this case is in sharp conflict and is considered here in the light most favorable to plaintiffs. Plaintiffs had contracted to buy two unimproved lots for $8,500 "subject to . . . a fill test to be made at buyer's expense." Plaintiff Joseph Billiet telephoned defendant that he had a contract to buy the lots but "would not proceed with the deal unless we had a test made for fill, and I told him if he would like to do it, I would like to have him handle it because he handled my work before, so he said, 'All right, I will take care of it.'" Billiet testified that between 1939 and 1942 defendant told him that it was his business to test soil for fill and that he employed defendant on four different occasions for that purpose. Defendant did not tell plaintiffs at any time that he was not a geologist or soil engineer or that plaintiff should get an engineer or city inspector to check the soil. Defendant fixed the price for his services at $10 per hour, which plaintiffs agreed to pay. On March 7, 1947, several days after this telephone conversation, defendant sent two employees and a drilling rig to plaintiffs' lots. Several holes had been drilled when Billiet arrived at the lots; defendant arrived shortly thereafter. Billiet testified that he remained on the sidewalk near the street while defendant picked up and examined samples of soil at each of the holes drilled. The location, depth, and number of holes to be drilled were entirely under the control of defendant. After defendant had examined samples of soil from each of the holes, he directed his employees to close the holes and told Billiet that he had "nothing to worry about here. It is perfectly okay. . . . You may go 12 to 16 inches but that is about all. . . . You have got a normal condition here, for about an 18-inch foundation." Defendant's employee in charge of the drilling rig testified, however, that he observed evidence of fill 4–5 feet deep in several of the holes, but did not inform either his employer or plaintiff of that fact. On March 17, 1947, in response to defendant's invoice, plaintiffs mailed defendant a check for $25 for his services and requested a letter from defendant stating his "findings" because it might be required by F.H.A. Defendant replied that "On March 7, 1947 we drilled five 16″ dia. test holes, . . . the holes were drilled to a depth of 5′ to 6′ deep, we did not find any evidence of fill other than on the surface for about 12″ to 16″." Defendant's invoice included the printed statement that among other things he did "test drilling." Billiet testified that in reliance on defendant's oral and written statements about the extent of the fill they bought the lots for $8,500 and that they would not have bought them had they known that defendant's statements were erroneous.

After purchasing the lots, plaintiffs decided to erect a two-story apartment building thereon. They entered into contracts for the construction of the building and for a loan to finance the construction. Plaintiffs' contract for the installation of the foundation at a cost of $3,121.40 was based on defendant's report that there was no fill below 16 inches and was expressly subject to an additional charge in the event the contractor encountered "unforeseen conditions such as fill and extra work is required. . . ." As the first foundation trench was being dug, it was discovered that the lot contained areas with 3 to 6 feet of fill. When notified by Billiet of this condition, defendant came to the site, looked at the trenches that had been dug, and stated that he had "evidently made a mistake." The depth of the fill required a much deeper foundation than defendant's report had led plaintiffs to expect. [The Los Angeles Municipal Code . . . requires the depth of the foundation for a two-story building to be 18 inches below undisturbed natural ground surface.]

Plaintiffs brought this action to recover the increased cost of installing the foundation. Their complaint stated three alternative theories of recovery: (1) breach of warranty, (2) deceit, and (3) negligence. The trial court made findings supporting a recovery on each of these theories. It found, among other things, that defendant held himself out as being qualified to make soil tests; that defendant represented and warranted to plaintiffs that there was no fill beyond 16 inches; that plaintiffs believed and acted in reliance on this representation and warranty, which was untrue; that defendant made his test for fill negligently and carelessly; that defendant had no reasonable grounds for believing his representation to be true; that the additional expenses plaintiffs incurred in the installation of the foundation were proximately caused by defendant's warranty, misrepresentation, and negligence; that plaintiffs did not know the true depth of the fill until the foundation trenches were being dug, and that had they known the true depth of the fill, they would not have purchased the lots. Judgment was entered awarding plaintiffs $3,093.65, the increased cost of installing the foundation. Defendant appeals. He challenges the insufficiency of the evidence to support the findings of fact and contends that the trial court did not apply the proper measure of damages. We have concluded that these contentions are, in part, well taken, and that the judgment must be reversed. . . .

The Cause of Action for Deceit:

(11–15) To be actionable deceit, the representation need not be made with knowledge of actual falsity, but need only be an "assertion, as a fact, of that which is not true, by one who has no reasonable ground for believing it to be true" . . . and made "with intent to induce (the recipient) to alter his position to his injury or his risk. . . ." Defendant's intent to induce plaintiffs to alter their position can be inferred from the fact that he made the representations with knowledge that plaintiffs would act in reliance on them. . . . The evidence discloses that defendant's statements were erroneous, that, as will be shown presently, defendant negligently performed the fill test, that his statement was therefore made without reasonable ground for believing it to be true . . . and that plaintiffs justifiably relied on his statement in purchasing the lots and in making their contracts for the erection of the building.

(16) Defendant contends, however, that even if his statement was erroneous, it was not a misrepresentation of fact, but was only a statement of opinion and thus cannot form the basis of an action for deceit. Defendant drilled the holes, examined the soil, and told Billiet that the fill was only 12–16 inches in depth. He did not give his statement in the form of an opinion but as a representation of fact. . . . His assertion was not a casual expession of belief, but a deliberate affirmation of the matters stated and was thus within the statute, which requires only that he assert, "as a fact . . . that which is not true. . . ."

(17, 18) Moreover, even if defendant's statement was an opinion, plaintiffs justifiably relied thereon. Defendant held himself out as an expert, plaintiffs hired him to supply information concerning matters of which they were ignorant, and his unequivocal statement necessarily implied that he knew facts that justified his statement. . . . The cause of action for deceit was therefore established by the evidence.

The Cause of Action for Negligence:

(19–22) The services of experts are sought because of their special skill. They have a duty to exercise the ordinary skill and competence of members of their profession, and a failure to discharge that duty will subject them to liability for negligence. Those who hire such persons are not justified in expecting infallibility but can expect only reasonable care and competence. They purchase service, not insurance. . . . Defendant's duty of care in performing the soil test was established by the testimony of his employee that the employee noticed evidence of fill 4–5 feet below the surface, as well as by the testimony of the persons who dug the foundation trenches. This testimony indicates that had defendant made his test with due care, he would have discovered the true extent of the fill, and it supports the inference that defendant made his test in a careless and negligent manner. Defendant's repeated assertion that he was qualified to test for fill, contrary to the testimony of his expert witness that laboratory tests were necessary, also indicate that defendant did not exercise the ordinary skill and competence of those in the business of soil testing. His failure to do so, as found by the trial court, supports the cause of action for negligence.

The Measure of Damages:

(23) The only question remaining is the measure of damages to be applied. Plaintiffs contend that the trial court correctly measured the damages by the difference between the actual cost of the foundation and what it would have cost had defendant's representations been true. This measure would have been a proper one had defendant undertaken to insure that the lots had no fill beyond 12–16 inches in depth. As indicated above, however, defendant's undertaking was limited to exercising due care to determine and report the extent of the fill, and the damages, whether for deceit or negligence, must be measured by the actual losses suffered because of the misrepresentation. . . .

(24) In reliance on defendant's information plaintiffs purchased the property. If the property was worth less than they paid for it, defendant is liable for the difference. On the other hand, if the lots were worth what plaintiffs paid for them, plaintiffs were not damaged by their purchase, for even though they would not have bought the lots had they known the truth, they nevertheless received property as valuable as that with which they parted.

(25) Plaintiffs also undertook to build on the property before they discovered the extent of the fill. At the time they discovered the truth, they were so far committed to their building project that it would be unreasonable to require them to terminate it to mitigate damages. . . .

(26) It may be assumed that lots with 3 to 6 feet of fill would not be as valuable as ones identical in other respects with only 12 to 16 inches of fill. Accordingly, by proving that the fill was deeper than defendant had reported, plaintiffs established that they were induced to buy lots that were less valuable than they had anticipated. As stated above, however, since they did not prove that the lots were worth less than they paid for them, they failed to establish damages flowing from their decision to buy. Similarly, if despite the additional cost, plaintiffs secured a building that was worth as much or more than it reasonably cost them to erect, no damages flowed from their decision to build. Plaintiffs did not prove that the extent of the fill made the lots unsuitable for their intended use, or that because of it, the reasonable cost of their building exceeded its value, and they successfully prevented defendant from introducing evidence that the value of the property as improved exceeded the amount plaintiffs invested in it. After plaintiffs purchased the lots they owned property that was suitable for the use they intended to make of it. Because of defendant's negligence plaintiffs erroneously believed that it was more suitable

for their purpose than it actually was. The additional expense they incurred, however, flowed from the condition of their land and not from defendant's report as to what that condition was. Thus, although they would not have undertaken to build had they known the truth, they have not proved any losses flowing from that decision.

The judgment is reversed.

EDMONDS, CARTER and SPENCE, JJ., and BRAY, J. pro tem., concur.
Three judges dissent.

✧

The student should recognize the negligence action here as essentially a run-of-the-mill malpractice suit. An individual holds himself out as an expert and, failing to live up to the normal standards *of his calling,* may be held liable in negligence.

The question of fraud is an interesting one. The problem centers around the question of intent to deceive. Intent to deceive is present in cases where a party asks if a sewer is hooked up; the other party knows it is not, but claims that it is. Courts also agree that intent to deceive is present when a party *claims* to know a fact is true, but in reality has *no idea* whether the statement is true or false. (See pages 280–281.) For example, to sell you a used car, I tell you the former owner was an elderly schoolteacher who only drove it on weekends under 40 mph. I have no idea whether this is true or not. I am claiming to know something I really don't know. In claiming to know, with no factual basis for the claim, I am guilty of a misrepresentation. The intent *is* to deceive.

The trouble with the case at hand is that the defendant had reason to believe what he said was true. He really felt that the facts were as reported and based them upon his soil tests, made in good faith even if not with skill. Therefore, there *was no* guilty knowledge or fraudulent intent as usually defined. For this reason, many, and perhaps most, courts would not find fraud in this type of case. He *was* negligent, even though honestly so, and recovery would succeed on that basis. But remember, being found guilty of fraud carries a moral stigma, and this is at least one reason why findings of fraud ought to be confined to cases involving actual guilty knowledge and intent. This would seem to be particularly true when the cases can be decided just as well on the ground of negligence.

Having found, at considerable length, that the defendant was guilty, the court found that there was no damage. The two measures of damage for fraud were discussed previously. If the "benefit of the bargain" theory had been in vogue in this jurisdiction, the plaintiff would have collected substantial damages. However, applying the "out-of-pocket-loss" theory, we arrive at a different answer. The court found that the plaintiff had paid

$8500 for two lots that were worth $8500. Therefore, how had the defendant's false report damaged them?

QUESTIONS

1. Would not almost any false statement used to induce a contract be fraud, if fraud encompasses both intentional and negligent misrepresentations?

2. If so, is there any difference between fraud and misrepresentation?

3. Are soil testers usually graduate engineers or geologists?

Duress and Undue Influence

On occasion a contract may be obtained without genuine assent by one party through threats of physical force, or, more often, through threats of a criminal prosecution instigated by the other party. If the threats are sufficiently frightening that they would intimidate a reasonable man, a contract secured in this way is said to be secured through duress, and is void.

Contracts may also be obtained without genuine assent from a weak, dependent party by someone in a dominating position. Usually the one in the dominating position bears a relationship, such as doctor or nurse to patient, guardian to ward, lawyer to client. When these conditions are present, the influence of the dominating party may in itself be enough to overcome the will of the dependent party. A contract secured through unfair pressure by a person in a dominating position is said to be secured through "undue influence" and is also void.

Many jurisdictions hold that contracts secured through moderate duress or undue influence, enough to affect a party's judgment, but not enough to deprive him of his own free will, result in a voidable contract rather than a void contract.

Obviously, both duress and undue influence are nothing more than further instances in which the claimed assent of one of the parties to a purported contract is in reality neither assent nor apparent assent.

CHAPTER NINETEEN

Mental and Legal Disability

> . . . *Mental and legal disability constitute instances in which manifestation of assent is not really the test. Even if a party under a disability does appear to assent to a contract, he may be able to avoid it in some instances.*

Mental Incapacity

To test the validity of an agreement we ask the question: did the parties appear (to a reasonable man) to have manifested mutual assent? This test is adequate to deal with the more usual contract problems, where two rational adults are bargaining honestly with one another on a matter that should have been properly understood between them.

This test does not provide an adequate means of deciding cases where one contracting party was completely devoid of his mental powers. Even if a party did appear to assent to a contract, if he was totally devoid of understanding, some departure from the test of apparent assent seems required.

As stated earlier (page 267) contracts with persons who have a mental or legal incapacity are usually voidable on the theory that the assent, although not necessarily made while under some misapprehension, was nevertheless ineffective. It should be stated in this connection that recognition by one party not under mental or legal disability that the other party *was* under a disability is not usually necessary to render the contract voidable (though this fact may be considered). Therefore, mental and legal disability constitute instances in which manifestation of assent is not really the test. Even if a party under a disability does appear to assent to a contract, he may be able to avoid it in some instances.

POOLE v. *HUDSON* (Delaware, 1951) 83 A2 703

> *Where a contract has been entered into with a person mentally incompetent, in good faith, without fraud or imposition, for a fair consideration, without notice of the incompetency, and has been executed in whole or in part, the contract will not be set aside unless the parties can be restored to their original position.*

The defendant wife filed an affidavit of defense in accordance with Rule 12(a) setting forth the following defense: "That she verily believes that she has complete defense to said action in that at the time she executed the purported bond and mortage she was in a hospital under the care of a Doctor and under the influence of opiates and did not know the nature and character of the papers she signed."

Plaintiff has moved for summary judgment against her. This motion was heard on the complaint, exhibit and the affidavits of demand and defense.

CAREY, J., sitting.

CAREY, J.

The question for decision is whether the defendant's affidavit "shows on its face a condition of facts which, if true, would constitute a legal defense" to plaintiff's action. More specifically, is it a complete defense in this case to show that Mrs. Hudson was "under the influence of opiates and did not know the nature and character of the papers she signed?"

The affidavit suggests, but does not expressly aver, mental incapacity at the time of the transaction. It was held in Delaware, at a very early date, that drunkenness, even though self-induced, may furnish a ground for avoiding a contract. *Dulany* v. *Greene.* Unquestionably, mental incapacity resulting from the use of drugs would likewise justify the same result. But, in every instance of mental impairment, regardless of its cause, if no circumstances of unfairness, fraud, duress or undue influence appear, the reasoning powers must be so impaired as to render the person actually incapable of comprehending and acting rationally in the particular transaction. . . . For example, merely being under the influence of intoxicating liquor is not enough to avoid a contract. The same is true of drugs. . . . Incapacity does not necessarily result from "being under the influence."

In this case, the affiant does not aver that her mind was influenced by the drug to the extent that she was incapable of understanding the transaction. The plaintiff should not be deprived of his foreclosure remedy simply because she did not know the nature of the papers she signed if her lack of knowledge was not due to a mental inability to comprehend their true character. We are not here concerned with a situation where inequitable conduct on the part of the plaintiff or any one else influenced the action of a person under some temporary mental impairment. No such case is made out and those authorities which deal with that type of situation have no present materiality. . . .

Assuming, however, that the affiant actually intended her words to mean that she *could not* understand the papers she signed, the result would be the same. The transaction would not be void, but voidable, at most. . . . Where a contract has been entered into with a person mentally incompetent, in good faith, without fraud or imposition, for a fair consideration, without notice of the incompetency, and has been executed in whole or in part, the contract will not be set aside unless the parties can be restored to their original position. *Poole* v. *Newark Trust Company,* supra. This principle, though of equitable origin, is today applied in most common law Courts. . . . It would be grossly unfair to allow a person to repudiate a contract without returning, or offering to return, the benefits which he received thereunder.

We have here, under the present assumption, nothing more than an averment of mental incapacity. The defendant does not say that the plaintiff had notice of her condition, or that she received no consideration, or that she was the victim of fraud or imposition, or that plaintiff was guilty of any bad faith. She does not say that she can and will return the consideration or has offered to return it.

The defendant's counsel questions the propriety of granting the present motion on the ground that all the pertinent facts are not before the Court, but he has not asked leave to file any further affidavits. Even if all of defendant's statements in the present record be true, no adequate defense is made out.

Plaintiff's motion must be granted.

✧

The plaintiff asked for a summary judgment—that is, a decision based solely upon the pleadings before the judge, without hearing the evidence in support of the pleadings. This procedure is similar to a trial upon a demurrer, because the issue is really whether the defense, even if proved, is legally sufficient to defeat the plaintiff's case.

In any case involving a voidable contract, there is, as mentioned earlier, an important difference between a contract that has been *executed* and an *executory* contract. For example, in the previous case, if the defendant had merely signed a mortgage agreement and was to borrow the money at some later date, probably the court would have permitted the defendant to avoid the agreement. No hardship against the plaintiff would have resulted. In this case, however, the defendant had already borrowed and evidently spent the money. The plaintiff is attempting to recover his money through foreclosure of the mortgage. (A mortgage entitles a lender to sell certain property of a borrower in the event the loan is not repaid.)

To void the contract in this case would impose an unwarranted hardship on the lender. Owing to the fact that the defendants had evidently received and spent the money lent to them, there would seem to be nothing unfair in holding them to the mortgage, even if a mental disability did exist as to the wife at the time of signing (though disability was not actually alleged or established in this case). The plaintiff did not know of the incapacity, if any, and did not take advantage of defendant in any way. His rights are as important as theirs.

QUESTIONS

1. Why not consider as valid all contracts made by persons suffering from a mental incapacity?

2. Why not treat all such contracts as completely void?

Minority

Though the legal incapacity of minors is similar in many respects to the allowance made for adults suffering from an actual mental incapacity, there are different problems involved, and we prefer to treat these two types of incapacity separately.

As to the drunk and the insane, the standard of "manifestation of assent" is applied unless the lack of understanding approaches total incapacity. The question is, does this person have enough mental capacity to be even slightly rational? Those who do not have sufficient understanding are not held, at least to executory agreements. In every case excused by this process, a factual finding must be made that the particular party in question lacked sufficient understanding. There is no blanket protection. Every case must be examined in the light of the characteristics of the alleged incompetent. On the other hand, in the case of minors, there *is* blanket protection from the consequences of the minor's contracts, extended automatically to everyone under 21 years of age. Any contract to which a minor is a party is automatically a special case. This is not only a part of the law of offer and acceptance, it is a reflection of much broader policies.

In nearly all fields of law the interests of the young (representing the hopes of tomorrow) are preferred, if necessary at the expense of the rest of society. In tort law, allowances are made for minority, though no arbitrary standard is imposed. The question is asked in every case in which a minor is charged with tortious conduct: did he have the understanding to appreciate the significance of his act? In the case of deliberate torts, minors as young as five or six have been held, though minors tend not be held for the tort of negligence until they are much older, nor to be barred in their own suit because of contributory negligence.

In the field of criminal law, minors below a certain age and maturity are not dealt with by the criminal courts but by special juvenile courts whose sole concern is the welfare of the minor, especially his rehabilitation.[1] Pro-

---

[1] The juvenile courts usually have jurisdiction of minors up to 16 or 18 years of age, though this jurisdiction may be waived by the court, based upon an evaluation of the minor's intellect, maturity, and the nature of his offense.

ceedings and disposition of cases in the juvenile court are not usually made a matter of public record, so that the minor involved does not acquire a criminal record as a result of the juvenile courts' disposition.

In divorce actions, and other cases involving the law of the family, most courts have enunciated the principle that the primary concern of the state is that the interests of minors be protected. Great, and perhaps in the eyes of some, unfair burdens may be imposed upon the adults if the court deems this necessary for the protection of children of divorced parents.[2]

As stated above, in contract law the protection afforded minors is arbitrarily applied to everyone under 21 years of age. No matter how shrewd and experienced a minor just under 21 may be, he is afforded the protection granted other minors. We need ask only one question to determine if a party is entitled to special protection. Is he under 21?

In justification of this approach, it may well be true that comprehension and judgment are two different things. Common experience tells us that many minors do tend to be erratic in their judgment. Judgment is built up through wide experience and observation, and the minor has not had the benefit of many years to season his thinking. Therefore, in his contractual relations, the minor is protected from his own folly.

The minor is protected by means of a special right given him to rescind his contracts. When he rescinds he must return any consideration remaining in his hand *if any still remains. But if he no longer has the consideration he received, he may still rescind.*

This point requires emphasis because it is so sweeping in implication that readers may fail to comprehend the full meaning. For example, if a minor buys a car and carelessly drives it off a cliff and destroys it, he may return what remains to the seller and get his money back. He may, in fact, buy a car, sell it, dissipate the proceeds, then rescind his original purchase of the car and get his money back. Some courts are fond of proclaiming that minority may be used as a shield to protect but not as a sword to secure unfair advantage: this must be regarded as a cliché. We have already observed the fact that the minor can take unfair advantage of his rights, to the ruin of others. There is virtually no limit to his ability to do so in the majority of states. (A minority of states do require a minor to return consideration received before he may disaffirm.) In a situation where the minor has misused his power against a seller of inferior intelligence and education, where the minor is 20 years and nine months old, and where the minor is rich and the victim is poor, where the minor has wasted the goods purchased, he may still rescind. Only his credit rating may be affected.

The results may seem shocking, but the policy of protecting the minor is carried out. The minor is thereby protected from almost any possible folly

---

[2] Thus, often the father is not guilty of conduct leading to a divorce yet is denied custody of the children and is required to support them.

on his part related to making contracts. However, merchants need not deal with minors if they prefer not, though in most states if the merchant believes a customer is an adult who is in fact a minor, the minor may still rescind. (In a small number of states a minor is prevented from recovering if he fraudulently misstates his age.) In practice, merchants tend to protect themselves by requiring a countersignature by an adult, who *can* be bound even if the minor disaffirms, when selling expensive items such as automobiles. The danger of much loss through selling small items would seem very slight, and most merchants are probably willing to take the risk. Probably other characteristics of an individual, notably his integrity and his financial standing, are at least as important as whether or not he is a minor in determining whether an individual will fulfill his promises. Our impression is that not very many contracts are disaffirmed because of minority, and those that are tend to be for large, expensive items. All the same, minors do possess a power that can be abused.

Harsh results could be avoided by dispensing with the objective test of "21 years" and instead applying a test based upon the degree of competence of the individual minor. The present rule has the advantage of being easy to apply but arbitrary; the alternative rule would be much more difficult to apply but more equitable. Because persons dealing with minors can, if they bother, protect themselves, there seems little reason to change the rules dealing with minority.

Our purpose in permitting minors to rescind their contracts is to protect them, and we have found, inconsistently enough, that in certain types of contracts they must be held to contracts for their own protection. As an illustration, suppose that a minor, orphaned but with funds of his own, consistently purchased food and then disaffirmed his contract. The time would come when he would have difficulty buying food, at least in a small town. For this reason, minors are held to the *reasonable value* of their necessities.[3] Necessities include food, lodging, clothing, reasonable education, and medical care, to state the most common examples. Even these things are necessities only to the extent that they are not provided for the minor by his parents or others. What is or is not a necessity has been held to depend to some extent upon the minor's social and economic position: the higher his position, the greater his needs are presumed to be.

As we know, any contract entered into during minority may be disaffirmed, except contracts for necessities (and these may be disaffimed to the extent that there is any excess in price above what is a reasonable price). Presumably, upon approaching his twenty-first birthday, the prudent minor will review all the contracts he has made during his lifetime to see which of these he wishes to disaffirm. The mere fact of reaching 21, however, does not

---

3 It would seem that this rationale is without much force in a large metropolitan center where most merchants and their customers are strangers.

instantly destroy the minor's rights to disaffirm contracts made during minority. The minor's contracts become binding when he has ratified them. Ratification is a question of intent, not real intent but apparent intent, which should by now be a familiar concept to the reader. It is impossible for a contract to be ratified during minority. The issue, then, upon a minor's reaching majority resolves itself into the question, has the former minor conducted himself in a manner after reaching 21 as to indicate an intent to be bound? If the answer is yes, a ratification will be found. The most obvious way to ratify a contract is to write the other party stating that the contract is thereby ratified, but this seldom happens. A payment of part or all of the purchase price after reaching the age of 21 is almost always found to constitute a ratification. Sooner or later use of an article, or even the mere expiration of time, must constitute a ratification, but how soon ratification would occur under these circumstances would be a question of fact, to be determined by a jury.

SNODDERLY v. BROTHERTON (Washington, 1933)
21 P 2d 1036

It is the general rule, announced and followed by a great majority of the courts in this country, that an infant, on disaffirming his contract, is required to return only so much of the consideration as remains in his hands in species, and is not required to make good to the other party the portion of the consideration that has been disposed of, lost or wasted during his infancy.

STEINERT, J.

This is an action brought on behalf of a minor, by his guardian, against the defendant to recover possession of a truck formerly owned by the minor and traded in by him as part of the purchase price of a new automobile; damages for detention of the truck are also sought in the complaint. The original transaction between the parties was evidenced by a conditional sale contract which the minor subsequently elected to disaffirm, preparatory to the bringing of this action. The cause was tried before the court, without a jury, resulting in findings of fact and conclusions of law favorable to the minor, followed by a judgment, from which defendant appeals.

The facts material to the consideration of the questions here involved are these: Appellant, Frank Brotherton, was at all times herein mentioned an automobile dealer at Walla Walla, Washington. Arthur D. Stradley, individually, conducted a mechanical and auto-trading business at Pomeroy, and in connection therewith was engaged in selling DeVaux automobiles for appellant on commission. Eugene Snodderly, who will hereinafter be referred to as respondent, was, on December 22, 1931, a minor, being then a few weeks over twenty years of age. For about five years previous to that time, respondent had been earning his own living by doing farm work and operating a truck which he had previously purchased. His earnings were retained by himself and used by him as he saw fit. He kept a bank account, on which he drew his personal checks. At one time, he had bought a Chevrolet car, but in the transaction his brothers had signed the necessary papers, on account of respondent's infancy. The Chevrolet car was later traded in on a truck, and again the brothers signed the papers.

A few years before, one Charles Snodderly, an uncle of the respondent, had died, leaving an estate to his nephews and nieces. From this estate, respondent was entitled to receive about four hundred dollars on reaching his majority, which was to occur on November 8, 1932. Mr. Stradley had known the respondent all his life and, in fact, was well acquainted with the various members of the family to which respondent belonged. He had had many dealings of a business nature with the respondent prior to the one here in question. He also knew that respondent would share in his uncle's estate.

On December 22, 1931, Stradley, as the agent of Brotherton, sold a new DeVaux automobile, on conditional sale contract, to respondent and one Ed Wise, an adult. By the terms of the contract, respondent's truck was taken in as a first payment of three hundred dollars; the balance was payable in monthly installments commencing April 1, 1932; the next to the last payment was to be in the sum of four hundred dollars payable November 1, 1932, which was just about the time that respondent was to receive his share of his uncle's estate; it was contemplated that this payment would come from that source. Wise paid nothing on the contract, but agreed to give a mortgage, as collateral to the conditional sale contract, on an estate in which he was personally interested. The mortgage, which was actually executed a few days subsequent to the conditional sale contract, ran to Stradley and was in the sum of $1,080, which covered the purchase price of the new car, together with interest and insurance. It was understood that out of this sum, when paid, respondent was to receive three hundred and fifty dollars and the balance was to be applied on the purchase price of the car.

The appellant, Brotherton, was not present while the sale of the car was being negotiated, the deal being handled between Stradley, his agent, and the two young men, respondent and Wise. Upon completion of preliminary negotiations, the conditional sale contract was signed by Brotherton as dealer and seller.

After purchasing the new DeVaux car, respondent and Wise used it jointly, as a pleasure conveyance, for about two months. Wise then disappeared, leaving the car with respondent; Wise has not been heard from since. Respondent continued to use the car until March 4, 1932, when he notified appellant that he had elected to disaffirm the contract, and at the same time demanded the return of his truck. Nothing had been paid on the contract except the initial payment of three hundred dollars, evidenced by the turn-in of the truck. The DeVaux car had then been run about twenty-one hundred miles, and had depreciated in value to the extent of two hundred and fifty dollars or more; one witness estimated the depreciation as high as five hundred dollars. In the meantime, appellant had expended $77.30 in overhauling and repairing the truck.

Two questions are presented upon this appeal, one of which is purely a question of law, and the other a mixed question of law and fact.

[1] The first question relates to the restoration to be made by a minor on disaffirming his contract. Rem. Rev. Stat., #5829, reads:

> A minor is bound, not only by contracts for necessaries, but also by his other contracts, unless he disaffirms them within a reasonable time after he attains his majority, and restores to the other party all money and property received by him by virtue of the contract, and remaining within his control at any time after his attaining his majority.

Respondent had not yet reached his majority when he declared his disaffirmance, nor at the time of the commencement of this action. It will be noted that the statute requires the minor to restore to the other party all money and other property received by him by virtue of the contract and *remaining* within his control. The statute does not require the restoration of the property in its original condition or in lieu thereof the payment of its equivalent in value, nor does it require the minor to compensate the other party for the use or depreciation of the property, but merely requires him to restore that which he retains or controls.

It is the general rule, announced and followed by a great majority of the courts in this country, that an infant, on disaffirming his contract, is required to return only so much of the consideration as remains in his hands in specie, and is not required to make good to the other party the portion of the consideration that has been disposed of, lost or wasted during his infancy. This is particularly true where the contract is for the purchase of personal property.

There are respectable authorities to the contrary, but they are in the minority. The reason given by the courts in these jurisdictions which have adopted the minority rule, is that a minor may not accept the benefit of a contract, fair upon its face and fair in its execution, without returning its equivalent in value to the other party; that, seeking equity, he must do equity. On the other hand, the reason underlying the majority rule is that the welfare of the infant is, in such cases, the first consideration of the law, and its policy is to protect the infant against improvidence and folly, because his mind and judgment are immature. The improvidence which the law contemplates is not simply the making of an unwise contract, but very often is the use or misuse to which the property is put after it is purchased. To deny the privilege or right of disaffirmance, when that improvidence or folly has become apparent, would permit the accomplishment of the very thing against which the law seeks to provide.

In some states, the statute compels the infant, upon disaffirmance, to restore the property received by him, or else to pay its equivalent in value. Our statute does not contain such alternative provision, but rests upon a broader policy. We conclude, here, that respondent fully complied with the statute above quoted and with the rule that conforms to the policy of the law in this state.

[2] The second question relates to the conditions under which a minor may disaffirm his contract. Rem. Rev. Stat., 5830, reads:

> No contract can be thus disaffirmed in cases where, on account of the minor's own misrepresentations as to his majority, or from his having engaged in business

as an adult, the other party had good reasons to believe the minor capable of contracting.

It will be noted from a reading of this section of the statute that, in order to prevent disaffirmance, there must be either an actual misrepresentation of age by the minor, or else an implied misrepresentation arising from his having engaged in business, whereby the other party has good reason to believe him to be capable of contracting. There is not a syllable of testimony nor a shred of evidence in the record that respondent actually misrepresented his age. We may, therefore, disregard that element. Whether respondent's former business activities and enterprises were such as to lead one generally to believe him capable of contracting, is immaterial in this case, because the court, in its memorandum opinion and also in its findings of fact, specifically found that Stradley, the agent of appellant, knew that respondent was not then of age. While there is some evidence to the contrary on this point, we think that the preponderance of the evidence as a whole supports the court's findings. We are not at liberty to upset those findings in the face of such preponderance. *Herz v. Ransom.* Inferences, though otherwise legitimate, cannot be drawn contrary to, and in the face of, actual knowledge.

In conclusion, we think that it is proper for us to say that we are satisfied that the contract between the parties was in all respects a fair one to the respondent, and that the appellant acted in all honesty and good faith, without any attempt to overreach the minor, but the law of this state and facts found by the court necessitate our holding against the contentions of appellant.

The judgment is affirmed.

BEALS, C.J., MAIN, TOLMAN, and BLAKE, JJ., concur.

❖

This case involves the interpretation of statutes, but these statutes are in turn a codification of the common law. The case is consistent with the majority rule throughout the United States. The one part that is not is the statutory provision that prohibits a minor from disaffirming when he has misrepresented his age, providing the other party is deceived. In most jurisdictions, the minor would be permitted to disaffirm even if he had misrepresented his age.

The basic policy question presented here is, how far will the rights of minors be preferred above those of the public at large? As we see, the answer is very far indeed. The reasons are set out in the case.

QUESTION

Some courts are fond of such expressions as "the defense of minority is a shield to protect the minor, not a sword to take unfair advantage." Would there seem to be any way of preventing a minor from using his protection as a sword?

SECTION FOUR

Limitations on the Right to Contract

CHAPTER TWENTY

The Need for Consideration

Contracts result only when one promise is extended in exchange for something in return. The something in return, in a general way, is what we mean by consideration.

Preface to the Study of Limitations on the Right to Contract

THE STUDY of contracts has been divided into two major headings: first, under the heading of "Intent in Contractual Relations" we have presented some principles helpful in understanding the nature of the agreement.

We have now reached the second major section, "Limitations on the Right to Contract." This section presents a study of various legal barriers that may prevent an agreement from being a contract even though it was intended by the parties to be a contract. These barriers involve questions both of abstract legal policy and of practical considerations.

Popular misconceptions concerning contract law often center around two premises: (1) the false assumption that informal agreements cannot create a contract, but rather that formal language, writing, or some other mumbo jumbo is invariably needed before legal rights may arise,[1] and (2) the equally false but perhaps even more common assumption that an agreement, clearly made, with express declarations of an intent to contract, will almost inevitably be valid if the parties so intend. Neither of these premises is necessarily true, even though in a particular case one or the other may be true.

[1] It is true that formalities are sometimes required. These are considered in Chapter 24.

The discussion relating to the nature of the agreement in Section One of this text should have demonstrated the invalidity of the first premise. In fact, the student is aware by now that agreements so informal that they are not even spoken, much less written, can result in a contract.

The second premise is also false. There are numerous reasons why an agreement though genuine may still not be enforceable. We will undertake a detailed examination of these factors in the text following.

Why Is Consideration Required as an Element of a Contract?

The requirement of consideration stems from policies based not so much on abstract morality as on practical grounds. We know from our study of offer and acceptance that a mere promise is not enforceable. There must be an *offer,* which is a promise conditional upon the making of a certain promise by the other party, and the offer must be accepted by a return promise.[2] We did not ask the question before, but why not enforce a promise without a promise in return?

The question to be put is, should casual promises to do favors or to bestow gifts on others result in legal obligations? Why not enforce an agreement in which *A* agrees to give something, and *B* agrees only to accept the gift? Morally, the point may be debatable, and surely in some particular cases a mere promise should be enforceable, but the answer of the common law to the question "Is the promise of a gift enforceable?"[3] has been an almost catagoric no. Contracts result only when one promise is extended in exchange for something promised in return. The something in return, in a general way, is what we mean by *consideration.*

Why has the policy of the common law required consideration? We do not suggest that life could not be lived if all promises were legally enforceable, but we submit that one would have to be very circumspect in everyday conversation if this were true. Here is a practical point worthy of thought. Would you care to be held on every promise you have made? Would this state of things be for the better or for the worse? Certainly it may be argued that promises made in the course of business should be, or at least could be, made enforceable under certain circumstances. This, in some respects, is the law under the Continental codes; it is true under narrow circumstances (to be considered later) in some American jurisdictions, and to some extent under the Uniform Commercial Code. Even so, most of us would probably prefer that only certain well-defined promises be legally enforceable.

2 Unilateral contracts substitute completion of acts for the return promise.

3 Not to be confused with a completed gift—that is, one in which a physical transfer of an object with intent that title pass to the donee has occurred.

The requirement of consideration limits the enforcement of promises to those in which each of the parties has bargained to give or surrender something. The fact that each party has agreed to give or surrender something suggests, if it does not verify, that the parties have devoted some reflection to the matter and that they seriously desire the promises to have legal consequences. Thus, only agreements with consideration extended by the parties are enforceable as contracts. The test is not perfect, but it is on the whole workable. When applied with ruthless logic, the concept of consideration may also lead to troublesome dilemmas, as we will see later. However, the same may be said of many other useful concepts, in law as well as elsewhere.

Definition of Consideration

Probably the oldest concept of *consideration* is the "benefit theory." As workable a definition of *benefit* as any is, "the promisor has, in return for his promise, acquired some legal right *to which he would not otherwise have been entitled.*" [4]

Benefit in this context refers to a legal right acquired under the contract that the party previously did not have. Usually, the promisor has in turn been promised something of value, and if each party makes such a promise in reliance upon that of the other, in the form of offer and acceptance, a contract results.

The benefit theory is somewhat difficult to follow in cases where, although a promisor may have in return for his own promise requested something of the promisee, the thing requested appears to be of no conceivable benefit to the promisor. One answer, of course, is that the promisor may be left to decide for himself what he feels is beneficial, but this distorts the ordinary meaning of benefit. We are therefore closer to reality in some cases when consideration is viewed as the promisee's giving something up—that is, suffering a detriment. Under this theory consideration for a promise is defined as "some loss or detriment to the promisee." [5]

Legal detriment refers to a legal right surrendered by the promisee in exchange for the promise of the promisor.

The two theories, "benefit" and "detriment," are merely different ways of looking at essentially the same things: the benefit theory looks to see that something was received by each party; the detriment theory looks to see that something (if only a legal right) was surrendered by each party.

[4] Henry Campbell Black, *Black's Law Dictionary* (4th ed.; St. Paul, Minn.: West Publishing Co., 1951), p. 200.

[5] *Corpus Juris Secundum* (Brooklyn, N.Y.: American Law Book Co., 1963) '17, p. 747.

Any promise to do something that a party was not previously obligated to do (as in the following case, to give up smoking cigars) is enough to constitute a detriment, and therefore it is easier in some cases to identify the consideration by the detriment theory than by the benefit theory.

We feel that, for whatever consolation it may provide to nonlawyers, either the benefit theory or the detriment theory describes the basic idea of consideration well enough to provide a guide in the majority of cases. Having long recognized that sometimes "benefit" and sometimes "detriment" provides the clearer basis for decision, courts have combined the two into one theory, stated more or less as follows: Consideration is a benefit to the promisor, or a detriment suffered by the promisee, in exchange for the promise of the promisor.

The Restatement of Contracts submits the following, more elaborate definition of consideration:

"Consideration for a promise is:

a) an act other than a promise,[6] or

b) a forbearance, or

c) the creation, modification or destruction of a legal relationship, or

d) a return promise.

Consideration may be given to the promisor or to some other person. It may be given by the promisee or some other person." [7]

One other aspect of consideration should be mentioned at this juncture, the fact that the concept of consideration is not altogether new to the student. The requirement of consideration is implicit in the legal definitions of the offer and the acceptance that have previously been considered. Remember that in the discussion of offer and acceptance, it was found that both the offer and the acceptance had to contain a promise to do something not previously required of the offeror and the offeree. At present we are merely examining the mutual promises to ascertain that they actually are promises in substance as well as being promises in form.

TALBOTT v. *STEMMONS' EXECUTOR* (Kentucky, 1889)
12 SW 297

> *If he has complied with his contract, although its performance may have proved otherwise beneficial, the performance on his part was a sufficient consideration for the promise to pay. The right to use and to enjoy the use of tobacco was a right that belonged to the plaintiff, and not forbidden by law . . . the abandonment of the use was a sufficient consideration to support the promise.*

---

[6] As in a unilateral contract.

[7] If given to a person other than the promisor, the contract is termed a *third-party beneficiary contract.*

PRYOR, J., delivered the opinion of the court.

This case comes from the superior court by an appeal. Mrs. Sallie D. Stemmons, the step-grandmother of the plaintiff, Albert R. Talbott, made with the latter the following agreement:

April 26th, 1880.

I do promise and bind myself to give my grandson Albert R. Talbott five hundred dollars at my death if he will never take another chew of tobacco or smoke another cigar during my life, from this date up to my death; and if he breaks this pledge, he is to refund double the amount to his mother.

(*Signed*)   Albert R. Talbott
Sallie D. Stemmons.

The grandmother died, and this action was instituted by the grandson against her personal representative to recover the $500, the plaintiff alleging that from the date of the agreement to the filing of this action by him he had not smoked a cigar or taken a chew of tobacco, etc.

A general demurrer was filed to the petition, that was sustained by the court below, and the action dismissed.

It is insisted by counsel for the personal representative that the agreement by the grandmother to pay the $500 is not based on a sufficient consideration, either good or valuable, and, being a mere gratuitous undertaking, cannot be enforced. There is nothing in such an agreement inconsistent with public policy, or any act required to be done by the plaintiff in violation of law; but, on the contrary, the step-grandmother was desirous of inducing the grandson to abstain from a habit, the indulgence of which she believed created a useless expense, and would likely, if persisted in, be attended with pernicious results. An agreement or promise to reform her grandson in this particular was not repugnant to law or good morals, nor was the use of what the latter deemed a luxury or enjoyment a violation of either; and so there was nothing in the case preventing the parties from making a valid contract in reference to the subject matter.

In the classification of contracts by the elementary writers, it is said: "An agreement by one party to give, in consideration of something to be done or forborne by the other party, or the agreement by one to do or forbear in consideration of something to be given by the other, are such contracts, when not in violation of law, as will be held valid." Whether the act of forbearance or the act done by the party claiming the money was or not of benefit to him is a question that does not arise in the case. If he has complied with his contract, although its performance may have proved otherwise beneficial, the performance on his part was a sufficient consideration for the promise to pay. The right to use and to enjoy the use of tobacco was a right that belonged to the plaintiff, and not forbidden by law. The abandonment of its use may have saved him money, or contributed to his health; nevertheless the surrender of that right caused the promise, and, having the right to contract with reference to the subject matter, the abandonment of the use was a sufficient consideration to support the promise.

Mr. Parsons, in his work on Contracts (vol. 1, 7th ed., 489) says: "The subject matter of every contract is something which is to be done, or which is to be omitted"; and, where the consideration is valuable, it need not be adequate. If, therefore, one parts with that he has the right to use and enjoy, the question of injury or benefit to the party seeking a recovery by reason of a full performance on his part will not be inquired into, because, if he had the legal right to use that which he has ceased to use by reason of the promise, the law attached a pecuniary value to it. If this was an action to recover such damages as the party had sustained by reason of the violation of the covenant or promise, the verdict or judgment would doubtless be nominal only; but where the parties have agreed on the amount to be paid on the performance of certain conditions, when a compliance with these conditions has been alleged and shown, the sum agreed on must be paid. Whether or not the mother of the young man would recover the penalty imposed on his failure to comply with his undertaking is not necessary to be decided. It is sufficient to say that the abandonment of the use of tobacco was such a consideration as authorized a recovery of the sum agreed on.

The judgment below is reversed, and remanded, with directions to overrule the demurrer, and for proceedings consistent with this opinion.

Petition for rehearing dismissed.

✧

The contract in this case is one that would be difficult to explain under the benefit theory. Strictly speaking, what benefit was it to the grandmother if the plaintiff gave up the various vices enumerated? By any ordinary definition there was no benefit to the grandmother, but there was a detriment to the grandson. He agreed to forfeit doing something that he otherwise could have done. He therefore surrendered a legal right, and this is consideration under the detriment theory.

This contract is unusual in another way, though the court doesn't discuss the problem. The grandmother is to pay $500 to the son if he lives up to his promise, and if he doesn't the son is to pay double that amount to the mother. Thus, the rights of the parties are to be determined by subsequent events—the event being whether or not the son lives up to his promise. Contracts in which the rights of the parties are determined by subsequent events are termed *aleatory* contracts. Other examples are fire insurance contracts, in which the obligation of the insurer to pay is incurred only in the event of a specified type of loss, or a grubstake contract in which *A* outfits *B*, who sets out in search of gold. If *B* fails to find gold, he owes *A* nothing; if he does, he owes *A* half of what he finds, even if he finds a million-dollar mine.

There is still another peculiar feature to this contract. Assuming that the son breaks his promise, he is obligated to pay $1,000, but not to his grandmother: he is to pay his mother. Contracts in which the consideration runs not to the promisor but to a third party are termed *third-party beneficiary contracts.*[8] The beneficiary of the contract is not a party to the contract, but is a third person designated by one of the parties. Life insurance contracts are a common example. A husband makes a contract with an insurance company by which he agrees to pay the company $100 a year, in return for the company's agreement to pay $10,000 in the event of his death, payment to be made to his wife. She is a third-party beneficiary. She could bring suit on the contract and recover, despite the fact that she is not a party to the contract.

In practically any contract, a promisor could specify that the return consideration be bestowed upon some third party. If this is done the motive is usually either to make a gift to that party or as a means of paying off some financial obligation to the third party. The third party has a right to bring suit on a contract of that kind, should the promise for his benefit not be fulfilled.

A final comment has no special bearing upon this case, but is a point worthy of emphasis, and one we hope the student will remember. The mutual promises *are,* in a sense, the consideration in a bilateral contract, and when the promises are made, a contract (other requirements being present) is formed. Therefore, when, as here, one or the other parties does not perform, this does not mean there was no contract. This means that the contract was broken, and the injured party is entitled to bring suit on the contract for his damages.

In determining whether or not a contract is enforceable, we do not usually have to wait to see if the respective obligations are actually performed. The exchange of the mutual promises in most cases binds the parties to the contract. The main exception is the unilateral contract, where the promisor is not bound until a certain act or acts requested by the promisor are actually performed.

QUESTIONS

1. What is the difference between the third-party beneficiary contract and other contracts?

2. The above dispute appears to arise in connection with the settlement of Sallie Stemmons estate. Why does plaintiff receive the $500, considering that this award was not made by will?

STELMACK ET AL. v. GLEN ALDEN COAL COMPANY
(Pennsylvania, 1940) 14 A 2d 127 (Part One)

> *If the promisor merely intends to make a gift to the promisee upon the performance of a condition, the promise is gratuitous and the satisfaction of the condition is not consideration for a contract.*

[8] See footnote 7, p. 308.

BARNES, J.

This is an appeal from the order of the court below entering judgment for the defendant in an action brought by plaintiffs to recover the cost of repairs to their building which was damaged as a result of mining operations conducted by the defendant. The suit is upon an oral agreement, and the sole question is whether the contract is supported by a consideration.

On July 3, 1962, plaintiffs purchased a certain lot of ground situated in the city of Scranton, upon which was erected a building containing stores and residential apartments.

[EDITOR'S NOTE: By the express terms of the deed by which the plaintiffs held their property, they did *not* have any right to recover for damage resulting from subsiding or shifting of the ground. This situation came about as follows. Originally, the surface rights and mineral rights were held by the same party. However, at some point, an owner of the entire bundle of rights sold the mineral rights, and along with them the right to surface support. From that time on, no owner of the surface rights could pass on the right to surface support to a subsequent buyer, for one cannot sell something he never owned.]

The defendant company is the present owner of the coal and mineral rights in the premises, and is actively engaged in mining operations. The plaintiffs aver that they were informed in 1927 by a duly authorized agent of the defendant that mining was about to begin under their property which would cause a subsidence of the soil. He is alleged to have made an oral agreement with them, on behalf of defendant, that if they would permit the coal company's employees to enter upon their land and prop up their building to prevent its collapse, or to minimize any damages that might occur, the company would make all repairs necessary to restore the property to its original condition.

Plaintiffs permitted ties and supports to be erected about their building which rendered it "unsightly" and resulted in some loss of rents, although it is not contended that the work was performed negligently. As mining operations continued during the period from 1928 to 1935, it became necessary, according to plaintiffs, to reconstruct the building due to the further subsidence of the surface. From time to time the defendant made repairs to the property, but later refused to restore it to its previous condition.

In the present action for the breach of the alleged oral agreement, plaintiffs seek to recover the sum of $3,185, representing the amount expended by them for the repair and restoration of their property. The court below excluded all evidence of the oral agreement, upon the ground that plaintiffs had failed to show that it was supported by a consideration and directed a verdict in favor of the defendant. From the order of the court in banc refusing a new trial, and entering judgment for the defendant, plaintiffs have taken this appeal.

Plaintiffs contend that (1) there was consideration for the oral agreement because of the detriment suffered by them in permitting the defendant to enter upon their land and place props and ties about their building; (2) the promise to repair was supported by a "moral consideration"; and (3) they are entitled to recover under the doctrine of promissory estoppel.

(1) That consideration is an essential element of an enforceable contract is

one of our fundamental legal concepts, and there are but few exceptions to the rule. "Consideration is defined as a benefit to the party promising, or a loss or detriment to the party to whom the promise is made." . . . The terms *benefit* and *detriment* are used in a technical sense in the definition, and have no necessary reference to material advantage or disadvantage to the parties.

(2) It is not enough, however, that the promisee has suffered a legal detriment at the request of the promisor. The detriment incurred must be the quid pro quo, or the "price" of the promise, and the inducement for which it was made. "Consideration must actually be bargained for as the exchange for the promise." . . . If the promisor merely intends to make a gift to the promisee upon the performance of a condition, the promise is gratuitous and the satisfaction of the condition is not consideration for a contract. The distinction between such a conditional gift and a contract is well illustrated in Williston on Contracts. Rec. Ed., Vol. 1, Section 112, where it is said: "If a benevolent man says to a tramp, 'If you go around the corner to the clothing shop there, you may purchase an overcoat on my credit,' no reasonable person would understand that the short walk was requested as the consideration for the promise, but that in the event of the tramp going to the shop the promisor would make him a gift."

(3) In the present case it clearly appears that the defendant's offer to repair the plaintiffs' building was entirely gratuitous. The permission to enter upon the land and to erect props and ties was sought by defendant merely for the purpose of conferring a benefit upon plaintiffs as a voluntary act, and not as the price or consideration of its alleged promise to restore the building to its original condition. The placing of supports about the structure was of no conceivable advantage to the defendant, for, as we have seen, it had no liability whatever "for any injury or damage that may be caused or done to the said surface or right of soil, or to the buildings or improvements" under the provisions of the deeds in plaintiffs' chain of title. The interest of plaintiffs alone was served by the defendant's efforts to prevent the collapse of the structure and to minimize the damages resulting from the mining operations. Because this was done at the expense of the defendant, and solely for the protection of the plaintiffs, we are unable to see how it could have constituted a consideration for the defendant's promise, and converted a purely gratuitous undertaking into a binding contract.

(This case is continued on pages 333 and 336.

✧

QUESTIONS

1. Why is not the agreement to permit the defendant to enter upon the premises for the purpose of shoring up the building valid consideration?

2. In this case does the requirement of consideration fulfill its function of restricting the enforcement of promises to those for which there is a good reason for enforcement?

Adequacy of Consideration

In surveying the law of consideration, two principles may be utilized as a frame of reference. These are (1) consideration is a requirement of a contract, and (2) the adequacy of the consideration is usually immaterial. The first of these has already been discussed.

So long as a promise can be found to represent any legal detriment, or any value at all, a contract may be found. The development of this rule probably reflects practical problems of judicial administration. Certainty of contract would be greatly reduced if, every time a party could demonstrate that his interests would be advanced only very little by a contract he had entered into, he could therefore renounce the contract. Judicial administration would become a nightmare if the courts were required to act as expert appraisers of the relative economic advantage of each side of every contract that might conceivably be "unfair." Finding no clear-cut basis for a halfway position, and faced with the choice of assessing all contracts, or none, as to adequacy of consideration, the courts traditionally have adopted the latter position. The parties themselves are held by the courts to be in the best position to estimate values as related to their own interests, and need not contract if they feel their interests are not well served.

Generally, therefore, "inadequacy of consideration" is no defense. Nevertheless, some courts have relieved parties from their contractual obligations on this ground in order to avoid hard cases, especially where a great inequality in competence and in economic power is present.

The trend in the development of the law shows signs of leaning toward a moderation of the strict approach to inadequacy. Between the alternatives of rescinding all or none of the contracts that might be deemed to be based upon inadequate consideration, the present rule is clearly preferable. However, this would seem to be an area of the law in which judgment may be used. Some courts have adopted this point of view and will give relief in cases of extreme hardship. In such cases, not only the relative value of the promises but the bargaining power and relative capacity of the parties is likely to be considered. Contrary to what some profess to believe, the uneducated, the elderly and feeble, and widows and orphans claiming hardship are more likely to receive the benefit of doubt than large corporations.

If the unfortunate contract was secured through misrepresentation or fraud, of course relief will be granted. But, in addition, proof of grossly unequal consideration is admissible as proof of misrepresentation or fraud. Grossly unequal consideration is by no means conclusive proof of fraud without additional evidence, but at least tends to bring the possibility of misrepresentations or fraud before the inquiry of the court.

It is also possible that grossly unequal consideration might provide some evidence of unilateral mistake. A victim of an unfortunate contract might, depending upon slight variations in the facts surrounding creation of the contract, claim either unilateral mistake or inadequacy of consideration. However, the cards are stacked heavily against him in either case, because neither theory is the basis for avoiding a contract without proof of some unusual factors.

Relief has also been granted under the doctrine of "commercial frustration." This doctrine has been applied in a few cases, as when the economic value of one party's legal benefit (or the other party's detriment) disappears due to later, unforeseeable events. For example, a party rented property on a certain day to witness the coronation parade of the King of England. The coronation was postponed, and the party renting the premises was able to avoid the contract because of commerical frustration.

A universal exception to the general rule in regard to adequacy applies when the consideration is an exchange of unequal but fixed sums of money. That is, a contract purportedly settling a debt by means of paying a smaller sum than is owed (at the time and place payment was agreed upon) can be avoided by the creditor. There is deemed to be no consideration on the part of the debtor, given in exchange for the reduction of the debt. The reason for this special exception is that all the usual problems discussed above are lacking. The court can tell at a glance that the economic benefits are unequal. With no reasons to support the usual rules as to inadequacy, those rules are simply not applied. This exception to the usual treatment of inadequacy naturally does not apply when the discrepancy in sums is derived from interest payments, or from payment in full at an earlier date than that required, or payment for some other type of economic benefit.

HODGKISS v. NORTHLAND PETROLEUM CONSOLIDATED ET AL. (Montana, 1937) 67 P 2d 811

There is no failure of consideration when one has received that which he intended to buy, although the thing bought should prove to be worthless. . . .

(8) The rule is that inadequacy of consideration, standing alone, is not a sufficient ground for refusing to enforce an agreement. . . .

The plaintiff testified that he received nothing for the execution of the oil and gas lease and the mineral deed. In his testimony, however, he later admitted that it was agreed at the time of their execution that he was to receive a certificate of interest of one unit in the trust. He also admitted receiving a memorandum stating that he was entitled to receive such a unit. He admitted that he had never made demand for the certificate of interest or unit, and that it was offered to him at the time he secured the release when he refused to accept it; it was also tendered to him in court. Evidence also appears in the record that the certificate was offered to him at an earlier date. The declaration of trust discloses that one thousand units might be issued at a par value of $100. The record is silent as to how many of these units or certificates of interest were ever issued.

It apparently was the theory of the pleader in the reply filed by plaintiff that the major consideration for these documents was the prospecting and development of the lands on which the defendants had oil and gas leases. It was recited in the declaration of trust at that time that the trust owned numerous other tracts of land under assignments of leases either in whole or in part, and that therefore, by reason of their failure to develop, the consideration for the lease and mineral deed failed.

(9–11) . . . Treating the pleading on behalf of plaintiff in his reply as a sufficient plea of failure of consideration, let us examine the proof to see whether the allegations of the reply were sustained. The plaintiff testified that the negotiations were conducted preliminary to the signing of the oil and gas lease and the mineral deed by one Hall, an agent of the trust or trustees. In response to an inquiry as to what statements were made by Hall before the signing of the instrument, plaintiff replied: "Mr. Hall said they are going to drill wells and develop the land and see if there is oil and gas on the land; that if they did not do so in five years, those leases would become null and void." Again, in response to a similar inquiry, he testified: "Mr. Hall said that the company agreed to drill wells; if they did not drill wells in five years leases would be no account and they went out of effect in five years time." This is the only testimony offered tending to prove what was referred to in the reply as an understanding or agreement for prospecting and development of the leased land. This proof falls far short of showing any such understanding or agreement. . . . No testimony was offered as to the value of the unit or certificate of interest other than plaintiff's assertion that he did not think it had any value. He did not undertake to say, however, that the unit was not what he bargained for. There is no failure of consideration when one has received that which he intended to buy, although the thing bought should prove to be worthless. . . .

(12–14) It is suggested that the unit or certificate of interest was practically worthless without development. Courts, however, must enforce contracts as made, not make new ones for the parties, no matter how unreasonable the terms may appear. . . . When plaintiff failed to prove his alleged agreement as set forth in his reply, he failed to sustain his pleading of failure of consideration, and when it appeared from the proof that the defendant at all times recognized his right to the unit in that it was attempted to be delivered to him—in fact, tendered to him—plaintiff failed to sustain his plea of want of consideration. The burden was not on the defendants to show that the unit had some value. The burden was on the plaintiff to show that there was no consideration.

✧

This plaintiff had entered into a promotional scheme in which he surrendered his gas, oil, and mineral rights in exchange for an interest in the entire scheme. He has received the trust certificate representing his interest. The court held that the fact that no actual development seems to have occurred cannot be considered failure of the consideration. The plaintiff's main problem seems to be an inability to prove any promise by the defendant beyond an agreement to organize the trust.

The argument was made that consideration in this case was inadequate. However, for all we know, the following year the trust developed its holdings and paid fabulous dividends. Many contracts are for types of consideration that are impossible for anyone but the person involved to adequately appraise. For example, how much is it worth to you to quit using tobacco? Might this not vary from person to person?

QUESTION

1. What problem necessarily arises when a jurisdiction adopts the position that inadequacy of consideration is a basis for setting aside a contract?

AMERICAN UNIVERSITY v. TODD (Delaware, 1938)
1 A 2d 595

> As a general rule, a court of law will not inquire into the adequacy or inadequacy of the consideration involved in a transaction. . . . But that rule does not usually apply when the consideration paid is of the same nature as the thing promised, and is equal or smaller in amount. A consideration of one dollar, therefore, will not usually support a promise to pay a larger sum of money. The reason for this exception is that in such cases, it is impossible for the law to indulge in the presumption of equivalence between the consideration and the promise.

Judgment was entered on the following instrument in writing, a copy of which was attached to its affidavit of demand:

Date: *March 27, 1928.* In consideration of one dollar in hand paid, receipt of which is hereby acknowledged, and also in consideration of my interest in Christian Education, and for and in consideration of the mutual promises of other subscribers to The American University Fund for Endowment, Buildings, Betterments, Equipment, Liquidation, and Expenses, I hereby promise and agree with said The American University, an educational corporation organized and existing by and under certain Acts of Congress, to pay to said University for its said Fund the sum of Five Thousand Dollars ($5,000.00), payment to be made to the Treasurer of said The American University, at Washington, District of Columbia, at my convenience. Given for a Scholarship. Name: *Mary T. Gambrill.*

This case is before us on the petition of William L. Todd, Executor of Mary T. Gambrill, deceased, to vacate a judgment for $5,000, entered against him, as executor, at the suit of "The American University." . . . The plaintiff's suit and the judgment entered in its favor was based on a written instrument, not under seal, dated March 27th, 1928, apparently signed by Mrs. Gambrill, and purporting, on its face, to be given "In consideration of one dollar in hand paid . . . and also in consideration of my [her] interest in Christian Education and for and in consideration of the mutual promises of other Subscribers to The American University Fund for Endowment, Buildings, Betterments, Equipment, Liquidation, and Expenses."

The American University, the plaintiff in the judgment, contends that Mrs. Gambrill, and after her death her executor, was bound to pay the $5,000 promised because the instrument sued on was given "In Consideration of the mutual promises of other subscribers to The American University Fund for Endowment, Buildings, Betterments, Equipment, Liquidation, and Expenses."

There undoubtedly are cases which hold that the mutual promises of the various subscribers to the same fund are a good and sufficient consideration to support a promise to pay. *University of Southern California* v. *Bryson.*

As Professor Williston says, however, "The difficulty with this view is its lack of conformity to the facts.

"It is doubtless possible for two or more persons to make mutual promises that each will give a specified amount to a charity or other object, but in the case of ordinary charitable subscriptions, the promise of each subscriber is made directly to the charity, or its trustees, and it is frequently made without any reference to the subscription of others. If induced at all by previous or expected subscriptions, this inducement only affects the motive of the subscriber; it cannot be said that the previous subscriptions were given in exchange for the later one. Indeed the earlier subscriptions would be open to the objection of being past consideration so far as a later subscription was concerned." 1 Willist. on Contracts (Rev. Ed.) Sect. 116, p. 406.

In the same section, Professor Williston, summing up what he had previously said, also adds: "On no reasonable interpretation of the facts can it be said that a subscriber in an ordinary charitable subscription makes his promise in exchange for the promises inducing other subscribers to subscribe."

This statement of Professor Williston is fairly applicable to this case, as notwithstanding the prior language used in the instrument sued on, not only the promise, but the alleged agreement of Mrs. Gambrill was made to and with The American University, and not to and with any other subscribers to its "Fund for Endowment, Buildings, Betterments, Equipment, Liquidation, and Expenses."

(7) It is not seriously contended that The American University bound itself by any promise to do anything, or that there was any consideration, whatever, supporting a contract between it and Mrs. Gambrill. See 1 Willist. on Contr. (Rev. Ed.) Sect. 113. In fact, as we have already pointed out, a memorandum written in ink on the face of the instrument, executed by her, states that the money which she promised to pay The American University was (to be) "Given for a Scholarship." That would seem to be strong evidence of the real intent of Mrs. Gambrill. See 1 Willist. on Contr. (Rev. Ed.) Sect. 116.

But whether or not that phrase, when read in connection with the other provisions of the instrument, can be said to indicate that the sum promised was intended to be a mere gift, and nothing more, the instrument shows on its face that it was without consideration. Even if the phrase "Given for a Scholarship" be regarded as a condition of the intended gift, there is still nothing on the face of the instrument to indicate that any promise, whatever, with reference thereto, that could possibly satisfy the essential elements of the consideration, was made by The American University, or by any other person, so that neither *Central Maine General Hospital* v. *Carter* . . . nor *New Jersey Orthopaedic Hospital, etc.* v. *Wright* . . . are in point. See 1 Willist. on Contr. (Rev. Ed.) Sect. 116.

(8) As Mr. Justice Holmes aptly said in *Martin* v. *Meles:* "Of course the mere fact that a promisee relies upon a promise made without other consideration does not impart validity to what before was void."

It is true that the instrument in question also purported to be "In Consideration of one dollar in hand paid, receipt of which is hereby acknowledged."

(9–11) As a general rule, a court of law will not inquire into the adequacy or inadequacy of the consideration involved in a transaction. 1 Willist. on Contr. (Rev. Ed.) Sect. 115. But that rule does not usually apply when the consideration paid is of the same nature as the thing promised, and is equal or smaller in amount. This is generally true where there is an exchange of money for a promise to pay money. A consideration of one dollar, therefore, will not usually support a promise to pay a larger sum of money. 1 Willist. on Contr. (Rev. Ed.) Sect. 115, p. 393. . . . The reason for this exception is that in such cases, it is impossible for the law to indulge in the presumption of equivalence between the consideration and the promise. 1 Willist. on Contr. (Rev. Ed.) Sect. 115.

(12) This case is within the reason of that rule, and the one dollar, payment receipted for, will not support Mrs. Gambrill's promise to pay $5,000. Nor does the fact that the promise was apparently made in Wilmington, Delaware, and payment was to be made in Washington, D.C., affect this conclusion. . . .

(13) Where the place of payment is an essential element of a contract, which changes prior rights in that respect, the payment of a smaller sum may support a promise to pay a larger sum. 1 Willist. on Contr. (Rev. Ed.) Sect. 121.

The text books, cited by the plaintiff's attorney (1 Willist. on Contr. (Rev. Ed.) Sect. 115, and note 20, and Restat. Laws of Contr. Sect. 76 (c)) refer to cases of that character. This is apparent on reference to 1 Willist. on Contr. (Rev. Ed.) Sect. 121. But, as we have already pointed out, this case involves very different facts.

For the reasons above given, the judgment in question must be, and hereby is, vacated.

✧

To understand this case, the student must be acquainted with the fact that there *is* a school of thought that holds as follows: A charity is seeking promises of financial support. I agree to pay $500, and then change my mind. The charity may then sue me for the $500. Why? Where is the consideration? The court (some courts only, to be sure) presume that some other mythical party, B, agreed to donate his $250 in return for my promise to donate $500, and vice versa. The mere fact that B and I are actually unaware of one another's existence, and that all the usual requirements of offer and acceptance are lacking, has not restrained the advocates of this point of view. They want to find consideration, and they do so.

This whole theory is a vast exercise in fantasy, as Professor Williston points out in the text of the case. Why do courts strive so desperately to invent nonexistent consideration? They are resorting to legal fiction in order to find a means whereby certain promises may be enforced. Charities are a commendable activity. The judge believes a public policy exists, or should exist, to assist charities in their financial affairs, and to support this policy a mere promise to donate funds is made a legal obligation.

If a public policy can be found in support of charities, why not merely hold, as a matter of common law, that a promise to a charity is one type of promise that is enforceable without consideration? Some courts do so. This is a more honest approach, and is less confusing. If we resort to the fiction described above, there is danger that the concept of consideration will be stretched so far out of shape as to be eventually unrecognizable. If, on the other hand, we candidly admit that a promise to pay a sum to a charity is not a contract, but is enforceable for reasons of public policy, everyone will understand, and the meaning both of consideration and of contract remains clear.

In earlier times, and even today in England, courts were less free to depart from precedent than are modern American courts. Therefore, when a new situation was recognized, more reliance had to be placed on inventing fictions to disguise change. Today, many of our courts are quite open in departing from precedent and forging new legal concepts to deal with new situations.

In this case, the student should have recognized that an interest in Christian education is no consideration because that "interest" did not constitute a benefit extended by the university in exchange for the promise of money, nor does it constitute the sacrifice of a legal right. The university promised nothing in exchange for the patron's promise to make a gift to the university. Lastly, one dollar is not adequate consideration for $5,000. One dollar is consideration for one dollar, leaving $4,999, without any consideration in return. This situation constitutes an exception to the general rule that the court will not evaluate the relative worth of the considerations being exchanged. The value of practically everything is more or less subjective, but money is an exception. One dollar is worth one dollar, by definition.

The problem in this case seems to have sprung from the fact that the promisor died. Very likely, if she had lived she would have proceeded to make good her promise. If she had included a provision in her will award-ing the $5,000 to the University, they would have received the money without difficulty. Or, if she had made a gift during her lifetime—that is, actually handed the University the $5,000—this would have been an ade-quate transfer. The trouble was that she neither willed nor transferred the money, nor was there an enforceable contract. She merely made a promise, and a promise is unenforceable, even if in writing.

QUESTION

1. Who might reasonably object if the executor of Mrs. Gam-brill's estate actually gave the money in question to the American University?

Some Common Problems Involving Consideration

OUTPUT AND REQUIREMENT CONTRACTS

A classic illustration of consideration consisting of something other than the agreement to give money or property (certainly these are the easiest types of consideration to visualize) is the requirement, or output, contract. This type of contract has already been referred to under the heading of "Certainty," and often an agreement of this type may be attacked on the ground of uncertainty as well as on the ground of lack of consideration.

These are the contracts discussed in which *A* agrees to provide *B* with all the gasoline he may require during a year at an agreed price. The con-sideration on the part of *A* is the agreement binding him to sell gasoline at an agreed price, which would prevent him from raising the prices he charges *B,* even if the general market price goes up. Most litigation has centered around the question, what consideration is extended by *B?* Admittedly he is not bound to buy any presently known amount of gasoline from *A.* However, if he agrees to buy all the gasoline he needs from *A,* he will be in breach of contract if he buys from anyone other than *A.* In other words, he has surrendered his legal right to buy gasoline from anyone whom he chooses. He is bound to buy only from *A.* He has also bound himself to pay the agreed price to *A,* which could be disadvantageous to him and advantageous to *A* if the general price level should drop.

This basic sort of pattern may be found with a number of variations. The factor essential to validity is that some definite obligation be imposed. If the contract reads, "*A* will provide *B* with all the gasoline *B* desires at a stated price, consideration is lacking because *B* is not legally bound to buy exclusively from *A,* as in the previous case. He had the right to buy "as much as he desired" before negotiation began. If he wished to bind *A* to sell at a certain price he must forego something himself, which could be done by agreeing, as in the previous example, to buy all he *requires* for a period of time.

[EDITOR'S NOTE: In addition to presenting questions relating to certainty, and to lack of consideration, output and requirement contracts often present close questions as to whether or not they are in violation of the Clayton Act (see page 575). If this type of contract favors one party over his competitors, as is generally the case, and if in addition the agreement affects interstate commerce, as is often not the case, the Clayton Act is probably being violated. A more detailed treatment of this question is presented in the section on business regulation.]

The UCC provisions dealing with this type of contract are as follows:

UCC—SECTION 2–306: Output, Requirements and Exclusive Dealings.
(1) A term which measures the quantity by the output of the seller or the requirements of the buyer means such actual output or requirements as may occur in good faith, except that no quantity unreasonably disproportionate to any stated estimate or in the absence of a stated estimate to any normal or otherwise comparable prior output or requirements may be tendered or demanded.
(2) A lawful agreement by either the seller or the buyer for exclusive dealing in the kind of goods concerned imposes unless otherwise agreed an obligation by the seller to use best efforts to supply the goods and by the buyer to use best efforts to promote their sale.

There is no great discrepancy between the general law of contracts and the UCC treatment of sales contracts based upon output, requirements, and exclusive dealings. Given certain minimum requirements these have been enforced under common law, under the Uniform Sales Act, and continue to be under the UCC. Perhaps the stated philosophy behind the UCC, with its emphasis upon the test of dealing in good faith, and reasonable conduct, may make some disputes over contracts of this sort easier to decide. The quantity either of output or of requirements to be tendered or demanded will be judged by reasonable expectations. In the event of sudden increase or decrease either in output or in requirements, the standard for judgment will be not only the reasonable expectations but the good faith of the parties.

DUBOFF v. MATAM CORPORATION (New York, 1947)
71 NYS 2d 134

The essence of any cause of action based on going out of business and ceasing to have requirements or an output is bad faith.

The complaint rests upon a contract between the parties by which plaintiffs were appointed sales agency for "all home appliance products produced" by defendant for a period of five years. The complaint alleges that during the five year period defendant breached the contract by notifying plaintiffs that it would not continue after April 25, 1947, to operate its manufacturing plant and would not manufacture or produce any articles of merchandise after that date but would liquidate its business and dispose of and sell its plant, machinery and assets and discontinue all future business. The damages claimed are future profits lost by this alleged anticipatory breach of contract.

It will be noted that the complaint in no way suggests bad faith on the part of the defendant or a purpose to evade its obligation. For aught that appears, and indeed does appear from the papers on the motion, the proposed cessation of business is a bona fide liquidation impelled by business conditions.

(1) While the cases are not in harmony as to the extent of the obligation entailed in a requirements or output contract, the weight of authority, as expressed in Matter of United Cigar Stores Co. of America, is that there is no implied obligation to continue in business. The contracting party is left free to do with his business as he may deem best provided his conduct is bona fide. Requirements or output may decrease or increase as business conditions fluctuate, and as the Circuit Court of Appeals for this Circuit said in the above cited case, there can be no rational distinction between decreases stopping short of extinction and those which do not.

(2) The essence of any cause of action based on going out of business and ceasing to have requirements or an output is bad faith. A complaint which wholly fails to indicate bad faith, as this complaint does, fails to state a cause of action. The order appealed from should be reversed with $20 costs and disbursements to the appellant and the motion to vacate the attachment granted.
GLENNON and VAN VOORHIS, JJ., concur.
DORE and COHN, JJ., dissent.

✧

OPTIONS

A type of case closely related to the foregoing illustration is the option. An option is an offer containing a promise that it will not be revoked for a period of time. *A* offers to sell *B* his automobile for $500, with the provision that this option will remain open to *B* for a period of two weeks only. One week later *A* cancels the option. May he do this? Again we are reviewing relationships in another context studied earlier in this text. (See page 216.)

The student will recall that an option may not only be terminated by a provision contained in the terms of the option but that it may also be re-voked by communicating notice of revocation any time before the terminat-ing provision occurs. The option is not binding, because there is a lack of consideration. There was nothing promised in return for the promise to hold the option open.

An option may easily be made an enforceable contract, by extending consideration in exchange for keeping the option open. Real-estate options are especially common. Often after long negotiation, *A* agrees to sell his property to *B* for $25,000 at any time within 3 months. *B* in return gives *A* $50 as consideration, binding *A* to his promise. Now, *A* may not withdraw his offer. This is an enforceable contract. Forfeiting the legal right to sell to anyone other than *B* for three months is consideration; so is a payment of $50. *B* has purchased an irrevocable option from *A*, good for three months.

The rule regarding revocation of offers to sell, under the UCC, has been modified so that some offers may not be withdrawn, even if without consid-eration.

UCC—SECTION 2–205: Firm Offers.
An offer by a merchant to buy or sell goods in a signed writing which by its terms gives assurance that it will be held open *is not revocable, for lack of consideration,* during the time stated or if no time is stated for a reasonable time, but in no event may such period of irrevocability ex-ceed three months; but any such term of assurance on a form supplied by the offeree must be separately signed by the offeror.

Though this proviso was discussed earlier in the context of offer and acceptance, the student will recognize that the problem presented, viewed through the glass of traditional contract law, is a lack of consideration.

Section 2–205 clearly and categorically dispels any confusion as to whether a firm offer may be enforceable. A firm offer is enforceable with-out consideration, subject to the mild restrictions of a three-month time limit, a writing, and a special signature if the proviso is part of the offeree's form.

PAST CONSIDERATION

The idea of an exchange is basic to bilateral contracts, each promise being given in reliance upon the other. Even in unilateral contracts, the ex-change is clear enough, an act being performed in response to a promise even though the promise does not become binding until the act is com-pleted.

Close questions may arise as to whether the promises were made with the intent (or more accurately, with the apparent intent) that they give rise to binding legal relations, but these are questions of fact. If a promise is given gratuitously, or solely because of a previous moral (not legal) obligation, that promise is not binding.

One pattern in which this happens is as follows: *A* gratuitously does *B* a favor. Later, *B* promises to give *A* $100 to show his gratitude for *A*'s favor. He never gives *A* the $100, and *A* sues on *B*'s promise. (Perhaps more commonly *B* dies, and *A* sues *B*'s estate.)

Here the benefit to *B* came *before B* made any promise to compensate *A*. Alleged consideration of this kind is sometimes called *past consideration,* but actually there was *no* consideration, and suits of this type fail. The fact that *A* did *B* a favor is a closed incident. *A* did not ask for anything in exchange for his favor, at least before he himself performed it, nor did *B* promise anything to induce the favor. Thus, although *B* may have a moral obligation, his own promise is not in exchange for any promise of a future legal detriment to *A*, and consequently is unenforceable for lack of consideration.

The reason behind our adherence to the concept of consideration is that it provides a rule whereby mere social and moral obligations may be distinquished from promises that most reasonable men would intend to have legal consequences. Therefore, despite occasional criticism on the ground that right does not always triumph when consideration is required, and despite an occasional case to the contrary, the doctrine of consideration appears to perform a useful function in helping distinguish moral from legal obligations. If strong sentiment ever develops for the enforcement of moral obligations, no doubt consideration will be dropped as a test. Meanwhile promises made without a promise given in return are usually not enforceable.

AN APOLOGY FOR CONSIDERATION [9]

If there has been any tendency of American courts to abandon, repudiate, or reform consideration, the present writer was unable to discover it. On the contrary, there was less judicial criticism of the doctrine than in the early part of this century.

The doctrine of consideration still rules us, and not from its grave. Vigorous attacks upon it began in the latter part of the nineteenth century, and continued well toward the middle of the twentieth century. Critical comments in judicial opinions were chiefly aimed at the corollaries or side-effects of the doctrine. Lord Dunedin's budding affection was nipped by the supposed corollary that consideration must move from the person to whom the performance of the promise is to be rendered, and in the United States two of the more striking castigations of the doctrine related to the pre-existing duty rule. Treatise and

[9] Edwin W. Patterson, "An Apology for Consideration," *Columbia Law Review* (1958), **58**, No. 7, pp. 929 ff.

periodical writers made a direct frontal assault on consideration and advocated the substitution of some basically different criteria of the legal enforceability of promises. The eminent English legal historian, Sir William Holdsworth, concluded that the tightening up of the doctrine of consideration during the last sixty years or more of the last century was a retrogression from the looser "moral obligation" test that Lord Mansfield tried (unsuccessfully) to introduce, and that a complete change-over to some test of enforceable promises adopted from one of the civil law systems would be preferable. Lord Wright in 1936 earnestly urged the complete abolition of the doctrine and the substitution of a test, did the promisor at the time of contracting do so with a deliberate mind to contract? . . .

This article was undertaken after a study of the controversial literature plus a thorough search by the present writer for American cases reported and digested during the period 1944–1957. If there has been any tendency of American courts to abandon, repudiate, or reform consideration, the present writer was unable to discover it. On the contrary, there was less judicial criticism of the doctrine than in the early part of of this century. Perhaps it was a bit naive to suppose that one would find any questioning of a doctrine that had received the approval of the *Restatement of Contracts*. In that learned treatise the statement of the rules as to consideration is somewhat intricate for the nonspecialist, and the judges prefer to quote the simpler and slightly rhetorical statement of "promissory estoppel" in Section 90. Still, the doctrine of consideration seems likely to be with us for a long time to come, and we shall therefore need to make the best of it.

While the utilitarians had the conception of promises giving rise to expectations in society and of the law as attaching remedies to nonfulfillment, they did not give us any criteria by which to determine what expectations under what circumstances and to what extent should be legally sanctioned. The choices are practically unlimited. One might decree that all promises accompanied by a handclasp, or all promises for the buying or selling of goods, or all promises for doing in exchange for giving, should be enforceable. The categories, no matter how numerous, would still seem rather arbitrary when placed in opposition to an emergent and unincluded type of promise which had aroused expectation. The Anglo-American legal systems have not escaped from this apparent arbitrariness (and as far as I know, no other system has). One conclusion seems certain, that not every promise, even though it may arouse some expectation, should be legally enforceable. As the late Professor Morris R. Cohen said:

> Many of us indeed would shudder at the idea of being bound by every promise no matter how foolish, without any chance of letting increased wisdom undo past foolishness. Certainly, some freedom to change one's mind is necessary for free intercourse between those who lack omniscience.

Professor Cohen apparently had in mind, in the excerpt quoted, that the promisor would be "bound" to the same extent as a promisor is bound in Anglo-American law, that is, very few "hard luck stories" will excuse non-performance. Regarded as a moral obligation, on the other hand, the extent of the obligation of the promisor is rather indefinite because it is limited by rather vague and unspecified excuses, such as "change of circumstances" or "'unforeseen disadvantages" or even, possibly, "conflicting but overlooked prior engagement." To the argument that promises so qualified by social conventions should not be legally enforceable it might be replied that the expectation created by such promises is, because of the vagueness and variety of excuses, less intense or firm than the expectation created by a valid business contract, and that accordingly every promise should be legally enforceable to the extent of the expectation (reasonably) aroused by it. However, such a criterion of enforceability would be so uncertain as to give little or no security to the promisee, and would impair the freedom from contract of all casual promisors.

If mere expectation is not enough, then what must be added? What justification can be given for holding a promisor legally bound (and therefore subject to a decree of specific performance or a judgment for damages) by a promise that he no longer is willing, or able, to fulfill? One requirement would seem to be that the promisor shall have a fair opportunity to choose or not choose to assume a binding obligation; another is that the promisee's expectation be augmented by something else done or left undone as a result of the promise. The former may be satisfied by any kind of formality that will definitely notify the promisor that he is assuming a legal obligation; such a kind of formality is very hard to find or invent in our present society. Even if such a red-light formality were found or invented, would we not have to ask the promisee to show some additional reason, other than his mere expectation, why the promisor's default and unwillingness to pay damages should entitle the promisee to recover damages? The question is not wholly rhetorical, because it is arguable that the expectation created by such a solemn formality of execution would greatly enhance the harm of nonperformance, as compared with "casual" promises. Yet the attitude of courts of equity toward the specific performance of gratuitous sealed promises indicates the insufficiency of such a basis for enforceability. The enforcement of gratuitous promises is, in most legal systems, hedged about with some formalities and often with registration requirements.

In a modern "free-enterprise" society of the eighteenth to the twentieth centuries, economic institutions supported and economic processes depended upon the market (i.e., a set of markets, for producer, grower, consumer, middleman, etc.) and the practice or habit of promise-making became a pattern of our culture. Since this promise-making occurred as a part of bargains, and as a means of controlling the future, a legal rule that bargained-for promises are enforceable serves to support and to reenforce the use of contract as an economic device, and thus serves the needs of society. Professor Karl N. Llewellyn stated a similar thesis at a somewhat higher level of generality:

Bargain is then the social and legal machinery appropriate to arranging affairs in any specialized economy which relies on exchange rather than tradition (the manor) or authority (the army, the U.S.S.R.) for apportionment of productive energy and of product.

Any promise that satisfies this test has a presumptive claim to the protection of the social interest in the security of transactions.

To these comments some objections may be noted. One is that bargaining is at best a crass materialistic process in which one side tries to cheat the other, and that the adoption of bargain as an exclusive test (which is not defended here) forces aunts to bargain with their nephews for attendance at funerals, and similar distortions of family or friendly relations. However, the European marriage settlement should destroy any delusion that materialism crept into family arrangements by the back stairs of consideration. The slightly ironic idealism of some discussions of consideration is wholly unjustified. Bargaining is an important pattern of conduct in economic activities that serve our material wants and many of our ideal wants (books, plays, concerts, records, etc.). Bargaining is an important means (though not the only means) to the creation and maintenance of a good society.

It may be pointed out, moreover, that bargaining gives greater freedom of individual choice than does either tradition (custom) or political authority. The promisor who attaches a condition of return-advantage to his promise can attain a greater freedom of choice as to the satisfaction of his wants than if he were dependent upon benevolent gifts in return; and at the same time he relieves his promisee of the tacit obligation imposed by a generous gift. The making of gifts between individuals in our society is accompanied normally by some expectation of a return gift. If I have invited you to dinner, I expect you to invite me to some similar social affair; if I have invited you several times and you have not invited me (without any apparent excuse) then I would ordinarily be demeaning myself to invite you again. Reciprocation is thus expected, *between equals* at least, in many of the social and nonlegal arrangements of life, and serves to preserve the independence and self-esteem of those who gratuitously reciprocate with benefits. One who lives wholly by soliciting gifts is a professional beggar. Reciprocal exchange is, then, a widely approved pattern of conduct in social relations outside of commerce and industry, and this makes the similar but narrower pattern required by consideration familiar and accessible to those who are unaware of legal consequences.

For whatever it may be worth, some evidence from anthropology supports these views. In the Trobriand Islands the late Professor Malinowski found that the coastal fisherman who with ostensible generosity regularly gave fish to the vegetable-growing tribe of the hill country expected return gifts of vegetables, and the vegetable-growers expected fish. Thus local usage, or what might better be called a "course of dealing," created expectations of reciprocal advantage like those of contract. By way of contrast, in another primitive society the giving of costly gifts or extravagant potlatch parties was one way of imposing upon a rival (of the donor) a crushing obligation to reciprocate. The latter was not, apparently, a happy use of reciprocity.

In the United States the bargain test leaves unenforceable very few business agreements that satisfy the other requirements, definiteness of mutual assent and of terms. It is significant that the draftsmen of the *Uniform Commercial Code* not only adopted a definition of contract as a bargain, but also found it necessary to make only a few types of promises enforceable without consideration. One was the promise forming part of a modifying agreement, which is now made enforceable (if contained in a signed writing) even though given in exchange for a promise of performance of the pre-existing duty of the latter promisor, or even though made gratuitously. A second is the firm-offer provision, which makes a promise not to revoke an offer effective if in a signed writing. A third is the letter of credit provison, which gives such a letter one of the characteristics of a negotiable instrument. The first two changes are substantially the same as those recommended by the Law Revision Commission and enacted in New York, and also recommended by the Law Revision Committee in England.

The role of contract in our (American) society is not the same as it used to be, and it may be argued, then, that some changes in our contract law will be needed in order to adapt it to the changed uses of contract. For instance, the development of cash-and-carry stores for certain kinds of merchandise has diminished the consumer credit in those lines; but for other lines (automobiles, television sets, household equipment) the volume of consumer credit has become vastly more important. The collective bargaining agreement diminishes the importance of the individual-employee contract and leaves the employer with a less effective means of coercing performance than was the "firing" of the individual employee; yet it does preserve "bargaining" as the pattern. "Compulsory contracts," the terms of which are specified by legislation, as in the case of insurance contracts, or in other cases by trade association rules, have reduced the scope of dickering over many details, yet with but few exceptions there is some competition as to price. Even if these transactions create only standardized relations, they fulfill the role and satisfy the requirements of contract. The integration of industries has brought together under one corporate ownership industrial units which provide materials or parts or services for other divisions of the same corporation; here to some extent authority and accounting supersede contract. Still, none of these changes portend the disappearance of contract as a social and economic device.

How well does the requirement of consideration protect the unwary signer or the casual promisor? Better, I think, than any formality, such as the seal, especially after it was turned into an (L.S.) on a printed form, and better than merely a signed writing, or that plus a statement of intent to be legally bound. Any of these can be ingeniously disguised by the printed form and thus be unnoticed. Consideration requires something to be done outside the writing and that is less easy to fake. The casual promisor who promises a generous gift to a wheedling relative might be hooked by a "signed writing," even by one containing Professor Williston's formula; the requirement of consideration has stopped a good many gift-promisees from collecting on benevolent, casual, improvident, or inchoate promises. It sometimes protects businessmen against liability on overly generous promises that they make to their complaining customers, yet it is arguable that in such a case the "past consideration" should be sufficient. It is also arguable that *some* means should be available to make gift-promises enforceable. This suggestion will be discussed below. The widespread prevalence of exaggerated or groundless claims based on the law of torts suggests what may happen if the possibility of holding alleged promisors on vague expressions of hope were extended. Those who, like the poet and composer, want to stay out of the bargaining process as far as possible should not be dragged into inadvertent contract-making.

While the proof of consideration is often less simple than in the case of a mere formality, it is more flexible and offers more weapons for enforcement by promisees who have conferred consideration yet have not sufficiently formalized it. Such proof is not confined to the express terms of the contract; it may be inferred from those terms, together with usage, course of dealing, and other circumstances outside the explicit utterances of the parties. . . .

Is proof of consideration the same as proof of agreement or "mutual assent" in the Anglo-American sense of offer and acceptance? One writer [10] who defends consideration maintains that:

> . . . consideration in its essential nature is an aspect merely of the fundamental notion of bargain, other aspects of which, no less but no more important, are offer and acceptance. Consideration, offer and acceptance are an indivisible trinity, facets of one identical notion which is that of bargain.

[10] See Hamson, *The Reform of Consideration,* 54 L.Q. Rev. 233 (1938), p. 234.

CHAPTER TWENTY-ONE

Promises Enforceable without Consideration

No one denies that in certain cases promises are enforced which do not fall within the usual definition of contract, and which lack consideration in the usual sense. [Thus] most courts are willing to enforce promises made in some types of charitable subscriptions. Some courts have tried valiantly to find a consideration present in these cases [through legal fictions]. . . . Many courts base their decision on what seems to be the real reason for this rule, namely, a public policy favoring charity, even to the extent of enforcing promises to charities made without consideration.

A Problem in Semantics

ANYONE FAMILIAR with contract law is aware that a considerable amount has been written in recent years concerning the "exceptions" to the doctrine of consideration. As may happen in the field of law, even the terminology defining the "exceptions" is not agreed upon.

Certainly one must observe that a number of isolated but clearly defined situations exist in which a *promise* may be enforced without consideration as defined by the "benefit or detriment" theory. The difference as to terminology centers initially around the definition of a contract. If we define a *promise* that is enforceable for any reason as a *contract,* we must then say that in a number of instances, "contracts" are enforceable without consideration in the "benefit-detriment" sense. If we pursue this logic further, and insist that every "contract"—as defined *in the previous sentence*—*does* have consideration, then, because there is no consideration in the benefit-detriment sense, we end up by describing some very peculiar and dissimilar relationships as "consideration." By this approach we end up by describing any reason for enforcing a promise as consideration.

We are aware that eminent writers take both sides on this question, and perhaps modesty should dictate silence. However, we will venture to express the opinion that communication between lawyers will be facilitated by the following approach: rather than bending the terms *contract* and *consideration* beyond recognition, we should confine our use of these terms to the traditional and well-defined meanings. Rather than calling all *enforceable promises* contracts, we should simply recognize that in special cases, reasons of policy or tradition call for the enforcing of certain categories of promise without a contract. Rather than calling these widely divergent reasons for enforcing promises "consideration" (which unless mixed with these other ideas *does* have a well-defined meaning), we should confine the meaning of consideration to the benefit-detriment relationship.

Restricting meanings to recognizable concepts will not restrict the evolution of the law, but will merely encourage the development of new terms as needed rather than using old terms as a rug under which to sweep all sorts of meanings.

The argument is one of semantics. No one denies that in certain cases promises are enforced that do not fall within the usual definition of contract and that lack consideration in the usual sense. But we prefer not to call these promises contracts. We will now examine some of these types of promises.

Revival of Duties Barred by the Statute of Limitations or by Discharge in Bankruptcy

There are instances in which the right to bring suit on a contract may be barred due to the operation of certain rules of law. Two examples of rules with this effect are the statute of limitations and discharge in bankruptcy.

Each of these is referred to elsewhere, bankruptcy on page 641 and the statute of limitations on page 286. These two defenses have much in common. Both are somewhat technical barriers to the collection of what is often a perfectly just claim. However, as has been explained in the earlier treatment of these defenses, there are valid reasons of public policy for both these defenses.

It happens that debts that are rendered uncollectible because of the statute of limitations or discharge in bankruptcy may be "revived" by the act of the debtor promising to pay the debt (usually the promise must be in writing) or by part payment after a debt is barred. The promise, or part payment, renders the entire debt collectible all over again.

Thus the well-intentioned debtor loses the legal protection provided by the statute of limitations or of the bankruptcy laws, when he makes such a promise in writing, or makes part payment, whereas the cynical, hard-boiled debtor who would never make such a promise or pay anything runs no risk.

We mention these rules here because some authorities consider these promises to be examples of contracts enforceable because of past consideration. Both the utility of these exceptions and the connection with the doctrine of considerations seem doubtful.

The reasons of policy behind extending a discharge based upon both limitations and bankruptcy seem sound enough. But what is the policy behind the exception mentioned above, that a written promise or part payment will render the debtor liable all over again? What is so magic about a written promise in this type of case? There is no requirement that the creditor should have in some way depended upon the promise; the rule is absolute. Both of these rulings may be argued on the basis of waiver, but why should a fiction such as waiver count more heavily than the sound reason behind granting a discharge?

One cannot help suspecting that an unstated rationale has been that, because the creditor let his guard down and was barred from suit by a mere technicality, maybe the debtor ought to have some technicalities to ensnare *him*. However, this is only an an unscientific guess. Decades of precedent lie behind the rules. And, at any rate, the exceptions do exist. The next question is, why discuss these exceptions in terms of consideration? By this analysis the original debt is deemed a moral obligation, and the promise to pay is deemed a moral consideration; a contract is said to result, and this is proof that moral consideration can be valid consideration.

We submit that the issue of consideration is not involved. A debt is rendered uncollectible through a technical bar—that is, limitations or bankruptcy. Surely the technical bar can be canceled out by another technicality, such as a promise to pay, assuming this is desirable. Then, why contrive an explanation based on consideration? To do so is, again, stretching the normal meaning of consideration out of recognition. This appears to be the only situation in which most courts do purport to recognize "moral consideration."

STELMACK ET AL. v. *GLEN ALDEN COAL COMPANY* (Pennsylvania, 1940) 14 A 2d 127 (Part Two)

A moral obligation is sufficient to support an express promise, where there has been a pre-existing obligation which has become inoperative by positive law.

[*See pages 311–312 for Part One of this case, in which the facts are stated.*]

Plaintiffs second point is also without merit. The principle asserted in some of our decisions that "moral consideration" will support a contract has no application to the situation here presented. The limitations upon this doctrine were clearly stated in *Stebbins* v. *County of Crawford* . . . where we said: "A moral obligation is sufficient to support an express promise, where there has been a pre-existing obligation which has become inoperative by positive law.[1] . . . In all these cases there is a moral obligation founded upon antecedent valuable consideration. Such promises, therefore, have a sound legal basis. They are not promises to pay something for nothing, not naked pacts, but the voluntary revival or creation of obligations which before existed in natural law, but which had been dispensed with, not for the benefit of the party obliged solely, but principally for the public convenience." . . . The authorities cited by plaintiffs plainly fall within this category.

(4) Here there was no pre-existing legal or equitable obligation which could serve as the foundation of a moral obligation. The plaintiffs and their predecessors in title were fully compensated, as expressly stated in the original deed, for any loss which might result from the withdrawal of surface support by the owner of the mining rights. The possibility of damage was reflected in the reduced purchase price paid for the property. Plaintiffs accepted the deed with full knowledge of the reservations and waiver of damages, and with the express stipulation that defendant should have no liability whatsoever for a subsidence of the land.

✧

According to this case, Pennsylvania courts recognize moral consideration in cases where a rule of law has barred a remedy, and a subsequent promise has been made to pay the debt. This case, however, did not fall within that narrow pattern, and no consideration was found here, despite that fact that defendant had made an express promise that was later repudiated.

QUESTION

1. Is repudiation of a promise to pay a debt barred by a rule of law necessarily a more grave moral offense than repudiation of other types of promises?

Charitable Subscriptions

Most courts are willing to enforce promises made in some types of charitable subscriptions. Thus, in a drive for hospital funds, parties promising sums to the drive and later refusing to pay may be held for the sum promised. Some courts have tried valiantly to find a consideration present in these cases, by such devices as pretending that *A* gave his promise in

---

[1] *Pre-existing obligation which has become inoperative by positive law* refers to discharge by statute of limitations or bankruptcy, just discussed.

consideration that other parties he had never heard of would do the same. Because typically there was no evidence that he really did give his contribution for that reason, the argument is hard to sustain. Many courts base their decision on what seems to be the real reason for this rule—namely, a public policy favoring charity, even to the extent of enforcing promises to charities made without consideration. (See *American University v. Todd,* page 317.)

Not all charities are thought sufficiently important to justify this type of ruling. The American University was not given the benefit of this theory. Hospitals are probably the most common beneficiaries of promises enforceable without consideration in return. Whether a particular charity will be permitted to recover on subscription promises is a matter to be decided in the individual jurisdiction.

Promissory Estoppel

Promissory estoppel is a basis for enforcing promises that has attracted considerable interest in recent years. In order to fully explain the term, we must begin by stating that "estoppel" is a concept of exceedingly broad dimensions in the field of law, and "promissory" estoppel is only one application of this concept. The general function of estoppel may be explained crudely in this fashion: "If you lure someone out on a limb, you can't saw the limb off." The elements of estoppel may be generalized as containing (1) creation of an appearance by one party with the knowledge that another party may rely on that appearance; (2) justifiable reliance by the second party upon the appearance created by the first party; (3) an attempt by the first party to deny the validity of the appearance he created, thereby injuring the second party. Upon proof of these facts, a court would intervene and prevent step 3. Thus the first party is being estopped—or in English "stopped"—from carrying out his unfair and injurious action in denying the validity of the appearance he has created.

Estoppel is used by some courts to prevent the unfairness stemming from some unilateral contracts (see page 215). When a party makes an offer of a unilateral contract, the other party begins to perform; then after the second party has undertaken performance, the first attempts to withdraw his offer (which, as we know, he could do at English common law), some courts will estop the first party from withdrawing his offer until the second party has had a reasonable opportunity to complete his performance. Fraud and estoppel are somewhat related concepts, except that in fraud some type of misrepresentation is present, whereas in estoppel there need not be any; it is the reversal of position following the other party's justifiable reliance that creates an estoppel. Estoppel and waiver are very similar, some differences being that waiver may be found regardless of any injury to another party; estoppel requires a prospective injury. In waiver the emphasis is on "voluntary surrender" of a right; in estoppel the emphasis is upon "inducing reliance" by the other party.

Promissory estoppel is a special form of estoppel, and arises when the deceptive appearance is created through a promise by one party. Promissory estoppel has the effect of preventing the party from withdrawing a promise made and relied upon by the other party, and thus, in effect, provides a rationale for requiring the promisor to perform the promise.

An exaggerated and imaginary case of promissory estoppel might be as follows: You promise your maiden aunt, who is in dire circumstances in some far-off state, that you will provide her housing on your own property. You request nothing of her, and you want nothing from her. If she were already in town things would be simpler, but because she isn't she has to hitch-hike across the country to take advantage of your promise. After a harrowing two-month hitch-hiking venture across the country, she presents herself tired, impoverished, and ill, at which point you inform her that you have changed your mind. In this case, some courts would enforce your promise on the ground of promissory estoppel.

STELMACK ET AL. v. GLEN ALDEN COAL COMPANY (Pennsylvania, 1940) 14 A 2d 127 (Part Three)

A promise which the promisor should reasonably expect to induce action or forbearance of a definite and substantial character on the part of the promises and which does induce such action or forbearance is binding if injustice can be avoided only by enforcement of the promise.

[See pages 311–312 and 333–334 for Parts One and Two of this case. The statement of facts is contained in Part One.

(5) Nor can plaintiffs' final contention that the defendant should be stopped from repudiating its promise be sustained. The doctrine of promissory estoppel, upon which they rely, may be invoked only in those cases where all the elements of a true estoppel are present, for if it is loosely applied any promise, regardless of the complete absence of consideration, would be enforceable. The principle involved is defined in the Restatement, Contracts, Section 90, in the following terms: "A promise which the promisor should reasonably expect to induce action of forbearance of a definite and substantial character on the part of the promisee and which does induce such action or forbearance is binding if injustice can be avoided only by enforcement of the promise." The subject is fully discussed in a recent decision of this court, *Fried* v. *Fisher*, . . . where the safeguards upon the application of the doctrine are clearly set forth.

(6, 7) Here no action was taken by plaintiffs in reliance upon the defendant's promise which resulted in disadvantage to them. They did not alter their position adversely or substantially. They have suffered no injustice in being deprived of a gratuitous benefit to which they have no legal or equitable right. We are satisfied that there is nothing in the present record to bring this case within any recognized exception to the well-settled principle of contract law, that a promise unsupported by consideration is nudum pactum, and unenforceable.

The judgment of the court below is affirmed.

✧

CHAPTER TWENTY-TWO

Contracts for Settling Disputes, and for Altering Existing Obligations

Because the terminology in this area is so confused in its application, we suggest that the student focus his attention on the process of discharge, particularly as affected by the intent of the parties, rather than on the terminology used to describe the process.

Compromise of Torts

A LEGAL DISPUTE may be compromised by a contract in which each party agrees to make some concession. Usually this is done by one party paying a sum of money in exchange for the other party's surrendering whatever legal claim he may have. (This is accomplished by the latter signing a paper termed a *release*.)

Contracts to compromise may terminate a dispute arising from either contract or tort, but because the process is more easily explained in the case of a tort, that form of compromise will be discussed first.

Practically any time a tort is claimed to have been committed, the parties involved have the decision to make: should they proceed to litigate the claim, or should they settle the claim out of court? Of course, either party by being stubborn can prevent settlement, but there are advantages to both parties in negotiating an out-of-court settlement if possible. Savings in time and emotional wear and tear can be substantial to say nothing of the savings in court costs, attorney fees, and costs of investigation. Parties may also wish to avoid the publicity inherent in a court determination.

The negotiation of tort settlements is extremely important to our casualty insurance companies, because almost every automobile accident gives rise to a tort claim against a negligent party and indirectly against his insurer.[1] The insurance adjuster is hired to negotiate the settlement of claims against his company. The fact that the overwhelming number of minor claims and most major claims are settled expediently out of court is a great economy to the insurers and to the public.

Few legal principles are involved in negotiating the compromise of a tort. The figure arrived at is almost entirely a question of bargaining, and could fall anywhere between the minimum verdict possible and the maximum verdict possible. If liability is unclear, but severe personal injuries are involved, the range of possible court awards might easily be from zero to $100,000. Generally, the plaintiff attempts to impress the defendant with the possibility of a fantastically high verdict, whereas the defendant attempts to impress the plaintiff with the possibility of no verdict, because of possible contributory negligence or some other defense. Many attorneys prefer to try an occasional case even if settlement could be obtained, in the hope of getting a huge verdict and thus impressing their opponents (the local insurance claims men) with their prowess—a valuable impression to carry into negotiation in future cases.

Many insurers like to try an occasional case in the hope of getting a defendant's verdict or a low jury award. Either of these can be highly embarrassing to the plaintiff's attorney, and will thus presumably impress other attorneys with the danger of not making prompt settlements in the future.

When a figure acceptable to both parties is determined, a binding contract is formed, the consideration being a release—that is, surrender of the right to sue in exchange for the payment of a sum of money. The practice is for the insurer to exchange a check for a signed release immediately upon agreement, the release being a document embodying all the terms of the contract of settlement.

Occasionally, a tort claim already compromised may be discovered to have been totally invalid. If the claim was fraudulent, the consideration given for the release may, of course, be recovered through rescission. If the claim was sincerely advanced even though it would not have supported a verdict, the courts have differed, but the more recent cases tend to hold that good faith on the part of the plaintiff is all that is required. Practically, this is the best solution.

Negligence cases are often very complex, and often there is some plausible argument to the effect that the defendant was not liable. The line between liability and no liability can be paper-thin and largely a question of

[1] Liability insurance protects the insured from one thing: legal liability. The insurer agrees to defend suits based on allegations that the insured defendant is legally liable and to pay up to the amount of the policy limits if the plaintiff wins.

subjective judgment until a case is tried and hindsight clarifies the situation. Why should the defendant be permitted to settle a doubtful case, then claim his money back on the ground of nonliability? The defendant always has the option to investigate, reflect on the evidence, reject a settlement, and defend in court if he wishes. It seems doubtful that he needs the protection of being able to overthrow his compromises except when he was misled by fraud. Here, as is normally the case, the adequacy of the consideration should be left to the parties to determine.

KELLER v. WOLF ET AL. (Minnesota, 1953)
58 NW 2d 891

> . . . *Whether a settlement of a claim for damages has been improvidently made is not to be determined by considering only the seriousness of the injuries and the extent of the damages. Plaintiff's likelihood of being able to establish a right of recovery against defendants must also be taken into consideration.*

Plaintiff, 23 years of age, was injured on the night of May 22, 1951, while walking on a public street in Long Prairie, Minnesota, when she was struck by an automobile driven by defendant Richard Wolf and owned by defendant George Wolf. Shortly thereafter, plaintiff retained Frank L. King as her attorney to institute a personal injury action. Subsequently, Logan O. Scow was substituted for King as her attorney. Before the action came on for trial, King filed a $2,000 lien for attorney's fees. The case was never tried on the merits since a stipulation for settlement was made on the afternoon of the day set for trial. The motion to set aside the stipulation was made almost two months later.

The law favors settlement of claims without recourse to litigation. . . . However, it is well settled that a stipulation for settlement may be set aside or avoided: (1) for fraud or collusion: (2) for mistake; or (3) where the stipulation was improvidently made and in equity and good conscience should not be allowed to stand. . . . Fraud and collusion have been expressly disclaimed by appellant's counsel and are not at issue here. There is no doubt that counsel for both parties acted with integrity and in good faith. The two grounds upon which counsel does claim that the release should be set aside are mistake and improvidence, both of which presented questions of fact which were determined by the trial court upon affidavits presented to it for consideration.

Plaintiff contends that she agreed to a settlement of $7,000 on the mistaken assumption that said sum was to be over and above any amount required to discharge the $2,000 lien of her prior attorney. She and her father, in their joint affidavit, alleged that Scow told her, prior to settlement, that she would receive the entire $7,000 amount. Scow's affidavit is directly to the contrary. Without doubt, plaintiff knew that the lien had been filed, and there is evidence that she knew that such lien would have to be satisfied out of the $7,000. The conflicting evidence without question sustains the trial court's finding the plaintiff was laboring under no mistake when she agreed to the settlement.

In any event, although in Minnesota the mistake need not be "mutual" in the sense that both parties are under a similar delusion, there must be concealment or, at least, knowledge on the part of one party that the other party is laboring under a mistake in order to set aside a release for unilateral mistake. . . .

Plaintiff here admitted at the hearing on the motion that there was no mistake on the part of defendants, nor did plaintiff claim that there was any concealment on the part of defendants or knowledge that plaintiff was laboring under any mistake. There appears, therefore, to be no evidence on which the release could be set aside on the grounds of mistake in any event.

We next come to the question whether the settlement of $7,000 was improvidently made. Improvidence in the making of a personal injury settlement imports an absence of calculation or a thoughtless exercise of discretion whereby a result is brought about which in equity and good conscience ought not to be allowed to stand.

With respect to plaintiff's injuries, her attending physician's affidavit—which is not seriously challenged—states:

> . . . that her injuries consisted of multiple fractures of the pelvis, compound fracture and dislocation of the right ankle, fractured rib and multiple bruises and that her condition was critical and she required blood transfusions and surgery of the ankle; that she was hospitalized for a long period of time and her hospital and doctor bill are approximately $900.00; that she is permanently crippled and will limp for the rest of her life, and that she will never be able to give normal birth to a child if the child weighs over four pounds . . . that said Pearl Keller has a 20 per cent disability in her said ankle and leg as a result of the injuries sustained. . . .

Her injuries are both serious and permanent. She has suffered considerable pain and has incurred much medical expense. There was a conflicting opinion in a letter introduced by defendants' counsel at the hearing, but there was an objection that the letter was a mere unsworn statement and, therefore, inadmissible. The objection was well taken, and the letter is not considered on this review. If no other factor were to be considered than the extent of plaintiff's injuries and damages, the settlement would clearly appear to have been improvidently made.

However, whether a settlement of a claim for damages has been improvidently made is not to be determined by considering only the seriousness of the injuries and the extent of the damages. Plaintiff's likelihood of being able to establish a right of recovery against defendants must also be taken into consideration. As the trial judge said in summarizing the instant situation:

> . . . They [plaintiff and her father] are apparently led by what they hear on the street—determined that they must have a very large sum in spite of the fact that the element of contributory negligence may bar recovery entirely.

Plaintiff's prospects regarding proof of negligence and contributory negligence *must* be considered and evaluated in determining whether a particular settlement is provident. It is defendant's contention that the settlement was provident since plaintiff's right of effecting any recovery at all was doubtful because of evidence of contributory negligence.

In his affidavit, counsel for defendants alleges that—

> . . . defendants' evidence would have shown that plaintiff was walking near the center line and some of defendants' evidence would have shown that she was on the wrong side of the road; . . . that there was a sidewalk for plaintiff to walk along and upon adjacent to the roadway; . . . that plaintiff was guilty of a violation of . . . [statute].

The affidavit also contains counsel's opinion that, in view of Minnesota law as applied to plaintiff's evidence, "it was very doubtful if the plaintiff would be entitled to recover from the defendants under the law."

The affidavit of the attorney who represented plaintiff at the settlement contains similar indications of what the evidence would have shown and that such evidence "might have warranted a jury finding that . . . [plaintiff] was contributorily negligent. . . ." This affidavit also mentions the delicate health of plaintiff and that counsel was advised by plaintiff's doctor that it would be to the best interest of plaintiff to avoid a trial.

The issue presented by the motion involved in this appeal is not plaintiff's contributory negligence as such but rather whether or not the settlement was provident in view of the *probable evidence* of plaintiff's contributory negligence. In deciding whether or not to settle for an amount less than the full measure of the damages an attorney must consider the probable evidence which will be presented and its potential effect on the jury. Such probable evidence may consist of physical exhibits, such as photographs, or it may involve facts which the witness has indicated to the attorney that he will testify to. Thus, in evaluating the latter type of evidence, the very statements of the witnesses as to what they will testify to are to be considered in determining the advisability of a settlement: that is, the fact that the statements were made, as distinguished from the truth of the statements, is an important consideration. The hearsay rule has no application where the fact that a person not a witness had made a statement is relevant and the statement is introduced merely to prove the fact of its being made and not to prove the facts stated. . . . It is the notice and knowledge acquired by the statements of the witnesses that must be employed in deciding whether a settlement for a certain amount is provident. It is counsel's action in the face of these statements that is being tested by the motion involved here. Of course, the accuracy of the attorney in summarizing the statements, the accuracy of the witness in relating the facts, and the possibility that the witness may change his testimony all are important in determining the weight of this evidence; but the statements themselves, as distinguished from the truth of the statements, are to be considered in deciding on a settlement and are admissible as evidence on the issue of the providence of that settlement. . . .

In view of the probability of adverse testimony as indicated in the affidavits of both counsel, the opinions of both counsel as set forth in the same affidavits, and the "facts" relating to the scene of the accident known to the attorneys together with the previous record of the jury which would decide the case, plaintiff's physical condition, and the competence of opposing counsel as expressed by plaintiff's attorney, it is our opinion that there is sufficient evidence to support the conclusion of the trial judge that the settlement was provident. The ruling did not involve any abuse of discretion.

Affirmed.

DELL, J., took no part in the consideration or decision of this case.

✧

A lien is an encumbrance upon property, the property being in this case the money extended by the insurance company as settlement of all claims. The effect of the lien in this case is to prevent the plaintiff from availing herself of the proceeds of her settlement until the claim of the lien-holder, King, her first attorney, is established and paid. However, merely because he has filed a $2,000 lien does not mean that she will have to pay $2,000. The reasonableness of the $2,000 fee is still a matter that may be litigated.

The issue of mistake should provide no problem, having been considered in detail earlier. Was the mistake here unilateral or bilateral?

Tort claims, even when liability is admitted, are about as unliquidated as a claim may get, because much of the claim involves such intangibles as pain and suffering, disabilities that may or may not turn out to be permanent, and future loss of wages. Considerable guesswork must always be involved in determinations of what is or is not a reasonable settlement. Where, as here, the liability is extremely doubtful because of evidence of contributory negligence, it may well be that any sum, even $5, would constitute a reasonable settlement. After all, the plaintiff might very well go to the expense of suit and recover nothing.

QUESTIONS

1. Should the amount of money a party wants be an important consideration in determining the amount for which a party should settle out of court?

2. What socially desirable purpose does the out-of-court settlement serve?

Settlement of Unliquidated Claims

As was true of tort claims, disputed contract claims may be settled by compromise. However, the compromise of contract is an area of much greater complexity than the compromise of torts. We will find a paradox when we attempt to apply the usual rules of consideration to some of these problems. In certain instances, the results are patently ridiculous; the cure, not so clear.

To facilitate the study of compromise of contracts, they are divided into two groups; liquidated and unliquidated. Liquidated contracts are those that may be reduced to a definite or logically ascertainable monetary sum. They call for the payment of a certain sum of money, or a sum of money calculable by some well-defined process, usually simple arithmetic. Thus, a claim for wages due for eight hours worked at $1.50 per hour is a liquidated claim of $12.

Unliquidated contracts are those that may not be reduced to a definite sum. A claim is considered unliquidated when a dispute, in which both parties are in good faith, exists either as to the validity of the claim or to the amount; as when one party asserts he is owed one amount and the other claims that he owes a lesser amount. In our last example, there might be a dispute in good faith over the hours actually worked, or the rate of pay agreed upon, which would render the claim unliquidated.

An unliquidated contract may be compromised in much the same fashion as a tort claim. Assuming two parties disagree on the amount due, an intermediate figure may be agreed upon, and a contract made to settle the dispute at this figure. The consideration extended is the surrender by a creditor of his claim for a higher amount in exchange for a surrender by the debtor of his claim that he owes a lesser amount. Thus a compromise entered into in good faith contains consideration on both sides. In cases of this type, obviously one party is often correct in his original claim and really is paying more, or receiving less, under the compromise than originally agreed. However, after compromise, the claim cannot be reopened without a showing of fraud by the opposite party. After all, the whole purpose of this type of agreement is to bring an end to disputes and litigation.

Other problems lurk within the facts of the typical settlement problem. When an agreement is made to settle a contractual dispute, when are the former claims actually discharged? Certainly two possibilities are apparent. The contract of compromise could be assumed to replace the previous contract immediately upon agreement, so that any recovery would not be limited to the terms of the compromise. Actually this would be a bilateral contract, being effective upon the exchange of promises. Or, the compromise could merely be considered as a tentative agreement, to serve as a discharge only when performed by payment, thus being a unilateral contract, requiring performance rather than mere agreement before taking effect.

Most courts decide the question as to when the second agreement supersedes the first purely on the basis of the apparent intent of the parties. If the parties seemed to intend the second agreement as canceling the first, the first is considered canceled. If they seemed to intend the second agreement to be effective as a discharge only when actually performed, the first would not be canceled until performance of the second, and meanwhile either party could change his mind.

Because in the usual situation neither party gave the slightest thought as to whether the new agreement was to cancel the old one immediately or upon performance, the interpretation of their "intent" leaves quite a lot of leeway to the discretion of the court.

When actual performance of the new agreement is required in order to discharge the original one, the new agreement is called the *accord* and the later performance the *satisfaction*. Thus, a completed performance is termed an *accord and satisfaction*. This terminology is also applied by some courts, but not by others, to the situation where a new agreement acts as an immediate discharge of a prior contract. Because the terminology in this area is so confused in its application, we suggest that the student focus his attention on the process of discharge, particularly as affected by the intent of the parties, rather than on the terminology used to describe the process.

OLSON v. *WILSON & COMPANY* (Iowa, 1953)
58 NW 2d 381

> *Accord and satisfaction is a method of discharging a contract or cause of action, whereby the parties agree to give and accept something in settlement of the claim or demand of the one against the other, and perform such agreement, the "accord" being the agreement, and the "satisfaction" its execution or performance.*

LARSON, J.

On or about August 1, 1951, the plaintiff sold thirty head of cattle, by oral contract, to the defendant, through defendant's agent, a Mr. Johnson. Plaintiff claimed he was to receive thirty-five cents a pound for the cattle, plus the excess if they were dressed out at a better grade. Defendant admits buying the cattle but denies plaintiff's claim as to the price agreed upon and contends that the cattle were purchased from plaintiff on a grade and yield basis in compliance with O.P.S. regulations. Under plaintiff's claim they amounted to $10,725.75. Under defendant's claim the amount due was $9,372.80.

After delivery of the cattle to defendant on August 6th, plaintiff received a draft in the net sum of $9,372.80, which was marked "in full payment of the above items." The items were listed as "cattle, 30 head, weight 30645, price $30.59, amount $9374.30, average test." On August 16th, through his attorney, plaintiff, by letter acknowledged receipt of the draft and advised defendant of his demand for $1351.45 in addition to the amount received. This letter stated, "Mr. Olson has not cashed this check and will not cash the check until he has been paid the additional sum of $1351.45 which is the amount owing him for thirty head of cattle at 35¢ per pound." Plaintiff also threatened the commencement of suit if the balance claimed was not received by August 30, 1951. Defendant replied by letter of August 23rd stating that they were making a "detailed investigation" of the matter in dispute and would advise plaintiff when it was completed.

On September 14, 1951, plaintiff through his attorney, again wrote the defendant company asking that defendant grant permission to plaintiff to cash the original draft without prejudice to plaintiff's claim for the balance, suggesting these words, "That Myrl Olson may endorse and cash Wilson & Co.'s Draft No. 9634, dated August 6, 1951, in the sum of $9372.80 without prejudice to any claim or rights he may have against your company, and that your company will not construe said endorsement and presentation for payment to be an admission by Mr. Olson that he has been paid in full for said 30 head of cattle weighing 30645 pounds."

On September 17, 1951 the defendant company wrote plaintiff's attorney advising him it had completed an investigation and was satisfied that there was no guaranteed price of thirty-five cents per pound, and that the draft represented a remittance on the basis of grade and yield of the cattle slaughtered, and that the plaintiff had received payment for their full value. This letter also stated: "Your communication of September 14th concerning the cashing of the check is, of course, a matter for the decision of Mr. Olson, since he was paid the full value of his cattle and this value was contained in our original remittance."

On October 1, 1951, the plaintiff through counsel again wrote defendant as follows:

> This letter is to advise you that today Myrl Olson presented for payment your draft No. 9634 in the sum of $9372.80. However, it is Mr. Olson's intention to consider this draft as only a partial payment on the 30 head of cattle sold to your company. It is not Mr. Olson's intention to accept this draft in full satisfaction of his claim against your company nor is the acceptance of this draft to be considered as an accord and satisfaction. . . . Mr. Olson does not intend to waive any rights or claims he may have for the balance in the sum of $1351.45. . . .

This letter was delivered to defendant two days later in Albert Lea, Minn. The draft was payable at First National Bank in Chicago, Illinois. Copies of the letters were filed as exhibits and were not denied. The present suit was commenced October 3, 1951, with plaintiff asking judgment against defendant for the sum of $1351.45.

Based upon the correspondence between the parties, the defendant, in addition to denying plaintiff's version of the contract, pleaded accord and satisfaction and asked dismissal of plaintiff's action. Defendant also made application to the court to adjudicate separately in advance of trial, in accordance with Rule 105, 58 I.C.A., the law issue of accord and satisfaction. The matter was submitted on the uncontroverted allegations of the pleadings on April 25, 1952 and the learned trial court in finding for the defendant held as a matter of law that there was an accord and satisfaction. We agree.

The only question before us is whether under the record there was an accord and satisfaction established as a matter of law.

The law looks with favor on the adjustment and settlement of controversies without resorting to court action. . . . Settlement by accord and satisfaction involves essentially a new contract or agreement, and the elements of a new contract must be found in the settlement to make it valid. . . . Obviously each case must be determined upon its own facts and circumstances. However, there are certain rules and decisions which guide and control transactions of this kind, such as those affecting liquidated and unliquidated claims, and the acts of the parties relating to intention, consideration, necessary implications, and bona fide disputes. We shall discuss them as they relate to this case, which is not complicated. It involves only a simple dispute between two parties over the terms of an oral agreement by which plaintiff sold and delivered cattle to the defendant.

There are many definitions of accord and satisfaction. "Accord and satisfaction is a method of discharging a contract or cause of action, whereby the parties agree to give and accept something in settlement of the claim or demand of the one against the other, and perform such agreement, the 'accord' being the agreement, and the 'satisfaction' its execution or performance."

In an early Iowa case, *Perin* v. *Cathcart,* Judge Deemer said: "But as an accord and satisfaction is an executed agreement whereby one of the parties undertakes to give, and the other to accept, in satisfaction of a claim arising either from contract or tort, something other or different from what he is or considers himself entitled to, no invariable rule can be laid down, with any degree of certainty, as to what constitutes such an agreement. Each case must be determined largely on its peculiar facts. To constitute a valid accord and satisfaction, not only must it be shown that the debtor gave the amount in satisfaction, but that it was accepted by the creditor as such. . . . The agreement need not be express, but may be implied from circumstances, as shown in the cases just cited. Where an offer of accord is made on condition that it is to be taken in full of demands, the creditor, doubtless, has no alternative but to refuse it or accept it upon such conditions. . . ."

While in the broad field of the law relating to accord and satisfaction, there has been much confusion and conflict, and all of the cases cannot be reconciled, the decisions of this court have been consistent and sound. This is especially true when such matters involve accord and satisfaction of single unliquidated claims, such as we have here presented to us.

Plaintiff and defendant entered into a contract for the sale and purchase of cattle, and the dispute centers upon the basis of the purchase. There is no dispute excepting the bona fide dispute as to the basis of the computation per pound for the cattle. Plaintiff contends it was on the basis of thirty-five cents a pound, plus the excess if they were dressed out at a better grade, and defendant contends the basis was on a grade and yield in compliance with O.P.S. regulation. This was the issue to be resolved in settlement.

According to Webster's New International Dictionary, a claim for debt or damage is "liquidated" in law when the precise amount thereof is fixed, or has been agreed upon. . . . "An unliquidated claim is one, the amount of which has not been fixed by agreement or cannot be exactly determined by the rules of arithmetic or of law."

Plaintiff's claim had not been and could not be exactly determined by the rules of arithmetic or by law. It had not been fixed by mutual agreement. We have said, "if it is admitted that one of two sums is due, but there is a dispute as to which is the proper amount, the demand is unliquidated within the meaning of accord and satisfaction."

1 C.J.S., Accord and Satisfaction, b. Dispute or controversy, 32, pp. 515, 519, states:

"In order that a claim or demand may be capable of being satisfied and discharged by the payment of a lesser amount than is claimed by the creditor, without any new or additional consideration, there must be a genuine dispute or controversy between the parties concerning either the amount due or the debtor's liability, or the claim must be unliquidated, for the only consideration for the accord and satisfaction, and the relinquishment of the unpaid balance of the claim, is the settlement of the dispute or the adjustment of the rights of the parties."

It is sufficient if the parties honestly believe in the correctness of their positions and assert their claim in good faith. "Thus, a claim is unliquidated, even if it appears that something is due, unless it further appears how much is due. . . ." That a bona fide dispute exists here there is no doubt.

It is correctly said that the intention of the parties must be determined in such matters. This court in passing on like facts in *Schultz* v. *Farmers Elevator Co.,* supra, said: "What was the effect of what he did say and what he did? . . . the evidence shows conclusively that he went to defendants to obtain a settlement for his corn. There was a dispute as to the amount due. Defendants say they paid him the amount of the check in settlement of his claim, and plaintiff took the check and used the money. We are of opinion that under the record there was a settlement and a complete accord and satisfaction."

In *Sparks* v. *Spaulding,* supra, it was held that where there is a dispute in good faith as to the amount due on any unliquidated claim, the defendant offered plaintiff a check in full satisfaction, and the plaintiff cashed it with full knowledge that it was tendered in full payment, it constituted an accord and satisfaction.

The intention of the parties is therefore an important factor. But intention is not alone determined by the words of a party, although they are sufficient for such determination in this case. It is often determined by his acts, the legal import of which he is held to know and expect others to believe.

Application of this rule to the facts before us leads to no other conclusion but that the offer to settle the bona fide dispute as to the terms of the sale by tendering the draft for $9372.80, together with the letter of September 17th refusing to allow the sum to be accepted under any condition but full payment, clearly expressed the intention of the defendant. That defendant's intention was fully understood by plaintiff there can be no doubt. Plaintiff presented the draft for payment fully aware of defendant's position as expressed in his letter of September 17th. Plaintiff's declaration in his letter of October 1st is of no avail, and even though defendant had received the letter in time to stop payment of the draft in Chicago, which is doubtful, it was under no duty to do so. By his acts plaintiff had accepted defendant's offer. The new agreement had been executed and accord and satisfaction determined upon the execution and presentment of the draft for payment. It was incumbent upon the plaintiff to get the defendant's consent to consider the draft as part payment before he cashed the draft.

Smith, C.J., and all Justices concur.

✧

QUESTIONS

1. Was the "contract of settlement" in this case unilateral or bilateral?

2. Was the case decided in accordance with the usual rules of offer and acceptance, as discussed earlier?

As is true of arbitration, settlement out of court through compromise, or accord and satisfaction, is encouraged by the courts. If parties seem to have entered into a contract in discharge of an earlier contract, the courts strive to give effect to the later agreement.

Here, as elsewhere in the law, intent is of primary importance. The sole question is, did the plaintiff, by accepting and cashing the defendant's draft, manifest an intent to contract according to the terms outlined by defendant regardless of the fact that plaintiff expressly stated he did not intend his acceptance of the check as a compromise?

At first glance, putting oneself in the plaintiff's position, the case may appear unreasonable. Having received the draft, why should he not be able to express his intent not to settle, then to go ahead and cash the draft? However, any proposition is apt to be too simple when only one side is considered.

Let us look at the dispute from the point of view of the defendant. It is, of course, possible that the defendant really is being overcharged. If this is the case, about his only bargaining strength lies in the fact that the plaintiff is eager for payment. Feeling that he is in the right, the defendant may withhold payment and wait for the plaintiff to litigate the matter. To show his good intentions (as well as to subject the plaintiff to some temptation to yield), there is no reason why the defendant should not be permitted to mail a draft to the plaintiff, with instructions that it may only be cashed as a settlement.

This is merely an offer of a unilateral contract. According to the terms of the offer, the act of cashing the check is an acceptance of the offer to settle. Why, therefore, should the plaintiff be able to accept the check (and the settlement), then turn around and repudiate his action by suing for the amount just surrendered? If the defendant has specified as one of the terms of his offer that acceptance of the check is to be deemed an acceptance of the offer, is it reasonable to permit the plaintiff to accept part of the offer and reject part? This agreement is somewhat similar in effect to that in the case of *Bellmore Dress Company* v. *Tanbro Fabrics Corporation,* page 233.

Settlement of Liquidated Claims

The problems of settlement when a liquidated sum is involved become more difficult. To begin this analysis, let us set forth some of the rules, already discussed, governing consideration: (1) consideration is required, (2) in general consideration will be deemed adequate, even though of little value, but (3) payment of a lesser sum of money to settle a debt for a larger sum, at the time and place due, will be deemed inadequate consideration to the extent of the difference between the sum paid and that owed.[2]

(1) Suppose that X owes Y $500. The amount is to be due June 1. On May 30, X informs Y that he has no property except $200 cash; he is leaving town to get another job, but if Y will give a release of the entire sum, X will give Y the $200 on June 1. As a practical businessman, faced with the choice of losing only $300 rather than the entire $500, Y might very well agree to this arrangement. As the law stands in most jurisdictions, even though Y does agree to forego the remainder of the debt, he is not bound by his word. If he is able to solve the practical, not legal, problems of locating X and some of his assets by which to satisfy the judgment, he may bring suit for the unpaid $300 and win. Why? Because as was said above, $200 is not adequate to meet a debt of $500. Only $200 of the total is discharged; $300 indebtedness is outstanding.

(2) But suppose that in the original facts, instead of merely paying $200, X gave Y $200 and his hunting dog Rover in exchange for discharge. Rover, as it happened, was afraid of wildlife and guns, but might reform and must be said to have some value. Because the question of whether or not Rover is worth $300 is a question that the courts would not entertain, leaving it to the judgment of the parties, the full debt is now settled. If Y should sue for any of the $300 he would lose. This arrangement is called a novation. A novation is the discharge of a contract by substituting a new contract, or new performance, in place of the old.

---

2 To the extent that this principle is ignored, as it is by a few courts, there is no particular problem in compromising liquidated contracts, and they may be treated exactly as the unliquidated contracts just discussed.

(3) We might further alter the facts by assuming that X made his proposition on May 1, rather than on June 1, when the debt was due. He offered immediate payment of $200 as settlement of the full payment of $500. Here again consideration for the entire $500 is present. Why? Because in paying one month before due, X is forfeiting a legal right he otherwise had, namely, of stalling payment until June 1. The monetary value of prepayment will not be appraised by the court, and could in fact be substantial to Y. (Suppose he needed $200 immediately to pay gambling debts, when failure to do so would result in "the boys" working him over?) Therefore, here again the full $500 debt is discharged.

Do not lose sight of the fact that in *any* compromise, both parties must agree. A debtor cannot announce that he is settling his $500 debt by giving the creditor his hunting dog. The creditor must agree to the suggested terms before a discharge can be claimed. But unless the liquidated debt is settled by some form of unliquidated payment, even *with* the agreement of the creditor, a settlement of less than the amount owed is not binding.

Other closely related problems present themselves frequently. Often, a long-term contract is made, but because of special circumstances, altering the contract on terms more favorable to only one of the parties seems mutually advantageous.

Two stock examples of this may be suggested. (1) During the depression many long-term leases were in effect, having been negotiated in more prosperous days. Often the tenant's business was unable to support the present rent, leaving the landlord with two alternatives: either lower the rent or face the possibility of the tenant's going bankrupt and vacating the premises when there is little chance of rerenting, considering business conditions. In such cases, wisdom may well decree a lowering of the rent for the remainder of the lease. A suit would probably yield less in the long run than would a somewhat lower rent. Yet legally, the promise to reduce rent lacks consideration and could be ignored, and the landlord could bring suit for back rent at a later date.

(2) A similar situation is presented when a key employee under long-term contract demands an immediate raise, under the threat of breaking his contract and going to work elsewhere at a higher rate. Certainly the employer could sue the employee if he breached his present contract, with every expectation of winning the suit. However, if the interest of the company is in retaining the employee despite his irritating qualities, wisdom may well decree a raise in salary. The previous salary was a liquidated amount, promised in exchange for the services to be performed by the employee. If the contract is changed by merely raising the salary, there is no consideration in return for the raise. If the employer later wished to avoid the substituted agreement, he could do so.

What would you suggest in order to overcome the lack of consideration in these two cases? There are at least two solutions to the problem. One, have the tenant assume some trivial duty, such as sweeping a hall used by both landlord and the tenant. Or, he could sacrifice some unimportant legal right. Either would constitute additional consideration extended by the tenant in return for the decrease in rent. Likewise, the employee could assume some additional, unimportant duty in exchange for his increase in pay. A second alternative would be a mutual rescission of the parties' present contract. (This would be supported by consideration: each party's surrender of rights being exchanged for the other party's surrender.) Then, with no contract in existence, they could proceed to negotiate a new one. True, in this event, after the first contract had been rescinded, neither party could hold the other to form a new contract. All previous promises are deemed wiped out by the rescission, and if following the rescission either party should then refuse to renew, he could do so. Under normal circumstances this would not seem a very great risk.

The student will also observe that the first solution proposed consists in meeting a liquidated obligation with an unliquidated consideration. This is the reverse of the situation in a compromise of a tort claim, where because the tort claim is unliquidated, any liquidated sum can settle the claim.

Thus it would appear that the informed debtor who knows he must give something of slight but unliquidated value to secure a valid release will succeed in getting his debt canceled, whereas the uninformed debtor will not. Law must be conceded to be in an undesirable state when it can be made to serve the purpose of one appraised of a technicality, but when it will serve to trap the uninitiated.

The unfortunate results follow *not* because any of the three principles originally postulated are lacking in sound policy. The reason is more general. Practically any principle in law or in other spheres of life, if followed blindly, will lead to logical extremes.

We have conceded that the law in regard to settlement of debts produces undesirable results. Perhaps one or the other of our initial principles should be modified in cases where the results do not meet the test of common sense.

Yet, before one concludes that the law regarding settlement of debts should be changed, he should consider other questions. First, which of our three premises shall we modify in order to effect a change, without confusing the law as it relates to other problems of consideration? Does a need for change really exist when the prudent person may obtain legal advice for a reasonable fee? Last, is there enough sentiment, or is the public benefit substantial enough, to warrant a departure from precedent? Enough so that we would sacrifice the present certainty of the law?

As far as we are concerned, the answer to all of these questions is, "We don't know." Some courts have abandoned the law as outlined here. The

UCC has discarded the entire concept of requiring consideration to support modification of a contract.[3]

DISTRICT BANK v. MORDECAI (Maryland, 1919)
105 A 586

A novation may be made by the substitution of a new obligation or contract between the same parties, with the intent to extinguish the old obligation or contract. . . .

[EDITOR'S NOTE: Defendant, Herbert Q. Mordecai, had issued promissory notes to two different banks. Upon being unable to pay them at maturity, an arrangement was made whereby certain claims of Mordecai, pending against the United States government and arising from damages inflicted during the Civil War, were to be assigned (transferred) to the creditors.

According to Mordecai, the assignment was made "providing the assignment would release [him] from all obligation" from payment of the notes. Subsequently, the United States government refused payment of the claims assigned.]

It is upon the facts stated above that we are to determine whether the court below correctly ruled in refusing to grant the prayers of the plaintiff asking for the instruction that there was no evidence, legally sufficient, to go to the jury tending to show a novation.

(1) A "novation" is a new contractual relation, and contains four essential requisites: (I) a previous valid obligation; (II) the agreement of all parties to the new contract; (III) the validity of such new contract; and (IV) the extinguishment of the old contract by the substitution for it of the new one. . . .

A novation may be made by the substitution of a new obligation or contract between the same parties, with the intent to extinguish the old obligation or contract; but it does not result from the substitution of one paper writing for another, or one evidence of debt for another, or one contract for another, unless such substitution is made with the intention of all the parties concerned to extinguish the old one.

(2) Therefore, in order to effect a novation, there must be a clear definite intention on the part of all concerned that such is the purpose of the agreement, for it is a well-settled principle that novation is never to be presumed. The intention of the obligor that the existing debt should be discharged by the new obligation must be concurred in by both debtor and creditor. The point in every case, then, is: Did the parties intend by their arrangement to extinguish the old debt or obligation and rely entirely on the new, or did they intend to keep the old alive and merely accept the new as further security, and this question of intention must be decided from all the circumstances. . . .

[3] See p. 357.

The question of intention in this case is one for the jury to decide, if the facts and circumstances reflecting upon such intention are legally sufficient to be submitted to the jury, as tending to show that it was the intention of the parties that the new agreement or assignment was to extinguish the old one. . . . Thus the only question that was before the lower court, in passing upon the plaintiff's first and second prayers, was the legal sufficiency of such evidence. . . .

It is claimed by the appellees, when the assignment was executed and delivered to the appellant, that it was understood and agreed that all other obligations given for the indebtedness here sought to be recovered were thereby extinguished; while it is claimed by the appellant that such was not the understanding or agreement, but that the assignment was only an additional security for the payment of said indebtedness.

In passing upon the question presented, we need only examine the evidence in support of the defendant's contention, which we are to assume to be true, and decide whether the same is legally sufficient to go to the jury. This we have done, and after fully considering said evidence, including the assignment itself, the conduct of the plaintiff upon the receipt of it, and the testimony of Henry Mordecai, one of the defendants, we have reached the conclusion that the court properly acted in submitting such evidence to the jury.

Finding no reversible errors, in the rulings of the court upon any of the exceptions taken, the judgment of the court below will be affirmed.

Judgment affirmed, appellant to pay the costs.

✧

Novation appears to be used by different authorities to mean different types of transaction. Some give the word a broad meaning, including as novation any scheme for terminating a contract by substituting a different contract or a different type of performance by one party. That is the way the word was used in the preceding case.

Other authorities confine the use of the word *novation* to mean the substituting of a new party in the place of an original party to the contract and releasing the original party from further liabilities. This is only one of many possible types of substitutions encompassed within the first use of the term.

Which usage one wishes to adopt does not matter, so long as the meaning is clear.

QUESTION

1. Did the previous case involve a substituted performance in the same sense that this one did? If not, explain the difference.

LEVINE v. BLUMENTHAL (New Jersey, 1936) 186 A 457

The payment of a part was not regarded in law as a satisfaction of the whole, unless it was in virtue of an agreement supported by a consideration. . . . The principle is firmly imbedded in our jurisprudence that a promise to do what the promisor is already legally bound to do is an unreal consideration. . . .

HEHLER, J.

By an indenture dated April 16, 1931, plaintiff leased to defendants, for the retail merchandising of women's wearing apparel, store premises situated in the principal business district of the city at Paterson. The term was two years, to commence on May 1 next ensuing, with an option of renewal for the further period of three years; and the rent reserved was $2,100 for the first year, and $2,400 for the second year, payable in equal monthly installments in advance.

The state of the case settled by the district court judge sets forth that defendants adduced evidence tending to show that, in the month of April, 1932, before the expiration of the first year of the term, they advised plaintiff that "it was absolutely impossible for them to pay any increase in rent; that their business had so fallen down that they had great difficulty in meeting the present rent of $175 per month; that if the plaintiff insisted upon the increase called for in the lease, they would be forced to remove from the premises or perhaps go out of business altogether"; and that plaintiff "agreed to allow them to remain under the same rental 'until business improved.'" While conceding that defendants informed him that "they could not pay the increase called for in the lease because of adverse business conditions," plaintiff, on the other hand, testified that he "agreed to accept the payment of $175 each month, on account." For eleven months of the second year of the term rent was paid by defendants, and accepted by plaintiff, at the rate of $175 per month. The option of renewal was not exercised; and defendants surrendered the premises at the expiration of the term, leaving the last month's rent unpaid. This action was brought to recover the unpaid balance of the rent reserved by the lease for the second year—$25 per month for eleven months, and $200 for the last month.

The district court judge found, as a fact, that "a subsequent oral agreement had been made to change and alter the terms of the written lease, with respect to the rent paid" but that it was not supported by "a lawful consideration," and therefore was wholly ineffective.

The insistence is that the current trade depression had disabled the lessees in respect of the payment of the full rent reserved, and a consideration sufficient to support the secondary agreement arose out of these special circumstances; and that, in any event, the execution of the substituted performance therein provided is a defense at law, notwithstanding the want of consideration. . . . It is said also that, "insofar as the oral agreement has become executed as to the payments which had fallen due and had been paid and accepted in full as per the oral agreement," the remission of the balance of the rent is sustainable on the theory of gift, if not of accord and satisfaction. . . .

. . . The point made by respondent is that the subsequent oral agreement to reduce the rent is nudum pactum, and therefore created no binding obligation.

(1–5) It is elementary that the subsequent agreement, to impose the obligation of a contract, must rest upon a new and independent consideration. The rule was laid down in very early times that even though a part of a matured liquidated debt or demand has been given and received in full satisfaction thereof, the creditor may yet recover the remainder. The payment of a part was not regarded in law as a satisfaction of the whole, unless it was in virtue of an agreement supported by a consideration. . . . The principle is firmly imbedded in our jurisprudence that a promise to do what the promisor is already legally bound to do is an unreal consideration. . . . It has been criticized, at least in some of its special applications, as "mediaeval" and wholly artificial—one that operates to defeat the "reasonable bargains of business men.". . . But these strictures are not well grounded. They reject the basic principle that a consideration, to support a contract, consists either of a benefit to the promisor or a detriment to the promisee—a doctrine that has always been fundamental in our conception of consideration. It is a principle, almost universally accepted, that an act of forbearance required by a legal duty owing to the promisor that is neither doubtful nor the subject of honest and reasonable dispute is not a sufficient consideration. . . .

Yet any consideration for the new undertaking, however insignificant, satisfied this rule. . . . For instance, an undertaking to pay part of the debt before maturity, or at a place other than where the obligor was legally bound to pay, or to pay in property, regardless of its value, or to effect a composition with creditors by the payment of less than the sum due, has been held to constitute a consideration sufficient in law. The test is whether there is an additional consideration adequate to support an ordinary contract, and consists of something which the debtor was not legally bound to do or give. . . .

And there is authority for the view that a payment of part of a debt, "accompanied by an agreement of the debtor to refrain from voluntary bankruptcy," is a sufficient consideration for the creditor's promise to remit the balance of the debt. But the mere fact that the creditor "fears that the debtor will go into bankruptcy, and that the debtor contemplates bankruptcy proceedings" is not enough; that alone does not prove that creditor requested the debtor to refrain from such proceedings. . . .

The cases to the contrary either create arbitrary exceptions to the rule, or profess to find a consideration in the form of a new undertaking which in essence was not a tangible new obligation or a duty not imposed by the lease, or, in any event, was not the price "bargained for as the exchange for the promise" . . . and therefore do violence to the fundamental principle. They exhibit the modern tendency, especially in the matter of rent reductions, to depart from the strictness of the basic common-law rule and give effect to what has been termed a "reasonable" modification of the primary contract. . . .

(6) So tested, the secondary agreement at issue is not supported by a valid consideration; and it therefore created no legal obligation. General economic adversity, however disastrous it may be in its individual consequences, is never a

warrant for judicial abrogation of this primary principle of the law of contracts.

(8) It is settled in this jurisdiction that, as in the case of other contracts, a consideration is essential to the validity of an accord and satisfaction. . . . On reason and principle, it could not be otherwise. This is the general rule. The cases cited by appellant . . . are not in point. It results that the issue was correctly determined.

Judgment affirmed, with costs.

✧

This case is similar to *American University* v. *Todd* in that both cases adhere to the rule that a small sum is not adequate consideration in exchange for a large sum of money.

The two cases differ in that *American University* v. *Todd* dealt only with the original agreement, which was deemed not a contract because of lack of consideration. In the Levine case, the original contract was valid. What failed was the attempt to amend the contract by reducing the obligation of the lessee, without additional consideration.

QUESTIONS

1. Make some intelligent speculation as to the legal, social, and economic consequences that would follow if the doctrine of consideration were completely discarded and in its place were substituted the test: "Viewing the agreement as a reasonable man, should it be enforced?"

2. What tests other than the one suggested above can you devise as a substitute for consideration?

Modification of Contract under the UCC

UCC—SECTION 2–209: Modification, Rescission and Waiver.
(1) An agreement modifying a contract within this Article needs no consideration to be binding.

In these few short words, the problems concerning alteration of contract with which we have been wrestling have been eliminated as regards sales contracts. Consistent with the policy of permitting the agreement between the parties to override the more technical legal requirements, the UCC permits modification of any sales contract without additional consideration.

As the law stands regarding sales contracts under the UCC, so long as both parties agree to a change in the obligation between the parties, there is no reason why the contract cannot be changed accordingly. This is true even though one party is relieved of much of his obligation, while the obligation of the other party remains as before. In effect, the latest agreement between the parties as to the terms of a contract will control. The concept of preexisting contractual obligation, with all its technical aspects previously discussed, means nothing under the UCC.

Yet, there are some limitations upon the ability of parties to change existing contracts. The parties must deal in good faith, and must adhere to reasonable commercial standards. These, of course, are factual considerations. The fact remains that there is no requirement as a matter of law under the UCC comparable to the requirement usually adhered to in ordinary contract law, that consideration be present on both sides before the obligation of one party may be modified.

Quite possibly, Section 2–302 (1) and 2–302 (2) (see page 590), dealing with unconscionable contracts, could be relied upon to avoid modifications induced through commercial blackmail or through other unfair means.

Another portion of this section permits limits to be placed by the parties upon the ease by which a sales contract may be modified.

UCC—SECTION 2–209: Modification, Rescission and Waiver.
(2) A signed agreement which excludes modification or rescission except by a signed writing cannot be otherwise modified or rescinded, but except as between merchants such a requirement on a form supplied by the merchant must be separately signed by the other party.

So, a provision restricting modifications to those that are agreed upon in writing is effective. Between merchants this type of provision may be included on a form supplied by one of the merchants. In dealing with nonmerchants, such a provision is not effective unless the term permitting only a written modification is separately signed by the nonmerchant. The device of requiring a special signature in order to bind is also required to render an irrevocable offer binding (see page 254) and in both cases has the effect of drawing particular attention to the provision in question.

CHAPTER TWENTY-THREE

Requirements of Form for Enforceable Contracts

Modern codes that specify the types of contract that must be in writing are usually little more than a rewording of the English Statute of Frauds, enacted by Parliament in 1677.

THE CODE OF HAMMURABI (2250 B.C.): FORMALITIES [1]

If a man purchase silver or gold, manservant or maidservant, ox, sheep or ass, or anything else from a man's son, or from a man's servant without witnesses or contracts, or if he receive (the same) in trust, that man shall be put to death as a thief.

✧

Significance

FORM and substance are not often easy to isolate from one another as separate qualities, and this is true in the study of contracts as well as elsewhere. For example, is the requirement of certainty of terms a requirement of form or of substance? Is not the emphasis on the objective test of assent essentially a matter of form that on occasion may lead to ignoring the substance of the "real" assent?

Whatever the answers to these questions, there are a number of requirements that are almost purely matters of form and that are necessary to the

[1] Robert Francis Harper, *The Code of Hammurabi* (Chicago: University of Chicago Press, 1904), p. 13.

enforceability of certain types of contracts. We have heaped them together in this chapter. These are properly regarded as potential restrictions upon the validity of an agreement. A contract will fail if the essentials of form to be discussed are not met, despite the presence of a clear agreement between the parties, just as one will fail for lack of consideration.

Nature of Restrictions

Some persons appear to have a built-in hostility toward devices that are purely matters of form. But the fact that a certain device may be categorized as "merely" a "formality" should not be grounds among open-minded persons for condemning the device as harsh, unreasonable, and outdated. There are often, though not always, good reasons for formalities. Most of the following section is devoted to formalities intended to simplify the process of proving terms of a contract, which is a worthy purpose. Objection may reasonably be made in instances where the formal requirements do not adequately carry out any clear-cut purpose, however commendable the original intent. This, unhappily, does seem to be true in certain instances.

The Statute of Frauds

We have heard the expression *An oral contract isn't worth the paper it isn't written on,* but this is not an accurate statement of the law. Generally, oral contracts are enforceable (for that matter, implied contracts are enforceable), the only problem with them being the practical question of proof. Proof may be obtained in a number of ways, but aside from presenting a signed document, the most common means is through oral testimony of witnesses, in open court, subject to cross-examination. Even if there are no independent witnesses to a contract, the party attempting to assert a contract may rely upon his own testimony as to the terms of the contract, though his testimony may be contradicted by the other party. Under these circumstances, in effect, one man's word is merely placed against another's, and a jury is only supposed to find for the plaintiff upon a preponderance of the evidence. Nevertheless, juries may and often do find a preponderance of evidence based on the fact that one party seemed to them much more credible than the other. For that matter, in criminal law, to obtain a conviction, the state has to prove its case beyond a *reasonable doubt.* Yet countless defendants have been convicted of a crime on nothing more than the sworn testimony of one prosecution witness. Notwithstanding the possible use of other evidence, however, the advantages in facilitating proof are in themselves enough to warrant putting most important contracts in writing.

Although the general rule of law is that oral testimony may be admitted into evidence, there are exceptions. Certain contracts may not be proved by oral testimony but on the contrary require as a matter of law a written, signed memorandum. Modern codes that specify the types of contract that must be in writing are usually little more than a rewording of the English Statute of Frauds, enacted by Parliament in 1677.

American jurisdictions have all adopted the general outlines of the statute of frauds, either by considering the statute as part of the common law of the state [2] or by enacting specific legislation. Only two sections of the original statute of frauds, the fourth and the seventeenth, have retained much significance. The fourth section is an enumeration of several types of contract with no particular common denominator except that they must be in writing or they are void. The seventeenth section relates to various types of sales contracts which, to be enforceable, must either be in writing or meet one of several alternative tests. If it does neither the contract is voidable but not void.

FOURTH SECTION OF THE STATUTE OF FRAUDS

SECTION 4 of the Statute of Frauds, an Act for Prevention of Frauds and Perjuries St 29 Car II c. 3 (1677)

IV. And be it further enacted by the authority aforesaid, That from and after the said four and twentieth day of June (1677) no action shall be brought (1) whereby to charge any executor or administrator upon any special promise, to answer damages out of his own estate; (2) or whereby to charge the defendant upon any special promise to answer for the debt, default or miscarriages of another person; (3) or to charge any person upon any agreement made upon consideration of marriage; (4) or upon any contract or sale of lands, tenements or heriditaments, or any interest in or concerning them; (5) or upon any agreement that is not to be performed within the space of one year from the making thereof; (6) unless the agreement upon which such action shall be brought, or some memorandum or note thereof, shall be in writing, and signed by the party to be charged therewith or some other person thereunto by him lawfully authorized.

The first part of this section of the statute of frauds concerns such an infrequent event as not to warrant mention. For those interested, outside research would illuminate this provision further. The third part of this section, relating to contracts in consideration of marriage, seems of little

---

[2] Most states, upon entering the union, adopted the common law and statutes of England as of various dates (often 1607 or 1776) to serve as a foundation upon which their courts could build. Many English statutes are embodied as a part of our common law. Some of the newer states adopted the common law of states admitted earlier.

practical import, because probably most marriages today are not made for consideration, but perhaps the human interest aspects merit comment. This part of the statute of frauds does not apply to mutual promises between girl and boy to marry. An oral contract of that type is enforceable in a few jurisdictions on a "breach of promise to marry" suit.

What is meant here is an agreement whereby one party promises to extend some other consideration, generally money or property, in exchange for a promise to marry. Premarital property settlements between prospective spouses are included in this category. Perhaps more common at the time the statute was devised was the situation in which Father promised a fortune and his daughter to an eligible young swain to persuade the latter to marry the daughter. We must infer that disputes over exactly what or how much was promised were frequent enough to have prompted Parliament in 1677 to do something to clear up these matters. It is interesting to speculate as to how many fathers, having reneged upon their promise to bestow a fortune upon a young bridegroom, consoled the latter with the advice that the bride was a real prize by herself. Divorce in those days was practically impossible.

The second part of the fourth section of the statute of frauds refers to contracts of guaranty or suretyship. The relationship under discussion is this: *A* agrees to pay *B*'s debt to *C, but only in the event B himself fails to pay.* The promise is secondary, in the sense that the first or primary obligation runs from *B* to *C. A*'s obligation comes into play only when the primary obligor, *B,* fails. The most important distinction to be made is in separating primary obligations (which need not be in writing) from secondary obligations (which usually must be in writing to be enforceable).

Consider the following situation: *B* goes to the restaurant *C,* but when he starts to pay his check he discovers he has forgotten his money, and *A* volunteers to pick up the check. Is this a secondary obligation? The answer is no. *A,* in effect, has made a gift to *B* (or perhaps even a loan). *A*'s contract with the restaurant was not conditioned by the *if*—that is, by the statement, *if B* does not pay, I will. *A*'s agreement was simply, "I will pay." If the agreement had been *A* will pay *if B* does not by tomorrow, the agreement would be secondary, and would therefore have to be in writing to be enforceable. An entire field of law is devoted to the exceptions and ramifications that result from variations in the factual and legal patterns in this type of contract. We do not feel that any rules of general significance may be revealed by pursuing this subject for a few more paragraphs, except for one last statement: even the generalizations we have used in the treatment of this subject are themselves subject to exceptions.

Contracts entered into for the sale of real property [3] remain today a

---

[3] Generally, land or buildings or other objects intended to remain permanently attached to the land is real property, while property intended to be movable is personal property.

species of contract that almost invariably must be in writing to be effective. This is no doubt true partly for historical reasons: in feudal England one's station in life depended upon the extent of land under one's domain, which in turn depended usually upon inheritance, or in other words, upon one's station in life. Real estate tended to mean castles and feudal domains. Aside from farm animals, suits of armor, and personal effects, personal property was practically nonexistent. The central importance of land in the development of English culture may be judged by the large amount of attention devoted to real property questions in early legal texts and collections of cases. Transactions of such paramount importance were reasonably enough treated with greater dignity and care than others, and a statutory requirement that these transactions should be in writing would logically follow.

With the proliferation of personal property in tangible form—for example, automobiles, airplanes, complex machinery, boats, appliances; and perhaps even more important, intangible personal property: stocks, bonds, bills of lading, and mortgages—the central importance of real property has been eclipsed.

Nevertheless, reasons remain for the requirement that contracts affecting interests in real estate be in writing. Owing to the nature of real estate, keeping track of the property rights involved is at the very least a complex, difficult business. Without scrupulous care to see that these interests are evidenced in writing, keeping tab would be all but impossible.

By the "nature" of real estate we mean the fact that it may not be moved about or readily put under lock and key. Most small articles of personal property are demonstrably yours either because you keep them on your person, you keep your eye on them, or you keep them locked up. None of these are convenient with regard to real estate in our present, complex property system. Some of your property may be in the hands of tenants, other parcels you may wish to mortgage to secure a bank loan, other parcels you may wish to leave vacant nine months of the year and use as a summer cottage. You cannot prove your interest in, and the exact boundaries of, these parcels of property very satisfactorily by word of mouth, nor could your tenant, nor could your mortgagee. A requirement that these interests be written seems essential to the orderly conduct of business affairs.

As the law stands all the documents used in transferring title to real property, transferring possession, and using the property as security for a debt must be evidenced in writing. In many jurisdictions, special requirements, such as a seal and witnesses, are also needed. Lawyers and legal questions tend to be more prominent in dealing with interests in real estate than in most areas of business. The complexity of the interests involved and the technical requirements to be dealt with explain why.

One isolated exception to the general rule that a real-estate transfer, to be effective, must be written is an equitable doctrine known as "part performance." If the following facts may be found, (1) a buyer is paid some or all of the purchase price under an oral contract to buy real property, (2) has taken possession of the real property, and (3) erected thereon substantial improvements, a court of equity will intervene. The seller cannot rescind the oral sale. On the contrary he will be forced to issue a deed to the buyer if the buyer has performed his side of the oral contract.

As the student will have observed, this is hardly more than a particular application of the doctrine of estoppel. But here the estoppel will not be found without all the above enumerated requirements being present. Therefore, the practice of making oral contracts for real estate, in the hope that a court will later enforce the contract through "part performance," is not recommended.

Contracts Requiring Over One Year for Performance

The remaining part of the fourth section of the statute of frauds deals with "any agreement that is not to be performed within the space of one year from the making thereof." The reasoning behind this requirement has been stated many times in such terms as, "the memory of man is short, and opportunities for misunderstanding multiply with the passage of time." Granting that the general idea behind this requirement is a good one, there are in fact difficult problems in administration.

How do we know when a contract is going to take a year to perform? Myriads of things could happen in the case of contracts that normally take six to nine months, to delay performance so that over a year is required. Should all oral contracts accidentally delayed over one year be voided? Would it have been rational to adopt a rule merely intended to facilitate proof which would result in the wholesale avoidance of contracts? If so, no one would know for sure whether a contract was enforceable or not, until either it was fully performed or the year was up. The rights of the parties would be in a state of suspended animation. An interpretation with this effect would promote neither the interests of ease of legal administration nor of society's ideas of justice.

Exactly what Parliament intended when they passed the statute probably no one will ever know. The usual interpretation applied by the courts, as we will see below, seems strained, perhaps even contrary to the plain meaning of the language, but workable. The difference between the strict wording and the judicial interpretations might very well reflect the differences between the well-intentioned but uninformed outlook of a legislator and the practical, problem-oriented approach of a judge.

First the test had to be one that could be applied as soon as the contract was formed. Having contracts in a state of suspended animation for a period of one year would have been intolerable. Therefore, whether or not the contract qualifies under the statute of frauds must be ascertainable as soon as the agreement is made. The test applied, although not phrased in these words, can be described as follows: "Is it *impossible by the terms of the contract* for the contract to be performed within a year?" If that is the case, it needs to be in writing. Otherwise the contract is void. But if there is no absolute impossibility of performing within a year, it need not be in writing.

Therefore, contracts that specify in their terms that they will be performed for a duration extending over more than one year must be in writing. A contract to perform an act after the lapse of more than a year must be in writing. A one-year contract, performance to start next week, would still not be fully performed a year from today, and must therefore be in writing. But a one-year contract, performance beginning now, could be performed within a year and would not need to be in writing. A contract to work for two succeeding winters would require more than one year and must be in writing, as would a contract to work until some predictable astronomic event due to happen more than one year off, such as the return of Haley's comet. Contracts to work in a capacity "for life" need not be in writing because death may occur in less than a year, in which case the contract would be performed.

A contract to clear timberland that normally would require more than a year could be performed in less time if sufficient personnel, machines, and other resources were devoted to the job. The same could be said for any type of building job. These contracts, therefore, would not need to be in writing. Current predictions are that more than 10 years will be required before man lands on the moon, but a contract made by a research corporation to place a man on the moon would not fail because of lack of writing, because there is no absolute prohibition to performance. We have been surprised enough times by the rapid conquest of space, and therefore few courts would be likely to deem performance within a year an absolute impossibility, even in the face of scientific opinion to the contrary.

An area in which judgment may be required still exists, because the question must still be answered "Is it *clearly impossible* to perform a contract in one year," or is performance merely "very unlikely." Yet the area subject to questions of judgment has been greatly reduced. This is an illustration of the ability of a rule of law to narrow disputes. Only an exceptional case will present difficulty under the current interpretation of this rule.

Although the ability to decide cases has been greatly facilitated by the judicial interpretation outlined above, we must recognize that the result is that many if not most contracts that actually do take more than a year do not need to be in writing. However, there is scant evidence to indicate that this presents any serious problem.

GRONVOLD v. WHALEY ET AL. (Washington, 1951) 237 P 2d 1026 (Part One)

> . . . The court will examine the surrounding circumstances to ascertain the terms of the contract and to determine whether, by those terms, the contract must of necessity require more than one year to perform. That the contract was not performed within a year is of no significance; nor does it matter that it was highly improbable that the contract would be performed within one year.

. . . The primary question posed by all three of appellant's assignments of error is whether the contract sued on falls within the purview of that portion of Rem. Rev. Stat. para. 5825, which reads: "In the following cases specified in this section, any agreement, contract and promise shall be void, unless such agreement, contract or promise, or some note or memorandum thereof, be in writing, and signed by the party to be charged therewith, or by some person thereunto by him lawfully authorized, that is to say: (1) every agreement that by its terms is not to be performed in one year from the making thereof; . . ."

It is appellant's position that Rem. Rev. Stat. para. 5825 (1) has application only where the contract, by its terms, cannot be performed within one year. Respondents, on the other hand, contend that the statute applied if, upon looking to the surrounding circumstances and considering the object contemplated by the contract, it can be determined that the parties intended that its performance should extend beyond one year from the making thereof. Both appellant and respondents cite decisions of this court in support of their respective positions.

. . . The rule in this jurisdiction is that a contract does not fall within Rem. Rev. Stat. para. 5825 (1) unless, by its terms, it cannot be performed within one year from its making. However, the court will examine the surrounding circumstances to ascertain the terms of the contract and to determine whether, by those terms, the contract must of necessity require more than one year to perform. That the contract was not performed within a year is of no significance; nor does it matter that it was highly improbable that the contract would be performed within one year. However, the performance required is actual performance; discharge by other means than performance is not sufficient to prevent the application of the statute. The rule of this jurisdiction is in accord with the weight of authority. . . .

The express terms of the contract in this case were as follows: Appellant and Hyneman were to develop and manage a transportation business and were to hold the stock until they had been repaid their investment out of the earnings of the business. The contract did not specify any definite amount of money which respondents agreed to furnish. When the amount advanced was so repaid, they were then to deliver half of the stock to appellant and Hyneman.

Respondents argue that the circumstances show that it was impossible to put the enterprise into actual operation until the completion of Bonneville dam and, since Bonneville dam was not expected to be completed, and was not in fact completed, until three years after the contract was entered into, the contract could not possibly have been performed within one year from its making. The gist of their position is that performance was made conditional upon an uncertain event, to wit, the return of respondents' investments out of the earnings of the joint venture and this condition could not possibly occur until after completion of the dam.

Although the data in the survey submitted to Whaley was based on conditions as they would exist after the completion of the dam, appellant testified that operation was to commence when temporary locks were completed. The evidence is that the temporary locks were not expected to be open, nor were they opened, until two years after the making of the contract. However, there is no evidence that the temporary locks could not possibly have been completed within one year. For example, the Army engineers in charge of the construction of the locks might have decided, for aught that appears in the record, to expedite the completion of the locks so as to be usable within one year. For the doing of a thing to be impossible it must be physically or legally incapable of being done.

Although it appears highly improbable that the contract could be performed within one year, we cannot say that the terms of the contract made performance impossible within that period; therefore it is our opinion that this contract is not void under the terms of Rem. Rev. Stat. para. 5825 (1).

❖

QUESTION

1. Do you think it would have made any difference if the dam had required five or six years for completion instead of three?

Formalities of the Sales Contract

We have already stressed the fact that the UCC–Sales is a highly flexible act, that one of the objectives of the act is to permit great informality in the formation of sales contracts. Nevertheless, in certain instances and for good reasons formal requirements are imposed.

Probably the most important of these is a lineal descendant of the seventeenth section of the original English Statute of Frauds. That Statute, passed in England in 1677, affected sales of over £10. As subsequently incorporated into the Uniform Sales Act, and enacted in all of the United States, the amount varied, but the remaining language varied only slightly from the original English draft, shown below. Further changes have been incorporated into the UCC version of the Statute, as, for example, the present minimum of a $500 price before a writing is required to validate a sales contract.

THE SEVENTEENTH SECTION OF THE STATUTE OF FRAUDS

SECTION 17 of the Statute of Frauds, An Act for Provision of Frauds and Perjuries St. 29 Car II c. 3 (1677)

XVII. And be it further enacted by the authority aforesaid, That from and after the said four and twentieth of June no contract for the sale of goods, wares and merchandise, for the price of ten pounds sterling or upwards, shall be allowed to be good, except the buyer shall accept part of the goods so sold, and actually receive the same, or give something in earnest to bind the bargain, or in part payment, or that some note or memorandum in writing of the said bargain be made and signed by the parties to be charged by such contract, or their agents thereunder lawfully authorized.

As incorporated into the UCC–Sales, the act was modified somewhat, reading at present as follows:

UCC—SECTION 2–201: Formal Requirements; Statute of Frauds.
(1) Except as otherwise provided in this section a contract for the sale of goods for the price of $500 or more is not enforceable by way of action or defense unless there is some writing sufficient to indicate that a contract for sale has been made between the parties and signed by the party against whom enforcement is sought or by his authorized agent or broker. A writing is not insufficient because it omits or incorrectly states a term agreed upon but the contract is not enforceable under this paragraph beyond the quantity of goods shown in such writing.

The UCC–Sales statute of frauds only applies to contracts for the sale of goods for the price of $500 or more. Below that amount, none of the provisions in this section are applicable. No writing or other formality is required for contracts below $500.

As for contracts of $500 or more, the code requires "some writing sufficient to indicate that a contract for sale has been made between the parties and signed by the party against whom enforcement is sought."

To be adequate under the UCC version of the Statute of Frauds, a writing does not need to contain all the terms of a contract, and may even contain inaccuracies, but a writing will not be enforceable for a greater quantity of goods than stated in the writing.

According to the official comment to the code, the only definite requirements to a writing are (1) it must indicate a contract for the sale of goods, (2) it must be "signed" (which includes any mark or initial intentionally used for the purpose of indicating assent), and (3) it must specify a quantity.

[UCC—SECTION 2–201 (cont.)]
(2) Between merchants if within a reasonable time a writing in confirmation of the contract and sufficient against the sender is received and the party receiving it has reason to know its contents, it satisfies the requirements of subsection (1) against such party unless written notice of objection to its contents is given within ten days after it is received.

Between merchants, and only between merchants, a signed confirmation of an order is effective as evidence of a contract against the *recipient* of the confirmation, unless the latter gives written notice of rejection within ten days after receiving the confirmation.

[UCC—SECTION 2–201 (cont.)]
(3) A contract which does not satisfy the requirements of subsection (1) but which is valid in other respects is enforceable
(a) if the goods are to be specially manufactured for the buyer and are not suitable for sale to others in the ordinary course of the seller's business and the seller, before notice of repudiation is received and under circumstances which reasonably indicate that the goods are for the buyer, has made either a substantial beginning of their manufacture or commitments for their procurement; or
(b) if the party against whom enforcement is sought admits in his pleading, testimony or otherwise in court that a contract for sale was made, but the contract is not enforceable under this provision beyond the quantity of goods admitted; or
(c) with respect to goods for which payment has been made and accepted or which have been received and accepted.

In summary, certain exceptions to the requirement of a writing are incorporated into the act, though somewhat different exceptions than those under the previous act. (1) A writing is not required if the goods are to be specially manufactured by the seller, and he has already undergone expense, or made a legal commitment in response to the order (nothing new). (2) An entirely new provision specifies that an unwritten contract will be enforceable to the extent that the opposite party admits its existence in court, but only for the amount of goods admitted. (3) Goods that have been either received and accepted or paid for need not be evidenced by a writing so long as they have been accepted by the buyer.

GRONVOLD v. WHALEY ET AL. (Washington, 1951)
237 P 2d 1026 (Part Two)

. . . The contract involved herein is not a contract to sell. . . .
No transfer of ownership was involved.

[See page 366 for facts of this case.]

Respondents argue that this contract falls within the purview of Rem. Rev. Stat. para. 5836–4, the pertinent portion of which reads: "(1) A contract to sell or a sale of any goods or choses in action exceeding the value of $50 shall not be enforceable by action unless the buyer shall accept part of the goods or choses in action so contracted to be sold or sold, and actually receive the same, or give something in earnest to bind the contract, or in part payment, or unless some note or memorandum in writing of the contract or sale be signed by the party to be charged or his agent in that behalf. . . ."

(6) We are of the opinion that Rem. Rev. Stat. para. 5836–4 does not apply for the reason that the contract involved herein is not a contract to sell. By the terms of the agreement, appellant was to have a twenty-five percent interest in the joint venture but all of the stock was to be held by Whaley and Dent until they had been repaid their investment. No transfer of ownership was involved.

QUESTION

1. What is required to constitute a contract to sell?

[EDITOR'S NOTE: This case was decided according to the terms of the Uniform Sales Act, rather than the more recent Uniform Commercial Code, upon which primary emphasis is placed in this text. However, as concerns the question of what does or does not constitute a sale, there is little difference between the two codes.]

The Parol Evidence Rule

Another rule involving questions of form is known as *the parol evidence rule*. This rule serves to facilitate the disposition of cases by the courts, and is of even wider application than the statute of frauds.

The parol evidence rule states that whenever a contract has been reduced to written form, oral testimony shall not be admitted into evidence to contradict the terms of the writing. The practical advantages of this rule are immediately obvious. Congested courts are either relieved from deciding, or if not, they are provided with a clear basis for deciding, multitudes of disputes over contractual terms. The written terms ordinarily prevail in case of a dispute. Contracts claimed to be uncertain are often by reference to the writing seen to be not uncertain, but merely undesirable from the petitioning party's point of view.

The disadvantages to the parol evidence rule are just as obvious as the advantages, and can be said to be those that are inherent in an arbitrary approach to any type of problem. Undoubtedly some people sign contracts without reading them, which is usually their fault, but sometimes they are told that the paper is a receipt for registered mail or something of the sort, which a reasonable person may well sign without reading. Sometimes the terms are obscure, even though in writing, and sometimes the contract, though written, has already been terminated by mutual agreement. These objections, however, have been largely met, as will be seen.

To liberalize the impact of the parol evidence rule (at the same time, however, increasing the difficulties of judicial decision) certain modifications to the rule have been evolved. These are the following: (1) Writings that are obviously intended as a bare skeleton of the agreement (whether this is the case is a decision made by the judge) may be filled in by the admission of oral testimony.[4] (2) Contracts that on their face appear to be ambiguous may be clarified by parol evidence.[5] (3) Contracts that were never intended as a contract at all—that is, jokes, and the like—may be proved as such by parol evidence.[6] By the same token other defenses—fraud, mistake, misrepresentation, illegality, undue influence—may be proved by the admission of parol evidence, and if a contract can be shown to be intended as effective only upon the occurrence of an oral contingency that has not occurred, this may be proved.[7] Mutual rescission of

---

[4] Charles T. McCormick, *Handbook of the Law of Evidence*, Hornbook Series (St. Paul, Minn.: West Publishing Co., 1954), p. 430. McCormick also points out in pages just preceding this that the propensity of the jury to favor the "underdog" is suggested as one reason for the development of the rule. Because the economic underdog is usually the party to assert oral evidence to overcome a written contract, it is suggested that judges developed the doctrine to keep oral (and often fabricated) evidence from the jury in order to minimize the prejudice usually directed at the "top dog."

[5] *Ibid.*, p. 446.

[6] *Ibid.*, p. 449.

[7] *Ibid.*, pp. 449–450. A contingency of this type is termed a *condition precedent*, which we have not studied yet but which will be covered in the following chapter. Note that the defenses enumerated are largely the "equitable defenses."

a written contract and substitution of another, different contract may also be shown.

Despite the seemingly vast array of modifications to the parol evidence rule, they *are* only modifications, and the burden of trying to establish an oral variation of a written contract is one a person should avoid placing upon his attorney.

The modifications discussed are rarely, if ever, direct contradictions of the parol evidence rule. We cannot say a written contract is being contradicted by parol evidence because the details were omitted and are allowed to be elaborated upon by oral testimony; nor may we say this as regards a contract that is ambiguous, nor may we say this about an apparent contract that was never intended as such, whether arising from fraud in the factum or jest.

Allegations that contradictory oral promises were made contemporaneously with the written contract, but were omitted therefrom, will not be admissible in court.

GLASCOE v. *MILETICH* (District of Columbia, 1951)
83 A 2d 587

> . . . The existence of a separate oral agreement as to any matter on which a written contract is silent, and which is not inconsistent with its terms, may be proved by parol, if under the circumstances of the particular case it may be inferred that the parties did not intend the writing to be a complete and final statement of the whole of the transaction between them.

HOOD, AJ.

Appellant is the executrix of the estate of her husband, who was engaged in the moving and storage business and who had received from appellee certain goods intended for shipment to Ottumwa, Iowa. The trial court found that the parties had agreed that the goods would not be shipped until notice from appellee but that without such notice the goods were shipped, and the court awarded appellee damages. Appellant does not question the award of damages for articles lost and damaged in transit but contends that other damages allowed on account of the premature or unauthorized shipment were erroneously awarded.

Appellant's argument is that the agreement to make the shipment only after notice from appellee was proved by parol evidence and had the effect of varying the written contract of the parties embodied in the bill of lading. The bill of lading acknowledged receipt of the goods from appellee, and provided that the carrier agreed to carry them to the destination indicated below which was written in as "Ottumwa, Iowa." The bill of lading contained no provision concerning when shipment would be made or when the goods would be delivered to their destination, except that in the printed terms and conditions on the reverse side there was the provision that the carrier was not bound to transfer the goods by any particular schedule or otherwise than "with reasonable dispatch."

As the bill of lading specified neither time of shipment nor time of delivery at destination and required only that the carrier act with reasonable dispatch, the oral agreement that shipment would not be made until notice from the shipper neither contradicted nor varied any term of the bill of lading. As was said by us in *Mitchell* v. *David*, "the existence of a separate oral agreement as to any matter on which a written contract is silent, and which is not inconsistent with its terms, may be proved by parol, if under the circumstances of the particular case it may properly be inferred that the parties did not intend the writing to be a complete and final statement of the whole of the transaction between them."

Furthermore, the oral agreement may be considered as a condition upon which the contract of shipment was made, namely, that it was not to become effective until notice from the shipper. A written contract may be made upon condition that it shall not become binding until some condition, resting in parol, shall occur. . . .

Affirmed.

QUESTION

1. If oral variation of written contracts were never permitted, no doubt attorneys would find it easier to predict the outcome of cases, and judges and juries would have an easier time deciding cases, both of which are desirable factors. Why then do we not adopt a rule of law barring any modification of written contracts?

UCC—SECTION 2–202: Final Written Expression: Parol or Extrinsic Evidence.

Terms with respect to which the confirmatory memoranda of the parties agree or which are otherwise set forth in a writing intended by the parties as a final expression of their agreement with respect to such terms as are included therein may not be contradicted by evidence of any prior agreement or of a contemporaneous oral agreement but may be explained or supplemented.

(a) by course of dealing or usage of trade (Section 1–205) or by course of performance (Section 2–208); and

(b) by evidence of consistent additional terms unless the court finds the writing to have been intended also as a complete and exclusive statement of the terms of the agreement.

The parol evidence rule as applied to sales, found in Section 2–202 of the UCC, is more flexible than the comparable rules of general contract law. Essentially, Section 2–202 states that a final, written expression of the intent of the parties "may not be contradicted by evidence of any prior agreement, or of a contemporaneous oral agreement." However, an agreement may be varied by course of dealing or usage of trade, or course of performance, as stated earlier in the code. And the writing may be varied by consistent additional terms, unless additional terms seemed to be excluded by the original writing.

We have found in other sections that as a general rule the parties may mutually rescind or alter a contract, without additional consideration under the UCC. The preceding statements do not deal with that question however, but merely prescribe what evidence may be admitted to prove additional terms, whether contemporaneous or subsequent to the original contract.

UCC—SECTION 2–203: Seals Inoperative.
The affixing of a seal to a writing evidencing a contract for sale or an offer to buy or sell goods does not constitute the writing a sealed instrument and the law with respect to sealed instruments does not apply to such a contract or offer.

CHAPTER TWENTY-FOUR

Problems Arising in the Performance, Breach, and Termination of Contracts

A partial failure of performance of a contract will not of itself give ground for its rescission, but may do so if it defeats the very object of the contract, or renders that object impossible of attainment, or if it concerns a matter of such prime importance that the contract would not have been made if default in that particular had been expected or contemplated, or is such that damages would be a wholly inadequate remedy.

Introduction

TWO SETS of problems are presented when a contract seems to have been breached. One set concerns the legal questions present in deciding whether a breach has occurred, and if it has what the proper legal remedy is. The other set of questions concerns the practical problem: what is the best course of action to take, assuming a breach has occurred?

It should be recognized that recourse to the courts is neither theoretically nor actually the necessary outcome of a breach of contract. The best course may be to forget the whole thing in some cases, in others to renegotiate the contract on terms more favorable to the other party, to compromise, and only as a last resort to sue.

Breach or termination of contract is a subject of exceedingly broad dimensions, including a wide array of diverse situations. Undoubtedly the usual contract is performed without serious dispute and soon forgotten.

375

Many another contract may go totally unperformed by one party under circumstances under which the other party couldn't care less, and may also be quickly forgotten. However, a variety of other contracts, ranging from one of slight significance to the man on the street to one of crucial importance to a major industrial concern, may result in litigation, perhaps before a justice of the peace, or perhaps ultimately before a state supreme court. Litigation may ensue almost before the ink is dry, or months or years later. The diverse characteristics a breach of contract may assume are practically without limit.

Anticipatory Breach

In some cases, when a party is not required to perform until some time in the future, but announces or through conduct indicates that when that time arrives he will not perform, the question naturally arises whether suit may be brought immediately or whether suit must be postponed until the actual breach occurs. This situation is termed *anticipatory breach*. Most courts hold that when the party commits an anticipatory breach, the other party has a choice. He may sue immediately, or he may postpone suit until the actual breach occurs, hoping that the breach will not occur. If he postpones suit and the contract is in fact performed, he then has no reason for taking legal action.

In order to bring a suit immediately upon learning that a contract will not be performed, the information leading to the belief that performance will not be forthcoming must be convincing. What is or is not convincing evidence of anticipatory breach is a matter of judgment. However, either words, or actions of the other party making his performance impossible, may constitute convincing evidence.

Dependent and Independent Promises

Let us consider the relative importance of the contractual term that is breached.

Up to this time the nature of contract has been somewhat oversimplified, because clear-cut contracts are better for purposes of illustration than complex and therefore confusing contracts. Most of the illustrations have been of contracts in which one simple promise has been exchanged for another simple promise. Many contracts are of this type. However, many others contain scores of terms. Some of the written terms of a contract may be considered only directive, expressing mere preferences of one party. Some are binding but of minor importance. Some are of critical importance. Should all of these be deemed of equal significance? *May* all of these be deemed of equal significance? The answer in each case requires some thought and study.

The breach of any term should entitle the other party to a remedy. The problem arises in tailoring the severity of the remedy to the significance of the breach. In a contract with many terms the breach of one term, if practically insignificant in the total picture, should not warrant nonperformance by the other party. Some of the flexibility needed to serve this purpose has been acquired by dividing contractual promises into two categories. If a promise is a dependent promise, it is a promise of such significance that, if not performed, the other party should be relieved of his obligations. Most promises are considered dependent. If a promise is an independent promise, a breach of that promise will give rise to an action for damages traceable to the breach, but the breach is not so important as to relieve the promisee from his obligation to extend his return performance.

The major promises going to the substance of a contract are by this dichotomy dependent, and the minor, relatively unimportant promises, independent. The question of which promises are so important that if not performed by the promisor the promisee is also excused from performance is a question of judgment. All the circumstances must be considered. The intentions of the parties (though mainly the offeror) as to the significance of the term or terms is of primary importance. In relatively simple contracts, where there are only one or two terms, there is no reason for requiring one party to perform unless it appears reasonably likely that the other will perform. In the more complex contracts, however, the more just solution is often to consider some minor, unperformed promises of a party independent, especially when the party has performed most of his bargain and when he is unable to fully perform the remainder of his bargain. In this way, the promisee would also be held to perform, but would be able to collect damages for any agreements not completed by the promisor. In some contracts, leases, for example, the promises of both parties are presumed to be independent.

WALTERS v. GOTCHER (Oregon, 1949) 211 P 2d 733

The provision relative to removal of debris was a dependent covenant which, when breached by the vendors, entitled the plaintiffs to rescind the contract to purchase the land. The covenant in question related to the whole consideration . . . "The true test, as to whether covenants of a contract are dependent or independent, rests on the intention of the parties, to be determined from the sense of the entire contract . . ."

BELT, J.

Plaintiffs, on August 30, 1946, commenced a suit to rescind a contract to purchase thirteen acres of land laying adjacent to what is commonly known as the "Columbia Slough" in Multnomah County, Oregon. From a decree dismissing the suit, the plaintiffs have appealed.

The plaintiffs, Hans Walters and his brother Arthur, for several years were engaged in the business of building small and medium-sized boats. During World War II the plaintiffs ceased building operations; but when it was over, they undertook to find a more suitable site for conducting their business. On the 5th day of April, 1946, the plaintiffs entered into a written contract with the defendants to buy—and the defendants agreed to sell—the thirteen-acre tract above mentioned at a price of $7,800.00. Five thousand dollars in cash was paid upon execution of the contract, and the balance of the purchase price namely, $2,800.00, was to be paid in monthly instalments of not less than $50.00 each. The defendants had operated a shingle mill on the premises in question until August 14, 1944, when the mill was virtually destroyed by fire. After the fire there remained on the land a great amount of scrap iron and sheet metal and two large boilers. There was also a large building 30 by 70 feet used as a dry kiln. Much of the land was covered by sawdust eight to ten feet deep. The plaintiffs, being anxious to construct a building on the premises in order to carry on their boat building operations, caused the following provision to be included in the contract of sale: "It is understood and agreed between the first and second parties that the seller is to clear off all debris—consisting of the scrap, boiler, and buildings, but that concrete foundations will not be removed —within ninety days from date of this contract."

It was further provided that: "Time and strict performance is of the essence of this agreement . . . ."

The defendants within the ninety days—which expired on July 4—removed the scrap iron. They also moved several truckloads of the sheet metal to another part of the premises, about 200 yards from the place where defendants thought the plaintiffs intended to build. The record is not clear when the boilers were removed. It is certain, however, that the large dry kiln building was not moved from the premises within the ninety-day period. As a matter of fact, the defendants, in the middle of August, were still engaged in their removal operations. The failure to move the dry kiln particularly deprived the plaintiff purchasers of their right to use the property and prevented them from commencing the building of their boat shop. Plaintiffs planned on burning the sawdust but, since it extended under a part of the dry kiln, could not do so without endangering such building. Plaintiffs deemed it to be hazardous to build over this deep layer of sawdust as a fire once started therein would have been very difficult to extinguish.

(1) There is much testimony about the high water of the Columbia River preventing the vendors from performing their part of the contract in reference to removal of the debris. It is common knowledge that the Columbia River each year commences to rise about the first part of June caused by melting snow in the high mountains along the upper reaches of the river. It is reasonable to assume that defendants "knew the river" and could reasonably have anticipated such condition. During 1946 there was no extraordinary flood stage of the water. If there was danger from high water, it should have been guarded against in the contract. Furthermore, there was no high water to interfere with removal

operations during the months of April and May. The plaintiff, Hans Walters, testified, in effect, that on several occasions he urged the defendants to get busy and clear the premises, but nothing was done about the matter.

The most that can be said for the defendants is that they partially performed their part of the contract. In our opinion, there was a failure of the defendants to perform those things of prime importance relating to the very substance of the contract. The rule applicable is thus stated in 1 Black on Rescission and Cancellation (2d ed.). . . . "A partial failure of performance of a contract will not of itself give ground for its rescission, but it may do so if it defeats the very object of the contract, or renders that object impossible of attainment, or if it concerns a matter of such prime importance that the contract would not have been made if default in that particular had been expected or contemplated, or is such that damages would be a wholly inadequate remedy."

In the instant case we think there was a substantial failure of performance. Plaintiffs were absolutely deprived of the use of the land by such failure of performance.

(2) It is well settled that a vendee, not in default, is entitled to rescind an executory contract for the purchase of land and recover money paid on the purchase price where a vendor has breached a material part of the contract. . . . It is not contended that the plaintiff vendees were in default.

(3) The provision relative to removal of debris was a dependent covenant which, when breached by the vendors, entitled the plaintiffs to rescind the contract to purchase the land. The covenant in question related to the whole consideration. . . . "The true test, as to whether covenants of a contract are dependent or independent, rests on the intention of the parties, to be determined from the sense of the entire contract rather than from any particular form of expression or the order in which the stipulations occur in the instrument; the order of time in which the intent of transaction requires performance being controlling. The intention must be gathered from the contract according to the ordinary rules of construction, on consideration of both its language and subject-matter."

(4) The time essence clause was applicable to both parties to the contract. . . . Plaintiffs first requested a thirty-day period in which the land was to be cleared, but defendants were not willing so to contract. Plaintiffs in all probability would not have entered into the contract to purchase the land had they known that the vendors would not substantially perform the covenant around which this controversy centers.

[EDITOR'S NOTE: As used here, the word *covenant* means one promise or provision of a contract.]

The decree dismissing the suit for rescission is reversed and the cause remanded with directions to enter a decree setting aside the contract and awarding plaintiffs judgment for the amount paid on the purchase price, together with interest thereon. Plaintiffs are entitled to recover costs and disbursements.

Conditions

Suppose Jones is negotiating a complex contract, and he knows that a number of the terms appear unimportant enough that a court would be apt to consider them independent promises. Yet to him these terms *are* important, and he emphatically wants these terms performed. May he make the entire contract dependent upon the performance of these minor terms? The best answer is that *perhaps* he may accomplish this purpose by using proper wording in the contract, but there are limits as to how far this process may go. Unless the promises appear to be of consequence by ordinary standards, the courts tend to place every obstacle available in the path of the party attempting to avoid a contract because of the other party's inexact performance.

A provision stating that one person's performance is dependent upon some future event (here, the performance of minor terms by the other) is called a condition. If the obligations making a condition are not performed, the mutual obligations are ordinarily terminated.

Two common types of condition are the condition precedent and the condition subsequent. A condition precedent is a condition in which the required event must occur before the liability of one of the parties to the contract is fixed. We have met one type of condition precedent before in the study of contracts: the requirement of full performance in the unilateral contract (page 214). Every unilateral contract is worded so that full performance by the promisee is required before the obligation of the promisor is fixed. However, the courts do not always enforce these contracts according to the full rigor of their terms, especially when great and unfair hardship (whatever that may mean) will result.

A condition subsequent is one in which the occurrence of an event terminates the obligations of one of the parties, when, had the event not occurred, he would have remained obligated. Perhaps the most common example of this type of condition is a provision contained in most casualty insurance contracts. The insurer is relieved of liability in the event that notice of a loss is not communicated within some period of time, often thirty days. Failure of notification for the stated period of time is the event that constitutes the condition subsequent, which upon occurrence releases the insurer from further obligation. However, many courts require a showing of actual prejudice against an insurer resulting from the delay before releasing the insurer from liability.

The reason conditions tend to be disfavored in court is that they often work an injustice against one of the parties. Although conditions are part of a contract and must be agreed to by the party against whom they operate, such contracts are often entered into under strong economic pressure. No doubt some feeling for the underdog has crept into the thinking in regard to conditions. Normally the underdog is the one needing a loan, an insurance contract, or is otherwise in an inferior bargaining position.

The most extreme forms of injustice arising from the use of conditions occur in situations where one party has performed expensive and complex tasks according to the contract but has nevertheless failed to satisfy a condition, thus losing not only his contract rights against the other party but possibly an enormous investment in the attempted performance. The loss of substantial rights in cases of this sort is termed a *forfeiture*. The courts are on record and attorneys on notice that conditions will be interpreted so as to avoid a forfeiture, if at all possible. Undoubtedly, if an unmet condition should reasonably be considered a dependent promise, courts will not be especially averse to enforcing it, but if the breach involves a minor sort of term that would ordinarily be considered an independent promise, chances of its finding favor in court are greatly reduced, especially if enforcement will result in a substantial foreefeiture by the other party.

ROYCE, INC. v. *UNITED STATES* (U.S. Court of Claims, 1954) 126 F. Supp. 196

Cases are legion holding that they abhor a forfeiture, and they will construe a clause as a covenant rather than a condition if at all possible. . . .

LARAMORE, J.

This action was instituted to recover (1) increased rentals as a result of an alleged breach of a lease between plaintiff and the Government wherein the Government allegedly assigned the occupation of a building to the Veterans' Administration in violation of the terms of the lease.

[EDITOR'S NOTE: The objection was to the use of the building by the Veterans' Administration, when the lease specifically provided the building would be used by the Department of the Army.]

(2) We believe that the use of the building by the Veterans' Administration did not violate or breach the terms of the lease between plaintiff and the Department of the Army.

Assuming that the use of the leased space by the Veterans' Administration was a violation of the terms of the lease, it is highly doubtful that such use would effect a termination and give the owner right of reentry.

[EDITOR'S NOTE: Reentry means forfeiture of the lease.]

(3, 4) The law recognized restrictions upon the use of property. They are . . . (2) a condition, and (3) a covenant. It does appear that plaintiff claims the lease created a condition. . . .

(5, 7) As stated supra the words "Military purposes" were descriptive and at most created a covenant. The general rule is that the breach by the lessee of the covenants or stipulations on his part contained in the lease does not work a forfeiture of the terms since the lessor's remedy is by way of a claim for damages. . . . Cases are legion holding that the courts abhor a forfeiture and they will construe a clause as a covenant rather than a condition if it is possible to do so. . . .

(8) We have found the value of the use of the leased space from June 15, 1947 to June 30, 1948 (the period of occupancy by the Veterans' Administration) to be $1,500 per month. The use by the Veterans' Administration was not more detrimental to the building and of substantially the same nature as the use by the Department of the Army. Even assuming there was a breach of the covenant, plaintiff has not shown any damages resulting from such breach.

❖

Perhaps the most common type of situation in which conditions may be found is in the ordinary lease for the rental of real estate. The advantage to the lessor (landlord) is that if a condition of the lease is violated, the lessor need not quibble at length with the lessee (tenant). Breach of a condition in a lease results in automatic forfeiture of the rights of the lessee, and the latter must simply move out.

However, because forfeiture is such a severe remedy, the courts strive not to find a breach of condition, and what's more, they admit it (see paragraph 5, 7 in the preceding case). In this case the lease specified that the premises of the lessor's building were to be used by the Department of the Army. The court had no problem in finding that (1) the clause was not one of such significance as to be termed a condition, and (2) if it was, the term was at any rate not breached.

CARTWRIGHT v. BARTHOLOMEW (Georgia, 1951)
64 SE 2d 323

> . . . Forfeiture of rights is not favored, and the courts will readily seize upon circumstances arising in the subsequent conduct or transactions of the parties, and imply a waiver. . . .

Drs. R. A. Bartholomew, E. D. Colvin, H. W. Grimes, Jr., and J. S. Fish, as an Obstetric Group, brought suit against William C. Cartwright in the Civil Court of Fulton County on an account stated in the sum of $120.00 plus interest. The defendant answered admitting a promise to pay the amount for which suit was brought but alleged that the plaintiffs' failure to perform their obligations under the contract resulted in damage to the defendant in more than the balance of the account due, for which reason the defendant is relieved from all liability. The answer further set up that the terms of the contract were that plaintiffs agreed to give the defendant's wife pre-natal care, attend the birth of the child, deliver the child, and give both mother and child post-natal care for six weeks following the birth of the child; that they agreed to use the "twilight sleep method," the same being the use of certain drugs to render the mother unconscious of pain, such drugs to be administered when labor pains began to occur at three-minute intervals; that the doctor on duty when defendant's wife entered the hospital would take charge and deliver the child; that at the time defendant's wife entered the hospital Dr. Grimes was on duty; that instead of remaining on duty to deliver the child he went off duty and was replaced by Dr. Fish; that Dr. Fish left shortly after 1:15 P.M. and did not return until after the birth of the child; that from 2:00 P.M., when labor pains began to occur at three-minute intervals until 4:20 P.M. there was on duty no doctor to administer the drugs as agreed; that the defendant's wife suffered excruciating pain needlessly as a result for a period of almost three hours, and for this reason the defendant is not indebted to plaintiff in any further amount.

(2–6) It is apparent from its terms that the agreement constituted an entire contract for a given price, the treatment to extend from the time of the agreement until six weeks after birth. So far as the testimony shows, this agreement was fulfilled by the plaintiffs, insofar as they were allowed to do so, for all of this period except two and one-half hours on the afternoon of the child's birth. It is true that the defendant's wife received only five days of the agreed six weeks post-natal treatment, but this was due to the defendant's action in removing his wife and child from the care of the clinic when they left the hospital. The contract was entire and not severable. . . . The defendant contends that, this being so, the plaintiff cannot recover unless he had performed all of the obligations imposed upon him under the terms of the contract, and that he did not perform all of its terms in that for the two-and-a-half-hour period in question, at a time when his wife most needed the services of the doctors, she did not receive them. . . . In the instant case granting that the failure of the doctors to appear during the time in question constituted a breach of the agreement, and that the defendant at that time could have refused all further services from them, procured another physician, and treated the contract as being at an end, . . . he did not do so, but accepted the doctors' services at 4:20 that afternoon, through the delivery of the child, and for five days thereafter, not releasing them until after the mother had left the hospital. . . . The court, quoting Story on Contracts, states as follows: "The entire fulfillment of the promise by either, in the absence of any agreement to the contrary, or waiver, is a condition precedent to the fulfillment of any part of the promise by the other." "Where a contract prescribes conditions precedent to a party's right to set up a cause of action or defense, and the terms are reasonable, the opposite party may usually successfully plead a failure to comply with the conditions as a reason for the court's refusal to entertain the action or defense; but forfeiture of rights is not favored, and the courts will readily seize upon circumstances arising in the subsequent conduct or transactions of the parties, and imply a waiver. . . ." Where a defendant accepts benefits arising under the contract, after discovery of the alleged breach, this will constitute a waiver of such breach. . . . While it is easily understandable that the defendant would not wish to employ a new physician on the very day his wife was in labor, nevertheless his conduct in retaining them throughout her subsequent stay in the hospital, and in having them proceed with the minor operation on the infant, constituted a waiver of his right to rely upon such breach for the purpose of rescinding the entire contract.

The parties sued upon an express contract, and stipulated at the trial of the case that testimony as to the range of charges or fees would not be introduced, but that the case would be submitted on the basis of a verdict of all or nothing. For this reason, the question of a reduction of fee based on partial failure of consideration is not before us.

The appellate division of the Civil Court of Fulton County did not err in affirming the judgment of the trial court directing a verdict in favor of the plaintiffs.

Judgment affirmed.

MacINTYRE, P.J., and GARDENER, J., concur.

The plaintiffs had promised to extend a series of medical services to the defendant, and the performance promised was entire, not severable (that is, divisible into parts). Performance according to the terms was therefore a condition precedent. However, surely the defendant, following a failure of strict performance early in the life of the contract, could not permit the plaintiff to extend further services, and then assert a breach of contract and claim a forfeiture as to all the services.

The plaintiff had a valid objection to the medical services offered when the physicians failed to appear during his wife's labor. He should have terminated their services at that point or reasonably soon after. Had he done so he would not have induced further benefits from the doctors. Because the defendants continued their services without objection by the defendant, the doctors have a right to be paid. This case illustrates one reason why courts are apt to seize upon a waiver; considering the lax conduct of the defendant, the plaintiffs now seem to have been more fair in their dealings than the defendant, regardless of the fact that the former did breach the contract.

Because the parties stipulated an all-or-nothing verdict, and the defendant, despite plaintiff's breach, waived the breach, the plaintiffs win the case.

QUESTIONS

1. What tort suit might have been brought under this set of facts by defendant's wife?

2. Assuming the existence of a tort, why is not the tort a valid defense to the plaintiff's contract action?

Operations of Some Typical Conditions

Construction contracts have already been mentioned in this discussion. They offer one of the most fruitful sources of problems involving conditions. Let us present as an actual illustration the following case: *A*, a physician, decided to have a house built. He proceeded to do extensive research in construction methods, and finally formulated a contract (which no doubt included consideration, legality, competent parties). This contract was a masterpiece of excruciating detail, specifying the number of nails per board, description of all materials, brand names, and nearly everything that could be imagined. The contract specified that any deviation from the specifications would be a breach, in which case he would owe the contractor nothing. He entertained his friends by enumerating the details he included, and everyone was surprised that the contractor signed.

In the event that the reader has been waiting for a punch line, there isn't any. So far as we know, the contract never went to court. No harm was done by submitting the overly detailed contract, and assuming the details really were important to the builder, perhaps some good was accomplished in making his wants known to the contractor and giving the latter notice he would have to toe the line.

Nevertheless, contrary to what the builder seemed to think, it was never true that he could have refused payment in the event that some of the details of the contract were not correctly performed.

In building contracts, a condition precedent is normally *not* given effect in cases where the deviation is unintentional and comparatively minor in effect. This rule is termed the doctrine of *substantial performance*. If minor but measurable harm results from an unintentional breach of condition, money damages equal to the amount of actual damage may be assessed against the contractor, but no more. Mere accidental substitution of one brand of material for another of equal grade would result in no money damages, nor would very minor deviations from plan. In the event of a deliberate deviation, the courts all state that they would permit the condition to operate, but in fact it is difficult to find a case where a condition is enforced against a contract without a *material* deviation. Intent in such a case would be hard to establish. If defects are material, there are good reasons for enforcing the condition; after all the builder has some rights.

The doctrine of substantial performance has been extended in application to other types of contracts in many jurisdictions.

Often a person contracting to have a building erected does not have the skill and knowledge necessary to determine whether or not the contractor is performing his obligations properly. Consequently, a condition is often included in the building contract requiring the contractor to secure a certificate of approval of his work from an architect agreed upon between the parties. This is designated as a condition precedent to payment of the contractor. This is not a provision that could be attacked as frivolous or of minor importance. There are sound reasons for requiring an architect's approval, and if the approval is withheld for just cause, the validity of this condition could hardly be questioned. Because most expressions of professional opinion are in the final analysis matters of judgment, even if there appears to be something to be said on either side, the decision of the architect would stand. The parties agreed by contract to abide by the architect's decision, and ordinarily his decision should be the last word. However, if the architect is acting out of malice, fraud, or collusion with the builder in withholding his certificate, most modern courts will relieve the contractor from performance of the condition. The most difficult situation, and one in which the courts are divided, is where the architect refuses the certificate in good faith but the evidence is overwhelming that his judgment is wrong. The student can see that a plausible argument might be advanced on either side of this question.

Another provision normally included in building contracts but also in many other contracts is one making time of performance a condition. (Generally, the designation of a certain time by which performance should be completed is presumed *not* to be a condition, but merely an independent promise meriting recovery for damages, if any.) In special cases, where the entire purpose of the contract will be defeated by a failure of performance by a certain time, a condition will be implied, and the other party discharged if performance is late. Performance can be made a condition in other cases by the use of proper wording, and the wording commonly used to express this purpose is, "Time is of the essence."

Leaving the subject of building contracts for a discussion of contracts in general, another common condition is that performance shall be "to the satisfaction" of one of the parties. Does this mean that a forfeiture may depend upon nothing more than the whim of one of the parties? In general the answer is no. Provisions of this type are construed to mean that performance must be acceptable to a reasonable man, and if the party involved happens to be a crank with excessively severe standards, his standards will not control. An exception has been recognized when the subject is primarily a matter of taste, to which personal preference is a question of opinion rather than of objective evidence. In that event personal standards apply, even if extreme, providing the party refusing performance is sincere in claiming he is dissatisfied. Obviously it would be very difficult to prove a party was not sincere in his claimed dissatisfaction.

Contracts that do not usually result from bargaining between the parties but that, on the contrary, are submitted on a completed form, to a party who has the option of taking the contract or leaving it, are termed *contracts of adhesion.* Examples are insurance contracts, lease-hold agreements (though some leases, to be sure, are the result of very hard bargaining indeed), and bills of lading. Contracts of adhesion are construed more critically, and more severely against the maker of the contracts. The rationale for this is usually stated to be that because the party furnishing the contract had the time and legal advice to draw up the agreement in exactly the form he wished, the slightest failure to resolve ambiguities or provide against eventualities must be construed against that party. The trouble with this view is that specific eventualities are bound to arise that no one could ever dream of happening, but which are still resolved against the party submitting the contract. Very likely another influence affecting the courts is that often the person submitting the contract has a bargaining position so strong the courts tend to view the inclusion of extreme terms as unfair.

ARD DR. PEPPER BOTTLING COMPANY v. *DR. PEPPER COMPANY* (CCA Mississippi, 1953) 202 F 2d 372

> *Courts are cautious in enforcing such contracts literally when to do so would result in injustice . . . courts tend to adopt an interpretation of the contract, wherever possible, requiring performance to the satisfaction of a reasonable man. After all is said and done, however, the question is one of construction or interpretation, and the contract, if not illegal or against public policy, must be enforced according to the actual or legally presumed intention of the parties.*

The complaint seeks the recovery of damages in the amount of $150,000.00 for the alleged wrongful, willful, and malicious breach of a bottler's license agreement entered into between Ard and Dr. Pepper in 1938. The answer admits the cancellation by Dr. Pepper of the license agreement on July 27, 1950, and alleges that Dr. Pepper in good faith determined that Ard had not complied with the terms and provisions of the license agreement, and that under the provisions of the agreement Dr. Pepper's determination as to these matters authorized it to cancel the agreement and was final and conclusive.

. . . The view of the district court is fairly summarized in the concluding paragraph of its charge to the jury:

> The Dr. Pepper Company, when it lets these contracts out, naturally is looking to the future. It puts at least a fair part of its business in the hands of its dealers and it, therefore, has the right to reserve unto itself the determination of whether or not the contract is being carried out to its satisfaction. The company, in good faith, and I think after a full and thorough investigation, and after an ample opportunity to Ard Dr. Pepper Bottling Company to take up the matter with it, determined that the contract was not being carried out to its satisfaction and, therefore, it had the right to cancel the contract. That being the law, it is the duty of the court to instruct the jury to return a verdict to find for the defendant.

By the bottler's license agreement entered into between Dr. Pepper and Ard on the 20th day of July, 1938, Dr. Pepper granted to Ard the exclusive license to bottle in a designated territory consisting of a number of counties in Mississippi a soft drink known as "Dr. Pepper," provided for the price and terms at which Dr. Pepper was to sell syrup to Ard, and agreed that "such exclusive license shall continue so long as Dr. Pepper Company, or its successors or assigns, continue the manufacture of Dr. Pepper syrup, unless sooner terminated under the provisions hereinafter set out."

Among Ard's agreements were the following (emphasis supplied):

(a) To accept Dr. Pepper as its leading drink. . . .

(b) To use modern, automatic and sanitary equipment throughout, of such character in all bottling operations *as are, or may be required and approved by the Grantor.*

(e) To at all times loyally and faithfully promote the sale of and secure thorough distribution of Dr. Pepper throughout every part of said territory and to all dealers therein, and to develop an increase in volume of sales of Dr. Pepper satisfactory to the Grantor. And in this connection, the Grantee agrees, represents and guarantees that the said territory included in this license, and every part thereof, and all dealers therein, can, and will be fully covered, solicited and worked by the Grantee in a systematic and business-like manner now, and at all times hereafter while this license agreement remains in effect. *The determination and judgment of Dr. Pepper Company as to whether or not this clause is being complied with when made in good faith, shall be sole, exclusive and final, and such determination by the Dr. Pepper Company that this clause is not being complied with shall in addition to any other grounds herein mentioned, be grounds for forfeiture of this license at the option of Grantor.*

The letter of cancellation dated July 27, 1950, fairly sets out the grounds upon which Dr. Pepper claimed the right to cancel and terminate the license agreement:

Your bottled Dr. Pepper has not been up to our required standard. Your bottling machinery and equipment are inadequate and insufficient and you have failed to use modern, automatic and sanitary equipment in your Dr. Pepper bottling operations, as you have been requested to do. The building in which you operate is wholly inadequate and improperly maintained for a modern, sanitary bottling plant.

You have failed to fully cover, solicit and work in a systematic and business-like manner for the promotion of Dr. Pepper the territory covered by your license agreement and all dealers therein. You have failed to at all times loyally and faithfully promote the sale of and secure thorough distribution of Dr. Pepper throughout every part of your territory and to all dealers therein, and you have failed to develop an increase in the volume of sales of Dr. Pepper satisfactory to the Dr. Pepper Company. You have failed to properly advertise Dr. Pepper in your territory.

You have failed within the judgment of Dr. Pepper Company to faithfully comply with the provisions of your license agreement and the Dr. Pepper Company hereby exercises its right to terminate the aforesaid Dr. Pepper Bottler's License Agreement.

There was substantial evidence of other breaches of the license agreement on the part of Ard. . . .

. . . In final analysis, the decision of the case depends upon the construction of those terms of the contract giving Dr. Pepper the right or option to terminate or cancel the license. The district court was of the opinion that, so long as Dr. Pepper's dissatisfaction was genuine and it acted in good faith, under the terms of the license agreement, Dr. Pepper's judgment was conclusive and, further, that there was no evidence of bad faith on the part of Dr. Pepper. We agree.

(3) Ard, having alleged that the contract was wrongfully terminated, had the burden of so proving. . . .

(4–6) It is, of course, elementary that competent persons ordinarily have the utmost liberty of contracting, and may enter into any agreement that they please so long as it is not illegal or violative of public policy. . . . A provision making the contract terminable at will would not have been illegal. . . . Indeed, Ard had the right to cancel the license, with or without cause, upon giving 90 days written notice to Dr. Pepper.

The present contract expressly provides that the determination of Dr. Pepper as to the failure of Ard to comply with any of the terms of the license agreement must be made in good faith. As said in *Goltra* v. *Weeks* . . . :

> The cases leave no doubt that such a provision for termination of a contract is valid, unless there is an absence of good faith in the exercise of the judgment. Here nothing of the kind is shown. Such a stipulation may be a harsh one, or an unwise one, but it is valid and binding if entered into.

(7, 8) So much has been written on the subject of contracts where performance by one party is conditioned on the satisfaction of the other party that there would be no point in our undertaking a restatement of the law on the subject. . . . Courts are cautious in enforcing such contracts literally when to do so would result in injustice. Dependent upon the subject matter of the contract and all of the circumstances surrounding the parties and particularly when a definite objective test of satisfaction is available, courts tend to adopt an interpretation of the contract, wherever possible, requiring performance to the satisfaction of a reasonable man. After all is said and done, however, the question is one of construction or interpretation, and the contract, if not illegal or against public policy, must be enforced according to the actual or legally presumed intention of the parties.

(9–11) The terms of the present contract in the light of its subject matter and of the circumstances of the parties leave little or no room for construction or interpretation. The impact upon Dr. Pepper's business of improper performance of a license agreement by a bottler could well be serious. Dr. Pepper was the party to be satisfied, not some imaginary reasonable person. It was not unreasonable for Dr. Pepper to reserve to its own business judgment the question of whether the agreement had been properly and faithfully performed. There was no evidence of actual ill will, nor of financial advantage to Dr. Pepper. The cancellation of the license agreement left Dr. Pepper without a distributor in the territory, and the place had not been filled. If Ard would make out his case by proof of performance, such proof must extend to such perfect performance as would negative Dr. Pepper's good faith. The proof in this case fails by a wide margin to meet that exacting standard. On the contrary, we, like the district court, are impressed that Dr. Pepper acted in the utmost good faith and indeed with patience and forbearance. The evidence did not authorize submission to the jury of the issue of Dr. Pepper's good faith and the judgment is therefore

Affirmed.

✧

Despite the usual reluctance of courts to set aside contracts merely because the test of "satisfaction" is not met, they have no reluctance in this case. This, of course, is a particularly strong case, for although in agency contracts the general rule is that the promisee's dissatisfaction alone is ground for terminating a relationship, here, we might surmise, any reasonable man might have been dissatisfied with the quality of performance.

QUESTIONS

1. Assuming the purpose of contracts is to carry out the intentions of the parties, could a contract carry out its purpose if conditions it contained were not enforced?

2. To what extent does the purpose of contracts as stated above seem open to question?

The Warranty

The case of *Gagne* v. *Bertran* was previously discussed in relation to the plaintiff's allegations of fraud and negligence. It happened that the plaintiff claimed another ground for recovery, for breach of warranty. The court discussed that issue as follows:

GAGNE v. *BERTRAN* (California, 1954) 275 P 2d 15
Part Two

> *Thus the general rule is applicable that those who sell their services for the guidance of others . . . are not liable in the absence of negligence or intentional misconduct.*

[See page 287 for facts of this case.]

THE CAUSE OF ACTION FOR BREACH OF WARRANTY

Plaintiffs contend that defendant undertook to guarantee the accuracy of the results of his test, not on the ground that there was an express warranty agreement, for there is no evidence of such an agreement, but on the ground that under the circumstances of this case the law imposes the strict liability of a warranty.

(1–8) For historical reasons warranties have become identified primarily with transactions involving the sale or furnishing of tangible chattels, . . . but they are not confined to such transactions. Strict liability has also been imposed for innocent misrepresentations of facts that the maker purported to know, that the recipient relied on in matters affecting his economic interests, and that the maker positively affirmed under circumstances that justify the conclusion that he assumed responsibility for their accuracy.

(9–10) The evidence in the present case does not justify the imposition of the strict liability of a warranty. There was no express warranty agreement, and there is nothing in the evidence to indicate that defendant assumed responsibility for the accuracy of his statements. He did not . . . tender plaintiffs an "absolute promise" that the results of his test would be accurate. He was not a seller of property who obligated himself as a part of his bargain to convey property in the condition represented. The amount of his fee and the fact that he was paid by the hour also indicate that he was selling service and not insurance. Thus the general rule is applicable that those who sell their services for the guidance of others in their economic, financial, and personal affairs are not liable in the absence of negligence or intentional misconduct.

✧

It may be seen from this language that a contractual proviso termed a *warranty,* somewhat similar to a condition, may come into play under certain circumstances. There are marginal instances in which the difference between the warranty and the condition is so vague as to be virtually indefinable. However, ordinarily the difference is this: the condition, as we have seen, may excuse performance (and under some circumstances give rise to an action in damages) when a stated event does or does not occur. The warranty is an assertion that some fact is true, with the additional understanding that if the assertion of fact is not true, if the warranty is breached, then the contract may be rescinded. In addition an action in damages will lie for all losses, probable or not, stemming from the breach of warranty. Unlike an action in fraud, no intent need be proved; consequently, a suit based upon breach of warranty is almost always easier to win than a suit based upon fraud or negligence.

As the case of *Gagne* v. *Bertran* illustrates, a promise is not ordinarily presumed to be a warranty without some affirmative showing that the promisor really was making an "absolute promise." However, there is an exception to the rule that is probably more important than the rule itself. This is in regard to the sales contract. Not only is practically any promise relating to the subject of a sale a warranty, but several warranties are implied by law to be attached to a sale even if not expressed. The treatment of warranties under the portion of the UCC relating to sales is considered below.

Section 2–313 of the Act provides the UCC definition of express warranties.

> UCC—SECTION 2–313: Express Warranties by Affirmation.
> Promise, Description, Sample.
> (1) Express warranties by the seller are created as follows:
>   (a) Any affirmation of fact or promise made by the seller to the buyer which relates to the goods and becomes part of the basis of the bargain creates an express warranty that the goods shall conform to the affirmation of promise.
>   (b) Any description of the goods which is made part of the basis of the bargain creates an express warranty that the goods shall conform to the description.
>   (c) Any sample or model which is made part of the basis of the bargain creates an express warranty that the whole of the goods shall conform to the sample or model.
> (2) It is not necessary to the creation of an express warranty that the seller use formal words such as "warrant" or "guarantee" or that he have a specific intention to make a warranty, but *an affirmation merely of the value of the goods or a statement purporting to be merely the seller's opinion or commendation of the goods does not create a warranty.*

By way of summary, UCC—Section 2–313 (1) tells us that an express warranty results when *any* one of the following, either a description of goods, or a sample or model, or an affirmation of fact, is made a part of the basis of the bargain.

Section (2) merely assures us that the word *warrant* or *guarantee* is not necessary to constitute a warranty. We are also informed that statements of opinion and value are not warranties. A merchant is free to indulge in trade puffs, and when so doing he is no more guilty of breach of warranty than he is of fraud, if he confines his comments to his opinions, and to expressions of monetary value.

Sales Warranties under the UCC

Under the older Uniform Sales Act a warranty was any affirmation, express or implied, tending to encourage the buyer to purchase the goods. In that act, however, as well as the present one, a number of warranties were usually "implied" as a matter of law. The beginning student may find it difficult to see how a warranty may be implied by law. Actually, an implied warranty of this kind is merely a command of the legislature, to the merchant, informing the latter that he provides a warranty as set out in the statute, whether he likes it or not. The warranty stems from the law and not from an act or even intention of the seller.

> UCC—Section 2-312: Warranty of Title and Against Infringement; Buyers Obligation Against Infringement.
> (1) Subject to subsection (2) there is in a contract for sale a warranty by the seller that
>> (a) the title conveyed shall be good, and its transfer rightful; and
>> (b) the goods shall be delivered free from any security interest or other lien or encumbrance of which the buyer at the time of contracting has no notice.

This language means that the buyer is assured as a matter of law, and without this being stated by the seller, that title to goods is clear at the time it is transferred. Occasionally, goods are sold to which the seller believes he has title, but is mistaken. On other occasions, there is some other type of claim, as when a bank holds a mortgage on property in security for payment of a debt by some third party.

Both of these contingencies are disposed of through this section. In either case, the seller is required to pass good and clear title to the buyer. Ignorance of a defect in the title is no excuse. Should the seller fail to transfer good and clear title, the buyer is provided with an action in breach of warranty by this section.

The seller is not obligated under this section if he has informed the buyer of a defect in the title prior to the sale. If the buyer had notice of the defect in title, he presumably offset the deficiency in title by paying a lower price, or at any rate he is presumably satisfied with the defective title at the bargained price. Even so, however, the language of subsection (2) quoted below indicates that the seller must use care to be sure that the buyer understands the defective title.

> [UCC—Section 2-312 (cont.)]
> (2) A warranty under subsection (1) will be excluded or modified *only by specific language or by circumstances* which give the buyer reason to know that the person selling does not claim title in himself or that he is purporting to sell only such right or title as he or a third person may have.

That the seller is not claiming to pass clear title to property that he sells *must* be evident for him to escape liability imposed by section (1). In situations of any ambiguity, the burden is upon the seller to make certain that the buyer understands the fact of unclear title.

Other defects in goods are dealt with in the following pages of rather technical reading. Broadly the question we are investigating now is, "for what types of defects in goods does the UCC prescribe an implied warranty?"

> UCC—SECTION 2–314: Implied Warranty: Merchantability; Usage of Trade.
> (1) Unless excluded or modified (Section 2–316), a warranty that the goods shall be merchantable is implied in a contract for their sale if the seller is a merchant with respect to goods of that kind. Under this section the serving for value of food or drink to be consumed either on the premises or elsewhere is a sale.

This paragraph requires that goods sold be of reasonably good quality, although what is reasonably good quality depends upon the contract and course of dealing between the parties. Goods of high quality for one purpose might be low quality for another, and even goods of a low quality for most purposes may be high-quality scrap.

Beyond a doubt this warranty is very broad in scope. It applies to every sales contract unless specifically abrogated under Section 2–316.

In order to define more specifically the meaning of merchantable, this section continues:

> [UCC—SECTION 2–314 (*cont.*)]
> (2) Goods to be merchantable must be at least such as
> (a) pass without objection in the trade under the contract description; and
> (b) in the case of fungible goods,[1] are of fair average quality within the description; and
> (c) are fit for the ordinary purposes for which such goods are used; and
> (d) run, within the variations permitted by the agreement, of even kind, quality and quantity within each unit and among all units involved; and

---

[1] Fungible goods are those dealt with by weight or measure as part of a common mass—for example, coal, sulphur, grain, and so on. To be fungible, every unit of weight or measure must be interchangeable with every other unit in the mass.

(e) are adequately contained, packaged, and labeled as the agreement may require; and

(f) conform to the promises or affirmations of fact made on the container and label if any.

(3) Unless excluded or modified (Section 2–316) other implied warranties may arise from course of dealing or usage of trade.

UCC—SECTION 2–315: Implied Warranty: Fitness for Particular Purpose. Where the seller at the time of contracting has reason to know any particular purpose for which the goods are required and that the buyer is relying on the seller's skill or judgment to select or furnish suitable goods, there is unless excluded or modified under the next section an implied warranty that the goods shall be fit for such purpose.

This warranty does not duplicate but rather supplements the previous warranty, for the following reason. Goods may well be of merchantable quality, and therefore not in violation of the previous warranty, yet goods may still not meet the particular purpose a buyer has in mind. This warranty, therefore, fills that loophole. This warranty is violated if goods are inadequate for a particular purpose, which is known, *or which should be known,* to the seller regardless of whether the goods are of merchantable quality.

Some difficulties are bound to result from ascertaining what is a particular purpose. The act envisions some purpose more narrow than the common, ordinary purpose for which the goods are customarily used. No doubt some borderline cases will arise on this point.

UCC—SECTION 2–316: Exclusion or Modification of Warranties.

(1) Words or conduct relevant to the creation of an express warranty and words or conduct tending to negate or limit warranty shall be construed wherever reasonable as consistent with each other; but subject to the provisions of this Article on parol or extrinsic evidence (Section 2–202) negation or limitation is inoperative to the extent that such construction is unreasonable.

Considerable confusion arises in construing some sales contracts as a result of the seller extending an express warranty in one paragraph, then denying it or even the implied warranties, in the next. This provision is a warning that unreasonable denial of warranties will be inoperative.

[UCC—SECTION 2–316 (*cont.*)]

(2) Subject to subsection (3), to exclude or modify the implied warranty of merchantability or any part of it the language must mention

merchantability and in case of a writing must be conspicuous, and to exclude or modify any implied warranty of fitness the exclusion must be by a writing and conspicuous. Language to exclude all implied warranties of fitness is sufficient if it states, for example, that "there are no warranties which extend beyond the description on the face hereof."

(3) (a) unless the circumstances indicate otherwise, *all* implied warranties are excluded by expressions like "as is," "with all faults" or other language which in common understanding calls the buyer's attention to the exclusion of warranties and makes plain that there is no implied warranty; and

(b) when the buyer before entering into the contract has examined the goods or the sample or model as fully as he desired or has refused to examine the goods there is no implied warranty with regard to defects which an examination ought in the circumstances to have revealed to him; and

(c) an implied warranty can also be excluded or modified by course of dealing or course of performance or usage of trade.

Clauses which are intended to restrict the applicability of warranties are termed *disclaimers*. Most of Section 2–316 is devoted to restriction of and amplification on the use of the disclaimer. This area of sales law has caused a good deal of confusion and litigation in the past. No doubt that is why the present act takes up the problem of disclaimer in such detail.

To summarize some of the sections of Section 2–315:

1. Language such as *as is* or *with all faults* will usually exclude the implied warranties.

2. An examination or opportunity for the buyer to examine will exclude the implied warranties, to the extent, but only to the extent, that defects could be discovered upon examination.

3. Implied warranties may be excluded in other cases by usage of trade, course of dealing, or course of performance. Making the determination of whether an implied warranty would be excluded under this provision would usually require an intimate knowledge of the trade practices in the industry, as well as of the details of the particular transaction and course of dealing.

4. Except by the means already itemized under 1, 2, and 3 above, an implied warranty of fitness may not be excluded except by writing that is conspicuous, though a general statement such as *There are no warranties that extend beyond the description on the face hereof* will exclude this warranty.

5. Except by the means already itemized under 1, 2, and 3 above, an implied warranty of merchantability may not be excluded without specific

mention of merchantability. The disclaimer of warranty need not be in writing, but if it is in writing, the writing must be conspicuous.

> UCC—SECTION 2–317: Cumulation and Conflict of Warranties Express or Implied.
>
> Warranties whether express or implied shall be construed as consistent with each other and as cumulative, but if such construction is unreasonable the intention of the parties shall determine which warranty is dominant. In ascertaining that intention the following rules apply:
>
> (a) Exact or technical specifications displace an inconsistent sample or model or general language of description.
>
> (b) A sample from an existing bulk displaces inconsistent general language of description.
>
> (c) Express warranties displace inconsistent implied warranties other than an implied warranty of fitness for a particular purpose.

Insurance Contracts

A number of factors are more or less uniquely true of insurance contracts: (1) they are contracts of adhesion, (2) in earlier days the insurance industry was guilty of abuses that attracted wide public attention, (3) it is common knowledge that this type of contract is almost never read by the insured, and if it is, is almost never understood, (4) and perhaps most important of all, the public feels an interest in seeing to it that widows and orphans and other likely beneficiaries of insurance policies receive the benefit of their policies rather than being left dependent upon public charity. Concern for the rights of insurance companies does not seem to have weighed too heavily in balancing this sentiment.

For these reasons, the interpretation of warranties and conditions in the insurance contract has become practically a law unto itself. For example, most states have drastically modified the common-law defenses of fraud, misrepresentation, and breach of warranty in life insurance contracts. An innocent misrepresentation by the insured is often no defense at all, and breach of warranty may be asserted by the insurer only when the warranty is established as material—that is, relating to something which, if the insurer had known about it, would have caused the policy not to be issued.

Even more drastic, no matter how grandiose the fraud practiced against the insurer in securing a life insurance contract, the defense of fraud is *completely* lost by the insurer after a period of time, usually two years after a policy was fraudulently procured. This provision, which most states require to be included in life insurance policies, is known as the *incontestable clause*. Attempts to provide against payment in the event of suicide of the insured have also been dealt with by statutes. Usually suicide is a ground for nonpayment if occurring within a year or two after taking of the policy. After that, it is no longer available to the insurer as a defense. In practice this has been sufficient protection for the insurer, because experience has demonstrated that most individuals taking out a policy with the intent of committing suicide fail to wait the designated period of time.

For all of the reasons stated, forfeiture in the case of insurance contracts is granted very grudgingly. The statement often made that in insurance contracts the contract is not made by the parties but by the courts appears to be a fair summary of the situation. This is despite the fact that insurance is a regulated industry in all of our states, and almost invariably, prospective contracts have to be screened by the state Insurance Commissioner before they may be issued. It is also true, however, that regulation is often lax and in some cases appears to be dominated by the industry supposedly regulated.

Discharge by Subsequent Agreement

An agreement between the parties that the performance owing under an unfulfilled contract shall be modified or superseded is generally enforceable (see Chapter 23), providing the requirement of consideration is met, and providing the subsequent agreement is not in conflict with the parol evidence rule (see Chapter 23).

Impossibility as a Defense

The circumstances under which impossibility of performance constitutes a defense to a suit based on nonperformance of contract vary widely. Perhaps the most important source of difference could be said to be one of definition: what do we mean by impossible?

Some courts require performance to be an absolute physical impossibility before the defense of impossibility may be successfully utilized, and require that the task be impossible not only for the party involved to perform but for anyone to perform. By this view, when a contract was made to provide a quantity of cans of oysters from a designated bay, and all the oysters from that bay became diseased and unfit for human consumption, impossibility constituted a defense. Impossibility would not have constituted a defense if the agreement had not been for the oysters to come from a particular bay. Then performance would still be possible. Difficult questions of fact often arise in deciding whether or not the intent of the parties did contemplate a particular source. If a particular *person* is necessary to performance, his death or illness will constitute a valid excuse for nonperformance.

Although any court would consider a case in which a necessary source of supply ceases to exist a valid excuse for nonperformance, other instances are more debatable. Strikes and wars, for example, offer real difficulties. Some courts refuse to consider impossibility caused by these events as a valid excuse, on the theory that the party should have had the foresight to specifically relieve himself of liability should he not wish to assume the risk of such an event. Others base their decision on whether a reasonable man could have foreseen the possibility of eventualities of that sort. Others take a more liberal view and hold that if, in fact, there is no way by which performance could be accomplished, the contract is terminated. Some courts discharge a party from further responsibility when a change in circumstances has merely made performance substantially more difficult than it otherwise would have been. If, for example, the cost of producing an article, due to a substantial increase in the cost of some component, be greatly increased, the more liberal courts would consider this a reason for nonperformance. Such views are no doubt in the minority.

As usual, the problem of lack of uniformity in decision stems from the fact that more than one consideration is involved. On the one hand, the interest of fairness would seem to militate against holding a party to a contract that through no fault of his own could not possibly be performed. The interest of preserving the integrity and meaning of contracts militates against making exceptions. The trend appears to be in the direction of relieving parties from liability in cases when in fact the contract could not be performed.

WASSERMAN THEATRICAL ENTERPRISE v. HARRIS
(Connecticut, 1950) 77 A 2d 329

> *One who engages for performance of such personal character that it can be performed only by a particular person is excused from liability by the physical incapacity of that person, before breach of the contract unless he has clearly assumed the risk of such incapacity.*

BROWN, CJ.

The plaintiff brought this action to recover damages for the defendant's failure to produce a theatrical performance as provided in a written contract between the parties. The court rendered judgment for the defendant and the plaintiff has appealed.

These facts are not in dispute: On October 30, 1946, the plaintiff entered into a contract with the defendant whereby the latter agreed to present Walter Huston in a theatrical performance entitled "The Apple of His Eye" at Worcester, Massachusetts, on the night of December 16, 1946. The contract contained this provision: "(T)his agreement and the terms hereof shall be subject to the customs governing uncontrollable circumstances, such as . . . illness of any of the chief artists of the said attraction and the like, and . . . upon the happening of any of such events no claim for compensation or damages shall be made by either party as against the other." The plaintiff which had been engaged in theatrical productions in Worcester for some eleven years had reason to anticipate a profit from the production and went to considerable expense and effort in preparing to stage it. On December 12, 1946, the defendant canceled the performance on the ground of Huston's illness. At the same time, bookings for Ithaca, Springfield and Rochester, scheduled to follow that for Worcester, were also canceled. The plaintiff has received nothing for its loss incident to the cancellation of the performance and has been at all times ready, able and willing to perform its obligations under the contract. The show, with Huston as leading man, had been on the road since the early fall of 1946. After eight performances a week had been given for four weeks in Boston, it opened in New Haven on December 12, 1946, for four performances and closed on December 14. As scheduled, the show opened for a month in Chicago on December 25. Huston participated in every performance given and had no understudy.

(1, 2) The defendant alleged as a special defense the provision of the contract quoted above, that Huston was the chief artist and essential performer in the production, and that by reason of his illness performance of the contract on December 16, 1946, was rendered impossible on the part of the defendant. Whether the court was warranted in sustaining this defense and, in reliance thereon, rendering judgment for the defendant is the question for determination. "One who engages for performance of such personal character that it can be performed only by a particular person is excused from liability by the physical incapacity of that person, before breach of the contract unless he has clearly assumed the risk of such incapacity. . . . Generally it is the promisor himself who is to render the personal services, but the principle is applicable to contracts where the promisor has agreed that a third person shall render such services and the latter becomes physically unable to do so. . . ." The quoted provision of the contract therefore is substantially declaratory of the condition which arises by implication in an agreement of this nature. An agreement for personal services, in the absence of a manifested contrary intention, is always subject to the condition, implied by law, that the person who is to render the services shall be able to perform at the appointed time. . . .

(3–5) In the view which we take of the case, the only conclusion of the court requiring consideration was that Huston's apprehension as to the state of his health was reasonable and reasonably justified the defendant in canceling the performance. The rule quoted is amplified by this further principle: "Where a promisor apprehends before . . . the time for performance of a promise in a bargain . . . that performance will seriously jeopardize his own life or health or that of others, he is not liable, unless a contrary intention is manifested or he is guilty of contributing fault, for failing to begin . . . performance, while such apprehension exists, if the failure to begin . . . performance is reasonable. . . . In determining whether a promisor's failure to begin . . . performance is reasonable . . . consideration is given to [a] the degree of probability, apparent from what he knows or has reason to know, . . . of physical or pecuniary harm or loss to himself or to others if he begins . . . performance, and (b) the extent of physical or pecuniary harm or loss to himself or to others likely to be incurred by attempting performance as compared with the amount of harmful consequences likely to be caused to the promisee by non-performance." Restatement, 2 Contracts, subsection 465.

Out of regard for human welfare the rule is often applicable . . . though performance is not only practicable but is not increased in difficulty. The possible consequences of performing may be so injurious as to free the promisor; and the fact that it later appears that no harmful consequences would have ensued does not alter the rule. The promisor is not bound to perform so long as failure to perform is reasonable because of existing grounds for apprehension." 2 id. subsection 465, comment b. "The extent of the harmful consequences apprehended, and the probability of their occurrence, involve questions of degree. Exact boundaries cannot be fixed, but the harm apprehended must be serious and the apprehension reasonable. . . .

(6) The further facts established by the finding as corrected and material upon this issue, which is sufficiently raised by the special defense, may be thus summarized: While playing in Boston, Huston, for some two weeks prior to December 12, experienced a tickling sensation in his throat, and during this time the condition became progressively worse. As often as two or three times during a performance he experienced a tightening of his throat. Although use of a medication afforded him temporary relief, he had similar difficulty while performing on the stage in New Haven on December 12, 13 and 14. His throat condition was a continuous and increasing cause of worry to him for he was constantly in fear during a performance that he would be unable to finish it. This fear did not affect him in social intercourse off the stage, but because of his apprehension that he could not go on with the show in the face of the recurring throat sensation he wanted to find out definitely the nature of his ailment. Had he kept the engagement in Worcester, and had his throat tightened, he probably could have completed the performance with the aid of lozenges. He had consulted a doctor in New York three or four times in the spring of 1946. The only doctor Huston consulted during November and December, 1946, was Dr. Loyal Davis, his personal friend, who, after hearing his symptoms, though no examination was made, advised him to go to Chicago for a complete and thorough examination and to have the condition attended to. Huston's throat attacks were becoming more frequent and he felt impelled to do something about them without delay. While he believed he could complete the New Haven engagement, he insisted upon canceling all performances for the week of December 16 in order to look after his throat condition immediately, for he believed it would be impossible for him to continue after concluding in New Haven. He was gravely concerned over the consequences of any delay in procuring medical attention.

From New Haven he proceeded to Chicago. A minor operation was performed on his throat at a hospital there and specimens of tissue were taken. The report that these disclosed no malignant condition relieved his mind, and he was able to resume his next scheduled performances in Chicago, where he played every performance. Huston was a man with a sincere desire to carry out his obligations. During his entire theatrical career of forty-five years, the only request which he had made for the cancellation of a performance was for the one at Worcester. The court's conclusion that Huston's fear and apprehension that his illness was of such a nature that it would, in the absence of immediate expert medical attention, seriously jeopardize his health and particularly his voice was a reasonable one and was warranted upon the facts set forth in the preceding paragraph. Under the principles recited above, it justified the further conclusion of the court that the defendant was not liable for the cancellation of the contract.

There is no error.

In this opinion the other judges concurred.

✧

The issue in this case appears to amount to this: Is the belief that performance will lead to injury or disability a reasonable ground for nonperformance? The court answers the question in the affirmative. Of course, this would be true only when performance required the services of that particular individual. Otherwise, someone else could be hired as a substitute. Obviously, acquiring an adequate substitute cannot ordinarily be done in the case of well-known actors.

SAFE HARBOR FISHING CLUB v. SAFE HARBOR REALTY COMPANY (Delaware, 1953) 107 A 2d 635

> *Mere inconvenience or substantial increase in the cost of compliance with a contract, though they might make compliance a hardship, cannot excuse a party from the performance of an absolute and unqualified undertaking to do a thing that is possible and lawful.*

On April 26, 1947, defendant Safe Harbor Realty Company, a corporation of the State of Delaware, and Safe Harbor Fishing Club, of the City of Chester, State of Pennsylvania, entered into a written agreement providing for the sale by the realty company to the fishing club of a certain land bordering on the Delaware Bay, in Kent County, near a place known as Pickering Beach, designated on the plot as 541 lots, a parking lot 700 feet long and 100 feet wide, and a tract of land on the shore of the Delaware Bay to be used as a club house. The agreement provided as a consideration for the sale of said lots that the plaintiff would pay to the corporate defendant the sum of $2,000; that the plaintiff would dredge a canal or creek and a basin for boats; that it would erect at the mouth of the creek a club house; that it would gravel the streets "that are laid out on the plot plan they are purchasing," and would pay to the defendant 50% of the sale of each lot until the said sum of $2,000 was fully paid to the corporate defendant; that in default of said agreement the plaintiff would forfeit all work done on said property as liquidated damages.

Plaintiff has requested that defendants be ordered and directed to construct a road leading to the club house site; that defendants return to plaintiff the sum of $6,500 which plaintiff spent in dredging the canal and yacht basin and that defendant corporation be directed to perform its obligations pursuant to the agreement of April 26, 1947.

Plaintiff contends that it was relieved from its duty to erect a club house on the club house site by reason of the excessive cost which would be entailed in the erection of a club house on that site and by reason of the serious difficulty, if not impossibility, of moving materials to the club house site in the absence of the construction of the road. Plaintiff entered into a building contract. At the time of the execution of the agreement there was no road leading to the club house site. From the testimony of the various witnesses it was obvious that a road leading to the site of the proposed club house would have to be constructed. Nevertheless, plaintiff executed an agreement which contained nothing relative to the construction of the road or as to whose responsibility its construction would be. . . .

(2) Plaintiff relies upon impossibility of performance and breach of the contract by the defendants in failing to construct the road. As to the road, I find no specific or implied obligation on the part of the defendants to construct it. It is undisputed that the excavation of the canal and yacht basin were to be at the expense of plaintiff and that the dirt obtained therefrom was to be used in the construction of the road. If there had been sufficient dirt obtained from the excavation work to use for the road, the cost of constructing the road would have been materially reduced. The difficulty arose when it was found that the dirt obtained was not sufficient for the purpose of making a roadbed. As the matter now stands, in order for work to proceed on the development as planned, it probably would be necessary to haul dirt for the purpose of making a roadbed. Plaintiff's inability to haul materials to its yacht club site by reason of the lack of a road does not make plaintiff's obligation to erect a club house on the club house site impossible of performance: it merely increases the difficulty and expense. I therefore do not find that the defendant corporation has breached the agreement by reason of its failure to construct the road.

(3) Plaintiff contends that in order to build a club house at the club house site it would be necessary to drive piling for a foundation for the building. There is testimony, which is not disputed, to the effect that this could be accomplished by using short piling for the foundation. This of course would increase the cost of the erection of the club house. It would not make the obligation of plaintiff to construct the club house impossible of performance.

(4–6) Mere inconvenience or substantial increase in the cost of compliance with a contract, though they might make compliance a hardship, cannot excuse a party from the performance of an absolute and unqualified undertaking to do a thing that is possible and lawful. Courts cannot alter contracts merely because they work a hardship. A contract is not invalid, nor is the obligor therein in any manner discharged from its binding effect, because it turns out to be difficult or burdensome to perform. See cases cited in 12 Am Jur., Contracts, Sec. 362, p. 928, n. 8. Mere inability to perform a contract will not alone relieve the defaulting party. . . . Accepting the testimony offered by plaintiff, it amounts, at most, to a substantial increase in cost of the erection of the club house by reason of necessity of using piling and by reason of the necessity of constructing a road to the club house site. As far as the club house site is concerned, it was a marshy formation. It was therefore obvious to plaintiff at the time of the execution of the contract that there might be considerable difficulty in erecting a club house on that site. Sufficient dirt for the construction of the road was not provided as a result of the excavation of the canal and yacht basin. It would be necessary in order to construct a road to haul additional dirt thereon. Admittedly, there is hardship, serious inconvenience, and a substantial increase in cost involved, but nothing more. I conclude that the erection of the club house on the club house site is not impossible of performance.

An order will be signed, upon notice in accordance with this opinion.

The concept of liquidated damages is mentioned in this case (see also page 260). A provision for liquidated damages is, in effect, a provision between the parties by which they agree in advance upon the damages to be awarded in the event of a breach.

Liquidated damages, like conditions, are looked upon with jaundiced eye by the courts, and for the same reasons. They are often extracted under coercion and often lead to hardship. The rule usually applied is that if the damages seem to bear a reasonable relationship to damages likely to arise upon breach, they will be enforced. If not, the entire provision is ignored.

The plaintiff relies upon mere difficulty as a basis for claiming impossibility. Although in some cases a discharge may be granted on the basis of impossibility when conditions have changed, even this is not uniformly true.

QUESTION

1. Considering that parties enter contracts because they wish either performance or a remedy in the event of nonperformance, why should not a party have the right to bring suit upon breach by the other even if performance is patently impossible?

Damages upon Breach

In the event of a breach of contract, the damages, strictly speaking, are not to put the plaintiff in as good a position as he was in before the contract was made but rather to put him in as good a position as he would be had the contract been performed. In other words, he is entitled to the profit the contract would have earned him, but the cost of his own performance must be considered also; therefore he is entitled only to the difference between what he would have received and what he would have expended.

It might be added that the plaintiff is not entitled to his attorney's fees or other expenses of collection, unless the original contract specified that these might be added to the judgment. (Many promissory notes include such a provision.) Consequently, in the usual case the plaintiff probably cannot recover the entire amount of his judgment free and clear. On the other hand, he often can clear *something*.

Proximate Cause in Breach of Contract

Although in a tort suit, the defendant is usually liable for all injuries proximately caused by his breach, in contracts the liability of the defendant is more narrowly circumscribed. Compensation is given for only those injuries that the defendant had reason to foresee as a probable result of his breach when the contract was made. Thus, losses stemming from some special cause known to the plaintiff but not to the defendant would not be chargeable to the latter. The only losses that could be charged to the defendant would be those that the defendant as a reasonable man should have realized would accrue at the time the contract was made. This rule gives the defendant the option of refusing to contract if he feels the damages might be too extravagant. He may, if he wishes, demand greater consideration in order to assume a dangerous contract. However, if he is aware of the risk, or should be, when the contract is made, there is no reason why he should not be held. This point is illustrated by the case of *Hadley* v. *Baxendale,* which is dear to the hearts of all law students.

HADLEY v. *BAXENDALE* (England, 1854), Court of Exchequer, 9 Exch. 341, 156 Eng. Rep. 145

> Where two parties have made a contract which one of them has broken, the damages which the other party ought to receive in respect of such breach of contract should be such as may fairly and reasonably be considered either arising naturally, i.e., according to the usual course of things, from such breach of contract itself, or such as may reasonably be supposed to have been in the contemplation of both parties, at the time they made the contract, as the probable result of the breach of it.

[EDITOR'S NOTE: Declaration in two counts by a shipper against a carrier for delay in negligence in the shipment of a crank shaft.]

At the trial before CROMPTON, J., at the last Gloucester Assizes, it appeared that the plaintiffs carried on an extensive business as millers at Gloucester;

and, that, on the 11th day of May, their mill was stopped by a breakage of the crank shaft by which the mill was worked. The steam engine was manufactured by Messrs. Joyce & Co., the engineers, at Greenwich. The fracture was discovered on the 12th, and on the 13th the plaintiffs sent one of their servants to the office of the defendants, who are the well-known carriers trading under the name of Pickford & Co., for the purpose of having the shaft carried to Greenwich. The plaintiffs' servant told the clerk that the mill was stopped, and that the shaft must be sent immediately; and in answer to the inquiry when the shaft would be taken, the answer was, that if it was sent up by twelve o'clock any day, it would be delivered at Greenwich on the following day. On the following day the shaft was taken by the defendants, before noon, for the purpose of being conveyed to Greenwich, and the sum of £21.4s. was paid for its carriage for the whole distance; at the same time the defendants' clerk was told that a special entry, if required, should be made to hasten its delivery. The delivery of the shaft at Greenwich was delayed by some neglect; and the consequence was that the plaintiffs did not receive the new shaft for several days after they would otherwise have done, and the working of their mill was thereby delayed, and they thereby lost the profits they would otherwise have received.

On the part of the defendants, it was objected that these damages were too remote, and that the defendants were not liable with respect to them. The learned Judge left the case generally to the jury, who found a verdict with £251. damages beyond the £251. amount paid into Court.

The judgment of the Court was now delivered by Alderson, B. We think that there ought to be a new trial in this case; but in so doing, we deem it to be expedient and necessary to state explicitly the rule which the Judge, at the next trial, ought, in our opinion, to direct the jury to be governed by when they estimate the damages.

Now we think the proper rule in such a case as the present is this:—Where two parties have made a contract which one of them has broken, the damages which the other party ought to receive in respect of such breach of contract should be such as may fairly and reasonably be considered either arising naturally, i.e., such as may reasonably be supposed to have been in the contemplation of both parties, at the time they made the contract, as the probable result of the breach of it. Now, if the special circumstances under which the contract was actually made were communicated by the plaintiffs to the defendants, and thus known to both parties, the damages resulting from the breach of such a contract, which they would reasonably contemplate, would be the amount of injury which would ordinarily follow from a breach of contract under these special circumstances so known and communicated. But, on the other hand, if these special circumstances were wholly unknown to the party breaking the contract, he at the most could only be supposed to have had in his contemplation the amount of injury which would arise generally, and in the great multitude of cases not affected by any special circumstances, from such a breach of contract. For, had the special circumstances been known, the parties might have specially provided for the breach of contract by special terms as to the damages in that case; and of this advantage it would be very unjust to deprive them. Now the above principles are those by which we think the jury ought to be guided in estimating the damages arising out of any breach of contract. It is said, that other cases such as breaches of contract in the non-payment of money, or in the not making a good title to land, are to be treated as exceptions from this, and as governed by a conventional rule. But as, in such cases, both parties must be supposed to be cognisant of that well-known rule, these cases may, we think, be more properly classed under the rule above enunciated as to cases under known special circumstances, because there both parties may reasonably be presumed to contemplate the estimation of the amount of damages according to the conventional rule. Now, in the present case, if we are to apply the principles above laid down, we find that the only circumstances here communicated by the plaintiffs to the defendants at the time the contract was made, were, that the article to be carried was the broken shaft of a mill, and that the plaintiffs were the millers of that mill. But how do these circumstances shew reasonably that the profits of the mill must be stopped by an unreasonable delay in the delivery of the broken shaft by the carrier to the third person? Suppose the plaintiffs had another shaft in their possession put up or putting up at the time, and that they only wished to send back the broken shaft to the engineer who made it; it is clear that this would be quite consistent with the above circumstances, and yet the unreasonable delay in the delivery would have no effect upon the intermediate profits of the mill. Or again, suppose that, at the time of the delivery to the carrier, the machinery of the mill had been in other respects defective, then, also, the same results would follow. Here it is true that the shaft was actually sent back to serve as a model for a new one, and that the want of a new one was the only cause of the stoppage of the mill, and that the loss of profits really arose from not sending down the new shaft in proper time, and that this arose from the delay in delivering the broken one to serve as a model. But it is obvious that, in the great multitude of cases of millers sending off broken shafts to third persons by a carrier under ordinary circumstances, such consequences would not, in all probability, have occurred; and these special circumstances were here never communicated by the plaintiffs to the defendants. It follows, therefore, that the loss of profits here cannot reasonably be considered such a consequence of the breach of contract as could have been fairly and reasonably contemplated by both parties when they made this contract. For such loss would neither have flowed naturally from the breach of this contract in the great multitude of such cases occurring under ordinary circumstances, nor were the special circumstances, which, perhaps, would have made it a reasonable and natural consequency of such breach of contract, communicated to or known by the defendants. The Judge ought, therefore, to have told the jury, that, upon the facts then before them, they ought not to take the loss of profits into consideration at all in estimating the damages. There must therefore be a new trial in this case.

✧

Some Practical Aspects of the Decision to Bring Suit

Presumably, everyone bringing suit in breach of contract expects to advance his interest in some way. The three most important considerations involved in bringing a suit are probably as follows: (1) emotional factors, (2) reasons of long-term strategy, and (3) (presumably the most frequent) purely financial considerations. We will discuss each of these in turn.

EMOTIONAL FACTORS

Suits are sometimes brought for spite, malice, or revenge. Although one cannot say when another person is getting his money's worth, one may rest assured that bringing a lawsuit is an expensive means of gaining personal satisfaction. As the economists would put it, the marginal utility of money spent on other forms of entertainment, say a vacation or a new hi-fi set, is apt to be higher. This is particularly true when the additional investment of endless conferences with attorneys, the anxieties of awaiting trial, and the trial itself are considered, completely aside from the financial investment.

Many attorneys absolutely refuse to take a case based purely on "principle," and probably no one should be encouraged to bring suit for this reason alone, even though a favorable verdict seems assured. In general, the greater wisdom will be to ignore some claims for very small sums of money, or for very minor irritations, even though legal action might be justified.

However, emotional considerations probably lead far more frequently to a party refraining from suit when from a strict financial point of view suit is called for. Whether a given amount of bother is worth a certain sum of money is a question that no one but the individual concerned can answer, and the relative amounts of bother as against money are always hard to estimate. Even so, one should not dismiss substantial legal rights merely because of the possible obstacles in enforcing them, without at least securing a professional opinion as to the actual extent of difficulties likely to be involved.

STRATEGIC FACTORS

In the class of strategic factors we would include suits against customers, brought not for the immediate gain, but to convince other customers that a concern means business and does not take breach of faith lightly. The government is probably following this sort of policy in the implementation of its notoriously rigorous enforcement against frauds directed against the United States. There is also the possibility that the mere act of filing suit will so intimidate a party that he is willing to perform his contract, recognizing that defending and ultimately losing a suit may be more burdensome than performing his contract.

However, there may be either positive or negative considerations, depending upon the situation. Banks and some other lending agencies are naturally concerned about their public image. They dislike being thought of as villains who enthusiastically foreclose upon widows and orphans and turn them out into the street. Consequently, banks often go to great lengths to work out a solution other than foreclosure of a home, to say nothing of a church.

Actually, both of the strategic considerations we have mentioned so far are concerned with the public image. The question is, what type of image best fits the needs of the enterprise faced with the decision. Some enterprises find a "hard but fair" image desirable, some a "soft" image.

In addition, the impact upon the other party of the decision to sue, or not to sue, must be considered. The question is not so much whether he will be angry—he probably will be—but rather how damaging his anger will be to the plaintiff. If the party in breach of contract is the plaintiff's principal customer, resort to suit is rather extreme medicine. Irritating though it may be, an unconditional surrender of legal rights might be preferable to losing an essential business relationship. If a party is faced with the long-term prospect of economic blackmail, perhaps the only alternatives may be diversification, going out of business, or merger with another concern, whichever is the least painful alternative.

If, however, the party who is in breach of contract is substantially dependent upon the other party to the contract, with patience, the former's enlightened self-interest should lead him to make an out-of-court settlement reasonably favorable to the interests of the wronged party. Pressure exerted too crudely may result in the loss of business relations with the party.

In summary, although there may be strategic reasons for bringing a suit when immediate profit will not result, there are also many instances when the better strategy would be to refrain from suit even though immediate profits may result.

FINANCIAL CONSIDERATIONS

In assessing the advantages or disadvantages of a suit from a purely financial point of view, an estimate must be made of the probable costs of suit. The biggest cost will usually be attorney fees, though travel expenses may be high, or even prohibitive, if the suit is to be tried far from the party's home. Costs of gathering evidence, especially expert witnesses, can also be substantial, and the possibility of loss of wages because of the time involved in trial should also be considered.

Perhaps we ought to interject here a word on behalf of attorneys. Many, and perhaps most, litigants feel there is a basic injustice in the fact that, when a party is damaged by another party to the tune of $2,000, it is impossible to make a net recovery of $2,000 because of the expenses, especially attorney fees. Whether this is just or not we would not venture to say; the fact is that attorneys like to be paid for their work, as does everyone else. Perhaps the situation is about as unjust as a person being afflicted with a disease, which then requires the services of a physician to cure. Attorneys and physicians are paid for essentially the same thing, the exercise of their professional skill and judgment, and the fee varies somewhat according to the size of the particular undertaking, the degree of skill required in the situation, and most important, the time involved.

Because, in fact, the costs can be high, the first question to consider is whether the probable recovery will exceed the probable cost. Although none of us can predict the future with certainty, a crude estimate is better than none at all. Furthermore, there are certain guidelines. If a claim is evidenced by a formal written contract on a fairly simple transaction, as a claim for goods sold or services rendered, and the other party has no reasonable defense, there is practically no limit to how small a claim may be to merit litigating.

A collection agency or young attorney may well be interested in pursuing the claim. The charge is often 50 percent of the value of the claim, but the other 50 percent is money that would otherwise not have been realized. Fees are usually a smaller percentage of larger claims.

If the claim is controversial, if the evidence is in sharp conflict, or if the law is hazy, and the other party seems determined to defend, the value of the claim would have to be higher to merit pursuing, but perhaps a compromise can be reached. If the claim is clear-cut but nonetheless the opposing party seems determined to defend, he may be bluffing or he may have an irrational desire to make things difficult for the plaintiff. His defending will cost both parties more attorney fees, but the problems remain the same. Are the probabilities of realizing a net sum, after paying all expenses, substantial? If so, is the probable net gain enough to make it worth while? If so, the decision to sue is proper.

Even if a case appears to be almost certain to be decided in the plaintiff's favor, and for a substantial amount, there is the question of whether the defendant's financial worth will permit recovery. One of the problems in our legal system is the fact that a judgment cannot be recovered from a defendant if he has no financial resources. The importance of this fact as a limitation upon the effectiveness of a legal remedy can hardly be overestimated. Although the sheriff will perform the duty of actually seizing property of the defendant and supervising a sale so that the proceeds may be applied to the judgment, the burden is upon the plaintiff or his attorney to locate assets for the sheriff to seize as well as to prepare the papers authorizing seizure. If the assets of the defendant are scant, what little he does have may not be worth the expense of tracing down and proceeding against. If the defendant owns real estate, however, the plaintiff is in a good position. A lien against the real estate is virtually automatic: the judgment need only be docketed (filed for record), and all real estate owned by the defendant within the jurisdiction of the court is automatically encumbered with a lien.

There is no way to collect a judgment awarded against a party having no money, property, or income. There is the possibility of holding the judgment until the party accumulates money or property or gets a job, but there are obvious defects with this course. One is that the possibility of his obtaining property is not necessarily large enough to merit the expense of suit; another is that the party may well vanish, with no forwarding address. Tracing vanished parties can usually be accomplished, but it is expensive; processing the judgment awarded in the original state through the courts of the state where the defendant is now located is an additional burden.

For these reasons, accepting an unfavorable compromise in which, nevertheless, the plaintiff gains something may be the best course when the defendant has very meager assets.

As a matter of fact, the overwhelming majority of legal disputes are settled out of court. Some disputes are disposed of through arbitration proceedings, but the vast majority are worked out through bargaining between the respective attorneys.

CHAPTER TWENTY-FIVE

Contracts Void
for Reasons
of Public Policy

The general rule is that contracts are void which require (1) a violation of the criminal law, (2) a violation of tort law, or (3) a violation of certain other established policies of the common law.

Contracts Opposed to Public Policy

IN OUR STUDY of contracts, we have attempted to show from time to time some of the reasons for the present state of the law. For example, due to the feeling that not all promises should be enforced, but only certain ones, the concept of consideration was devised. Because of the difficulties in deciding cases according to a secret assent, we rely upon the manifestations of assent in determining whether or not there is an agreement.

In this section we will deal with reasons that are more immediate. Here we find contracts rendered void not because of some long-range, over-all policy but simply because our society believes the subject matter of the particular contract under scrutiny is, in a moral sense, bad. It may be bad for several reasons. The general rule is that contracts are void which require (1) a violation of the criminal law, (2) a violation of tort law, or (3) a violation of certain other established policies of the common law. In fact, some (and very likely all) courts will declare a contract void if it runs strongly contrary to our generally accepted ideas of morality, even if there is no previously stated policy against such contracts.

Of course, the fact that certain acts are recognized as torts or crimes in

412

itself demonstrates that these acts are contrary to public policy, and therefore the entire section could be summarized as a discussion of contracts unenforceable for various reasons of public policy. So long as we do not lose sight of this fact, however, analysis is facilitated by subdividing the discussion into the three mentioned groups: contracts to commit a crime, contracts to commit a tort, and contracts otherwise contrary to public policy.

Contracts to Commit a Crime or a Tort

Not much imagination is required to see that the purposes of law would be defeated by enforcing contracts requiring the commission of a crime. If A hires B to murder someone and pays him $1,000 in advance, no court will say B should either go ahead and commit murder or return the $1,000. Obviously, a court could not decide that B was wrong in not committing the murder and should therefore return the $1,000. Admittedly B is dishonest in keeping the $1,000, but under the circumstances there is clearly nothing a court could do to support the agreement. Although the example is extreme, it illustrates the reason for the general rule, which in many cases is not so clear, that in the event a contract involves doing something that is illegal, the courts will not only refuse to enforce it but will not even order the return of money or property that one party might have obtained as a result of his illegal dealing. The court leaves both parties in whatever mess it finds them.

For the same reasons that contracts requiring commission of a crime are in most cases unenforceable, contracts requiring commission of a tort are also unenforceable. Because a tort is by definition a wrong, the court could not place itself in the position of assessing damages against the party who refused to commit the wrong.

Though the previous analysis is clear when applied to the common-law crimes, such as murder, robbery, and burglary, the situation becomes much more complicated when acts contrary to some types of legislation become involved. We find thousands of prohibited activities listed in our statute books. Often they bear no relation to right or wrong in the most commonly accepted sense, nor even in some cases to the protection of the public. Much legislation involves matters of minor importance and is designed to ease the chores of public administrators or to secure revenue. Nonetheless, most of this law is, in form, criminal law, often dispensing with the element of intent. These "crimes" are termed *malum prohibita,* meaning, the act is wrong not because of any moral transgression but merely because a legislature or some other authorized body has said it is wrong. These are apt to

be misdemeanors, punishable by fine or at most a relatively short confine-
ment in the city or county jail. Crimes involving an act that is considered
morally wrong are called *malum in se:* the examples given above, murder,
robbery and burglary, are malum in se. These are felonies, punishable by
long terms in the state penitentiary, or even death.

Some courts will enforce contracts involving certain types of provisions
which, though illegal, are merely malum prohibita. Licensing requirements,
if merely revenue-producing and not designed to protect the public, may be
treated in this way. A license is usually designed to raise revenue if anyone
willing to pay the fee will be given a license without further qualification.

There are other exceptions to the general rule that contracts contrary to
law will not be enforced. Several exceptions are grounded on the common-
sense observation that in certain instances the public welfare is not advanced by placing both parties beyond the pale of the courts.

Sometimes the obvious purpose of a statute will not be promoted by refusing enforcement of contracts that are in violation of the statute. If a corporation in interstate commerce hires employees to work for less than the
minimum wage law, this should not bar the employee from recovery. As a
matter of fact an employee may recover (in this case the remedy is statutory) triple damages. The reason is that the employee is the party being
protected by the statute. The desired policy is facilitated by encouraging
suit, not by denying the employee the right to sue. We have included in the
cases a number of similar situations.

Another exception, related to the one just discussed and applied even to
crimes malum in se, is the defense "not in pari delicto." *Pari delicto* means
"equal guilt." The most clear-cut instance of this defense occurs when a
party performs an act that normally would not be a crime at all but that,
because of facts unknown to him, is a crime in the particular setting. For
example, a mover under contract with another party transports household
furniture to another state. Unknown to the mover the furniture had been
stolen; therefore a statute prohibiting interstate transportation of stolen
goods had been violated. Due to the mover's lack of knowledge of the
crime, recovery could be obtained by him for his service despite the obvious illegal nature of the contract. Because the mover had no guilty knowledge, he was not in "pari delicto." Usually only misapprehensions of fact,
not mistakes as to the state of the law, will excuse a party. (Ignorance of
the law is no excuse, as the saying goes.)

The defense "not in pari delicto" has on some occasions been applied
where both parties had some knowledge of illegality. On analysis, many
such cases are really instances in which the court is carrying out the policy
of a statute in protecting certain parties. One illustration is this: the victim
of a confidence game, in which a professional criminal involves a respectable citizen in an illegal scheme to get rich quick, borrows money from the

citizen to help carry out the scheme and then escapes with the money. The victims are the ones the law is trying to protect, and the professional con men cannot be readily apprehended unless the victims are willing to come forward. Considering the embarrassment in being found susceptible to the lure of ill-gotten gain, and being gullible besides, there is little to induce victims to come forward unless they have at least some hope of recovering their money.

A few cases have held that if one party withdraws from an agreement before any illegal acts have been performed, he may still sue to recover consideration conveyed to the other party. This qualification is somewhat of a reversal of the basic rule. Surely no court would let our man who made a contract to have another killed recover because he changed his mind before the deed was performed.

One might conclude that a wide range of discretion is employed by courts in deciding cases involving illegal contracts. This seems justified. There seems to be no way of laying out a black-and-white rule defining when the public policy will be advanced by enforcing an illegal contract. However, we have seen that cases of this kind do arise. If in particular cases the public interest is served by permitting a party to recover, or to enforce a contract involving illegality, no one can reasonably complain.

FONG ET AL. v. MILLER (California, 1951) 223 P 2d 606

As a general rule, to which there are exceptions, a party to an illegal contract can neither recover damages for breach nor by rescinding recover the performance that he has rendered or its value . . .

VAN DYKE, J.

On January 1, 1946, Horace Fong and Fulton Fong, predecessor in interest of Lily Fong, entered into a contract with Ruby Miller. The contract recited that Miller was the owner of a cafe known as the Gate Inn, situated at Jackson, California, consisting of a bar for the sale of liquor, and a restaurant; that Miller desired to obtain the services of the Fongs to manage and operate the restaurant and that the Fongs were willing to undertake such services upon the following terms: That any additional equipment or construction added to the restaurant would be paid for by the Fongs, which additions would remain their property, except where the removal of them would damage the building in which they were located; that all licenses for the conduct of Miller's business should be taken out and maintained in her name, but that the Fongs would pay to her as rental for the restaurant premises a sum equal to one-half of the total of all license fees required for the operation of all businesses conducted upon the premises; that the Fongs would pay all expenses due to operation of the restaurant; that they should receive as compensation for their services all pro-

ceeds from the restaurant, and in addition thereto one-fourth "of the net revenue derived from the operation of the bar and amusement machines." The
Fongs improved the restaurant by spending over $4,000 in additional equipment
and over $1,000 in constructing living quarters to be used by their help. They
then began the operation of the restaurant as agreed upon. Differences arose
between the parties and about two months after the Fongs moved in Miller
locked them out. Treating this as an eviction from leased premises, the Fongs
brought this action to recover the amounts so expended in connection with the
restaurant and $15,000 additional, demanded as compensation for loss of pro-
spective profits. At the trial of the action the Fongs waived their claim for
damages for prospective profits. The parties stipulated that the "amusement
machines" referred to in the contract which were being operated by Miller were
in fact slot machines, punchboards, a roulette table and a blackjack table and
that the term used in the contract was so understood. The trial court, deeming
the contract to be tainted with illegality, denied relief to plaintiffs upon that
ground. From the judgment entered that they take nothing plaintiffs present this
appeal.

(1, 2) We think the trial court was correct in its analysis of the contract and
in its conclusions that no relief could be granted appellants, notwithstanding the
respondent alleged wrongful acts. As a general rule, to which there are exceptions, a party to an illegal contract can neither recover damages for breach nor
by rescinding recover the performance that he has rendered or its value. . . .
Under certain conditions, notwithstanding that one is a party to an illegal
bargain, relief may be accorded if such party be not in pari delicto, but we are
unable to conceive how appellants here could claim that they occupied that
innocent position. Under the contract they were to operate the restaurant and to
receive as their compensation therefor not only the profits from the restaurant,
but in addition thereto a share of the profits from the bar and from the gambling
devices. What they did in operating the restaurant may have been honest enough,
but when they agreed that they were to be given for their services 25% of the
profits derived from gambling they tainted their contract with illegality. This
made it to their interest that the gambling should flourish in order that their
profits therefrom might be enhanced. To say that such a consideration could be
valid and that a contract requiring its payments would not be unlawful would
be to say that a laborer might, because his labor was honest, lawfully agree that
he should be paid from the profits of a crime which the parties contemplated his
employer would engage in. The trial court correctly held that the appellants
were in pari delicto and that the contract was unlawful and that the court
should leave the parties where it found them.

Appellants argue that this contract possessed a dual nature and that one part
of it, which they call a lease, could be completely separated from the unlawful
agreement to receive a share in the profits of crime. But we think that the
contract cannot receive such construction. Notwithstanding the agreement was
to last for five years, with option for renewal for a second five years, and
assuming that the appellants might lawfully receive the proceeds from the
operation of the restaurant, it is yet quite clear from the terms of the contract
itself that such profits were not the sole consideration moving to the appellants
under the agreement. In addition to the profits from the restaurant, they were to

receive a share in the profits of contemplated illegal action. That provision rendered the contract void. The contract made it clear that the consideration moving to respondent was the operation by appellants of the restaurant in connection with her liquor-selling and gambling business. "If any part . . . of several considerations for a single object, is unlawful, the entire contract is void." Civ. Code §1608.

(3) Appellants urge that by waiving their claim for future profits and confining their demands to the cost of their added equipment and reconstruction they freed their contract of the taint of illegality. But these things did not change the nature of the contract nor relieve the appellants of the rule invoked against them by the trial court. Appellants bitterly complain that the court's action leaves the respondent unjustly enriched. The complaint is a familiar one and is generally made by those who, deeming themselves wronged by their companions in illegal venture, find themselves denied any right to enforce their unlawful agreements. Their pleas have always been unavailing. "This rule is not generally applied to secure justice between parties who have made an illegal contract, but from regard for a higher interest—that of the public, whose welfare demands that certain transactions be discouraged." . . .

The judgment appealed from is affirmed. The purported appeal from the order denying motion for new trial is dismissed.

The Fongs were no more guilty than Ruby Miller. Both parties had agreed to the operation of gambling devices in the cafe. However, the Fongs had no standing in court, despite the fact that perhaps most of their profits were to come from a legal enterprise—that is, operating the cafe.

QUESTION

1. Evidently, one party to an illegal contract is often in a position to make a sizable profit at the expense of the other party. What is the purpose in permitting this?

CHEMICAL BANK & TRUST COMPANY v. PRUDENCE-BONDS (New Corporation) et al. (CCA New York, 1954) 213 F 2d 443

In order to determine whether a contract made contrary to a penal statute is illegal and void, the statute must be considered as a whole to ascertain whether it was the intention of the Legislature that the statute have such effect. . . .

Appellant relies upon the specific wording of Section 9592–21 (h), which it contends makes illegal any contract of insurance issued by an insurance company which has not complied with the filing requirements of Section 9591–21(a), which appellee admits it had not done.

(2) It is agreed between the parties that the business of insurance is affected with a public interest and subject to regulation by the State. But we do not agree with appellant's contention that it necessarily follows that a failure to comply with the provisions of a regulatory statute relating to insurance renders null and void a policy of insurance freely entered into by the parties. In order to determine whether a contract made contrary to a penal statute is illegal and void, the statute must be considered as a whole to ascertain whether it was the intention of the Legislature that the statute have such effect. . . .

There is no express provision in the foregoing sections of the Ohio General Code which states that a failure to comply with any of the provisions contained therein renders an insurance contract void. If such was the intent of the Legislature it could easily have said so in express words. On the contrary, the statute provides a $500.00 fine for a willful violation of the Act and that the license of any insurer who fails to comply with an order of the superintendent may be suspended. The provisions of Section 9592–35 calling for a liberal interpretation of the Act, and the provisions of Section 9592–33 dealing with the procedure by which the license of an insurer may be suspended, indicate regulation of the insurance business rather than prohibition against engaging in such business. In our opinion, a consideration of the several provisions of the Code results in the conclusion that it was the purpose of the Legislature to regulate the insurance business by the imposition of a penalty rather than by declaring illegal and void such contracts of insurance as might be issued while the insurer was not in compliance with the provisions of the statute. This conclusion is in accord with the rulings of the Ohio Supreme Court . . . ; which we consider controlling on the issue. . . .

(3, 4) Nor do we consider the contract as void as against public policy. A contract is not void as against public policy unless it is injurious to the public or contravenes some established interest of society. . . . The insurance contract involved in this case, under which appellant has had the benefit of full performance by the appellee, is clearly not of that nature. . . .

The judgment of the District Court is affirmed.

✧

Here is a case in which blind adherence to the general rule that a party to an illegal contract may not enforce it in court would lead to a preposterous result. Statutes regulating insurance companies are devised to protect the general public. This being so, the desired end obviously cannot be achieved if, in cases where an insurer fails to comply with regulations, the insured rather than the insurer is penalized. Consequently, the commonsense approach of permitting the insured to recover on his policy is used to decide this case.

QUESTION

1. Suppose suit were brought by one of the parties to whom the insurer had sold a policy, asking that his contract of insurance be rescinded. Would the suit succeed under the circumstances found in the above case?

RUBIN v. DOUGLAS (District of Columbia, 1948)
59 A 2d 690

. . . Even though a party be considered technically in pari delicto he may be permitted to recover if the law in question was passed for his protection and it appears that the purposes of the law will be better effectuated by granting relief than by denying it.

HOOD, AJ.

Plaintiff sued to recover money which she had paid defendant under the following circumstances. Plaintiff, who suffered from arthritis, at the suggestion of a third person went to see defendant and informed him of her condition. Defendant who employed the title "professor," agreed to give plaintiff a series of treatments at a cost of $440. According to plaintiff defendant stated these treatments would cure her; according to him he told her he believed they would be of help to her. The treatments, consisting of massaging and rubbing in of an ointment, were given, and plaintiff paid $160 on account. She refused to pay the balance, and brought this action to recover that which had been paid. Defendant filed a counterclaim for the balance of $280. The trial court awarded plaintiff judgment on her claim and denied recovery on the counterclaim.

Plaintiff's claim for recovery is based on the contention that the treatments administered by defendant were in violation of the Healing Arts Practice Act. This Act, with certain exceptions not here material, prohibits the practice of the healing art by anyone not licensed in accordance with the Act. Defendant was not so licensed. The definition given "the healing art" by the Act includes "relieving, correcting, or curing" or "attempting to prevent, relieve, correct, or cure any disease." The Act exempts from its provisions "the practice of massage . . . under the direction of a person licensed to practice the healing art"; but no contention is made here that the treatments given by defendant were under the direction of a person so licensed. We think it plain that the treatments by defendant, who was neither licensed nor acting under direction of a licensed person, were in violation of the Act; whether such treatments were given in an attempt to cure or to help plaintiff's complaint the defendant was criminally charged with violation of the Act and he pleaded guilty.

Considering first the counterclaim of defendant for the balance of his agreed fee, it is clear that the trial court correctly ruled that no recovery could be allowed. "The general rule is that an illegal contract, made in violation of a statutory prohibition designed for police or regulatory purposes, is void and confers no right upon the wrongdoer." . . .

With respect to plaintiff's claim for recovery of the sum paid by her, the defendant's contention is that if the contract was in violation of the statute, then no recovery can be had for money paid for illegal services which have been rendered. The rule contended for has been applied in many cases but is not of universal application. "It has long been the law that, where an action is founded upon an unlawful contract, the court will not interfere to relieve either of the parties thereto in an action against the other from the results thereof."

However, if the parties are not in pari delicto, and one of them has not been guilty of serious moral turpitude, he may repudiate the contract and recover what he has paid under it. . . . And even though a party be considered technically in pari delicto he may be permitted to recover if the law in question was passed for his protection and it appears that the purposes of the law will be better effectuated by granting relief than by denying it. . . .

In the present case we do not consider plaintiff in pari delicto with defendant, but even if she were it is apparent that the law was passed for the protection of the public, including plaintiff, and that the purposes of the Act will not be effectuated by permitting defendant to retain that which he ought not to have received. The public interests, in our opinion, are best served by requiring defendant to pay back the fruits of his illegal agreement.

Affirmed.

✧

Although in this case the court speaks of pari delicto, the rationale is actually the same as in the previous case. Acts regulating unlicensed physicians are directed toward protecting the public, not punishing the gullible. This being the case, a member of the public who has been victimized is not barred from suit.

Examples of Contracts Illegal As Against Public Policy

Contracts may be adjudged illegal merely because part of the consideration on one side or the other constitutes a gross violation of generally accepted ideas of morality or because some aspect seems to be clearly opposed to the long-range interests of society.

For example, there is a well-defined public policy within our law favoring marriage. Therefore, contracts in which a party agrees to postpone marriage for an unreasonable period of time are traditionally illegal and void. (For the same reason, provisions in wills that bestow favors conditioned upon a party refraining from marriage are void. Usually such invalid provisions of a will are ignored, and the party is given the benefit of the will free from strings.) The historical reasons for this policy are said to be the feeling that a high birth rate was desirable as a means of increasing the local lord's armed strength, as well as that of the nation. In earlier times, birth rates and death rates were almost balanced, and perhaps infringements upon marriage, if widely imposed, might conceivably have had an adverse effect upon society. In these days of exploding populations, the peril does not seem imminent. Another reason for opposing restraints upon marriage is the fear that adults contractually bound to remain in the single state might be tempted into the paths of immorality. Perhaps this is a reasonable concern.

There is a policy making void contracts in which one party agrees to obtain a divorce in exchange for cash or other consideration. Divorce, under the Christian ethic, has always been considered an evil.

These examples, however, are merely illustrative of a facet or two of the relations between public policy and illegality of contract. Many other well-recognized doctrines that may render a contract void may be found incorporated within the common law. Probably it may be stated that almost any act that is widely condemned by society is apt, if prescribed by contract, to result in the contract being illegal.

Contracts in Restraint of Trade

Possibly the most common type of case in which public policy is a ground for setting aside a contract is found in the case of the contract in restraint of trade. Contracts in which one party agrees not to enter into competition with another are against public policy and void. The same is true if two parties, already in the same business, agree to fix prices so as not to compete or if they agree to bind together to drive a third party out of business so they will then have local control of a phase of business or industry. An agreement by an artisan not to practice his trade is also usually unenforceable. These two types of agreements have been void at common law for centuries except under special circumstances, described below.

The public policy opposed to all of these agreements is centered around the recognition of the importance of business activity to the community at large. Our economic welfare depends upon the division of labor, the creation and exchange of goods and services—that is, upon business. This was true of England earlier than of most Western nations, because England emerged from feudalism to become a mercantile power comparatively early. The economy cannot operate at its best, so the common law holds, with restrictions upon entry into business or upon workmen from entering into their trade. Nor is the community usually well served when competition is artificially restricted.

Agreements in restraint of trade are permitted when the agreement is not intended to restrain trade but serves some other reasonable purpose in carrying out a contract. The usual illustration involves the selling of business goodwill. A small hot dog stand may have very minor physical assets. Because of the patronage built up with a steady group of customers, the stand may have quite a high income. In order for the owner to sell the stand at a price reflecting its *earning capacity,* which in turn depends upon the habit of the customers in going to that stand, the seller would have to agree not to reopen at another nearby location. If he did open nearby, his former customers would probably follow him, and the main asset of the buyer would be lost. Therefore, an agreement by the seller of a going concern not to enter into competition against the buyer is permissible if the restrictions do no more than reasonably protect the buyer. Reasonableness as to the limitations of time before the seller may reopen, and the geographic bounds within which the seller is forbidden to open, will vary infinitely, depending upon the nature of the business. Some businesses compete internationally, others not even locally. Every case presents a question of judgment. This exception to the general rule regarding competition carries out the policy of promoting commerce. Business is encouraged, not restricted, by this exception.

Skilled artisans who have acquired trade secrets from an employer may be hired under the condition that if they leave that employer they may not secure similar work elsewhere for a period of time. The purpose in this is to encourage the discovery of new processes by giving the discoverer reasonable protection against disclosure of his trade secrets. Agreements of this nature are construed very narrowly, however, and are not extended in duration beyond what is absolutely necessary to the reasonable protection of trade secrets.

The common-law policy against restraint of trade is interesting primarily because this was the seed, in a historical sense, of our present antimonopoly legislation. Where the common law merely refused to enforce contracts in restraint of trade, however, federal legislation provides both criminal and civil penalties for forming monopolies and otherwise inhibiting competition. In addition to outright agreements to fix prices, other methods that tend to restrain trade are now contrary to law under certain circumstances, depending largely upon their effect upon commerce.

LOBEK v. *GROSS* (New Jersey, 1949) 65 A 2d 745

> . . . *The cause of action was based upon an agreement in restraint of marriage and consequently void as contrary to the public policy of this state.*

It is alleged in the amended bill that the agreement sought to be performed was made on or about May 15, 1939 and provided that the appellant would be nurse and companion of the said Koretsky as long as he lived and that she would not marry as long as he lived and that in consideration of the above promise by the appellant it was agreed by Koretsky that he would devise one-half of his entire estate to the appellant. The bill then recites performance by appellant from that date until the death of Koretsky on January 7, 1946. Subsequent to his death Koretsky's will was admitted to probate by the former Prerogative Court and the present defendants qualified as executors and trustees thereunder. No mention of appellant is made in the will.

Subsequent to the institution of the suit the defendants caused interrogatories to be served upon the appellant which were admitted into evidence together with the answers thereto. Interrogatory No. 5 and the answer thereto by appellant are as follows:

"5. What specifically was the service which the complainant undertook to render to Israel Koretsky as a companion pursuant to the terms of the agreement alleged in the amended bill of complaint?"

Answer: "5. As a companion, complainant was to travel with Israel Koretsky, attend social functions with him, attend plays, theatres, movies, cocktail parties; to be his hostess, and to entertain for him at social functions for his friends; to play gin rummy and other card games with him, and further agreed not to marry so long as the said Israel Koretsky remained living."

The Vice Chancellor advised a dismissal of the bill upon the ground that the cause of action was based upon an agreement in restraint of marriage and consequently void as contrary to the public policy of this state. With this reasoning we concur. The case is substantially identical to *Lowe* v. *Doremus* . . . in which case the Court of Errors and Appeals held a similar agreement void. The Lowe case is controlling and dispositive.

The appellant has urged that since the contract was made in the state of Illinois and that since such a contract is valid in that state . . . it is enforceable in this state under the principles of comity. This argument overlooks the rule that a contract valid where made will not be enforced in this state if it contravenes the public policy thereof. . . .

. . . By her own admission in the answer to interrogatories the appellant has placed the agreement in the realm of illegal contracts. Since she is therefore not entitled to recover in any event it is pointless to consider the remaining questions.

The decree of the former Court of Chancery is affirmed.

For affirmance: Chief Justice VANDERBILT and Justices CASE, HEHER, WACHENFELD, BURLING and ACKERSON—6.

For reversal: None.

✧

Beyond much doubt, the original reasons for declaring illegal agreements not to marry have ceased to exist. The population explosion might even suggest an opposite approach. Therefore, many states have begun to depart from older precedents and to hold agreements not to marry as being valid.

The intriguing question here is whether the court would have held this agreement valid had it *not* contained the provision against marriage. Our guess is that it would have declared the contract void even without the provision against marriage, although that provision gave the court a well-established basis for making its decision.

The contract might be decribed as one in which the appellant agreed to be a sort of private geisha girl in exchange for one half of Koretsky's estate.

It is likely that most states would find this contract contrary to public policy aside from the ground on which this decision was based. Here there was no need for the court to embark upon this less tangible basis for decision when precedents existed to justify nonenforcement of the contract because of the provision against marriage.

JOHNSON v. SENEGAL (Massachusetts, 1952)
109 NE 2d 467

> *Conduct which is not criminal may nevertheless be so unlawful that it will vitiate a contract which calls for it. . . . The test of invalidity "is whether the underlying tendency of the contract under the conditions described was manifestly injurious to the public interest and welfare."*

The question to be determined is whether a contract of partnership which contemplates the furnishing of entertainment to public officers as a means of carrying on the business is legal and enforceable.

The testimony of the plaintiff on the question of the legality of the purposes of the partnership was in substance that the partners, in their efforts to sell parking meters, entertained with food and liquor the municipal officers having power to purchase them for the municipality, and that such entertainment was "one of the very purposes of the partnership." But the plaintiff testified that no gift was made to any official apart from such entertainment. Because such entertainment was one of the very purposes of the partnership, the case is not governed by *Barry* v. *Capen,* relied on by the plaintiff, where HOLMES, J., said, "The plaintiff may have rendered illegal services, and yet the defendant's promise may have been in consideration of the plaintiff's promising to perform or performing legal ones only. If the contract was legal, it would not be made illegal by misconduct on the part of the plaintiff in carrying it out." . . .

. . . the crime of bribery is defined as the giving to a public officer of "any gift or gratuity whatever," with intent to influence him in his official capacity. It has been held elsewhere that furnishing food and drink to a public officer by way of entertainment, to be consumed by that officer presently, while wholly bad in morals, is not bribery under a statute like ours. If we assume in this case that the partnership was not engaged in bribery, it does not follow that its purposes were lawful. Conduct which is not criminal may nevertheless be so unlawful that it will vitiate a contract which calls for it. In *Fuller* v. *Dame,* in which the opinion was written by Chief Justice SHAW, notes given by the owner of land to a stockholder in a railroad corporation to be paid when the railroad should locate its warehouse near the land, were held invalid. The Chief Justice said that the law "avoids contracts and promises made with a view to place one under wrong influences, those which offer him temptation to do that which may injuriously affect the rights and interests of third persons." In accord is *Guern-*

sey v. *Cook.* In *Frost* v. *Inhabitants of Belmont,* although the decision was rested in part upon the want of authority of the town to pay for expenses incurred in attempting to procure from the Legislature an act of incorporation, this court said, "The practice of procuring members of the legislature to act under the influence of what they have eaten and drunk at houses of entertainment tends to render those of them who yield to such influences wholly unfit to act in such cases. They are disqualified from acting fairly towards interested parties, or towards the public. The tendency and object of these influences are to obtain by corruption what it is supposed cannot be obtained fairly."

In *Adams* v. *East Boston Company,* it was said that the test of invalidity "is whether the underlying tendency of the contract under the conditions described was manifestly injurious to the public interest and welfare. . . . It is sufficient if the contract when applied to the facts inevitably tends to results which impair not merely the character of the Legislature, but the public confidence in its integrity." In *Noble* v. *Mead-Morrison Manufacturing Company,* RUGG, C.J., said, "A contract respecting public service and public welfare is illegal, which by its express terms, by its inherent tendency, or by the means necessarily or by fair implication to be employed in its execution, requires the performance of acts corrupt in themselves or inclining toward the pollution of public or private honesty and integrity of purpose." The Restatement . . . declares that "A bargain to influence or to attempt to influence a legislative body or members thereof, otherwise than by presenting facts and arguments to show that the desired action is of public advantage, is illegal. . . ." And in the Restatement . . . it is said that "A bargain to endeavor to secure a public contract by presenting to the official having power to make the contract inducements except such as relate to the desirability on public grounds of entering into the contract is illegal. . . ."

In the opinion of a majority of the court the contract of partnership in this case was illegal, and the plaintiff has no right to an accounting of profits received under it. The final decree is reversed, and a new final decree is to be entered, dismissing the bill with costs.

So ordered.

✧

As was true in the previous case, here the contract was illegal despite the fact that it did not require commission of a crime or a tort. The court considered the contract contrary to the public welfare, and on the ground of public policy, held the contract void.

QUESTION

1. Is it necessary that a precedent or statute be found to support a decision based upon public policy for the decision to be legally binding?

SHELLY v. *KRAEMER,* 334 U.S. 1, 1948

> *These are not cases, as has been suggested, in which the States have merely abstained from action, leaving private individuals free to impose such discriminations as they see fit. Rather, these are cases in which the States have made available to such individuals (signers of restrictive covenants) the full coercive power of government to deny to petitioners, on the grounds of race or color, the enjoyment of property rights.*

[EDITOR's NOTE: There were two cases under consideration by the United States Supreme Court in this matter, one from Missouri and one from Michigan. This *Shelley* v. *Kraemer* decision relates to both. The portion of the facts quoted below pertains only to the Michigan case.]

Mr. Chief Justice VINSON delivered the opinion of the Court. . . .

In June, 1934, one Ferguson and his wife, who then owned the property located in the city of Detroit which is involved in this case, executed a contract providing in part:

> This property shall not be used or occupied by any person or persons except those of the Caucasian race. It is further agreed that this restriction shall not be effective unless eighty percent of the property fronting on both sides of the street in the block where our land is located is subjected to this or a similar restriction.

The agreement provided that the restrictions were to remain in effect until January 1, 1960. The contract was subsequently recorded; and similar agreements were executed with respect to eighty percent of the lots in the block in which the property in question is situated.

By deed dated November 30, 1944, petitioners, who were found by the trial court to be Negroes, acquired title to the property and thereupon entered into its occupancy. On January 30, 1945, respondents, as owners of property subject to the terms of the restrictive agreement, brought suit against petitioners in the Circuit Court of Wayne County. After a hearing, the court entered a decree directing petitioners to move from the property within ninety days. Petitioners were further enjoined and restrained from using or occupying the premises in the future. On appeal, the Supreme Court of Michigan affirmed, deciding adversely to petitioners' contentions that they had been denied rights protected by the Fourteenth Amendment.

[EDITOR's NOTE: This refers to Section 1 of the Fourteenth Amendment, which is quoted at the end of this case.]

Petitioners have placed primary reliance on their contentions, first raised in the state courts, that judicial enforcement of the restrictive agreements in these cases has violated rights guaranteed to petitioners by the Fourteenth Amendment of the Federal Constitution and Acts of Congress passed pursuant to that Amendment. Specifically, petitioners urge that they have been denied the equal protection of the laws, deprived of property without due process of law, and have been denied privileges and immunities of citizens of the United States. We pass to a consideration of those issues. . . .

The restriction of the covenant in the Michigan case seeks to bar occupance by persons of the excluded class. It provides that "This property shall not be used or occupied by any person or persons except those of the Caucasian race."

It should be observed that these covenants do not seek to prescribe any particular use of the affected properties. Use of the properties for residential occupancy, as such, is not forbidden. The restrictions of these agreements, rather, are directed toward a designated class of persons and seek to determine who may and who may not own or make use of the properties for residential purposes. The excluded class is defined wholly in terms of race or color; "simply that and nothing more."

It cannot be doubted that among the civil rights intended to be protected from discriminatory state action by the Fourteenth Amendment are the rights to acquire, enjoy, own and dispose of property. Equality in the enjoyment of property rights was regarded by the framers of that Amendment as an essential pre-condition to the realization of other basic civil rights and liberties which the Amendment was intended to guarantee. Thus, Sec. 1978 of the Revised Statutes, derived from Sec. 1 of the Civil Rights Act of 1866 which was enacted by Congress while the Fourteenth Amendment was also under consideration, provides:

All citizens of the United States shall have the same right, in every State and Territory, as is enjoyed by white citizens thereof to inherit, purchase, lease, sell, hold, and convey real and personal property.

This court has given specific recognition to the same principle. . . .

[The present case does] not involve action by state legislatures or city councils. Here the particular patterns of discrimination and the areas in which the restrictions are to operate, are determined, in the first instance, by the terms of agreements among private individuals. Participation of the State consists in the enforcement of the restrictions so defined. The crucial issue with which we are here confronted is whether this distinction removes these cases from the operation of the prohibitory provisions of the Fourteenth Amendment.

Since the decision of this Court in the Civil Rights Cases, 109 U.S. 3 (1883), the principle has become firmly embedded in our constitutional law that the action inhibited by the first section of the Fourteenth Amendment is only such action as may fairly be said to be that of the States. The Amendment erects no shield against merely private conduct, however discriminatory or wrongful. We conclude, therefore, that the restrictive agreements standing alone cannot be regarded as violative of any rights guaranteed to petitioners by the Fourteenth Amendment. So long as the purposes of those agreements are effectuated by voluntary adherence to their terms, it would appear clear that there has been no action by the State and the provisions of the Amendment have not been violated. . . .

But here there was more. These are cases in which the purposes of the agreement were secured only by judicial enforcement by state courts of the restrictive terms of the agreements. The respondents urge that judicial enforcement of private agreements does not amount to state action; or, in any event, the participation of the State is so attenuated in character as not to amount to state action within the meaning of the Fourteenth Amendment. Finally, it is suggested, even if the States in these cases may be deemed to have acted in the constitutional sense, their action did not deprive petitioners of rights guaranteed by the Fourteenth Amendment. We move to a consideration of these matters. . . .

. . . We are called upon to consider whether enforcement by state courts of the restrictive agreements in these cases may be deemed to be the acts of those States; and, if so, whether that action has denied these petitioners the equal protection of the laws which the Amendment was intended to insure. We have no doubt that there has been state action in these cases in the full and complete sense of the phrase. The undisputed facts disclose that petitioners were willing purchasers of properties upon which they desired to establish homes. The owners of the properties were willing sellers; and contracts of sale were accordingly consummated. It is clear that but for the active intervention of the state courts, supported by the full panoply of state power, petitioners would have been free to occupy the properties in question without restraint.

These are not cases, as has been suggested, in which the States have merely abstained from action, leaving private individuals free to impose such discriminations as they see fit. Rather, these are cases in which the States have made available to such individuals the full coercive power of government to deny to petitioners, on the grounds of race or color, the enjoyment of property rights in premises which petitioners are willing and financially able to acquire and which the grantors are willing to sell. The difference between judicial enforcement and non-enforcement of the restrictive covenants is the difference to petitioners between being denied rights of property available to other members of the community and being accorded full enjoyment of those rights on an equal footing. . . .

For the reasons stated, . . . the judgment of the Supreme Court of Michigan must be reversed.

Reversed.

Mr. Justice REED, Mr. Justice JACKSON, and Mr. Justice RUTLEDGE took no part in the consideration or decision of these cases.

[EDITOR's NOTE: Section 1 of the Fourteenth Amendment to the Constitution of the United States:

All persons born or naturalized in the United States, and subject to the jurisdiction thereof, are citizens of the United States and of the State wherein they reside. No State shall make or enforce any law which shall abridge the privileges or immunities of citizens of the United States; nor shall any State deprive any person of life, liberty, or property, without due process of law; nor deny to any person within its jurisdiction the equal protection of the laws.]

✧

This historic decision is interesting for reasons going beyond its holding that restrictive covenants that discriminate against racial, ethnic, or religious groups are contrary to the Fourteenth Amendment and therefore illegal and unenforceable. It may be considered the first of a series of cases in which the Supreme Court began to take a more positive stand regarding racial questions, culminating in the famous school desegregation case.

Legal
Responsibility for
the Acts of Others

CHAPTER TWENTY-SIX

Introduction to Agency and Employment Relationships

> . . . We very frequently find the employee combining in one person the "servant" and the "agent." The existence of this situation presents the possibility that the employer may be legally responsible for torts of the employee . . . or that the employer may be legally responsible for contracts made by the employee. . . .

THERE SEEMS little question but that the common-law view of man embraces the idea of what we normally refer to as free will. By this view, each man is in control of his own actions and is therefore accountable for them. Perhaps it is true, as findings in the social sciences may indicate, that this view is oversimplified at the very least and that all of us to some degree and many of us to a large degree are constitutionally unable to control some aspects of behavior, even under threat of punishment. Nevertheless, most of us are able to meet most of the demands that society and the law impose upon us. Logically there must be some relationship between the demands we, who make up society, impose upon ourselves through our law and our capacity to meet these demands.

Whether everyone is able to follow all of the dictates of the law or not, it would seem that those who are able are on the whole better off to do so, and those who are unable must take the consequences. Aside from occasional allowances made for the insane, or more frequently, the young, the law views with disfavor claims for special exceptions to its dictates grounded upon irresponsibility.

Although this problem is usually thought of in the context of the criminal law, the problem also concerns the law of torts and contracts as well as other areas of the private law. A party must be held for the torts he com-

433

mits, and a party must be held accountable for his contracts. If only those persons were held responsible for torts or contracts who, on reflection, wished to be held, there would be no purpose in having law governing these relationships. We may therefore consider it a general principle, with only rare exceptions, that a person is held accountable for his actions in all of his contacts with the law.

If it is true that a person is accountable for his actions, is the reverse true, namely, that a person is not responsible for the actions of others? Before the criminal law one is usually not legally responsible for the actions of others unless he in some way instigated or encouraged those actions. In our private law, the situation differs. Here we find many instances in which a person does bear legal responsibility for the actions of others. This fact is so significant that we will explore various aspects of this vicarious liability at length. This chapter, then, discusses the extent of and the limits of our responsiblity for the acts of others.

Not only is it possible, it is common, for a party to be responsible in damages either for contracts made by another party or for torts committed by another party. This is because most economic activity today is carried on by parties in the employ of others rather than by self-employed proprietors. The latter, in fact, constitute an almost insignificant portion of the total work force of modern America. Corporations are staffed by persons employed by the corporation. In the final analysis, the corporation is identifiable only as a piece of paper. Everyone on the payroll from the president on down is an employee of the corporation. Even in the case of proprietorships and partnerships, much of the everyday work is usually performed by employees of the proprietor or of the partners. Obviously, the business organization is and must be accountable to some degree for the actions of those in its employ.

Problems in Terminology

The legal terminology applied to problems in this area is rather confusing. Those who adhere to the most precise usage refer to a person who performs physical *tasks* for another as a *servant,* and the person for whom the servant is doing the tasks as the *master.* Persons who represent other persons (most commonly by making contracts for them) are *agents,* the person represented being the *principal.* So we have two parallel but decidedly overlapping fields of law, that of master–servant and that of principal–agent, dealing with what the man in the street would consider to be similar aspects of employer–employee relationships.

In all probability the reasons for this division are almost purely historic in origin. Legal arrangements by which one person, the slave or the serf, worked in some menial capacity for another, date back so far into the mists of time that it is difficult to estimate when such institutions first appeared. And it is not so very long since these institutions have disappeared, even in Western society, especially the United States. Even when these institutions did disappear, whether the descendants of the serf continued tilling someone else's soil or worked as a domestic servant or whether with the advent of the Industrial Revolution he secured a subsistence toiling in a factory, neither his social nor his economic status was yet very high.

On the other hand, the personnel relied upon by the landed gentry to perform the supervisory, the financial, and the legal transactions necessary to the sound management of the landed estate did enjoy very respectable, if not the highest, social and economic standing. After all, at least in some periods of history, these managers could read, write, and calculate, and often their employers could not.

The legal relations governing the first group evolved into the law of master–servant. It was unthinkable that a servant would be representing his master: the servant performed tasks under the supervision of his master or the master's agent. Therefore the legal problems encountered between master and servant did not involve making contracts, but were concerned almost exclusively with liability for torts of the servant.

Relations with the second group were governed by the law of principal–agent. It was unlikely that the agent would be performing tasks under the direct supervision of his principal. Mainly he negotiated contracts for his principal, perhaps related to managing the principal's landed estate or his mill.

Both the station in life and the legal problems involving these two groups were so different, in earlier times, that it is no wonder that two separate bodies of law developed, to a large extent independent of one another. But times have changed, and the lines of separation are no longer clear. Socially, what used to be the difference between a place near the top of the social pyramid and one at rock bottom has now become a rather mixed situation. It is debatable whether or not a machinist necessarily enjoys a lower social and economic status than a salesman. Even more important, however, the two previously separate functions of servant and agent have become hopelessly intermingled in the course of modern employment.

Today, the employee of either a proprietorship, a partnership, or a corporation is very likely both to perform tasks under the supervision of the employer and on occasion to represent the employer. In other words, we very frequently find a person, in his capacity as employee, combining in one person the servant and the agent. The existence of this situation presents the possibility that the employer may be legally responsible for torts of the employee occurring in connection with the tasks the employee is performing or that the employer may be legally responsible for contracts made by the employee, while the latter is acting for the employer.

Many employees have this dual character. The clerk in the men's department is acting as a servant when rearranging merchandise or creating displays, and his master is exposed to liability in tort if the servant should carelessly injure someone while so doing. At the same time, the clerk is acting as an agent when contracting to sell merchandise to a customer, and if he contracts to sell at a lower price than authorized, his principal will probably be bound, regardless of the agent's lack of actual authority. In these instances, the master and the principal are one and the same party: the employer.

Probably most store clerks, route salesmen, bill collectors, many truck drivers, and even quite a few factory workers fall within the limits of this dual, servant-agent capacity.

Although it seems clear that all servants are employees in the sense discussed above, not all agents are employees. For example, the real-estate broker, the stockbroker, the lawyer are not ordinarily employees of the persons they represent: they are independent agents. The clients for whom one of these agents act will usually reserve no right to supervise the activities of the agent, except in unusual circumstances, and therefore the client is not ordinarily exposed to tort liability. In other words, an agent may or may not be an employee, and his power to act for someone else does not depend upon an employment relationship. For this reason, we believe that the traditional terms *principal* and *agent* are the better terms to use when discussing the power and authority of one person to make contracts or otherwise represent another.

The interrelationship and overlap among the concepts of master–servant, principal–agent, and employer–employee present difficulties in terminology. There is some temptation to treat all of these relationships merely as particular variations of the broadest category, and refer in all instances to employer–employee so long as an employment situation exists. This is particularly tempting because the term *servant* is no longer descriptive in the popular mind of the status of employees, and the terms *master–servant* have been abandoned in popular usage. However, the fact that all agents are not employees makes this usage unwieldy.

On the other hand, precision is facilitated by examining separately the liability for torts of servants and the liability for contracts made by agents, whether employee-agents or independent-agents.

For these reasons, we believe that the traditional terms master–servant and principal–agent are the better terms and will be used henceforth except in special cases. The reader is asked to bear in mind that the same party often fills a dual role as master-principal or servant-agent, and that in most instances we are concerned with parties who would ordinarily be referred to as employer–employee.

Formation of the Principal–Agent and the Master–Servant Relationships

Theoretically, the agency relationship is founded upon nothing more than the consent of the principal for the agent to act as agent and the consent of the agent to so act. The same is true of the master as regards his servant. Stated otherwise, a contract is not necessarily required. Occasionally it may happen that you ask a friend of yours to purchase something for you, making him your agent, or that you ask him to help you move a piece of furniture and he agrees, making him your servant. All the legal incidents of these relationships follow, despite the lack of a contract.

However, to terminate our discussion of the theoretical and to commence some discussion of the practical, it will be helpful at the outset to recognize that in most instances these relationships are based upon contract and that the relationships that produce legal disputes are overwhelmingly those based upon contract. Most agents and servants are being paid for their services.

Yet, even though most of the more important of these relationships are based upon contract, very often these contracts are very informal. In fact, generally such contracts need not be in writing. Some states require agents, who are supposed to make written contracts for their principal, to be authorized by a written contract. (This is called the *equal dignity rule*.)

Aside from special requirements of this sort, the agent or the servant may be retained through oral contract or even by an implied contract.

The requirements necessary to become a principal and to appoint an agent are not very imposing. Anyone with the authority to make contracts for himself may make contracts through an agent. And anyone able to contract is entitled to hire a servant to assist him.

The requirements for being an agent or servant are, if possible, even less imposing. Any person with the mental capacity to carry out the instructions assigned to him for performance may be an agent or servant. A minor may be an agent or servant. The fact of an agent being a minor does not constitute ground for the principal to escape a contract with a third party.

Liability for the Torts of Others

The agent, merely because he has the capacity to contract for his principal, does not necessarily expose his principal to liability in tort. But often, as said earlier, the agent is also a servant. If so, as tested below, the master–principal may be held for the servant–agent's tort.

The master is liable for the torts committed by his servant so long as the servant was acting within the scope of his authority at the time the tort was committed. This general rule is known as the doctrine of *respondeat superior*. What are the reasons for this doctrine? Several have been advanced. First, that the master is reaping the advantages of conducting a business, in the form of making a profit, with the assistance of servants; therefore, he should bear some of the social burdens that arise from conducting a business through servants, including the burden of reimbursing innocent victims of those servants. Second, that the master is the one with the authority to discipline the servants and hence with the power to prevent or at least discourage their wrongful acts. He is able to lay down rules of conduct that he may enforce under threat of fine or dismissal; the member of the general public who is the victim of such a tort has no such authority. Whatever rationale may be correct, the rule is well established.

Of course, the master is not liable for all wrongful acts of his servant. If an employee should go home after work in an angry mood and beat his wife, he is not then acting within the scope of his employment and there is no rational basis for holding the master liable.[1] Essentially, the question is, was the servant pursuing his employment at the time he committed a tort? There is no cut-and-dried means of answering the question of whether a servant was or was not acting within the scope of his employment. Factory hands, having left their machines temporarily to engage in horseplay with the intent of returning to work in a short time, have been held to be within the scope of their employment. A truck driver, carrying a load composed mostly of illegal cargo for his own purposes, but at the same time running an errand for his master, was held to be in the scope of his employment, as was another truck driver who had left his prescribed route for private reasons at the time of an accident but had intended to return to his route in a short time. As a matter of fact, the most important considerations in determining whether the servant is within the scope of his employment appear to be: are the servant's intentions in some way related to performing some task for the master, and does the activity engaged in at the time the tort was committed bear a close relationship to the master's business.

The fact that a servant has been specifically instructed not to engage in an activity does not mean that his master will escape liability if the employee nevertheless violates the instruction. Otherwise, a master could simply instruct the servant not to do anything wrongful, and thereby escape all liability to the public.

Some cases have relieved the master from liability for *deliberate* wrongs of their servants, such as wrongfully hitting someone (assault and battery), even if committed while pursuing the master's business objectives. Probably the majority of states hold otherwise, and there seems to be no good

1 This example is from Floyd R. Mechem, *Outlines of the Law of Agency* (Chicago: Callaghan & Company, 1952), p. 246.

reason why they should not. The public would seem to need as much protection from deliberate wrongs by servants as from any other wrongs, and presumably the master is as influential in preventing his employees from committing this type of wrong as he is in preventing unintentional wrongs.

M. J. ULINE COMPANY v. *CASHDAN* (CCA Washington, D.C., 1948) 171 F 2d 132

. . . A principal is not liable for his agent's tort unless it is within the scope of the agent's employment.

EDGERTON, C. J.

Appellee Genevieve Cashdan was struck and injured by a hockey stick during a game at which she was a spectator. She and her husband had paid for and were occupying front seats. They have recovered judgment against appellant, the corporation that owned the hockey rink and employed one of the teams. One of appellant's players raised his stick above his head and tried to strike a member of the other team. Beyond the fact that a hockey game was in active progress, there was nothing to show what the culprit's motive was. He missed his opponent and struck appellee. There was testimony that the game had been rough and that the referee had not been calling fouls.

The court instructed the jury that ". . . the player who struck the plaintiff Genevieve L. Cashdan was acting as a servant, agent, or employee of the defendant, M. J. Uline Company, Incorporated, and within the scope of his employment at the time the plaintiff was injured. Therefore, the acts and omissions of the said player were, in contemplation of law, the acts and omissions of the defendant. . . ."

(1–4) As we said in the Park Transfer Company case, "A principal is not liable for his agent's tort unless it is 'within the scope of the agent's employment.' It is not within the scope of the employment if it is done for the agent's purposes only. Unless an assault, or other tort, is actuated in part at least by a purpose to serve a principal, the principal is not liable." . . . It is possible that in trying to inflict serious bodily harm on an opponent the culprit was actuated in part by a purpose to win the game, or to make it interesting, and so to serve the appellant. If this was the fact, the blow was "within the scope of the agent's employment" and the appellant was liable. The court was therefore right in declining to direct a verdict for the appellant. But the suggested conclusion as to the agent's purpose is not the only one at which a jury might reasonably have arrived. The culprit may have been, at the moment when he struck the blow, completely indifferent to the work he was employed to do and actuated only by anger or hostility toward the man he tried to injure. It follows that the question whether or not the blow was within the scope of the agent's employment should have been submitted to the jury.

Reversed.

❖

The question remains, why, when an employee carrying out his work injures someone because of momentary inattention, the employer may be held; but when the employee carrying out his work injures someone because of momentarily losing his temper, the employer may not be held, unless it can be shown that the employee was attempting to further the employer's interests by committing assault and battery. Does not the employer have a responsibility to screen hostile as well as inattentive employees from his employ, particularly in employment well calculated to raise an employee's temper? Does not the employer have an opportunity to discipline an employee who violates instructions not to batter opponents? Should not such instructions be given? Does not the employer make a profit from the public, made possible by the employment relationship? Might the employer reasonably be held for damages made possible by the employment relationship, even if the damages are immediately caused by the employee's "anger and hostility"?

WOLFORD v. SCOTT NICKELS BUS COMPANY
(Kentucky, 1953) 257 SW 2d 594

> . . . to establish liability of the owner . . . for damages arising from the operation of a motor vehicle . . . where the vehicle is operated by a person other than the owner, the relationship of master and servant or principal and agent is necessary . . .

DUNCAN, J.

Appellee, Scott Nickels Bus Company, recovered judgment against Robert Wolford and Omer Wolford for $2,600, representing damages to its bus sustained in a collision with a truck owned by Robert Wolford and driven by Omer Wolford. The appeal is by Robert Wolford alone, who insists that he was entitled to a peremptory instruction because there was no evidence establishing the fact that Omer Wolford was either his agent or servant at the time of the collision.

Omer Wolford, who seems to have neither a permanent residence or employment, is a brother of Robert Wolford. Although usually residing elsewhere, Omer had been residing in the home of his mother, which was near Robert's home, for approximately a week before the accident. On the day of the collision, Omer, accompanied by his son Bronson Wolford, went to Robert's home, procured the truck and took it to Williamson, West Virginia, where it was placed in the garage of Mingo Motor Company for repairs. While the repairs were being made, Omer apparently spent a good part of his time drinking beer, which he says was recommended by his doctor. About 5 o'clock in the afternoon, he got the truck out of the garage and started the return trip to the home of his mother. During the course of his return, the accident in question occurred.

Robert states emphatically that he did not direct Omer to take the truck to Williamson on this occasion nor did he consent for him to do so. He states that the truck had been left at his home the night before, apparently with the keys in it; that he went to work the next morning about 6:30, leaving the truck at his home, and that he had no knowledge that the truck had been taken until he returned that evening. Upon learning that Omer had taken it, he immediately began searching and finally found the truck at the place of the collision in a wrecked condition. He states that a day or so before the accident he was discussing with Omer a mechanical defect in the truck, at which time Omer stated he would take it to Williamson and have it repaired. Robert states that he told Omer he did not want it taken to Williamson because he had all of his work done at another garage located nearer his home.

Omer admits that he took the truck without either the knowledge or consent of his brother. He admits that when he arrived at Robert's home for the purpose of getting the truck he did not see Robert at or about his home.

(1) Liability for damages arising from the operation of a motor vehicle must rest on something more than mere ownership. Where the vehicle is operated by a person other than the owner, the relationship of master and servant or principal and agent is necessary to establish liability of the owner. . . .

(2) There is no basic fundamental distinction to be drawn between the liability of a master for the tortious act of his servant and a principal for the tortious act of agent. In both cases, the liability is grounded upon the maxim of respondeat superior. A distinction based upon the difference in control has been suggested, but it has not been maintained by modern authority, which has taken agents and servants to be in coextensive categories as far as the question of their control by the employer is concerned. In each case, the relationship must exist at the time and in respect to the thing causing the injury and at a time while the agent or servant is acting within the scope of his agency or employment.

(3, 4) Where the facts are in dispute and the evidence is contradictory or conflicting, the question of agency, like other questions of fact, is to be determined by a jury. However, where the facts are undisputed, the question becomes one of law for the court. . . . Inasmuch as there is no contradiction of the testimony of appellant, we must accept his statement that his truck was being operated on the occasion of the collision without his knowledge or consent. Obviously, the relationship of master and servant or principal and agent did not exist between the owner and operator of the vehicle.

❖

Had the appellant asked his brother to drive the car to a garage for repairs and had his brother then become involved in a collision, this would have presented an example of employment by mere consent. Obviously, there is no consideration to support a contract in such an arrangement. But without some form of employment relationship, there is no basis for liability against appellant.

A few states have statutes that create a presumption that anyone driving another person's car is acting for the owner. So far as this writer has been able to determine no state does more than create a presumption, which may be rebutted by evidence such as used in this case. It seems rather improbable that any jurisdiction would go so far as to make the owner liable in the event that a car involved in an accident was stolen or borrowed without the permission of the owner.

Liability on Contracts Made by Others

The liability of a principal for contracts made in his name by his agent or his alleged agent is somewhat similar to the situation regarding liability of the master for the torts of his servant. The general rule as to contracts is that the principal is bound to a contract so long as the agent making the contract is within the scope of the authority to contract given to him by his principal. However, in somewhat the same fashion that a master may find himself liable for the tort of his servant, even when the servant is acting in an unauthorized manner, or contrary to instructions, the agent may sometimes bind his principal in contract even though the contract is unauthorized, or contrary to instructions.

Thus, it becomes necessary to draw a distinction between the authority of the agent, meaning the sum total of acts that the principal has expressly or impliedly permitted the agent to perform, and the *power* of the agent to bind the principal to contract. The power to bind the principal in certain cases extends beyond acts the principal has permitted or authorized the agent to perform.

REAL AUTHORITY

The authority that a principal has actually granted to an agent is termed *real authority*. Real authority may be granted in two ways: it may be specifically bestowed upon an agent through written or oral communication. Authority bestowed in this manner is aptly termed *express authority*.[2] In addition, instead of being expressly granted, authority of an agent may result from circumstances. A pattern of behavior may arise in which it becomes tacitly understood between principal and agent that the agent may make certain types of contracts. Authority that arises in this way is termed *implied authority*.

Implied authority may arise in different ways. For one thing, no set of instructions, no matter how detailed, may enumerate exactly not only all the things an agent is supposed to do, but in addition, how he is supposed

---

2 The power of attorney, an impressive-sounding name for what is often an impressive-looking document, is nothing more than a formal, express grant of authority, signed by the principal and used by the agent as evidence of his powers.

to do them. Few agency contracts in fact expressly catalog all or even most of the things the agent is supposed to do.[3]

Thus, practically every agency situation automatically implies a certain quantum of authority along with the authority expressly stated. Although the term *implied authority* would seem adequate to describe authority of this nature, the term *incidental authority* is also used and is applied to this and only this type of authority. Mechem prefers this usage.[4]

A somewhat different though perhaps overlapping use of the words *implied authority* arises in cases where the means of communicating the extension of a measure of authority is neither oral nor written, but rather through acts. In this usage, even though the means of communication is neither oral nor written, all the same there is communication, usually by example. This may happen when one long-term agent assumes the duties of another, being already familiar through ordinary observation with the latter's duties and authority. The difference between this type of implied authority on the one hand and express authority on the other is the same as the difference between an implied contract and an express contract (see page 206). The difference is purely in the manner of communication. Mechem believes that the term *implied authority* should be restricted to this usage.[5] Finally there are the relatively rare cases involving emergencies, in which, in order for the agent to cope reasonably with an emergency, the agent must perform almost unprecedented acts. This type of authority arises only when the agent has no opportunity to contact the principal and to request instructions. Inevitably this type of situation does sometimes arise, and the authority of the agent to take reasonable measures to meet the emergency is implied because of the unusual circumstances. Sometimes this form of implied authority is termed *authority by necessity*. It must be admitted that this form of implied authority is conveyed somewhat less directly from principal to agent than the other forms discussed. Rather, the reasoning seems to be that if the agent could have given the authority in a situation of this type, he would have, and therefore the court does not permit the actual lack of communication to stand in its way in finding implied authority.

[3] Basically, the same problem is the source of much dispute in the realm of constitutional law: the constitution delineates certain broad powers to be assumed by each branch of the government. However, necessarily, each branch has had to find implied powers in addition to those expressly stated. In the case of Congressional power, these implied powers are at least hinted at in the "necessary and proper" clause referred to in this text. When, however, this clause was interpreted to mean what it had to mean in order for the federal government to function, *McCulloch v. Maryland,* 1819 (4 Wheat 316, 4 L Ed 579), a storm of protest arose.

[4] Philip Mechem, *Outlines of the Law of Agency* (4th ed.; Chicago: Callaghan & Company, 1952).

[5] Mechem, *op. cit.*

Both express authority and the various forms of implied authority are forms of *real authority,* meaning that an agent acting under one of these forms of authority is authorized, at least impliedly, to perform the act in question.

APPARENT AUTHORITY

The important thing to remember concerning both express and implied authority is that they both require a finding by a court that authority was, or at least would have been, extended (in the case of authority by necessity) by the principal. The essential difference between express and implied authority is the manner in which this authority is extended to the agent.

Apparent authority is a different matter. This form of authority, if it may be called that, arises in situations roughly comparable to those in which an employee has the capacity to render the employer liable for his (the employee's) torts. As we have seen, the employee is almost never authorized to commit a tort. Yet, the employer is often liable when the employee does commit a tort. The fact that the employee violated instructions does not necessarily exempt the employer from liability. The case of apparent authority is analogous in the sense that when apparent authority is present, it is assumed that the agent did *not* have the real authority to make a contract; in other words he is acting contrary to his instructions, but nonetheless, the principal is liable on the contract.

Generally speaking, when an appearance has been created by the principal that his agent has a certain measure of authority, and relying upon this appearance a third party enters into a contract, the principal will be liable for this apparent authority even if he has instructed the agent not to make that very sort of contract.

The result of apparent authority, that one person is bound on a contract he never wished to make, is distasteful enough that there must be compelling reasons in favor of this result. It may be argued that the policies behind apparent authority are similar to those of estoppel. Estoppel was discussed earlier in this text as embracing the idea "if you lure a person out on a limb, you can't saw the limb off." How does this pertain to apparent authority? Just this. If you create an appearance that reasonably leads another to believe your agent has the authority to make contracts for you, you cannot deny this authority when a third person relies upon this appearance by making a contract with that agent.

Looking at the reasons from a broader perspective, the policy behind apparent authority is of a practical nature. Remember that almost all business is carried on by agent. If business firms could avoid their contracts merely by denying the authority of their agent in a particular case, almost no contract would be enforceable. Business as it is known in the modern world could not be conducted. Because of these pragmatic considerations, the opposite approach is taken. Businessmen are entitled to assume that an agent has the authority that his principal causes him to appear to have.

For all of these reasons therefore, a contract negotiated by an agent whom the principal has clothed with an appearance of authority may be enforced just as if the agent actually had the real authority he appeared to have. Nothing *requires* the principal to clothe his employee with the appearance of having authority to contract, but if he does, the agent may contract just as if he had real authority.

Perhaps the simplest manner in which a principal may create apparent authority is merely by telling a third party that the agent has greater authority than he has actually granted to the agent. However, sometimes a title or a position carries a degree of authority with it as a matter of custom in a particular trade, so that merely giving the agent that title or position automatically gives him a measure of apparent authority. A store manager, for example, is assumed in many trades to have rather broad powers to contract. Therefore, naming an agent as manager but secretly limiting his authority to an unusual degree will result in his having an area of apparent authority. Of course this will not be true if the principal communicates the fact to the third party that the agent does *not* have the authority customarily held by persons with that title.

The test for determining whether an appearance of authority has been conveyed is simply this: would a reasonable person assume, on the basis of the appearances created by the principal, or permitted by him to stand uncontradicted, that the agent is authorized to contract? If a reasonable person would assume from the evidence that the principal had extended this authority to the agent, though he actually had not, apparent authority almost surely exists.

On the other hand, the mere assertion by the agent that he has a certain measure of authority does not create apparent authority. The source of the apparent authority *must be traceable to some deed or word* of the principal. Were this not the case, any of us could assume the power to contract for almost any principal, merely by telling third parties that we possessed the authority to do so. Obviously, there would be no reason for holding the principal to contracts made under circumstances of this kind. This sort of thing is beyond the control of any principal. And therefore, the burden is placed upon the third party to ascertain that there is reasonably convincing evidence, stemming from circumstances, a statement, or an impression that *stem from the principal,* that the agent does have authority for his act.

Usually a party having apparent authority is an agent of the principal who finds himself bound, but as we see from the following case this is not necessarily true. It can happen that a complete stranger may take advantage of an appearance created or permitted by the principal, thus assuming the appearance of authority.

What about a party who, deciding to make a dishonest living, forges identification papers and manages to convince some victims that he represents a prominent magazine company. He proceeds to sell fake "subscriptions" and pocket the proceeds. Has he apparent authority, so as to bind the magazine company on the "subscriptions"? The answer, of course, is no, because the appearance of authority was not created or tolerated by the publisher. The culprit was acting strictly on his own, and the third parties who were taken in cannot reasonably argue that the publisher, who had no knowledge of the impostor, is at fault.

It is, in fact, a general rule of agency law that the statements of the agent as to his authority may not be relied upon by the third party. Appearances created or tolerated by the principal may be relied upon; those created by the agent, including his own statements, may not be relied upon. If an impostor does persuade a third party that he is the representative of someone else, and arrange a contract when in reality there is not even apparent authority, the impostor himself is the only party who may be held in damages for his contract. Of course, impostors of this sort are usually difficult to locate, but the same rule would apply to ordinary agents who make contracts for which they have neither real nor apparent authority, and for the same reasons.

What about the liability of an agent who has apparent authority but (as would naturally follow) does not have real authority? May the agent be held liable by the principal for reimbursement of losses that result from his binding the principal to an unauthorized contract? Clearly this should be, and is, the case. The same rule prevails when the servant commits a tort for which the master is sued; the master may secure reimbursement from the servant. Suits of this kind do not appear to be very common, however, perhaps because often the servant does not have sufficient assets to make a suit against him worth-while.

If an agent, or one purporting to be an agent arranges a contract for a principal when he lacks real or apparent authority to do so, of course the principal cannot be held. The agent may be held personally responsible for performance or for damages on non-performance of the contract by the third party. On the other hand, should the principal wish to do so, he may ratify the unauthorized contract. This subject is dealt with at greater length later in this section.

GENERAL AND SPECIAL AGENTS

Some authorities attach great significance to the distinction between "special" and "general" agency arrangements, the special agent being an agent who is empowered to perform only one transaction or at most a limited number of transactions encompassing a narrow range of activities. A general agent presumably has broad authority and in some instances almost unlimited authority. In other words, the difference between the two is based upon a question of degree. The objection to this dichotomy as an analytic tool is that the usual question of fact to be determined in solving a problem involving agency is "What *is* the extent of the authority of the agent?" Knowing that a special agent has little power and that a general agent has much is no aid to determining what in fact the power of a particular agent actually may be. Upon determining what the bounds of the agent's authority are, then and only then may one neatly classify him as a special or general agent. By this time the fact we were trying to determine is usually already determined, and we are not helped much in being able to tag a name on our agent after the problem is already solved.

There may be some utility in knowing merely that an agent has been *designated* a special agent by his principal. However, regardless of his designation, his power will be determined by the scope of the authority actually or apparently granted, and not, as already said, by the tag attached. He may be called a special agent, but if in fact he is given broad powers, he is a general agent.

Yet, perhaps occasionally, the fact that a person is known as a general agent causes him to have apparent authority beyond his real authority, and perhaps occasionally the fact that a person is known as a special agent prevents the appearance of authority, and thus does limit that agent's power. In such a case, the tag, admittedly, is significant.

KANELLES v. *LOCKE* (Ohio, 1919) 12 Ohio Appellate Reports 210

> . . . *We think that she by her voluntary act, or by her negligent act, had placed someone in a position where it would appear to anyone coming in to become a guest at the hotel that he was properly in charge, and that therefore she made herself by her conduct responsible for his acts, acting with the apparent scope of a clerk or employe in a hotel, to receive property of her guests.*
> . . .

D. Kanelles brought an action to recover the sum of $744, being the amount of money and valuables that he deposited with a man in charge of the Hotel Ohio, owned and operated by Mrs. Ida J. Locke, the defendant, in which action he failed.

It seems that Mrs. Locke was running the Hotel Ohio, in 1627 Prospect Avenue, Cleveland; that on the 23rd of December, 1918, at the hour of one o'clock in the morning, Mr. Kanelles applied, with a friend, and was received as a guest in said hotel, and paid the sum of $2 for a room, to which they were assigned; that in the hotel were notices posted as is required of innkeepers under the law of Ohio; that after they were shown to a room Kanelles told the man who appeared to be in charge, and who showed them to the room, that he desired to leave his money and valuables with the hotel proprietor for the night, whereupon they all returned to the office and the man in charge wrote out a receipt describing $484 in currency, a diamond stickpin and two checks for $5 each; that the man signed this receipt with the name of the proprietress of the hotel, Mrs. Locke, by him, and gave it to Kanelles, after which he, Kanelles, retired; that in the morning he presented the receipt to Mrs. Locke and requested the return of his money and valuables, whereupon he learned that this man who apparently was in charge of the office was not in the employ of Mrs. Locke at all, and, as she claimed, had no authority to receive the money or valuables; that upon going to the room of this man Mrs. Locke found that he had absconded, taking the money and valuables with him; and that Mrs. Locke refused to make good the loss to her guest and the action was brought, resulting in a verdict for the defendant.

We have gone over this bill of exceptions carefully, and it shows that this man who signed the receipt, J. C. Clemens, was and had been for some time a roomer in this hotel. We further find that the hotel was open to receive visitors at this time in the morning, or night, and that no one was in the office to take charge of guests who might arrive except this person Clemens and a young lady who was also a boarder or lodger in the hotel; that when the plaintiff entered with his friend and asked for a room, Clemens, who appeared to be in charge, got up and went behind the counter, had them register, got the key from its proper place, assigned them to a room, and took them to their room; and that after they had gone to the room, when the plaintiff requested that the hotel take charge of his valuables, they went down to the office, and with the help of the young lady wrote a receipt which at first was not satisfactory, and then wrote the receipt of which the following is a copy:

Mr. D. Kanalos, Man in Room 111 Gave me 1 Diamond pin and $484.00 in bills and 2 $5.00 checks.

Mrs. Locke
Hotel Ohio
per J. C. Clemens.

During this time the only person who appeared in charge of the office was this man Clemens. Whether Mrs. Locke had turned over the office to him to do these things we are not able to determine; but the fact remains that he was the only person there, apparently in charge of a public office that was receiving guests at that time in the morning or night, and that plaintiff became a guest and had a right to turn his valuables over to the hotel for safe-keeping, in accordance with the notices published in the hotel. We think the plaintiff was warranted in believing that this man in charge was the duly authorized agent for the purpose of receiving guests and receiving for safe-keeping valuables of the guests.

It is claimed by the defendant that this man was not her agent and had no authority to receive valuables or do anything around the hotel, and that therefore she was not responsible for any money or valuables that might be deposited with him. We can not acquiesce in this doctrine. An agency may be created by estoppel, and that estoppel may be allowed on the ground of negligence or fault on the part of the principal, *upon the principle that when one of two innocent parties must suffer loss, the loss will fall on him whose conduct brought about the situation.* 2 Corpus Juris, 462, and cases cited.

Here the proprietress of this hotel left this man in the office either designedly or negligently, clothed with apparent authority to do what hotel clerks usually do, and one who came in for the purpose of becoming a guest, and did become a guest, might reasonably conclude that he had *apparent* authority to do what clerks under similar circumstances would have a right to do.

In *Curtis* v. *Murphy,* 64 Wis., at page 4, we find this doctrine:

A traveler who goes to a hotel at night and finds a clerk in charge of the office, assigning rooms, etc., has the right to assume that such clerk represents the proprietor and has authority to take charge of money which may be handed him for safe-keeping.

And in that case the supreme court of Wisconsin held the hotelkeeper responsible under circumstances similar to those in the case at bar.

In the case at bar Mrs. Locke, the defendant, had complied with all the requirements of the statute to relieve innkeepers from liability by posting the notices required by law, and we think that she was an innkeeper within the meaning of the law; we think that she by her voluntary act, or by her negligent act, had placed someone in a position where it would appear to anyone coming in to become a guest at the hotel that he was properly in charge, and that therefore she made herself by her conduct responsible for his acts, acting with the apparent scope of a clerk or employe in a hotel, to receive property of her guests; and we think the court was clearly wrong in holding that there was no responsibility and in rendering a judgment against the plaintiff for costs. For these reasons the case will be reversed and remanded to the municipal court for further proceedings in accordance with law.

Judgment reversed, and cause remanded.

DUNLAP, P.J., and WASHBURN, J., concur.

✧

One interesting aspect of this case is the finding that Clemens, the thief, was found to have apparent authority when he not only did not have the real authority but was not, in fact, an agent, servant, or employee of the defendant in any way, shape, or form. Nevertheless, the decision seems reasonable considering the peculiar facts.

Observe that this case seems to consider apparent authority as a form of estoppel. Most cases do not consider the two concepts identical, though the similarity is widely recognized. Before an estoppel may be found, the party in whose favor the estoppel operates must be faced with a loss, caused by the other person's misleading appearance or change of position. The plaintiff in this case was, of course, faced with such a loss. However, in some instances a contract is made by one having the appearance of authority, under circumstances in which the only loss is the loss of whatever benefit the contract might have given a party. The provable financial benefit may be little or nothing. Such contracts are enforceable under the doctrine of apparent authority, but with little or no actual loss attributable to a repudiation of the contract, estoppel is not a satisfactory explanation. The more pragmatic explanation that simple business necessity requires the result is a better explanation.

SOUTHERN ELECTRICAL CORPORATION v. ASHLEY-CHICOT ELECTRICAL COOPERATIVE, INC.
(Arkansas, 1952) 251 SW 2d 813

A principal is . . . bound by all acts of a general agent which are within the apparent scope of his authority. . . .

Appellant, the Southern Electrical Corporation, Inc., is engaged in selling, among other things, materials such as cables and accessories for electrical installation, and appellee, The Ashley-Chicot Electrical Cooperative, Inc., is engaged in furnishing electricity to homes in the counties indicated by its name. This suit was brought in the Circuit Court of Ashley County by appellant to recover the sum of $2,406.32. After the introduction of all the evidence both sides asked for an instructed verdict, whereupon the Court, sitting as a jury, found in favor of appellee, hence this appeal.

An outline of the facts and circumstances out of which the litigation arose is as follows: On December 29, 1948, Pentecost, who at that time was and for several years previously had been manager of appellee, ordered from appellant, at a price agreed on between the two, a quantity of conductor or cable including accessories. On January 11, 1949, this order was shipped by appellant, under invoice number 3723 which referred to appellee's order number 00035. It was received by appellee in due course, and it was paid for in full on the 20th by company check in the amount of $11,374.60. Following this, other shipments were made and paid for in like manner. One such shipment of material, which precipitated this controversy, was made on May 6, 1949, amounting to $8,-519.69, which is not questioned in any way by appellee, but on May 13th its board of directors instructed its new manager (who had replaced Pentecost) to deduct the amount of $2,406.32 and to remit only $6,113.37, all of which was done that same day. Appellant refused to accept the check as payment in full and brought suit as stated above.

Appellee's reason for withholding payment of the balance of $2,406.32 due on the May 6th shipment involves the issues in this suit. It is contended by appellee that this amount was overpaid on the shipment first made on January

11th; that its manager, Pentecost, had no authority to make full payment on the first shipment; and that the excess charge for the conductor made by appellant was in violation of a written contract governing the price, which contract was entered into by both parties prior thereto and to which contract the Rural Electrification Association was also a party.

The lower Court, sitting as a jury, in refusing recovery to appellant, based its holding, in a short statement, on the ground that such a price contract was entered into on December 17, 1947, that appellant knew it was bound by it, and that both parties tried in vain to get the R.E.A. to change it.

(1, 2) Conceding there was a written contract between the parties governing the price of materials, they still had a right to change that contract by mutual agreement. All the evidence shows that the contract was changed in this instance by agreement, between appellant, on the one hand, and Pentecost, as manager of appellee, on the other hand. It is insisted by appellee, however, that Pentecost had no authority to agree to such a change. We see no merit in this contention. The well-established rule by which we must be guided here is briefly stated in *Chalmers & Son* v. *Bowen,* . . . from which opinion we quote:

> A principal is not only bound by the acts of the agent done under express authority, but he is also bound by all acts of a general agent which are within the apparent scope of his authority, whether they have been authorized by the principal or not, and even if they are contrary to express directions. The principal in such case is not only bound by the authority actually given to the general agent, but by the authority which the third person dealing with him has a right to believe has been given to him.

(3) As we view the record there is no evidence to show that Pentecost was not acting "within the apparent scope of his authority" when he agreed, on behalf of appellee, to the change in price, but there is abundant evidence to show he was so acting. Without encumbering this opinion by detailing the evidence, it is deemed sufficient to point out: that Pentecost had been the manager for several years, clothed with full apparent authority to transact business of this same character for appellee; he had formerly made similar purchases from appellant; he wrote checks on his company and none were turned down; and his transactions were only supervised by the board of directors meeting for an hour or two each month, at which time they scarcely, if ever, made any objections or even checked over his records.

(5) In addition to what we have already said, even if it were not clearly shown that Pentecost had apparent authority to bind appellee in this instance, we are convinced from the uncontradicted evidence that the sale was ratified both by the actions and the lack of action on the part of the board of directors. In this connection the evidence shows that at least one of the directors knew the terms and conditions of the transaction before shipment was made; that full payment by check signed by Pentecost and one director was made on January 20th; that the material was accepted by and used to the advantage of appellee; that the board of directors met (with Pentecost) and had opportunity to raise objections in February, March and April, but it failed to do so.

For the reasons stated and since there is no dispute over the amount in controversy, the judgment of the lower Court is reversed and remanded to the trial Court with directions to enter judgment in favor of appellant in the amount sued for.

✧

In the final analysis, the apparent authority in this case stems from the title *general manager* and the fact that the party holding this title had in fact acted for several years as though he had the customary authority of a general manager.

The case may well have been decided in the same way if the party holding the title had not actually acted as manager for a long period of time. Though that evidence certainly helped, third parties would ordinarily be entitled to assume that even a newly appointed general manager would have the usual authority of a general manager in the particular trade or business involved.

CHAPTER TWENTY-SEVEN

Additional Topics on Principal and Agent

The agency problems dealing with ratification are usually based upon a claim by the third party that the conduct *of the principal demonstrated ratification. In other words, the usual claim is that the intent necessary for ratification may reasonably be implied from the acts of the principal.*

The Undisclosed Principal

SUPPOSE THAT a manufacturing concern wishes to build a factory in an area presently devoted to agricultural uses. Under these circumstances, the manufacturer would probably wish to buy up that land quietly if at all possible. Otherwise, as soon as the identity of the buyer, and the purpose of his purchases became known, the price demanded would be likely to skyrocket. Landowners would reason, correctly, that for the land to have been selected for the purpose contemplated there must be characteristics about the land or its location that make it more valuable than the general run of farm land. It would be assumed that the manufacturer would be willing to pay more than the prevailing price, and the landowners concerned would probably not be ashamed to demand a considerable premium. Needless to say, from the manufacturer's point of view, this would be an undesirable state of affairs. Inevitably, the thought would occur to the manufacturer, as it probably already has to the reader: why not send around agents to buy up the land in their own name but with the plan of conveying title to the manufacturer at an appropriate time?

A scheme of this sort may (or may not) sound like shady tactics, but legally it may be done, though practically it is nonetheless difficult to pull off without someone suspecting the facts. An agent who operates under his

453

own name for a secret principal is termed, logically enough, an agent for an undisclosed principal.

Granting that this device seems a little irregular because the third party is in effect dealing with someone other than the person he assumes he is dealing with, why is this arrangement tolerated? The primary reason is probably that the same effect could be reached by other routes anyway, and these other routes are so basic and so essential to modern commerce that they could not effectively be blocked. One such route is the assignment, considered on page 484. Is there any reason why certain parties could not go out and purchase a number of desired properties, then assign their interest to their "principal" at some later date? It might be argued that a large number of simultaneous assignments to one party might be a distinctive enough event to merit a special rule prohibiting such a transaction, but if this rule were adopted, the assignments could merely be spaced more discretely. Another device by which the same effect could be realized, not considered elsewhere in this text and therefore not further elaborated upon, is to have agents purchase legal title to desired property, then hold it in trust for another party.

It would seem almost certain that the inconveniences in administering the law would outweigh any benefits that would be derived from outlawing the right of agents to act as undisclosed principals. And it may be debatable whether or not this arrangement is really so insidious after all.

Incidents of the Relationship between Undisclosed Principal, His Agent, and the Third Party

RIGHTS OF THIRD PARTY

The most significant aspect concerning the position of the undisclosed principal has already been mentioned, this being that he may remain unknown to third parties, and yet may have contracts made for his benefit by his agents. These contracts will ordinarily be valid regardless of the fact that the third party is completely unaware of the identity of the principal with whom he is actually dealing.

In a few types of situations this will not be true. If the third party will be materially prejudiced by the fact that he is dealing with an undisclosed principal, he will not be held to the resulting contract. Of course, this statement is meaningless without some idea of what is and is not considered material prejudice. Consider, for example, the earlier example concerning land purchased by agents for a factory site. Ignorance of the identity of the actual buyer may well have affected the seller's asking price but would not constitute material prejudice.

A contract will be considered as materially prejudicial if it requires the third party to perform personal services for one whom he finds personally distasteful. Prejudice will also be found if, in fact, the third party actually inquired of the agent as to whether the agent was representing any undisclosed principal, and the agent denied that he was. This, of course, would amount at least to misrepresentation and possibly to fraud. Either would be a basis for avoiding the contract. The first of these two instances of material prejudice, relating to personal services, is merely another illustration of the special treatment given personal services in almost every contact with the law. Parallel instances discussed in this text are found relating to the assignment of contracts (contracts for the performance of personal services may not be assigned) and relating to specific performance (specific performance may not be obtained to enforce a contract for personal services). The second exception is merely a particular application of the usual rules relating to misrepresentation and fraud.

When the third party makes a contract with the agent for an undisclosed principal, he is under the impression that the agent is the real party in interest. What happens if the agent discovers that his principal will not perform the contract? The agent may, of course, suggest to the third party that the principal is the real party in interest. He may also broadly hint that the principal is the more solvent of the two and would be the better party to sue. However, if the third party does not take the hint, or does not even wish to respond to a direct suggestion, he may hold the agent to the contract. The agent is the party upon whom the third party originally relied, and the third party may collect damages from the agent. If recovery is actually realized against the agent, the agent is entitled to be indemnified by the principal, however.

Because the principal is the real party in interest, and can hold the third party to a contract made by the agent, the third party has the reciprocal right to hold the principal to the contract should he learn the identity of the principal. This seems inconsistent with the third party's right to hold the agent. Does this suggest that the third party may recover twice? Of course this could not be. But the third party does have the right to pursue his rights against both parties until that time when he has made an election to confine his recovery to one party or the other. Various jurisdictions differ as to the exact point in the proceedings at which the third party will be held to have made an election. Probably the most usual ruling provides that when the third party knows of the existence of the principal, actually securing judgment against either principal or agent will constitute an election. If, at that time, the third party was unaware of the existence of the principal, and had secured judgment against the agent, election would not have occurred. It is difficult to see why obtaining a judgment against either principal or agent, which turns out to be uncollectable, should constitute an election, and some jurisdictions hold that an election has not been made until judgment is actually satisfied.

RIGHTS AGAINST THE THIRD PARTY

As we have seen, in the event of dispute, the third party to a contract made by the agent for an undisclosed principal may bring suit against either the principal or the agent. Does the reverse hold true? That is, may the third party be sued by either principal or agent? This would seem to follow, and it does. That the principal may hold the third party under these circumstances would seem to follow almost inexorably from the basic policy of recognizing contracts made for undisclosed principals. Some of the reasons supporting this policy were discussed earlier. Assuming the recognition of the fact that an undisclosed principal may be the real party in interest, it would manifestly make no sense to deny him the right to assert his interest in court.

Reasons for granting the agent the power to sue are equally straightforward. The undisclosed principal has the right to remain undisclosed throughout the life of a transaction, should he wish to do so. But unless the agent has the power to bring suit in his own name, the principal would be unable to bring suit without revealing his true identity. Thus, for the relationship to accomplish its ends, the agent must be entitled to bring suit in his own name.

PARTIALLY UNDISCLOSED PRINCIPAL

It is entirely possible that an agent may make contracts for a principal, under circumstances in which the third person is aware that the agent does represent a principal, but in which the identity of the principal is unknown. Under these circumstances the principal is sometimes referred to as a partially disclosed principal. Under normal circumstances, there is no difference between the rules applicable to the undisclosed principal on the one hand and the partially disclosed principal on the other. The few instances in which there is some difference are so narrow and particular as to be beyond the scope of this text.

ROGALSKY v. *RYAN* (New York, 1948) 80 NYS 2d 564

> *It is true that plaintiff Rogalsky was acting for Cornell University, but he signed the agreement as a principal and is liable as a principal whether or not the defendants believed him to be acting as agent or principal. . . . The agreement does not fail of its effect though one who is described as a principal or who assumes a principal's obligation is in truth an agent only.*

CRIBB, J.

Plaintiffs bring this action in Equity Court to compel specific performance of a written agreement executed by plaintiff Rogalsky and defendants on the 19th day of June, 1947, whereby Rogalsky agreed to purchase and defendants agreed to sell and convey to him certain therein briefly described farm lands consisting of about 223 acres with two houses and out-buildings. The purchase price was $21,000, of which amount $2,000 was paid to the defendants upon the execution of the agreement. The balance of the purchase price was to be paid "on the closing, which will be as soon as the necessary legal papers can be drawn and submitted to my attorney for a reasonable examination."

Subsequently, on the 19th day of June, 1947, plaintiff Rogalsky assigned to plaintiff Cornell University all of his rights and obligations contained in said agreement.

Defendants by their answer admit the making and execution of the contract by the respective parties and the receipt by them of $2,000 on the purchase price at the time of its execution, and the assignment by Rogalsky to Cornell University. They set up, however, three separate defenses. First, that Rogalsky was acting as agent for Cornell University and that he obtained the agreement from defendants through fraud and misrepresentation in that he told them that any "income tax due by reason of gain made by the defendants on the sale would be assumed and paid by the plaintiffs." Second, that plaintiffs have an adequate remedy at law.

(1–3) As to the first defense alleging fraud on the part of Rogalsky in obtaining defendants' written acceptance of the offer to purchase, no evidence whatever was offered upon the trial in support of the allegation of fraud, and counsel for defendants made no reference to this alleged fraud in his brief. It is true that plaintiff Rogalsky was acting for Cornell University, but he signed the agreement as a principal and is liable as a principal whether or not the defendants believed him to be acting as agent or principal. He is one of the plaintiffs in this action. The agreement does not fail of its effect though one who is described as principal or who assumes a principal's obligation is in truth an agent only. "The authority of the agent may be shown by parol, and the principal for whom he acts, . . . may sue and be sued as if his name had been disclosed." *Irvmor Corporation* v. *Rodewald,* 253 N.Y. 472, 475, 171 N.E. 747, 748, 70 A.L.R. 192. Upon cross examination Rogalsky frankly stated that he was not authorized by Cornell University in writing to act as its agent in purchasing defendants' farm. Counsel for the defendants therefore maintains that the agreement is void under Section 259 of the Real Property Law because the agreement in effect grants to the defendants a lease of the house for a period of five years, and that Rogalsky was acting as agent of Cornell University without written authority therefor. Section 259 reads as follows: "A contract for the leasing for a longer period than one year, or for the sale, of any real property, or an interest therein, is void, unless the contract, or some note or memorandum thereof, expressing the consideration, is in writing, subscribed by the party to be charged, or by his lawful agent thereunto authorized by writing." It seems clear that this contention of defendants' counsel is without merit. The offer to purchase was in writing and subscribed by the party to be charged, namely, Rogalsky who signed as principal. It also provided the terms upon which defendants were to occupy the house for five years.

(4) It seems that the second defense set up must fail. Cornell University did not seek the purchase of the Ryan farm for ordinary farming activities, but rather for specific experimental purposes. The testimony discloses that the Department of Agronomy in the State College of Agriculture at Cornell University received an appropriation from the State Legislature to carry on important research in connection with so-called limestone soils for the benefit of some three or four million acres of land lying between Albany and Buffalo; that representatives of the Department examined a large area in an effort to locate a farm in reasonable proximity to Cornell University, having sufficient acreage, contours, drainage, types of soil—all as required for the experimental work contemplated—and which could be purchased. Professor Cline testified that the Ryan farm was the only one found meeting all these requirements. This Court believes that it would be most difficult, if not impossible, to compensate Cornell University in money damages for the loss it would sustain if defendants failed to convey the farm lands as provided by the contract in question.

Plaintiffs are entitled to judgment directing the specific performance of the contract as demanded in the complaint, together with costs of this action.
Findings and proposed judgment may be submitted accordingly.

✧

Fraud would have been found here had the defendant inquired of Rogalsky if he was acting for an undisclosed principal and Rogalsky had flatly denied that this was the case. However, defendants did not inquire of Rogalsky relating to his status. It is firmly established that the agent for an undisclosed principal is in no way at fault for not revealing his identity as an agent.

Ratification

It should be evident to the student by this time that agents do not always do what they are supposed to do; specifically they do not necessarily follow their instructions, and in fact they do not necessarily stay within their power. We have already discussed the situations that arise when an agent goes beyond his instructions but remains within his power. These boundaries describe the area of apparent authority. In other instances, however, the agent attempts to bind his principal when he is beyond even his apparent authority. In other words, he is without any power whatever to bind the principal on the contract purportedly made for the benefit of the principal. The agent's liability in cases of this kind is discussed in detail in a following section. The principal is not liable on a contract of this nature, and the agent is liable to the third party for any damages resulting from failure of the principal to perform.

Nevertheless, there are circumstances under which the principal may be held. First let us examine some aspects of the position of the principal in a case where his agent, lacking any power, has nonetheless made a contract. May the principal claim the benefit of the contract? In a formal legal sense, we are again faced with a situation in whch ordinary principles of assignment would provide a ready answer. There is ordinarily no reason why the agent could not assign his contract with the third party to the principal, if the latter is willing to accept the assignment. Because the end could be effected anyway, there is surely no reason why the end should not be accomplished more directly. The legal concept of ratification is in fact relied upon.[1] If the principal wishes to ratify an unauthorized contract of the agent he is entitled to do so. But even this approach, though logical, is a little unrealistic. For we must observe that in most instances the third party has no means of knowing whether the contract made by the agent is authorized by instructions from the principal or not. Although legally he is not entitled to rely upon a statement of the agent as to what his authority is, actually he often does. Suppose the agent has persuaded the third party that the contract is authorized, when actually the agent lacks the authority, or in an extreme case is an impostor and not an agent for the principal at all. Nevertheless, suppose the agent or impostor goes to the principal and explains what he has done. If the principal wishes the contract to be binding, in a practical sense he need not do anything. The third party has assumed all along that the contract was authorized, and has hardly any means of ascertaining that it was not. Probably in most instances of this nature, the principal quietly proceeds as though there was never any question as to the contract's validity, and indeed it would be difficult to establish that there ever was.

For these reasons, the question as to what a principal must do to prove that he has ratified an unauthorized contract rarely is presented. The question is almost invariably framed in the context of the principal's denying the authority of an agent or purported agent to make a contract, and of the third party insisting that the contract was in some way ratified by the principal.

REQUIREMENTS FOR RATIFICATION

In order for ratification to be even possible, certain requirements must be present. These are as follows:[2] (1) The contract for which ratification is sought to be proved must be a contract that would have been valid

---

[1] Previously met in the section on fraud: A contract induced by fraud may nonetheless be ratified, and a minor upon reaching his majority may ratify the contracts made during minority.

[2] Philip Mechem, paraphrased from *Outlines of the Law of Agency* (Chicago: Callaghan & Company, 1952), pp. 129–134.

had the agent had the authority at the time he purported to bind the principal. (2) The principal must have the present ability to authorize the act when the alleged ratification occurs. (3) The contract must have purported to be on behalf of the principal. (4) The principal must have knowledge (or at least an opportunity to learn) of the material facts of the contract in order for him to be held to have ratified it. The legal result of ratification is that a present act is recognized as binding retroactively. When viewed in this light, the requirements listed above seem reasonable. For example, it would not be reasonable to observe that an authorized act was illegal but to extend legal sanction retroactively to that same illegal act. If illegal when performed, the lapse of a period of time would not render that act any more legal *when it was performed,* even if the law might have changed in the meantime. It also seems reasonable that a principal must have the present power to authorize an act in order to ratify the act. For example, if this power stems from a position of authority in a corporation, but at the time when ratification is attempted the principal no longer fills the position of authority in the corporation, he no longer has the legal capacity to ratify.

If the original contract did not purport to bind the principal, the situation in which ratification is alleged (remembering that in the overwhelming majority of cases plaintiff is a third party claiming that the principal has ratified) requires that the party said to be an agent has acted under circumstances in which there is neither express, implied, nor apparent authority. This situation is to be distinguished from the case of the agent for an undisclosed principal, in which the authority of the agent to act for the principal does exist, although the principal has not been revealed as the real party in interest. For ratification to be even considered as a possibility, that agent must have claimed to be acting for the principal. Otherwise, why should the alleged principal be involved any more than anyone else?

Finally, it seems reasonable that in order to hold the principal to a ratification, he must have had some opportunity to know just what it is he is supposed to be ratifying.

THE PROCESS OF RATIFICATION

We have mentioned earlier in this section that the process of ratification is not confined in its application to the law of agency, but has application in many fields of law and has already been treated in the sections on contract, in the context of ratification of fraud, and ratification of a contract by a former minor who has just attained his majority.

The essence of proving ratification lies in showing convincing evidence of an intent of the principal to take advantage of, and therefore a showing of his agreeing to be held to, a contract. The most clearly defined instances of ratification naturally arise, therefore, when there is an unequivocal statement by a party that he wishes the contract in question to be binding upon him. However, this rarely happens in any context, and as stated earlier, in agency problems the usual patterns involve a claim by a third party that the unauthorized act of the agent was in some way agreed to by the principal.

The agency problems dealing with ratification are usually based upon a claim by the third party that the *conduct* of the principal demonstrated ratification. In other words, the usual claim is that the intent necessary for ratification may reasonably be implied from the acts of the principal. The sort of act that is most frequently alleged to constitute a ratification is accepting benefits of the agent's contract by the principal. To the extent that an acceptance of benefits may be shown, this is indeed rather strong evidence of a ratification. It is well established that a party may not accept some of the benefits of a contract while rejecting others. Either the contract is accepted in its entirety or rejected, and acceptance of any portion will constitute an acceptance and therefore a ratification of the entire contract. Earlier cases, in which the same basic principle was applied to other sorts of contract problems, may be found on page 299.

STANDARD OIL COMPANY OF TEXAS v. MANLEY
(Texas, 1949) 178 F 2d 136

> *Generally, in order to have a ratification, an agent must purport to do something in behalf of his principal, and the principal, with full knowledge of all the material facts, must do something to evidence an intent to approve the unauthorized act.*

This action originated as a suit in trespass to try title of an oil-and-gas leasehold estate in Grayson County, Texas, held by appellant, a Delaware corporation. All parties claim from a common source, namely, The Grand High Court Heroines of Jericho of Texas and Jurisdiction, a Negro fraternal lodge, hereinafter referred to as the Grand High Court. Appellant bases its claim on an oil-and-gas lease from the Grand High Court dated February 19, 1945.

The Grand High Court, from which the claim of all parties in this case emanates, is an unincorporated fraternal organization, composed of female relatives of Negro Masons. There are about 440 local lodges known as Local Courts of Heroines, which are subordinate to the Grand High Court. The latter, composed of officers of the local courts, constitutes the Grand Lodge of this organization, which is governed by a written constitution, and has its headquarters in Fort Worth, Texas. In 1940, the constitution of this organization was amended so as to allow the Grand High Court to convey or transfer property by warranty deed or bill of sale, provided the instrument conveying the property was signed by the Most Worshipful Grand Joshua; the Most Ancient Grand Matron; and the Most Ancient Grand Secretary, whose duty it was to affix the official seal.

The lease under which appellant asserts its claim was acquired for H. H. Coffield (appellant's agent) by Jack Campbell, who was one of many persons hired to contact property owners for the purpose of acquiring oil-and-gas leases. It was purported to have been signed on behalf of the Grand High Court by William M. McDonald, Grand Joshua; R. A. Winn, Most Ancient Grand Matron; and N. S. Mosely, Most Ancient Grand Secretary. The acknowledgment was taken in statutory form by Zalee A. Payne, under her seal, and dated February 21, 1945. It was duly filed for record in the proper office of Grayson County, Texas, and was later assigned by H. H. Coffield to the appellant; the latter paying a $43 bonus, which was accepted by William M. McDonald for the Grand High Court. Appellant also paid the Grand High Court two annual delay rentals of $43 each. These delay rentals were to be paid each year to the lessor if the appellant did not drill for oil.

On October 16, 1947, William M. McDonald, acting for the Grand High Court, conveyed the same property to W. H. Harvey, pursuant to a resolution of the Grand High Court passed at a meeting in June, 1947, authorizing him to sell the land by warranty deed. On November 13, 1947, the Grand High Court, by letter, attempted to return to appellant its check for $129. The latter refused to accept it, and returned the check on November 21, 1947. Harvey then executed an oil-and-gas lease to appellee Hubbard, who in turn assigned it to appellees Manley and Roberts.

(1) The lower court found that the lease on which appellant predicates its claim was invalid; and we think this finding was correct, because there was ample evidence to sustain it. It is true that the lease was signed by the Grand Joshua, William M. McDonald, but the Most Ancient Grand Matron and the Most Ancient Grand Secretary did not sign it. The evidence is that the daughter of said secretary signed the lease for her mother, who was ill at the time. The name of the Most Ancient Grand Matron was placed on the lease by Zalee A. Payne, who had no authority to do so. The only method by which property could be conveyed by the Grand High Court was for the deed or other instrument to be signed by three specified officers. In the instant case, only one of these officers signed the lease; and, by virtue of this fact, no title passed to the appellant unless the Grand High Court in some way ratified this unauthorized act of its members. The lower court found that there was no such ratification; we differ from it on this point, in that we are convinced from the acts and conduct of the parties subsequent to the execution of the lease that there was a ratification of such a character as to import validity to the lease, irrespective of the defects in its execution.

(2, 3) The general rule is that, in order to have a ratification, an agent must purport to do something in behalf of his principal; and the principal, with full knowledge of all the material facts, must do something to evidence an intent to approve the unauthorized act. In applying these elements of ratification to this case, we think the Grand High Court did ratify the lease that McDonald purported to make. Undoubtedly, in signing the lease, McDonald purported to act as agent of the Grand High Court; and the latter, by accepting the bonus payment and delay rentals, evidenced an intent to approve McDonald's act. Approval of the unauthorized act may be express or implied; receipt of such benefits from the unauthorized transaction, with full knowledge of the facts, is sufficient approval to meet the test of this particular element of ratification. The only real question of ratification in the instant case is whether or not the Grand High Court had knowledge of all the material facts. In determining whether such knowledge existed, we must take into consideration the peculiar nature of this association. It would be unreasonable to require that each member of the Grand High Court should have had such knowledge.

Grand Secretary of said court, on January 21, 1946, drew a draft for $43 on the Merchants and Planters National Bank of Sherman, Texas, which was the depository bank named in the lease. The Secretary carried this on her records as "total collected from oil lease, Sherman Farm."

The minutes of each meeting of the Grand High Court for 1945, 1946, and 1947, in the Grand Secretary's report, and in the Auditor's report, show receipt of $43 payments as "total collected from oil lease, Sherman Farm." These reports, having been read aloud in open session, were all specifically approved and adopted by the official sessions of the Grand High Court. After each session of said court, the minutes, including the secretary's and auditor's reports, were printed, bound in paperbacked volumes, made available to all members, and sent to each local court.

(4) We are of the opinion that these acts of the Grand High Court amounted to a ratification of the invalid lease, and that it was error to overrule the motion of appellant for an instructed verdict. The judgment appealed from is reversed, and the cause remanded for further proceedings not inconsistent with this opinion.

Reversed.

✧

When, as in this case, the principal conducts himself (or itself) in a manner completely inconsistent with disapproval of the agent's act and quite consistent with approval, ratification has occurred. Compare this set of facts with those of the following case, where despite the fact that the principal did not repudiate the purported agent's acts, nonetheless the failure to repudiate those acts was reasonably explained on grounds other than approval of the acts. Under these circumstances, ratification was not found to have occurred.

WOLFORD v. *SCOTT NICKELS BUS COMPANY* (Kentucky 1953) 257 S.W. 2d 594 (Part Two) (See p. 440 for facts in this case.)

> *It is generally true that any act which may be authorized in the first instance may be ratified by the principal, in which event the principal becomes bound by the ratification.*

The evidence discloses that the repairs to appellant's truck on the day of and before the collision were made by Mingo Motor Company, of Williamson, amounting to $36.46. Appellant paid for the repairs some three or four months after the collision. Appellee insists that even if Omer Wolford was without authority to take the truck to Williamson on the day of the collision his unauthorized act was ratified by payment for the repairs.

(5) It is generally true that any act which may be authorized in the first instance may be ratified by the principal, in which event the principal becomes bound by the ratification. However, there are certain requisites of ratification which we do not think are present here. In order that the ratification may be effective, there must be an intention to ratify, although the intention may be inferred from the facts and circumstances. As a consequence, ratification cannot be inferred from acts which may be readily explained without involving any intent to ratify. . . .

(6) In this case, appellant explains his payment for the repairs by stating that he did not want to have any trouble with the garage over the account. The amount involved is hardly sufficient to justify the trouble and expense which would have been incurred in contesting a claim asserted by the garage for the repairs. Other reasonable explanations for the payment of the account might also be suggested which are entirely consistent with the theory of nonratification of the unauthorized act of Omer in taking the truck to the garage.

We do not think the payment of the garage bill incurred on the unauthorized trip which resulted in this collision amounted to a ratification by appellant. From what we have said, it follows that the court should have directed a verdict for Robert Wolford.

The judgment is reversed for proceedings consistent with this opinion.

❖

Relations between Principal and Agent

TERMINATION OF AGENCY

The relation between principal and agent is based upon the consent of both. Therefore, it is axiomatic that the relationship may be terminated any time either party (or both by agreement) withdraws his consent. Beyond any question, this is the means by which most agency agreements are terminated. It should be noted that even if a contract between the parties should specify that an agency agreement should continue for a stated period of time, neither party can be forced to continue against his will. The party in breach of contract may, however, be held for damages.

However, there are other means by which a termination may be effected. In some instances, the original agreement may contain the seed of its own termination. Whether a particular objective is contemplated, with the proviso that the principal–agent relationship will terminate upon attaining that objective, or a definite time period is set upon the expiration of which the agency will terminate, in either case the original agreement effects the termination. In addition, often the accomplishment of an objective will terminate the relationship even though the agreement did not specify that termination would automatically follow. For example, if principal hires agent to sell principal's white elephant, and agent does, it seems reasonably obvious that the agency has terminated, even though nothing specifically provided that the sale would have this effect.

A number of events will result in termination of an agency as a matter of law. These events bear a strong resemblance to those which terminate an offer as a matter of law, and for the same reasons. Death or insanity of either the agent or the principal, or bankruptcy of the principal, or destruction of the subject matter—all will terminate an agency as a matter of law.

NOTICE OF TERMINATION

If an agent is widely known to have the authority to bind his principal one day, and the next day this authority is revoked, it goes without saying that considerable confusion would be the lot of third parties relying upon their understanding of the agent's authority. Apparent authority is one device utilized to protect the third party in cases of this sort: an agent who has been dealing with customers of the principal but who is suddenly deprived of his real authority, continues to hold a degree of apparent authority until the customers are informed that the real authority of the agent no longer exists. As to those third parties with whom the agent has had previous dealings, the principal must give personal notice of the termination of the agency in order to destroy the power (as distinct from the authority) of the agent to make binding contracts. But, this rationale has no place as to third parties who have not had direct dealings with the agent. They, presumably, have no basis for a belief that the agent does have authority to represent the principal, and consequently they have no need for personal notice that the agent in fact does not. As to these parties, the principal need merely give constructive notice through a newspaper notice.

Obligations of the Agent Owed to the Principal
(as Well as of the Servant to the Master)

It is the view of this writer that the discussion concerning the obligations of the agent to the principal is presented in an unduly fragmented manner in many sources. Indeed, sometimes the presentation bears a remarkable resemblance to the Boy Scout Law.[3] The *basic* obligations of the agent are essentially twofold. He owes a duty of absolute loyalty to the principal and to the interests of the principal, and he owes a duty to follow the instructions of the principal. No doubt even the duty to follow the instructions of the principal may be considered as merely a particular statement of one aspect of the agent's duty of loyalty.

True, the cases dealing with the agent's obligation of loyalty have fallen into certain fairly well-defined patterns, and these may be profitably explored. For one, it is decidedly a disloyal act for the agent to purport to act for two principals at the same time, without informing each party of this conflict in interest and without securing the permission of each to proceed under this arrangement. Any compensation received by an agent from a competing, undisclosed second principal may be recovered by the original principal, through suit if necessary. The obvious reason for this rule is the widely appreciated fact that no one can serve two masters, with contrary interests, loyally, at the same time.

It would naturally follow, and need hardly be mentioned, that the agent is also precluded from pursuing his own interests at the expense of his principal. Again, it may be doubted if anyone, when he places himself in the position in which his business interests compete with those of his principal, can under these circumstances serve the interests of the principal with absolute loyalty.

If an agent owes a duty of absolute loyalty, he obviously may not be tapping the principal's till when, or even if, the opportunity presents. From this observation, we may extract several subsidiary rules: First that the agent is obligated to account for money or other articles of value that belong to the principal but find their way into the agent's custody. Second, consistent with this duty, the agent must keep records showing the various sums of money or other articles of value he has received. And third he must not commingle his and his principal's assets.

Finally, the agent must be scrupulously careful to inform the principal of any significant aspect of the principal's business that may come to the agent's attention. The reasons for this are not hard to discover. For one thing, the agent is the eyes and ears of the principal. Only through the

---

[3] A scout is trustworthy, loyal, helpful, friendly, courteous, kind, obedient, cheerful, thrifty, brave, clean, and reverent.

senses of the agent, in most instances, may the principal discover the information he needs to carry on his business. Moreover, the principal is in fact held legally accountable for all information that is or even should be known to the agent. Serious, even disastrous, consequences can therefore befall the principal when the agent has or should have vital information, but does not pass this information on to the principal.

RIANDA v. SAN BENITO TITLE GUARANTEE COMPANY
(California, 1950) 217 P 2d 25

> *Defendant's duty to plaintiffs is to be determined by the application of ordinary principles of agency. . . . It is the duty of an agent to obey the instructions of his principal and exercise in his employment reasonable skill and ordinary diligence, and, if defendant violated instructions or acted negligently . . . it would ordinarily be liable for any loss occasioned by its breach of duty.*

GIBSON, CJ.

Plaintiffs appeal from a judgment for defendant in an action to recover damages arising from the alleged negligence of defendant in failing to present for payment a check delivered to it in connection with a real estate transaction.

On July 3, 1946, Marian Jublit, a real estate agent and one of the plaintiffs herein, wrote a letter to defendant at Hollister requesting it to "prepare title search, necessary deed and deed of trust etc. covering the sale of 608 acres in San Benito County by Harry Rianda to Nick Daskarolis." She enclosed an unsigned copy of a "Deposit Receipt" or sales agreement on which the names of Daskarolis and plaintiff Rianda were typed after the word "signed" at the appropriate places for their signatures. Under the terms of the agreement, the total sales price was $91,200, payable $30,000 within 60 days, and the balance by installment note secured by a deed of trust. The agreement acknowledged receipt of a deposit of $5,000. (This sum was apparently retained by plaintiffs as a forfeiture and is not involved in this action.) The agreement further provided that the deposit should be increased to 10% of the purchase price upon "acceptance by purchaser," and that any payments could be converted into cash, if made in other than lawful money, and could be retained by the seller in case of default.

On July 5, Hublit sent defendant a $5,000 check drawn by Daskarolis on a Hollister bank. This check, which named defendant as payee, was not accompanied by any explanations or instructions. Although the check may have been given in pursuance of the agreement that the deposit was to be increased to 10% of the purchase price, defendant was not informed that such was its purpose, and the check was for $880 in excess of the amount required to complete the necessary deposit of $9,120. Defendant's manager endorsed the check, "Pay to the order of the Hollister National Bank 12 Hollister, Cal. Escrow Account San Benito Title Guarantee Co.," and placed it in defendant's files with other papers relative to the transaction.

A few days later Hublit told defendant that Daskarolis' wife was to be named as a grantee in the deed from Rianda, that the cash payment was to be $27,000 rather than $30,000, and that the amount of the note secured by trust deed was to be correspondingly increased to $64,200. Defendant made a title search and prepared a deed, note, deed of trust and proposed escrow instructions. No reference was made in these instructions to the $5,000 payment mentioned in the deposit receipt, nor to the $5,000 check made payable to defendant. The seller's instructions, which were signed by Rianda, authorized defendant to deliver the deed to the grantees upon the payment to the defendant of the sum of $27,000 plus the note and deed of trust for $64,200. The buyer's instructions were never delivered to or signed by Daskarolis, and he never gave defendant any instructions, oral or written, with respect to the transaction. Although he inspected the note and trust deed at defendant's office, he did not sign them.

In a letter to defendant dated August 23, Rianda's attorney, whose office was in San Jose, demanded that defendant forward $5,000 to Rianda "covering" the amount deposited with defendant, stating that Daskarolis had indicated his intention not to complete the purchase. On Monday, August 26, Daskarolis withdrew $5,000 from his commercial account with the drawee bank, leaving a balance insufficient to cover the check, and orally informed defendant that he had "stopped payment" on the check. It does not appear when the letter from Rianda's attorney was received but defendant answered it on August 26, informing the attorney of the action taken by Daskarolis. The time set for performance of the contract by Daskarolis passed, and plaintiffs brought this action seeking to recover the amount of the check on the theory that defendant was negligent in failing to cash or deposit the check promptly. The title company defended on the ground that it had received no instructions from either party to cash or deposit the check and that it was not guilty of negligence in failing to do so.

The court found that defendant had not been negligent, and the question to be determined is whether there is evidence to support this finding.

(1, 2) Defendant's duty to plaintiffs is to be determined by the application of ordinary principles of agency, whether defendant be considered as escrow holder with duties to both Rianda and Daskarolis or as agent of plaintiffs alone. It is the duty of an agent to obey the instructions of his principal and exercise in his employment reasonable skill and ordinary diligence, and, if defendant violated instructions or acted negligently in retaining the check in its files, it would ordinarily be liable for any loss occasioned by its breach of duty.

(3) Plaintiffs contend that the terms of the sales agreement relating to the seller's option to retain all amounts paid in the event of default, and authorizing the seller to convert into cash all payments made in other than lawful money, constituted instructions to cash the check or at least put defendant on notice of facts sufficient to place it under a duty to present the check promptly. We cannot agree, however, that mere knowledge of the terms of the unsigned copy of the agreement placed defendant under such a duty, and, moreover, it is difficult to see how the agreement can be construed as a direction to defendant

to cash the check. It does not mention defendant or provide for an escrow, and it does not require anyone to cash checks received from the buyer. Nor is any reference made in the agreement to the check which was subsequently delivered to defendant without instructions. There is nothing in the agreement or elsewhere in the record to show that it was intended or understood as an instruction to defendant to do anything with the check. There was no evidence that defendant was ever informed that the sales agreement had been signed by the parties or that there was a binding contract, and, as we have seen, the instruction signed by Rianda did not follow the terms of the agreement, but contained different provisions as to the amount of the cash payment, the principal of the note and trust deed, and the parties to be named as grantees. Furthermore, defendant was not informed that the check was a part of a deposit which was then due and which might be forfeited in the event of default by Daskarolis. In this connection, it is significant that, as before stated, the amount of the check did not conform to the amount of the deposit required by the terms of the agreement. It is likewise significant that, although Daskarolis made the check payable to defendant, he never gave defendant any instructions concerning it.

(4) It is argued that the letter of August 23, notifying defendant of Daskarolis' contemplated default and demanding payment of $5,000, placed defendant under a duty to present the check for payment. Even if we assume that the letter might have placed defendant under such a duty, the record does not show that defendant had any opportunity to act before Daskarolis made the withdrawal from his bank account. There was no proof as to when the letter was mailed, where it was mailed, when it was received, or when it should have been delivered to defendant in Hollister in the ordinary course of the mails. All that the record shows is that the letter was dated at San Jose, August 23, which was a Friday, and that it was answered by defendant by a letter dated August 26, which was a Monday. Neither was there any evidence as to what time of day on Monday, August 26, Daskarolis withdrew the money or notified defendant that he had "stopped payment" on the check. Under these circumstances the trial court was not compelled to find that the defendant received notice of plaintiffs' claim in time to act.

We cannot say as a matter of law that defendant was guilty of any breach of duty in failing to cash or deposit the check.

The judgment is affirmed.

❖

The obligation on the part of an agent to follow instructions is crystal clear, as is his liability in the event his failure to follow instructions results in a loss to the principal. Unfortunately, the instructions here were anything but clear, and the evidence that the agent received them in time to act thereon was, if anything, even less clear. The agent is not required to be a mind reader in order to avoid liability for failure to obey instructions.

Obligations of the Master to the Servant
(and of Principal to the Agent)

Earlier, the point was emphasized that the overlapping relationships under discussion, principal-agent, and master-servant may or may not be founded upon contract. More to the immediate point, the services rendered pursuant to each of these relationships may or may not be performed in the expectation of compensation. But in the overwhelming majority of instances, there is an expectation of compensation, and this expectation is based upon an express or implied contract.

Therefore, the master has an obligation to extend whatever compensation he has expressly or impliedly contracted to extend. Whether this obligation stems from some principle inherent in the law of agency or whether this obligation is merely one application of the law of contract is a moot point. Why any explanation beyond the fact that there is a contract should be necessary, however, is difficult to see.

Being a personal relationship, the employment contract may not be specifically enforced against either party, and either party may break the contract. Should this occur, the other party may bring suit in damages, but at the same time, each party has the obligation of minimizing his own damages. In other words, if an employee is fired, contrary to the provisions of his employment contract, he has an obligation to seek comparable employment elsewhere. His damages will be limited to the difference between what he would have received from the defendant employer, less what he received in his new employment. If he failed to make a reasonable effort to secure new employment, evidence will be admitted to shed light on the question of what he *could* have received had he tried to secure employment. Whatever sum the fact finders conclude that he could have received had he made a reasonable effort to do so will be deducted from his damages.

By the same token, if an employee should leave his employment contrary to his contract, the employer must attempt to minimize his damages by hiring a replacement if possible and may not merely sit back, permit damages to multiply, and present the bill to the departed employee.

Consistent with the general rules of contract, if the employee is guilty of breach of contract, the employer will have the benefit of the usual rules concerning termination upon breach. (See page 376.) See also, the treatment of "permanent employment" (page 256).

Reimbursement and Indemnity of Agent or Servant

Not surprisingly, the employer owes the employee a duty to make good any sums of money that the employee has expended for the benefit of the employer. By the same token, the employer owes the employee a duty to make good sums extracted from the employee by lawsuit—for example, stemming from authorized acts performed by the employee in the scope of his employment and for which he himself was not at fault. Though obviously closely related, the employer's duty to make good sums expended on day-to-day business for his benefit is termed the *duty of reimbursement*. The employer's duty to make good on such extraordinary claims as judgments against the employee is termed the *duty to indemnify*. In either case, the employer's duty extends only to cases in which the payment was incurred in the furtherance of the employer's interest, the payment must have been reasonable, and the payment must not have resulted solely from the employee's mistake or misdeed.

Both as to this heading and that immediately preceding, the liability of the principal to the agent is exactly as outlined above. Thus, whether an agent is also an employee, or whether he is an independent agent, paid by fee, the same incidents as outlined above remain applicable.

CHAPTER TWENTY-EIGHT

The Independent
Contractor

Normally we think of the pants presser and the brain surgeon as running their own trade or profession. They are subject to their own working rules rather than yours or mine. . . . Parties with these characteristics are termed independent contractors, *rather than servants.*

O RDINARILY, the employment agreement is based upon contract. Throughout the preceding pages, attention has been devoted to the liability attaching to the master that may result from acts of his servant. Possibly, though hopefully not, the student may have concluded at this point that anyone hired to perform work for another party will necessarily expose the latter party to liability for the torts of the former. This discussion, though usually presented earlier in a discussion of agency, provides an excellent vehicle for the purpose of bringing the forest back into focus, in the event that it has been lost for the trees.

Everyone who performs work that is useful to us is not our servant. Whether we order our pants pressed by the dry cleaner, a suit made by the tailor, plans prepared by our architect, or a frontal lobotomy performed by a brain surgeon, it seems clear that in none of these cases will we be liable for torts perpetrated by one of the craftsmen or professional men. Even if the tort in some way was involved in the performance of the work we requested, there is still no liability on our part. Why not? Because in none of these cases is it understood that we will or even may act in a supervisory capacity over the subject rendering the performance. In the final analysis the distinction stems from the relationships between the parties. Normally we think of the pants presser and the brain surgeon as running their own trade or profession. They are subject to their own working rules rather than yours or mine. They begin and end their working days in accordance with their own decision rather than yours or mine. Parties with these characteristics are termed *independent contractors,* rather than servants. They are, quite literally, independent parties with whom we may contract.

In any particular case, a member of any of the vocational groups mentioned above could be a servant. Some wealthy persons may hire one individual to do all of their clothes pressing. If so, the chances are that hours and working conditions are set by the person receiving the service, the master, and the party performing the service is a servant, not an independent contractor. Sometimes architects are hired as servants of large corporations, and many others are hired as instructors in educational institutions. Doctors are also hired by educational and research institutions. Under these circumstances, the doctors and architects would be servants, not independent contractors.

Consequently, the primary distinction between the servant and the independent contractor is in the relationship between the party providing services and the one receiving them. The most important aspect of this relationship is whether in fact the party receiving the services also reserves the right to control the working conditions. If so, whether this control is exercised to any great extent or not, there exists a master–servant relationship. The master is liable for the torts of the servant committed within the scope of employment. If the party performing services is not a servant he is an independent contractor, and the party receiving the services is not ordinarily liable for the torts of the independent contractor.

One other factor, of secondary importance in determining whether a person is a servant or an independent contractor, is the degree of skill, knowledge, and experience necessary to perform certain tasks. Until fairly recently, those performing tasks requiring exceedingly complex skills and considerable knowledge, as the doctor or architect, were almost automatically held to be independent contractors, whereas those performing very simple tasks were almost automatically held to be servants.

Those performing tasks requiring complex skills and considerable knowledge are no longer necessarily independent contractors, as discussed above, but those performing the most simple tasks are even today likely to be considered servants under almost any circumstances. Thus, even though you contract with the housemaid to clean your house for a set price, or bargain with a neighbor boy to mow your lawn at a contract price, and set no special conditions of employment, these are likely to be considered employees rather than independent contractors.

Dangerous Activities

Earlier, mention was made of the fact that in certain instances one is responsible in tort for the activities of his independent contractor, despite the fact that the general rule is to the contrary. These exceptions are grounded upon the theory that one engaging in dangerous activities cannot avoid his responsibility to the public merely by shifting the burdens onto an independent contractor (who, by the way, might not be financially responsible).

The most obvious instances of dangerous activities involve such activities as blasting, maintaining wild animals, or handling poisonous chemicals. Naturally, what is or is not so inherently dangerous as to bind the employer in negligence, even though the actual negligence is on the part of an independent contractor, is a question that must be determined, for the most part at least, by the particular facts of a case.

Apparent Employment

There is another pattern of cases in which one may be held liable for the activities of an independent contractor. Suppose a department store leases out a certain section of the store to an independent contractor, often a jewelry department or shoe department. There is no employer–employee relationship between the owner of the store and the independent contractor. Nevertheless appearances are to the contrary, and the department store does appear to own the business actually owned and operated by the independent contractor. In this and in similar cases, where a business appears to the general public to be part of a responsible, known business organization but is in fact an independent contractor, the apparent owner, the department store in our example, may be held liable for torts of the actual owner and operator of the leased department. Of course, the independent contractor is liable for his own tort. The issue is likely to be important when the independent contractor is not financially responsible. The rationale behind this rule is that the customer, when he decides to trade with the particular business organization, does so in part because of his confidence in that organization. In other words, the appearance that he was dealing with a widely known concern led him to trade with that concern. Presumably (if we are to relentlessly carry this idea to its logical conclusion) we must assume that the customer felt that if he were the victim of a tort, the business organization he believed he was patronizing would be financially able and perhaps willing to pay his claim. On this theory the apparent owner on whom the customer relied may be held liable. It might well be argued that most shoppers do not calculate the probable ability of a retail outlet to meet their tort claims in the event they are injured, before deciding to patronize the establishment. On the other hand, in a rather vague sense shoppers probably do consider the image of stability and reputation for fair dealing, as against small, unknown, and possibly fly-by-night outfits. If this is true, the apparent owner should be held for lending its name (for a price) to the less well established.

RHONE v. TRY ME CAB COMPANY (District of Columbia, 1933) 65 F 2d 834

> . . . We now have in Washington hundreds of taxicabs engaged very literally—in a public calling . . . holding out to the public an illusion of incorporated responsibility which they do not possess; painted, named, and numbered to heighten that illusion; each cab constituting a potential danger both to its passengers and to the public, yet having no financial responsibility. . . .

HITZ, AJ.

This case comes here by writ of error to the Municipal Court of the District of Columbia and presents a question of some public importance, touching the operation of taxicabs in Washington, under the present system of control, or the lack of it.

The plaintiff in error, who was plaintiff below, was a passenger in a taxicab and claims to have been injured by negligence of its driver.

The declaration names as defendants Williams, the driver; Jackson, registered as owner of the cab; and the Try Me Cab Company, a corporation, applicant for registration of the cab and whose name it bore on the occasion in question.

No process was served upon Williams, and the action was abandoned as to him, though he appeared as a witness for the defense at the trial.

The declaration was in familiar form, claiming damages from the cab company and Jackson, or either of them, as owners or operators of the cab for the personal injuries caused by negligence of the driver alleged to be the servant or agent of the owners or operators.

The two defendants by their pleas denied liability for the driver, asserting that he was an independent contractor with the passenger, and in sole control of the cab at the time of the alleged accident.

The plea of the cab company further denied that it is engaged in carrying passengers for hire; that it ever received the plaintiff as a passenger; that it owns this cab, or any other cab; or that it exercised any control or management of the cab at the time in question.

Jackson's plea admitted ownership of the cab, but asserted that he had no liability therefor at the time of accident because of a contractual arrangement between himself and Williams, the driver, by which he received a daily compensation for the cab, of which Williams had full control.

No question was raised against the pleadings; the case was tried on the merits; and at the conclusion of all the evidence the defendants moved for a directed verdict, which was granted; and the main question presented here concerns the correctness of that ruling.

The bill of exceptions states that there was testimony regarding negligence of the driver and resulting injury to the plaintiff sufficient to raise substantial questions for the jury on those issues, but that the case was decided on the legal relations of the parties as disclosed by the evidence.

The plaintiff testified that prior to the occurrence a printed card had been left at her door advertising the Try Me Cab Company; that she had read other advertisements in the telephone directory reading: "Metropolitan, 1911—Try Me Cab Company—A careful and courteous service. Special rates by the hour, day, or week. We go anywhere—reliable chauffeurs. Try Me Cab Company, Metropolitan, 1911." Being induced by these advertisements, she telephoned to the cab company at its advertised office, asking for a cab; that in response a cab was sent to her house marked "Try Me Cab Company," and that she embarked in it, to her injury.

Another witness testified to knowledge of these facts, saying that the cab was marked "Try Me Cab Company, Number 7."

An agent of the director of traffic testified that the official records showed 106 cabs registered under applications of the Try Me Cab Company; that such applications were not required to be made by the owner; that the record relating to the cab in question shows in the space for applicant "Try Me Cab Company." In the space for the signature of the owner appears in typewriting "Try Me Cab Company," in handwriting, "Walter Jackson."

The vice president of the cab company testified that it is a nonprofit-sharing corporation, incorporated under the laws of the District of Columbia for the purpose of furnishing its members a telephone service and the advantages offered by use of the corporate name, while the company did not own this cab or any other cab. The defendant Jackson testified that he owned the cab; that he had licensed and registered it as a taxicab; that the name of Try Me Cab Company had been placed on the record because of an inquiry at the license office as to the name of the company in which it was to be used; that he had personally operated the cab until he became ill shortly before the accident, he collecting and retaining all earnings without accounting to the company.

Jackson further testified that, at the time of the accident, he had rented the car to Williams, the driver, for $3.50 per day; that Williams was operating the car under this arrangement on the occasion of the accident, but also under the taxicab permit issued to Jackson, paying the daily rental, exercising full control, and retaining all receipts with no accounting to the company or to him.

Williams corroborated Jackson in all matters, admitting that he was driving at the time of the accident and in full charge of the cab.

The counsel stipulated that the advertisements mentioned by the plaintiff were authorized by the cab company, and that Jackson was the owner of the car.

In this state of case, the defendants contended that the company was not liable for the plaintiff's injuries because Jackson owned the car; and that Jackson was not liable because he rented the car to the driver, who emerges from their dealings inter sese as an independent contractor with the customers of the company and solely responsible for their injuries, if any one is. It is further contended that no relation of master and servant or principal and agent existed among the parties, since the driver was a bailee with control of the bailment, and that the reliable chauffeurs of the company, who go anywhere, go upon their own, with no accountability to the company and no liability to the passenger, beyond the personal responsibility of the driver.

The trial court accepted this view of the situation and directed a verdict for both defendants.

(1) But we find it clear that the cab was engaged in a public calling; under license of public authority; issued upon the joint application of the cab company and Jackson; that at the time of the accident it bore the name of the company; was sent out by the company in response to an application induced by its advertisements; that it was made available for that purpose by Jackson; and operated by a driver furnished by Jackson, under a public vehicle license issued to Jackson.

Upon this showing we are of opinion that both the company and Jackson are estopped to deny liability to a passenger so induced to employ the cab and injured by negligence of the driver sent to operate it. . . .

(2) In the trial court the plaintiff asked the vice president of the company on cross-examination three questions tending to bring out the preceise relations of the company to the owner and the driver of this cab, namely:

1. What agreement was there between the owner of this cab and the Try Me Cab Company, with respect to the operation of the cab?

2. What could the Try Me Cab Company do to the driver of such a cab as this if he refused to go in response to a call received at the office of the company?

3. Did the Try Me Cab Company provide a garage for the repair of such cabs as the one here involved?

Objections to these questions were sustained, and they were excluded. But we consider them material to the full development of the case, especially in view of the elaborate and detailed averments of the pleas, and if the case should be retried we are of opinion that these questions might well be admitted, if again presented.

Shortly after the record of this case was filed in this court, the two appellees joined in a motion for leave to file typewritten briefs instead of the usual printed briefs, on the ground of their financial inability to pay for the printing.

This motion was supported by an affidavit of poverty, and was therefore granted.

So this case proceeds in this court in forma pauperis on all sides, which serves to emphasize the public interest and private hardship frequently appearing in such litigation in this jurisdiction.

For we now have in Washington hundreds of taxicabs engaged—very literally—in a public calling; performable only upon the public streets under public license; holding out to the public an illusion of incorporated responsibility which they do not possess; painted, named, and numbered to heighten that illusion; each cab constituting a potential danger both to its passengers and to the public, yet having no financial responsibility to either beyond an equity of redemption in some used motor car.

In this case, even that is absent, for while Jackson asserted his ownership of the car at the license office and in his testimony, and while his ownership was stipulated by counsel, his motion papers show that he never had any interest in the car beyond attempting to buy it under a conditional sales contract subsequently forfeited.

While the cab company apparently never owned any cab, nor anything else, beyond a chartered misnomer which it leased to cab drivers, and through which it called itself a cab company when in fact it was a cab calling company.

The present methods of selling motorcars and licensing public vehicles lead naturally to the present situation of cutthroat irresponsibility in a public service of great importance and daily danger to many persons.

While our duty is to apply the law as we find it, in this respect we find it so unsatisfactory that we feel impelled to suggest that some change should be made, either by legislative enactment or municipal regulation.

Perhaps an improvement of this situation can be found in a system of compulsory insurance preliminary to the license and running in rem with the car in favor of any one injured by its negligent operation under any arrangement with the licensee, such as many of our states now have and such as appears to have covered hackney coaches in London for a hundred years.

The judgment of the Municipal Court is reversed, and the cause remanded.

Reversed.

✧

When retail establishments appear to be run by a prominent organization but actually are not, there may sometimes be reasonable doubt as to whether or not the patrons really were induced to trade by a feeling that if they were injured the prominent name would be financially responsible.

Accidents in most retail establishments are not common, and it may be doubted if many individuals even think about the possibility of injury when entering department stores, for example. However, this case is exceptional.

The fact that automobile accidents are not uncommon is well established, and the suspicion exists in the minds of many that taxis may be more accident-prone than other passenger vehicles. Therefore, it seems quite likely that passengers would in fact rely upon the appearance of corporate ownership.

Even when the reliance of a customer is less-well-established than in this case, however, the apparent owner is very often held on the basis of having created a deceptive appearance.

SECTION SIX

The Transfer of Intangible Legal Rights

(Herein of Assignment and the Negotiable Instrument)

CHAPTER TWENTY-NINE

Preface to the Study of Assignment and Negotiation

. . . There soon grew up an organization of international bankers having agents or correspondents in the principal commercial centers, and these firms, instead of actually delivering coins of one type in exchange for coins of another, would write a letter of exchange to their correspondents, effecting the transfer purely on paper.[1]

The Transfer of a Claim in Earlier Days: A Fictitious Account

VICTORE DE SALVATORE was a prosperous merchant in sixteenth-century Venice. He had many dealings with suppliers in Greece. Early in his career it was necessary for him to carry gold personally to Greece in order to effect a purchase of merchandise. However, his credit was now well established, and to pay for merchandise ordered from Greece he would request a letter of advice from a local Venetian banker. This letter would be sent to the banker's correspondent in Greece. The letter would request the correspondent to pay the designated sum in gold to Salvatore's supplier. Lorenzo, Salvatore's courier would deliver the letter and select the merchandise to be purchased. On receipt of the letter of advice the correspondent would pay the supplier, the supplier would ship the merchandise, and after receipt, Salvatore would pay his banker.

When in the course of business a Greek merchant wished to order goods from Venice, he would obtain a letter of advice drawn by *his* banker upon the Venetian bank, and the two letters would cancel each other out. Of

---

[1] Theodore F. T. Plucknett, *A Concise History of the Common Law*, 5th ed. (Boston: Little, Brown and Co., 1956), p. 667.

course, the transactions between the bankers were many and frequent, and the balance of credit would fluctuate from day to day. In the event one bank built up a substantial balance at the expense of the other, it was possible that the debtor bank might have a large credit balance built up in a bank near the creditor bank. If so, a shipment of gold between these two nearby banks could settle the accounts all around. By this and similar transactions, large shipments of gold, over long distances, could be avoided.

One day, Lorenzo, Salvatore's courier, was crossing the Tyrrhenian Sea when unfortunately the sloop on which he had taken passage was intercepted by a pirate corsair. Suspecting Lorenzo of being an agent for a rich merchant, the pirates searched him for the gold they felt he should have been carrying. They found nothing but papers. Some of the pirates wished to hold him for ransom and others to sell him into slavery, but the pirate captain was so furious at Lorenzo's utter and inexcusable lack of gold that he hurled him into the sea.

Eventually the parties concluded that Lorenzo's ship was lost, so Salvatore requested a duplicate letter, located another, more dependable courier at one half the salary Lorenzo had been paid, and the letter of advice reached the correspondent Greek banker without incident. It was a little late but the story had a happy ending, because by using notes instead of gold, nobody lost a penny on the deal.

HISTORICAL DEVELOPMENT OF THE BILL OF EXCHANGE [2]

Already in the fourteenth century . . . the formal deed began to be replaced by the informal letter of advice which accompanied it; it is this letter of advice which eventually grew into the modern bill of exchange.

All through the middle ages attempts were being made to make debts assignable and if possible payable to anyone who was the bearer of a document. The principle was widespread; in the year 771 a monk gave to a church, "or the bearer of this document," the right of avenging his death and collecting the *wer* if he were murdered; in 1036 a man left by his will the guardianship of his wife to two relatives "or to whoever shall bear this writing." In mercantile affairs this device became a common feature of sealed promises to pay. They were first drawn in favour of a named payee "or his attorney," and in such cases a formal deed of attorney would be necessary to entitle anyone except the payee to sue upon the instrument. Documents of this type were common in the thirteenth and fourteenth centuries, for in fact they were simply the bond under seal

2 *Ibid.,* pp. 665–667.

which figures in countless actions of debt. Debtors were careful not to pay even an attorney except in return for the original bond, for payment was no defence if the creditor still held the sacred document. It therefore naturally followed that a debtor was safe in paying anyone who returned him his deed. Later still, therefore, the mere production of the document was accepted as sufficient authority entitling the bearer to sue, at first in the name of the payee, and later in his own name. In the fifteenth century the validity of written promises to pay made out in this form was questioned, save in the single instance where the bearer was the properly constituted attorney of the payee.

The future lay rather in the development of "exchange" than in the promise to pay or the "writing obligatory." "Exchange" was at first the simple process of changing coins of one currency against those of another, but there soon grew up an organization of international bankers having agents or correspondents in the principal commercial centres, and these firms, instead of actually delivering coins of one type in exchange for coins of another, would write a letter of exchange to their correspondents, effecting the transfer purely on paper. With an international organization they quickly realized that the transfer of money between various countries could be effected by merely transferring balances, setting off a credit balance in one country against a debit balance in another. A merchant who wished to remit money abroad would therefore address himself most usually to one of these bankers. The remitter A. therefore secures from his banker B. (in exchange for money paid to him) a bill drawn in foreign currency by B. upon C., payable to D. B. and C. are very often partners or agents of the same international bank. Under the ordinary form this arrangement would be embodied in a formal deed. Already in the fourteenth century, however, the formal deed began to be replaced by the informal letter of advice which accompanied it; it is this letter of advice which eventually grew into the modern bill of exchange.

✧

CHAPTER THIRTY

Assignments

. . . The assignee has the same rights to performance as the assignor . . . had. Assuming the contract is one that may be assigned, and that the third party has no defense, the assignee may recover against the party owing the performance.

The Assignment of Benefits under a Contract

ALL OF US are aware that the ownership of tangible property may be transferred from one person to another. For example, transfers of property are most frequently by gift, or sale, or inheritance. However, some of our most valuable rights are often not in the form of tangible property, but rather consist in rights to some future benefit, assured us through a contract. Is it not reasonable to inquire whether or not the expected benefits of one's contract may likewise be transferred? The answer is that many types of future benefit assured by a contract may be transferred, and the transfer of one's benefit under a contract is termed an *assignment* of those benefits. An assignment of a contract benefit may be made as a gift, or may be made in exchange for some consideration (making the transfer, in effect, a sale of the expected contract benefit). In the commercial world, most assignments are made in exchange for consideration.

From what has been said, it should be evident that an assignment always requires the existence of a contract in the first instance. The assignment is the process by which rights accruing under the contract are then transferred from one of the original parties (an assignor) to another party (an assignee).

A simple illustration of a contractual assignment is the transfer of rights provable by an IOU: Jones owes Smith $20 as a result of a prior contract, and has expressed his promise to repay by giving Smith an IOU for that amount. Smith, however, needs funds immediately after this transaction, so he sells the IOU to Brown. Let us say Brown pays $18—having demanded a $2 discount because of the inconvenience and uncertainty of collection. (There need not be any discount. The price is purely a matter of bargaining.) Brown, having bought the IOU, now has the right to collect the original $20, no more and no less, from Jones. Just to make sure no misunderstanding will arise, Brown should advise Jones of the assignment. (Otherwise Jones could hardly be blamed for making payment to the original party to the contract, Smith, and should Smith then disappear, Brown, not Jones, would have to bear the loss.) Upon notification of the assignment of the IOU, Jones is obligated to pay Brown rather than Smith when the payment is due. Brown has legal standing to recover from Jones on the assignment through a contract action, if necessary, to secure collection.

Observe in this case that the similarity between the IOU and personal property is very striking. In one case, we are selling an IOU worth $20; in another case Smith could sell a watch worth $20. The only difference is that the holder probably wishes to convert the IOU to cash and he might be content to keep the watch. If he bought the watch and the IOU both on speculation, either one could be sold to a third party. Sooner or later, however, the IOU will be presented to Jones for payment. The watch need be presented to no one, having value and utility in itself.

The situation is not much more complicated when an IOU is not relied upon as evidence of a debt. Assume Jones and Smith have made a contract in which Smith agrees to deliver a load of corn to Jones, and Jones agrees to pay $20 for the corn. Again, Smith may transfer his right to receive the $20 to Brown, for whatever Brown will pay; let us say $18. Again, the right to receive the $20 from Jones is a clear-cut contract right, assigned to Brown, and operates in exactly the same fashion as the last example. A written instrument, such as an IOU is not essential to effect an assignment, but is often used as a matter of convenience.

How about Jones' side of the contract? Jones has the right to receive a quantity of corn. Could this right be assigned by Jones to some other party? The answer is yes. Most contractual rights may be assigned, although there are exceptions.

The first exception to the general rule that contract rights may be assigned is that rights to personal performance may not be assigned. As an extreme case, the romantic stories in which the prospective bridegroom loses his right to his fiancee's hand in a poker game, and obligates her to marry some lucky winner, never had any legal basis. A promise to marry simply cannot be assigned. Contracts to perform surgical operations and legal or other professional services may not be assigned, nor may an agreement to perform services as a butler, nor for that matter may any form of employment be assigned. So far as the person supposed to perform personal services is concerned, the policy behind this exception is the same as the policy mentioned earlier, forbidding specific performance of personal services. Assignment of personal service contracts would be a form of human bondage, forcing individuals to work for parties for whom the individual might never have contracted to work on his own volition. Inevitably a point is reached where it becomes a question of judgment as to whether services are actually personal services or not. A contract calling for delivery of a load of corn obviously is not a contract involving a personal service, because the corn, not delivery by any particular person, is all that is desired. A contract to act as a butler obviously does require the personal service of a particular person. Contracts involving some types of construction work, as, for example, plumbing or electrical installation, might be viewed as personal services, because a particular individual was named, or as merely contracts in which a particular end is desired that could be produced by any competent workman, depending upon the details.

Another restriction upon the assignment of contract benefits is that any time a contract specifically states that the benefits may not be assigned, this provision will be given effect. Here, then, is a second major limitation upon assignment. Furthermore, the person supposed to perform cannot be held to any duties as a result of an assignment that he was not required to perform for the original party to the contract. Having made his contract in the first instance, the rights of the party required to perform may not be altered by solitary action of the opposite party to the original contract, nor to any other party to whom the benefits may be assigned. In the contract for the sale of corn, Jones, who had the obligation to deliver the corn to Smith, may not be required to deliver the corn to some point more distant than originally agreed upon.

Rights and Duties under an Assignment

What happens if the party to whom the assignment is made (hereafter the assignee) is met by a stubborn refusal to perform on the part of the party owing the obligation? The general rule is that the assignee has the same rights to performance as the assignor (the party who made the assignment) had. Assuming the contract is one that may be assigned, and that the third party has no defense, the assignee may recover against the party owing the performance.

If, on the other hand, the party supposed to have a duty of performance really does not owe any duty because the contract was procured by the original assignor through fraud, duress, or some other contract defense, *the assignee has only the rights of the original assignor.* Stating this general proposition differently, *whatever defenses are good against the assignor are also good against any assignee.*

The next question is, what about the rights of the assignee, who pays for a benefit that turns out to be uncollectible? May he recover against the assignor? At first glance, it would seem that the assignor should be liable, but further consideration suggests that this is not necessarily true. In many instances, both the assignor and the assignee recognize that the claim being assigned may in a practical sense be uncollectible. For example, claims are often assigned to a collection agency for a fraction of their face value, for the very reason that the assignor has been unable to realize upon the claim, and the assignee, the collection agency, well knew this fact at the time it accepted the assignment. There is no reason in this case why the assignor should be held in the event collection is impossible. In the usual case the only warranties that are implied by the assignor are that the right was legally valid, that it was not obtained through fraud, duress, or the like and that he knows of no defenses. In cases where one of these warranties is breached by the assignor, suit by the assignee should be successful. Of course, in cases where an assignment is not transferred for a consideration, but was merely a gift to the assignee from the assignor, no suit would lie against the assignor if the assigned right were uncollectible. The beneficiary may not look the gift horse in the mouth.

Up to this time the discussion has involved the transfer only of contractual benefits. This accounts for only half the picture. In every contract, each party is promised a benefit (the consideration extended by the opposite party), but also each party promises to perform a duty (the consideration he promised to extend to the opposite party). In our last example, Smith had the benefit, a right to receive $20, but had the duty to deliver his load of corn. The question often arises, may Smith transfer his *duty* to deliver the corn to Black? In a sense this may be done, but only within strict limits. This process is called a *delegation*. It is the opposite of an assignment, in the sense that through an assignment a right is transferred to another, whereas through a delegation a *duty* is transferred to another. We will use our previous example to illustrate some problems of delegation.

Smith and Jones have a contract by the terms of which Smith agrees to deliver a load of corn to Jones, and Jones agrees to pay Smith $20. Jones pays Smith $20, fulfilling his obligation under the contract. Smith delegates his duty to Black, agreeing to pay Black in return for Black's promise to deliver the load of corn to Jones. But assuming that Black has agreed to deliver the corn to Jones—does this in itself discharge Smith? To put it another way, if I owe you money, may I cancel my debt merely by getting some third party to *agree* to pay you? May the obligation between two parties to a contract be altered by a later agreement (not yet fulfilled) between one of the parties and some third person?

Clearly this could not be. Contracts would not be worth making if either party could escape responsibility merely by delegating their duties to a party who in turn may never perform. In our example, the situation would be this: Smith may delegate the duty to deliver the corn—that is, Black may agree to deliver the corn for Smith. If Black *does* perform, the contract between Jones and Smith is terminated by performance. If Black does *not* perform, Smith is still liable for his promise to Jones. Stating this as a principle, performance of a contract may be delegated, but the delegation in no way alters the original responsibility of the delegating party. As in the case of assignment, there are many types of contracts that may not be delegated. Professional services of all types are entered into, based upon a favorable opinion as to the special competence of the party engaged, and this performance may not be delegated to some other professional. This, of course, again involves personal service. In any case in which the quality of performance would probably be affected by the characteristics of the individual supposed to perform, the contract may not be delegated. But contracts in which the obligation is merely to deliver a commodity, as Jones' corn or other articles, usually may be delegated.

We have now considered both the assignment of Smith's right to receive $20 from Jones and the delegation of his duty to deliver the corn. Is there any reason why Smith may not simply turn both his rights and duties over to a third party? Suppose he desires to terminate his business. Could he not assign Black the right to the $20, and in addition delegate to Black the duty to deliver the corn? He could, and this is often done. This type of transaction is termed *an assumption* by Black of Smith's contract. However, in some contexts this type of transaction is termed simply an *assignment,* even though it should be distinguished from the usual assignment, which consists only of a transfer of benefits.

Because an assumption merely combines the assignment and the delegation there is nothing new to explain concerning the assumption. Having been assigned the benefits under the original contract, Black would be entitled to recover the payment of $20. Having been delegated the duty to perform, Black is obligated to deliver the corn. Should he fail in the latter, however, Smith is still obligated, because he cannot escape from his responsibility to Jones merely by delegating it to Black.

A common situation, often referred to as an assignment, but really an assumption, is the "assignment" of a lease. Suppose an agreement is entered into by which Smith agrees to pay rent at so much per year to Jones, and in turn he has the right to occupy certain premises. Later, Smith may wish to move elsewhere. Smith and Black may reach an agreement by which Black may assume the lease, receiving the benefits of occupancy and accepting the duty of paying rent to Jones, the landlord. If Black fails to make payment, however, Smith, the original lessee, may be held.

A somewhat different arrangement may be agreed upon between the parties when an operating business is sold. In this case the person selling the business will usually have both debtors and creditors. The buyer may assume all of the debts and receive an assignment of all the credits. The consideration the buyer pays for the business will be related to the relative amounts of debts and credits as well as to the value of the physical assets. Of course, an estimate as to the collectibility of the credits must also be made. Here, as in all the previous examples, the purchaser has the same rights as the seller to collection of the credits assigned. And, if the purchaser fails to pay the outstanding debts he agreed to pay, the seller of the business remains liable on them.

CHAPTER THIRTY-ONE

An Introduction to the Negotiable Instrument

Although most of us, when we dream of wealth, tend to dream of money rather than of negotiable instruments, the truth is that far more wealth is in the form of negotiable instruments than in the form of money. . . .

The Negotiable Instrument: Its Relationship to Contract Law

THE ASSIGNMENT is a process that effects the transfer of ordinary contract rights. Negotiation is also a process that effects the transfer of legal rights, but it is a different process. Only certain distinct types of legal instruments are negotiable. The negotiable instrument is a very special type of contract. In this respect the relationship between the law of negotiable instruments and the law of contracts is somewhat the same as the relationship between the law of sales and the law of contracts: both sales and negotiable instruments build upon the law of contracts, but each has special rules of its own. Each is treated in the UCC. It must be admitted that the law of negotiable instruments is the more specialized of the two; it is more a law unto itself. The negotiable instrument may be described as a network of contractual relationships, tying both the immediate parties and subsequent transferees together into its web of contractual duties.

The Purposes of the Negotiable Instruments

Negotiable instruments have been used in commerce for centuries. Today, they serve two main functions: as substitutes for money, which is

490

the usual function of checks (as well as of bills of exchange, with which the student may not be familiar), and as a means of securing a loan of money, the usual function of a promissory note.

Although most of us, when we dream of wealth, tend to dream of money rather than of negotiable instruments, the truth is that far more wealth is in the form of negotiable instruments than in the form of money. Most of us receive our salary in the form of a negotiable instrument (a check), which we usually deposit in a bank, withdrawing a small amount of cash for pocket money. We pay our bills by check. When we borrow from the bank, we sign a negotiable instrument (a promissory note). The bank then deposits the money we borrowed into a bank account, which again we spend by check. Similar practices are followed by business firms, large and small, and by government at all levels. Profits and losses appear as balances in the bank, usually resulting from check deposits, rather than as a wad of money in some huge corporate safe.

The concept of negotiation has been extended to many types of documents used throughout the commercial world, far beyond its original application to checks, bills of exchange, and notes. For example, most corporate stocks, bills of lading, and warehouse receipts employ the essential principles of negotiability in their transfer procedures, though there are minor differences in the application of these principles in particular cases. In summary, the financial transactions of our economy are performed largely through the use of negotiable instruments.

Through a study of the most fundamental principles of the basic negotiable instruments: the check, the bill of exchange, and the note, a general idea of the implications of negotiability may be gained. This core of understanding will provide a framework which in turn will greatly simplify further study of related problems—for example, the transfer of stocks or bills of lading and warehouse receipts. There are a wide variety of special applications of the general principles of negotiation, but a basic core of central principle. Therefore, this treatment is confined to a discussion of the characteristics of the basic negotiable instruments: the check, the bill, and the note. If these are understood, the variations incorporated into other instruments can be readily learned.

The Comparative Advantages and Disadvantages:
Assignments Versus Negotiable Instruments
Versus Money

Money, a medium of exchange, is issued by national governments. An important characteristic of money is that anyone having possession, whether or not he has the right (that is, title) to the money, may *transfer* title to an innocent party, by simple transfer of possession of the money. This is not true of most forms of property. Normally, a person in possession of property can pass no better title than he has. Title to stolen money may be transferred by a thief to an unsuspecting party even though the thief himself lacks legal title.

This ease of transfer is an advantage in many respects. A merchant acquires title to money received in payment of goods he sells even if the customer has stolen or found the money (unless the merchant has actual notice that the money came to the buyer illegally). This would be true even though the rightful owner of the money could later identify it by serial number or by markings on the bills. The rightful owner could recover the stolen money from the thief himself if it were still in the possession of the thief, but he could not recover it from an innocent third party who had accepted it. The fact that an innocent receiver of money can be certain that he has title renders money highly acceptable in day-to-day business. Yet the very ease of transfer, which is money's great advantage, is also at times a disadvantage. The same merchant who receives money that, unknown to him, has been stolen may himself be the victim of theft or loss, and his claim to his own money is lost as soon as it is transferred to another innocent recipient. For this reason sums of money must be handled with great care. Money has other disadvantages in being clumsy to handle, in requiring careful counting, and in not providing any proof of payment in itself.

We have found that some rights may be transferred by assignment. An assignment has few of the disadvantages of money, but it also has few of the advantages. A simple contractual promise to pay, an IOU, cannot be utilized very well as a substitute for money. An IOU could be assigned from one party to another, and presented for payment to the promisor by the ultimate assignee. The trouble with assignments, as we have seen, is that through an assignment, the assignee gets *only* the rights of the assignor. Any defenses that bar collection by the assignor will also bar collection by any subsequent assignee. Therefore, a merchant will not ordinarily accept an assignment in payment for goods. In order to be safe in accepting an assignment as payment, a merchant would have to inquire carefully into the nature of the transaction between the original parties to the contract. Even then there may be a defense, such as fraud practiced upon the signer of the IOU, not yet revealed but which could rear its ugly head later.

All the same we should not lose sight of a desirable feature of the assignment, which is that transfer may only be made through an *intentional* delivery. A thief or finder of an IOU acquires nothing of value to him because the promisor who issued the IOU is entitled to ask how the holder came into possession, and need not pay if the IOU was lost by, or stolen from, any rightful holder.

This brings us to the principal advantage in the use of negotiable instruments; they provide a means of transfer of rights which is similar to an assignment but in which a third party recipient *usually acquires better rights to collection* than the party who took under the original contract. If a third party can be reasonably sure that he will have the right to collect on an instrument, regardless of disputes between the original parties to the contract, third parties will be much more likely to accept the instrument than they would an ordinary assignment. This is, in essence, what a negotiable instrument does. The gist of a negotiable instrument is that an innocent third party (termed a *holder in due course*) who takes a negotiable instrument without knowledge of any defects has *greater* rights to collection than the party to whom the instrument is first given (called *the payee*). Regardless of a breach of contract or other similar defense by the party to whom the instrument is issued, the third party (holder in due course) is entitled to collect upon his instrument.

Other advantages in the use of negotiable instruments are that their use largely eliminates the dangers of loss or theft that exist when using money; and the burdensome housekeeping chores of counting money and providing physical storage are reduced. A check for $11,433.12 provides in itself assurance that it is for that exact amount much more readily than a pile of currency and coin. This amount is represented by one small piece of paper, and it need not be counted. There is no limit to how much currency may be represented by a small, convenient slip of paper. It can be in a form whereby, if lost or stolen, it will be uncollectible by the thief or finder. In addition, a negotiable instrument, when paid, acts as a receipt for payment of a transaction. Probably all of us have at one time or another dug through our canceled checks to establish that a questionable charge had indeed been paid. In the case of other types of negotiable instruments, it is the normal procedure for a note to be stamped "paid" and returned to the party obligated when his obligation is discharged. The returned instrument will always act as a receipt of payment, and return of an instrument must, therefore, always be insisted upon when payment is made.

CHAPTER THIRTY-TWO

When Is an Instrument Negotiable?

. . . The form of an instrument determines whether or not it is negotiable. If it is, all the special incidents of a negotiable instrument come into play. If the third party is a holder in due course, he can overcome most defenses based upon the contract between the original two parties.

Introduction: The Development of Ideas in This and Succeeding Chapters

BECAUSE the unique characteristic of a negotiable instrument is in providing certain third-party holders of an instrument with special rights to collection, the concern of most fundamental importance is to know when a third party may have this unusual and significant right. In order to answer this question we need to know three things. First, is a legal instrument in the form required to make it negotiable? (The balance of this chapter will deal with this question.) Second, did the circumstances surrounding the transfer of the instrument from the payee to the third person satisfy the legal requirements of a negotiation? (This process of transfer is considered in Chapter 33, which follows.) Third, and finally, assuming the form of the instrument to be correct, and the method of transfer to be proper, what additional circumstances must be present for a party to have the rights of a holder in due course? (This is considered in Chapter 34 of this section.)

These three questions form a theoretical framework upon which the student may fit more detailed information. There are many facts to be learned about negotiable instruments. Yet facts unrelated to a logical framework but merely considered as isolated bits of information are worthless.

494

Requirements of Form

Some definite means must be provided for distinguishing which instruments are negotiable and which are not. The means used to distinguish negotiable instruments from nonnegotiable instruments is by requiring that instruments, in order to be negotiable, adhere to a certain form. An instrument, when created according to the set form, *will* be negotiable, regardless of what the creator may have intended. The form of an instrument, then, determines quite arbitrarily the incidents that follow.

COMMERCIAL CREDIT CORPORATION v. *ORANGE COUNTY MACHINE WORKS* (California, 1949) 208 P 2d 780

> *The application of the rules applicable to negotiable instruments . . . sometimes causes hardship. . . . But the primary purpose of the law-merchant is to make commercial paper serve in lieu of money.*

[EDITOR'S NOTE: The cases in this section refer to the Uniform Negotiable Instruments Law (hereafter abbreviated NIL in the text following), which was formerly in force in all states but has been superseded by the UCC in those states adopting the latter act. Differences between the two acts are not very great, and lacking many decided cases under the UCC, cases decided under the NIL will in most instances serve just as well to illustrate the issues of law here involved.]

(3, 4) The second contention (that the instrument was not negotiable) fails also because in applying the law-merchant, codified in California in our Civil Code, and generally following the Negotiable Instruments Law now adopted by every state in the Union, certain arbitrary rules must be applied. The application of the rules applicable to negotiable instruments in particular cases sometimes causes hardship and loss to individuals, as defendant earnestly argues to be the fact in this case. But the primary purpose of the law-merchant is to make commercial paper serve in lieu of money. This being the case, when one executes and delivers an instrument containing the elements of negotiability as prescribed by the Negotiable Instruments Law, and when that instrument passes into the hands of a holder in due course, it is the making of the instrument and the placing of it in the channels of commerce which set in motion a chain of circumstances peculiar to the law-merchant. In this case the defendant made, executed, and delivered the promissory note—put it into circulation as a substitute for money.

✧

As this case demonstrates, the form of an instrument determines whether or not it is negotiable. If it is, all the special incidents of a negotiable instrument come into play. If the third party is a holder in due course (discussed in detail in Chapter 34, he can overcome most defenses based upon the contract between the original two parties. These would include breach of contract or fraud in securing the contract, by the original party to the contract who received the negotiable instrument in payment. Lacking some reason for doubting the validity of the instrument, the holder will be assumed to be a holder in due course (until proved otherwise), and the fact that the *original* transaction is still only executory (that is, has not been performed) is no defense.

Two-Party and Three-Party Instruments

Negotiable instruments are divisible into two major categories: two-party instruments and three-party instruments. The oldest and most important two-party instrument is the promissory note.[1] The person issuing the note is called the *maker,* and the person to whom the note is made is called the *payee.*

Bills of exchange and drafts (hereafter collectively termed *bills*) are different names for one form of three-party instrument. The check is the other form of three-party instrument. Bills are instruments in which one party, termed the *drawer,* orders another, termed the *drawee,* to pay a third party, the *payee.* The same parties appear on a check, the basic distinction being that the drawee of a check is always a bank.

The basic types of instruments and the parties to each *must be learned* before further progress in understanding negotiable instruments may be made.

The various types of negotiable instrument are described in the UCC as follows:

UCC—SECTION 3–104: . . . "Draft"; "Check"; "Certificate of Deposit"; "Note."
(2) A writing which complies with the requirements of this section is
(a) a "draft" ("bill of exchange") if it is an order;
(b) a "check" if it is a draft drawn on a bank and payable on demand;
(c) a "certificate of deposit" if it is an acknowledgment by a bank of receipt of money with an engagement to repay it;
(d) a "note" if it is a promise other than a certificate of deposit.

---

[1] The bond, including the corporate bond, is merely a variation of the note. Bonds are distinguished only in that we usually think of them as being issued in large offerings, and usually have the general assets of a corporation behind them. The certificate of deposit is another form of two-party instrument. This instrument is issued by a bank following the deposit of funds for a period of time. Should the depositor wish to make use of the funds, he may negotiate the certificate of deposit to a third party, instead of withdrawing the money from the bank.

Rules for Drafting a Negotiable Instrument

The requirements to which any negotiable instrument, whether two-party or three-party, must adhere are set out in the following section of the UCC:

> UCC—SECTION 3–104: Form of Negotiable Instruments; . . .
> (1) Any writing to be a negotiable instrument within this Article must
> (a) be signed by the maker or drawer; and
> (b) contain an unconditional promise or order to pay a sum certain in money and no other promise, order, obligation or power given by the maker or drawer except as authorized by this Article; and
> (c) be payable on demand or at a definite time; and
> (d) be payable to order or to bearer.

A negotiable instrument must be in writing, must be payable in money, and must be signed by the person putting it into circulation, the maker or drawer, and the promise to pay must be unconditional. If the instrument is a two-party instrument, the issuing party is the maker, and he must promise unconditionally to pay the face value. If a three-party instrument, the issuing party is the drawer, and he must unconditionally order the drawee to pay the face value.

UNCONDITIONAL PROMISE OR ORDER TO PAY

Mere expressions of intention by a maker to pay his note or a mere request of a drawee to pay a bill are not unconditional, and therefore such wording will not create a negotiable instrument. Many difficult and important problems arise concerning other aspects of the question as to whether a promise is unconditional. Doubt frequently arises when detailed statements of the transaction under question are attached to the instrument. So ... statements attached do not restrict the rights of a holder in any ... special conditions to collection, the instrument is ... when reference is made to other ... that the rights of a holder are ... dered nonnegotiable. This is be- ... cannot fully ascertain his rights ... s, which in turn inhibit free circu- ... y not have access to the extrane- ... be able to ascertain his rights to ... be determinable, as to their obliga-

UCC—Section 3–105: When Promise or Order Unconditional.

(1) A promise or order otherwise unconditional is not made conditional by the fact that the instrument

(a) is subject to implied or constructive conditions; or

(b) states its consideration, whether performed or promised, or the transaction which gave rise to the instrument, or that the promise or order is made or the instrument matures in accordance with or "as per" such transaction; or

(c) refers to or states that it arises out of a separate agreement; or

(d) states that it is drawn under a letter of credit; or

(e) states that it is secured, whether by mortgage, reservation of title or otherwise; or

(f) indicates a particular account to be debited or any other fund or source from which reinbursement is expected; or

(g) is limited to payment out of a particular fund or the proceeds of a particular source, if the instrument is issued by a government or governmental agency or unit; or

(h) is limited to payment out of the entire assets of a partnership, unincorporated association, trust or estate by or on behalf of which the instrument is issued.

(2) A promise or order is not unconditional if the instrument

(a) states that it is subject to or governed by any other agreement; or

(b) states that it is to be paid only out of a particular fund or source except as provided in this section.

OBLIGATIONS MUST BE FOR A SUM CERTAIN IN MONEY

The first of these requirements, that the obligation be for a sum certain, is imposed for the simple reason that obligations could hardly be transferable were they not for some definite sum. The second has given rise to more dispute, some cases under the NIL holding that obligations due in foreign money were negotiable, and should be paid off in the appropriate foreign money. The UCC position on this question, enumerated below, serves the function of settling this question in a reasonable way, and in a way convenient to those engaged in commerce.

UCC—Section 3–106: Sum Certain.

(1) The sum payable is a sum certain even though it is to be pai[d]

(a) with stated interest or by stated installments; or

(b) with stated different rates of interest before and after de[fault or] a specified date; or

(c) with a stated discount or addition if paid before or a[fter the date] fixed for payment; or

(d) with exchange or less exchange, whether at a fixed rate or at the current rate; or

(e) with costs of collection or an attorney's fee or both upon default.

(2) Nothing in this section shall validate any term which is otherwise illegal.

UCC—SECTION 3–107: Money.

(1) An instrument is payable in money if the medium of exchange in which it is payable is money at the time the instrument is made. An instrument payable in "currency" or "current funds" is payable in money.

(2) A promise or order to pay a sum stated in a foreign currency is for a sum certain in money and, unless a different medium of payment is specified in the instrument, may be satisfied by payment of that number of dollars which the stated foreign currency will purchase at the buying sight rate for that currency on the day on which the instrument is payable, or, if payable on demand, on the day of demand. If such an instrument specifies a foreign currency as the medium of payment the instrument is payable in that currency.

OBLIGATIONS PAYABLE ON DEMAND OR AT A DEFINITE TIME

Although there need not be any statement on the instrument as to when payment will take place, payment may not be made conditional upon events that are not certain to happen. If no time is stated, it is presumed payable on demand. A statement promising payment when one fulfills his contract with another party makes payment conditional (it is not *certain* to happen) and renders an instrument nonnegotiable.

Many negotiable instruments contain a provision that if some event occurs, the face amount of the instrument will become payable immediately upon that occurrence. Often the designated event is failure to make a payment of principal or interest on the instrument or upon the loss or destruction of security. A provision of this type is termed an *acceleration clause*. Although some types of acceleration clause were the subject of considerable debate under the NIL, under the UCC an acceleration clause does not render an instrument nonnegotiable as not being due at a fixed time. These clauses are viewed as being payable, at the outside, on the date stated by the instrument, with the possibility existing that a holder may be entitled to payment earlier—that is, should the clause go into effect. In that event it merely becomes a demand instrument.

UCC—SECTION 3–108: Payable on Demand.

Instruments payable on demand include those payable at sight or on presentation and those in which no time for payment is stated.

UCC—Section 3–109: Definite Time.

(1) An instrument is payable at a definite time if by its terms it is payable

(a) on or before a stated date or at a fixed period after a stated date; or

(b) at a fixed period after sight; or

(c) at a definite time subject to any acceleration; or

(d) at a definite time subject to extension at the option of the holder, or to extension to a further definite time at the option of the maker or acceptor or automatically upon or after a specified act or event.

(2) An instrument which by its terms is otherwise payable only upon an act or event uncertain as to time or occurrence is not payable at a definite time even though the act or event has occurred.

PAYABLE TO ORDER OR TO BEARER

To be negotiable, a legal instrument must be made payable ". . . to order of" or ". . . to bearer." These are termed the *words of negotiation.* The presence of these words indicates an intent that the instrument be negotiable, and failure to include these words indicates the opposite.

There is an important difference between instruments payable "to bearer" and those payable "to order." Instruments payable to bearer on their face are transferred in the same way as money. Title may pass by simple delivery to another party, and an innocent transferee gains title even though the transferor himself had no title. An instrument payable to order requires the indorsement of the payee before it may be negotiated. If lost or stolen before indorsed, legal title to the instrument will not pass. A forged indorsement is of no more value to the transferee of the instrument than is counterfeit money.

The following sections of the UCC explain, qualify, or elaborate upon the requirement that a negotiable instrument must be payable to order or to bearer. No doubt the most usual situation involving order instruments is that mentioned below at (1)(c).

UCC—Section 3–110: Payable to Order.

(1) An instrument is payable to order when by its terms it is payable to the order or assigns of any person therein specified with reasonable certainty, or to him or his order, or when it is conspicuously designated on its face as "exchange" or the like and names a payee. It may be payable to the order of

(a) the maker or drawer; or

(b) the drawee; or

(c) a payee who is not maker, drawer or drawee; or

(d) two or more payees together or in the alternative; or

(e) an estate, trust or fund, in which case it is payable to the order of the representative of such estate, trust or fund or his successors; or

(f) an office, or an officer by his title as such in which case it is payable to the principal but the incumbent of the office or his successors may act as if he or they were the holder; or

(g) a partnership or unincorporated association, in which case it is payable to the partnership or association and may be indorsed or transferred by any person thereto authorized.

(2) An instrument not payable to order is not made so payable by such words as "payable upon return of this instrument properly indorsed."

(3) An instrument made payable both to order and to bearer is payable to order unless the bearer words are handwritten or typewritten.

UCC—SECTION 3–111: Payable to Bearer.

An instrument is payable to bearer when by its terms it is payable to

(a) bearer or the order of bearer; or

(b) a specified person or bearer; or

(c) "cash" or the order of "cash," or any other indication which does not purport to designate a specific payee.

BADER v. WILLIAMS (District of Columbia, 1948)
61 A 2d 637

> *The Code requires that a negotiable promissory instrument contain an unconditional promise or order to pay a certain sum in money on demand or at a fixed or determinable future time to order or to bearer. While some courts have held to the contrary, the general rule is that an instrument which does not contain these essentials is merely an acknowledgment of a debt and not a good negotiable instrument.*

Appellant sued appellee for the full amount of an "I.O.U." signed by appellee and her husband on account of money previously advanced as part of the purchase price of a restaurant business to be conducted as a joint enterprise by the husband and appellant. The case was tried to a jury, but at the close of the evidence the trial court directed a verdict for appellee. This appeal is from the judgment entered on such directed verdict.

The "I.O.U." sued upon was as follows:

Glenn E. Bader
April 12, 1947
I.O.U. 2165.55 for
Business Expense at
4408 Arkansas Ave.
(Signed) Carl N. Williams
(Signed) Frances H. Williams

(1, 2) Appellant urges, first, that the instrument sued on was a negotiable promissory instrument so as to make applicable the provision of the Uniform Negotiable Instruments Law providing that such an instrument is deemed prima facie to have been issued for a valuable consideration. We can not agree with this contention. The Code requires that a negotiable promissory instrument contain an unconditional promise or order to pay a certain sum in money on demand or at a fixed or determinable future time to order or to bearer. While some courts have held to the contrary, the general rule is that an instrument which does not contain these essentials is merely an acknowledgment of a debt and not a good negotiable instrument. As the instrument here in question does not comply with these requirements, none of the statutory presumptions of the Negotiable Instruments Act, such as that of valuable consideration urged by appellant, are applicable in this case.

This case illustrates one important difference between a negotiable instrument and a simple acknowledgment of indebtedness. Had this instrument been in negotiable form, the presumption would have been that the note had been issued for consideration, and lack of consideration would have had to be proved by the defendant. Not being negotiable, the existence of consideration must be proved by the plaintiff. Thus, the burden of proof as to consideration is shifted when a note is negotiable.

Had this instrument been negotiable, but in the hands of a holder in due course, the issue of consideration would be immaterial. The holder in due course of a *negotiable* instrument may recover even if a contract defense between the maker and payee (such as lack of consideration) is proved.

Considering that the maker of a negotiable instrument is in effect waiving many possible defenses, why would a party issue a negotiable instrument? He would *seem* to be in a better position issuing a nonnegotiable instrument, and this is, in fact, true. However, most businessmen would ordinarily refuse to accept any instrument other than one that is negotiable. They would naturally prefer to avail themselves of the special benefits a negotiable instrument provides a holder.

QUESTIONS

1. What would you think of the advisability of accepting an instrument worded identically to the one here in question, with the statement added "This instrument is negotiable."

2. Why does not the law simply consider every commercial instrument negotiable?

CHAPTER THIRTY-THREE

Requirements of Issue, Transfer, and Negotiation

The main significance of being a holder is that, if certain additional conditions are fulfilled, the holder may be a holder in due course. If the transferee is not a holder, he cannot be a holder in due course. The key to determining whether or not a negotiation has occurred, and therefore whether the transferee is a holder, lies in understanding when an indorsement is necessary to negotiation, and when it is not.

Transfer

AS WE HAVE SEEN, the first question to be asked in any problem dealing with the collectibility of a negotiable instrument should be "Is the instrument negotiable in form?" Assuming that this question is answered in the affirmative, the next question is "Has the instrument actually been negotiated?"

Negotiation takes place when an instrument, negotiable in form, is transferred from one party to another, and when the circumstances surrounding that transfer meet a number of special requirements. Therefore, once it is established that an instrument is negotiable, the study of negotiation revolves around the question, what special requirements must be met for a transfer to constitute a negotiation, and have these requirements been met?

Strangely the word *transfer* is not defined at all in the UCC, though the word is frequently used. Possibly *transfer* is not defined because it is used in an ordinary, nontechnical sense. As used in the UCC *transfer* seems to have the broadest meaning, encompassing several processes by which an instrument is intentionally conveyed from one person to another. And although it is not defined, the ramifications of transfer are elaborated upon, as follows:

503

UCC—Section 3–201: Transfer.
(1) Transfer of an instrument *vests in the transferee such rights as the transferor has therein,* except . . . [the exception will be considered later].

So we may assume that ordinarily, no matter what the form of transfer, the transferee gains at least the right, if any, of the transferor. We will find that often the transferee gains greater rights than those of the transferor.

Let us proceed from the general term *transfer* to more particular types of transfer. The first of these is *issue.*

ISSUE

Ordinarily the process of getting a negotiable instrument into the hands of a holder in due course is a two-step process. The first step generally involves a transfer between the maker (of a note) or drawer (of a bill or check) or an authorized agent for either, and the payee. This process is known as the *issue of a negotiable instrument.*

UCC—Section 3–102: Definitions and Index of Definitions.
(1) an "Issue" means the *first* delivery [1] of an instrument to a holder or remitter.

All that is required for a proper issue is a physical transfer to the payee plus, ordinarily, the intent to transfer.

Although is is possible for an instrument to be made up and in some way transferred to a payee unintentionally, thus presenting the question of whether or not a valid issue has occurred, this is a problem that is so rare we may leave the problem for attorneys to solve when and if it does arise. This problem will not arise if order instruments are not prepared until immediately before delivery to the payee, and if bearer instruments are kept in the possession of the maker or drawer, until he is ready to deliver them. In addition, one might carefully scrutinize one's business operation to determine if there is not some way by which order instruments, which are by far the more safe, might not serve in place of bearer instruments.

Another question concerning issue is, may the payee ever be a holder in due course? He may, but we are getting ahead of ourselves. This subject will be dealt with after we have discussed the topics of the holder, of negotiation, and of the holder in due course.

---

[1] Delivery is defined by the UCC as follows (Section 1–201. General Definitions): "(14) 'Delivery' with respect to instruments, . . . means *voluntary* transfer of possession." (Italics ours.)

NEGOTIATION

We now turn from issue to still another, and highly significant, form of transfer, the negotiation. *Negotiation* is defined by the UCC as follows:

UCC—SECTION 3–202: Negotiation.

(1) Negotiation is the transfer of an instrument in such a manner that the transferee becomes a holder. If the instrument is payable to order it is negotiated by delivery with any *necessary* (italics ours) indorsement; if payable to bearer it is negotiated by delivery.

(2) An indorsement must be written by or on behalf of the holder and on the instrument or on a paper so firmly attached thereto as to become a part thereof.

THE HOLDER

Thus, several new terms are closely related. Negotiation is a process, achieved in some instances by delivery of an instrument with a *necessary* indorsement, and in other instances by delivery *without* an indorsement. Further discussion is necessary to delineate when an indorsement is necessary and when it is not. But if the requisites of negotiation are present, the person taking through this process is a holder.

The main significance of being a holder is that, if certain additional conditions are fulfilled, the holder may be a holder in due course. If the transferee is not a holder, he cannot be a holder in due course. The key to determining whether or not a negotiation has occurred, and therefore whether the transferee is a holder, lies in understanding when an indorsement is necessary to negotiation and when it is not. We shall therefore turn our attention to this subject.

Indorsements

An indorsement is necessary to effect a negotiation when the instrument is (1) an order instrument on its face—that is, when the wording on the face of the instrument reads "pay to the order of Jones"—and when the instrument has no indorsements on the back. To negotiate this instrument, not only must it be indorsed, but it must be indorsed by one specific person, Jones, and this means the Jones the maker or drawer had in mind. The signature of this Jones, therefore, is a necessary indorsement, as referred to in UCC—SECTION 3–202.

Presumably, an instrument of this kind would be placed in the hands of the payee, Jones. In order for this instrument to be negotiated on to another party, Jones would have to indorse the instrument.

THE SPECIAL INDORSEMENT

(2) Another instance in which an indorsement is *necessary* for negotiation, under UCC—SECTION 3–202 arises when an instrument *whether bearer on its face or order on its face* has as its last (most recent) indorsement a special indorsement. An indorsement "Pay to the order of J. Jones" on the back of an instrument would constitute a special indorsement.

The presence of this form of indorsement means that someone's indorsement will be necessary before further negotiation will be possible, regardless of whether the instrument was order or bearer on its face.

> UCC—SECTION 3–204: Special Indorsement.
> (1) A special indorsement specifies the person to whom or to whose order it makes the instrument payable. Any instrument specially indorsed becomes payable to the order of the special indorsee and may be further negotiated only by his indorsement.

The purpose of the special indorsement is to provide a means by which an instrument may be negotiated while at the same time preserving its "order" character (assuming the instrument was an order instrument before the special indorsement). If an instrument was a bearer instrument prior to the special indorsement, the special indorsement provides a means by which the instrument may be negotiated while at the same time converting the instrument to an order instrument. The advantage to either maintaining the "order" character of the instrument, or to changing the instrument from "bearer" to "order," is that when it is "order" even if the instrument is lost or stolen only the party to whom it is indorsed may transfer it further. His is the indorsement necessary to further negotiation. A bearer instrument may be negotiated without indorsement.

THE RESTRICTIVE INDORSEMENT

(3) The third instance in which an indorsement is necessary for negotiation under UCC—SECTION 3–202 arises when an instrument, whether bearer on its face or order on its face has as its last indorsement a restrictive indorsement. The restrictive indorsement is peculiar in a number of respects. For one thing, the necessary indorsement may not require the signature of a particular individual, but may merely call for someone in a particular position. An indorsement "pay to any bank or banker" is a restrictive indorsement, but any bank or banker can provide the necessary

indorsement. In general, restrictive indorsements are used with the intent that the circulation of the instrument be limited, though as seen below a restrictive indorsement does not absolutely guarantee this will be the case. (See UCC—SECTION 3–206.) Thus, after a bank or banker took the instrument indorsed "pay to any bank or banker" he could theoretically negotiate the instrument on to anyone willing to accept it. In practice, however, the bank almost invariably would send the instrument through banking channels to the drawee bank for collection.

UCC—SECTION 3–205: Restrictive Indorsements.
An indorsement is restrictive which either
(a) is conditional; or
(b) purports to prohibit further transfer of the instrument; or
(c) includes the words "for collection," "for deposit," "pay any bank," or like terms signifying a purpose of deposit or collection; or
(d) otherwise states that it is for the benefit or use of the indorser or of another person.

One common form of restrictive indorsement is used by a party wishing his check to be deposited to his account in a particular bank.

For deposit only, in the First National Bank of Podunk
/s/ John Jones

With this indorsement, one may safely mail the check to the bank for deposit, though one should never mail a check with a blank indorsement.

An even more common type of restrictive indorsement, the example given earlier, is used by a bank accepting and paying a check drawn on another bank. Often checks will go through one or more intermediate banks before accounts are settled between the bank paying the check to the holder and the bank holding the drawer's account. For this reason, the bank paying the check usually stamps the check with the restrictive indorsement:

Pay to any bank or banker
First National Bank of Podunk

Each succeeding bank usually indorses checks received and sent on to other banks in this fashion, until the check reaches the drawer's bank for collection.

The restrictive indorsement prevents *the first taker* from becoming a holder in due course unless he meets the terms of the restriction. Thus, in our first example above, the parties who might qualify as a holder in due course are limited to those who are banks or bankers. It is important to remember that only the first taker is inhibited by a restrictive indorsement. This is logical, because almost any taker, even a bank other than the depositor's bank, is going to wish to negotiate the instrument on for purposes of collection. If a restrictive indorsement forbade negotiation beyond the first taker, he would have no assurance of recovering the value of the instrument. This point is emphasized because there had been considerable confusion as to the rights of the taker of a restrictive indorsement under the older Negotiable Instruments Law.

UCC—SECTION 3–206: Effect of Restrictive Indorsement.

(1) No restrictive indorsement prevents further transfer or negotiation of the instrument.

.   .   .

(3) Except for an intermediary bank, any transferee under an indorsement which is conditional or includes the words "for collection," "for deposit," "pay to any bank," or like terms . . . must pay or apply any value given by him for or on the security of the instrument consistently with the endorsement and to the extent that he does so he becomes a holder in due course if he otherwise complies with the requirements of . . . a holder in due course.

(4) . . . A later holder for value is neither given notice nor otherwise affected by such restrictive indorsement unless he has knowledge that a fiduciary or other person has negotiated the instrument in any transaction for his own benefit or otherwise in breach of duty. . . .

To recapitulate, an indorsement *is necessary* (1) when an instrument is an order instrument on its face and has never been indorsed; (2) when the latest indorsement was a special indorsement no matter whether the instrument is bearer or order on its face; (3) when the latest indorsement was a restrictive indorsement no matter whether order or bearer on its face.

THE BLANK INDORSEMENT

Let us now turn to the instances in which an indorsement is *not necessary* in order to effect a negotiation, and therefore to constitute the transferee a holder. The first instance is when the instrument is a bearer instrument on its face and has never been indorsed. As stated earlier, a bearer instrument resembles currency, in that negotiation consists in mere delivery to a third party. Any transferee of a bearer instrument is a holder.

The second instance in which indorsement is not necessary in order to effect a negotiation, and therefore to constitute the transferee a holder, arises *any time* the latest indorsement is in blank, or "to order of bearer," no matter whether the instrument is bearer or order on its face. The blank indorsement is treated as follows in the UCC.

> UCC—SECTION 3–204: Blank Indorsement.
> (2) An indorsement in blank specifies no particular indorsee and may consist of a mere signature. An instrument payable to order and indorsed in blank becomes payable to bearer and may be negotiated by delivery alone until specially indorsed.

A blank indorsement consists of a signature only, with no further qualifying words. Thus *John A. Jones* is a blank indorsement. The effect of the last indorser's indorsing an order instrument in blank is to change it from an order instrument into a bearer instrument. Everyone knows this in a general way. The student has no doubt been warned not to indorse his check until he is ready to cash it. The effect of indorsing the check in blank is to change it to a bearer instrument, and a bearer instrument, it will be recalled, can be negotiated onto succeeding parties by mere delivery, just like money. It may also be negotiated by a thief or a finder. A bearer instrument will, of course, continue to be a bearer instrument if the last indorsement is in blank.

The requirements necessary to constitute a transferee a holder are summarized by the UCC as follows:

> UCC—SECTION 1–201: General Definitions.
> (20) "Holder" means a person who is in possession of . . . an instrument . . . drawn, issued, or indorsed to him or to his order or in blank.

All of what has been said relating to indorsements is summarized in these few words, but without some elaboration, these few words are not so self-explanatory as to adequately convey the concepts involved.[2]

---

[2] [*Editor's Note:* Although the matter is discussed elsewhere, it is reasonable for an alert student to inquire at this juncture, what happens if an instrument is stolen and a necessary indorsement is forged? A forgery may result in transfer of the instrument in a physical sense, but not in the taker being a holder, as defined by SECTION 3–202. The rightful holder, who has been deprived of the instrument prior to his indorsing, should report the loss to the drawee or maker. The drawee or maker will then refuse to pay the instrument upon presentment. It doesn't matter *who* presents the instrument when the forgery comes to light. No one tracing their title back to the forger can claim valid title. If several successive parties have negotiated the instrument following the forgery, each holder can demand repayment from an earlier holder, until the instru-

One might well inquire why (if as recently stated) a bearer instrument need not be indorsed at all in order to negotiate it to a holder, it is still sometimes indorsed in blank. Although an indorsement is not necessary for the purpose of negotiation, nevertheless certain other incidents stem from the act of indorsement. Specifically, an indorsement extends some warranties (considered later) to all subsequent parties to the instrument. Therefore, the quality of any instrument, bearer, or order is improved by each indorsement. Many and probably most transferees of a bearer instrument will therefore insist upon having the indorsement of the transferor, even though negotiation may be accomplished without indorsement.

Summarizing the relationship between the indorsement and the original character of the instrument—that is, whether order or bearer on its face—the original character will control until there is an indorsement. However, regardless of whether order or bearer on its face, the latest indorsement will be controlling and will determine whether or not at that time a further indorsement will be necessary to effect a negotiation, and thereby render the transferee a holder.

Possibly a word should be interjected at this point to bring one issue into perspective: what exactly is the significance of being a holder in due course rather than merely a holder? In the ordinary case, where all parties have dealt honestly and without misunderstanding, the difference will probably not be important. The holder will be able to collect on his instrument. It is only the exceptional case, where the party expected to pay asserts a defense against the holder that the difference becomes important. In that event, however, a mere holder may well not succeed in collecting, and a holder in due course probably will. It is exactly this type of situation which provides the rationale behind the concept of negotiation.

THE PROBLEM OF THE IMPOSTOR

A source of perplexing problems that caused much difference in opinion and in judicial decision under the NIL has hopefully been settled by the following sections of the UCC. A number of important business problems may be involved. Perhaps the most serious situation arises when an employee with access to payroll records manages to include the names of a number of nonexistent persons on a corporate payroll, along with addresses from which the employee may secure the paychecks when mailed.

---

ment is back in the hands of the party who took from the forger. He can demand payment from the forger, but usually the forger is difficult to locate. Thus, the party accepting an instrument from a forger is usually the party to absorb the loss. This is one reason behind the slogan "Know Your Indorser." The party from whom the instrument was stolen, or who lost it, is entitled to the instrument, and is entitled to collect when due from the drawee or maker.]

The employee, of course, then indorses the checks as payee, using the opportune name, and retains the proceeds. The question is, should the signature of a nonexistent person (if there really is such a person as named, he is certainly not the one the employer had in mind) be considered a forgery? A forgery does not pass title, and the effect of considering a signature of this sort a forgery would be to throw the loss upon the transferee. The trouble with this approach, in turn, would be that the employer, in failing to maintain internal controls adequate to discover defalcations of his employees, and proceeding to issue an instrument to a party not even an employee, is more at fault than the transferee who accepts the instrument from the bogus payee. For this reason, the burden of any losses is placed upon the employer issuing the instrument, and as a matter of law the effect is easily reached merely by treating the indorsement of the dishonest employee as being effective.

This situation is dealt with in UCC—Section 3–405 (c). A variation of the pattern occurs when the plot becomes thicker, and the party actually authorized to make out the employer's negotiable instruments makes them out to nonexistent parties and then negotiates them himself. Finally, there is the situation in which a party acts in a more straightforward manner as an impostor. He merely states he is the Mr. Smith to whom a check is owed, which is then handed to him by a payroll check; or he effects the same result through the mail or by telephone. Under these circumstances, his indorsement will constitute a valid transfer of the instrument. The reason is the same: again the transferee taking from the impostor is far less culpable than the party whose negligence made the deception against the taker possible.

These questions are treated by the UCC as follows:

UCC—Section 3–405: Impostors; Signature in Name of Payee.
(1) An indorsement by any person in the name of a named payee is effective if
(a) an impostor by use of the mails or otherwise has induced the maker or drawer to issue the instrument to him or his confederate in the name of the payee; or
(b) a person signing as or on behalf of a maker or drawer intends the payee to have no interest in the instrument; or
(c) an agent or employee of the maker or drawer has supplied him with the name of the payee intending the latter to have no such interest.
(2) Nothing in this section shall affect the criminal or civil liability of the person so indorsing.

CHAPTER THIRTY-FOUR

The Holder in Due Course: His Rights and Rights Deriving from Him

Negotiable instrument probably would not in many cases be acceptable to third parties at all if it were not for the protection afforded by their being a holder in due course.

Qualifications of a Holder in Due Course

LET US NOW shift our attention back to the holder, the party who holds an instrument as a result of a negotiation. What are his rights? To answer this question we need still more information. If a holder meets certain tests he is a *holder in due course*. The holder in due course has the special rights we have referred to previously. He is able to sue and collect against the maker or drawee [1] of a negotiable instrument, and to recover, despite a defense based upon the contract between the maker (or drawer) and the payee, even though the defense would be an effective defense if the suit were brought against the maker (or drawee) by a holder *not* a holder in due course.

How does one qualify as a holder in due course? Essentially he must be innocent in the sense of not being aware of any wrongful conduct on the part of previous parties to the instrument and of being unaware of any defects or irregularities in the instrument. He must also have given some value for the instrument, but need not have paid the face value. The requirements of the holder in due course are set out in the UCC as follows.

[1] A discussion as to who is liable on a bill is taken up in the following chapter. Usually the drawee is liable; but at other times the drawer or an indorser is.

512

UCC—SECTION 3–302: Holder in Due Course.
(1) A holder in due course is a holder who takes the instrument
(a) for value; and
(b) in good faith; and
(c) without notice that it is overdue or has been dishonored or of any defense against or claim to it on the part of any person.
(2) A payee may be a holder in due course.

These few provisions must be considered one of the two key sections of the act (the other key section being that describing the requirements of a negotiable instrument, UCC—SECTION 3–104). Almost every problem involving negotiable instruments will bring these two key sections into play, and few problems can be found that will involve neither one of these.

SECTION 3–202 is brief. As is true of many brief statements that are applied to innumerable situations, each with its own peculiar shading of fact and circumstance, standing by itself this section would be subject to a proliferation of differing interpretations. In order to avoid this sort of confusion, each of the provisions of this section is in turn elaborated upon in great detail in later sections of the act.

Taking a Negotiable Instrument "for Value"

Let us turn first to the questions presented by UCC—SECTION 3–302. To be a holder in due course one must take the instrument "(a) for value." But what is value? As further elaborated upon in UCC—SECTION 3–303 (see Act in appendix for the exact wording of this section), this is a complex concept. In particular it is *not* synonomous with merely having promised consideration in exchange for an instrument. If the holder's contract with his transferor is executory, he has not irrevocably exposed himself to a loss, because he may rescind his contract. Under these circumstances what is the most equitable means of settling a controversy when the party issuing an instrument raises a defense? This point is best explained through an illustration. Suppose A is the maker of a note, and A issues the note to B. B is guilty of fraud in procuring the note from A, but B transfers the note to C. C does not pay for the instrument, but promises to deed a vacant lot to B at some later date, in exchange for the note. In shorthand, we may view the situation thus:

Maker   Payee   Holder
$A \longrightarrow$ (Fraud) $\longrightarrow B \longrightarrow C$ (value not yet irrevocably given)

Assuming that A's defense is valid, that B is guilty of fraud in having procured the instrument from A, and that C has not yet transferred the lot to B, why should not C rescind his contract with B? He may return the note to B, who is subject to A's defense, and A may avoid the loss he would otherwise suffer. C may keep his lot.

The obvious justice in not making C a holder in due course unless he has irrevocably extended value before receiving notice of a defect, and thereby not permitting B to profit from his wrongdoing and not causing A to suffer a loss needlessly, are adequate explanations of the purpose in requiring value in exchange for an instrument beyond a mere executory agreement.

We may cite another common example of a situation which, before the UCC, caused much controversy but is now settled by the UCC: what about the payee who deposits a check into his checking account? Later it is determined that the payee secured the check from the drawer through fraud. Then the payee's bank attempts to collect the check from the drawer's bank. The drawer has already stopped payment by his own bank and announces his intention to defend if the payee's bank wishes to sue him on the check. Here again, the payee's bank is not a holder in due course unless the account has actually been withdrawn by the payee-depositor. The payee's bank has not parted with value if all it has to do is to return the check to the payee and to deduct the amount of the check from the payee-depositor's account. The bank is no worse off, and an injury to an innocent party, the drawer, will be avoided. Of course, it would have been another story if the bank had credited the payee-depositor's account, but before the bank received notice of any defense the payee had closed out his account and departed. In that event the bank would have taken the check for value, and would (presuming the other requirements were met) be a holder in due course.

Probably, by this time, the point is made: *for value* presupposes some tangible, irrevocable commitment given in exchange for the instrument. Normally the value given is simply a sum of money given the previous holder.

However, any irrevocable commitment to a third person is considered as value. A negotiable instrument, given in exchange for a negotiable instrument, is considered as value because it may be made irrevocable merely by transfer to a holder in due course, and whether this is done is not within the control of the maker or drawer. The same is true of a letter of credit given for a negotiable instrument.

Value is also present when an instrument is given in payment for a debt already in existence. Thus, X, being a holder of an instrument given him by some other party, indorses the instrument over to Y, who has previously sold X merchandise. X instructs Y to apply the instrument to X's account. Y is a holder in due course of the instrument. However, one who goes through the legal process of attaching an instrument—in order to satisfy a judgment, for example—is not a holder in due course.

There is no requirement that the value extended in exchange for an instrument need be for the face value of the instrument. By agreement of the parties, the instrument may be discounted, and often instruments are discounted in commercial practice.

Taking a Negotiable Instrument in "Good Faith"

The second requirement for qualification as a holder in due course is that he take the instrument "(b) in good faith." *Good faith* is not defined specifically in relation to negotiable instruments in Section 3 of the UCC. However, these words are defined in their general application to the entire act in UCC—SECTION 1–201 (19) like this: 'Good faith' means honesty in fact in the conduct or transaction concerned."

Further insight as to the intended meaning of *good faith* may be obtained through an examination of the usage of this term under the earlier NIL. To begin with, good faith is a question of fact, and therefore, if the case is not heard in equity, good faith is a jury question. Good faith does not necessarily imply a lack of negligence (though some kinds of negligence may bar one from being a holder in due course under the provisions of (c) below). In the final analysis, the question as to whether a person is dealing honestly or dishonestly reduces itself to the determination of that person's intent. Quite possibly a taker of an instrument with the best intentions might have been exposed to information which, had he analyzed the information correctly, would have led to the conclusion that there was a defense to the instrument. On this information, the taker could nonetheless be found to be in good faith.

Taking a Negotiable Instrument without Notice of Defect

The third requirement for qualifications as a holder in due course is that he has taken the instrument "(c) without notice that it is overdue or has been dishonored or of any defense against or claim to it on the part of any person."

This section too is elaborated upon, in this case in UCC—SECTION 3–304: Notice to Purchaser. According to the provisions of this section, the purchaser is deemed to have notice of a "claim or defense" if the instrument would seem to be of questionable validity for the following reasons, each of which is a matter of degree: (1) incompleteness of the instrument, and (2) visible evidence of forgery or alteration.

The fact of an instrument being incomplete or altered may or may not be notice of infirmity. It seems rather incredible at first thought that an alteration might *not* constitute a fatal infirmity, but the following illustration, taken from the comment on the UCC, clarifies the point.[2]

Consider the example of a check dated January 2, 1948, written on January 2, 1949. Few readers can claim that they have never mistakenly used the wrong year, during the first few days of a new year, even when writing a check. It would seem reasonable for a purchaser to assume permission to correct what was almost certainly a minor error of this kind, and a later purchaser would not be on notice of a claim or defense on that basis alone. The same would be true concerning blank spaces. Certain spaces are often left blank, especially the designation of the payee (because many merchants prefer to stamp in their official business title). Although one or perhaps two blanks may not necessarily put a purchaser on notice, at some inexact point too many blanks will. In summary, the determination of whether the fact of blank spaces, or of alteration, is notice depends upon questions of degree. Evidently a test not unlike that of the reasonable man of tort law will be used to determine this question.

Another reason noted above whereby the purchaser may have notice of a claim or defense is "visible evidence of forgery." Conjuring up an instance in which visible evidence of a forged signature would not be notice is beyond the imagination of this writer. Presumably, evidence of a forged signature would be notice in any circumstance. Of course, there might be questions of degree as to whether in fact a particular instrument *did* or did not show evidence of forgery.

All of the above instances, and any other irregularity such "as to call into question its validity, terms, or ownership or create an ambiguity as to the party to pay" will constitute notice of a defense, and will therefore disqualify the holder from being a holder in due course.

The second reason given whereby a purchaser may be said to have had notice of a claim or defense to an instrument, as stated in UCC—SECTION 3–304, is "if the purchaser has notice that the obligation of any party is voidable in whole or in part, or that all parties have been discharged."

The third reason stated in UCC—SECTION 3–304 for considering a purchaser to have had "notice of a claim or defense" is if the purchaser has notice that either a payment on the principle of an instrument is overdue, or that another instrument in the same series is overdue, either of which would constitute notice that the instrument is overdue. However, the fact that interest payments are behind is not notice, because the practice of permitting interest payments to remain unpaid and not forcing payment is widespread.

2 *Uniform Commercial Code, 1958 Official Text with Comments* (The American Law Institute, 1958), p. 273.

An instrument is overdue if acceleration has been made, if demand has already been made upon a demand instrument, or if an instrument remains in circulation more than a reasonable time after its issue. A "reasonable time" for a check . . . is presumed to be 30 days.

SALITAN v. *DIVELBISS* (Oklahoma, 1955) 286 P 2d 724

> *The principal complaint made by defendant in the case at bar is that plaintiffs did not acquire the trade acceptances in good faith . . . as provided under Section 122 . . . and were therefore not "holder(s) in due course." And, not being holders in due course, the trade acceptances were subject to the same defenses as if they were non-negotiable. . . .*

The plaintiffs in error brought an action to recover a money judgment against the defendant in error on three trade acceptances. The jury returned a verdict in favor of the defendant and the judgment of the trial court was in accord with the verdict. The plaintiffs have appealed.

The instruments in this suit are three original trade acceptances, payable to the order of Sterling Materials Company, Inc., all of which are dated May 18, 1951, at Medford, Oklahoma, and addressed to Ray Divelbiss and due respectively September 1, 1951, October 1, 1951, and November 1, 1951. The first two are in the sum of $307 each and the third is for $308.30. All were accepted at Medford, Oklahoma, on May 25, 1951, and made payable at the Grant City Bank, Medford, Oklahoma and allegedly purchased from the Sterling Materials Company, Inc. May 29, 1951, by Samuel S. Salitan and David Little, Copartners, d/b/a Credit Industrial Company, by reason of which Credit Industrial Company allegedly became "holder in due course" of said instruments.

(1) The instruments are in the form of "Trade Acceptances." A trade acceptance is a draft or bill of exchange drawn by the seller on the purchaser of goods sold, and accepted by such purchaser, *Atterbury* v. *Bank of Washington Heights* . . . and governed generally by the rules of law applicable to negotiable instruments.

The right to recover, if any, is dependent upon whether Credit Industrial Company was an innocent purchaser for value, without notice of any defect (that is, was it a holder in due course?) of the trade acceptances which had been endorsed by the payee and delivered to it. Credit Industrial Company contends that it so purchased the instruments. . . .

The undisputed facts developed in the case from defendant's evidence are substantially that Sterling Materials Company, through its representatives, made arrangements with defendant, Divelbiss, for the sale of a roofing compound manufactured by Sterling Materials Company by the trade name of "Asbestolene." As part of this arrangement the defendant was promised an exclusive countywide dealership for the product, a progressive advertising campaign to be conducted by Sterling Materials Company, and a sales force from Sterling Materials Company to sell the product in the county.

Subsequently, the "Asbestolene," when applied to a roof by a customer, proved worthless and the defendant refunded the amount of the sale and tendered the remainder of the roofing materials on hand as the company's dealer back to Sterling Materials Company. Other dealerships were granted by Sterling Materials Company within the county, without the knowledge or consent of defendant; the advertising campaign promised defendant was never conducted; and the sales force of the company made but one appearance in the county in an effort to sell the product.

The plaintiffs' action was based upon the trade acceptances, which were payable to order of Sterling Materials Company, Inc. The trade acceptances were attached to plaintiffs' petition as Exhibits A–1, A–2 and A–3 as required by 12 O.S. 1951 subparagraph 296 and made a part thereof. None of the exhibited trade acceptances bore an endorsement from the payee, Sterling Materials Company, to the plaintiffs, such as would constitute them holders in due course of said trade acceptances; consequently, the terms and provisions of the exhibits should govern. . . . However, (over defendant's objections) upon the trial of the case, the trade acceptances were admitted as evidence upon oral proof that the plaintiff had, before maturity, acquired the trade acceptances from the payee giving a check therefor, which (check was not introduced in evidence) was purportedly duly paid in its regular course of business of purchasing commercial paper at discount. . . .

The principal complaint made by defendant in the case at bar is that plaintiffs did not acquire the trade acceptances in good faith . . . as provided for under Section 122 . . . and were therefore not "holder(s) in due course." And, not being holders in due course, the trade acceptances were subject to the same defenses as if they were non-negotiable. . . .

The facts hereinbefore narrated tend to prove that plaintiffs did not purchase the trade acceptances outright and in good faith, but were merely carrying out an understanding had with payee company to assist in collecting the trade acceptances. There are facts and circumstances in evidence, which indicate that payee is the real party in interest instead of plaintiffs. The evidence and permissible inferences tended to establish defendant's contention that plaintiffs were not holders in due course of the trade acceptances and did not buy the trade acceptances in good faith nor pay value therefor so as to constitute them holders in due course, all of which raised issues of fact to be determined by the jury under proper instructions. The jury having determined the questions in favor of defendant, and being sustained by competent evidence, the jury's findings on the issues are binding on this Court on appeal. *Stevens* v. *Wey,* supra.

Finding no substantial errors in the record, and holding that the judgment is sustained by the evidence and not contrary to law, the judgment is affirmed.

WILLIAMS, V.C.J., and WELCH, CORN, BLACKBIRD and JACKSON, JJ., concur.

This case revolves about an issue of fact: was the Credit Industrial Company merely the plaintiff's agent for purposes of collection, or had a valid sale of the instrument been effected? If a valid sale of the instrument had been effected, and if taker had not known of the claimed defenses at the time of receiving the instrument, the taker would have qualified as a holder in due course. However, upon hearing the facts, the jury found the taker was not actually a purchaser but was merely acting on behalf of plaintiff. Assuming this to be true the Credit Industrial Company was not a holder in due course.

Rights of a Holder in Due Course

We have stated before, and we believe it worth stating again, that the main paths to understanding the negotiable instrument lie in finding (1) if an instrument is in the form required to make it negotiable, (2) if the circumstances surrounding the transfer of the instrument satisfy the legal requirements of negotiation, and (3) if the additional circumstances necessary to make the holder a holder in due course are satisfied. These questions have now been explored. We now come to the crucial question: what are the special rights given the holder in due course or his assignee?

> UCC—SECTION 3–305: Rights of a Holder in Due Course.
> To the extent that a holder is a holder in due course he takes the instrument free from
> (1) all claims to it on the part of any person; and
> (2) all defenses of any party to the instrument with whom the holder has not dealt except . . .[3]

There are some defenses that may be valid against the holder in due course, and they are considered below, but they are not very frequently encountered. What is most important is that in the usual case, the information in (1) and (2) above is the information that counts. The holder in due course usually takes the instrument free from defenses, in a practical sense, simply because the most usual defenses are barred by (1) or (2) above. The first, (1) above, refers to assertions by a party that he has a claim such as a lien or an ownership interest in the instrument. The second, (2) above probably covers the majority of cases that arise. With a very few exceptions discussed below, all defenses asserted by parties with whom the holder has not dealt, are cut off.

The most usual pattern in which that happens is as follows: A, a maker

[3] These defenses are the real defenses enumerated on page 520. They will render any instrument uncollectible against the party who issued, or purportedly issued, the instrument.

or drawer, gives an instrument to B, the payee. B was guilty in his dealings with A of fraud, misrepresentation, breach of contract, or one of a variety of other acts that might constitute a defense to an ordinary contract. But this will not constitute a defense against C, a taker from B and a holder in due course, because, in the words of 3–305(2), "all defenses of any party to the instrument with whom the holder has not dealt" are cut off. Exceptions are discussed below.

Defenses Effective against a Holder in Due Course

Let us now turn to those defenses that are effective against a holder in due course. These are termed real defenses.

UCC—SECTION 3–305: Rights of a Holder in Due Course.
To the extent that a holder is a holder in due course he takes the instrument free from . . .
(2) all defenses of any party to the instrument with whom the holder has not dealt except . . .
(a) infancy, to the extent that it is a defense to a simple contract; and
(b) such other incapacity, or duress, or illegality of the transaction, as renders the obligation of the party a nullity; and
(c) such misrepresentation as had induced the party to sign the instrument with neither knowledge nor reasonable opportunity to obtain knowledge of its character or its essential terms; and
(d) discharge in insolvency proceedings; and
(e) any other discharge of which the holder has notice when he takes the instrument.

INFANCY AND INCAPACITY

The treatment of (a) infancy and (b) incapacity, duress, and illegality is necessarily phrased in qualified language. This is a matter of necessity, because, remember that although the UCC is a uniform act, it is not within the realm of federal law. The UCC has been and is being adopted by the legislatures of the several states. Each state has its own existing law concerning the extent to which infancy, incapacity, duress, and illegality constitute defenses. There are rather substantial variations from state to state as concerns the operation of these defenses. Consequently, about all the framers of the UCC could do was, in effect, to relate the operation of each of these defenses back to the law of the particular state.

Examining these defenses more carefully we observe that infancy is given special treatment above: In cases when infancy is a defense against a simple contract, infancy is also a defense against a holder in due course of a negotiable instrument. The reasons of policy behind the defense of infancy have been explored earlier in the section on contracts. The remaining defenses, also dealt with in the section on contracts, will in some instances render an ordinary contract void and in other instances voidable. If the defense would render a contract void, the defense also renders a negotiable instrument void—that is, even a holder in due course is barred from collecting. If the defense would merely render a contract voidable, the defense would not prevent collection by a holder in due course.

Finally, we wish to emphasize that although these defenses do exist, they are rather infrequently encountered. Cases involving incapacity, duress, and illegality are rare in themselves. Cases in which these are present to a degree or under circumstances sufficient to render a contract void are likely to be practically collectors' items. Probably of those so far mentioned, minority would be the most common defense.

MISREPRESENTATION

Although UCC—SECTION 3–305, subsection 2, part C (the section on defenses) uses the term *misrepresentation,* it seems clear from the wording used, and especially from the comments, that in this context, *misrepresentation* refers to fraud.

Under special circumstances, fraud will be a defense effective against a holder in due course. These instances occur when the fraud practiced is fraud in the factum. Fraud in the inducement does not constitute a defense against the holder in due course.[4] Fraud in the factum consists in certain types of fraud in which there is no knowledge or intent by the issuing party that an instrument be created. Clever substitution of a negotiable instrument in the place of some altogether different paper that a party intended to sign is an example of this type of fraud.

INSOLVENCY

Discharge in insolvency is always a defense to a contract claim. Some of the incidents of this defense are outlined briefly on pages 332 and 640.

As a poignant contrast to the happy position of the holder in due course, we might scan the position of the holder who does not have the rights of the holder in due course.

UCC—SECTION 3–306: Rights of One Not Holder in Due Course.
Unless he has the rights of a holder in due course any person takes the instrument subject to

---

[4] Both of these forms of fraud were discussed in the sections on contracts.

(a) all valid claims to it on the part of any person; and
(b) all defenses of any party which would be available in an action on a simple contract; and
(c) the defenses of want or failure of consideration, nonperformance of any condition precedent, non-delivery, or delivery for a special purpose . . . ; and
(d) the defense that he or a person through whom he holds the instrument acquired it by theft, or that payment or satisfaction to such holder would be inconsistent with the terms of a restrictive indorsement. The claim of any third person to the instrument is not otherwise available as a defense to any party liable thereon unless the third person himself defends the action for such party.

FORGERY

One other defense ought to be mentioned. This is the defense of forgery. Nothing in the UCC sections just quoted relates to this defense. Perhaps the reason for this is that an instrument with the drawer's name forged is not even a valid instrument so far as the reputed drawer is concerned. As to him it is a nullity from the time of inception. On the other hand, the instrument is valid against the forger, despite the fact that he uses the wrong name. A holder in due course of a forged instrument would be able to collect against the forger. There is a rather substantial problem so far as subsequent parties are concerned; namely, that forgers tend to be difficult to locate.

The following section relates not only to forgers but to any person who purports to sign for another but who actually lacks the authority. It is possible in some instances for an employee to misunderstand the limits of his authority, and therefore to sign an instrument without the necessary authority, but also without any criminal intent. In cases of this sort, the chances of collecting from the party responsible for the unauthorized signature might be good.

UCC—SECTION 3–404: Unauthorized Signatures.
(1) Any unauthorized signature is wholly inoperative as that of the person whose name is signed unless he ratifies it or is precluded from denying it.

Finally, why is not the fact that a necessary indorsement was forged, or merely not obtained, listed as being a defense against the holder in due course? The question and the answer are mainly a matter of semantics. Remember, in order for a party to qualify even as a holder, previous *neces-*

sary indorsements must be obtained. If a necessary indorsement has been forged it obviously has not been obtained. Therefore, a person in possession of an instrument with a forged indorsement is not even a holder, much less a holder in due course. Not being even a holder, the party in possession has no right to enforce collection.

Defenses that are good against a holder in due course are often referred to as the real defenses. Those that might be good against a holder but are cut off against a holder in due course are referred to as the *personal defenses*.

The Payee as a Holder in Due Course

We may now consider the question previously alluded to (page 504) presented by UCC—Section 2–302 of the UCC, which reads: "(2) A Payee may be a holder in due course."

How may this come about? Basically, the question is, why shouldn't a payee qualify as a holder in due course? If he meets the requirements of Section 3–302 he will so qualify. However, ordinarily a payee against whom there is some defense will not take "in good faith" and "without notice . . . of any claim to it on the part of any person." For example, if there is fraud in procuring a negotiable instrument from maker or drawer, usually the fraud is perpetrated by the payee.

If there is a defense against the payee, such as misrepresentation, fraud, duress, or breach of contract, that payee will usually know about it. He will usually be the guilty party. But, there are occasional situations in which a payee may take innocently, despite the fact that there is a defense based upon the contract, and in this rare case, the payee may be a holder in due course. To repeat, the test is simply whether in fact the payee can meet the requirements of UCC—Section 3–302, and—though this is unlikely—if he can, he is a holder in due course.

Seven different situations in which the payee might be a holder in due course are listed in the comment to the official text of the Uniform Commercial Code.[5] There seems no need for the student to become a specialist on this point, but to illustrate that the possibility exists we may quote one example from that source: "*A* defrauds the maker into signing an instrument payable to *P*(ayee). *P*(ayee) pays *A* for it in good faith and without notice, and the maker delivers the instrument directly to *P*(ayee)." [6] The payee may be a holder in due course because he was in good faith. *A* was the party guilty of fraud.

[5] *Uniform Commercial Code, ibid.,* pp. 268–269.
[6] *Uniform Commercial Code, ibid.,* p. 268.

BRANZ v. *STANLEY* (Maine, 1947) 51 A 2d 192

> *For it is well settled in this jurisdiction that if not intending to sign a promissory note she was by fraud and deceit and without negligence on her own part tricked into signing that which afterwards proved to be a note the instrument is void as to all parties.*

In this action upon a promissory note against Carlton H. Stanley and Alice F. Stanley at the close of the evidence the jury was instructed to return a verdict against both defendants. Carlton H. Stanley abides the verdict. Alice F. Stanley reserved exceptions.

The case reported shows that Carlton H. Stanley, having wrecked his Studebaker, on October 30, 1945, purchased and received delivery of a used Terraplane from Samuel Silverman doing business as Sam's Used Car Lot, traded in his old car and gave his negotiable installment note of even date for $275 in part payment of the balance of the purchase price. On the same or following day the payee having indorsed the note for transfer, offered it for discount to Maurice A. Branz doing business as the Guardian Acceptance Co. but he refused to finance the paper without another signer and a representative apparently of the payee carried the note to the home of Carlton H. Stanley and his wife Alice F. Stanley signed it as a comaker. Five days later the note still bearing its original date and indorsement for transfer was delivered to Maurice A. Branz who sent his check for $250 to Samuel Silverman for it and when the first installment was not paid sued the signers jointly for the full amount of the note.

The exceptant Alice F. Stanley, however, stated at the trial that on November 5, 1945, a man whom she did not know brought papers to her home which her husband Carlton H. Stanley asked her to hurry and sign and on her inquiry as to what they were told her that they were just about the car, which she thought referred to the wrecked Studebaker and not to the Terraplane just bought, and without knowing their contents she wrote her name on two papers where the man who had kept them folded up lifted the corners for her to sign. She insisted that she did not know she had signed a note and conditional sales agreement which the papers proved to be, or even that her husband had made the instruments until later he told her what she had done and made known his intention to desert her and let her pay for the car. And she says that when a few weeks later he did abandon her she notified the holder of the note she would not be responsible for it.

(1, 2) The exceptant's account of what took place when she signed the note in suit is partially confirmed by her housekeeper and not clearly contradicted in the record. And improbability does not compel its rejection as unworthy of belief. If found to be true, which we think it could be, . . . and if that defense is not barred by her own negligence she is not liable on it in this action. For it is well settled in this jurisdiction that if not intending to sign a promissory note she was by fraud and deceit and without negligence on her own part tricked into signing that which afterwards proved to be a note the instrument is . . .

void as to all parties. And whether she is estopped by her own negligence from denying her signature was a question for the jury. . . .

We are of opinion that the charge of fraud made here raises issues of facts which should have been submitted to the jury and the ruling below directing a verdict against the exceptant was error. On this ground, without consideration of other questions argued on the briefs, the exceptions are sustained.

Exceptions sustained.

✧

Just as a manifestation of assent is a requirement of any contract, intent *to issue* an instrument is a requirement for a valid negotiable instrument. Issuance of a negotiable instrument while harboring a mistaken impression as to the nature of the contract for which the instrument was given would not invalidate the instrument. Here, however, the party may have been unaware she was signing a negotiable instrument, and if so, this condition was caused by another party's fraud.

If there was no intent to sign the instrument, the signature is not valid, and the instrument, so far as the misled signer is concerned, is a nullity.

Rights of Successors in Title to the Holder in Due Course

What about a party who takes from a holder in due course but who, because of having heard of some defense before taking the instrument, or for any other reason, is not a holder in due course *himself?* The obvious way to decide such a situation would be to hold that this party, not being a holder in due course, should have no special rights. In fact, however, a holder taking an instrument from a holder in due course receives *the same rights* as that holder in due course had. Why? The reason is because the policy behind the creation of negotiable instruments requires that result. The purpose of negotiable instruments, one must remember, is to provide a means of strengthening the rights of distant holders of instruments. The holder in due course, as we have seen, is given certain rights, so that he may feel secure in accepting a negotiable instrument. But suppose a holder in due course accepts a negotiable instrument which does not become due for a long period of time. How can he recover upon such an instrument? If he is not in a position to wait until the instrument matures (and some notes run for as long as 50 years), his only means of liquidating the instrument is to recover the value by negotiating it on to another party, often a bank. Were there no special provisions in the law, a holder in due course would find it impossible to negotiate such an instrument, if it became generally known after he took it in good faith, that there was some contract defense to the instrument. (A transferee taking with knowledge of a defense can-not, by definition, be a holder in due course.)

Under these circumstances, the only way a holder in due course might collect on the instrument would be to wait until the instrument matured, meanwhile leaving the holder's capital tied up. But this is not the law. To avoid the situation described, *any holder taking from a holder in due course is given the same rights as the holder in due course himself had* (except those holders actually participating in some fraud concerning the instru-ment).

Another rationale for the same result is based upon the reasoning that the holder in due course may assign the rights he has acquired, and the holder receiving the assignment of those rights may enforce them.

The importance of this provision is easily underestimated. Although re-quiring only a few words to explain, this provision is a major exception to the general rule that one must be a holder in due course to overcome con-tract defenses.

UNITED STATES v. *SKINNER* (USDC Idaho, 1956) 137 F Supp. 234

The United States, having derived its title through Continental Bank and Trust Company, a holder in due course, has all of the rights of the former holder and is subject only to the de-fenses the maker would have against the Continental Bank and Trust Company. . . .

This is an action brought by the United States against the defendants, hus-band and wife of Preston, Idaho, on a note in the amount of $1,074.90, dated November 9, 1951, executed by the defendants in favor of Averitt and Jacob Company, Salt Lake City, Utah. The note was signed as consideration for the purchase of materials for use on the defendants' home. November 9, 1951, the note was purchased by Continental Bank and Trust Company, Salt Lake City, Utah. June 9, 1953, the note was assigned to the United States under the terms of the bank's insurance contract with the Government wherein the United States insured payment of loans made pursuant to the National Housing Act, 12 U.S.C.A. subparagraph 1701 et seq. No payments were made other than the down payment of $110.50.

The Government has moved for summary judgment based upon the plead-ings on file herein. Briefs have been filed and the Court has heard oral argu-ment.

Defendants contend that Continental Bank and Trust Company, at the time it assigned the note, was not a holder in due course, and therefore was subject to any defenses the defendants might have had against the original payee. This is based on defendants' claim that the materials furnished by Averitt and Jacob

Company were so defective that they could not be used for the purpose for which they were purchased.

(1, 2) It appears from the pleadings and papers on file herein that the bank had no knowledge of any alleged defects in the materials furnished until after it took the note, which would have no effect on its status of a holder in due course, inasmuch as whether or not the bank was a holder in due course must be determined as of the time it took the note. The note was a negotiable instrument under Idaho law. . . . Idaho Code defines a holder in due course as one who takes the instrument under the condition that the instrument is complete and regular on its face; that he became the holder of it before it was overdue and without notice that it had been previously dishonored; he took it for value and in good faith, and that at the time it was negotiated to him he had no notice of any infirmity in the instrument or defect in the title of the person negotiating it.

The affidavit of one J. J. Gustafson, an officer of the said bank, which is undisputed in the record, shows that all of the above conditions were met at the time the note was negotiated to it, making it the holder in due course.

(4) In order to defeat the right of a purchaser of a note to recover it is necessary to either show actual knowledge of the defect or notice of such facts and circumstances as would charge him with actual bad faith in taking the paper without investigating the circumstances. . . . The facts show that the Continental Bank had no actual knowledge of a defect of the note and that the bank acted in good faith in accepting the note. Further, this court finds no such defect in the completion certificate as to put the bank on notice in that respect.

(5) The United States, having derived its title through Continental Bank and Trust Company, a holder in due course, has all of the rights of the former holder and is subject only to the defenses the maker would have against the Continental Bank and Trust Company. . . .

For these reasons it appears to the Court that the Motion for Summary Judgment should be granted. Counsel for Plaintiff may prepare and submit Judgment.

✧

This case might well be contrasted with the one on page 517. In that case there was, and in this case there may well have been, a potential defense based upon the contract between the original parties. In neither of these two cases was the party bringing suit a holder in due course. The difference in outcome is attributable entirely to the fact that in this case the holder had derived his title *through* a holder in due course, whereas in the earlier case the holder had not done so.

CHAPTER THIRTY-FIVE

Determining Liability for Payment of a Negotiable Instrument

In addition to the liability of general indorsers to make good on an instrument if it is not paid, all indorsers to a negotiable instrument, general and qualified alike, make certain warranties which are somewhat similar to the implied warranties of sale in the sales contract.

Primary Liability

WHO IS LIABLE for payment of a negotiable instrument? This depends upon the type of instrument. In the case of a note, the maker is the party who in the ordinary course of events is expected to pay. Therefore the maker is said to be "primarily" liable. If the maker refuses to pay, unless he has a defense he may be successfully sued by the holder. Even if he does have a defense, the maker may be successfully sued by a holder in due course, unless the defense is one of the real defenses.

The situation is more complex in the case of a check or draft. No doubt the payee of one of these instruments generally assumes that the drawee will pay. However, it is not correct to assume that the drawee is legally bound to pay. There is no binding legal relationship between a drawee and a payee merely because the drawer has filled in the drawee's name on a draft. Conceivably the drawee might be a complete stranger to the other parties. As a matter of fact there is nothing to prevent the drawer from selecting his drawee at random from a telephone directory. Of course, such a drawee will not pay. Or, in case the instrument is a check, and the drawee is a bank, merely because a drawer uses a check from a particular bank is no assurance that the bank actually has the drawer's funds on deposit. If they do not have the drawer's funds on deposit they will not pay the check except, perhaps, through error.

If the drawee is not necessarily liable, how do we determine whether or

528

not he may be held? The only way of determining this is to present the instrument to the drawee and ask him either for payment, in the event it is payable on sight, or for a written promise to pay the instrument when due if it is payable at some later date. This process of the payee is called *presentment,* and if the drawee either pays, or notes on the instrument that he will pay when due, this act constitutes *acceptance.* If he declines acceptance, the instrument is said to be dishonored, and no liability attaches to the dishonoring drawee.[1]

Upon acceptance, the liability of the drawee becomes legally fixed. He is known at this point as the *acceptor* or *drawee-acceptor,* as he will be referred to herein. Of course, if acceptance is by the simple act of payment (as *is* almost always the case upon presenting a check to a bank) the same act is both an acceptance and a discharge of the drawee's obligations. When acceptance is not by payment, but rather by a promise to pay when due, then after acceptance the drawee-acceptor is legally liable and if he refuses to pay upon presentment on the due date he may be successfully sued upon the instrument. This is true even (surprisingly) if the drawer's signature was forged on the face of the instrument.[2]

The named drawer could not be charged in this event, since he has no means of preventing a forger from using his name on an instrument. The drawee is only authorized to pay out the drawer's funds according to the drawer's order, and may not pay out the drawer's funds to a forger. Nor may the drawee charge the drawer's account when an instrument is presented containing a forged indorsement on the back. However, the drawee may recover his money from the party who presented the defective instrument if he has already paid the latter. Then each taker may recover in turn from an earlier taker, leaving the party who took from the forger to locate and collect from the forger if he can. Usually he cannot.

The drawee-acceptor may therefore be the party "primarily" liable on a three-party instrument, but if the drawee does not accept when first presented, strictly speaking no one is primarily liable.

Certification of a check by the drawee bank is a special form of accept-

[1] Although prior to acceptance there is not necessarily an obligation between drawee and the holder, often there will be a prior contract between drawee and drawer by which the drawee promises in advance to pay according to the order of the drawer. If the drawee dishonors, he may be in breach of a contract with the drawer. This is, in fact, the case when a bank refuses to honor the order of the drawer to pay out his funds to the payee. The payee has no legal recourse against the drawee bank, but the drawer may bring suit against the bank, based upon the injury the dishonor has done to the drawer's credit.

[2] The drawee may not be held, if he has unknowingly accepted an instrument with a forged necessary *indorsement* (as distinguished from a forged *signature* on the face), because he has no way of knowing the signature of indorsers, whereas he is expected to know the signature of the drawer, and for this reason is held if he accepts or pays a check on which the drawer's signature is forged.

ance. There is no basic difference between this form of acceptance and any other. The effect is to render the bank primarily liable and subject to a suit by the holder if payment is refused when due. Ordinarily the bank has no liability to the holder, though it does have a contractual obligation with the drawer to pay out funds at the demand of the drawer. Certification of a check is discussed under the UCC as follows:

UCC—SECTION 3–411: Certification of a Check.

(1) Certification of a check is acceptance. Where a holder procures certification the drawer and all prior indorsers are discharged.

(2) Unless otherwise agreed a bank has no obligation to certify a check.

(3) A bank may certify a check before returning it for lack of proper indorsement. If it does so the drawer is discharged.

Secondary Liability

LIABILITY OF DRAWER ON A THREE-PARTY INSTRUMENT

What other recourse does the holder have in the event of dishonor of an instrument by the maker or drawee? The drawer on a three-party instrument and the indorsers on any instrument are said to be secondarily liable—that is, *liable only* after presentment has been made upon the maker or drawee and after a dishonor by him. The drawer's liability is described as follows:

UCC—SECTION 3–413: Contract of Maker, Drawer and Acceptor.

(2) The drawer engages that upon dishonor of the draft and any necessary notice of dishonor or protest [3] he will pay the amount of the draft to the holder or to any indorser who takes it up. . . .

UCC—SECTION 3–508: Notice of Dishonor.

(1) Notice of dishonor may be given to any person who may be liable on the instrument by or on behalf of the holder or any party who has himself received notice, or any other party who can be compelled to pay the instrument. In addition an agent or bank in whose hands the instrument is dishonored may give notice to his principal or customer or to another agent or bank from which the instrument was received.

(2) Any necessary notice must be given by a bank before its midnight deadline and by any other person before midnight of the third business day after dishonor or receipt of notice of dishonor.

---

[3] Protest is a procedure for giving formal notice of dishonor. In that protest is required by the UCC only for instruments that appear on their face to be drawn outside the United States and its territories, we do not deal with this further.

(3) Notice may be given in any reasonable manner. It may be oral or written and in any terms which identify the instrument and state that it has been dishonored. A misdescription which does not mislead the party notified does not vitiate the notice. Sending the instrument bearing a stamp, ticket or writing stating that acceptance or payment has been refused or sending a notice of debit with respect to the instrument is sufficient.
(8) Notice operates for the benefit of all parties who have rights on the instrument against the party notified.

This is just about what we would expect as a matter of common sense. On the one hand it would make no sense to hold the drawer primarily liable. He has given his instrument, and the payee has received it, with the understanding that for reasons of convenience to one or both parties, a third party will exchange the instrument for cash. It would be inconsistent to permit the payee to turn around and demand cash from the drawer. Yet, if the drawee, the party who would ordinarily make payment, refuses to do so, it would certainly seem inconsistent *not* to require the drawer, who presumably received benefits that prompted him to issue the instrument, to make good. Therefore, upon dishonor by the drawee, the holder may assert his rights against the drawer. In order to hold any secondary party, actual notice (written or oral) of the dishonor must be extended to the party sought to be held.

LIABILITY OF INDORSERS

The position of the indorser may also be explained as a matter of common sense. Remember that the indorser normally indorses upon transfer of the instrument to some other party in payment for goods or services, or in exchange for cash. The person receiving the instrument does so because he believes it represents cash value and that ultimately the cash value can be realized. By indorsing the instrument, the indorser is, according to a contract implied by law, contracting that the cash value can indeed be realized. If cash value cannot indeed be realized by the transferee, the indorser is liable under the implied contract to return the cash he received from that transferee. Sometimes there is more than one indorser. The transferee may hold any earlier indorser [4] if the transferee has presented the instrument to the maker or drawee and it has been dishonored, and if prompt notice of presentment and dishonor has been given to the indorser one wishes to hold. However, the best practice is to notify promptly *all* indorsers and the drawer, if any. If one indorser will not pay without suit, there is still the hope that another may.

This contract, implied by law, that the indorser will make good on the instrument in the event it is dishonored, is extremely important in its bear-

[4] The special liability of the qualified indorser is explained below.

ing upon the rights of holders. For various reasons, even when an instrument is valid, a party primarily liable to pay might not do so. He might be insolvent; he might have disappeared, or he might simply refuse to pay for no logical reason. At best, under these circumstances, someone is faced with a lawsuit, and at worst, collection from the party primarily liable may be impossible. Therefore, the implied contract referred to above, making it the obligation of the indorser to pay following presentment, dishonor, and notice, is of great importance to a transferee. It simply means that the transferee has the option of recovery against the earlier indorsers.

> UCC—SECTION 3–411: Contract of Indorser; Order of Liability.
> (1) Unless the indorsement otherwise specified (as by such words as "without recourse") every indorser engages that upon dishonor and any necessary notice of dishonor . . . he will pay the instrument according to its tenor at the time of his indorsement to the holder or to any subsequent indorser who takes it up. . . .
> (2) Unless they otherwise agree, indorsers are liable to one another in the order in which they indorse, which is presumed to be the order in which their signatures appear on the instrument.

THE QUALIFIED INDORSER

Subsection (1) above delineates one exception to the pattern of liability previously discussed. An indorser may disclaim his liability by adding the words *without recourse* to his indorsement, whether it is special or in blank. Such an indorsement is termed a *qualified indorsement* and releases the indorser from the obligation to pay upon dishonor of an otherwise valid instrument. The distinction here is, if an instrument is fundamentally defective, the qualified indorser is liable, but he does not give blanket guarantee against nonpayment of a valid instrument.

Any indorsement, whether blank, special, or restrictive, may have added the words *without recourse* and therefore constitute a qualified indorsement. For the purpose of determining the liability of an indorsement under the implied contract, indorsements are divided into qualified indorsements and general indorsements; the latter includes all indorsements *not* containing the words *without recourse*.

Because the liability of the qualified indorser is less than the liability of the general indorser, one might expect that the qualified indorsement would almost always be used. Why is this not done? The reason probably is that transferees are loathe to accept a qualified indorsement. There is little point in attempting to negotiate by qualified indorsement if this is going to frighten the transferee into refusing to accept the instrument. In fact, the use of qualified indorsement is fairly infrequent.

Transferors of a bearer instrument by delivery without the holder's indorsement (whether bearer on its face, or order on its face but indorsed in blank by a prior holder) are held only to the liability of a qualified indorsement (described above). Moreover, when a bearer instrument is transferred only by delivery, without indorsement, the transferor is liable only to his immediate transferee. All indorsers on the other hand are liable to any subsequent transferee, whether of order or bearer instruments. [5] This is the reason that takers of a bearer instrument usually require an indorsement. Even though the indorsement is not essential to negotiation, it lends the credit of the indorser to subsequent holders. Therefore, those holders may hold the indorsement for payment under his implied contract.

It is sometimes said that each additional indorsement improves the quality of a negotiable instrument. In a sense this is true. The more indorsers, the broader the choice of the holder in selecting an indorser to make good on the instrument should the party primarily liable dishonor. Any general (that is, unqualified) indorser may be held by a holder. Of course, the holder may only recover once.

How would a reasonable holder proceed in determining the indorser or other party secondarily liable from whom to demand payment? He would attempt to select the one most likely to pay with the minimum of effort. When the holder is paid, he in turn gives the instrument to the indorser (or other party) who paid him. That party is now the holder; (if an indorser) he now has the same rights as did the previous holder against earlier indorsers as well as against the drawer or maker. Of course when the instrument is paid by a drawer or maker, this process ends.

CHANEY v. HAMM (Ohio, 1952) 119 NE 2d 95

> In Elworthy v. Helwick . . . the Court held that when a note is made payable in installments the promise to pay each installment is a separate note in itself; therefore . . . the (indorser) was discharged by reason of the failure to receive notice of the nonpayment.

This is a law appeal from the judgment of the Common Pleas Court finding for the plaintiff for the sum of $1,701 with interest and costs of suit. The action was brought by the plaintiff-appellee as endorsee of (a) . . . promissory note. . . . (Defendant-appellant was an indorser.)

The case was submitted to the Court without the intervention of a jury, upon an agreed statement of facts, which may be epitomized as follows:

(1–3) The plaintiff-appellee is a holder in due course of the said promissory

[5] When an order instrument is made bearer by a blank indorsement, other holders may transfer by delivery, just as any other bearer instrument.

note; that when the first installment became due on May 24, 1949, the same was not presented for payment in accordance with G. C. subparagraph 8175, but that the maker was called on the telephone and told that the note was due; that the indorser of the note was not notified of the nonpayment of the same until June 10th. Counsel for the plaintiff-appellee admits the statutory requirements with reference to presentment for payment and notice of dishonor but urges that this was not necessary as the note did not become due until May 24, 1950; that the first installment only was due and the statutory requirements had no application. We cannot concur in this conclusion. In *Elworthy* v. *Helwick* . . . the Court held that when a note is made payable in installments the promise to pay each installment is a separate note in itself; therefore, the defendant-appellant (indorser) was discharged by reason of the failure to receive notice of the nonpayment. (Defendant *was* held for payment of the remaining installments.)

We therefore hold that the Court properly rendered judgment for the defendant upon the first installment of the note and for the plaintiff for the balance due.

Finding no error in the record, the judgment will be affirmed.

HORNBECK, P.J., and WISEMAN and MILLER, J.J., concur.

An interesting aspect of this case is that it would not have been decided the same way today. Although under the NIL notice of dishonor had to be given in writing, under the UCC notice may be given by any reasonable means, and presumably a telephone call would be considered a reasonable means. See UCC—SECTION 3–508 (3) in Appendix. But it remains true that prompt notice in some form must be given to hold those who are secondarily liable.

INDORSEMENT FOR ACCOMMODATION

Although a person ordinarily indorses a negotiable instrument for the purpose of negotiating it onto another taker, there is another reason for indorsing an instrument.

A person otherwise unconnected with an instrument may indorse for the purpose of lending his credit to the instrument. Such an indorser is termed an *accommodation indorser*. Ordinarily, this type of indorsement would be obtained when the present owner of the instrument, be he drawer, payee, or a later holder, finds it difficult to persuade someone to purchase the instrument from him. The latter may be willing to purchase, however, if another party in whom he has confidence will act as accommodation indorser. Then, if the other parties primarily or secondarily liable on the instrument turn out to be bankrupt, departed, or otherwise difficult to collect from, the accommodation indorser may be held. The provisions of UCC—SECTION 3-411 apply to accommodation indorsers just as to all other indorsers: in other words, these indorsers will be treated in all respects as any other indorser. The motive of the indorser, whether he indorses to accommodate some friend or business associate, or to negotiate his own instrument to a new taker, makes little difference.

The accommodation indorsement may be blank, special, or restrictive and may be qualified or general. It would seem that a discriminating taker might be dubious about a qualified accommodation indorsement.

One other section of the UCC is pertinent to this topic:

UCC—SECTION 3-415:
(5) An accommodation party is not liable to the party accommodated, and if he pays the instrument has a right of recourse on the instrument against such party.

Accommodation parties may lend their credit not only by indorsement but also in the capacity of an additional maker, drawer, or drawee.

Warranties of Indorsers

In addition to the liability of general indorsers to make good on an instrument if it is not paid, all indorsers to a negotiable instrument, general and qualified alike, make certain warranties that are somewhat similar to the implied warranties of sale in the sales contract.

Naturally, a student encounters some difficulty in distinguishing the legally imposed contract of the indorser as discussed above, from the warranties of the indorser presently under discussion. At first glance it might even seem that the warranties are merely an extension of the remedies imposed by the implied contract, and that the two sets of remedies might be compiled into one list. Unfortunately this is not the case. In the first place, the prerequisites to bringing a claim under the two sets of remedies are not the same. In order to claim under the implied contract, prompt presentment and notice of dishonor must be given to the indorsers and the drawer. None of these steps is required as a prerequisite to suit under the warranties: all that is necessary is proof that one of the warranties has been breached. In addition, the qualified indorser is excluded from liability under the implied contract, but remains liable for most of the warranties. Finally the implied contract mainly concerns the question of whether a valid instrument is paid. The warranties mainly concern the question of whether or not the instrument is defective. If there is no defect in the instrument or the circumstances surrounding its issue, there is no suit under the warranties even if the instrument is not paid. The warranties are as follows:

UCC—SECTION 3–417: Warranties on . . . transfer.
(2) Any person who transfers an instrument and receives consideration warrants to his transferee and if the transfer is by indorsement to any subsequent holder who takes the instrument in good faith that
(a) he has a good title to the instrument . . .[6]
(b) all signatures are genuine or authorized; and
(c) the instrument has not been materially altered; and
(d) no defense of any party is good against him; and
(e) he has no knowledge of any insolvency proceeding instituted with respect to the maker or acceptor or the drawer of an unaccepted instrument.

The variations applicable to the qualified indorser are described as follows:

(3) By transferring "without recourse" the transferor limits the obligation stated in subsection (2) (d) to a warranty that he has no knowledge of such a defense.

Thus *any* indorser warrants good title, the validity of the signatures, that there has been no material alteration, that there are no defenses to the instrument (a qualified indorser warrants only that he has *no knowledge* of defenses), and that he knows of no insolvency proceedings against the party primarily liable.

There is no particular time period short of the statute of limitations, or perhaps short of acts that might constitute a waiver or estoppel against the transferee, during which suit must be brought upon a breach of one of these warranties.

[EDITOR'S NOTE: There would be no reason to deal with the following question, except that almost every year it is asked by at least one student. In the chart below each arrow indicates a transfer for value to the party to the right. The question is, upon dishonor, can an indorser recover against parties to his right as well as to his left?

Maker → Payee-Indorser → Indorser → Indorser → Indorser
                    #1   #2   #3   #4

The question betrays a basic lack of understanding of the process involved. Each indorser, as he transfers to a later indorser (represented by a transfer to the right), is selling something. He is selling a note, probably in exchange for cash. If the note

[6] The balance of this sentence concerns the special status of agents who are indorsing instruments in the name of a principal.

is uncollectible, the transferee demands his money back from his seller, the party to his left. Obviously, therefore, an indorser may only demand his money back from the party to his left, the party who sold to him. To suppose otherwise would be comparable to supposing that after defective merchandise was returned to the seller, the seller could return the goods and demand a second payment from the buyer who had previously returned the goods.

This diagram also helps to illustrate why a transferee may skip his immediate indorser and collect from an earlier indorser. Whether the note goes from 4 to 3 to 2 to 1, or directly from 4 to 1, the rights of the parties remain the same: each party is back where he started from except 1, who must still recover against the maker before he is restored to his original position.]

FIRST DISCOUNT CORPORATION v. HATCHER AUTO SALES (Ohio, 1951) 102 NE 2d 4

> *The plaintiff had no notice of any incapacity, by reason of minority, of the maker of the note. By paying the defendant for the note, it is clear that the plaintiff relied on the defendant's warranty that the maker did have the capacity to contract. It necessarily follows that the plaintiff may, as a holder of the note although not a holder in due course, enforce the defendant's liability on the warranty. . . .*

On July 25, 1946, Charles V. Lynch executed and delivered to the defendant, the Hatcher Auto Sales, Inc., a . . . promissory note in the sum of $391.92 payable in monthly installments on the purchase price of an automobile.

On the following day the defendant for a valuable consideration indorsed the note to the plaintiff, The First Discount Corporation, without recourse.

Lynch made no payment on the note.

As the holder of the note, the plaintiff company then instituted an action against Lynch. However, the discovery was made that although Lynch had answered a questionnaire by giving his age as 21 years, he was in fact a minor at the time the note was executed. Hence, by reason of this defense the plaintiff was unable to recover a judgment against him.

Thereupon the plaintiff notified the defendant company of these facts and demanded payment of the note by reason of the defendant's indorsement thereon. Payment was refused by the defendant, and the plaintiff then instituted the instant suit in the Municipal Court of Dayton.

A judgment was rendered against the defendant by the trial court.

By reason of the provisions of Section 8170, General Code, the defendant warranted "That all prior parties had capacity to contract."

The statutory language used in that section of the Uniform Negotiable Instruments Act clearly indicates that the right to enforce that warranty may be asserted by a holder who is not a holder in due course.

Thus, Section 8170, General Code, provides in part:

"*Every person negotiating an instrument* by delivery or by a qualified indorsement *warrants:*

"3. That all prior parties had capacity to contract.

"4. That he has no knowledge of any fact which would impair the validity of the instrument or render it valueless.

"But when the negotiation is by delivery only, the warranty extends in favor of no *holder* other than the immediate transferee. . . ."

On the other hand, Section 8171, General Code, provides in part:

"Every indorser who indorses without qualification, *warrants, to all subsequent holders in due course;*

"1. The matters and things mentioned in paragraphs numbered one, two and three of the next preceding section.

"2. That the instrument is at the time of his indorsement valid and subsisting.

"In addition, he engages that . . ."

It is obvious from a comparison of the two foregoing sections of the General Code that the warranties provided for in Section 8170, General Code, are available to other holders than those in due course. Section 8170, General Code, states that every person negotiating an instrument "warrants" and also recognizes the warranty as extending in favor of a "holder," whereas Section 8171, General Code, states that the more extensive warranties there involved are only to "holders in due course." There is no language in Section 8170, General Code, which indicates that the warranties there provided for are only to holders in due course.

As the majority opinion states, the plaintiff had no notice of any incapacity, by reason of minority, of the maker of the note. By paying the defendant for the note, it is clear that the plaintiff relied on the defendant's warranty that the maker did have capacity to contract. It necessarily follows that the plaintiff may, as a holder of the note although not a holder in due course, enforce the defendant's liability on the warranty provided for by Section 8170, General Code; and that therefore the judgment must be affirmed.

Thus it may be seen that a taker other than a holder in due course may be able to secure repayment from his indorser, even if the taker could not prevail against a primary party having a contract defense.

This case, like the others in this section, was decided under the NIL. Under the UCC, the liability of the qualified indorsement (for such this was) warrants that "no defense of any party is good against him." This warranty would be broken in a case with circumstances similar to this case, arising under the UCC.

Discharge

A negotiable instrument, whether a bill, a note, or a check, is issued so that in some way it may serve as a substitute for money.

When a negotiable instrument is issued, it is contemplated that sooner or later a holder will present the instrument to the party primarily liable for payment. Even if there is dishonor and an indorser is forced to pay, that party retains rights against the maker or drawee-acceptor, if any.

When the instrument finally is paid by the party primarily liable, or by the drawer, the life of the instrument has run its course. It was originally issued to the payee as a substitute for money; on payment the money is returned in exchange for the instrument. The instrument is thereupon discharged. Upon a discharge of this sort, the party paying the holder should make sure to receive the instrument back. Otherwise, the instrument can be negotiated on to a holder in due course, and payment could be demanded all over again. The negligence of the party paying off the instrument, in not securing the instrument back, is not a defense against a holder in due course. A tender of payment (which consists in an offer to pay, combined with actual display of the cash, to demonstrate that the offer to pay is no idle brag) will operate to terminate further accumulation of interest, and to discharge the party making tender from attorney fees or costs. A tender does not discharge principal or interest already owing, however, even though the holder should refuse to accept payment.

Although payment is the usual means of discharge, there are various others. A note may be canceled, for example, by a party wishing to make a gift or do a favor to the primary obligee. Cancellation may be effected by deliberate destruction of the instrument, or by the holders plainly noting on the instrument his intention to cancel.

There are other, less frequently encountered means by which secondary parties to an instrument may be discharged. A holder's releasing the security of an instrument will discharge the party or parties secondarily liable, for the excellent reason that his act of doing so makes it much more likely that recovery cannot be obtained from the party primarily liable, which in turn would make it more likely that recourse against other parties would be necessary, were that permitted. Because the act of the holder has prejudiced the secondary parties, they are discharged from the burdens that the holder's act would have imposed upon them.

A material alternation, if fraudulent, by the holder will discharge a party whose contract is changed thereby; the instrument is enforceable against the original parties as it was before the alteration. An acceptance of a bill by the drawee-acceptor that varies from the terms of the instrument may be treated by the holder as a dishonor, should he wish to do so, but if he accedes in this variant acceptance, he discharges all other parties.

Finally, it has already been observed that delay in presentment or notice of dishonor will result in the discharge of the indorsers.

SECTION SEVEN

Business Regulation

CHAPTER THIRTY-SIX

History and Special Problems in the Regulation of Business

Proliferation of regulation is in main the result of greater complexity of and interdependence among the cogs and wheels of our industrial machine and greater interdependence between the latter and the public.

W E ARE ALL aware that our political and economic life, and probably life in general, is becoming progressively more complex. During days when business firms were small, the economy of a village could be nearly independent. Products were crude and readily inspected and reputations well known within the confines of a locale. Under these conditions elaborate regulation was less necessary to protect the consumers from the businessman and to protect competing businessmen from one another.

Even so, contrary to what many appear to believe, business regulation is not a product of the New Deal or of the twentieth century. Records of fifteenth- and sixteenth-century English parliaments show that much legislation was enacted for the regulation of merchants and artisans. Apparently, commerce was regulated in England and elsewhere for hundreds of years, without ever raising serious questions as to whether or not it was a proper subject of governmental activity. Only in comparatively recent times did the doctrine of laissez-faire appear, and in its wake, the attitude that government control over business is inherently bad. That period in which our government was striving to avoid regulation, if it ever did exist, was short and has ended. The memory lingers on.

At the present time our immense body of regulatory law presents a number of difficult problems both to the businessman and to the lawyer. Perhaps the first problem to consider is simply the vast extent of regulatory law. This body of law includes regulation imposed by the city, the county, the state, and the federal government, and by numerous separate administrative agencies at each level. The United Nations are not yet directly involved, so far as we know, but the fact is that treaties with foreign powers are law and thus binding upon citizens within the United States, to the point of overriding state legislation running to the contrary.

One problem presented by the enormous scope of business regulation is briefly enough stated: finding what one may legally do is no longer an easy matter. There is great danger to the businessman of his overlooking some prohibition of which he has never heard; indeed, perhaps imposed by some government agency of which he has never heard.

Unfortunately, there is no villain at whom to point our finger. Proliferation of regulation is in main the result of greater complexity of and interdependence among the cogs and wheels of our industrial machine and greater interdependence between the latter and the public. Changing philosophies concerning the responsibilities owed the public by holders of great economic power may be a cause for increased regulation, but probably changes in philosophy as to the need for regulation are grounded to some extent on a recognition of the facts and problems resulting from changed conditions.

Leaving the problems of proliferation of business regulation, another problem may be described as that of inefficient or inappropriate law. Although some forms of business regulation have been with us for centuries, many aspects of business regulation reflect recent developments, and there has not been time for much experimentation with different legal approaches.

Problems concerning big business, and the corresponding rise of big government to deal with these problems, are relatively new. By contrast, our common-law crimes—murder, burglary, and larceny, for example—are not basically different today than they were three hundred years ago. There has been plenty of time for the law relating to these crimes to work out acceptable precedents for dealing with practically every legal problem that might arise. The fact that many problems of business regulation are new, implies in itself that the most efficient or most appropriate solutions may not yet have been discovered, and may not be discovered without the benefit of more experience. Yet, even the fact that many problems of business regulation are relatively new does not exhaust the difficulties in lawmaking and administration. To make matters worse the needs of business regulation continue to change and expand very rapidly.

Probably the greatest problem, however, in devising a coherent scheme of business regulation is the enormous conflict in underlying philosophy as to what economic or political ends ought to be promoted by regulation. A consensus of feeling that the acts prohibited by the common-law crimes are wrong and should be discouraged by direct action of the government is a part of our cultural heritage. Views as to what and how extensive the role of government should be in regulating economic activity enjoys no such consensus. Furthermore, unlike the prosecution of common-law crime, the regulation of business unavoidably becomes a political issue. We are all affected in about the same way by the fact of murder being a crime. But only certain clearly defined groups are directly affected by most types of business regulation. Naturally, groups with special interests tend to bind together and exercise what political influence they can to promote their mutual interests. In addition, many people lacking any financial interest nevertheless have a powerful emotional attachment to certain views concerning the proper role of government in regulating business. As a consequence, any law relating to this subject is apt merely to reflect the outcome of the latest battle between proponents of opposing political or economic doctrines, and may be valid only until some other group mobilizes its heavy guns and renews the battle by electing or influencing legislators or influencing public opinion. Not only may the letter of the law change in response to political conditions, but the policies behind the administration of the law may change. Enforcement, for example, may be hamstrung by a legislature voting inadequate funds to an agency given the responsibility for enforcement, or through deliberate nonenforcement by decision of the executive department. And there is always the possibility of lower-echelon enforcement officers' holding views in conflict with those of their own superiors. This discussion by no means exhausts the difficulties inherent in the attempt to regulate business, but should suffice to demonstrate that the problems are more imposing than in more settled areas of our law.

CHAPTER THIRTY-SEVEN

The Legal Machinery for Regulating Business

It is . . . small wonder that the ordinary channels of law enforcement are not very effective in securing strict enforcement of business regulation.

Introduction

THE LEGAL STRUCTURES through which the power of government is brought to bear upon the business world are exceedingly diverse. The arrangements by which government may regulate a particular business are often arrived at through a consideration of pragmatic factors, including special characteristics of the business involved, the nature and extent of existing legal structures, and the strength of public sentiment and of political power supporting proposed regulation.

An analysis of all the different arrangements presently implementing business regulation would be impossible, and would serve no useful purpose. The following treatment explores two modal approaches to the regulation of business. These are (1) regulation through traditional procedures of the criminal law, and (2) regulation by the administrative agency.

This classification is less than perfect, because there is a good deal of overlap between these two forms of organization. Technically, the city police or the office of the county prosecutor may be administrative agencies, depending, of course, upon how the latter is defined. However, there *are* important differences in powers and procedures between the police and the prosecutor, on the one hand, and such agencies as the independent regulatory agencies of the federal government, as well as many agencies at the state level, on the other. The purpose of the ensuing discussion is to

546

show in what ways the powers given some agencies—the independent regulatory agencies, for example—represent a departure from the usual procedures of law enforcement, and the reasons for these departures.

Regulation Through Traditional Procedures
of the Criminal Law

The procedures by which we administer our criminal law are largely descended from the English common law, though there are many latter-day American modifications. Today crimes are almost always specifically defined in the criminal codes, even though the statutes in turn may be interpreted through criteria embodied in our common law. Because it is generally felt that a person should not be branded a criminal unless he at least has some theoretical means of knowing that his act is a crime, the statutes defining crime tend to be as specific as possible. Furthermore, criminal statutes are strictly interpreted by the courts; in the event of an ambiguity as to whether an act is a crime or not, the ambiguity will be resolved in favor of the defendant.

Probably these features of our criminal law are as they should be when the outcome of a decision determines whether a person is to be hanged or sent to prison. These features of our criminal law are not necessarily desirable when the outcome of a decision merely determines whether or not one may conduct business in a certain way. In fact, the requirements that legislation be very specific, and that the courts construe the legislation strictly, make business regulation through the procedures of the criminal law difficult, because often a course of action prohibited by legislation can be altered just enough to circumvent the legislation, without substantially altering the practices sought to be condemned. Amending the legislation in response is usually very cumbersome, and in any event, new circumventions may be quickly devised.

There are a number of other difficult problems in enforcing business regulation through the procedures of the criminal law. Assuming certain business practices are outlawed by the legislature, the burden is upon the police to discover violations of the law and upon the prosecutor to secure a conviction in a jury trial. Actually, it is doubtful if the policeman on the beat will ever hear of new regulatory legislation. The policeman feels, probably with ample justification, that his main job is to keep the peace, which is accomplished by enforcing our laws concerning major felonies, as well as public misdemeanors: assault and battery, drunk in public, disorderly conduct, and so forth. In addition the police are responsible for traffic regulation, which alone probably absorbs more time and energy than any other phase of police activity. More than likely the policeman is doing very well if he can keep up with our highly complex and rapidly changing law of arrest, search, and seizure, and he may be forgiven if he does not keep abreast of all other laws the legislature may enact.

Much the same things may be said of the prosecuting attorney. He too is apt to view his job as prosecuting major criminals, or minor criminals who visibly affect the public safety, as, for example, traffic offenders. He is not likely to divert time from these duties to go searching for indications of crime of which no one has complained (often the case concerning business regulation), and if he does, he is apt to look for crime more sensational than a dry, undramatic violation of some business code.

Much business regulation requires technical competence to understand and therefore to administer. Food and drug laws often require competence in medicine or chemistry, for example. Other areas may require special competence in economics, engineering, or even agriculture. The ordinary prosecutor is not an expert in all these disciplines himself, nor is anyone else, and he usually does not have the financial resources to enlist experts as investigators. To the extent that these conditions are present, they practically foreclose the possibility of enforcement in areas requiring technical competence.

The potential or actual violators of business regulation are apt to be persons whom no one, including the police, would think of as criminals in the ordinary sense. They are not the type of chronic troublemakers that become well-known police characters, nor the type of person that other citizens frequently report to the police. They are, in fact, likely to be respectable citizens in the ordinary sense of these words and often unaware themselves of the business codes they may be violating. Under these conditions, police and prosecutor are probably willing to look the other way, or content themselves with a warning instead of more vigorous prosecution when they do find violations of business codes. And very likely they are correct in the sense of reflecting overall community standards. If so, a jury would be loathe to convict even if an indictment were brought.

It is therefore small wonder that the ordinary channels of law enforcement are not very effective in securing strict enforcement of business regulation.

[EDITOR's NOTE: An example of an area in which state regulatory legislation is widespread, fairly uniform, but almost totally unenforced is that of false and misleading advertising. The basic statute is termed the "Printers Ink Model Statutes," *Printers Ink* being the advertising trade journal for which the statute was drafted. Most states have adopted the statute with or without modification. The statute is directed against the person submitting the advertisement rather than the publication in which it appears. The originator of the advertisement is held absolutely liable for any false or misleading advertisements made with the intent of promoting sales of goods or services. Remedies are through the usual criminal procedures.

Although the act is in most respects a good one, and has been widely adopted, convictions under it have been so rare as to be practically collector's items, due to defects in enforcement we have already mentioned. These statutes are supplementary to the common-law remedies in fraud or breach of contract. Possibly in some instances private suits are initiated instead of criminal prosecuton being brought under this act.]

Regulation by the Administrative Agency

Modern business conditions are not amenable to the type of regulation just described. It is no doubt desirable to assign lawmaking, law-interpret- ing, and law-enforcing functions to distinct and separate legislative, judicial, and executive bodies to the extent that it is possible to do so. However, the complexity of modern conditions makes effective business regula- tion most difficult. When the objective of law is the supervision of whole industries, for a dozen different reasons of social policy, it seems necessary to utilize forms of legal organizations that blend the three traditional branches of government.

Supervising a business or economic group on a day-to-day basis, which is the essence of a rational scheme of regulation, is almost an impossible task for either a court or a legislature. A court makes decisions based upon the merits of some occurrence past. The legislature seeks to guide conduct through broad precepts addressed to the future. What is needed for the task of regulation is an organization with the facilities to keep in touch with day- to-day events over a broad range of activities. There must be a permanent staff of experts engaged in investigating and fact finding, as well as formu- lating new plans, policies, and procedures by which to best utilize the in- formation obtained. The experts must be given the power to implement their plans and policies. To do this they need a measure of legislative power, and to enforce their legislative pronouncements, they need a meas- ure of judicial power.

Our modern administrative agency is the organization that has been de- vised to assume these extensive powers, and thereby to fill the gap result- ing from the limitations of the traditional branches of government.

Administrative agencies may be, and in fact are, created at all levels of the government, but they are usually created by the act of some legislative body.[1] The legislative act defines the purposes and powers of the agency, votes it a budget, and either designates the head of the agency or provides some means for selection of the head. After selection of the head, whether an individual or a board, then clerks and experts in appropriate disciplines are hired, lines of authority within the agency are drawn, and the agency is ready to proceed with the business of recommending and implementing regulatory activities.

[1] See page 186 for a discussion of the administrative agency set up by the State of New York for the purpose of implementing workmen's compensation legislation.

The tasks of the administrative agency usually consist in giving practical effect to some policy set out by the legislature as expressed by statute. One reason the administrative agency is an effective instrument is that by creating an agency or modifying an existing agency by statute, the agency may be tailored by the legislature to fit the particular types of problems with which the agency is supposed to deal. The agency becomes a specialist in dealing with certain more or less specific types of problems. The traditional law-enforcement agencies are generalists, devoting their energies over a wide variety of law-enforcement problems.

Another important advantage in regulating through administrative agencies is that the mass of detail involved in many types of economic regulation is of such magnitude that only a well-organized bureaucracy could cope with the detail. There must be thousands, or tens of thousands, of different railroad rates set by the Interstate Commerce Commission (ICC), taking into account various types of commodities for which rates are set and the different routes by which different commodities may be sent. It would seem unworkable to leave the enormous burden of rate-making with Congress. If Congress set railroad rates it could not possibly do much else, and would probably not even be able to keep up on its rate-making.

Because administrative agencies are created to administer activities that are very complex, the legislature usually grants the agency the power to fill in the details of a rather broad legislative mandate by instructing the agency to issue its own supplementary rules and regulations. These rules and regulations have the force of law in their own right, without the necessity of further approval by the legislature. In other words, the legislature may set up a standard or policy as a guide to the agency, but the agency is then expected to draw up rules and regulations to implement the standard or policy set by the legislature. Thus, many administrative agencies, though technically a part of the executive branch, wield broad legislative powers. Experts are given these powers because the experts in an administrative agency are presumed (and indeed hired to be) better qualified to write coherent and appropriate rules and regulations within their field of technical competence than are legislators. As one may see, the agency can meet the problem of evasion that often renders legislation ineffective: an agency can promulgate new rules and regulations as fast as means can be found to evade them.

In addition, the administrative agency often has very broad judicial powers. The agency itself determines whether or not its rules and regulations are being violated. If a party charged with being in violation of an agency rule denies the charge, he is usually entitled to a hearing in which to establish his innocence but—the hearing will be before the agency. Both prosecutor and judge will be members of the agency, and there will be no jury. The agency will determine the facts. Eventually, after all appeals within the agency have failed, an accused usually, though not always, may appeal to the courts for review. It should, of course, be mentioned that death or imprisonment of an accused is not involved in an administrative hearing. Most frequently the question involves whether some commercial practice may be continued or not. However, large sums of money often do hinge upon the determination by an administrative agency, and usually the agency determination is final for practical purposes because appeal to the courts is so expensive and because chances for success of such an appeal are small owing to various presumptions entertained by the courts that favor the agency.

Administrative agencies are given broad judicial powers for the same sort of reasons they are given broad legislative powers. The experts of the administrative agency are hired because of their expertise, and are therefore presumed better qualified to make determinations of fact involving complex technical issues, than are judges. They are also presumed to be particularly qualified in interpreting their own rules and regulations, on the common-sense theory that if they, the administrators, drew them up, presumably they have a better idea than outsiders of what the rules and regulations are supposed to mean. In the usual case, the only basis for appeal to the courts will be upon a question purely of law.

In summary, it is not going too far to say that administrative agencies, although performing an executive function, nevertheless often have broad legislative and judicial powers. However, administrative agencies provide a means, and perhaps the only means at our disposal, for devising and implementing systematic regulation where the problem of burdensome detail, the requirement of expert knowledge, and the need for continuing supervision cannot be met through traditional structures of the legislative, executive, and judiciary branches.

CHAPTER THIRTY-EIGHT

Growth of the Administrative Agency and Limitations on Its Power

If administrative action must be based upon enabling legislation, it follows that administrative action may in some instances be challenged on the ground that the action is not within the scope of the enabling legislation.

History of Administrative Agencies

JUST AS it is false, though widely believed, that business regulation is a new development, it is also false, as some believe, that administrative agencies are a product of the twentieth century, or more specifically, of the 1930's. Administrative law is in fact probably the oldest form of law, undoubtedly antedating formal legislation. The King's Council of medieval England, for example, was a form of administrative agency. It derived its power from the king, and its functions were to take a part in creating legislation and to supervise and enforce that legislation under the general guidance of the king. One difference between modern dictatorships and modern democracies would seem to be that the former govern almost entirely through administrative bodies, largely unchecked, whereas the latter rely on administrative bodies only when necessary, and provide legislative and judicial checks on the power bestowed.

At the present time, in America, administrative agencies may be found at all levels of government, but no doubt the best known are those of our federal government. One set of agencies are the traditional departments of the President's Cabinet: State; Defense; Treasury; Justice; Commerce;

Agriculture; Labor; Post Office; Health, Education, and Welfare; and Interior. Some of these are as old as the federal government itself, and all are headed by an appointee directly responsible to the President. Their power is largely determined by Congress, in the sense that in most cases the activities of the department are authorized by legislation, directing the department to undertake regulation or supervision of a certain area. Of course, the President often takes a strong hand in obtaining such legislation.

The next major group of agencies are the independent regulatory agencies, the Interstate Commerce Commission, Federal Communication Commission, Security Exchange Commission, National Labor Relations Board, Maritime Commission, and Civil Aviation Board, for example, though there are many others. These vary in structure, some being headed by several commissioners, others headed by a single person. They are not directly responsible to the President, and are at least supposed to be independent of both executive and legislature. Most of the heads are appointed by the President, with the advice and consent of the Senate, and are often appointed for a fixed term. Of course, often their policies can be influenced by Congress or the President, by, for example, cuts or threatened cuts in appropriations.

State governments have sets of agencies somewhat comparable to the federal government. Often, however, a large number of department heads at the state level are elected directly by the electorate.

Power wielded by an administrative agency must be justified through some grant of power by the legislature. Possibly the simplest model for this process would consist of a simple legislative act that creates an agency, specifies the boundaries within which the agency is supposed to administer, and also specifies the general purpose of the rules the agency may set up to implement the legislation.

Actually, of course, most of the federal agencies have been in existence for years, and recent legislation has usually extended or redefined the powers of particular agencies. For example, taxes and agricultural policy are revised almost every year and result in minor shifts in the operation of the Departments of the Treasury and of Agriculture, respectively.

If administrative action must be based upon enabling legislation, it follows that administrative action may in some instances be challenged on the ground that the action is not within the scope of the enabling legislation. As a matter of fact, this type of challenge has been made. It has on some occasions been successful, but it is clearly more difficult to succeed in such a challenge today than it was in the past. The increased difficulty lies both in the use of more careful wording by Congress in its enabling legislation, and in a more tolerant attitude of the courts toward delegation of legislative power.

The objection to delegation of power from legislature to administrative

agency has always been that a delegation violates the traditional concept of
the division of powers between executive, legislative, and judiciary. In
challenging the delegation of legislative power, we are concerned with a
question of degree. How much power may be delegated? In earlier days, attempts were made to restrict delegation as narrowly as possible, perhaps to
the point of only permitting certain specified acts to be delegated. As the
complexity of government has increased, the necessity of delegation has increased correspondingly, due to the inability of Congress to deal effectively
and in detail with more widely assorted matters of administration. The
degree to which legislative power may be delegated has more or less consistently increased with the passage of time, since the early days of the
republic, and the end of the process is not necessarily in sight. Originally, a
statutory standard by which administrative rules might be measured was
required for delegation to be valid. This was broadened so that rules made
consistent with a *policy* set out in an act are permissible. Considering that
the only policy set out in some legislative grants is that regulation be imposed to "further the public interest," it is doubtful whether even a policy
in the usual sense of the term is required at the present time.

Owing to the fact that today delegation may be very broad, and that
rules promulgated by the agency may likewise be very broad, the possibility
of challenging administrative activity on the ground of its being outside the
scope of the enabling act is naturally diminished. However, the fact remains that no agency is given a blank check to regulate everything in any
way it would like. There are limitations upon the subject matter under any
agency's jurisdiction, and no doubt an agency occasionally does exceed its
intended powers. When this is the case, an act of an agency may still be
voided by an appeal to the proper court.

Limitations on the Power of Administrative Agencies

The exercise of power by an administrative agency is usually through
one of two legal forms. One is the *rule* (or regulation), which consists in a
standard of conduct laid down by the agency, addressed to a group within
the jurisdiction of the agency. Thus, the rule has the effect of legislation.
Second is the *order,* which requests action of a specific party, usually an
individual or a firm. Thus the order has the effect of a judicial decision.

At the very least, any exercise of power by an agency—that is, a rule or
an order—must meet the minimum requirements of due process under the
Fifth or Fourteenth amendments.[1] Unfortunately, no general rule can be

[1] The Fifth Amendment to the Constitution of the United States of America provides in part: "No person shall . . . be deprived of life, liberty, or property, without
due process of law; . . . It restrains the *federal* government.
The Fourteenth Amendment repeats these words, though it contains a number of

advanced to define when an administrative action has met the require-ments of due process. The sum of possible actions of all possible agencies adds up to a series of patterns of fact far too complex to be amenable to general rules. Probably it is safe to say that notice of a proposed rule or order to the parties affected is always an important factor to a finding of due process. The greater the extent to which a decision is based upon an impartial hearing upon the evidence, or the greater the opportunity for judicial review, the less possibility there is that an action might not be found to meet the requirements of due process. In most instances, either an adequate hearing or adequate judicial review will be enough to constitute due process.

The federal agencies must (with certain exceptions) meet procedural rules imposed by the Administrative Procedure Act (hereafter referred to as the APA). This act, passed in 1946, was intended to impose some stand-ards of uniformity upon the welter of federal administrative agencies and to define limitations upon their powers. Most authorities do not feel that the act accomplished a great deal in this respect, but perhaps it does at least define the basic rights of those regulated by federal agencies within the act. (Some federal agencies are not covered by the act.) The procedural re-quirements under the act are probably somewhat more stringent than those imposed by the Fifth Amendment. Because the APA provides the nearest thing we have to a common denominator to the legal limitations governing administrative agencies, we will direct our attention to it. The APA does not apply to state administrative agencies.

LIMITATIONS ON RULE MAKING
RULE MAKING

APA—SECTION 4.

(a) *Notice*—General notice of proposed rule making shall be published in the Federal Register [2] . . . and shall include (1) a statement of the time, place, and nature of public rule making proceedings; (2) reference to the authority under which the rule is proposed; and (3) either the terms of substance of the proposed rule or a description of the subject and issues involved . . . where notice or hearing is required by statute (this subsec-tion shall not apply . . . in any situation in which the agency for good

other provisions. Interpretations of these clauses are extremely voluminous, both as to their general application and their application to certain specific problems of ad-ministrative law. It restrains the *state* governments.

[2] The introductory paragraph of Section 4 of the APA excludes the following sub-jects from these provisions: "(1) any military, naval, or foreign affairs function of the United States or (2) any matter relating to agency management or personnel or to public property, loans, grants, benefits, or contracts. . . ."

cause finds . . . that notice and public procedure thereon are impracticable, unnecessary, or contrary to the public interest).

(b) *Procedures*—After notice required by this section, the agency shall afford interested persons an opportunity to participate in the rule making through submission of written data, views, or arguments with or without opportunity to present the same orally in any manner; and, after consideration of all relevant matter presented, the agency shall incorporate in any rules adopted a concise general statement of their basis and purpose. *Where rules are required by statute to be made on the record after opportunity for an agency hearing, the requirements of sections 7 and 8 [3] shall apply in place of the provisions of this subsection.*

Note that two requirements are imposed: (1) notice of a proposed rule, of the terms of the rule, and of the hearing (if any); and (2) some provision for receiving the views of interested parties, but *this need not necessarily include provision for a formal hearing, including the right to present views orally and to examine witnesses.* Stated otherwise, a provision enabling interested parties to write an agency and express their views would be sufficient under the act in many instances. Note that in the last lines under (b) Procedures . . . the act specifies the instances in which a formal hearing is required—that is, when the enabling statute [4] specifies that a formal hearing is required. Last, there are several instances in which no notice or hearing is required. (See footnote 1.)

REQUIREMENTS CONCERNING HEARINGS

Aside from the requirements of notice and of hearing, an administrative act is more likely to be found Constitutional when challenged as a violation of due process if there is some established procedure provided for securing judicial review. The question of judicial review will be considered in the following section. This is suggested in the following provision of the APA:

ADJUDICATION

APA—SECTION 5.

In every case of adjudication required by statute to be determined on the record after opportunity for an agency hearing . . . [5]

---

[3] Sections 7 and 8 are set out in detail in the Appendix.

[4] *Statute* means the legislative act to which the agency traces its power. If that act specifies that notice and hearing are required, the agency must meet these requirements.

[5] Certain exceptions are noted, the most important being when a trial de novo is provided for.

(a) *Notice:* Persons entitled to notice of an agency hearing shall be timely informed of (1) the time, place, and nature thereof; (2) the legal authority and jurisdiction under which the hearing is to be held, and (3) the matters of fact and law asserted. In instances in which private parties are the moving parties, other parties to the proceeding shall give prompt notice of issues controverted in fact of law; and in other instances agencies may by rule require responsive pleading. . . .

(b) *Procedure:* The agency shall afford all interested parties opportunity for (1) the submission and consideration of facts, arguments, offers of settlement, or proposals of adjustment where time, the nature of the proceeding, and the public interest permit, and (2) to the extent that the parties are unable so to determine any controversy by consent, hearing, and decision upon notice and in conformity with sections 7 and 8.[6]

It must be emphasized again that this section, as did the section dealing with rule making, only requires a formal procedure in cases that require a hearing according to the enabling act. However, as said previously, there is a possibility that orders that afford *neither* notice that an order was under consideration *nor* a provision by which the person affected may be heard might be unconstitutional as lacking due process, even when no hearing is required under the enabling act.

JUDICIAL REVIEW

Assuming one is dissatisfied with the action of an administrative agency, to what extent is one entitled to challenge this action in the courts? Generally speaking, judicial review is required under the APA, though the act provides that this right may be precluded by a particular statute.

JUDICIAL REVIEW

APA—SECTION 10.

Except so far as (1) statutes preclude judicial review or (2) is by law committed to agency discretion—(a) RIGHT OF REVIEW.—Any person suffering legal wrong because of any agency action, or adversely affected or aggrieved by such action within the meaning of any relevant statute, shall be entitled to judicial review thereof.

The general rule, therefore, is that judicial review of an administrative action may be obtained. There are special cases in which review is denied, and in these cases review is not a matter of right. However, even when not

[6] Section 7 provides ground rules for hearings under the APA, and Section 8 provides certain procedures to which the agency must adhere in arriving at decisions. Sections 7 and 8 are set out in detail in the Appendix.

available as a review of the correctness of administrative proceedings, there is the possibility of challenging administrative actions on Constitutional grounds, especially due process, or challenging whether the action falls within the area of jurisdiction provided in the enabling act.

Limitations upon Judicial Review

Although the denial of judicial review by statute may be important in certain cases, probably of more importance is a rather wide variety of limitations relating to the type of question that will be reviewed, or to the circumstances under which a question will be reviewed.

As a general proposition, it seems clear that some limitations upon review by courts must be imposed; after all, if every case were subject to complete retrial before judge and jury, there would be no point in assigning certain types of problems to administrative agencies. Practically every adverse decision of an agency might well be appealed, with the court in every case being called upon to substitute its own judgment for the expert knowledge of the agency. This would not be a workable arrangement for reasons previously discussed.

On the other hand, some review must be afforded if the agencies are not to become dictators. Absolute power appears to encourage arbitrary use of that power, and surely some legal check on the exercise of power by administrative agencies is in order.

The balance struck between these competing demands reflects an attempt to give as much leeway as possible to the agencies in the determination of factual matters, and matters requiring expert knowledge, at the same time permitting a review of essentially legal questions. The main problem in applying a formula of this type is that there is no clear line between factual matters and those requiring expert knowledge on one hand, and legal questions on the other. However, a vague guide is doubtless better than none at all. Several specific rules are in use, all of which serve to limit the possibility of judicial review.

The first of these is the rule that before recourse to the courts may be sought, all possible remedies available from the agency must be exhausted. Thus, in the usual proceeding, a hearing may first be conducted before a trial examiner. Following an unfavorable decision before the trial examiner, there is still ordinarily the possibility of appeal directly to the head of the agency. Until such an appeal is requested, and acted upon, there is no right to judicial review. Of course, if an agency is unduly slow in making a final decision, the unnecessary delay may in itself be a basis for appeal to the courts.

Any special requirements imposed by an agency as a condition precedent to final hearing must be met, assuming they are reasonable. For example, an agency may require that a petition to appeal to the head of the

[D]PPING THE FOURTH BRANCH [8]

The six powerful commissions that referee the nation's business competition do guard the public's interest in a majority of cases. But it is fair to ask whether a majority is enough. A high court is expected to be ethically unassailable in all cases. And one of the roles of the fourth branch agencies is to act as a kind of high court over business, in the public interest.

[...] continue to pop to the surface of the news as congressional [...]uice around in the quiet recesses of the federal regulatory agen[...]

[...]gs in proper perspective, it should be emphasized that the standard [...]his so-called "fourth branch of government" is generally high. The [...] commissions that referee the nation's business competition do [...]blic's interest in a majority of cases.
[...] fair to ask whether a majority is enough. A high court is expected to [...] to act as a kind of high court over business, in the public interest. [...]ce peddlers do not phone justices of the Supreme Court to argue or [...] a case before the jurists. They do not do so because (1) the tradition [...]ial inviolability, though not absolute, is at least very strong; and [...]n selected for top judicial posts are generally above reproach. [...] question is what props may be used to help establish similar traditions [...]itudes for the fourth branch.
[...]st, it seems reasonable to ask Congress to pass a minimal code of ethical [...]ards. This should include a requirement, under threat of penalty, that all [...]ersations or letters on a case under adjudication be made a part of the [...]rd.
[...] is, of course, impossible to legislate honesty. But such a requirement would [...] the well-intentioned commissioner, who might be tempted to make excep- [...]ns for friendship's sake, chapter and verse to quote on why he has to enter [...] friend's conversation in the official record.
Second, it is sensible to seek means of assuring that all presidential selections [...]or these posts are men of the highest caliber and strictest ethical character [...] these posts are men of the highest caliber and strictest ethical character. Bu[...]

Many of the present commissioners on the six agencies are such men. Bu[...] "many" are not enough.

We agree with the suggestions made recently by Judge Henry Friendly of th[...] Second Circuit Court of Appeals. He urged that Presidents give the sam[...] attention to appointments for these posts that they do for supreme judici[...] appointments; that law groups keep a sharp watch on the posts; and that Co[...] gress indicate in advance what qualifications are expected in the men it mu[...] approve.

It is under such men that the tradition of inviolability will grow.

✧

agency be filed within a certain period of time after the first hearing. If the time period lapses, the complainant may find he is foreclosed from further legal action.

Two rules of thumb used by courts as a basis for limiting review of administrative agency decisions apply to the area of decisions of fact, and are closely related. One of these is that decisions confined solely to findings of fact will normally be accepted. A rather crude analogy may be made between the function of the jury in an ordinary jury trial at law, whose findings of fact are ordinarily accepted, and the agency, whose findings are ordinarily accepted on review. The other rule relating to this question is little more than a clarification of the agency's role in fact determination, and this is known as the substantial evidence rule. This rule holds that following an examination of the facts of a case, though they may be in dispute, the agency may not be overruled in its finding of fact if there is substantial evidence in support of the agency finding. This does *not* mean overwhelming evidence; it means, in effect, that when there is evidence, but the evidence is reasonably subject to dispute, the agency can resolve the dispute according to its own judgment.

Two other rules dealing with the acts of an agency closely parallel one another. One of these is that acts that fall purely within the discretion of the agency may not be appealed. It is impossible to specify what may or may not be within the agency's discretion lacking a specific context. In general, however, one might say that the purposes and goals to be served by an agency are not matters of discretion, they depend upon statute, but the organizational methods and the means selected to implement goals are generally matters of discretion. The other rule, closely related to the rule of agency discretion, is that matters purely within the expertise of the agency may not be appealed. There is clearly a substantial overlap between these two rules. How the purposes of the agency are to be implemented would tend to be matters of expertise, and it would seem to be difficult to distinguish the two concepts. After all, an agency is given discretion mainly for the purpose of exercising its expertise.

INTEGRITY OF SECURITIES AND EXCHANGE COMMISSION GUARDED: TRADITION SET [7]

> *Somehow or other the SEC (Securities and Exchange Commission) has created an atmosphere around itself like the Supreme Court: . . . These [early] leaders allowed no monkey business —they created an aura of cool integrity that pretty well continues to this day.*

Among the recent shocking disclosures of influence peddling and hidden pressure upon the regulatory agencies in Washington, the Securities and Exchange Commission looks clean and unsullied. Why?

Some think the answer goes to the heart of the problem of the great regulatory commissions: the "fourth branch of government" which determines such intimate matters as the price you pay for an interstate bus ticket or the channel on which you hear your favorite program.

Somehow or other the SEC has created an atmosphere around itself like the Supreme Court: nobody offers free airplane rides to the members of the Supreme Court; it would be unthinkable for litigants to call up Supreme Court justices to plead their side. (Something very much like this has been done in the Federal Power Commission and Federal Communications Commission.)

Not the SEC.

PATTERN SET AT START

Why this difference? Primarily, observers think, because of the kind and caliber of men on the SEC, and particularly those at its start. They set a pattern. They established a tradition.

The regulatory agencies are policemen—just as real as the uniformed patrolman on the corner beat. Politics and apathy can demoralize a police force. They can do the same thing to a federal regulatory commission.

The first head of the SEC in 1934 was Joseph P. Kennedy, New England financier; the second, James M. Landis; the third, William O. Douglas, present member of the Supreme Court. Like a Vermont block of granite, Judge Robert E. Healy, an initial member of the SEC, strengthened the structure. These leaders allowed no monkey business—they created an aura of cool integrity that pretty well continues to this day.

BIZARRE FINDINGS

There is a tendency of federal regulatory agencies after they have been set up by a reform wave to be neglected and forgotten, a home of political hacks. Often they seem to become the agents of the interests they are supposed to regulate. After years of journalistic criticism, Congress finally set up an investigation in 1957 and it has produced some of the most spectacular sequels and bizarre episodes of the Eisenhower administration, including the fall of Sherman Adams.

There has been repeated evidence that Congress itself has been embarrassed by the genie it has released out of the bottle, *for some of the strongest behind-the-scenes pressure upon weak regulatory agencies comes from congressmen themselves.*

Practically everything the original subcommittee touched upon under the short-lived tenure of counsel Bernard Schwartz, and the later committee under Chairman Oren Harris (D) of Arkansas, produced an explosion. There have been the payola hearings, the spectacular disclosures of rigged quiz shows, the discovery of gifts from Bernard Goldfine, the resignation and indictment of FCC Commissioner Richard A. Mack, the recent resignation of FCC Chairman John Doerfer, and now new questions and charges.

PROBES CAL

Most sophisticated

What it disclosed cer
seemed sporadic and r
needed into what is real

Why have not men of h
promised to bring the "best
inseparable part of these poli
public?

Right at present here are thre

a. The payola inquiry will sho
idol of teenage millions.

b. Thomas G. Corcoran, one-time
on private talks he had with three me
on a gas utility rate case after the public

c. Rep. Oren Harris himself is unde
having approved in advance the accepta
members of the FPC of a free airplane ri
member, at the expense of a gas-pipeline c
before the commission.

The bewildered public asks: What are the e
agencies, business world, and of Congress itself

A startling explanation of the Corcoran epis
approaches to regulatory agencies are "accepted pr

Again, Chairman Harris, himself attempting to
federal agencies, now supports the acceptance of f
sioners on the ground that it was "an errand of mercy."

NEW CODE DEMANDED

The payola and rigged quiz inquiries disclosed a cyn
norance by the FCC of what was going on under its nose.

The Harris subcommittee in its 1959 report proposed a
practice to prevent the agencies from becoming "a headless fo
government."

But the nation knows that it is not any written code that ke
Court incorruptible—it is simply a tradition that any other cours
merely intolerable but unthinkable. In general, this has applied
too.

The Harris subcommittee added that appointment of men "of u
ability and character" would be "one of the most effective steps"
standards on the commissions. Most observers here agree that what is
is not an absence of ethical guidelines but a lapse of morale, and abo
human failure.

❖

Indiscretions
investigators s
cies.

To put thin
of ethics in t
six powerfu
guard the p

But it is
be ethicall
agencies i

Influen
cajole or
of judic
(2) me

The
and at

Fir
stand
conv
reco

I
giv
ti
th

f

REGULATORY IRREGULARS [9]

*Only the appointment of dedicated and courageous commission-
ers, knowledgeable in the field they must referee, can assure safeguarding of the public interest.*

Last week President Eisenhower promised the nation "a better man" to fill a
crucial post on the Federal Power Commission.

Had he produced such a better man—or indeed appointed such men to all of
the regulatory posts he has filled recently—we would have applauded him. For
it is in the field of "better men" that most can be done to improve the "fourth
branch of government." As it is he has failed to grasp this opportunity for
propping that sagging branch.

There are good men in the six commissions that oversee transport, securities,
communications, trade and advertising, aeronautics, and power supplied in the
interest of the public and of a healthy balance in these industries. But there are
not enough.

And the President's recent appointments—with the exception of his new
Federal Communications Commission chairman—have not improved the situation.

We do not agree that the President's failure to reappoint the courageous,
consumer-minded power commissioner, William Connole, was automatically a
bad decision. We do not believe in indispensable men. But when Mr. Connole
was not replaced with an appointee of equal vigor and consumer orientation,
this dropping of Connole did become regrettable.

With variations, the same can be said of new appointments to the Interstate
Commerce Commission and to the Civil Aeronautics Board.

Certainly none of these newly designated commissioners are bad men. They
are, indeed, men of capability in certain fields. But none are clearly qualified as
the "better men" needed in the specific fields involved. And none have shown
marked understanding of consumer interests.

This clearly is a problem that rests in the executive department's lap.
Codes of ethics can set minimum standards of conduct for the regulators.
Congressional investigation can bring about cautious adherence to the letter of
these standards. But these are negative virtues.

Only the appointment of dedicated and courageous commissioners, knowledgeable in the field they must referee, can assure safeguarding of the public
interest. The Senate can reject bad men. It can do little, however, to influence
the appointment of "better men" instead of those who are simply "not bad."
That is the President's job.

✧

Mention should be made of certain differences between the courts and the regulatory agencies which are overlooked in the above readings.

First, a regulatory agency of necessity works with a particular industry, and therefore, with particular leaders of that industry. Dealings with them are apt to be both frequent and continuous over a period of years. This is inevitable, because in order to regulate intelligently, the regulators must keep in touch with the activities of the regulated.

The courts deal with a wide variety of problems, with a diffuse clientele having nothing resembling a common background. They are therefore not apt to build up acquaintanceships with those appearing before them; in fact, if a case involving an acquaintance should arise, it is easy enough for a judge to disqualify himself.

The regulatory agencies have a much more positive lawmaking job than do the courts, and it is impossible for them to seal themselves off from contacts among the regulated, as the courts both can and do. Granted that the administrator must keep in contact, it then becomes most difficult to draw the line as to whether a friendly drink, a friendly dinner, or a free airplane ride is permissible or not. These are activities that our legislators may engage in without much hesitation as to the ethics of the situation.

CHAPTER THIRTY-NINE

An Illustration of the Problems of Business Regulation —The Antitrust Laws

The Sherman Act demonstrates a recognition that competition is important and that affirmative action by the government is necessary and desirable in order to maintain competition. Yet in many areas of the economy, competition is not required, and indeed, has been abolished by law.

Who Must Compete?

EARLIER IN THIS TEXT the statement was made that law tends to be at its most confused when the underlying policies to be implemented are none too clear. The segment of business regulation designed to enforce competition provides good examples of competing, contradictory policies that are reflected by competing, contradictory rules of law.

The history of business regulation reveals wide fluctuation in policy concerning competition. In early times, restrictions upon competition through devices such as price-fixing by guilds, by legislation, and by government patents and monopolies were common throughout Europe. At a later date competition came to be regarded as desirable, and in England agreements between competitors by which they agreed not to compete were usually considered contrary to public policy and unenforceable at common law. However, at no time were agreements not to compete a criminal offense at common law. They merely could not be enforced through the courts in the event one party violated the agreement.

We must bear in mind that our dedication to competition is based upon reasons; mainly the belief that competition serves the end of protecting the

565

public. Prices cannot be raised to unconscionable heights, nor quality lowered, while other businessmen are offering more reasonably priced products of better quality. The least efficient competitors are eliminated. The market tends to serve as a regulator.

From this reasoning it follows that when the market cannot operate effectively, because competition is lacking, other types of controls must be substituted to protect the public interest. This is precisely the line of development that American business regulation has tended to follow.

The problem facing legislators attempting to maintain competition between business concerns has been, first, to identify the devices by which erstwhile business concerns become cooperators or otherwise avoid the rigors of competing. Next, the legislators have attempted to devise statutes that would forbid the practices that had restrained and were restraining competition.

The Sherman Antitrust Act [1] was the first federal antimonopoly legislation. It was enacted by Congress in 1890. Congress derived its Constitutional authority under the power to regulate interstate commerce (Article I, Section 8, of the Constitution), and the provisions apply only when interstate commerce is affected.

SHERMAN ANTITRUST ACT [EXCERPTS]

1. Every contract, combination in form of a trust or otherwise, or conspiracy, in restraint of trade or commerce among the several states, or with foreign nations, is declared to be illegal.
2. Every person who shall monopolize, or attempt to monopolize, or combine or conspire with any person or persons to monopolize any part of the trade or commerce among the several states or with foreign nations, shall be deemed guilty of a misdeameanor.

The act provides a maximum fine of $5,000 and imprisonment up to one year as criminal penalties; for injunctions against further abuses; and in addition for civil suits by private parties injured by unfair restraints, for which treble damages may be awarded.

The means of avoiding competition that were identified and prohibited by the Sherman Antitrust Act are three. The first devices prohibited are *restrictive agreements* between competing business concerns. These agreements might be to divide up markets—by geographic area, for example—or competitors might simply set prices at a uniform level, usually but not necessarily at an artificially high level; or agreements might be made *not* to alter production, improve quality or design, or expand sales efforts.

The second devices prohibited are *restrictive combinations*. These are

[1] 15 USCA 1–7.

usually accomplished by combining two or more concerns into one large enough to dominate a market, or at least large and powerful enough to restrain competition. Many of our present industrial giants, if not most, were formed in this way.

The third (although the dimensions of this prohibition have not been well defined even today), *monopolizing,* or attempting to monopolize without engaging in activities enumerated above. This question involves the effect of size and economic power per se, even if acquired through both fair and legal means, as, for example, growth.

The Application of Antitrust Legislation

Let us see how the Sherman Act has succeeded in dealing with the three categories of practices enumerated above.

(1) *Restrictive agreements* have been found to be per se violations of the act, and, in fact, when price changes of competing firms have been concerted over a period of time courts have been willing to imply an illegal agreement without direct proof that such an agreement actually existed. Trade associations of some industries have been subject to particular scrutiny regarding price setting activities under the Sherman Act. The most recent headlines featuring this type of violation have been the startling revelation of collusive price fixing in the electrical industry.

(2) *Restrictive combinations* (mergers and consolidations being the most common type) present much greater difficulties. How should *combination . . . in restraint of trade* be interpreted? Every merger or consolidation will restrain trade to some extent: the two or more competitors who joined hands will no longer be competing with one another. Yet there was no indication that every merger or consolidation was intended to be illegal. Sound economic considerations may dictate merger or consolidation. Most types of manufacturing enterprise must achieve a certain minimum size to reach optimum efficiency. Merger is a quick way to reach optimum size.

The test quite properly applied to combination cases has been termed the *rule of reason.*[2] Is the restraint, created by a combination, reasonable? This test has been criticized, especially as applied to some of the older cases, as overlooking by definition a certain degree of monopolization. In fact, some cases did express a rather tolerant attitude toward anything short of total domination of a market. However, the problem was not in the test but in the specific application of the test.

[2] The *rule of reason* applies to all types of restraints, but price-fixing agreements have been held unreasonable per se, thus restricting the significance of the rule of reason to cases involving combinations. (Source: Arthur T. Dietz, *An Introduction to the Anti-Trust Laws* (Middleton, Conn.: Bookman Associates, 1951), pp. 8, 9.

As the student has discovered, there are usually only two types of test by which a legal decision can be made. One, a mechanical test, whereby a very precise and objective fact determines the result of a case. (For example, a contract is formed when the acceptance is placed in the hands of the offeror's agent of communication. The mere fact of doing so determines when a contract was formed: a more mechanical test could not be imagined.) Many questions, however, are matters of degree, and must be decided by weighing the evidence and applying judgment. (Whether a contract is sufficiently *certain* to be enforced is a question of this type.) Practically every question in tort law is determined by judgment, or stated otherwise, reasonableness considering the circumstances. A mechanical test is impossible when no one objective fact can offer a basis for decision. Therefore, whether adequate or not, some statement of whether or not a combination is reasonable will remain the test of guilt or innocence in antitrust prosecution regarding combinations for the foreseeable future. This will be true until the science of economics can devise a test by which harmful combinations can be separated from beneficial or at least harmless combinations, by reference to some objective, ascertainable fact.

Statutory Supplement to the Anticombination Provision

Due mainly to weaknesses in the anticombination provision, the Sherman Act was supplemented in certain respects by the Clayton Act of 1914.[3] Section 7 of the Clayton Act, as amended in 1950, contains a provision preventing the acquisition of stock, or assets of another corporation, ". . . where the effect of the acquisition might be substantially to lessen competition, or to create a monopoly."

All mergers [4] or consolidations involve an acquisition of stock by one company or both and therefore fall within the above provisions. Some originally unforeseen loopholes in the Sherman Act were plugged by this act. Control of a corporation could be obtained through a purchase of a controlling interest in the voting stock, and thus not be a combination under the Sherman Act but still result in restraint of competition. Or one corporation could sell out its assets to another corporation, in effect removing itself as a competitor, but not technically constituting a combination of the two. These practices were not prohibited under the Sherman Act. They are now covered by the above language of the Clayton Act as amended.

[3] 15 USCA 12 ff.

[4] Mergers are accomplished by Company *A* issuing its own stock to the stockholders of Company *B* in exchange for the entire business structure of Company *B*. *B* ceases to exist; *B* has been swallowed up by *A*, but, of course, the former *B* stockholders are now stockholders of *A*. Consolidations follow a similar pattern except that a new corporation *C* is formed, and *C* stock is given to stockholders of *A* and *B* in exchange for their present holdings. Then *A* and *B* cease to exist.

Furthermore, the language of the Clayton Act, "the effect . . . *might* be substantially to lessen competition," appeared to be a mandate by the legislature to place greater weight on effects, and less on intent and other considerations favoring the combining corporations. In other words, *judgment* (or the rule of reason) remained the test, but the balance was shifted to place greater emphasis on results in the interest of preserving competition.

Interlocking directorates, a means by which joint action of corporations may be secured by having the same directors on the boards of two or more companies, are prohibited by the Clayton Act, but this provision may be circumvented in so many ways that the provision is practically a dead issue.

Enforcement of the Sherman Act has always been through the Antitrust Division of the Justice Department, relying upon traditional procedures of the criminal law, or of equity. The supplementary legislation added by the Clayton Act and its amendments is enforced by the Federal Trade Commission, an administrative agency. The advantages of an administrative agency, from the point of view of law enforcement, have been discussed in a prior section.

(3) *Monopolizing* in itself is the third practice forbidden by the Sherman Act. This is outlined in Section 2 of the Act. Although most violations of Section 2 of the Sherman Act would tend also to be violations of Section 1, conceivably one might monopolize without actually intending to do so. At one point Alcoa produced 90 percent of the virgin aluminum ingot production in the United States, and prosecution was begun under Section 2. However, World War II interrupted prosecution, and during the war two other aluminum companies had reached a competitive position. Alcoa's dominance was reduced, and a final decision on the case was postponed for five years, then for an additional five years. The court seemed to hold that size and success alone might not be considered an antitrust violation, but that size plus any abuse of the power size bestowed would be a violation of Section 2. Presumably, then, Section 2 may become an issue when for some reason, even unusual efficiency, a concern's growth is so rampant it virtually controls a market. The test in this type of case appears to be a "control-plus" test. If a firm is big enough to exert market control, and if in any way it exerts this market control to secure some advantage, the possession of power is abused and subject to penalty. There is admittedly an inconsistency in encouraging competition until the unsure line is reached at which a business becomes dominant, then, in effect, requiring it to assume an essentially noncompetitive, public-oriented attitude. To put the dilemma another way, we might say that competition is a good thing except when one competitor is altogether too successful.

Limitations upon the right of a concern to do business as it may please have often been imposed when competition itself would no longer function as a regulator. The situation presented by a giant concern with almost total economic control over certain commodities would be similar to that presented by utilities. Should antitrust prosecution be abandoned as a restraint in favor of more detailed regulations of a few industrial giants? It is doubtful if any theory provides an adequate answer. In any event, however, monopolization as such, without other illegal activities, has not to this day been the basis for a successful prosecution under the Sherman Act.

Countercurrents in Antitrust Policy

Although there have been additional and supplementary acts, the Sherman Act may be said to represent one current in the treatment of the problems involving competition. The Sherman Act demonstrates a recognition that competition is important and that affirmative action by the government is necessary and desirable in order to maintain competition.

Yet in many areas of the economy competition is not required, and indeed has been abolished by law. We shall attempt to explore some of these conflicting currents in the paragraphs below. All of the exceptions probably have one common denominator. In order to be exempt from what might be termed the basic philosophy of the Sherman Act, each interest must have mobilized substantial political power. Basically, the decision as to what activity is or is not required to compete is a political decision. However, this is not to say that there are not in most instances important economic reasons for exempting an economic activity from the rigors of competition.

It seems rather clear that at common law, workers were expected to compete against one another for the opportunity of selling their services. Indeed, agreements between workers to withhold their services unless their demands were met was the *one* type of agreement not to compete that was not only unenforceable but was prosecuted as a criminal offense. This type of agreement was considered a criminal conspiracy, aimed at injuring the employer.

The concept of workers organizing and going on strike gradually gained acceptance. Without tracing the details of the union movement, we know that eventually the right to join a union and the right to strike not only became tolerated, but are today protected by federal statute. One may rationalize this development on the basis that the disparity in bargaining power between an individual employee and a modern business enterprise is usually too great, unless the worker is permitted to organize. Unrestrained competition between workers for available jobs resulted in wages and working conditions that were in the long run unacceptable to our society. Accordingly, adjustments were made in the legal structure, and workmen were permitted to bargain as a group.

Even prior to the Wagner Act (1935), which first regulated employers and prevented certain means of their discouraging union membership among their employees, the Sherman Act was not widely applied against unions. Theoretically, it would seem that any agreement to bargain as a member of a union would constitute a contract in restraint of trade. Actually, the mere act of forming a union or even of striking has never been held to be a violation of the Sherman Act, though on one or two occasions strikes that resulted in significant interference in interstate commerce were so held. Eventually, with the passage of the Taft–Hartley Act, regulation of unions was placed almost exclusively in the hands of the NLRB.

Although labor was permitted by law to limit the competition for jobs, and to organize to meet the superior economic power of big employers, before long, government regulation of big labor was found to be necessary. At the present time, a broad range of labor-management problems are dealt with by the National Labor Relations Board, a federal administrative agency, regulating both management and unions in their conduct of labor relations in interstate commerce.

It is all very well to argue that when competition produces desired results as a regulator, it will be relied upon, and when not, controls that prevent abuses by those not competing will be imposed. But there is no small problem in determining when competition does produce desired results as a market regulator and when it does not.

If wage earners may organize because, in the long run, their competing against each other for jobs is undesirable, how about other types of workers? How about the proprietors of one-man barber shops? Should they not be permitted to organize for the same reasons? We know as a matter of common observation that they do. The argument in favor of their organizing runs the same; unrestricted price-cutting among competing barbers would reduce wages to an unconscionably low level. The same argument is used by plumbers and other types of proprietors.[5]

By the same token, lawyers have seen to it that they are required, as a matter of professional ethics, to adhere to minimum fee schedules. Comparable sanctions are imposed by other professional groups. This approach is rationalized as necessary to protect the public; if a lawyer is unable to make a decent living, the temptation to engage in ambulance chasing and other forms of unethical conduct is increased. The logic may be valid, but if so, we cannot assume that competition is necessarily in the public interest in other contexts.

The small retailer, the druggist, the neighborhood grocer, and the corner haberdasher do not see why these considerations do not apply to him. Is the fact that one group provides services exclusively, whereas the other,

[5] Organization among such other groups appears to be fairly common, though presumably the Sherman Act would be violated if interstate commerce were involved.

besides serving customers and designing attractive displays, also sells property so significant? Again the line is gray, not black or white.

It is partly because of the very real question as to whether competition does always protect the public, in a particular situation, that the goals of business regulation often seem contradictory. Partly the contradiction stems from political decisions that really are contradictory; that is, on some occasions proponents of competition have obtained legislation favorable to their point of view, and on other occasions the opponents of competition have been successful.

In response to the plea of small retailers for a device to protect the public from the evils of chain stores, especially their habit of lowering prices and employing "loss leaders," legislation has been passed in many states permitting "retail price-maintenance agreements." These agreements permit the owner of a trademark, normally the manufacturer or wholesaler, to provide by contract, or in some cases practically to dictate the price at which items carrying the trademark may be sold. Thereby, *price* competition on these items is abolished. Needless to say, the small retailers attempt to persuade or pressure manufacturers to initiate price-maintenance agreements.

Statutes permitting retail price maintenance are termed *fair trade laws*. One important statutory mechanism by which fair trade laws authorize manufacturers practically to dictate prices is termed the *nonsigner clause,* and it operates as follows: a contract between a manufacturer and any *one* retailer naming the price at which a trade-marked item may be sold is, if nonsigner clauses are recognized in that state, binding upon *all other* retailers in the state. Certainly, a contract between two parties does not *normally* bind every other party in a state who might sell a certain product, therefore these statutes introduce a real novelty into the law. True, the right to change law through legislation is broad, but holding parties to a contract they did not make is a rather drastic step. Many state supreme courts have declared legislation creating a nonsigner clause unconstitutional.

As a matter of fact, it was recognized by the United States Congress that fair trade laws probably violated the Sherman Antitrust Act. Consequently, the Sherman Act was amended by the Miller–Tydings Act to exempt state fair trade legislation from the provisions of the Sherman Act. When the United States Supreme Court held that the Miller–Tydings Act did not permit the nonsigner clause, the McGuire Act [6] was passed, providing that nonsigner clauses are valid in any state that does not forbid them.

The justification that is put forth by the supporters of fair trade is that our economic system depends upon competition; the giant food and drug chains would drive the independents out of business if allowed to sell at

[6] 15 USC 45(5).

very low prices; driving the independents out of business would reduce competition; therefore, price-maintenance agreements are not a means of reducing competition but of maintaining competition. The plausibility of the argument demonstrates that the question is not as simple as it first appears. Some courts have rejected the nonsigner clause, the heart of fair trade legislation, as opposed to public policy, holding that although competition specifically designed to ruin a competitor is unfair, and could be enjoined, mere "stiff" competition is desirable. The reasoning is that if a concern is not efficient enough to buck the competition, there is no economic justification for its existence. This presents the broad policy question of whether or not there is an intrinsic value in such enterprises as the neighborhood grocery, the small farm, or the corner drug store if indeed they cannot compete economically. There is no ultimate answer, because the question is one of personal values.

Let us continue to examine the continuum of instances in which competition is modified by statute. Having started at one end of our spectrum with laborers, who should not or at any rate most clearly are not required to compete, we have progressed through "service-proprietors," such as barbers and plumbers, and professional men, who are also often relieved from the rigors of competition, though on somewhat less clear-cut theoretical, if not legal, grounds. Then we arrived at a middle area, small retailers of various sorts who in most states are provided some protection from competition on trade-marked items, though in some states are not. As we proceed on our scale from the individual laborer, the small business, to the opposite extreme and investigate large industrial enterprises, we would perhaps expect to find a clearly defined situation in which competition always (1) can, and (2) should, be enforced. If this was anticipated, the reader will be disappointed. To the contrary, some of our most difficult problems in formulating sound policy are found in this area.

In examining big business, we find many instances in which government regulation, rather than competition, is relied upon almost exclusively to protect the public interest. The best examples are the "natural monopolies" —public utilities, for example. Railroads, airlines, telephone and telegraph facilities, radio and TV stations, and power companies are usually granted virtual monopolies within a territory, or if not, entry is restricted so that competition is confined to only a few concerns. The reason for this preferential treatment is based upon simple economy. In these lines, required investment is so great that duplication would be a waste of national resources. Or, as is true of television channels, there are facilities for only a few concerns within an area. In return for the quasi-monopoly, the owners and managers of these concerns submit to thorough and far-reaching governmental regulation. The license or certificate necessary to operate must be obtained from the government; existing services may not be terminated even if unprofitable nor may services be extended into new territory without permission. Rates are set by the government, and all aspects of service held to the test of the public interest.

As illustrations of this type of regulation, the Interstate Commerce Commission (the first of the independent regulatory agencies) regulates the railroads and trucklines. The Civil Aeronautics Board regulates airlines. The Federal Power Commission regulates the electric power industry. The Federal Communication Commission regulates radio and television. The list could go on to great length; the main point we wish to make is that the industries included within the designation of "natural monopolies" gain something: a measure of freedom from competition, while they yield something: freedom of operation. They are supervised more closely than other concerns. Competition cannot act as a check; therefore regulation must.

Even aside from the countercurrents in antitrust policy enumerated in the previous section (unions, fair trade legislation, and regulated industries) there is a further contradiction in the implementation of the policy favoring competition.

Businessmen are required to compete with one another, but they are *not permitted* to compete ruthlessly. Thus we have the possibility of a mythical (maybe or maybe not) businessman, prosecuted under the Sherman or Clayton acts for such practices as engaging in a pricing scheme or refusing to invade territories dominated by other concerns in return for like favors in his own territory. Having fought an embarrassing and expensive suit brought by the government, and resolved to go forth and sin no more, our hero energetically strives to demonstrate his competitive instinct by crushing his competitors. He may soon find himself being prosecuted for unfair competitive practices.

Unfair Competition

The last area of business regulation we shall discuss will be in the area of unfair competition. This tends to break down into two types of practices: (1) those that are substantially designed to protect one competitor from another, and (2) those that are geared as much to protecting consumers from unfair practices as to preserving competition. We will discuss only the first, the second being too broad a subject for this text.

The purpose of much of the Clayton Act was to prevent squeezing out of competitors by "dirty tactics." Perhaps the most significant of these provisions is Section 2 of the Clayton Act, as amended by the Robinson–Patman Act, which prohibits price discrimination ". . . where the effect of such discrimination may be substantially to lessen competition or tend to create a monopoly in any line of commerce" or to thereby injure competitors or customers. Thus, quantity discounts to customers may be justified only by (1) *proof* of actual differences in the sellers costs between high- and low-volume purchasers, or (2) proof that interstate commerce is not affected. In addition, a showing that a party is merely meeting competition is a defense. Proof being difficult and expensive to collect, the end effect is pressure upon all businessmen to sell to all other businessmen at the same price, whether justifiable economically or not.

Even where economically justifiable, and this is proved, the FTC may outlaw quantity discounts where to do so may promote monopoly—that is, squeeze out an inefficient competitor. The Robinson–Patman amendment originated in investigations of chain stores, and is considered by some to be parallel in motive and effect to the fair trade laws. The purpose is to save the small, inefficient competitor from the large, efficient competitor. This is surely a countercurrent against the trend of the antitrust laws. It also illustrates a fact of business regulation that we will mention only briefly but that can hardly be overestimated in importance. A very large volume of business regulation today is initiated *not* by government or consumer groups but by special business interests. The objectives may be to see that their competitor who is operating above board is harassed by regulation, or to forbid "dirty tactics," or to get a subsidy or other forms of economic assistance. Tariffs and crop allowances serve as examples.

Exclusive dealerships, where a purchaser must buy all of an item from a seller if he wishes to buy any; or tying agreements—contracts in which a customer, to obtain one product by lease or purchase, must agree to buy other products from the seller or lessor are prohibited. Tying agreements are clearly a form of economic coercion upon buyers, and few arguments can be marshaled to defend them.

Another Robinson-Patman amendment of the Clayton Act prohibits a purchaser from paying his seller a fee for brokerage, commissions, or other similar pretexts. The seller is also forbidden from receiving fees of this nature. The purpose of this provision was to prevent the seller from extorting kickbacks, especially from the smaller and weaker firms. A commission to the *seller* can hardly amount to anything other than a kickback, or a discount to the favored buyers, *not* required to pay the fee, who are usually larger than those required to pay the fee.

All the Robinson–Patman amendments are controversial—as for that matter to a lesser degree is the whole area of government regulation of business.

There are well-informed persons, both economists and lawyers, who feel that the complex provisions of the Robinson–Patman amendments make no sense. As put by Donald Dewey: ". . . in short, the Robinson–Patman Act, on its face, outlaws all bargaining as the process is understood in the business world. Congress, of course, contemplated no such quixotic crusade but merely intended to soften, in some measure, the competition waged by a few large firms that had injured politically influential retailers and wholesalers. (One can make a good case that the law was aimed specifically at three companies, Sears Roebuck, Goodyear Tire and Rubber, and the A & P.) This object could probably have been realized had Congress limited itself to giving the Federal Trade Commission small appropriations and broad hints as to the firms they should have been used against." [7]

It is important to remember that exclusive franchises, or output or requirement contracts, almost always present some question of violation of this section of the Clayton Act. Careful draftsmanship and diligent study must be employed before making contracts of this nature, in order to ascertain that they are not in violation of the law.

We will not venture a final value judgment as to whether enforcement of competition is a realistic approach to business regulation, or whether more, or perhaps even less, drastic measures are necessary. Authorities on one side of the fence point to great concentrations of economic power as proof that antitrust has failed. On the other side, equally reputable authorities point out that the antitrust division of the Department of Justice and the Federal Trade Commission has been chronically underfinanced, and often supervised by administrations indifferent to antitrust. These political limitations present another question: to what degree has the policy of antitrust actually been accepted? The answers, if any, are not simple ones.

[7] Donald Dewey, *Monopoly in Economics and Law* (Chicago: Rand McNally & Co., 1959), pp. 196–197.

APPENDIX

Uniform Commercial Code

ARTICLE 1: GENERAL PROVISIONS

PART 1
Short Title, Construction, Application and Subject Matter of the Act

§1–101. **Short Title.** This Act shall be known and may be cited as Uniform Commercial Code.

§1–102. **Purposes; Rules of Construction; Variation by Agreement.** (1) This Act shall be liberally construed and applied to promote its underlying purposes and policies.

(2) Underlying purposes and policies of this Act are

(a) to simplify, clarify and modernize the law governing commercial transactions;

(b) to permit the continued expansion of commercial practices through custom, usage and agreement of the parties;

(c) to make uniform the law among the various jurisidictions.

(3) The effect of provisions of this Act may be varied by agreement, except as otherwise provided in this Act and except that the obligations of good faith, diligence, reasonableness and care prescribed by this Act may not be disclaimed by agreement but the parties may by agreement determine the standards by which the performance of such obligations is to be measured if such standards are not manifestly unreasonable.

(4) The presence in certain provisions of this Act of the words "unless otherwise agreed" or words of similar import does not imply that the effect of other provisions may not be varied by agreement under subsection (3).

(5) In this Act unless the context otherwise requires

(a) words in the singular number include the plural, and in the plural include the singular;

(b) words of the masculine gender include the feminine and the neuter, and when the sense so indicates words of the neuter gender may refer to any gender.

§1–103. **Supplementary General Principles of Law Applicable.** Unless displaced

577

by the particular provisions of this Act, the principles of law and equity, including the law merchant and the law relative to capacity to contract, principal and agent, estoppel, fraud, misrepresentation, duress, coercion, mistake, bankruptcy, or other validating or invalidating cause shall supplement its provisions.

§1–104. **Construction Against Implicit Repeal.** This Act being a general act intended as a unified coverage of its subject matter, no part of it shall be deemed to be impliedly repealed by subsequent legislation if such construction can reasonably be avoided.

§1–105. **Territorial Application of the Act; Parties' Power to Choose Applicable Law.** (1) Except as provided hereafter in this section, when a transaction bears a reasonable relation to this state and also to another state or nation the parties may agree that the law either of this state or of such other state or nation shall govern their rights and duties. Failing such agreement this Act applies to transactions bearing an appropriate relation to this state.

(2) Where one of the following provisions of this Act specifies the applicable law, that provision governs and a contrary agreement is effective only to the extent permitted by the law (including the conflict of laws rules) so specified:

Rights of creditors against sold goods. Section 2–402.

Applicability of the Article on Bank Deposits and Collections. Section 4–102.

Bulk transfers subject to the Article on Bulk Transfers. Section 6–102.

Applicability of the Article on Investment Securities. Section 8–106.

Policy and scope of the Article on Secured Transactions. Sections 9–102 and 9–103.

§1–106. **Remedies to Be Liberally Administered.** (1) The remedies provided by this Act shall be liberally administered to the end that the aggrieved party may be put in as good a position as if the other party had fully performed but neither consequential or special nor penal damages may be had except as specifically provided in this Act or by other rule of law.

(2) Any right or obligation declared by this Act is enforceable by action unless the provision declaring it specifies a different and limited effect.

§1–107. **Waiver or Renunciation of Claim or Right After Breach.** Any claim or right arising out of an alleged breach can be discharged in whole or in part without consideration by a written waiver or renunciation signed and delivered by the aggrieved party.

§1–108. **Severability.** If any provision or clause of this Act or application thereof to any person or circumstances is held invalid, such invalidity shall not effect other provisions or applications of the Act which can be given effect without the invalid provision or application, and to this end the provisions of this Act are declared to be severable.

§1–109. **Section Captions.** Section captions are parts of this Act.

PART 2

General Definitions and Principles of Interpretation

§1–201. **General Definitions.** Subject to additional definitions contained in the subsequent Articles of this Act which are applicable to specific Articles or Parts thereof, and unless the context otherwise requires, in this Act:

(1) "Action" in the sense of a judicial proceeding includes recoupment, counterclaim, set-off, suit in equity and any other proceedings in which rights are determined.

(2) "Aggrieved party" means a party entitled to resort to a remedy.

(3) "Agreement" means the bargain of the parties in fact as found in their language or by implication from other circumstances including course of dealing or usage of trade or course of performance as provided in this Act (Sections 1–205 and 2–208). Whether an agreement has legal consequences is determined by the provisions of this Act, if applicable; otherwise by the law of contracts (Section 1–103). (Compare "Contract.")

(4) "Bank" means any person engaged in the business of banking.

(5) "Bearer" means the person in possession of an instrument, document of title, or security payable to bearer or indorsed in blank.

(6) "Bill of lading" means a document evidencing the receipt of goods for shipment issued by a person engaged in the business of transporting or forwarding goods, and includes an airbill. "Airbill" means a document serving for air transportation as a bill of lading does for marine or rail transportation, and includes an air consignment note or air waybill.

(7) "Branch" includes a separately incorporated foreign branch of a bank.

(8) "Burden of establishing" a fact means the burden of persuading the triers of fact that the existence of the fact is more probable than its non-existence.

(9) "Buyer in ordinary course of business" means a person who in good faith and without knowledge that the sale to him is in violation of the ownership rights or security interest of a third party in the goods buys in ordinary course from a person in the business of selling goods of that kind but does not include a pawnbroker. "Buying" may be for cash or by exchange of other property or on secured or unsecured credit and includes receiving goods or documents of title under a pre-existing contract for sale but does not include a transfer in bulk or as security for or in total or partial satisfaction of a money debt.

(10) "Conspicuous": A term or clause is conspicuous when it is so written that a reasonable person against whom it is to operate ought to have noticed it. A printed heading in capitals (as: NON-NEGOTIABLE BILL OF LADING) is conspicuous. Language in the body of a form is "conspicuous" if it is in larger or other contrasting type or color. But in a telegram any stated term is "conspicuous." Whether a term or clause is "conspicuous" or not is for decision by the court.

(11) "Contract" means the total legal obligation which results from the parties' agreement as affected by this Act and any other applicable rules of law. (Compare "Agreement.")

(12) "Creditor" includes a general creditor, a secured creditor, a lien creditor and any representative of creditors, including an assignee for the benefit of creditors, a trustee in bankruptcy, a receiver in equity and an executor or administrator of an insolvent debtor's or assignor's estate.

(13) "Defendant" includes a person in the position of defendant in a cross-action or counterclaim.

(14) "Delivery" with respect to instruments, documents of title, chattel paper or securities means voluntary transfer of possession.

(15) "Document of title" includes bill of lading, dock warrant, dock receipt, warehouse receipt or order for the delivery of goods, and also any other document which in the regular course of business or financing is treated as adequately evidencing that the person in possession of it is entitled to receive, hold and dispose of the document and the goods it covers. To be a document of title a document must purport to be issued by or addressed to a bailee and purport to cover goods in the bailee's possession which are either identified or are fungible portions of an identified mass.

(16) "Fault" means wrongful act, omission or breach.

(17) "Fungible" with respect to goods or securities means goods or securities of which any unit is, by nature or usage of trade, the equivalent of any other like unit. Goods which are not fungible shall be deemed fungible for the purposes of this Act to the extent that under a particular agreement or document unlike units are treated as equivalents.

(18) "Genuine" means free of forgery or counterfeiting.

(19) "Good faith" means honesty in fact in the conduct or transaction concerned.

(20) "Holder" means a person who is in possession of a document of title or an instrument or an investment security drawn, issued or indorsed to him or to his order or to bearer or in blank.

(21) To "honor" is to pay or to accept and pay, or where a credit so engages to purchase or discount a draft complying with the terms of the credit.

(22) "Insolvency proceedings" includes any assignment for the benefit of creditors or other proceedings intended to liquidate or rehabilitate the estate of the person involved.

(23) A person is "insolvent" who either has ceased to pay his debts in the ordinary course of business or cannot pay his debts as they become due or is insolvent within the meaning of the federal bankruptcy law.

(24) "Money" means a medium of exchange authorized or adopted by a domestic or foreign government as a part of its currency.

(25) A person has "notice" of a fact when

(a) he has actual knowledge of it; or

(b) he has received a notice or notification of it; or

(c) from all the facts and circumstances known to him at the time in question he has reason to know that it exists.

A person "knows" or has "knowledge" of a fact when he has actual knowledge of it. "Discover" or "learn" or a word or phrase of similar import refers to knowledge rather than to reason to know. The time and circumstances under which a notice or notification may cease to be effective are not determined by this Act.

(26) A person "notifies" or "gives" a notice or notification to another by taking such steps as may be reasonably required to inform the other in ordinary course whether or not such other actually comes to know of it. A person "receives" a notice or notification when

(a) it comes to his attention; or

(b) it is duly delivered at the place of business through which the contract was made or at any other place held out by him as the place for receipt of such communications.

(27) Notice, knowledge or a notice or notification received by an organization is effective for a particular transaction from the time when it is brought to the attention of the individual conducting that transaction, and in any event from the time when it would have been brought to his attention if the organization had exercised due diligence.

(28) "Organization" includes a corporation, government or governmental subdivision or agency, business trust, estate, trust, partnership or association, two or more persons having a joint or common interest, or any other legal or commercial entity.

(29) "Party," as distinct from "third party," means a person who has engaged in a transaction or made an agreement within this Act.

(30) "Person" includes an individual or an organization (see Section 1–102).

(31) "Presumption" or "presumed" means that the trier of fact must find the existence of the fact presumed unless and until evidence is introduced which would support a finding of its non-existence.

(32) "Purchase" includes taking by sale, discount, negotiation, mortgage, pledge, lien, issue or re-issue, gift or any other voluntary transaction creating an interest in property.

(33) "Purchaser" means a person who takes by purchase.

(34) "Remedy" means any remedial right to which an aggrieved party is entitled with or without resort to a tribunal.

(35) "Representative" includes an agent, an officer of a corporation or association, and a trustee, executor or administrator of an estate, or any other person empowered to act for another.

(36) "Rights" includes remedies.

(37) "Security interest" means an interest in personal property or fixtures which secures payment or performance of an obligation. The retention or reservation of title by a seller of goods notwithstanding shipment or delivery to the buyer (Section 2–401) is limited in effect to a reservation of a "security interest." The term also includes any interest of a buyer of accounts, chattel paper, or contract rights which is subject to Article 9. The special property interest of a buyer of goods on identification of such goods to a contract for sale under Section 2–401 is not a "security interest," but a buyer may also acquire a "security interest" by complying with Article 9. Unless a lease or consignment is intended as security, reservation of title thereunder is not a "security interest" but a consignment is in any event subject to the provisions on consignment sales (Section 2–326). Whether a lease is intended as security is to be determined by the facts of each case; however, (a) the inclusion of an option to purchase does not of itself make the lease one intended for security, and (b) an agreement that upon compliance with the terms of the lease the lessee shall become or has the option to become the owner of the property for no additional consideration or for a nominal consideration does make the lease one intended for security.

(38) "Send" in connection with any writing or notice means to deposit in the mail or deliver for transmission by any other usual means of communication with postage or cost of transmission provided for and properly addressed and in the case of an instrument to an address specified thereon or otherwise agreed, or if there be none to any address reasonable under the circumstances. The receipt

of any writing or notice within the time at which it would have arrived if properly sent has the effect of a proper sending.

(39) "Signed" includes any symbol executed or adopted by a party with present intention to authenticate a writing.

(40) "Surety" includes guarantor.

(41) "Telegram" includes a message transmitted by radio, teletype, cable, any mechanical method of transmission, or the like.

(42) "Term" means that portion of an agreement which relates to a particular matter.

(43) "Unauthorized" signature or indorsement means one made without actual, implied or apparent authority and includes a forgery.

(44) "Value." Except as otherwise provided with respect to negotiable instruments and bank collections (Sections 3–303, 4–208 and 4–209) a person gives "value" for rights if he acquires them

(a) in return for a binding commitment to extend credit or for the extension of immediately available credit whether or not drawn upon and whether or not a charge-back is provided for in the event of difficulties in collection; or

(b) as security for or in total or partial satisfaction of a pre-existing claim; or

(c) by accepting delivery pursuant to a pre-existing contract for purchase; or

(d) generally, in return for any consideration sufficient to support a simple contract.

(45) "Warehouse receipt" means a receipt issued by a person engaged in the business of storing goods for hire.

(46) "Written" or "writing" includes printing, typewriting or any other intentional reduction to tangible form.

§1–202. **Prima Facie Evidence by Third Party Documents.** A document in due form purporting to be a bill of lading, policy or certificate of insurance, official weigher's or inspector's certificate, consular invoice, or any other document authorized or required by the contract to be issued by a third party shall be prima facie evidence of its own authenticity and genuineness and of the facts stated in the document by the third party.

§1–203. **Obligation of Good Faith.** Every contract or duty within this Act imposes an obligation of good faith in its performance or enforcement.

§1–204. **Time; Reasonable Time; "Seasonably."** (1) Whenever this Act requires any action to be taken within a reasonable time, any time which is not manifestly unreasonable may be fixed by agreement.

(2) What is a reasonable time for taking any action depends on the nature, purpose and circumstances of such action.

(3) An action is taken "seasonably" when it is taken at or within the time agreed or if no time is agreed at or within a reasonable time.

§1–205. **Course of Dealing and Usage of Trade.** (1) A course of dealing is a sequence of previous conduct between the parties to a particular transaction which is fairly to be regarded as establishing a common basis of understanding for interpreting their expressions and other conduct.

(2) A usage of trade is any practice or method of dealing having such regularity of observance in a place, vocation or trade as to justify an expectation that it will be observed with respect to the transaction in question. The existence

and scope of such a usage are to be proved as facts. If it is established that such a usage is embodied in a written trade code or similar writing the interpretation of the writing is for the court.

(3) A course of dealing between parties and any usage of trade in the vocation or trade in which they are engaged or of which they are or should be aware give particular meaning to and supplement or qualify terms of an agreement.

(4) The express terms of an agreement and an applicable course of dealing or usage of trade shall be construed wherever reasonable as consistent with each other; but when such construction is unreasonable express terms control both course of dealing and usage of trade and course of dealing controls usage of trade.

(5) An applicable usage of trade in the place where any part of performance is to occur shall be used in interpreting the agreement as to that part of the performance.

(6) Evidence of a relevant usage of trade offered by one party is not admissible unless and until he has given the other party such notice as the court finds sufficient to prevent unfair surprise to the latter.

§1–206. Statute of Frauds for Kinds of Personal Property Not Otherwise Covered. (1) Except in the cases described in subsection (2) of this section a contract for the sale of personal property is not enforceable by way of action or defense beyond five thousand dollars in amount or value of remedy unless there is some writing which indicates that a contract for sale has been made between the parties at a defined or stated price, reasonably identifies the subject matter, and is signed by the party against whom enforcement is sought or by his authorized agent.

(2) Subsection (1) of this section does not apply to contracts for the sale of goods (Section 2–201) nor of securities (Section 8–319) nor to security agreements (Section 9–203).

§1–207. Performance or Acceptance Under Reservation of Rights. A party who with explicit reservation of rights performs or promises performance or assents to performance in a manner demanded or offered by the other party does not thereby prejudice the rights reserved. Such words as "without prejudice," "under protest" or the like are sufficient.

§1–208. Option to Accelerate at Will. A term providing that one party or his successor in interest may accelerate payment or performance or require collateral or additional collateral "at will" or "when he deems himself insecure" or in words of similar import shall be construed to mean that he shall have power to do so only if he in good faith believes that the prospect of payment or performance is impaired. The burden of establishing lack of good faith is on the party against whom the power has been exercised.

ARTICLE 2: SALES

PART 1
Short Title, General Construction and Subject Matter

§2-101. Short Title. This article shall be known and may be cited as Uniform Commercial Code–Sales.

§2-102. Scope; Certain Security and Other Transactions Excluded from This Article. Unless the context otherwise requires, this Article applies to transactions in goods; it does not apply to any transaction which although in the form of an unconditional contract to sell or present sale is intended to operate only as a security transaction nor does this Article impair or repeal any statute regulating sales to consumers, farmers or other specified classes of buyers.

§2-103. Definitions and Index of Definitions. (1) In this Article unless the context otherwise requires

(a) "Buyer" means a person who buys or contracts to buy goods.

(b) "Good faith" in the case of a merchant means honesty in fact and the observance of reasonable commercial standards of fair dealing in the trade.

(c) "Receipt" of goods means taking physical possession of them.

(d) "Seller" means a person who sells or contracts to sell goods.

(2) Other definitions applying to this Article or to specified Parts thereof, and the sections in which they appear are:

"Acceptance." Section 2–606.
"Banker's credit." Section 2–325.
"Between merchants." Section 2–104.
"Cancellation." Section 2–106 (4).
"Commercial unit." Section 2–105.
"Confirmed credit." Section 2–325.
"Conforming to contract." Section 2–106.
"Contract for sale." Section 2–106.
"Cover." Section 2–712.
"Entrusting." Section 2–403.
"Financing agency." Section 2–104.
"Future goods." Section 2–105.
"Goods." Section 2–105.
"Identification." Section 2–501.
"Installment contract." Section 2–612.
"Letter of Credit." Section 2–325.
"Lot." Section 2–105.
"Merchant." Section 2–104.
"Overseas." Section 2–323.
"Person in position of seller." Section 2–707.
"Present sale." Section 2–106.
"Sale." Section 2–106.
"Sale on approval." Section 2–326.

"Sale or return." Section 2–326.

"Termination." Section 2–106.

(3) The following definitions in other Articles apply to this Article:

"Check." Section 3–104.

"Consignee." Section 7–102.

"Consignor." Section 7–102.

"Consumer goods." Section 9–109.

"Dishonor." Section 3–507.

"Draft." Section 3–104.

(4) In addition Article 1 contains general definitions and principles of construction and interpretation applicable throughout this Article.

§2–104. Definitions: "Merchant"; "Between Merchants"; "Financing Agency." (1) "Merchant" means a person who deals in goods of the kind or otherwise by his occupation holds himself out as having knowledge or skill peculiar to the practices or goods involved in the transaction or to whom such knowledge or skill may be attributed by his employment of an agent or broker or other intermediary who by his occupation holds himself out as having such knowledge or skill.

(2) "Financing agency" means a bank, finance company or other person who in the ordinary course of business makes advances against goods or documents of title or who by arrangement with either the seller or the buyer intervenes in ordinary course to make or collect payment due or claimed under the contract for sale, as by purchasing or paying the seller's draft or making advances against it or by merely taking it for collection whether or not documents of title accompany the draft. "Financing agency" includes also a bank or other person who similarly intervenes between persons who are in the position of seller and buyer in respect to the goods (Section 2–707).

(3) "Between merchants" means in any transaction with respect to which both parties are chargeable with the knowledge or skill of merchants.

§2–105. Definitions: Transferability; "Goods"; "Future" Goods; "Lot"; "Commercial Unit." (1) "Goods" means all things (including specially manufactured goods) which are movable at the time of identification to the contract for sale other than the money in which the price is to be paid, investment securities (Article 8) and things in action. "Goods" also includes the unborn young of animals and growing crops and other identified things attached to realty as described in the section on goods to be severed from realty (Section 2–107).

(2) Goods must be both existing and identified before any interest in them can pass. Goods which are not both existing and identified are "future" goods. A purported present sale of future goods or of any interest therein operates as a contract to sell.

(3) There may be a sale of a part interest in existing identified goods.

(4) An undivided share in an identified bulk of fungible goods is sufficiently identified to be sold although the quantity of the bulk is not determined. Any agreed proportion of such a bulk or any quantity thereof agreed upon by number, weight or other measure may to the extent of the seller's interest in the bulk be sold to the buyer who then becomes an owner in common.

(5) "Lot" means a parcel or a single article which is the subject matter of a

separate sale or delivery, whether or not it is sufficient to perform the contract.

(6) "Commercial unit" means such a unit of goods as by commercial usage is a single whole for purposes of sale and division of which materially impairs its character or value on the market or in use. A commercial unit may be a single article (as a machine) or a set of articles (as a suite of furniture or an assortment of sizes) or a quantity (as a bale, gross, or carload) or any other unit treated in use or in the relevant market as a single whole.

§2–106. Definitions: "Contract"; "Agreement"; "Contract for Sale"; "Sale"; "Present Sale"; "Conforming" to Contract; "Termination"; "Cancellation." (1) In this Article unless the context otherwise requires "contract" and "agreement" are limited to those relating to the present or future sale of goods. "Contract for sale" includes both a present sale of goods and a contract to sell goods at a future time. A "sale" consists in the passing of title from the seller to the buyer for a price (Section 2–401). A "present sale" means a sale which is accomplished by the making of the contract.

(2) Goods or conduct including any part of a performance are "conforming" or conform to the contract when they are in accordance with the obligations under the contract.

(3) "Termination" occurs when either party pursuant to a power created by agreement or law puts an end to the contract otherwise than for its breach. On "termination" all obligations which are still executory on both sides are discharged but any right based on prior breach or performance survives.

(4) "Cancellation" occurs when either party puts an end to the contract for breach by the other and its effect is the same as that of "termination" except that the cancelling party also retains any remedy for breach of the whole contract or any unperformed balance.

§2–107. Goods to Be Severed From Realty: Recording. (1) A contract for the sale of timber, minerals or the like or a structure or its materials to be removed from realty is a contract for the sale of goods within this Article if they are to be severed by the seller but until severance a purported present sale thereof which is not effective as a transfer of an interest in land is effective only as a contract to sell.

(2) A contract for the sale apart from the land of growing crops or other things attached to realty and capable of severence without material harm thereto but not described in subsection (1) is a contract for the sale of goods within this Article whether the subject matter is to be severed by the buyer or by the seller even though it forms part of the realty at the time of contracting, and the parties can by identification effect a present sale before severance.

(3) The provisions of this section are subject to any third party rights provided by the law relating to realty records, and the contract for sale may be executed and recorded as a document transferring an interest in land and shall then constitute notice to third parties of the buyer's rights under the contract for sale.

PART 2
Form, Formation and Readjustment of Contract

§2–201. **Formal Requirements; Statute of Frauds.** (1) Except as otherwise provided in this section a contract for the sale of goods for the price of $500 or more is not enforceable by way of action or defense unless there is some writing sufficient to indicate that a contract for sale has been made between the parties and signed by the party against whom enforcement is sought or by his authorized agent or broker. A writing is not insufficient because it omits or incorrectly states a term agreed upon but the contract is not enforceable under this paragraph beyond the quantity of goods shown in such writing.

(2) Between merchants if within a reasonable time a writing in confirmation of the contract and sufficient against the sender is received and the party receiving it has reason to know its contents, it satisfies the requirements of subsection (1) against such party unless written notice of objection to its contents is given within ten days after it is received.

(3) A contract which does not satisfy the requirements of subsection (1) but which is valid in other respects is enforceable

(a) if the goods are to be specially manufactured for the buyer and are not suitable for sale to others in the ordinary course of the seller's business and the seller, before notice of repudiation is received and under circumstances which reasonably indicate that the goods are for the buyer, has made either a substantial beginning of their manufacture or commitments for their procurement; or

(b) if the party against whom enforcement is sought admits in his pleading, testimony or otherwise in court that a contract for sale was made, but the contract is not enforceable under this provision beyond the quantity of goods admitted; or

(c) with respect to goods for which payment has been made and accepted or which have been received and accepted (Section 2–606).

§2–202. **Final Written Expression: Parol or Extrinsic Evidence.** Terms with respect to which the confirmatory memoranda of the parties agree or which are otherwise set forth in a writing intended by the parties as a final expression of their agreement with respect to such terms as are included therein may not be contradicted by evidence of any prior agreement or of a contemporaneous oral agreement but may be explained or supplemented

(a) by course of dealing or usage of trade (Section 1–205) or by course of performance (Section 2–208); and

(b) by evidence of consistent additional terms unless the court finds the writing to have been intended also as a complete and exclusive statement of the terms of the agreement.

§2–203. **Seals Inoperative.** The affixing of a seal to a writing evidencing a contract for sale or an offer to buy or sell goods does not constitute the writing a sealed instrument and the law with respect to sealed instruments does not apply to such a contract or offer.

§2–204. **Formation in General.** (1) A contract for sale of goods may be made in any manner sufficient to show agreement, including conduct by both parties which recognizes the existence of such a contract.

(2) An agreement sufficient to constitute a contract for sale may be found even though the moment of its making is undetermined.

(3) Even though one or more terms are left open a contract for sale does not fail for indefiniteness if the parties have intended to make a contract and there is a reasonably certain basis for giving an appropriate remedy.

§2–205. **Firm Offers.** An offer by a merchant to buy or sell goods in a signed writing which by its terms gives assurance that it will be held open is not revocable, for lack of consideration, during the time stated or if no time is stated for a reasonable time, but in no event may such period of irrevocability exceed three months; but any such term of assurance on a form supplied by the offeree must be separately signed by the offeror.

§2–206. **Offer and Acceptance in Formation of Contract.** (1) Unless otherwise unambiguously indicated by the language or circumstances

(a) an offer to make a contract shall be construed as inviting acceptance in any manner and by any medium reasonable in the circumstances;

(b) an order or other offer to buy goods for prompt or current shipment shall be construed as inviting acceptance either by a prompt promise to ship or by the prompt or current shipment of conforming or non-conforming goods, but such a shipment of non-conforming goods does not constitute an acceptance if the seller seasonably notifies the buyer that the shipment is offered only as an accommodation to the buyer.

(2) Where the beginning of a requested performance is a reasonable mode of acceptance an offeror who is not notified of acceptance within a reasonable time may treat the offer as having lapsed before acceptance.

§2–207. **Additional Terms in Acceptance or Confirmation.** (1) A definite and seasonable expression of acceptance or a written confirmation which is sent within a reasonable time operates as an acceptance even though it states terms additional to or different from those offered or agreed upon, unless acceptance is expressly made conditional on assent to the additional or different terms.

(2) The additional terms are to be construed as proposals for addition to the contract. Between merchants such terms become part of the contract unless:

(a) the offer expressly limits acceptance to the terms of the offer;

(b) they materially alter it; or

(c) notification of objection to them has already been given or is given within a reasonable time after notice of them is received.

(3) Conduct by both parties which recognizes the existence of a contract is sufficient to establish a contract for sale although the writings of the parties do not otherwise establish a contract. In such case the terms of the particular contract consist of those terms on which the writings of the parties agree, together with any supplementary terms incorporated under any other provisions of this Act.

§2–208. **Course of Performance or Practical Construction.** (1) Where the contract for sale involves repeated occasions for performance by either party with knowledge of the nature of the performance and opportunity for objection to it by the other, any course of performance accepted or acquiesced in without objection shall be relevant to determine the meaning of the agreement.

(2) The express terms of the agreement and any such course of performance, as well as any course of dealing and usage of trade, shall be construed whenever reasonable as consistent with each other; but when such construction is unreasonable, express terms shall control course of performance and course of performance shall control both course of dealing and usage of trade (Section 1–205).

(3) Subject to the provisions of the next section on modification and waiver, such course of performance shall be relevant to show a waiver or modification of any term inconsistent with such course of performance.

§2–209. Modification, Rescission and Waiver. (1) An agreement modifying a contract within this Article needs no consideration to be binding.

(2) A signed agreement which excludes modification or rescission except by a signed writing cannot be otherwise modified or rescinded, but except as between merchants such a requirement on a form supplied by the merchant must be separately signed by the other party.

(3) The requirements of the statute of frauds section of this Article (Section 2–201) must be satisfied if the contract as modified is within its provisions.

(4) Although an attempt at modification or rescission does not satisfy the requirements of subsection (2) or (3) it can operate as a waiver.

(5) A party who has made a waiver affecting an executory portion of the contract may retract the waiver by reasonable notification received by the other party that strict performance will be required of any term waived, unless the retraction would be unjust in view of a material change of position in reliance on the waiver.

§2–210. Delegation of Performance; Assignment of Rights. (1) A party may perform his duty through a delegate unless otherwise agreed or unless the other party has a substantial interest in having his original promisor perform or control the acts required by the contract. No delegation of performance relieves the party delegating of any duty to perform or any liability for breach.

(2) Unless otherwise agreed all rights of either seller or buyer can be assigned except where the assignment would materially change the duty of the other party, or increase materially the burden or risk imposed on him by his contract, or impair materially his chance of obtaining return performance. A right to damages for breach of the whole contract or a right arising out of the assignor's due performance of his entire obligation can be assigned despite agreement otherwise.

(3) Unless the circumstances indicate the contrary a prohibition of assignment of "the contract" is to be construed as barring only the delegation to the assignee of the assignor's performance.

(4) An assignment of "the contract" or of "all my rights under the contract" or an assignment in similar general terms is an assignment of rights and unless the language or the circumstances (as in an assignment for security) indicate the contrary, it is a delegation of performance of the duties of the assignor and its acceptance by the assignee constitutes a promise by him to perform those duties. This promise is enforceable by either the assignor or the other party to the original contract.

(5) The other party may treat any assignment which delegates performance

as creating reasonable grounds for insecurity and may without prejudice to his rights against the assignor demand assurances from the assignee (Section 2–609).

PART 3
General Obligation and Construction of Contract

§2–301. General Obligations of Parties. The obligation of the seller is to transfer and deliver and that of the buyer is to accept and pay in accordance with the contract.

§2–302. Unconscionable Contract or Clause. (1) If the court as a matter of law finds the contract or any clause of the contract to have been unconscionable at the time it was made the court may refuse to enforce the contract, or it may enforce the remainder of the contract without the unconscionable clause, or it may so limit the application of any unconscionable clause as to avoid any unconscionable result.

(2) When it is claimed or appears to the court that the contract or any clause thereof may be unconscionable the parties shall be afforded a reasonable opportunity to present evidence as to its commercial setting, purpose and effect to aid the court in making the determination.

§2–303. Allocation or Division of Risks. Where this Article allocates a risk or a burden as between the parties "unless otherwise agreed," the agreement may not only shift the allocation but may also divide the risk or burden.

§2–304. Price Payable in Money, Goods, Realty, or Otherwise. (1) The price can be made payable in money or otherwise. If it is payable in whole or in part in goods each party is a seller of the goods which he is to transfer.

(2) Even though all or part of the price is payable in an interest in realty the transfer of the goods and the seller's obligations with reference to them are subject to this Article, but not the transfer of the interest in realty or the transferor's obligations in connection therewith.

§2–305. Open Price Term. (1) The parties if they so intend can conclude a contract for sale even though the price is not settled. In such a case the price is a reasonable price at the time for delivery if

(a) nothing is said as to price; or

(b) the price is left to be agreed by the parties and they fail to agree; or

(c) the price is to be fixed in terms of some agreed market or other standard as set or recorded by a third person or agency and it is not so set or recorded.

(2) A price to be fixed by the seller or by the buyer means a price for him to fix in good faith.

(3) When a price left to be fixed otherwise than by agreement of the parties fails to be fixed through fault of one party the other may at his option treat the contract as cancelled or himself fix a reasonable price.

(4) Where, however, the parties intend not to be bound unless the price be fixed or agreed and it is not fixed or agreed there is no contract. In such a case the buyer must return any goods already received or if unable so to do must pay their reasonable value at the time of delivery and the seller must return any portion of the price paid on account.

§2–306. Output, Requirements and Exclusive Dealings. (1) A term which measures the quantity by the output of the seller or the requirements of the buyer means such actual output or requirements as may occur in good faith, except that no quantity unreasonably disproportionate to any stated estimate or in the absence of a stated estimate to any normal or otherwise comparable prior output or requirements may be tendered or demanded.

(2) A lawful agreement by either the seller or the buyer for exclusive dealing in the kind of goods concerned imposes unless otherwise agreed an obligation by the seller to use best efforts to supply the goods and by the buyer to use best efforts to promote their sale.

§2–307. Delivery in Single Lot or Several Lots. Unless otherwise agreed all goods called for by a contract for sale must be tendered in a single delivery and payment is due only on such tender but where the circumstances give either party the right to make or demand delivery in lots the price if it can be apportioned may be demanded for each lot.

§2–308. Absence of Specified Place for Delivery. Unless otherwise agreed

(a) the place for delivery of goods is the seller's place of business or if he has none his residence; but

(b) in a contract for sale of identified goods which to the knowledge of the parties at the time of contracting are in some other place, that place is the place for their delivery; and

(c) documents of title may be delivered through customary banking channels.

§2–309. Absence of Specific Time Provisions; Notice of Termination. (1) The time for shipment or delivery or any other action under a contract if not provided in this Article or agreed upon shall be a reasonable time.

(2) Where the contract provides for successive performances but is indefinite in duration it is valid for a reasonable time but unless otherwise agreed may be terminated at any time by either party.

(3) Termination of a contract by one party except on the happening of an agreed event requires that reasonable notification be received by the other party and an agreement dispensing with notification is invalid if its operation would be unconscionable.

§2–310. Open Time for Payment or Running of Credit; Authority to Ship Under Reservation. Unless otherwise agreed

(a) payment is due at the time and place at which the buyer is to receive the goods even though the place of shipment is the place of delivery; and

(b) if the seller is authorized to send the goods he may ship them under reservation, and may tender the documents of title, but the buyer may inspect the goods after their arrival before payment is due unless such inspection is inconsistent with the terms of the contract (Section 2–513); and

(c) if delivery is authorized and made by way of documents of title otherwise than by subsection (b) then payment is due at the time and place at which the buyer is to receive the documents regardless of where the goods are to be received; and

(d) where the seller is required or authorized to ship the goods on credit the credit period runs from the time of shipment but post-dating the invoice or delaying its dispatch will correspondingly delay the starting of the credit period.

§2–311. Options and Cooperation Respecting Performance. (1) An agreement for sale which is otherwise sufficiently definite (subsection (3) of Section 2–204) to be a contract is not made invalid by the fact that it leaves particulars of performance to be specified by one of the parties. Any such specification must be made in good faith and within limits set by commercial reasonableness.

(2) Unless otherwise agreed specifications relating to assortment of the goods are at the buyer's option and except as otherwise provided in subsections (1) (c) and (3) of Section 2–319 specifications or arrangements relating to shipment are at the seller's option.

(3) Where such specification would materially affect the other party's performance but is not seasonably made or where one party's cooperation is necessary to the agreed performance of the other but is not seasonably forthcoming, the other party in addition to all other remedies

(a) is excused for any resulting delay in his own performance; and

(b) may also either proceed to perform in any reasonable manner or after the time for a material part of his own performance treat the failure to specify or to cooperate as a breach by failure to deliver or accept the goods.

§2–312. Warranty of Title and Against Infringement; Buyer's Obligation Against Infringement. (1) Subject to subsection (2) there is in a contract for sale a warranty by the seller that

(a) the title conveyed shall be good, and its transfer rightful; and

(b) the goods shall be delivered free from any security interest or other lien or encumbrance of which the buyer at the time of contracting has no knowledge.

(2) a warranty under subsection (1) will be excluded or modified only by specific language or by circumstances which give the buyer reason to know that the person selling does not claim title in himself or that he is purporting to sell only such right or title as he or a third person may have.

(3) Unless otherwise agreed a seller who is a merchant regularly dealing in goods of the kind warrants that the goods shall be delivered free of the rightful claim of any third person by way of infringement or the like but a buyer who furnishes specifications to the seller must hold the seller harmless against any such claim which arises out of compliance with the specifications.

§2–313. Express Warranties by Affirmation, Promise, Description, Sample. (1) Express warranties by the seller are created as follows:

(a) Any affirmation of fact or promise made by the seller to the buyer which relates to the goods and becomes part of the basis of the bargain creates an express warranty that the goods shall conform to the affirmation or promise.

(b) Any description of the goods which is made part of the basis of the bargain creates an express warranty that the goods shall conform to the description.

(c) Any sample or model which is made part of the basis of the bargain creates an express warranty that the whole of the goods shall conform to the sample or model.

(2) It is not necessary to the creation of an express warranty that the seller use formal words such as "warrant" or "guarantee" or that he have a specific intention to make a warranty, but an affirmation merely of the value of the goods or a statement purporting to be merely the seller's opinion or commendation of the goods does not create a warranty.

§2–314. Implied Warranty: Merchantability; Usage of Trade. (1) Unless excluded or modified (Section 2–316), a warranty that the goods shall be merchantable is implied in a contract for their sale if the seller is a merchant with respect to goods of that kind. Under this section the serving for value of food or drink to be consumed either on the premises or elsewhere is a sale.

(2) Goods to be merchantable must be at least such as

(a) pass without objection in the trade under the contract description; and

(b) in the case of fungible goods, are of fair average quality within the description; and

(c) are fit for the ordinary purposes for which such goods are used; and

(d) run, within the variations permitted by the agreement, of even kind, quality and quantity within each unit and among all units involved; and

(e) are adequately contained, packaged, and labeled as the agreement may require; and

(f) conform to the promises or affirmations of fact made on the container or label if any.

(3) unless excluded or modified (Section 2–316) other implied warranties may arise from course of dealing or usage of trade.

§2–315. Implied Warranty: Fitness for Particular Purpose. Where the seller at the time of contracting has reason to know any particular purpose for which the goods are required and that the buyer is relying on the seller's skill or judgment to select or furnish suitable goods, there is unless excluded or modified under the next section an implied warranty that the goods shall be fit for such purpose.

§2–316. Exclusion or Modification of Warranties. (1) Words or conduct relevant to the creation of an express warranty and words or conduct tending to negate or limit warranty shall be construed wherever reasonable as consistent with each other; but subject to the provisions of this Article on parol or extrinsic evidence (Section 2–202) negation or limitation is inoperative to the extent that such construction is unreasonable.

(2) Subject to subsection (3), to exclude or modify the implied warranty of merchantability or any part of it the language must mention merchantability and in case of a writing must be conspicuous, and to exclude or modify any implied warranty of fitness the exclusion must be by a writing and conspicuous. Language to exclude all implied warranties of fitness is sufficient if it states, for example, that "There are no warranties which extend beyond the description on the face hereof."

(3) Notwithstanding subsection (2)

(a) unless the circumstances indicate otherwise, all implied warranties are excluded by expressions like "as is," "with all faults" or other language which in common understanding calls the buyer's attention to the exclusion of warranties and makes plain that there is no implied warranty; and

(b) when the buyer before entering into the contract has examined the goods or the sample or model as fully as he desired or has refused to examine the goods there is no implied warranty with regard to defects which an examination ought in the circumstances to have revealed to him; and

(c) an implied warranty can also be excluded or modified by course of dealing or course of performance or usage of trade.

(4) Remedies for breach of warranty can be limited in accordance with the provisions of this Article on liquidation or limitation of damages and on contractual modification of remedy (Sections 2–718 and 2–719).

§2–317. Cumulation and Conflict of Warranties Express or Implied. Warranties whether express or implied shall be construed as consistent with each other and as cumulative, but if such construction is unreasonable the intention of the parties shall determine which warranty is dominant. In ascertaining that intention the following rules apply:

(a) Exact or technical specifications displace an inconsistent sample or model or general language of description.

(b) A sample from an existing bulk displaces inconsistent general language of description.

(c) Express warranties displace inconsistent implied warranties other than an implied warranty of fitness for a particular purpose.

§2–318. Third Party Beneficiaries of Warranties Express or Implied. A seller's warranty whether express or implied extends to any natural person who is in the family or household of his buyer or who is a guest in his home if it is reasonable to expect that such person may use, consume or be affected by the goods and who is injured in person by breach of the warranty. A seller may not exclude or limit the operation of this section.

§2–319. F.O.B. and F.A.S. Terms. (1) Unless otherwise agreed the term F.O.B. (which means "free on board") at a named place, even though used only in connection with the stated price, is a delivery term under which

(a) when the term is F.O.B. the place of shipment, the seller must at that place ship the goods in the manner provided in this Article (Section 2–504) and bear the expense and risk of putting them into the possession of the carrier; or

(b) when the term is F.O.B. the place of destination, the seller must at his own expense and risk transport the goods to that place and there tender delivery of them in the manner provided in this Article (Section 2–503);

(c) when under either (a) or (b) the term is also F.O.B. vessel, car or other vehicle, the seller must in addition at his own expense and risk load the goods on board. If the term is F.O.B. vessel the buyer must name the vessel and in an appropriate case the seller must comply with the provisions of this Article on the form of bill of lading (Section 2–323).

(2) Unless otherwise agreed the term F.A.S. vessel (which means "free alongside") at a named port, even though used only in connection with the stated price, is a delivery term under which the seller must

(a) at his own expense and risk deliver the goods alongside the vessel in the manner usual in that port or on a dock designated and provided by the buyer; and

(b) obtain and tender a receipt for the goods in exchange for which the carrier is under a duty to issue a bill of lading.

(3) Unless otherwise agreed in any case falling within subsection (1) (a) and (c) or subsection (2) the buyer must seasonably give any needed instructions for making delivery, including when the term is F.A.S. or F.O.B. the loading berth of the vessel and in an appropriate case its name and sailing date. The seller may treat the failure of needed instructions as a failure of cooperation under

this Article (Section 2–311). He may also at his option move the goods in any reasonable manner preparatory to delivery or shipment.

(4) Under the term F.O.B. vessel or F.A.S. unless otherwise agreed the buyer must make payment against tender of the required documents and the seller may not tender nor the buyer demand delivery of the goods in substitution for the documents.

§2–320. C.I.F. and C. & F. Terms. (1) The term C.I.F. means that the price includes in a lump sum the cost of the goods and the insurance and freight to the named destination. The term C. & F. or C.F. means that the price so includes cost and freight to the named destination.

(2) Unless otherwise agreed and even though used only in connection with the stated price and destination, the term C.I.F. destination or its equivalent requires the seller at his own expense and risk to

(a) put the goods into the possession of a carrier at the port for shipment and obtain a negotiable bill or bills of lading covering the entire transportation to the named destination; and

(b) load the goods and obtain a receipt from the carrier (which may be contained in the bill of lading) showing that the freight has been paid or provided for; and

(c) obtain a policy or certificate of insurance, including any war risk insurance, of a kind and on terms then current at the port of shipment in the usual amount, in the currency of the contract, shown to cover the same goods covered by the bill of lading and providing for payment of loss to the order of the buyer or for the account of whom it may concern; but the seller may add to the price the amount of the premium for any such war risk insurance; and

(d) prepare an invoice of the goods and procure any other documents required to effect shipment or to comply with the contract; and

(e) forward and tender with commercial promptness all the documents in due form and with any indorsement necessary to perfect the buyer's rights.

(3) Unless otherwise agreed the term C. & F. or its equivalent has the same effect and imposes upon the seller the same obligations and risks as a C.I.F. term except the obligation as to insurance.

(4) Under the term C.I.F. or C. & F. unless otherwise agreed the buyer must make payment against tender of the required documents and the seller may not tender nor the buyer demand delivery of the goods in substitution for the documents.

§2–321. C.I.F. or C. & F.: "Net Landed Weights"; "Payment on Arrival"; Warranty of Condition on Arrival. Under a contract containing a term C.I.F. or C. & F.

(1) Where the price is based on or is to be adjusted according to "net landed weights," "delivered weights," "out turn" quantity or quality or the like, unless otherwise agreed the seller must reasonably estimate the price. The payment due on tender of the documents called for by the contract is the amount so estimated, but after final adjustment of the price a settlement must be made with commercial promptness.

(2) An agreement described in subsection (1) or any warranty of quality or condition of the goods on arrival places upon the seller the risk of ordinary

deterioration, shrinkage and the like in transportation but has no effect on the place or time of identification to the contract for sale or delivery or on the passing of the risk of loss.

(3) Unless otherwise agreed where the contract provides for payment on or after arrival of the goods the seller must before payment allow such preliminary inspection as is feasible; but if the goods are lost delivery of the documents and payment are due when the goods should have arrived.

§2–322. **Delivery "Ex-Ship."** (1) Unless otherwise agreed a term for delivery of goods "ex-ship" (which means from the carrying vessel) or in equivalent language is not restricted to a particular ship and requires delivery from a ship which has reached a place at the named port of destination where goods of the kind are usually discharged.

(2) Under such a term unless otherwise agreed

(a) the seller must discharge all liens arising out of the carriage and furnish the buyer with a direction which puts the carrier under a duty to deliver the goods; and

(b) the risk of loss does not pass to the buyer until the goods leave the ship's tackle or are otherwise properly unloaded.

§2–323. **Form of Bill of Lading Required in Overseas Shipment; "Overseas."** (1) Where the contract contemplates overseas shipment and contains a term C.I.F. or C. & F. or F.O.B. vessel, the seller unless otherwise agreed must obtain a negotiable bill of lading stating that the goods have been loaded on board or, in the case of a term C.I.F. or C. & F., received for shipment.

(2) Where in a case within subsection (1) a bill of lading has been issued in a set of parts, unless otherwise agreed if the documents are not to be sent from abroad the buyer may demand tender of the full set; otherwise only one part of the bill of lading need be tendered. Even if the agreement expressly requires a full set.

(a) due tender of a single part is acceptable within the provisions of this Article on cure of improper delivery (subsection (1) of Section 2–508); and

(b) even though the full set is demanded, if the documents are sent from abroad the person tendering an incomplete set may nevertheless require payment upon furnishing an indemnity which the buyer in good faith deems adequate.

(3) A shipment by water or by air or a contract contemplating such shipment is "overseas" insofar as by usage of trade or agreement it is subject to the commercial, financing or shipping practices characteristic of international deep water commerce.

§2–324. **"No Arrival, No Sale" Term.** Under a term "no arrival, no sale" or terms of like meaning, unless otherwise agreed,

(a) the seller must properly ship conforming goods and if they arrive by any means he must tender them on arrival but he assumes no obligation that the goods will arrive unless he has caused the non-arrival; and

(b) where without fault of the seller the goods are in part lost or have so deteriorated as no longer to conform to the contract or arrive after the contract time, the buyer may proceed as if there had been casualty to identified goods (Section 2–613).

§2–325. **"Letter of Credit" Term; "Confirmed Credit."** (1) Failure of the buyer seasonably to furnish an agreed letter of credit is a breach of the contract for sale.

(2) The delivery to seller of a proper letter of credit suspends the buyer's obligation to pay. If the letter of credit is dishonored, the seller may on seasonable notification to the buyer require payment directly from him.

(3) Unless otherwise agreed the term "letter of credit" or "banker's credit" in a contract for sale means an irrevocable credit issued by a financing agency of good repute and, where the shipment is overseas, of good international repute. The term "confirmed credit" means that the credit must also carry the direct obligation of such an agency which does business in the seller's financial market.

§2–326. Sale on Approval and Sale or Return; Consignment Sales and Rights of Creditors. (1) Unless otherwise agreed, if delivered goods may be returned by the buyers even though they conform to the contract, the transaction is

(a) a "sale on approval" if the goods are delivered primarily for use, and

(b) a "sale or return" if the goods are delivered primarily for resale.

(2) Except as provided in subsection (3), goods held on approval are not subject to the claims of the buyer's creditors until acceptance; goods held on sale or return are subject to such claims while in the buyer's possession.

(3) Where goods are delivered to a person for sale and such person maintains a place of business at which he deals in goods of the kind involved, under a name other than the name of the person making delivery, then with respect to claims of creditors of the person conducting the business the goods are deemed to be on sale or return. The provisions of this subsection are applicable even though an agreement purports to reserve title to the person making delivery until payment or resale or uses such words as "on consignment" or "on memorandum." However, this subsection is not applicable if the person making delivery

(a) complies with an applicable law providing for a consignor's interest or the like to be evidenced by a sign, or

(b) establishes that the person conducting the business is generally known by his creditors to be substantially engaged in selling the goods of others, or

(c) complies with the filing provisions of the Article on Secured Transactions (Article 9).

(4) Any "or return" term of a contract for sale is to be treated as a separate contract for sale within the statute of frauds section of this Article (Section 2–201) and as contradicting the sale aspect of the contract within the provisions of this Article on parol or extrinsic evidence (Section 2–202).

§2–327. Special Incidents of Sale on Approval and Sale or Return. (1) Under a sale on approval unless otherwise agreed

(a) although the goods are identified to the contract the risk of loss and the title do not pass to the buyer until acceptance; and

(b) use of the goods consistent with the purpose of trial is not acceptance but failure seasonably to notify the seller of election to return the goods is acceptance, and if the goods conform to the contract acceptance of any part is acceptance of the whole; and

(c) after due notification of election to return, the return is at the seller's risk and expense but a merchant buyer must follow any reasonable instructions.

(2) Under a sale or return unless otherwise agreed

(a) the option to return extends to the whole or any commercial unit of the goods while in substantially their original condition, but must be exercised seasonably; and

(b) the return is at the buyer's risk and expense.

§2–328. **Sale by Auction.** (1) In a sale by auction if goods are put up in lots each lot is the subject of a separate sale.

(2) A sale by auction is complete when the auctioneer so announces by the fall of the hammer or in other customary manner. Where a bid is made while the hammer is falling in acceptance of a prior bid the auctioneer may in his discretion reopen the bidding or declare the goods sold under the bid on which the hammer was falling.

(3) Such a sale is with reserve unless the goods are in explicit terms put up without reserve. In an auction with reserve the auctioneer may withdraw the goods at any time until he announces completion of the sale. In an auction without reserve, after the auctioneer calls for bids on an article or lot, that article or lot cannot be withdrawn unless no bid is made within a reasonable time. In either case a bidder may retract his bid until the auctioneer's announcement of completion of the sale, but a bidder's retraction does not revive any previous bid.

(4) If the auctioneer knowingly receives a bid on the seller's behalf or the seller makes or procures such a bid, and notice has not been given that liberty for such bidding is reserved, the buyer may at his option avoid the sale or take the goods at the price of the last good faith bid prior to the completion of the sale. This subsection shall not apply to any bid at a forced sale.

PART 4

Title, Creditors and Good Faith Purchasers

§2–401. **Passing of Title; Reservation for Security; Limited Application of This Section.** Each provision of this Article with regard to the rights, obligations and remedies of the seller, the buyer, purchasers or other third parties applies irrespective of title to the goods except where the provision refers to such title. Insofar as situations are not covered by the other provisions of this Article and matters concerning title become material the following rules apply:

(1) Title to goods cannot pass under a contract for sale prior to their identification to the contract (Section 2–501), and unless otherwise explicity agreed the buyer acquires by their identification a special property as limited by this Act. Any retention or reservation by the seller of the title (property) in goods shipped or delivered to the buyer is limited in effect to a reservation of a security interest. Subject to these provisions and to the provisions of the Article on Secured Transactions (Article 9), title to goods passes from the seller to the buyer in any manner and on any conditions explicitly agreed on by the parties.

(2) Unless otherwise explicitly agreed title passes to the buyer at the time and place at which the seller completes his performance with reference to the physical delivery of the goods, despite any reservation of a security interest and even though a document of title is to be delivered at a different time or place; and in particular and despite any reservation of a security interest by the bill of lading

(a) if the contract requires or authorizes the seller to send the goods to the buyer but does not require him to deliver them at destination, title passes to the buyer at the time and place of shipment; but

(b) if the contract requires delivery at destination, title passes on tender there.

(3) Unless otherwise explicitly agreed where delivery is to be made without moving the goods,

(a) if the seller is to deliver a document of title, title passes at the time when and the place where he delivers such documents; or

(b) if the goods are at the time of contracting already identified and no documents are to be delivered, title passes at the time and place of contracting.

(4) A rejection or other refusal by the buyer to receive or retain the goods, whether or not justified, or a justified revocation of acceptance revests title to the goods in the seller. Such revesting occurs by operation of law and is not a "sale."

§2–402. **Rights of Seller's Creditors Against Sold Goods.** (1) Except as provided in subsections (2) and (3), rights of unsecured creditors of the seller with respect to goods which have been identified to a contract for sale are subject to the buyer's rights to recover the goods under this Article (Sections 2–502 and 2–716).

(2) A creditor of the seller may treat a sale or an identification of goods to a contract for sale as void if as against him a retention of possession by the seller is fraudulent under any rule of law of the state where the goods are situated, except that retention of possession in good faith and current course of trade by a merchant-seller for a commercially reasonable time after a sale or identification is not fraudulent.

(3) Nothing in this Article shall be deemed to impair the rights of creditors of the seller

(a) under the provisions of the Article on Secured Transactions (Article 9); or

(b) where identification to the contract or delivery is made not in current course of trade but in satisfaction of or as security for a pre-existing claim for money, security or the like and is made under circumstances which under any rule of law of the state where the goods are situated would apart from this Article constitute the transaction a fraudulent transfer or voidable preference.

§2–403. **Power to Transfer; Good Faith Purchase of Goods; "Entrusting."** (1) A purchaser of goods acquires all title which his transferor had or had power to transfer except that a purchaser of a limited interest acquires rights only to the extent of the interest purchased. A person with voidable title has power to transfer a good title to a good faith purchaser for value. When goods have been delivered under a transaction of purchase the purchaser has such power even though

(a) the transferor was deceived as to the identity of the purchaser, or

(b) the delivery was in exchange for a check which is later dishonored, or

(c) it was agreed that the transaction was to be a "cash sale," or

(d) the delivery was procured through fraud punishable as larcenous under the criminal law.

(2) Any entrusting of possession of goods to a mechant who deals in goods of

that kind gives him power to transfer all rights of the entruster to a buyer in ordinary course of business.

(3) "Entrusting" includes any delivery and any acquiescence in retention of possession regardless of any condition expressed between the parties to the delivery or acquiescence and regardless of whether the procurement of the entrusting or the possessor's disposition of the goods have been such as to be larcenous under the criminal law.

(4) The rights of other purchasers of goods and of lien creditors are governed by the Articles on Secured Transactions (Article 9), Bulk Transfers (Article 6) and Documents of Title (Article 7).

PART 5
Performance

§2–501. Insurable Interest in Goods; Manner of Identification of Goods. (1) The buyer obtains a special property and an insurable interest in goods by identification of existing goods as goods to which the contract refers even though the goods so identified are non-conforming and he has an option to return or reject them. Such identification can be made at any time and in any manner explicitly agreed to by the parties. In the absence of explicit agreement identification occurs

(a) when the contract is made if it is for the sale of goods already existing and identified;

(b) if the contract is for the sale of future goods other than those described in paragraph (c), when goods are shipped, marked or otherwise designated by the seller as goods to which the contract refers;

(c) when the crops are planted or otherwise become growing crops or the young are conceived if the contract is for the sale of unborn young to be born within twelve months after contracting or for the sale of crops to be harvested within twelve months or the next normal harvest season after contracting whichever is longer.

(2) The seller retains an insurable interest in goods so long as title to or any security interest in the goods remains in him and where the identification is by the seller alone he may until default or insolvency or notification to the buyer that the identification is final substitute other goods for those identified.

(3) Nothing in this section impairs any insurable interest recognized under any other statute or rule of law.

§2–502. Buyer's Right to Goods on Seller's Insolvency. (1) Subject to subsection (2) and even though the goods have not been shipped a buyer who has paid a part or all of the price of goods in which he has a special property under the provisions of the immediately preceding section may on making and keeping good a tender of any unpaid portion of their price recover them from the seller if the seller becomes insolvent within ten days after receipt of the first installment on their price.

(2) If the identification creating his special property has been made by the buyer he acquires the right to recover the goods only if they conform to the contract for sale.

§2–503. Manner of Seller's Tender of Delivery. (1) Tender of delivery requires that the seller put and hold conforming goods at the buyer's disposition and give the buyer any notification reasonably necessary to enable him to take delivery. The manner, time and place for tender are detemined by the agreement and this Article, and in particular

(a) tender must be at a reasonable hour, and if it is of goods they must be kept available for the period reasonably necessary to enable the buyer to take possession; but

(b) unless otherwise agreed the buyer must furnish facilities reasonably suited to the receipt of the goods.

(2) Where the case is within the next section respecting shipment tender requires that the seller comply with its provisions.

(3) Where the seller is required to deliver at a particular destination tender requires that he comply with subsection (1) and also in any appropriate case tender documents as described in subsections (4) and (5) of this section.

(4) Where goods are in the possession of a bailee and are to be delivered without being moved

(a) tender requires that the seller either tender a negotiable document of title covering such goods or procure acknowledgment by the bailee of the buyer's right to possession of the goods; but

(b) tender to the buyer of a non-negotiable document of title or of a written direction to the bailee to deliver is sufficient tender unless the buyer seasonably objects, and receipt by the bailee of notification of the buyer's rights fixes those rights as against the bailee and all third persons; but risk of loss of the goods and of any failure by the bailee to honor the non-negotiable document of title or to obey the direction remains on the seller until the buyer has had a reasonable time to present the document or direction, and a refusal by the bailee to honor the document or to obey the direction defeats the tender.

(5) Where the contract requires the seller to deliver documents

(a) he must tender all such documents in correct form, except as provided in this Article with respect to bills of lading in a set (subsection (2) of Section 2–323); and

(b) tender through customary banking channels is sufficient and dishonor of a draft accompanying the documents constitutes non-acceptance or rejection.

§2–504. Shipment by Seller. Where the seller is required or authorized to send the goods to the buyer and the contract does not require him to deliver them at a particular destination, then unless otherwise agreed he must

(a) put the goods in the possession of such a carrier and make such a contract for their transportation as may be reasonable having regard to the nature of the goods and other circumstances of the case; and

(b) obtain and promptly deliver or tender in due form any document necessary to enable the buyer to obtain possession of the goods or otherwise required by the agreement or by usage of trade; and

(c) promptly notify the buyer of the shipment.

Failure to notify the buyer under paragraph (c) or to make a proper contract under paragraph (a) is a ground for rejection only if material delay or loss ensues.

§2–505. Seller's Shipment Under Reservation. (1) Where the seller has identified goods to the contract by or before shipment:

(a) his procurement of a negotiable bill of lading to his own order or otherwise reserves in him a security interest in the goods. His procurement of the bill to the order of a financing agency or of the buyer indicates in addition only the seller's expectation of transferring that interest to the person named.

(b) a non-negotiable bill of lading to himself or his nominee reserves possession of the goods as security but except in a case of conditional delivery (subsection (2) of Section 2–507) a non-negotiable bill of lading naming the buyer as consignee reserves no security interest even though the seller retains possession of the bill of lading.

(2) When shipment by the seller with reservation of a security interest is in violation of the contract for sale it constitutes an improper contract for transportation within the preceding section but impairs neither the rights given to the buyer by shipment and identification of the goods to the contract nor the seller's powers as a holder of a negotiable document.

§2–506. Rights of Financing Agency. (1) A financing agency by paying or purchasing for value a draft which relates to a shipment of goods acquires to the extent of the payment or purchase and in addition to its own rights under the draft and any document of title securing it any rights of the shipper in the goods including the right to stop delivery and the shipper's right to have the draft honored by the buyer.

(2) The right to reimbursement of a financing agency which has in good faith honored or purchased the draft under commitment to or authority from the buyer is not impaired by subsequent discovery of defects with reference to any relevant document which was apparently regular on its face.

§2–507. Effect of Seller's Tender; Delivery on Condition. (1) Tender of delivery is a condition to the buyer's duty to accept the goods and, unless otherwise agreed, to his duty to pay for them. Tender entitles the seller to acceptance of the goods and to payment according to the contract.

(2) Where payment is due and demanded on the delivery to the buyer of goods or documents of title, his right as against the seller to retain or dispose of them is conditional upon his making the payment due.

§2–508. Cure by Seller of Improper Tender or Delivery; Replacement. (1) Where any tender or delivery by the seller is rejected because non-conforming and the time for performance has not yet expired, the seller may seasonably notify the buyer of his intention to cure and may then within the contract time make a conforming delivery.

(2) Where the buyer rejects a non-conforming tender which the seller had reasonable grounds to believe would be acceptable with or without money allowance the seller may if he seasonably notifies the buyer have a further reasonable time to substitute a conforming tender.

§2–509. Risk of Loss in the Absence of Breach. (1) Where the contract requires or authorizes the seller to ship the goods by carrier.

(a) if it does not require him to deliver them at a particular destination, the risk of loss passes to the buyer when the goods are duly delivered to the carrier even though the shipment is under reservation (Section 2–505); but

(b) if it does require him to deliver them at a particular destination and the goods are there duly tendered while in the possession of the carrier, the risk of loss passes to the buyer when the goods are there duly so tendered as to enable the buyer to take delivery.

(2) Where the goods are held by a bailee to be delivered without being moved, the risk of loss passes to the buyer

(a) on his receipt of a negotiable document of title covering the goods; or

(b) on acknowledgment by the bailee of the buyer's right to possession of the goods; or

(c) after his receipt of a non-negotiable document of title or other written direction to deliver, as provided in subsection (4) (b) of Section 2–503.

(3) In any case not within subsection (1) or (2), the risk of loss passes to the buyer on his receipt of the goods if the seller is a merchant; otherwise the risk passes to the buyer on tender of delivery.

(4) The provisions of this section are subject to contrary agreement of the parties and to the provisions of this Article on sale on approval (Section 2–327) and on effect of breach on risk of loss (Section 2–510).

§2–510. **Effect of Breach on Risk of Loss.** (1) Where a tender or delivery of goods so fails to conform to the contract as to give a right of rejection the risk of their loss remains on the seller until cure or acceptance.

(2) Where the buyer rightfully revokes acceptance he may to the extent of any deficiency in his effective insurance coverage treat the risk of loss as having rested on the seller from the beginning.

(3) Where the buyer as to conforming goods already identified to the contract for sale repudiates or is otherwise in breach before risk of their loss has passed to him, the seller may to the extent of any deficiency in his effective insurance coverage treat the risk of loss as resting on the buyer for a commercially reasonable time.

§2–511. **Tender of Payment by Buyer; Payment by Check.** (1) Unless otherwise agreed tender of payment is a condition to the seller's duty to tender and complete any delivery.

(2) Tender of payment is sufficient when made by any means or in any manner current in the ordinary course of business unless the seller demands payment in legal tender and gives any extension of time reasonably necessary to procure it.

(3) Subject to the provisions of this Act on the effect of an instrument on an obligation (Section 3–802), payment by check is conditional and is defeated as between the parties by dishonor of the check on due presentment.

§2–512. **Payment by Buyer Before Inspection.** (1) Where the contract requires payment before inspection non-conformity of the goods does not excuse the buyer from so making payment unless

(a) the non-conformity appears without inspection; or

(b) despite tender of the required documents the circumstances would justify injunction against honor under the provisions of this Act (Section 5–114).

(2) Payment pursuant to subsection (1) does not constitute an acceptance of goods or impair the buyer's right to inspect or any of his remedies.

§2–513. **Buyer's Right to Inspection of Goods.** (1) Unless otherwise agreed and subject to subsection (3), where goods are tendered or delivered or identified to the contract for sale, the buyer has a right before payment or acceptance to inspect them at any reasonable place and time and in any reasonable manner. When the seller is required or authorized to send the goods to the buyer, the inspection may be after their arrival.

(2) Expenses of inspection must be borne by the buyer but may be recovered from the seller if the goods do not conform and are rejected.

(3) Unless otherwise agreed and subject to the provisions of this Article on C.I.F. contracts (subsection (3) of Section 2–321), the buyer is not entitled to inspect the goods before payment of the price when the contract provides

(a) for delivery "C.O.D." or on other like terms; or

(b) for payment against documents of title, except where such payment is due only after the goods are to become available for inspection.

(4) A place or method of inspection fixed by the parties is presumed to be exclusive but unless otherwise expressly agreed it does not postpone identification or shift the place for delivery or for passing the risk of loss. If compliance becomes impossible, inspection shall be as provided in this section unless the place or method fixed was clearly intended as an indispensable condition failure of which avoids the contract.

§2–514. **When Documents Deliverable on Acceptance; When on Payment.** Unless otherwise agreed documents against which a draft is drawn are to be delivered to the drawee on acceptance of the draft if it is payable more than three days after presentment; otherwise, only on payment.

§2–515. **Preserving Evidence of Goods in Dispute.** In furtherance of the adjustment of any claim or dispute

(a) either party on reasonable notification to the other and for the purpose of ascertaining the facts and preserving evidence has the right to inspect, test and sample the goods including such of them as may be in the possession or control of the other; and

(b) the parties may agree to a third party inspection or survey to determine the conformity or condition of the goods and may agree that the findings shall be binding upon them in any subsequent litigation or adjustment.

PART 6
Breach, Repudiation and Excuse

§2–601. **Buyer's Rights on Improper Delivery.** Subject to the provisions of this Article on breach in installment contracts (Section 2–612) and unless otherwise agreed under the sections on contractual limitations of remedy (Sections 2–718 and 2–719), if the goods or the tender of delivery fail in any respect to conform to the contract, the buyer may

(a) reject the whole; or

(b) accept the whole; or

(c) accept any commercial unit or units and reject the rest.

§2–602. **Manner and Effect of Rightful Rejection.** (1) Rejection of goods must be within a reasonable time after their delivery or tender. It is ineffective unless the buyer seasonably notifies the seller.

(2) Subject to the provisions of the two following sections on rejected goods (Sections 2–603 and 2–604),

(a) after rejection any exercise of ownership by the buyer with respect to any commercial unit is wrongful as against the seller; and

(b) if the buyer has before rejection taken physical possession of goods in which he does not have a security interest under the provisions of this Article (subsection (3) of Section 2–711), he is under a duty after rejection to hold them with reasonable care at the seller's disposition for a time sufficient to permit the seller to remove them; but

(c) the buyer has no further obligations with regard to goods rightfully rejected.

(3) The seller's rights with respect to goods wrongfully rejected are governed by the provisions of this Article on Seller's remedies in general (Section 2–703).

§2–603. Merchant Buyer's Duties as to Rightfully Rejected Goods. (1) Subject to any security interest in the buyer (subsection (3) of Section 2–711), when the seller has no agent or place of business at the market of rejection a merchant buyer is under a duty after rejection of goods in his possession or control to follow any reasonable instructions received from the seller with repect to the goods and in the absence of such instructions to make reasonable efforts to sell them for the seller's account if they are perishable or threaten to decline in value speedily. Instructions are not reasonable if on demand indemnity for expenses is not forthcoming.

(2) When the buyer sells goods under subsection (1), he is entitled to reimbursement from the seller or out of the proceeds for reasonable expenses of caring for and selling them, and if the expenses include no selling commission then to such commission as is usual in the trade or if there is none to a reasonable sum not exceeding ten per cent on the gross proceeds.

(3) In complying with this section the buyer is held only to good faith and good faith conduct hereunder is neither acceptance nor conversion nor the basis of an action for damages.

§2–604. Buyer's Options as to Salvage of Rightfully Rejected Goods. Subject to the provisions of the immediately preceding section on perishables if the seller gives no instructions within a reasonable time after notification of rejection the buyer may store the rejected goods for the seller's account or reship them to him or resell them for the seller's account with reimbursement as provided in the preceding section. Such action is not acceptance or conversion.

§2–605. Waiver of Buyer's Objections by Failure to Particularize. (1) The buyer's failure to state in connection with rejection a particular defect which is ascertainable by reasonable inspection precludes him from relying on the unstated defect to justify rejection or to establish breach

(a) where the seller could have cured it if stated seasonably; or

(b) between merchants when the seller has after rejection made a request in writing for a full and final written statement of all defects on which the buyer proposes to rely.

(2) Payment against documents made without reservation of rights precludes recovery of the payment for defects apparent on the face of the documents.

§2–606. What Constitutes Acceptance of Goods. (1) Acceptance of goods occurs when the buyer

(a) after a reasonable opportunity to inspect the goods signifies to the seller that the goods are conforming or that he will take or retain them in spite of their non-conformity; or

(b) fails to make an effective rejection (subsection (1) of Section 2–602), but such acceptance does not occur until the buyer has had a reasonable opportunity to inspect them; or

(c) does any act inconsistent with the seller's ownership; but if such act is wrongful as against the seller it is an acceptance only if ratified by him.

(2) Acceptance of a part of any commercial unit is acceptance of that entire unit.

§2–607. Effect of Acceptance; Notice of Breach; Burden of Establishing Breach After Acceptance; Notice of Claim or Litigation to Person Answerable Over. (1) The buyer must pay at the contract rate for any goods accepted.

(2) Acceptance of goods by the buyer precludes rejection of the goods accepted and if made with knowledge of a non-conformity cannot be revoked because of it unless the acceptance was on the reasonable assumption that the non-conformity would be seasonably cured but acceptance does not of itself impair any other remedy provided by this Article for non-conformity.

(3) Where a tender has been accepted

(a) the buyer must within a reasonable time after he discovers or should have discovered any breach notify the seller of breach or be barred from any remedy; and

(b) if the claim is one for infringement or the like (subsection (3) of Section 2–312) and the buyer is sued as a result of such a breach he must so notify the seller within a reasonable time after he receives notice of the litigation or be barred from any remedy over for liability established by the litigation.

(4) The burden is on the buyer to establish any breach with respect to the goods accepted.

(5) Where the buyer is sued for breach of a warranty or other obligation for which his seller is answerable over

(a) he may give his seller written notice of the litigation. If the notice states that the seller may come in and defend and that if the seller does not do so he will be bound in any action against him by his buyer by any determination of fact common to the two litigations, then unless the seller after seasonable receipt of the notice does come in and defend he is so bound.

(b) if the claim is one for infringement or the like (subsection (3) of Section 2–312) the original seller may demand in writing that his buyer turn over to him control of the litigation including settlement or else be barred from any remedy over and if he also agrees to bear all expense and to satisfy any adverse judgment, then unless the buyer after seasonable receipt of the demand does turn over control the buyer is so barred.

(6) The provisions of subsections (3), (4) and (5) apply to any obligation of a buyer to hold the seller harmless against infringement or the like (subsection (3) of Section 2–312).

§2–608. Revocation of Acceptance in Whole or in Part. (1) The buyer may revoke his acceptance of a lot or commercial unit whose non-conformity substantially impairs its value to him if he has accepted it

(a) on the reasonable assumption that its non-conformity would be cured and it has not been seasonably cured; or

(b) without discovery of such non-conformity if his acceptance was reasonably induced either by the difficulty of discovery before acceptance or by the seller's assurances.

(2) Revocation of acceptance must occur within a reasonable time after the buyer discovers or should have discovered the ground for it and before any substantial change in condition of the goods which is not caused by their own defects. It is not effective until the buyer notifies the seller of it.

(3) A buyer who so revokes has the same rights and duties with regard to the goods involved as if he had rejected them.

§2–609. **Right to Adequate Assurance of Performance.** (1) A contract for sale imposes an obligation on each party that the other's expectation of receiving due performance will not be impaired. When reasonable grounds for insecurity arise with respect to the performance of either party the other may in writing demand adequate assurance of due performance and until he receives such assurance may if commercially reasonable suspend any performance for which he has not already received the agreed return.

(2) Between merchants the reasonableness of grounds for insecurity and the adequacy of any assurance offered shall be determined according to commercial standards.

(3) Acceptance of any improper delivery or payment does not prejudice the aggrieved party's right to demand adequate assurance of future performance.

(4) After receipt of a justified demand failure to provide within a reasonable time not exceeding thirty days such assurance of due performance as is adequate under the circumstances of the particular case is a repudiation of the contract.

§2–610. **Anticipatory Repudiation.** When either party repudiates the contract with respect to a performance not yet due the loss of which will substantially impair the value of the contract to the other, the aggrieved party may

(a) for a commercially reasonable time await performance by the repudiating party; or

(b) resort to any remedy for breach (Section 2–703 or Section 2–711), even though he has notified the repudiating party that he would await the latter's performance and has urged retraction; and

(c) in either case suspend his own performance or proceed in accordance with the provisions of this Article on the seller's right to identify goods to the contract notwithstanding breach or to salvage unfinished goods (Section 2–704).

§2–611. **Retraction of Anticipatory Repudiation.** (1) Until the repudiating party's next performance is due he can retract his repudiation unless the aggrieved party has since the repudiation cancelled or materially changed his position or otherwise indicated that he considers the repudiation final.

(2) Retraction may be by any method which clearly indicates to the aggrieved party that the repudiating party intends to perform, but must include any assurance justifiably demanded under the provisions of this Article (Section 2–609).

(3) Retraction reinstates the repudiating party's rights under the contract with due excuse and allowance to the aggrieved party for any delay occasioned by the repudiation.

§2–612. "Installment Contract"; Breach. (1) An "installment contract" is one which requires or authorizes the delivery of goods in separate lots to be separately accepted, even though the contract contains a clause "each delivery is a separate contract" or its equivalent.

(2) The buyer may reject any installment which is non-conforming if the non-conformity substantially impairs the value of that installment and cannot be cured or if the non-conformity is a defect in the required documents; but if the non-conformity does not fall within subsection (3) and the seller gives adequate assurance of its cure the buyer must accept that installment.

(3) Whenever non-conformity or default with respect to one or more installments substantially impairs the value of the whole contract there is a breach of the whole. But the aggrieved party reinstates the contract if he accepts a non-conforming installment without seasonably notifying of cancellation or if he brings an action with respect only to past installments or demands performance as to future installments.

§2–613. Casualty to Identified Goods. Where the contract requires for its performance goods identified when the contract is made, and the goods suffer casualty without fault of either party before the risk of loss passes to the buyer, or in a proper case under a "no arrival, no sale" term (Section 2–324) then

(a) if the loss is total the contract is avoided; and

(b) if the loss is partial or the goods have so deteriorated as no longer to conform to the contract the buyer may nevertheless demand inspection and at his option either treat the contract as avoided or accept the goods with due allowance from the contract price for the deterioration or the deficiency in quantity but without further right against the seller.

§2–614. Substituted Performance. (1) Where without fault of either party the agreed berthing, loading, or unloading facilities fail or an agreed type of carrier becomes unavailable or the agreed manner of delivery otherwise becomes commercially impracticable but a commercially reasonable substitute is available, such substitute performance must be tendered and accepted.

(2) If the agreed means or manner of payment fails because of domestic or foreign governmental regulation, the seller may withhold or stop delivery unless the buyer provides a means or manner of payment which is commercially a substantial equivalent. If delivery has already been taken, payment by the means or in the manner provided by the regulation discharges the buyer's obligation unless the regulation is discriminatory, oppressive or predatory.

§2–615. Excuse by Failure of Presupposed Conditions. Except so far as a seller may have assumed a greater obligation and subject to the preceding section on substitute performance:

(a) Delay in delivery or non-delivery in whole or in part by a seller who complies with paragraphs (b) and (c) is not a breach of his duty under a contract for sale if performance as agreed has been made impracticable by the occurrence of a contingency the non-occurrence of which was a basic assumption on which the contract was made or by compliance in good faith with any applicable foreign or domestic governmental regulation or order whether or not it later proves to be invalid.

(b) Where the causes mentioned in paragraph (a) affect only a part of the seller's capacity to perform, he must allocate production and deliveries among his customers but may at his option include regular customers not then under contract as well as his own requirements for further manufacture. He may so allocate in any manner which is fair and reasonable.

(c) The seller must notify the buyer seasonably that there will be delay or non-delivery and, when allocation is required under paragraph (b), of the estimated quota thus made available for the buyer.

§2–616. **Procedure on Notice Claiming Excuse.** (1) Where the buyer receives notification of a material or indefinite delay or an allocation justified under the preceding section he may by written notification to the seller as to any delivery concerned, and where the prospective deficiency substantially impairs the value of the whole contract under the provisions of this Article relating to breach of installment contracts (Section 2–612), then also as to the whole,

(a) terminate and thereby discharge any unexecuted portion of the contract; or

(b) modify the contract by agreeing to take his available quota in substitution.

(2) If after receipt of such notification from the seller the buyer fails so to modify the contract within a reasonable time not exceeding thirty days the contract lapses with respect to any deliveries affected.

(3) The provisions of this section may not be negated by agreement except in so far as the seller has assumed a greater obligation under the preceding section.

PART 7
Remedies

§2–701. **Remedies for Breach of Collateral Contracts Not Impaired.** Remedies for breach of any obligation or promise collateral or ancillary to a contract for sale are not impaired by the provisions of this Article.

§2–702. **Seller's Remedies on Discovery of Buyer's Insolvency.** (1) Where the seller discovers the buyer to be insolvent he may refuse delivery except for cash including payment for all goods theretofore delivered under the contract, and stop delivery under this Article (Section 2–705).

(2) Where the seller discovers that the buyer has received goods on credit while insolvent he may reclaim the goods upon demand made within ten days after the receipt, but if misrepresentation of solvency has been made to the particular seller in writing within three months before delivery the ten day limitation does not not apply. Except as provided in this subsection the seller may not base a right to reclaim goods on the buyer's fraudulent or innocent misrepresentation of solvency or of intent to pay.

(3) The seller's right to reclaim under subsection (2) is subject to the rights of a buyer in ordinary course or other good faith purchaser or lien creditor under this Article (Section 2–403). Successful reclamation of goods excludes all other remedies with respect to them.

§2–703. **Seller's Remedies in General.** Where the buyer wrongfully rejects or revokes acceptance of goods or fails to make a payment due on or before delivery or repudiates with respect to a part or the whole, then with respect to any goods directly affected and, if the breach is of the whole contract (Section 2–612), then also with respect to the whole undelivered balance, the aggrieved seller may

(a) withhold delivery of such goods;

(b) stop delivery by any bailee as hereafter provided (Section 2–705);

(c) proceed under the next section respecting goods still unidentified to the contract;

(d) resell and recover damages as hereafter provided (Section 2–706);

(e) recover damages for non-acceptance (Section 2–708) or in a proper case the price (Section 2–709);

(f) cancel.

§2–704. Seller's Right to Identify Goods to the Contract Notwithstanding Breach or to Salvage Unfinished Goods. (1) An aggrieved seller under the preceding section may

(a) identify to the contract conforming goods not already identified if at the time he learned of the breach they are in his possession or control;

(b) treat as the subject of resale goods which have demonstrably been intended for the particular contract even though those goods are unfinished.

(2) Where the goods are unfinished an aggrieved seller may in the exercise of reasonable commercial judgment for the purposes of avoiding loss and of effective realization either complete the manufacture and wholly identify the goods to the contract or cease manufacture and resell for scrap or salvage value or proceed in any other reasonable manner.

§2–705. Seller's Stoppage of Delivery in Transit or Otherwise. (1) The seller may stop delivery of goods in the possession of a carrier or other bailee when he discovers the buyer to be insolvent (Section 2–702) and may stop delivery of carload, truckload, planeload or larger shipments of express or freight when the buyer repudiates or fails to make a payment due before delivery or if for any other reason the seller has a right to withhold or reclaim the goods.

(2) As against such buyer the seller may stop delivery until

(a) receipt of the goods by the buyer; or

(b) acknowledgment to the buyer by any bailee of the goods except a carrier that the bailee holds the goods for the buyer; or

(c) such acknowledgment to the buyer by a carrier by reshipment or as warehouseman; or

(d) negotiation to the buyer of any negotiable document of title covering the goods.

(3) (a) To stop delivery the seller must so notify as to enable the bailee by reasonable diligence to prevent delivery of the goods.

(b) After such notification the bailee must hold and deliver the goods according to the directions of the seller but the seller is liable to the bailee for any ensuing charges or damages.

(c) If a negotiable document of title has been issued for goods the bailee is not obliged to obey a notification to stop until surrender of the document.

(d) A carrier who has issued a non-negotiable bill of lading is not obliged to obey a notification to stop received from a person other than the consignor.

§2–706. Seller's Resale Including Contract for Resale. (1) Under the conditions stated in Section 2–703 on seller's remedies, the seller may resell the goods concerned or the undelivered balance thereof. Where the resale is made in good faith and in a commercially reasonable manner the seller may recover the difference between the resale price and the contract price together with any incidental damages allowed under the provisions of this Article (Section 2–710), but less expenses saved in consequence of the buyer's breach.

(2) Except as otherwise provided in subsection (3) or unless otherwise agreed resale may be at public or private sale including sale by way of one or more contracts to sell or of identification to an existing contract of the seller. Sale may be as a unit or in parcels and at any time and place and on any terms but every aspect of the sale including the method, manner, time, place and terms must be commercially reasonable. The resale must be reasonably identified as referring to the broken contract, but it is not necessary that the goods be in existence or that any or all of them have been identified to the contract before the breach.

(3) Where the resale is at private sale the seller must give the buyer reasonable notification of his intention to resell.

(4) Where the resale is at public sale

(a) only identified goods can be sold except where there is a recognized market for a public sale of futures in goods of the kind; and

(b) it must be made at a usual place or market for public sale if one is reasonably available and except in the case of goods which are perishable or threaten to decline in value speedily the seller must give the buyer reasonable notice of the time and place of the resale; and

(c) if the goods are not to be within the view of those attending the sale the notification of sale must state the place where the goods are located and provide for their reasonable inspection by prospective bidders; and

(d) the seller may buy.

(5) A purchaser who buys in good faith at a resale takes the goods free of any rights of the original buyer even though the seller fails to comply with one or more of the requirements of this section.

(6) The seller is not accountable to the buyer for any profit made on any resale. A person in the position of a seller (Section 2–707) or a buyer who has rightfully rejected or justifiably revoked acceptance must account for any excess over the amount of his security interest, as hereinafter defined (subsection (3) of Section 2–711).

§2–707. "Person in the Position of a Seller." (1) A "person in the position of a seller" includes as against a principal an agent who has paid or become responsible for the price of goods on behalf of his principle or anyone who otherwise holds a security interest or other right in goods similar to that of a seller.

(2) A person in the position of a seller may as provided in this Article withhold or stop delivery (Section 2–705) and resell (Section 2–706) and recover incidental damages (Section 2–710).

§2–708. Seller's Damages for Non-acceptance or Repudiation. (1) Subject to subsection (2) and to the provisions of this Article with respect to proof of market price (Section 2–723), the measure of damages for non-acceptance or repudiation by the the buyer is the difference between the market price at the time and place for tender and the unpaid contract price together with any incidental damages provided in this Article (Section 2–710), but less expenses saved in consequence of the buyer's breach.

(2) If the measure of damages provided in subsection (1) is inadequate to put the seller in as good a position as performance would have done then the measure of damages is the profit (including reasonable overhead) which the seller would have made from full performance by the buyer, together with any incidental damages provided in this Article (Section 2–710), due allowance for costs reasonably incurred and due credit for payments or proceeds of resale.

§2–709. **Action for the Price.** (1) When the buyer fails to pay the price as it becomes due the seller may recover, together with any incidental damages under the next section, the price

(a) of goods accepted or of conforming goods lost or damaged within a commercially reasonable time after risk of their loss has passed to the buyer; and

(b) of goods identified to the contract if the seller is unable after reasonable effort to resell them at a reasonable price or the circumstances reasonably indicate that such effort will be unavailing.

(2) Where the seller sues for the price he must hold for the buyer any goods which have been identified to the contract and are still in his control except that if resale becomes possible he may resell them at any time prior to the collection of the judgment. The net proceeds of any such resale must be credited to the buyer and payment of the judgment entitles him to any goods not resold.

(3) After the buyer has wrongfully rejected or revoked acceptance of the goods or has failed to make a payment due or has repudiated (Section 2–610), a seller who is held not entitled to the price under this section shall nevertheless be awarded damages for non-acceptance under the preceding section.

§2–710. **Seller's Incidental Damages.** Incidental damages to an aggrieved seller include any commercially reasonable charges, expenses or commissions incurred in stopping delivery, in the transportation, care and custody of goods after the buyer's breach, in connection with return or resale of the goods or otherwise resulting from the breach.

§2–711. **Buyer's Remedies in General; Buyer's Security Interest in Rejected Goods.** (1) Where the seller fails to make delivery or repudiates or the buyer rightfully rejects or justifiably revokes acceptance then with respect to any goods involved, and with respect to the whole if the breach goes to the whole contract (Section 2–612), the buyer may cancel and whether or not he has done so may in addition to recovering so much of the price as has been paid

(a) "cover" and have damages under the next section as to all the goods affected whether or not they have been identified to the contract; or

(b) recover damages for non-delivery as provided in this Article (Section 2–713).

(2) Where the seller fails to deliver or repudiates the buyer may also

(a) if the goods have been identified recover them as provided in this Article (Section 2–502); or

(b) in a proper case obtain specific performance or replevy the goods as provided in this Article (Section 2–716).

(3) On rightful rejection or justifiable revocation of acceptance a buyer has a security interest in goods in his possession or control for any payments made on their price and any expenses reasonably incurred in their inspection, receipt, transportation, care and custody and may hold such goods and resell them in like manner as an aggrieved seller (Section 2–706).

§2–712. "Cover"; Buyer's Procurement of Substitute Goods. (1) After a breach within the preceding section the buyer may "cover" by making in good faith and without unreasonable delay any reasonable purchase of or contract to purchase goods in substitution for those due from the seller.

(2) The buyer may recover from the seller as damages the difference between the cost of cover and the contract price together with any incidental or consequential damages as hereinafter defined (Section 2–715), but less expenses saved in consequence of the seller's breach.

(3) Failure of the buyer to effect cover within this section does not bar him from any other remedy.

§2–713. Buyer's Damages for Non-Delivery or Repudiation. (1) Subject to the provisions of this Article with respect to proof of market price (Section 2–723), the measure of damages for non-delivery or repudiation by the seller is the difference between the market price at the time when the buyer learned of the breach and the contract price together with any incidental and consequential damages provided in this Article (Section 2–715), but less expenses saved in consequence of the seller's breach.

(2) Market price is to be determined as of the place for tender or, in cases of rejection after arrival or revocation of acceptance, as of the place of arrival.

§2–714. Buyer's Damages for Breach in Regard to Accepted Goods. (1) Where the buyer has accepted goods and given notification (subsection (3) of Section 2–607) he may recover as damages for any non-conformity of tender the loss resulting in the ordinary course of events from the seller's breach as determined in any manner which is reasonable.

(2) The measure of damages for breach of warranty is the difference at the time and place of acceptance between the value of the goods accepted and the value they would have had if they had been as warranted, unless special circumstances show proximate damages of a different amount.

(3) In a proper case any incidental and consequential damages under the next section may also be recovered.

§2–715. Buyer's Incidental and Consequential Damages. (1) Incidental damages resulting from the seller's breach include expenses reasonably incurred in inspection, receipt, transportation and care and custody of goods rightfully rejected, any commercially reasonable charges, expenses or commissions in connection with effecting cover and any other reasonable expense incident to the delay or other breach.

(2) Consequential damages resulting from the seller's breach include

(a) any loss resulting from general or particular requirements and needs of which the seller at the time of contracting had reason to know and which could not reasonably be prevented by cover or otherwise; and

(b) injury to person or property proximately resulting from any breach of warranty.

§2–716. Buyer's Right to Specific Performance or Replevin. (1) Specific performance may be decreed where the goods are unique or in other proper circumstances.

(2) The decree for specific performance may include such terms and conditions as to payment of the price, damages, or other relief as the court may deem just.

(3) The buyer has a right of replevin for goods identified to the contract if after reasonable effort he is unable to effect cover for such goods or the circumstances reasonably indicate that such effort will be unavailing or if the goods have been shipped under reservation and satisfaction of the security interest in them has been made or tendered.

§2–717. Deduction of Damages From the Price. The buyer on notifying the seller of his intention to do so may deduct all or any part of the damages resulting from any breach of the contract from any part of the price still due under the same contract.

§2–718. Liquidation or Limitation of Damages; Deposits. (1) Damages for breach by either party may be liquidated in the agreement but only at an amount which is reasonable in the light of the anticipated or actual harm caused by the breach, the difficulties of proof of loss, and the inconvenience or non-feasibility of otherwise obtaining an adequate remedy. A term fixing unreasonably large liquidated damages is void as a penalty.

(2) Where the seller justifiably withholds delivery of goods because of the buyer's breach, the buyer is entitled to restitution of any amount by which the sum of his payments exceeds

(a) the amount to which the seller is entitled by virtue of terms liquidating the seller's damages in accordance with subsection (1), or

(b) in the absense of such terms, twenty per cent of the value of the total performance for which the buyer is obligated under contract or $500, whichever is smaller.

(3) The buyer's right to restitution under subsection (2) is subject to offset to the extent that the seller establishes

(a) a right to recover damages under the provisions of this Article other than subsection (1), and

(b) the amount or value of any benefits received by the buyer directly or indirectly by reason of the contract.

(4) Where a seller has received payment in goods their reasonable value or the proceeds of their resale shall be treated as payments for the purposes of subsection (2); but if the seller has notice of the buyer's breach before reselling goods received in part performance, his resale is subject to the conditions laid down in this Article on resale by an aggrieved seller (Section 2–706).

§2–719. Contractual Modification or Limitation of Remedy. (1) Subject to the provisions of subsections (2) and (3) of this section and of the preceding section on liquidation and limitation of damages,

(a) the agreement may provide for remedies in addition to or in substitution for those provided in this Article and may limit or alter the measure of damages recoverable under this Article, as by limiting the buyer's remedies to return of the goods and repayment of the price or to repair and replacement of non-conforming goods or parts; and

(b) resort to a remedy as provided is optional unless the remedy is expressly agreed to be exclusive, in which case it is the sole remedy.

(2) Where circumstances cause an exclusive or limited remedy to fail of its essential purpose, remedy may be had as provided in this Act.

(3) Consequental damages may be limited or excluded unless the limitation or exclusion is unconscionable. Limitation of consequential damages for injury to the person in the case of consumer goods is prima facie unconscionable but limitation of damages where the loss is commercial is not.

§2–720. **Effect of "Cancellation" or "Rescission" on Claims for Antecedent Breach.** Unless the contrary intention clearly appears, expressions of "cancellation" or "rescission" of the contract or the like shall not be construed as a renunciation or discharge of any claim in damages for an antecedent breach.

§2–721. **Remedies for Fraud.** Remedies for material misrepresentation or fraud include all remedies available under this Article for non-fraudulent breach. Neither rescission or a claim for rescission of the contract for sale nor rejection or return of the goods shall bar or be deemed inconsistent with a claim for damages or other remedy.

§2–722. **Who Can Sue Third Parties for Injury to Goods.** Where a third party so deals with goods which have been identified to a contract for sale as to cause actionable injury to a party to that contract

(a) a right of action against the third party is in either party to the contract for sale who has title to or a security interest or a special property or an insurable interest in the goods; and if the goods have been destroyed or converted a right of action is also in the party who bore the risk of loss under the contract for sale or has since the injury assumed that risk as against the other;

(b) if at the time of the injury the party plaintiff did not bear the risk of loss as against the other party to the contract for sale and there is no arrangement between them for disposition of the recovery, his suit or settlement is, subject to his own interest, as a fiduciary for the other party to the contract;

(c) either party may with the consent of the other sue for the benefit of whom it may concern.

§2–723. **Proof of Market Price: Time and Place.** (1) If an action based on anticipatory repudiation comes to trial before the time for performance with respect to some or all of the goods, any damages based on market price (Section 2–708 or Section 2–713) shall be determined according to the price of such goods prevailing at the time when the aggrieved party learned of the repudiation.

(2) If evidence of a price prevailing at the times or places described in this Article is not readily available the price prevailing within any reasonable time before or after the time described or at any other place which in commercial judgment or under usage of trade would serve as a reasonable substitute for the one described may be used, making any proper allowance for the cost of transporting the goods to or from such other place.

(3) Evidence of a relevant price prevailing at a time or place other than the one described in this Article offered by one party is not admissible unless and until he has given the other party such notice as the court finds sufficient to prevent unfair surprise.

§2–724. **Admissibility of Market Quotations.** Whenever the prevailing price or value of any goods regularly bought and sold in any established commodity market is in issue, reports in official publications or trade journals or in newspaper or periodicals of general circulation published as the reports of such market shall be admissible in evidence. The circumstances of the preparation of such a report may be shown to affect its weight but not its admissibility.

§2–725. **Statute of Limitations in Contracts for Sale.** (1) An action for breach of any contract for sale must be commenced within four years after the cause of action has accrued. By the original agreement the parties may reduce the period of limitation to not less than one year but may not extend it.

(2) A cause of action accrues when the breach occurs, regardless of the aggrieved party's lack of knowledge of the breach. A breach of warranty occurs when tender of delivery is made, except that where a warranty explicitly extends to future performance of the goods and discovery of the breach must await the time of such performance the cause of action accrues when the breach is or should have been discovered.

(3) Where an action commenced within the time limited by subsection (1) is so terminated as to leave available a remedy by another action for the same breach such other action may be commenced after the expiration of the time limited and within six months after the termination of the first action unless the termination resulted from voluntary discontinuance or from dismissal for failure or neglect to prosecute.

(4) This section does not alter the law on tolling of the statute of limitations nor does it apply to causes of action which have accrued before this Act becomes effective.

ARTICLE 3: COMMERCIAL PAPER

PART 1
Short Title, Form and Interpretation

§3–101. **Short Title.** This Article shall be known and may be cited as Uniform Commercial Code—Commercial Paper.

§3–102. **Definitions and Index of Definitions.** (1) In this Article unless the context otherwise requires

(a) "Issue" means the first delivery of an instrument to a holder or a remitter.

(b) An "order" is a direction to pay and must be more than an authorization or request. It must identify the person to pay with reasonable certainty. It may be addressed to one or more such persons jointly or in the alternative but not in succession.

(c) A "promise" is an undertaking to pay and must be more than an acknowledgment of an obligation.

(d) "Secondary party" means a drawer or endorser.

(e) "Instrument" means a negotiable instrument.

(2) Other definitions applying to this Article and the sections in which they appear are:

"Acceptance." Section 3–410.

"Accommodation party." Section 3–415.

"Alternation." Section 3–407.

"Certificate of deposit." Section 3–104.

"Certification." Section 3–411.

"Check." Section 3–104.

"Definite time." Section 3–109.

"Dishonor." Section 3–507.

"Draft." Section 3–104.

"Holder in due course." Section 3–302.

"Negotiation." Section 3–202.

"Note." Section 3–104.

"Notice of dishonor." Section 3–508.

"On demand." Section 3–108.

"Presentment." Section 3–504.

"Protest." Section 3–509.

"Restrictive Indorsement." Section 3–205.

"Signature." Section 3–401.

(3) The following definitions in other Articles apply to this Article:

"Account." Section 4–104.

"Banking Day." Section 4–104.

"Clearing house." Section 4–104.

"Collecting bank." Section 4–105.

"Customer." Section 4–104.

"Depositary Bank." Section 4–105.

"Documentary Draft." Section 4–104.

"Intermediary Bank." Section 4–105.

"Item." Section 4–104.

"Midnight deadline." Section 4–104.

"Payor bank." Section 4–105.

(4) In addition Article 1 contains general definitions and principles of construction and interpretation applicable throughout this Article.

§3–103. **Limitations on Scope of Article.** (1) This Article does not apply to money, documents of title or investment securities.

(2) The provisions of this Article are subject to the provisions of the Article on Bank Deposits and Collections (Article 4) and Secured Transactions (Article 9).

§3–104. **Form of Negotiable Instruments; "Draft"; "Check"; "Certificate of Deposit"; "Note."** (1) Any writing to be a negotiable instrument within this Article must

(a) be signed by the maker or drawer; and

(b) contain an unconditional promise or order to pay a sum certain in money and no other promise, order, obligation or power given by the maker or drawer except as authorized by this Article; and

(c) be payable on demand or at a definite time; and

(d) be payable to order or to bearer.

(2) A writing which complies with the requirements of this section is

(a) a "draft" ("bill of exchange") if it is an order;

(b) a "check" if it is a draft drawn on a bank and payable on demand;

(c) a "certificate of deposit" if it is an acknowledgment by a bank of receipt of money with an engagement to repay it;

(d) a "note" if it is a promise other than a certificate of deposit.

(3) As used in other Articles of this Act, and as the context may require, the terms "draft," "check," "certificate of deposit" and "note" may refer to instruments which are not negotiable within this Article as well as to instruments which are so negotiable.

§3–105. When Promise or Order Unconditional. (1) A promise or order otherwise unconditional is not made conditional by the fact that the instrument

(a) is subject to implied or constructive conditions; or

(b) states its consideration, whether performed or promised, or the transaction which gave rise to the instrument, or that the promise or order is made or the instrument matures in accordance with or "as per" such transaction; or

(c) refers to or states that it arises out of a separate agreement; or

(d) states that it is drawn under a letter of credit; or

(e) states that it is secured, whether by mortgage, reservation of title or otherwise; or

(f) indicates a particular account to be debited or any other fund or source from which reimbursement is expected; or

(g) is limited to payment out of a particular fund or the proceeds of a particular source, if the instrument is issued by a government or governmental agency or unit; or

(h) is limited to payment out of the entire assets of a partnership, unincorporated association, trust or estate by or on behalf of which the instrument is issued.

(2) A promise or order is not unconditional if the instrument

(a) states that it is subject to or governed by any other agreement; or

(b) states that it is to be paid only out of a particular fund or source except as provided in this section.

§3–106. Sum Certain. (1) The sum payable is a sum certain even though it is to be paid

(a) with stated interest or by stated installments; or

(b) with stated different rates of interest before and after default or a specified date; or

(c) with a stated discount or addition if paid before or after the date fixed for payment; or

(d) with exchange or less exchange, whether at a fixed rate or at the current rate; or

(e) with costs of collection or an attorney's fee or both upon default.

(2) Nothing in this section shall validate any term which is otherwise illegal.

§3–107. Money. (1) An instrument is payable in money if the medium of exchange in which it is payable is money at the time the instrument is made. An instrument payable in "currency" or "current funds" is payable in money.

(2) A promise or order to pay a sum stated in a foreign currency is for a sum certain in money and, unless a different medium of payment is specified in the instrument, may be satisfied by payment of that number of dollars which the stated foreign currency will purchase at the buying sight rate for that currency on the day on which the instrument is payable or, if payable on demand, on the day of demand. If such an instrument specifies a foreign currency as the medium of payment the instrument is payable in that currency.

§3–108. **Payable on Demand.** Instruments payable on demand include those payable at sight or on presentation and those in which no time for payment is stated.

§3–109. **Definite Time.** (1) An instrument is payable at a definite time if by its terms it is payable

(a) on or before a stated date or at a fixed period after a stated date; or

(b) at a fixed period after sight; or

(c) at a definite time subject to any acceleration; or

(d) at a definite time subject to extension at the option of the holder, or to extension to a further definite time at the option of the maker or acceptor or automatically upon or after a specified act or event.

(2) An instrument which by its terms is otherwise payable only upon an act or event uncertain as to time of occurrence is not payable at a definite time even though the act or event has occurred.

§3–110. **Payable to Order.** (1) An instrument is payable to order when by its terms it is payable to the order or assigns of any person therein specified with reasonable certainty, or to him or his order, or when it is conspicuously designated on its face as "exchange" or the like and names a payee. It may be payable to the order of

(a) the maker or drawer; or

(b) the drawee; or

(c) a payee who is not maker, drawer or drawee; or

(d) two or more payees together or in the alternative; or

(e) an estate, trust or fund, in which case it is payable to the order of the representative of such estate, trust or fund or his successors; or

(f) an office, or an officer by his title as such in which case it is payable to the principal but the incumbent of the office or his successors may act as if he or they were the holder; or

(g) a partnership or unincorporated association, in which case it is payable to the partnership or association and may be indorsed or transferred by any person thereto authorized.

(2) An instrument not payable to order is not made so payable by such words as "payable upon return of this instrument properly indorsed."

(3) An instrument made payable both to order and to bearer is payable to order unless the bearer words are handwritten or typewritten.

§3–111. **Payable to Bearer.** An instrument is payable to bearer when by its terms it is payable to

(a) bearer or the order of bearer; or

(b) a specified person or bearer; or

(c) "cash" or the order of "cash," or any other indication which does not purport to designate a specific payee.

§3–112. Terms and Omissions Not Affecting Negotiability. (1) The negotiability of an instrument is not affected by

(a) the omission of a statement of any consideration or of the place where the instrument is drawn or payable; or

(b) a statement that collateral has been given for the instrument or in case of default on the instrument the collateral may be sold; or

(c) a promise or power to maintain or protect collateral or to give additional collateral; or

(d) a term authorizing a confession of judgment on the instrument if it is not paid when due; or

(e) a term purporting to waive the benefit of any law intended for the advantage or protection of any obligor; or

(f) a term in a draft providing that the payee by indorsing or cashing it acknowledges full satisfaction of an obligation of the drawer; or

(g) a statement in a draft drawn in a set of parts (Section 3–801) to the effect that the order is effective only if no other part has been honored.

(2) Nothing in this section shall validate any term which is otherwise illegal.

§3–113. Seal. An instrument otherwise negotiable is within this Article even though it is under a seal.

§3–114. Date, Antedating, Postdating. (1) The negotiability of an instrument is not affected by the fact that it is undated, antedated or postdated.

(2) Where an instrument is antedated or postdated the time when it is payable is determined by the stated date if the instrument is payable on demand or at a fixed period after date.

(3) Where the instrument or any signature thereon is dated, the date is presumed to be correct.

§3–115. Incomplete Instruments. (1) When a paper whose contents at the time of signing show that it is intended to become an instrument is signed while still incomplete in any necessary respect it cannot be enforced until completed, but when it is completed in accordance with authority given it is effective as completed.

(2) If the completion is unauthorized the rules as to material alteration apply (Section 3–407), even though the paper was not delivered by the maker or drawer; but the burden of establishing that any completion is unauthorized is on the party so asserting.

§3–116. Instruments Payable to Two or More Persons. An instrument payable to the order of two or more persons

(a) if in the alternative is payable to any one of them and may be negotiated, discharged or enforced by any of them who has possession of it;

(b) if not in the alternative is payable to all of them and may be negotiated, discharged or enforced only by all of them.

§3–117. Instruments Payable With Words of Description. An instrument made payable to a named person with the addition of words describing him

(a) as agent or officer of a specified person is payable to his principal but the agent or officer may act as if he were the holder;

(b) as any other fiduciary for a specified person or purpose is payable to the payee and may be negotiated, discharged or enforced by him;

(c) in any other manner is payable to the payee unconditionally and the additional words are without effect on subsequent parties.

§3–118. **Ambiguous Terms and Rules of Construction.** The following rules apply to every instrument:

(a) Where there is doubt whether the instrument is a draft or a note the holder may treat it as either. A draft drawn on the drawer is effective as a note.

(b) Handwritten terms control typewritten and printed terms, and typewritten control printed.

(c) Words control figures except that if the words are ambiguous figures control.

(d) Unless otherwise specified a provision for interest means interest at the judgment rate at the place of payment from the date of the instrument, or if it is undated from the date of issue.

(e) Unless the instrument otherwise specifies two or more persons who sign as maker, acceptor or drawer or indorser and as a part of the same transaction are jointly and severally liable even though the instrument contains such words as "I promise to pay."

(f) Unless otherwise specified consent to extension authorizes a single extension for not longer than the original period. A consent to extension, expressed in the instrument, is binding on secondary parties and accommodation makers. A holder may not exercise his option to extend an instrument over the objection of a maker or acceptor or other party who in accordance with Section 3–604 tenders full payment when the instrument is due.

§3–119. **Other Writings Affecting Instrument.** (1) As between the obligor and his immediate obligee or any transferee the terms of an instrument may be modified or affected by any other written agreement executed as a part of the same transaction, except that a holder in due course is not affected by any limitation of his rights arising out of the separate written agreement if he had no notice of the limitaton when he took the instrument.

(2) A separate agreement does not affect the negotiability of an instrument.

§3–120. **Instruments "Payable Through" Bank.** An instrument which states that it is "payable through" a bank or the like designates that bank as a collecting bank to make presentment but does not of itself authorize the bank to pay the instrument.

§3–121. **Instruments Payable at Bank. Note:** *If this Act is introduced in the Congress of the United States this section should be omitted. (States to select either alternative)*

Alternative A—

A note or acceptance which states that it is payable at a bank is the equivalent of a draft drawn on the bank payable when it falls due out of any funds of the maker or acceptor in current account or otherwise available for such payment.

Alternative B—

A note or acceptance which states that it is payable at a bank is not of itself an order or authorization to the bank to pay it.

§3–122. **Accrual of Cause of Action.** (1) A cause of action against a maker or an acceptor accrues

(a) in the case of a time instrument on the day after maturity;

(b) in the case of a demand instrument upon its date or, if no date is stated, on the date of issue.

(2) A cause of action against the obligor of a demand or time certificate of deposit accrues upon demand, but demand on a time certificate may not be made until on or after the date of maturity.

(3) A cause of action against a drawer of a draft or an indorser of any instrument accrues upon demand following dishonor of the instrument. Notice of dishonor is a demand.

(4) Unless an instrument provides otherwise, interest runs at the rate provided by law for a judgment

(a) in the case of a maker of a demand note, from the date of demand;

(b) in all other cases from the date of accrual of the cause of action.

PART 2

Transfer and Negotiation

§3–201. **Transfer: Right to Indorsement.** (1) Transfer of an instrument vests in the transferee such rights as the transferor has therein, except that a transferee who has himself been a party to any fraud or illegality affecting the instrument or who as a prior holder had notice of a defense or claim against it cannot improve his position by taking from a later holder in due course.

(2) A transfer of a security interest in an instrument vests the foregoing rights in the transferee to the extent of the interest transferred.

(3) Unless otherwise agreed any transfer for value of an instrument not then payable to bearer gives the transferee the specifically enforceable right to have the unqualified indorsement of the transferor. Negotiation takes effect only when the indorsement is made and until that time there is no presumption that the transferee is the owner.

§3–202. **Negotiation.** (1) Negotiation is the transfer of an instrument in such form that the transferee becomes a holder. If the instrument is payable to order it is negotiated by delivery with any necessary indorsement; if payable to bearer it is negotiated by delivery.

(2) An indorsement must be written by or on behalf of the holder and on the instrument or on a paper so firmly affixed thereto as to become a part thereof.

(3) An indorsement is effective for negotiation only when it conveys the entire instrument or any unpaid residue. If it purports to be of less it operates only as a partial assignment.

(4) Words of assignment, condition, waiver, guaranty, limitation or disclaimer of liability and the like accompanying an indorsement do not affect its character as an indorsement.

§3–203. **Wrong or Misspelled Name.** Where an instrument is made payable to a person under a misspelled name or one other than his own he may indorse in that name or his own or both; but signature in both names may be required by a person paying or giving value for the instrument.

§3–204. **Special Indorsement; Blank Indorsement.** (1) A special indorsement specifies the person to whom or to whose order it makes the instrument payable. Any instrument specially indorsed becomes payable to the order of the special indorsee and may be further negotiated only by his indorsement.

(2) An indorsement in blank specifies no particular indorsee and may consist of a mere signature. An instrument payable to order and indorsed in blank becomes payable to bearer and may be negotiated by delivery alone until specially indorsed.

(3) The holder may convert a blank indorsement into a special indorsement by writing over the signature of the indorser in blank any contract consistent with the character of the indorsement.

§3–205. **Restrictive Indorsements.** An indorsement is restrictive which either

(a) is conditional; or

(b) purports to prohibit further transfer of the instrument; or

(c) includes the words "for collection," "for deposit," "pay any bank," or like terms signifying a purpose of deposit or collection; or

(d) otherwise states that it is for the benefit or use of the indorser or of another person.

§3–206. **Effect of Restrictive Indorsement.** (1) No restrictive indorsement prevents further transfer or negotiation of the instrument.

(2) An intermediary bank, or a payor bank which is not the depositary bank, is neither given notice nor otherwise affected by a restrictive indorsement of any person except the bank's immediate transferor or the person presenting for payment.

(3) Except for an intermediary bank, any transferee under an indorsement which is conditional or includes the words "for collection," "for deposit," "pay any bank," or like terms (subparagraphs (a) and (c) of Section 3–205) must pay or apply any value given by him for or on the security of the instrument consistently with the indorsement and to the extent that he does so he becomes a holder for value. In addition such transferee is a holder in due course if he otherwise complies with the requirements of Section 3–302 on what constitutes a holder in due course.

(4) The first taker under an indorsement for the benefit of the indorser or another person (subparagraph (d) of Section 3–205) must pay or apply any value given by him for or on the security of the instrument consistently with the indorsement and to the extent that he does so he becomes a holder for value. In addition such taker is a holder in due course if he otherwise complies with the requirements of Section 3–302 on what constitutes a holder in due course. A later holder for value is neither given notice nor otherwise affected by such restrictive indorsement unless he has knowledge that a fiduciary or other person has negotiated the instrument in any transaction for his own benefit or otherwise in breach of duty (subsection (2) of Section 3–304).

§3–207. **Negotiation Effective Although It May Be Rescinded.** (1) Negotiation is effective to transfer the instrument although the negotiation is

(a) made by an infant, a corporation exceeding its powers, or any other person without capacity; or

(b) obtained by fraud, duress or mistake of any kind; or

(c) part of an illegal transaction; or

(d) made in breach of duty.

(2) Except as against a subsequent holder in due course such negotiation is in an appropriate case subject to rescission, the declaration of a constructive trust or any other remedy permitted by law.

§3–208. **Reacquisition.** Where an instrument is returned to or reacquired by a prior party he may cancel any indorsement which is not necessary to his title and reissue or further negotiate the instrument, but any intervening party is discharged as against the reacquiring party and subsequent holders not in due course and if his indorsement has been cancelled is discharged as against subsequent holders in due course as well.

PART 3
Rights of a Holder

§3–301. **Rights of a Holder.** The holder of an instrument whether or not he is the owner may transfer or negotiate it and, except as otherwise provided in Section 3–603 on payment or satisfaction, discharge it or enforce payment in his own name.

§3–302. **Holder in Due Course.** (1) A holder in due course is a holder who takes the instrument

(a) for value; and

(b) in good faith; and

(c) without notice that it is overdue or has been dishonored or of any defense against or claim to it on the part of any person.

(2) A payee may be a holder in due course.

(3) A holder does not become a holder in due course of an instrument:

(a) by purchase of it at judicial sale or by taking it under legal process; or

(b) by acquiring it in taking over an estate; or

(c) by purchasing it as part of a bulk transaction not in regular course of business of the transferor.

(4) A purchaser of a limited interest can be a holder in due course only to the extent of the interest purchased.

§3–303. **Taking for Value.** A holder takes the instrument for value

(a) to the extent that the agreed consideration has been performed or that he acquires a security interest in or a lien on the instrument otherwise than by legal process; or

(b) when he takes the instrument in payment of or as security for an antecedent claim against any person whether or not the claim is due; or

(c) when he gives a negotiable instrument for it or makes an irrevocable commitment to a third person.

§3–304. **Notice to Purchaser.** (1) The purchaser has notice of a claim or defense if

(a) the instrument is so incomplete, bears such visible evidence of forgery or alteration, or is otherwise so irregular as to call into question its validity, terms or ownership or to create an ambiguity as to the party to pay; or

(b) the purchaser has notice that the obligation of any party is voidable in whole or in part, or that all parties have been discharged.

(2) The purchaser has notice of a claim against the instrument when he has knowledge that a fiduciary has negotiated the instrument in payment of or as security for his own debt or in any transaction for his own benefit or or otherwise in breach of duty.

(3) The purchaser has notice that an instrument is overdue if he has reason to know

(a) that any part of the principal amount is overdue or that there is an uncured default in payment of another instrument of the same series; or

(b) that acceleration of the instrument has been made; or

(c) that he is taking a demand instrument after demand has been made or more than a reasonable length of time after its issue. A reasonable time for a check drawn and payable within the states and territories of the United States and the District of Columbia is presumed to be thirty days.

(4) Knowledge of the following facts does not of itself give the purchaser notice of a defense or claim

(a) that the instrument is antedated or postdated;

(b) that it was issued or negotiated in return for an executory promise or accompanied by a separate agreement, unless the purchaser has notice that a defense or claim has arisen from the terms thereof;

(c) that any party has signed for accommodation;

(d) that an incomplete instrument has been completed, unless the purchaser has notice of any improper completion;

(e) that any person negotiating the instrument is or was a fiduciary;

(f) that there has been default in payment of interest on the instrument or in payment of any other instrument, except one of the same series.

(5) The filing or recording of a document does not of itself constitute notice within the provisions of this Article to a person who would otherwise be a holder in due course.

(6) To be effective notice must be received at such time and in such manner as to give a reasonable opportunity to act on it.

§3–305. **Rights of a Holder in Due Course.** To the extent that a holder is a holder in due course he takes the instrument free from

(1) all claims to it on the part of any person; and

(2) all defenses of any party to the instrument with whom the holder has not dealt except

(a) infancy, to the extent that it is a defense to a simple contract; and

(b) such other incapacity, or duress, or illegality of the transaction, as renders the obligation of the party a nullity; and

(c) such misrepresentation as has induced the party to sign the instrument with neither knowledge nor reasonable opportunity to obtain knowledge of its character or its essential terms; and

(d) discharge in insolvency proceedings; and

(e) any other discharge of which the holder has notice when he takes the instrument.

§3–306. **Rights of One Not Holder in Due Course.** Unless he has the rights of a holder in due course any person takes the instrument subject to

(a) all valid claims to it on the part of any person; and

(b) all defenses of any party which would be available in an action on a simple contract; and

(c) the defenses of want or failure of consideration, non-performance of any condition precedent, non-delivery, or delivery for a special purpose (Section 3–408); and

(d) the defense that he or a person through whom he holds the instrument acquired it by theft, or that payment or satisfaction to such holder would be inconsistent with the terms of a restrictive indorsement. The claim of any third person to the instrument is not otherwise available as a defense to any party liable thereon unless the third person himself defends the action for such party.

§3–307. **Burden of Establishing Signatures, Defenses and Due Course.** (1) Unless specifically denied in the pleadings each signature on an instrument is admitted. When the effectiveness of a signature is put in issue

(a) the burden of establishing it is on the party claiming under the signature; but

(b) the signature is presumed to be genuine or authorized except where the action is to enforce the obligation of a purported signer who has died or become incompetent before proof is required.

(2) When signatures are admitted or established, production of the instrument entitles a holder to recover on it unless the defendant establishes a defense.

(3) After it is shown that a defense exists a person claiming the rights of a holder in due course has the burden of establishing that he or some person under whom he claims is in all respects a holder in due course.

PART 4
Liability of Parties

§3–401. **Signature.** (1) No person is liable on an instrument unless his signature appears thereon.

(2) A signature is made by use of any name, including any trade or assumed name, upon an instrument, or by any word or mark used in lieu of a written signature.

§3–402. **Signature in Ambiguous Capacity.** Unless the instrument clearly indicates that a signature is made in some other capacity it is an indorsement.

§3–403. **Signature by Authorized Representative.** (1) A signature may be made by an agent or other representative, and his authority to make it may be established as in other cases of representation. No particular form of appointment is necessary to establish such authority.

(2) An authorized representative who signs his own name to an instrument

(a) is personally obligated if the instrument neither names the person represented nor shows that the representative signed in a representative capacity;

(b) except as otherwise established between the immediate parties, is personally obligated if the instrument names the person represented but does not show that the representative signed in a representative capacity, or if the instrument does not name the person represented but does show that the representative signed in a representative capacity.

(3) Except as otherwise established the name of an organization preceded or followed by the name and office of an authorized individual is a signature made in a representative capacity.

§3–404. **Unauthorized Signatures.** (1) Any unauthorized signature is wholly inoperative as that of the person whose name is signed unless he ratifies it or is precluded from denying it; but it operates as the signature of the unauthorized signer in favor of any person who in good faith pays the instrument or takes it for value.

(2) Any unauthorized signature may be ratified for all purposes of this Article. Such ratification does not of itself affect any rights of the person ratifying against the actual signer.

§3–405. **Impostors; Signature in Name of Payee.** (1) An indorsement by any person in the name of a named payee is effective if

(a) an impostor by use of the mails or otherwise has induced the maker or drawer to issue the instrument to him or his confederate in the name of the payee; or

(b) a person signing as or on behalf of a maker or drawer intends the payee to have no interest in the instrument; or

(c) an agent or employee of the maker or drawer has supplied him with the name of the payee intending the latter to have no such interest.

(2) Nothing in this section shall affect the criminal or civil liability of the person so indorsing.

§3–406. **Negligence Contributing to Alteration or Unauthorized Signature.** Any person who by his negligence substantially contributes to a material alteration of the instrument or to the making of an unauthorized signature is precluded from asserting the alteration or lack of authority against a holder in due course or against a drawee or other payor who pays the instrument in good faith and in accordance with the reasonable commercial standards of the drawee's or payor's business.

§3–407. **Alteration.** (1) Any alteration of an instrument is material which changes the contract of any party thereto in any respect, including any such change in

(a) the number or relations of the parties; or

(b) an incomplete instrument, by completing it otherwise than as authorized; or

(c) the writing as signed, by adding to it or by removing any part of it.

(2) As against any person other than a subsequent holder in due course

(a) alteration by the holder which is both fraudulent and material discharges any party whose contract is thereby changed unless that party assents or is precluded from asserting the defense;

(b) no other alternation discharges any party and the instrument may be enforced according to its original tenor, or as to incomplete instruments according to the authority given.

(3) A subsequent holder in due course may in all cases enforce the instrument according to its original tenor, and when an incomplete instrument has been completed, he may enforce it as completed.

§3–408. **Consideration.** Want or failure of consideration is a defense as against any person not having the rights of a holder in due course (Section 3–305), except that no consideration is necessary for an instrument or obligation thereon given in payment of or as security for an antecedent obligation of any kind. Nothing in this section shall be taken to displace any statute outside this Act under which a promise is enforceable notwithstanding lack or failure of consideration. Partial failure of consideration is a defense pro tanto whether or not the failure is in an ascertained or liquidated amount.

§3–409. **Draft Not an Assignment.** (1) A check or other draft does not of itself operate as an assignment of any funds in the hands of the drawee available for its payment, and the drawee is not liable on the instrument until he accepts it.

(2) Nothing in this section shall affect any liability in contract, tort or otherwise arising from any letter of credit or other obligation or representation which is not an acceptance.

§3–410. **Definition and Operation of Acceptance.** (1) Acceptance is the drawee's signed engagement to honor the draft as presented. It must be written on the draft, and may consist of his signature alone. It becomes operative when completed by delivery or notification.

(2) A draft may be accepted although it has not been signed by the drawer or is otherwise incomplete or is overdue or has been dishonored.

(3) Where the draft is payable at a fixed period after sight and the acceptor fails to date his acceptance the holder may complete it by supplying a date in good faith.

§3–411. **Certification of a Check.** (1) Certification of a check is acceptance. Where a holder procures certification the drawer and all prior indorsers are discharged.

(2) Unless otherwise agreed a bank has no obligation to certify a check.

(3) A bank may certify a check before returning it for lack of proper indorsement. If it does so the drawer is discharged.

§3–412. **Acceptance Varying Draft.** (1) Where the drawee's proffered acceptance in any manner varies the draft as presented the holder may refuse the acceptance and treat the draft as dishonored in which case the drawee is entitled to have his acceptance cancelled.

(2) The terms of the draft are not varied by an acceptance to pay at any particular bank or place in the continental United States, unless the acceptance states that the draft is to be paid only at such bank or place.

(3) Where the holder assents to an acceptance varying the terms of the draft each drawer and indorser who does not affirmatively assent is discharged.

§3–413. **Contract of Maker, Drawer and Acceptor.** (1) The maker or acceptor engages that he will pay the instrument according to its tenor at the time of his engagement or as completed pursuant to Section 3–115 on incomplete instruments.

(2) The drawer engages that upon dishonor of the draft and any necessary notice of dishonor or protest he will pay the amount of the draft to the holder or to any indorser who takes it up. The drawer may disclaim this liability by drawing without recourse.

(3) By making, drawing or accepting the party admits as against all subsequent parties including the drawee the existence of the payee and his then capacity to indorse.

§3–414. **Contract of Indorser; Order of Liability.** (1) Unless the indorsement otherwise specifies (as by such words as "without recourse") every indorser engages that upon dishonor and any necessary notice of dishonor and protest he will pay the instrument according to its tenor at the time of his indorsement to the holder or to any subsequent indorser who takes it up, even though the indorser who takes it up was not obligated to do so.

(2) Unless they otherwise agree indorsers are liable to one another in the order in which they indorse, which is presumed to be the order in which their signatures appear on the instrument.

§3–415. **Contract of Accommodation Party.** (1) An accommodation party is one who signs the instrument in any capacity for the purpose of lending his name to another party to it.

(2) When the instrument has been taken for value before it is due the accommodation party is liable in the capacity in which he has signed even though the taker knows of the accommodation.

(3) As against a holder in due course and without notice of the accommodation oral proof of the accommodation is not admissible to give the accommodation party the benefit of discharges dependent on his character as such. In other cases the accommodation character may be shown by oral proof.

(4) An indorsement which shows that it is not in the chain of title is notice of its accommodation character.

(5) An accommodation party is not liable to the party accommodated, and if he pays the instrument has a right of recourse on the instrument against such party.

§3–416. **Contract of Guarantor.** (1) "Payment guaranteed" or equivalent words added to a signature mean that the signer engages that if the instrument is not paid when due he will pay it according to its tenor without resort by the holder to any other party.

(2) "Collection guaranteed" or equivalent words added to a signature mean that the signer engages that if the instrument is not paid when due he will pay it according to its tenor, but only after the holder has reduced his claim against the maker or acceptor to judgment and execution has been returned unsatisfied, or after the maker or acceptor has become insolvent or it is otherwise apparent that it is useless to proceed against him.

(3) Words of guaranty which do not otherwise specify guarantee payment.

(4) No words of guaranty added to the signature of a sole maker or acceptor affect his liability on the instrument. Such words added to the signature of one of two or more makers or acceptors create a presumption that the signature is for the accommodation of the others.

(5) When words of guaranty are used presentment, notice of dishonor and protest are not necessary to charge the user.

(6) Any guaranty written on the instrument is enforceable notwithstanding any statute of frauds.

§3–417. **Warranties on Presentment and Transfer.** (1) Any person who obtains payment or acceptance and any prior transferor warrants to a person who in good faith pays or accepts that

(a) he has a good title to the instrument or is authorized to obtain payment or acceptance on behalf of one who has a good title; and

(b) he has no knowledge that the signature of the maker or drawer is unauthorized, except that this warranty is not given by a holder in due course acting in good faith

(i) to a maker with respect to the maker's own signature; or

(ii) to a drawer with respect to the drawer's own signature, whether or not the drawer is also the drawee; or

(iii) to an acceptor of a draft if the holder in due course took the draft after the acceptance or obtained the acceptance without knowledge that the drawer's signature was unauthorized; and

(c) the instrument has not been materially altered, except that this warranty is not given by a holder in due course acting in good faith

(i) to the maker of a note; or

(ii) to the drawer of a draft whether or not the drawer is also the drawee; or

(iii) to the acceptor of a draft with respect to an alteration made prior to the acceptance if the holder in due course took the draft after the acceptance, even though the acceptance provided "payable as originally drawn" or equivalent terms; or

(iv) to the acceptor of a draft with respect to an alteration made after the acceptance.

(2) Any person who transfers an instrument and receives consideration warrants to his transferee and if the transfer is by indorsement to any subsequent holder who takes the instrument in good faith that

(a) he has a good title to the instrument or is authorized to obtain payment or acceptance on behalf of one who has a good title and the transfer is otherwise rightful; and

(b) all signatures are genuine or authorized; and

(c) the instrument has not been materially altered; and

(d) no defense of any party is good against him; and

(e) he has no knowledge of any insolvency proceeding instituted with respect to the maker or acceptor or the drawer of an unaccepted instrument.

(3) By transferring "without recourse" the transferor limits the obligation stated in subsection (2) (d) to a warranty that he has no knowledge of such a defense.

(4) A selling agent or broker who does not disclose the fact that he is acting only as such gives the warranties provided in this section, but if he makes such disclosure warrants only his good faith and authority.

§3–418. **Finality of Payment or Acceptance.** Except for recovery of bank payments as provided in the Article on Bank Deposits and Collections (Article 4) and except for liability for breach of warranty on presentment under the preceding section, payment or acceptance of any instrument is final in favor of a holder in due course, or a person who has in good faith changed his position in reliance on the payment.

§3–419. **Conversion of Instrument; Innocent Representative.** (1) An instrument is converted when

(a) a drawee to whom it is delivered for acceptance refuses to return it on demand; or

(b) any person to whom it is delivered for payment refuses on demand either to pay or to return it; or

(c) it is paid on a forged indorsement.

(2) In an action against a drawee under subsection (1) the measure of the drawee's liability is the face amount of the instrument. In any other action under subsection (1) the measure of liability is presumed to be the face amount of the instrument.

(3) Subject to the provisions of this Act concerning restrictive indorsements a representative, including a depositary or collecting bank, who has in good faith and in accordance with the reasonable commercial standards applicable to the business of such representative dealt with an instrument or its proceeds on behalf of one who was not the true owner is not liable in conversion or otherwise to the true owner beyond the amount of any proceeds remaining in his hands.

(4) An intermediary bank or payor bank which is not a depositary bank is not liable in conversion solely by reason of the fact that proceeds of an item indorsed restrictively (Sections 3–205 and 3–206) are not paid or applied consistently with the restrictive indorsement of an indorser other than its immediate transferor.

PART 5
Presentment, Notice of Dishonor and Protest

§3–501. When Presentment, Notice of Dishonor, and Protest Necessary or Permissible. (1) Unless excused (Section 3–511) presentment is necessary to charge secondary parties as follows:

(a) presentment for acceptance is necessary to charge the drawer and indorsers of a draft where the draft so provides, or is payable elsewhere than at the residence or place of business of the drawee, or its date of payment depends upon such presentment. The holder may at his option present for acceptance any other draft payable at a stated date;

(b) presentment for payment is necessary to charge any indorser;

(c) in the case of any drawer, the acceptor of a draft payable at a bank or the maker of a note payable at a bank, presentment for payment is necessary, but failure to make presentment discharges such drawer, acceptor or maker only as stated in Section 3–502(1) (b).

(2) Unless excused (Section 3–511)

(a) notice of any dishonor is necessary to charge any indorser;

(b) in the case of any drawer, the acceptor of a draft payable at a bank or the maker of a note payable at a bank, notice of any dishonor is necessary, but failure to give such notice discharges such drawer, acceptor or maker only as stated in Section 3–502(1) (b).

(3) Unless excused (Section 3–511) protest of any dishonor is necessary to charge the drawer and indorsers of any draft which on its face appears to be drawn or payable outside of the states and territories of the United States and the District of Columbia. The holder may at his option make protest of any dishonor of any other instrument and in the case of a foreign draft may on insolvency of the acceptor before maturity make protest for better security.

(4) Notwithstanding any provision of this section, neither presentment nor notice of dishonor nor protest is necessary to charge an indorser who has indorsed an instrument after maturity.

§3–502. **Unexcused Delay; Discharge.** (1) Where without excuse any necessary presentment or notice of dishonor is delayed beyond the time when it is due

(a) any indorser is discharged; and

(b) any drawer or the acceptor of a draft payable at a bank or the maker of a note payable at a bank who because the drawee or payor bank becomes insolvent during the delay is deprived of funds maintained with the drawee or payor bank to cover the instrument may discharge his liability by written assignment to the holder of his rights against the drawee or payor bank in respect of such funds, but such drawer, acceptor or maker is not otherwise discharged.

(2) Where without excuse a necessary protest is delayed beyond the time when it is due any drawer or indorser is discharged.

§3–503. **Time of Presentment.** (1) Unless a different time is expressed in the instrument the time for any presentment is determined as follows:

(a) where an instrument is payable at or a fixed period after a stated date any presentment for acceptance must be made on or before the date it is payable;

(b) where an instrument is payable after sight it must either be presented for acceptance or negotiated within a reasonable time after date or issue whichever is later;

(c) where an instrument shows the date on which it is payable presentment for payment is due on that date;

(d) where an instrument is accelerated presentment for payment is due within a reasonable time after the acceleration;

(e) with respect to the liability of any secondary party presentment for acceptance or payment of any other instrument is due within a reasonable time after such party becomes liable thereon.

(2) A reasonable time for presentment is determined by the nature of the instrument, any usage of banking or trade and the facts of the particular case. In the case of an uncertified check which is drawn and payable within the United States and which is not a draft drawn by a bank the following are presumed to be reasonable periods within which to present for payment or to initiate bank collection:

(a) with respect to the liability of the drawer, thirty days after date or issue whichever is later; and

(b) with respect to the liability of an indorser, seven days after his indorsement.

(3) Where any presentment is due on a day which is not a full business day for either the person making presentment or the party to pay or accept, presentment is due on the next following day which is a full business day for both parties.

(4) Presentment to be sufficient must be made at a reasonable hour, and if at a bank during its banking day.

§3–504. **How Presentment Made.** (1) Presentment is a demand for acceptance or payment made upon the maker, acceptor, drawee or other payor by or on behalf of the holder.

(2) Presentment may be made

(a) by mail, in which event the time of presentment is determined by the time of receipt of the mail; or

(b) through a clearing house; or

(c) at the place of acceptance or payment specified in the instrument or if there be none at the place of business or residence of the party to accept or pay. If neither the party to accept or pay nor anyone authorized to act for him is present or accessible at such place presentment is excused.

(3) It may be made

(a) to any one of two or more makers, acceptors, drawees or other payors; or

(b) to any person who has authority to make or refuse the acceptance or payment.

(4) A draft accepted or a note made payable at a bank in the continental United States must be presented at such bank.

(5) In the cases described in Section 4–210 presentment may be made in the manner and with the result stated in that section.

§3–505. **Rights of Party to Whom Presentment Is Made.** (1) The party to whom presentment is made may without dishonor require

(a) exhibition of the instrument; and

(b) reasonable identification of the person making presentment and evidence of his authority to make it if made for another; and

(c) that the instrument be produced for acceptance or payment at a place specified in it, or if there by none at any place reasonable in the circumstances; and

(d) a signed receipt on the instrument for any partial or full payment and its surrender upon full payment.

(2) Failure to comply with any such requirement invalidates the presentment but the person presenting has a reasonable time in which to comply and the time for acceptance or payment runs from the time of compliance.

§3–506. **Time Allowed for Acceptance or Payment.** (1) Acceptance may be deferred without dishonor until the close of the next business day following presentment. The holder may also in a good faith effort to obtain acceptance and without either dishonor of the instrument or discharge of secondary parties allow postponement of acceptance for an additional business day.

(2) Except as a longer time is allowed in the case of documentary drafts drawn under a letter of credit, and unless an earlier time is agreed to by the party to pay, payment of an instrument may be deferred without dishonor pending reasonable examination to determine whether it is properly payable, but payment must be made in any event before the close of business on the day of presentment.

§3–507. **Dishonor; Holder's Right of Recourse; Term Allowing Re-Present-ment.** (1) An instrument is dishonored when

(a) a necessary or optional presentment is duly made and due acceptance or payment is refused or cannot be obtained within the prescribed time or in case of bank collections the instrument is seasonably returned by the midnight deadline (Section 4–301); or

(b) presentment is excused and the instrument is not duly accepted or paid.

(2) Subject to any necessary notice of dishonor and protest, the holder has upon dishonor an immediate right of recourse against the drawers and indorsers.

(3) Return of an instrument for lack of proper indorsement is not dishonor.

(4) A term in a draft or an indorsement thereof allowing a stated time for representment in the event of any dishonor of the draft by nonacceptance if a time draft or by nonpayment if a sight draft gives the holder as against any secondary party bound by the term an option to waive the dishonor without affecting the liability of the secondary party and he may present again up to the end of the stated time.

§3–508. Notice of Dishonor. (1) Notice of dishonor may be given to any person who may be liable on the instrument by or on behalf of the holder or any party who has himself received notice, or any other party who can be compelled to pay the instrument. In addition an agent or bank in whose hands the instrument is dishonored may give notice to his principal or customer or to another agent or bank from which the instrument was received.

(2) Any necessary notice must be given by a bank before its midnight deadline and by any other person before midnight of the third business day after dishonor or receipt of notice of dishonor.

(3) Notice may be given in any reasonable manner. It may be oral or written and in any terms which identify the instrument and state that it has been dishonored. A misdescription which does not mislead the party notified does not vitiate the notice. Sending the instrument bearing a stamp, ticket or writing stating that acceptance or payment has been refused or sending a notice of debit with respect to the instrument is sufficient.

(4) Written notice is given when sent although it is not received.

(5) Notice to one partner is notice to each although the firm has been dissolved.

(6) When any party is in insolvency proceedings instituted after the issue of the instrument notice may be given either to the party or to the representative of his estate.

(7) When any party is dead or incompetent notice may be sent to his last known address or given to his personal representative.

(8) Notice operates for the benefit of all parties who have rights on the instrument against the party notified.

§3–509. Protest; Noting for Protest. (1) A protest is a certificate of dishonor made under the hand and seal of a United States consul or vice consul or a notary public or other person authorized to certify dishonor by the law of the place where dishonor occurs. It may be made upon information satisfactory to such person.

(2) The protest must identify the instrument and certify either that due presentment has been made or the reason why it is excused and that the instrument has been dishonored by nonacceptance or nonpayment.

(3) The protest may also certify that notice of dishonor has been given to all parties or to specified parties.

(4) Subject to subsection (5) any necessary protest is due by the time that notice of dishonor is due.

(5) If, before protest is due, an instrument has been noted for protest by the officer to make protest, the protest may be made at any time thereafter as of the date of the noting.

§3–510. **Evidence of Dishonor and Notice of Dishonor.** The following are admissible as evidence and create a presumption of dishonor and of any notice of dishonor therein shown:

(a) a document regular in form as provided in the preceding section which purports to be a protest;

(b) the purported stamp or writing of the drawee, payor bank or presenting bank on the instrument or accompanying it stating that acceptance or payment has been refused for reasons consistent with dishonor;

(c) any book or record of the drawee, payor bank, or any collecting bank kept in the usual course of business which shows dishonor, even though there is no evidence of who made the entry.

§3–511. **Waived or Excused Presentment, Protest or Notice of Dishonor or Delay Therein.** (1) Delay in presentment, protest or notice of dishonor is excused when the party is without notice that it is due or when the delay is caused by circumstances beyond his control and he exercises reasonable diligence after the cause of the delay ceases to operate.

(2) Presentment or notice or protest as the case may be is entirely excused when

(a) the party to be charged has waived it expressly or by implication either before or after it is due; or

(b) such party has himself dishonored the instrument or has countermanded payment or otherwise has no reason to expect or right to require that the instrument be accepted or paid; or

(c) by reasonable diligence the presentment or protest cannot be made or the notice given.

(3) Presentment is also entirely excused when

(a) the maker, acceptor or drawee of any instrument except a documentary draft is dead or in insolvency proceedings instituted after the issue of the instrument; or

(b) acceptance or payment is refused but not for want of proper presentment.

(4) Where a draft has been dishonored by nonacceptance a later presentment for payment and any notice of dishonor and protest for nonpayment are excused unless in the meantime the instrument has been accepted.

(5) A waiver of protest is also a waiver of presentment and of notice of dishonor even though protest is not required.

(6) Where a waiver of presentment or notice of protest is embodied in the instrument itself it is binding upon all parties; but where it is written above the signature of an indorser it binds him only.

PART 6
Discharge

§3–601. **Discharge of Parties.** (1) The extent of the discharge of any party from liability on an instrument is governed by the sections on
    (a) payment or satisfaction (Section 3–603); or
    (b) tender of payment (Section 3–604); or
    (c) cancellation or renunciation (Section 3–605); or
    (d) impairment of right of recourse or of collateral (Section 3–606); or
    (e) reacquisition of the instrument by a prior party (Section 3–208); or
    (f) fraudulent and material alteration (Section 3–407); or
    (g) certification of a check (Section 3–411); or
    (h) acceptance varying a draft (Section 3–412); or
    (i) unexcused delay in presentment or notice of dishonor or protest (Section 3–502).
    (2) Any party is also discharged from his liability on an instrument to another party by any other act or agreement with such party which would discharge his simple contract for the payment of money.
    (3) The liability of all parties is discharged when any party who has himself no right of action or recourse on the instrument
    (a) reacquires the instrument in his own right; or
    (b) is discharged under any provision of this Article, except as otherwise provided with respect to discharge for impairment of recourse or of collateral (Section 3–606).

§3–602. **Effect of Discharge Against Holder in Due Course.** No discharge of any party provided by this Article is effective against a subsequent holder in due course unless he has notice thereof when he takes the instrument.

§3–603. **Payment or Satisfaction.** (1) The liability of any party is discharged to the extent of his payment or satisfaction to the holder even though it is made with knowledge of a claim of another person to the instrument unless prior to such payment or satisfaction the person making the claim either supplies indemnity deemed adequate by the party seeking the discharge or enjoins payment or satisfaction by order of a court of competent jurisdiction in an action in which the adverse claimant and the holder are parties. This subsection does not, however, result in the discharge of the liability
    (a) of a party who in bad faith pays or satisfies a holder who acquired the instrument by theft or who (unless having the rights of a holder in due course) holds through one who so acquired it; or
    (b) of a party (other than an intermediary bank or a payor bank which is not a depositary bank) who pays or satisfies the holder of an instrument which has been restrictively indorsed in a manner not consistent with the terms of such restrictive indorsement.
    (2) Payment or satisfaction may be made with the consent of the holder by any person including a stranger to the instrument. Surrender of the instrument to such a person gives him the rights of a transferee (Section 3–201).

§3–604. **Tender of Payment.** (1) Any party making tender of full payment to a holder when or after it is due is discharged to the extent of all subsequent liability for interest, costs and attorney's fees.

(2) The holder's refusal of such tender wholly discharges any party who has a right of recourse against the party making the tender.

(3) Where the maker or acceptor of an instrument payable otherwise than on demand is able and ready to pay at every place of payment specified in the instrument when it is due, it is equivalent to tender.

§3–605. **Cancellation and Renunciation.** (1) The holder of an instrument may even without consideration discharge any party

(a) in any manner apparent on the face of the instrument or the indorsement, as by intentionally cancelling the instrument or the party's signature by destruction or mutilation, or by striking out the party's signature; or

(b) by renouncing his rights by a writing signed and delivered or by surrender of the instrument to the party to be discharged.

(2) Neither cancellation nor renunciation without surrender of the instrument affects the title thereto.

§3–606. **Impairment of Recourse or of Collateral.** (1) The holder discharges any party to the instrument to the extent that without such party's consent the holder

(a) without express reservation of rights releases or agrees not to sue any person against whom the party has to the knowledge of the holder a right of recourse or agrees to suspend the right to enforce against such person the instrument or collateral or otherwise discharges such person, except that failure or delay in effecting any required presentment, protest or notice of dishonor with respect to any such person does not discharge any party as to whom presentment, protest or notice of dishonor is effective or unnecessary; or

(b) unjustifiably impairs any collateral for the instrument given by or on behalf of the party or any person against whom he has a right of recourse.

(2) By express reservation of rights against a party with a right of recourse the holder preserves

(a) all his rights against such party as of the time when the instrument was originally due; and

(b) the right of the party to pay the instrument as of that time; and

(c) all rights of such party to recourse against others.

PART 7

Advice of International Sight Draft

§3–701. **Letter of Advice of International Sight Draft.** (1) A "letter of advice" is a drawer's communication to the drawee that a described draft has been drawn.

(2) Unless otherwise agreed when a bank receives from another bank a letter of advice of an international sight draft the drawee bank may immediately debit the drawer's account and stop the running of interest pro tanto. Such a debit and any resulting credit to any account covering outstanding drafts leaves in the drawer full power to stop payment or otherwise dispose of the amount and creates no trust or interest in favor of the holder.

(3) Unless otherwise agreed and except where a draft is drawn under a credit issued by the drawee, the drawee of an international sight draft owes the

drawer no duty to pay an unadvised draft but if it does so and the draft is genuine, may appropriately debit the drawer's account.

PART 8
Miscellaneous

§3–801. **Drafts in a Set.** (1) Where a draft is drawn in a set of parts, each of which is numbered and expressed to be an order only if no other part has been honored, the whole of the parts constitutes one draft but a taker of any part may become a holder in due course of the draft.

(2) Any person who negotiates, indorses or accepts a single part of a draft drawn in a set thereby becomes liable to any holder in due course of that part as if it were the whole set, but as between different holders in due course to whom different parts have been negotiated the holder whose title first accrues has all rights to the draft and its proceeds.

(3) As against the drawee the first presented part of a draft drawn in a set is the part entitled to payment, or if a time draft to acceptance and payment. Acceptance of any subsequently presented part renders the drawee liable thereon under subsection (2). With respect both to a holder and to the drawer payment of a subsequently presented part of a draft payable at sight has the same effect as payment of a check notwithstanding an effective stop order (Section 4–407).

(4) Except as otherwise provided in this section, where any part of a draft in a set is discharged by payment or otherwise the whole draft is discharged.

§3–802. **Effect of Instrument on Obligation for Which It Is Given.** (1) Unless otherwise agreed where an instrument is taken for an underlying obligation

(a) the obligation is pro tanto discharged if a bank is drawer, maker or acceptor of the instrument and there is no recourse on the instrument against the underlying obligor; and

(b) in any other case the obligation is suspended pro tanto until the instrument is due or if it is payable on demand until its presentment. If the instrument is dishonored action may be maintained on either the instrument or the obligation; discharge of the underlying obligor on the instrument also discharges him on the obligation.

(2) The taking in good faith of a check which is not postdated does not of itself so extend the time on the original obligation as to discharge a surety.

§3–803. **Notice to Third Party.** Where a defendant is sued for breach of an obligation for which a third person is answerable over under this Article he may give the third person written notice of the litigation, and the person notified may then give similar notice to any other person who is answerable over to him under this Article. If the notice states that the person notified may come in and defend and that if the person notified does not do so he will in any action against him by the person giving the notice be bound by any determination of fact common to the two litigations, then unless after seasonable receipt of the notice the person notified does come in and defend he is so bound.

§3–804. **Lost, Destroyed or Stolen Instruments.** The owner of an instrument which is lost, whether by destruction, theft or otherwise, may maintain an action in his own name and recover from any party liable thereon upon due proof of his ownership, the facts which prevent his production of the instrument and its terms. The court may require security indemnifying the defendant against loss by reason of further claims on the instrument.

§3–805. Instruments Not Payable to Order or to Bearer. This Article applies to any instrument whose terms do not preclude transfer and which is otherwise negotiable within this Article but which is not payable to order or to bearer, except that there can be no holder in due course of such an instrument.

SECTIONS 7 AND 8 OF THE ADMINISTRATIVE PROCEDURE ACT 60 STAT. 237 (1946), 5 U.S.C. SUBSECTIONS 1001–1011

Hearings

§7. In hearings which Section 4 or 5 requires to be conducted pursuant to this section—

(a) Presiding Officers. There shall preside at the taking of evidence (1) the agency, (2) one or more members of the body which comprises the agency, or (3) one or more examiners appointed as provided in this Act; but nothing in this Act shall be deemed to supersede the conduct of specified classes of proceedings in whole or part by or before boards or other officers specially provided for by or designated pursuant to statute. The functions of all presiding officers and of officers participating in decisions in conformity with section 8 shall be conducted in an impartial manner. Any such officer may at any time withdraw if he deems himself disqualified; and, upon the filing in good faith of a timely and sufficient affidavit of personal bias or disqualification of any such officer, the agency shall determine the matter as a part of the record and decision in the case.

(b) Hearing Powers. Officers presiding at hearings shall have authority, subject to the published rules of the agency and within its powers, to (1) administer oaths and affirmations, (2) issue subpenas authorized by law, (3) rule upon offers of proof and receive relevant evidence, (4) take or cause depositions to be taken whenever the ends of justice would be served thereby, (5) regulate the course of the hearing, (6) hold conferences for the settlement or simplification of the issues by consent of the parties, (7) dispose of procedural requests or similar matters, (8) make decisions or recommend decisions in conformity with Section 8, and (9) take any other action authorized by agency rule consistent with this Act.

(c) Evidence. Except as statutes otherwise provide, the proponent of a rule or order shall have the burden of proof. Any oral or documentary evidence may be received, but every agency shall as a matter of policy provide for the exclusion of irrelevant, immaterial, or unduly repetitious evidence and no sanction shall be imposed or rule or order be issued except upon consideration of the whole record or such portions thereof as may be cited by any party and as supported by and in accordance with the reliable, probative, and substantial evidence. Every party shall have the right to present his case or defense by oral or documentary evidence, to submit rebuttal evidence, and to conduct such cross examination as may be required for a full and true disclosure of the facts. In rule making or determining claims for money or benefits or applications for initial licenses any agency may, where the interest of any party will not be prejudiced thereby, adopt procedures for the submission of all or part of the evidence in written form.

(d) Record. The transcript of testimony and exhibits, together with all papers and requests filed in the proceeding, shall constitute the exclusive record for decision in accordance with Section 8 and, upon payment of lawfully prescribed costs, shall be made available to the parties. Where any agency decision rests on official notice of a material fact not appearing in the evidence in the record, any party shall on timely request be afforded an opportunity to show the contrary.

Decisions

§8. In cases in which a hearing is required to be conducted in conformity with Section 7—

(a) Action by Subordinates. In cases in which the agency has not presided at the reception of the evidence, the officer who presided (or, in cases not subject to subsection (c) of Section 5, any other officer or officers qualified to preside at hearings pursuant to Section 7) shall initially decide the case or the agency shall require (in specific cases or by general rule) the entire record to be certified to it for initial decision. Whenever such officers make the initial decision and in the absence of either an appeal to the agency or review upon motion of the agency within time provided by rule, such decision shall without further proceedings then become the decision of the agency. On appeal from or review of the initial decisions of such officers the agency shall, except as it may limit the issues upon notice or by rule, have all the powers which it would have in making the initial decision. Whenever the agency makes the initial decision without having presided at the reception of the evidence, such officers shall first recommend a decision, except that in rule making or determining applications for initial licenses (1) in lieu thereof the agency may issue a tentative decision or any of its responsible officers may recommend a decision, or (2) any such procedure may be omitted in any case in which the agency finds upon the record that due and timely execution of its functions imperatively and unavoidably so requires.

(b) Submittals and Decisions. Prior to each recommended, initial, or tentative decision, or decision upon agency review of the decision of subordinate officers, the parties shall be afforded a reasonable opportunity to submit for the consideration of the officers participating in such decisions (1) proposed findings and conclusions, or (2) exceptions to the decisions or recommended decisions of subordinate officers or to tentative agency decisions, and (3) supporting reasons for such exceptions or proposed findings or conclusions. The record shall show the ruling upon each such finding, conclusion, or exception presented. All decisions (including initial, recommended, or tentative decisions) shall become a part of the record and include a statement of (1) findings and conclusions, as well as the reasons or basis therefor, upon all the material issues of fact, law, or discretion presented on the record; and (2) the appropriate rule, order, sanction, relief, or denial thereof.

A BRIEF DISCUSSION OF BANKRUPTCY AND OF PROBATE PROCEDURES

In a very general way, the procedures followed upon death are similar to those relating to bankruptcy; that is, the decedent's assets and his legal liabilities are calculated, and the assets are applied to payment of the liabilities.

Introduction

Probably one may say that the fundamental areas of the private law are tort and contract, assuming *fundamental* to mean those areas that provide many concepts widely drawn upon in other areas of the law and applied in a wide variety of differing types of problem. However, it is desirable to acquaint the student with some basic notions involved in two other areas. These are bankruptcy and probate procedures.

The purpose of including a brief description of some aspects of these areas is to provide the student with necessary background information. Questions of inheritance and bankruptcy are often involved in contract questions. Very often an agreement must be analyzed to determine whether or not it is a binding contract before a party may secure payment from a decedent's estate or from the assets of a bankrupt. No attempt is made to explore the details within these areas of the law but merely to describe some of the processes involved.

Bankruptcy

As a matter of social policy, it became clear at a rather late date in the evolution of our law that a person who had become hopelessly in debt was never likely to recover financially. This was recognized as an undesirable result. Aside from the fact that it condemned a useful citizen and his family to endless poverty, it also deprived the community of the best services of some of its most capable members. Not infrequently the person who became insolvent was one of the more enterprising and energetic members of the community, who had simply suffered fortuitous losses.

In addition, insolvency presented serious difficulties to the creditors. Sometimes an insolvent party continued operating his business at a loss despite the fact that the situation was hopeless, thus progressively reducing the assets from which his creditors might recover. Furthermore, the creditors themselves were tempted to compete with one another, sometimes unfairly, in an attempt to secure payment of outstanding debts at the expense of other creditors. In addition this situation often tempted the debtor to secrete remaining assets, or give them away, or otherwise defraud the creditors.

In order to avoid these effects, the idea of a discharge in bankruptcy was evolved. Upon insolvency (being unable to meet debts as they accrue or arriving at a point where total liabilities exceed total assets), a debtor may voluntarily petition a federal district court to initiate bankruptcy proceedings (termed *voluntary bankruptcy*), or a creditor may petition that the debtor be declared bankrupt (termed *involuntary bankruptcy*).

Greatly oversimplifying the process, what then occurs is that the bankrupt's assets and liabilities are ascertained, and the assets are divided up among the bankrupt's creditors. A factor that greatly complicates the process is that certain claims are given a priority, meaning that these claims will be paid in full before creditors with claims of lower priority may receive anything. Taxes, and claims for wages, for example, have a high priority. Certain property, such as the tools of the bankrupt's trade, and enough clothes to keep him covered, may not be taken at all. After his assets are distributed to the creditors, usually many creditors are not fully paid. Often they receive only a few cents on every dollar owed and sometimes nothing. Nevertheless, when the debtor has given all that he must give according to law, he is then discharged from further obligation to pay his debts. The debts are rendered uncollectible in the same fashion as debts barred by the statute of limitations.

Students often fail to appreciate the importance of the institution of bankruptcy to the decision-making processes of businessmen. Actually, the credit—the ability and willingness of potential customers to pay—is a prime consideration to the businessman in planning his business policies and procedures. If an obligee has no assets with which to pay an obligation, there is no way of collecting upon the obligation, even if the obligee would like to pay. This is the reason that mortgages and other forms of security are so important to business and indirectly why credit agencies are given special protection by the law.[1]

A valid mortgage is an arrangement in which a debtor gives the creditor the exclusive right to recover against certain property of the debtor. In the event of bankruptcy the creditor may satisfy his entire debt from the mortgaged property. Any excess of value above that owed the creditor is then distributed among the other creditors.

Inheritance

In a very general way, the procedures followed upon death are similar to those relating to bankruptcy—that is, the decedent's assets and his legal liabilities are calculated, and the assets are applied to payments of the liabilities. Of course, any similarity usually ends there. For example, in the bankruptcy situation the problems usually arise because there are not enough assets to pay all the creditors, whereas in the present case there are usually enough assets to pay the claims. Therefore in settling estates there are usually no problems of priority of creditors. The procedures are quite different in detail.

After payment of a decedent's liabilities from his assets, the disposition of the remainder of the assets will be according to one of two schemes. If the decedent has made a valid will, ordinarily the terms of the will are given

---

[1] See Chapter 11 on defamation.

effect and his property is distributed according to those terms. The actual transactions surrounding this process are performed by a party designated the *executor,* who is usually named in the will. If an executor is not named in the will, the court will appoint one. Usually the executor is someone near the decedent, often the spouse. The executor is the party responsible for winding up an estate, but in practice, of course, relies heavily upon legal advice. When a party dies without making a will, an *administrator* is appointed, and his functions are the same as the executor's; the only significance to the difference in terms is that in one case distribution is according to a will; in the other case it is not. These are common terms, however, and the student should remember them.

The question naturally arises, what is required for a will to be valid, and why should there be special requirements for the transfer of property after death? The special requirements of a will are imposed in order to make sure that the intent of the decedent is given effect. The will requires special technicalities—for example, that it be signed before at least two witnesses who have in turn witnessed each other sign the will. The purposes of the technicalities are twofold. First, to combat the danger of forgery or alteration of a will. This is a fairly substantial danger, or would be if just any informal scrap of paper would be given legal effect. Probably many persons close to an elderly person would be able to acquire a signature, and type in favorable terms of a will above it, or as a last resort copy a signature. Very likely there are those who believe they know better than an elderly person how the latter person's property ought to be distributed, because, in fact, persons have been known to attempt to alter or forge wills.

Second, the formality of signing a will makes it clear to a testator that this expression of his desires is the official version and the one that will be given legal effect. It is not unusual for an older person in circumstances of moderate wealth to make written promises to give the same property to a number of persons, either by letter or by notes left around and discovered after death. Frequently these are not only contradictory but they are undated, so there is no way of knowing which expresses the most recent intent of the decedent. If such communications were legally valid, distributions of decedent's property on death would often be hopelessly confusing and the primary purpose stated above, carrying out the intent of the decedent, would probably not be accomplished.

Therefore such writings are given no legal effect. There is a systematic means by which a person may express his intentions as to the disposition of his property after death. This means is through a valid will and only through a valid will. This rule carries with it the unfortunate but unavoidable fact that decedents who leave only some note or scrap of paper indicating how they wish their property to be distributed will be frustrated in their intentions. Therefore it is to the interest of anyone with much property to have a will drawn.

Another problem that must be considered is that of mental incapacity. No matter how scrupulously one may adhere to the formal requirements of a will, it seems evident that the will should not be considered effective if the testator is completely devoid of his senses. Unfortunately, neither psychology nor law has been able to devise any exact definition or measurement by which a person may be categorically proved sane or insane. Insanity (or psychosis, to use the nearest equivalent from the science of psychology) is a matter of degree. Obviously, however, whether a decision as to a party's sanity is always correct or not, decisions have to be made as to whether a testator had the mental capacity to make a will. Ultimately, a jury decides on the basis of the evidence. The important fact is that some reasonable degree of rationality at the time of making a will is required in order for the will to be valid.[2]

One other important qualification should be mentioned: It is impossible to completely disinherit one's widow. Aside from the obvious injustice of this act, the effect would be to place the burden of supporting the widow upon public charitable institutions, when by conventional standards the obligation is that of the decedent. Most states have statutes providing that the widow may elect between taking a certain share of the estate or accepting whatever provision is made for her by will. If the will provides for less than her statutory share, she may take that share regardless of the terms of the will.

The only way for the husband to avoid this difficulty is through a contract with the wife by which she agrees to accept less than the share provided for her by statute. However, such agreements are scrutinized very closely by the courts and tend to be rejected if challenged, for obvious reasons.

One other way to avoid the problem is for the testator to dissipate his estate by riotous living as he feels death approaching. A penniless old age is the obvious hazard, however, if he is wrong in his estimate of his own life span.

Supposing a person owning property dies without making a will? We have already indicated that such evidence as letters, notes, or even statements as "You may have this when I am gone" do not effect a transfer of property. (None of these would be considered gifts because there is neither an intent to make a present transfer nor a transfer of possession.) What does happen when a person dies intestate—that is, without a will?

Every state has passed legislation which deals with this problem. The statutes specify a number of differing situations, and the share of an estate that various parties get in each of these situations. For example, if a wife is the sole survivor of a decedent, normally all the property goes to her. If a wife and one child remain, often the estate is split between them, and if more than one child remains, often the wife gets one third, and the remainder is split between the other children. These proportions vary from state to state. All sorts of other possibilities are usually provided for. If no relatives remain, the property goes to the state. (This is termed *escheat*.)

The important thing to remember concerning these statutes is that although they do divide the property among those whom the decedent would probably want it to, only by sheer chance would the scheme of distribution be exactly as the decedent preferred. For persons with minor children the scheme is apt

[2] Technically stated, the mental capacity required is that a testator "be able to understand the nature of a will, that he should remember generally the nature and extent of his property and the persons who are the natural objects of his bounty and that he should be able to conceive an intelligent scheme of disposition of his estate." 57 American Jurisprudence, Wills 63–67.

to be particularly awkward, because a fixed proportion of the estate will generally go to the minor children, usually requiring some sort of formal guardianship and careful accounting to ascertain that each full share really was spent on *each particular* child. Most parents with minor children expressly disinherit the children by will and make the surviving parent sole heir, so that the surviving parent can have a free hand in apportioning the money between the children as circumstances dictate.

Index of Cases

Index of Readings

Subject Index